Barclay's

APOLOGY

IN MODERN ENGLISH

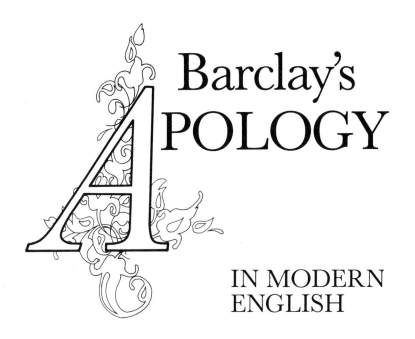

Barclay's APOLOGY

IN MODERN ENGLISH

EDITED BY DEAN FREIDAY

BARCLAY'S APOLOGY IN MODERN ENGLISH

©1967 by Dean Freiday

©1991 by The Barclay Press

International Standard Book Number:
0-913342-69-6 paper
0-913342-72-6 library binding

Library of Congress Catalog Card Number: 67-18796

First printing 1967
Second printing 1969
Third printing 1980
Fourth printing 1991
Fifth printing 1998

Printed on acid-free recycled paper

Published by THE BARCLAY PRESS
110 S. Elliott Rd., Newberg, Oregon 97132 U.S.A.

Contents

Copyright Permissions

Notes identified as *Encyc. Brit.* are from the *Encyclopaedia Britannica,* and with the exception of two especially indicated as from the 11th ed, are from the 1958 ed. Quotations are used by permission of the Encyclopaedia Britannica.

(3) For a variety of sources ranging from Bible dictionaries and handbooks of denominations, or works on comparative ecclesiology, to specific treatises on individual theologians or aspects of Quakerism, I am indebted to the following:

Abingdon Press for the quotations from the 1956 ed of the *Handbook of Denominations in the United States* by Frank S. Mead; and also *The Interpreter's Bible.*

William H. Allen, Bookseller, Philadelphia, for permission to quote from Wilson Frescoln's *Voltaire's Letters on the Quakers.*

Howard Brinton for quotations from his *Friends for 300 Years.*

Henry J. Cadbury for quotations from his *Annual Catalogue of George Fox's Papers.*

T. & T. Clark of Edinburgh for the quotation from the Marcus Dods translation of Augustine's *City of God,* also used in the *Great Books of the Western World* series published by Encyclopaedia Britannica.

Doubleday & Company, Inc. for the quotations from John H. Leith's *Creeds of the Churches.*

Gerald Duckworth & Co. Ltd. of London for the quotations from *Quaker Women 1650-1690* by Mabel R. Brailsford.

Encyclopaedia Britannica for permission (with T. & T. Clark of Edinburgh) to quote from the Marcus Dods translation of Augustine's *City of God,* vol 18 of *Great Books of the Western World.*

Epworth Press, London, for the quotation from vol 1 of *A History of the Methodist Church in Great Britain,* Rupert Davies and Gordon Rupp, general editors.

Fortress Press for the quotations from *Three Treatises* of Martin Luther.

Wilson Frescoln for the use of his translation of *Voltaire's Letters on the Quakers* quoted in the introduction.

Friends Journal for permission to reprint part of Thomas Kelly's "The Gathered Meeting," which originally appeared in *The Friend* (Philadelphia) and is currently included in the London Discipline and in the recently published (posthumous) collection of Thomas Kelly's writings, *The Eternal Promise.*

Funk & Wagnalls Company, Inc. for the quotations from *A New Standard Bible Dictionary* (1926), ed by Jacobus, Nourse, and Zeno; also the *New Schaff-Herzog Encyclopedia of Religious Knowledge* (1908).

Harper & Row, Publishers, Inc. for "The Gathered Meeting," from *The Eternal Promise,* the posthumous collection of Thomas Kelly's writings; for part of Dorothy Canfield Fisher's introductory essay on Quaker humor from *Friendly Anecdotes,* by Irvin C. and Ruth V. Poley; *A History of Christianity,* by Kenneth Scott Latourette; and *Calvin, The Origins and Development of His Religious Thought,* by Francois Wendel.

Herder and Herder for the quoted sections of the article, "Justification," in the *Theological Dictionary* of Karl Rahner and Herbert Vorgrimler © 1965 Herder KG.

Acts 24:14 NEB: "But this much I will admit: I am a follower of the new way (the 'sect' they speak of), and it is in that manner that I worship the God of our fathers; for I believe all that is written in the Law and the prophets, . . ."

Titus 2:11-14 NEB: "For the grace of God has dawned upon the world with healing for all mankind; and by it we are disciplined to renounce godless ways and worldly desires, and to live a life of temperance, honesty, and godliness in the present age, looking forward to the happy fulfillment of our hopes when the splendour of our great God and Saviour Christ Jesus will appear. He it is who sacrificed himself for us, to set us free from all wickedness and to make us a pure people marked out for his own, eager to do good."

1 Thes 5:21 Cath-CCD: ". . . Test all things; hold fast that which is good."

(The dedicatory address to Charles II has been omitted as primarily of historical interest.)

ABOUT THE BIBLICAL CITATIONS

The biblical quotations in the English edition of the *Apology* were originally from the Authorized, or King James, Version of the Bible. In the present edition (with some rare exceptions) one of three recent widely accepted English versions has been selected: Revised Standard Version (RSV), New English Bible (NEB), or New American Catholic Edition — Confraternity of Christian Doctrine Translation (Cath-CCD). Unfortunately the Old Testament was completely unavailable, as yet, in the New English Bible, and this was partially true of the New American Catholic Edition. For the few books of the latter where the Douay Version was cited the abbreviation used is Cath-Douay rather than Cath-CCD.

With regret, the J. B. Phillips version of the New Testament has been avoided because of disagreement among Bible authorities on various points of scholarship. It would not be right, however, to ignore the popular acceptance this version has received because of its movingly contemporary language.

ABBREVIATIONS USED IN THIS WORK

a	article	Ezek	Ezekiel	Phil	Philippians
art	article			Prov	Proverbs
Assoc.	Association	ff	and following	pp	pages
		fl	flourished		
biog	biographical	fn	footnote	q	question
Brit.	Britannica			quest	question
		Gal	Galatians		
Cat.	Catalogue	Gen	Genesis	Rel.	Religious
Cath.	Catholic			Rev	Revelation
c.	century	Hab	Habakkuk	rev	revised
c.	circa	Heb	Hebrews	Rom	Romans
c	chapter	Hist.	History		
cap	chapter			s	section
ch	chapter	ibid	the same work	1 Sam	1 Samuel
chap	chapter	Id.	the same work	sect	section
1 Chron	1 Chronicles	Isa	Isaiah	sects	sections
				ser	series
Col.	Columbia	Jer	Jeremiah	Ses.	Session
Col	Colossians			S. J.	Society of
1 Cor	1 Corinthians	1	book		Jesus (Jesuits)
2 Cor	2 Corinthians	Lev	Leviticus	s.v.	under the word
corr	corrected	lib	book	sv	under the word
		loc cit	place cited		
d.	died			1 Thes	1 Thessalonians
Deut	Deuteronomy	Mat	Matthew	2 Thes	2 Thessalonians
Dict.	Dictionary	MS	manuscript	1 Tim	1 Timothy
DNB	Dictionary	MSS	manuscripts	2 Tim	2 Timothy
	of National	Mus.	Museum	tom	tome, section
	Biography			tract	tractate, treatise
ed	edition	Neh	Nehemiah		
Ed.		NT	New Testament	v	volume
	editor's comment			vol	volume
Encyc.		O.D.C.C.	Oxford Dictionary of the Christian Church		
	Encyclopedia	O.E.D.	Oxford English Dictionary	WCC	World Council of Churches
Engl.	English	op cit	work cited		
Eph	Ephesians	OT	Old Testament		
et seq	and following			Zech	Zechariah
Ex	Exodus	p	page	Zeph	Zephaniah
Exod	Exodus	1 Pet	1 Peter		
		2 Pet	2 Peter		

FOOTNOTES in the same type size as the text are Barclay's own. Those in smaller type have been added by the present editor.

PERSONAL ACKNOWLEDGMENTS

My greatest debt in this work is unquestionably to Trinity Parish Library in New York City. This was originally established for the use of the clergy in Trinity's seven constituent churches. The staff not only tolerated me for days on end, but tactfully schooled me in the complex bibliographical routes of theological literature. The librarian during most of this time, who has since left the premises for the marital state, Mrs. Alice Erlander Wilcox, spent untold hours in helping me track down obscure allusions. Her Lutheran background and knowledge of sources on seventeenth century Anglican church history were invaluable in supplying leads to explanatory material. By far the great majority of the questions raised were answered with the resources of Trinity's fine collection.

The stubborn remainder wore trails in several directions. Another Episcopal institution, General Theological Seminary, was an invaluable source of seventeenth century materials, and has such an excellent bibliographic and biographical collection that all but roughly a dozen of the remaining references to various periods of church history were annotated there. I am particularly indebted to Mr. Duncan Thomas of that institution. Several of the most difficult biographical finds I owe to Prof. George A. Barrois of Princeton Theological Seminary, a specialist in the Reformation era. Others were located at Union Theological Seminary, and one in a German encyclopedia on Protestantism at the Jewish Theological Seminary.

On Quaker fine points, Lewis Benson, an unequalled authority on the writings of George Fox, and Edmund Goerke, a voracious reader of early Quaker literature with an indexing mind, spent days of seeking. They supplied some of the fine quotations included in notes of that type.

Quaker Henry J. Cadbury brought to bear his remarkable range of knowledge on Quaker history and his unrivalled biblical scholarship (RSV Bible Committee, *Interpreter's Bible*, etc.) for a critical reading of the entire manuscript. Gerald W. Dillon, pastor of First Friends Church, Portland, Oregon, performed a like service and made helpful comments with which I endeavored to take into account the views of Evangelical Friends.

Two non-Quakers performed unusual services: Rev. Frank S. Mead, the Methodist author of the *Handbook of Denominations in the United States,* made a valiant effort to find a commercial publisher for this work. Rev. David J. Bowman, S. J., the first Roman Catholic to occupy a staff position with the National Council of Churches (Faith and Order Department, August, 1966), made helpful suggestions on the notes pertaining to points of Catholic doctrine in this immediate post-Conciliar era when evaluations are particularly difficult.

D. Elton Trueblood, who is shortly to publish a long-awaited biography of Barclay (at present there is no definitive study), gave an over-all evaluative reading, as did Frederick B. Tolles, the Quaker historian, and William Hubben, Quaker editor and author of a number of philosophical studies. John McCandless, who did the printing, made many helpful typographical and editorial suggestions.

Pearl Hall, co-director of Powell House retreat center, proofread the entire work and asked that the cost of her labors be contributed to the Powell House development fund. I am grateful for all of these helpful services. Any responsibility for errors or omissions, however, is mine.

D. F.

BIOGRAPHICAL NOTE

Robert Barclay (1648-1690) was born at Gordonstown, Morayshire, in the north of Scotland, where his father and mother were temporarily residing.

His father, David Barclay (1610-1686), was the first of the family not to live at Kirtounhill, formerly the family seat. His own father's "pecuniary embarrassments" had made it necessary to dispose of the estate of Mathers, which had been in the family for over 300 years. After David Barclay's education was completed, he became a volunteer in the army of Gustavus Adolphus in the Thirty Years War. He returned to Scotland on the outbreak of the Civil War and soon became a colonel of a cavalry regiment in the Royalist army. When Cromwell came into power, he was dismissed from his post and lived at Gordonstown for several years. After a time he purchased the estate of Ury, near Aberdeen. He sat in several successive parliaments and was one of the Trustees of forfeited lands in Scotland.

David Barclay became a Quaker in 1665, partly through the help of an old comrade in arms, John Swinton, 19th baron of that name, who shared a room with him when they were both confined in Edinburgh Castle for political reasons. Lord Swinton had accepted Quakerism a short time before, and although he had been "processed" by the synod of Moray and excommunicated in 1651 by the Commission of the General Assembly at Perth apparently for favoring "sectarian errors," he had been "one formerly cried up for his piety." This sentence was inexplicably relaxed "without personal compearance."

Robert Barclay's mother was Catherine Gordon, daughter of Sir Robert Gordon of Gordonstown, who was first Knight Baronet of Scotland and son of the Earl of Sutherland. She was thus a member of the powerful Gordon clan, and also a cousin of Charles II, king of England. It was because of her deathbed plea to her husband that Robert Barclay, eldest of their five children, was called home from Paris in 1663, at the age of fifteen.

Robert had been learning "a little grammar," as he modestly described his education, which included Latin and French, and apparently enough Greek, Hebrew, church history, and patristics for him later to pursue his own studies in those fields. This was at the Roman Catholic Scots College in Paris, where the contemporary Anglican Bishop of Edinburgh also received "a little grammar" as well as his higher education. His uncle (also named Robert Barclay), the principal, was responsible for his being weaned from the strict Calvinism of his youth[1] to Roman Catholicism. He had also promised him his estate if he would but remain in France and complete his Catholic education.

David Barclay made no attempt to influence his children's views, and for a time young Robert used this liberty to hear from several faiths. While his father was imprisoned in Edinburgh Castle, the governor forbade visits from his son for several months; but his father's example, discussions with Lord Swinton,[2] and his attendance at the meetings of the Quakers began to have an effect on him.

Several of the steps leading to what Budge[3] has described as the experience in which "the Saviour revealed Himself to

[1] Robert Barclay, the *Apologist*, says in his treatise on *Universal Love* (included in the incomplete collection of his publications known as *Truth Triumphant*, London, 1692, and hereafter cited as *Works*; the location is p 678): "My first education, from my infancy up, fell among the strictest sort of Calvinists; those of our country being generally acknowledged to be the severest of that sect; in the heat of zeal surpassing not only Geneva (from whence they derive their pedigree) but all other Reformed Churches abroad."
The rigidness of Presbyterian church discipline had given Scotland's national church what Richard Baxter (see biog fn p 149) called "godliness without sects."

[2] John Swinton, who is frequently considered one of the earliest of the Quaker "mystics," may have been the person whose message greatly impressed Barclay at the first meeting he attended. This message was expressed in an oxymoron which has been passed down through the centuries: "In stillness there is fullness. In fullness there is nothingness. In nothingness there are all things."

[3] Frances Anne Budge, *The Barclays of Ury*, London, Harris, 1881. This sketch, reprinted from the *Friends Quarterly Examiner*, has been a principal source for this biographical note. Others have been John Barclay, *Diary of Alexander Jaffray* (and *Memoirs* of the history of Friends in the North of Scotland), 2nd ed, London, Darton & Harvey, 1834; and William C. Braithwaite, *The Second Period of Quakerism*, 2nd ed, prepared by Henry J. Cadbury, Cambridge University Press, 1961.

his seeking soul" are probably described in the *Apology*.[4] Budge also accents the astonishment there must have been when first the widely known and respected father, and then his "highly-gifted intellectual son," whose family armorial bearings included the mitre of Aberbrothwick, fell into "the scandalous errors of Quaquerism." Thus had the Presbytery of Brechin in the diocese of David Barclay's brother-in-law, Bishop Strachan, viewed the new appearance on the Scots religious horizon.

Robert Barclay's "convincement" was in 1666. Just four years later he and Christian Molleson were married "after the manner of Friends," as the standard phrasing now has it. She was the daughter of Gilbert Molleson, a merchant and bailie of Aberdeen. There was considerable furore over the marriage, which was the first in that city to take place in Quaker fashion by the mutual exchange of vows, after the marriage had been "allowed" by the meeting, and without an officiating clergyman.[5] The marriage was but one issue in the persecution and disturbance of meetings that was then at a high point in Aberdeen. Some idea of the over-all extent of Quaker persecution is given by the fact that at least 4,200 Friends (by conservative computation) were simultaneously in prison in 1661, and many counties were completely empty of adult male Friends.[6]

The year of Christian Molleson and Robert Barclay's wedding was also that of the publication of *Truth Cleared of Calumnies*, the first of a ten-year series of polemical and apologetic publications. In the meantime Barclay had travelled widely "in the interest of Truth." Later, in 1677, he accompanied William Penn, George Fox, George Keith, and others during part of a religious visit to Holland and Germany, which included a great gathering at Amsterdam. It was on this trip that he and Penn established a religious friendship with the Princess Elizabeth of the Palatinate and Barclay began a correspondence with her that is still preserved. She was one of

[4] The passage about the secret power that touched his heart in the silent assemblies of God's people has become a "classic" quotation among Friends; it appears on p 254.

[5] "The public preachers of the place thought their authority so slighted by this act, and were so exasperated at it, that by the Bishop's means they procured letters to summon Robert Barclay before the Privy Council for an unlawful marriage. 'This matter was however so overruled of the Lord,' as the Friends of Ury expressed it, 'that they never had power to put their summons into execution, so as to do us any prejudice' " — John Barclay, *Diary of Alexander Jaffray*, etc., p 297.

[6] Braithwaite, *Second Period of Quakerism*, pp 9 and 114.

the two great women intellectuals for whom he served as a spiritual confidante.[7] A distant cousin, the Princess Elizabeth was a sister of Prince Rupert and a close friend of Descartes. On one of the Quaker visits to Heidelberg, she was living in that city, and Braithwaite states,[8] "her singular breadth of intellect must have exerted powerful influence in the Court" of the Prince Elector. It was he who had been responsible for inviting Spinoza to occupy the chair of philosophy at the University of Heidelberg.

In 1679 Robert Barclay again visited the Netherlands. This was also the year in which Charles II constituted the lands at Ury a free barony with civil and criminal jurisdiction,[9] and in which the Duke of York appointed Barclay a member of the Scots Privy Council.

George Fox's great plan for a series of Quaker proprietary colonies in America must have been taking shape then, too, for it is believed to have been conceived on Fox's wide travels there in 1672 and 1673.[10] West Jersey was the first of these, when Byllynge, whose feudal manor at Salem was in financial straits, agreed to a Quaker settlement at Burlington in 1677, arranged by his bankruptcy trustees: William Penn, Gawen Lawrie, and Nicholas Lucas. Penn's acquisition of Pennsylvania in 1681 and its settlement in 1682 were next, followed within a few months by the acquisition of East Jersey by Penn and eleven others, ten of whom were Quakers.

Almost immediately Robert Barclay and eleven additional proprietors were brought into the picture to make East Jersey a haven for persecuted Scots groups. Barclay's uncle, Robert

---

[7] The other was Lady Conway of Ragley, Worcestershire. When this learned and philosophical viscountess (the daughter of Speaker Finch) became a Quaker, Henry More (1614-1687), the Cambridge Platonist, was sorely grieved that she had joined "the most melancholy sect that ever was in the world." — Edward Grubb, "The Early Quakers," ch 4, vol 8, p 126, of *The Cambridge History of English Literature*, Putnam, 1912. See also the *Conway Letters.* ed by Marjorie Hope Nicolson, London, Oxford Univ. Press, 1930. Specific reference to Barclay is on pp 435ff.

[8] *Beginnings of Quakerism,* p 414.

[9] These privileges were retained until the tenure of all such grants in Scotland was ended during the reign of George II.

[10] The steps leading to the acquisition of these four middle colonies (Delaware was the last, a gift from King James to William Penn) were clearly outlined for the first time in John E. Pomfret, *The Province of East New Jersey 1609-1702*, Princeton Univ. Press, 1962, particularly pp 130-134. (*The Province of West New Jersey 1609-1702* had been issued by the same author and publisher in 1956.)

Gordon, and his relatives, the earls of Perth and Melfort, were the only non-Quakers in the new group. By special provision for his benefit, and at their instigation, Barclay was elected non-resident governor of East Jersey for life, and this was confirmed by Charles II. One brother, John, settled in East Jersey and had an active part in the proprietorship. His younger brother, David, died at sea en route there. Robert Barclay's close friend George Keith, a partner in a number of theological dialogues,[11] also migrated there and became the first Surveyor General. His maps, preserved at Perth Amboy, N. J., are still the basis of many land titles.

In 1686, one year after the death of Robert's brother David, their father died at Ury. Robert Barclay's own death, hastened perhaps by the heavy responsibilities in connection with East Jersey and his efforts at James' court with Penn on behalf of Quaker toleration, followed four years later. The immediate cause was a violent fever contracted on a religious visit to some parts of the north of Scotland. His seven children were all alive fifty years later, and there were between sixty and seventy descendants at that time. The family is also remarkable for the number of outstanding Quakers who were produced generation after generation.

D. F.

[11] Barclay owes some debt for his own doctrinal development (notably in the areas of Inward Revelation and the Scriptures) to Keith, but the dependence is not great. J. Philip Wragge, *The Faith of Robert Barclay*, London, Friends Home Service Committee, 1948, is a competent examination of the matter. However, Henry J. Cadbury feels a closer indebtedness is demonstrated in Wragge's unpublished study, "The Debt of Robert Barclay to George Keith" (1946).

ABOUT THE APOLOGY

"Not long after I had received and believed the Testimony I now bear," Barclay says in the preface to his *Catechism and Confession of Faith*, dated 1673, "I had in view both the possibility and facility [i.e., feasibility] of such a work."

His introductory statements to the *Apology* do not indicate a similar long-standing urge, but stress instead his humility before the task which he has undertaken "in confidence that with God's help there is nothing that I cannot do," and to which he has "devoted myself and all that is mine." In view of the unexpected widespread response to the Theological Theses, "it seems appropriate," he says, "to explain them more fully at this time, and to defend them with certain arguments." "According to the grace that has been given me as one of several whom God has chosen to be dispensers of this Gospel, it seemed good, and appropriately my duty..."

When one examines the *Apology's* place in the sequence of his works included in *Truth Triumphant* (published in 1692 and hereafter referred to as his *Works*, although additional unpublished items exist) it seems to be the apex of a series begun in 1670, less than four years after his "convincement." No doubt his spiritual advisors had fostered his "concern" for this type of work, recognizing the value of his Catholic (see Note, p xli) training in Latin, theology, and patristics. The *Apology* is also uniquely personal in being a "thinking through" of his own religious journey from the strict Calvinism of his youth, to the Roman Catholicism of his schooling, and finally to his Quaker convincement.

WHAT THE APOLOGY COVERS

It has been a frequent custom to construct systematic theologies around a readily recognizable pattern. The Apostle's Creed has been a favorite choice. Barclay chose instead the familiar sequence of the Westminster Shorter Catechism, known not only to him but to the great majority of the citizens of his native Scotland. The dependence is not close. Only a few of the same questions are covered. Many are not considered at all, and there is no attempt to give the same prominence to each subject that is given there. This had also been the pattern of Barclay's own *Catechism*.

In assessing the *Apology*, it is frequently overlooked that it is not a complete statement of the Quaker faith, although as Howard Brinton says[1] it "affords the most complete interpretation that we have of Quakerism as *thought about.*" It contains almost nothing on Quaker polity. Barclay had already dealt fully with that in his *Anarchy of the Ranters* (1674). The Quaker marriage ceremony is not even mentioned, although this has been one of the most obvious points of Quaker "differentness" through the years, and one of its best-known features.[2]

There is no systematic treatment of such "notional" Christian doctrines as the Atonement, although the casual references are consistent with the belief of the early Quakers that it was a basic presupposition of the whole personal process of conversion and growth in perfection. Quakers believed, too, in a Triune God, although they disliked the use of the word "persons" and some other aspects of standard Trinitarian doctrine.[3]

The *Apology* does examine thoroughly most of what was at issue between the Quakers and the major contemporary denominations. Some historians have classed Quakerism as radical Puritanism, and some have tried to derive it from continental mysticism, or noted the analogies with Anabaptism. Still others have pictured it as one of the hundreds of sects that sprang up in seventeenth century England,[4] and Braithwaite

---

[1] Introduction to his *Friends for 300 Years*, N. Y., Harper & Bros., 1952, p viii.

[2] Barclay did touch briefly on it in his *Anarchy of the Ranters*.

[3] Article IV of Barclay's *Confession of Faith* affirms the full biblical doctrine of the divinity and "pre-existence" of Christ in whom "dwelleth all the fulness of the God-head bodily," *Works*, p 162.
The doctrine of the Trinity is dealt with in the first 25 pages of Thomas Evans, *An Exposition of the Faith of the Religious Society of Friends*. A 4th ed was published in 1828, although there are earlier ones.
A reaction to anthropomorphism in views of the deity is also suggested as a factor in the objections to Trinitarian doctrine by William Penn's comment that Lodowick Muggleton of the contemporary "Muggletonians" preached a "six-foot God." — Quoted by Umphrey Lee, *The Historical Backgrounds of Methodist Enthusiasm*, N. Y., Columbia, 1931, p 56.

[4] According to Lee, op cit, *Gangraena*, published in London in 1645 by Thomas Edwards (1599-1647), a Presbyterian who zealously collected all of the information to the discredit of the sects that he could find, catalogues 176 "errors," "heresies," "blasphemies," which he classified in sixteen groups. Some modern studies have placed the number much higher.

has documented some of its debt to these minor groups,[5] but it certainly did not consider itself one of them. In Fox's view — and in Barclay's — Quakerism was a fresh blossoming of the apostolic church as it had existed before the dark night of apostasy which had lasted nearly 1400 years. While it was by no means a slavish primitivism, it nevertheless considered itself faithful to the apostolic concept of Christianity and the Church.

Most denominations held that Christian prophecy ceased about the second century, and that revelation was confined to the prophets and apostles and perhaps a few charismatic leaders — usually the founding fathers of the denomination. Over against this view, Quakers did and do believe that "revelation" (in a sense which the biblical use of the term allows) continues. This is partially covered by what other terminology would recognize as "illumination" (but not "illuminism"). And it is most certainly "in the vein of" (to avoid comparison of details) the Roman Catholic concept of "private revelation." It generally leads more to an applicational or interpretive insight — an unfolding, or "opening," of Truth — rather than to any "novel doctrine," as Barclay so clearly points out.

THE QUAKER VIEW OF SCRIPTURE

The *Apology* was written at a time when the recent decision of the Anglican Archbishop of Armagh, James Ussher (1581-1656), that the world was created in precisely 4004 B. C., was being sufficiently "canonized" for it to be included in the marginal notations of the King James version of the Bible from 1701 on. Many Established Churchmen, and others, held to the sacredness of every comma and period — the punctuation, as well as the "letter," of the text. In such an age, Quakers made at least a 200-year leap into the future in their view of scripture. As opposed to literal and proof-text-based interpretations, they adopted a synoptic and situational approach. *All* biblical statements on a certain subject had to be harmonized. While "key passages" were admitted, there was no patience with isolated "proof texts" which clearly contradicted other biblical evidence.

---

[5] William C. Braithwaite also cites *Gangraena*, on "The Puritan Revolution," in *The Beginnings of Quakerism*. One of the Rowntree series on Quaker history, Braithwaite's work was first published in 1912 and reprinted in 1923. The 2nd ed, revised by Henry J. Cadbury, was published by Cambridge Univ. Press in 1955 and reprinted in 1961.

The "automatic penmanship" theory had no place in this sophisticated view of the Bible. Variations in texts, missing books, and corruptions in transmission were all allowed for. There was even a glimmer of modern "form criticism." Nevertheless, in interpreting a text the emphasis was placed upon the "plain and naked import of the words" and allegorical or figurative interpretations were abstained from wherever possible.[6] In applying biblical statements theologically, "twining" and "wresting"[7] were to be avoided and the "plain doctrines there delivered" were to be used "without niceties and School distinctions."[8] Demythologizing was unheard of. But such usages as "day" to mean "time" in the concept of a "day of visitation" suggest that there may even have been some of that kind of interpretation for passages which are — now at least — in conflict with scientific knowledge.

Quakers also took a different view of scriptural authority. Alone of surviving groups they insisted on the primacy of the Holy Spirit as the authority and the source of revelation. Luther had raised the watchword of "scripture alone," and Catholic doctrine in the Counter-Reformation became distorted from a "two source" (tradition and scripture) foundation to a defensive position of almost "tradition alone." Barclay refuted both concepts. He said that it is the Holy Spirit to which all Christians ultimately appeal for guidance. Catholic Ecumenical Councils and Synods pray that they may be led by the Spirit. Most Protestants insist that the scriptures have meaning because of the response invoked in the hearts and minds of readers by the Spirit.[9] Quakers go a step further and say that it is the Spirit who reveals to us both the Word and the Son, and they point out, as is sometimes forgotten, that Christ himself, not the scriptures, was the Word.

Quakers alone based their ministry and worship, as well as their concepts of revelation, reconciliation, sanctification, and

[6] *Works,* p 112.

[7] ibid, p 76.

[8] ibid, p 112.

[9] Fox was somewhat more Christocentric on "authority" than Barclay. He tended to see the Spirit more as the agent by whom Christ was revealed and made present, and by whom he ruled directly in his church.

Umphrey Lee has summarized the major Protestant interpretations as: "Luther insisted that the Spirit follows the Word and the sacraments; and Calvin held that the Spirit accompanies the Word, testifying to its truth, and enforcing it upon the heart of the believer." — op cit, p 36.

regeneration, on the work of the Spirit. Even the condition of man, when he was under the judgment of God for his progenitor's disobedience, required the true grace of God, transmitted by the Spirit, to free him from evil, rather than any "natural" light. Yet this redemption, which was purchased by Christ's death, was considered universal. Every man, everywhere, not merely "all kinds of men" in Christendom, as others maintained, was enlightened by a saving and spiritual Light. The extent to which pagans knew the difference between right and wrong was the work of the Spirit of Christ in their hearts and consciences. Men could not come to such decisions in their "natural state" without the help of the Spirit. But even "Japonians, Brasilians, Cannibals"[10] could find its leadings accessible to their consciences. Thus pagan "moral sense" was considered an encounter with a divine imperative which informed the conscience. It was not the work of conscience itself.

This is one of the most significant portions of the *Apology*. Its doctrine ran directly counter to Calvin's double-predestination, and in Methodist hands (John Wesley adopted it bodily[11]) it has largely triumphed over it. In English-speaking countries it has replaced "election" to eternal damnation or eternal bliss in even the Calvinist-derived churches, and in Europe and elsewhere it is still penetrating them. This and the Quaker doctrine of perfection together became cornerstones of Methodism.

Howard Brinton has defined the Quaker position[12] by saying that Calvinistic theology "emphasizes human depravity and insists that salvation is the miracle of God's grace in which man, as man, because of the evil of his nature, can perform no part." "The position of Robert Barclay, who set the pattern for early Quaker thought," he says, "was intermediate between the two poles of Hegelian idealism and neo-Calvinism. Barclay was pessimistic regarding what he called 'natural' man's present condition, but optimistic in respect to man's capacity for regeneration and union with God even in this life. He thought that with divine help, man might, as God's creation, become perfected here and now."

Luther's primarily three-pronged assault on the faith of Roman Catholicism (justification by faith, an emphasis on

---

[10] As John Brown, the Congregationalist, grouped them in his *Quakerisme, the Path-way to Paganisme*, Edinburgh, Cairns, 1678.

[11] See p xxxv.

[12] In his Introduction, op cit, p ix.

preaching, and denial of all but three sacraments[13]) found as little reception in Quakerism as Quakerism has had in Lutheran countries.[14] Although twentieth-century Quakers talk little about justification, nevertheless Barclay's treatment of the subject is a review of the whole controversy in the century following Luther's battlecry. Justification through the righteousness of Christ might well be the name for the Quaker version of this doctrine (as indeed it was called by Samuel Fisher in 1660). This made room for the Atonement, and shifted the emphasis from the antagonism over works, placing it instead in sanctification, or holiness of life — what modern Quakers probably mean when they state the possibility of making all of life sacramental.

[13] He originally included penance. On p 132 of *The Babylonian Captivity of the Church*, he says: "To begin with, I must deny that there are seven sacraments, and for the present maintain there are but three: baptism, penance, and the bread." However, by p 258 he had decided to restrict the term "sacrament" to "those promises which have signs attached to them," and limited these to "baptism and the bread." Page references are to *Three Treatises*, Martin Luther, © 1960 by The Fortress Press, Philadelphia.

[14] Lutheranism had its own spiritual reformation in the movement called Pietism which bore some superficial resemblances to Quakerism. But apparently neither movement owes much, if anything, to the other. Philip Jacob Spener's *Pia Desideria*, which sparked it, was published in 1675, a year before Barclay's *Apology*.

Theodore G. Tappert, who translated it into English for the first time, in an edition published by Fortress Press, Philadelphia, 1964, ignores Quakerism in his discussion of the "revival of moral and religious earnestness" of the 17th and 18th c., even though he considers English Puritanism, Roman Catholic Jansenism, and Hasidist Judaism as evidences of this. He also considers John Bunyan, the Dutch Reformed Willem Teelinck, Zinzendorf, Wesley, Gilbert Tennant, and the Roman Catholic Blaise Pascal "participants in a common historical climate." The only reference to Quakers in the introduction is the statement that Spener was called "a Quaker, a Rosicrucian, a chiliast, a fanatic" because he was reluctant to disown the radical excesses of the extremists in his movement. Spener himself says in the text (p 47) that he is "alarmed and ashamed" that "the teaching of an earnest, inner godliness" is so strange and unfamiliar that those who cultivate it are suspected of being "secret papists, Weigelians, or Quakers."

The deadness of Lutheran churches of the period was so great that a distinguished theologian received express praise in his funeral service "for never having slept in church" (quoted by Tappert from Paul Grünberg's 3-vol study of Spener, Göttingen, 1893-1906, vol 1, p 27).

Luther had rigorously stamped out any emphasis upon inwardness or mysticism, saying: "Try not to see even Jesus in glory until you have seen Him crucified" and "as He was and walked on earth" (Lee, op cit, p 33). When a band of three Zwickau prophets visited him, and appealed to the Spirit as authority, he answered (ibid, p 32) in his more characteristic vernacular: "I slap your spirit on the snout."

THE DOCTRINE OF PERFECTION

Barclay's doctrine of perfection and its correlative, perseverance, were adopted by a major part of English-speaking Protestantism — partly through Methodism, partly through the British "Higher Life Movement" and the more or less parallel Keswick movement, and partly through fresh contacts with Quakerism. Warfield's monumental study of perfectionism[15] says of the Quaker variety that "that taught by Wesley shows such similarity, even in details and modes of expression that a mistaken attempt has been made to discover an immediate genetic connection between them." In view of Wesley's other appropriations, which were not as widely admitted in Warfield's day,[16] the search does not seem as "mistaken" now, although it should be pointed out that Quakerism stressed corporate, as well as personal, obedience.

Warfield does specifically credit Quakerism for much of the "mystical perfectionism" that continually arose in nineteenth century America. He terms it "direct infection." However, he finds it difficult to determine how much stemmed from reading Barclay's *Apology* "which had long since become the Quaker 'classic,' and was not suffered to mold on dusty shelves, or from contact with those who carried forward his teachings in living tradition. Barclay was not the first to frame them, nor the only accessible source from which they could be derived. And this may illustrate the difficulty in determining how far Quaker influences co-operated in producing the perfectionism of nineteenth century America. It was there. It was *vera causa;* but the extent of its contribution to the effect is indeterminate."[17]

[15] Benjamin Breckenridge Warfield was Professor of Didactic and Polemic Theology at Princeton Theological Seminary. His 2-vol *Perfectionism,* N. Y., Oxford, 1931, posthumously published, reprinted articles on various aspects of the subject which originally appeared in theological journals. This quotation is from vol 1, p 3, on "Ritschl the Rationalist." A one-volume 464-page abridgment published by the Presbyterian and Reformed Publishing Co., Philadelphia, 1958, unfortunately omits much of the fairly extensive Quaker material found in the 2-vol ed.

[16] See fn p xxxiv. In addition to the borrowings indicated there, the recent *History of the Methodist Church in Great Britain,* Rupert Davies, Gordon Rupp, general editors, London, Epworth, 1965, vol 1, p 239, suggests that John Wesley's "knowledge of Quaker organization" may have been responsible for the quarterly circuit assemblies, although trimestrial oversight of the Methodist societies and gatherings of society stewards had been held for some time.

[17] Warfield, op cit, vol 2, p 340.

Ministry and worship, as described in the *Apology*, represent a radical reorientation in relation to both Protestant and Catholic forms, which early Quakerism considered equally apostate. Although Quaker analysts differ as to the degree to which that worship is primitivism, nonetheless it is closest to the only worship actually described in the New Testament. Whether this is because the NT record is fragmented, or because this was the only form of NT worship there was, is still open to conjecture. Certainly there are good rational reasons for considering the Johannine gospel largely liturgical in intent or derivation (as Oscar Cullman does[18]). But the stubborn fact remains that traditional Quaker worship is the closest to what is actually described in the Pauline epistles, 1 Cor 14:26-33 and elsewhere.[19]

In making comparisons with forms of worship that have evolved in other churches, one cannot ignore the semi-contemplative method which the individual Quaker worshipper employs, but under a sense of inward communion and with prophetic expectation. This is a roundabout way of stating that there seem to be points of Roman Catholic contact in the "method" and "sense" of worship, if not in the expectation.

When it came to ministry, the lay-clerical dichotomy was ignored by the Quakers. They observed that the concepts of "laity" and "clergy" are unscriptural. The Greek *laos* meant "people" and was generally used to refer to all of the people of God, and the single NT use of the word *kleros* in 1 Pet 5:3 is translated "heritage" in the KJ ("those in your charge," in the RSV, "charges" in the Cath-CCD, and "those who are allotted to your care" in the NEB). The passage advocates example, rather than domineering. Quakers noted the increasing "clericalization" of the church in history and set up instead a "universal ministry." The present writer has seen nothing which claims that this was derived from Luther's doctrine of "the priesthood of all believers." Although Fox's terminology comes close, the context seems to indicate little dependence.

Quakerism also had a "specialized ministry" — those particularly gifted, who were called, ordained, prepared, and supplied unmediatedly by the Holy Spirit — which was surely

[18] *Early Christian Worship*, Studies in Biblical Theology No. 10. London, SCM Press, 1953.

[19] As the *Interpreter's Bible* duly notes in Clarence Tucker Craig's exegesis and John Short's exposition of 1 Cor 14:26-33.

unique in concept. While some Protestants have emphasized
the divine call to the ministry, this has almost always been
coupled with professionalized training and ecclesiastical ordination. The relatively recent sacralization of professional edu-
cators as especially equipped for ministry among Friends is
more difficult to explain in a group which began with such
high praise for the ministry of illiterate men. Under present
economic stresses "part-time ministry" or ministry as a second
vocation may seem less "practical" than it did, but it is certainly no less relevant. The insistence that ministry is the work
of all of the people of God has been re-emphasized both by
the World Council of Churches' Faith and Order statements
and by Vatican II. Quakerism is finding increasing need for
executive or administrative assistance for the laity, and Protestantism is stressing the equipping function of the "professional"
ministry.[20] To that extent, they are coming together, but it
would seem unfortunate to lose a living demonstration that an
all-lay church can function.

The Quaker position on the sacraments, shared to some
extent by Salvationists, who also have no outward baptism and
communion, is now in the ecumenical forefront. At first glance
it seems "heretical" to more traditional Christians, but nonetheless challenges them on the significance of these rites. Whether
it will eventually prevail over the varying interpretations of the
number and significance of outward sacraments is a matter for
determination by the Holy Spirit. Although many a modern
mind balks at the idea of outward sacraments,[21] many a modern ecclesiast seems equally adamant about reinterpretation.
Roman Catholic sacramental theology, however, has recently
come alive and is doing some of the most constructive study
and rethinking in this area.[22]

[20] That is, that the chief function of the clergy is to equip the laity
for their ministry, both "in the world" and in the church.

[21] Emil Brunner's *Our Faith* is apologetic on this subject in both
senses of the word, starting the treatment of sacraments with a long defense against those who find them meaningless.

[22] The Jesuits Bernard Cooke and Bernard Leeming, the French Ora-
torian Louis Bouyer, and the Dutch Dominican Edward Schillebeeckx have
been particularly constructive in this field and have extensive bibliogra-
phies. *Transignification* is being examined at the hypothetical level, and
although the much-discussed encyclical *Mysterium Fidei* (1965) re-
established *transubstantiation* as the norm for the faithful, it looked with
favor upon further examination by theologians.

THE ROLE OF CONSCIENCE IN THE STATE AND CHURCH

At a time when church and state are striking a new balance in most countries, and Christendom (where Christianity has been the "dominant" faith) is a thing of the past, Barclay's fourteenth proposition is of particular interest. So, too, is the content on the role of the individual conscience in relation to the state, as well as that on the centrality of conscience as it applies to morality and ethics. The role of the religious group with reference to the individual is dealt with — yet the old, old stereotype of Quakerism as rampant individualism still dies hard.

Nevertheless, in spite of all the "checks and balances" and the guidance which a group can provide, the individual conscience in those pioneering souls who are willing to step out ahead of society in general is the growing edge in the applicational aspects of faith. This is equivalent to saying that in the seventeenth century casuistry had already yielded to contextualism for Quakers. Broad principles — and the guidance and counsel of the church — were the framework in which the individual found his "concerns," and his rationale for day to day existence.

Tenderness of conscience toward all aspects of life and all of humanity frequently gave the Quaker earlier awareness than his mainstream Christian brethren of the problems old and new which human beings face, and led to "concern" to do something about them.[23] Empathy was an unknown word, but not an unknown emotion, among early Friends. The flexibility of behavior which in nearly every situation demanded a reflection on ultimate principles sometimes led to apparently contradictory acts, but it almost never led to a faith that was lacking in the application of Christian love.

Barclay's final proposition covers what one Quaker commentator has so far misunderstood as to call the "trivialities" of Quaker behavior. Hat honor, honorifics, the taking of oaths,

---

[23] Friends' concern for the abolition of slavery in America began at least as early as 1688 with a minute of the German Quakers in Germantown, Pa. Howard Brinton, op cit, documents the steps leading to complete elimination of slave-holding among Friends themselves, and then from society in general. This was achieved by Friends in Pennsylvania and New Jersey by 1776 and by other Friends groups in America soon afterward.

The part played by Friends in England is well documented in the article, "antislavery," in the 14th ed of the *Encyc. Brit.*

and objection to tithes may seem dated and quaint today, but this strange bundle is still a never-ending call to integrity in all aspects of human relations. These facets of Quaker "character" were also responsible for swinging the pendulum of individual freedom in Restoration England back toward democracy at a time when Puritan excesses seemed the ideal justification for aristocratic reassertion. Indeed, every effort was being made then to return to the pre-Cromwellian elegances and dominances.

To this, Quakers offered a stiff-necked but non-violent resistance. Imprisonments, distraints of property, death, and all manner of sufferings could not sway them from treating all persons with equal courtesy. Hats stayed on even before kings, and if "O, King" was respectful enough a salutation for the biblical kings, it was good enough for King Charles II or King James II.

While the question of establishment, disestablishment, and anti-disestablishmentarianism (long reputed the longest word in the dictionary) is still being argued and is an issue in some current church-union proposals in Great Britain, the tithing aspect — the tax rock upon which the establishment rested and foundered — was settled earlier. Exemption for nonconformists, and, in time, abolition, evolved from the Quaker refusals to pay. The fury which Quaker behavior could unleash was never greater, according to Barclay, than when the clergy tried to enforce the collection of tithes. They became livid with rage when they found themselves in opposition to an unyielding group of people who allowed their property to be confiscated, their meeting houses to be torn down, and their bodies to be put in unbelievably filthy prisons.

The final proposition also deals with war, which is once again an issue for Christians. While Barclay deals at greater length with it in his treatise *On Universal Love,* the brief material in the *Apology* is good. One of Cadoux's studies on pacifism[24] names the *Apology* as the second major work in "what may be called the modern interest in the early Christian attitude to war." It was preceded only by the great *De Jure Belli ac Pacis* of Hugo Grotius, published in 1625.

[24] Cecil John Cadoux, *The Early Christian Attitude to War; a contribution to the history of Christian ethics,* London, Headley, 1919, p 6.
Roland Bainton's *Christian Attitudes Toward War and Peace,* N. Y., Abingdon, 1960, is a more recent definitive study.

REACTIONS OF OTHERS TO THE QUAKER POSITION

One of the best brief summations of the points at issue between Quakers and other Christians in the seventeenth century is by Henry J. Cadbury.[25] Although he was using the Quaker example as an analogy to explain the relationship of Jesus to Judaism, perhaps this can be reversed. Of the conflict that developed between Jesus and the temple authorities over the law, he says: "They knew they were defending the law, but Jesus hardly knew he was attacking it," and his followers "found themselves left with an unresolved problem on their hands in the matter of the scope and extent of Old Testament authority in the new movement.... Jesus most likely combined, much as the early Quakers did, an *independence of judgment* with a sense of *complete fidelity* to the official scriptures and their generally accepted authority [italics mine].

"In both instances," he continues, "their critics could not reconcile the two aspects of the combination and made the most of every implicit belittling of the traditional standard." The early Friends "criticized much in the Christianity around them, but they had no thought of condemning the Bible or of setting up the Light within as a separate or superior standard. To their opponents the situation appeared quite otherwise. The Protestants not only regarded the Bible as sacred but associated with its sacredness much of their own belief and practice. The Quaker attack on their churches, or sacraments, or ministry, or tithes, or saints' days seemed tantamount to attacking the Bible, while the independent teaching of the Quakers, no matter how much the Bible itself was quoted in their support, seemed the arrogant and blasphemous assertion of individual opinion."[26]

It was not of the Quakers, but of the 1640's and the multitude of dissenting groups that arose then in England, that

---

[25] The sequence of the quotations has been rearranged to reverse the analogy. They are from *The Peril of Modernizing Jesus*, London, S.P.C.K., 1962 (first published in 1937 by Macmillan), pp 173-174.

[26] The next two sentences, although not pertinent to the 17th c., are certainly applicable to the 20th: "The Quakers denied any conflict or contradiction but they left an unresolved problem to trouble their followers in later generations. On the other hand at various times individuals were driven almost to the extremes to which their enemies' suspicions thought they were tending, and they claimed the immediate and supreme authority for what they believed and practiced, irrespective of any scriptural sanction."

Thomas Comber (1645-1699), Dean of Durham, spoke when he referred to "those late unhappy times when Hell was broke loose." The first attack on the Quakers (whose genesis for tercentenary purposes was fixed at 1652, although there were earlier "events") was by John Bunyan of *Pilgrim's Progress* fame. He was a Baptist when he directed his first book, *Some Gospel Truths Opened*, against them in 1656.[27] Bunyan maintained that the Quakers ignored the historical Jesus, and he attacked their concept of universal grace. Edward Burrough answered in what Braithwaite has well classed as an "impassioned rhetorical style." In 1659 George Fox "made rejoinder to over a hundred pamphlets directed against Friends."

The next major dialogue was that in 1660 of Quaker Samuel Fisher with four eminent theologians: John Owen, D. D., late Dean of Christ's Church College, Oxford; Thomas Danson, M. A., onetime Fellow of Magdalene College, Oxford; John Tombes, B. D.; and one of the truly great ministers of the English Reformation, Richard Baxter.[28] Fisher titled his reply *Rusticus ad Academicos*, but out-academicized his opponents in nearly 800 closely-printed, well-documented and theologically astute, but incredibly boring quarto pages.[29] Edward Grubb has praised Fisher's view of scripture, particularly good on the canon. Some of the apocryphal books referred to are now discredited, but the references form an interesting sidelight on the knowledge of the time.[30] When one compares the literary

[27] Braithwaite, *Beginnings of Quakerism*, pp 286-288, gives some of the details of the charges and their defense by Edward Burrough.
Edward Grubb, "The Early Quakers," *Cambridge History of English Literature*, N. Y., Putnam, 1912, chap 4, vol 8, says that Quakers were not mentioned by name, but were the obvious target.
The volume of early Quaker literature is astounding. Luella M. Wright, *The Literary Life of the Early Friends 1650-1725*, N. Y., Columbia, 1932, p 8, has assembled some statistics based on known surviving material. She states that "within seven decades after 1653," 440 Quaker propagandists produced 2.678 separate titles varying in length from folio volumes of 1,000 pages to single broadsheets. She also notes the progressive multiplication of Quaker tracts from 23 in 1653, to 43 in 1654, and 70 in 1655, with the total number of titles mounting to "468 before the Restoration." She further states that the total number of copies circulated before 1725 has been estimated at 2,500,000 tracts by some and over 4,000,000 by others.

[28] See p 149 for biographical note.

[29] Fisher greatly overworked his favorite device, alliteration, with such gems as "talking of trivial temporal tittles" (p 46, 1677 ed), and "lightless labyrinths of your learning" (p 48).

[30] They are mentioned in Braithwaite, and Henry J. Cadbury has written on them, "Early Quakerism and Uncanonical Lore," *Harvard Theological Review*, vol 40, 1947, pp 177-204.

styles of this material, it is not difficult to see why Barclay's work achieved immediate recognition and why his *Apology* has remained the Quaker classic in its field.

George Eliot (1819-1880) considered the *Apology* "among the richest gems of our language," one which "touches our hearts fully as much as it pleases our fancy and our reason."[31] Voltaire's own comment is as cryptic as the comment of Andrew Pitt, which he quotes, is jejune. Voltaire called it "quite as good a work as it could be."[32] He remarks that the dedicatory epistle to Charles II, whose substance he skillfully compresses into a brief paragraph, "contains no base flatteries, but bold truths, and just counsels." He finds it "particularly astonishing" that even though the letter was written by an "obscure individual" (actually the Barclays were at least "petty nobility" and Barclay's mother, a Gordon, was a cousin of King Charles II) its purpose was achieved, and the persecution of Friends was halted for a time. Czar Peter the Great took a copy of the *Apology* to Russia to have it translated, although this was not done.[33]

By no means has all of the comment on the *Apology* been by way of literary appraisal. Sir Leslie Stephen, president of the Ethical Society and editor of the *Dictionary of National Biography*, called it "in many respects one of the most impressive theological writings of the century."[34] It has stood the test of time well enough for the Rev. T. A. Bampton of Frome, writing in 1940, to state that "among the stars of the theological firmament Robert Barclay may be reckoned one of the first

[31] *Journal of the Friends Historical Society*, vol 11, 1914, p 18, quoted from the 3-vol biography edited by her husband, J. W. Cross, vol 1, p 275 and p 18.

[32] Pitt called it "one of the best books that ever came out of the hand of man." The version used for all quotations is the critical translation by Wilson Frescoln, *Voltaire's Letters on the Quakers*, Philadelphia, Wm. H. Allen, 1953, pp 20 (Voltaire) and 11 (Pitt). The four letters on the Quakers are the first of his *Lettres sur les Anglais, ou lettres philosophiques*, written between 1726 and 1730 or 1731.

[33] See William Hubben, "Quakerism in Russia," *Friends Intelligencer*, vol 105, 6th month 19, 1948, pp 352-353. The article says of Peter the Great: "...when a delegation of Friends visited him — Gilbert Mollison and Thomas Story were among them — he condemned the Friends harshly for their pacifism. At the same time he promised to have Barclay's *Apology* translated into Russian, a project which was never carried out."

[34] In the item on Barclay, over his signature, in the *DNB*, vol 3, p 169, of the N. Y., Macmillan, 1885 ed.

magnitude."[35] The finest compliment of all came from Barclay's contemporary, the last of the Cambridge Platonists, John Norris (1657-1711), the rector of Bremerton, near Salisbury, who stated in his *Two Treatises Concerning the Divine Light* (1692):[36] "1 had rather engage against an hundred Bellarmins, Hardings, or Stapletons than with one Barclay."

Nonetheless, many were ready to pick up the challenge. Presbyterian John Brown wrote a railing and bitterly invective reply, which as Barclay rightly remarked was longer than the *Apology* itself. Brown admitted that "some will think I am too large" in answering everything "that he belched out against the truth," but knowing how these Quakers gloat over anything that is unanswered, he left "nothing untouched." Brown was so eager to get it into print (1677) that Barclay accused him of beguiling "those who pin their faith upon the Clergy's sleeve" by answering a book written in Latin that was "not extant in their mother tongue." Thus he may "pervert words as he will, draw consequences at pleasure, and make to himself what monsters best please his fancy."[37] He says that this made him "hasten an English edition" not one sheet of which was committed to the press until several weeks after Brown's book came out.

Brown charged that the "ministry of these locusts" is "Antichristian enmity to our Lord Jesus, his person, office, work, institutions, and to the whole of the blessed gospel." He alternated between laughter at the "presumptuous and ridiculously confident assertions" of the Quakers, and bemoaning this judgment of God upon his own denomination. About the only place he seems to have agreed with Barclay was in condemning Scholastic theology, which he said was "spun out by light, audacious, and too too philosophical brains."

Even before the Latin edition of the *Apology* had come off the press, Nikolaus Arnold, a "double Calvinist" of the Netherlands, had engaged in dialogue with Barclay's *Theological Theses*. There are a number of references to this *Exercitation* woven into the *Apology*, and Barclay's printed Latin reply is

[35] This is the opening sentence of his article, "Barclay on War," *Congregational Quarterly*, vol 18, pp 401-405. He is described as a Baptist in the *Bulletin of the Friends Historical Association* notice.

[36] Cited by Braithwaite, *Second Period of Quakerism*, as p 250 of the 2nd ed, 1727. Those named were outstanding Catholic apologists. Bellarmine is the best known (see biog fn p 133).

[37] Introduction to his own vindication of his *Apology*, *Works*, pp 722-723.

also extant, but the Arnold portion — which may have existed only in manuscript form — is apparently lost, in spite of the fact that Arnold's books are quite common in theological collections. Another dialogue with Adrian Paets, an Ambassador to Spain and an official of the Dutch East India Company, whom Barclay termed "a man of no mean account both in the learned and political" worlds is included in the printed *Works,* which also includes the Barclay portions of several other exchanges of a doctrinal nature. But perhaps the most effective dialogue that Barclay was to enter was posthumous — that with John Wesley.

THE RELATIONSHIP OF QUAKERISM TO METHODISM

The effect of the Methodist Revival of the late nineteenth century on Friends is well known. The introduction of pastors and "programmed worship" (now adopted by approximately two-thirds of the Quaker meetings in the United States) is generally attributed to the mass evangelization by the Methodists of that era, particularly in the Midwest. Less known is the earlier influence of Quakerism on Methodism, much of which resulted from Barclay's *Apology.*

Although John Wesley was by no means a mere copyist, he did reprint a couple of Quaker items, one of which he claimed as his own at several places in his writings.[38] This was Anthony Benezet's (1713-1784) *Some Historical Account of Guinea,* which this close associate of John Woolman in the Quaker anti-slavery movement had published in 1771 in Philadelphia. Wesley issued it in abridged form in 1774 under the title *Thoughts Upon Slavery.* It was reprinted and widely distributed in England and America. Outler states that Wesley made its "vivid sentiments" his own, and that Wesley's own part in the abolition of slavery was not inconsiderable.

Wesley referred to Barclay's *Apology* as "that solemn

---

[38] Albert C. Outler, *John Wesley,* N. Y., Oxford, 1964, deals with this in a fn pp 85-86 and cites *Letters,* VIII, 6, 7, 276 as evidence. This form of literary borrowing was not uncommon in that era and was considered a form of endorsement. Wesley according to Outler also reprinted without credit a *Calm Address to Our American Colonies* (1775); borrowed from Samuel Johnson, *A Treatise on Baptism* ... and *A Roman Catechism* abridged from a treatise of a similar title by Bishop John Williams of Chichester (1686).

trifle."[39] And although he told one person who joined the Quakers that he had "an honest heart but a weak head,"[40] he admitted in his *Journal*[41] that in London, at least, many "who once seemed to be pillars" had been shaken and were "hugely in love" with "that solemn trifle," and that he and his brother "were at the pains of reading [it] over ... with them" to re-settle them in the truth.

In his *Letter to a Person Lately Join'd with the People Call'd Quakers* (1748) he distinguishes between Quakers and their opinions. He says: "I do by no means intend to deny that many Quakers (so termed) are real Christians, men who have the mind that was in Christ. With some of them I count it a blessing to converse, and cannot but esteem them very highly in love." A rather generous estimate in an age that stressed polemics!

In spite of his general estimate of the *Apology*, Wesley by no means considered Barclay's thoughts on Calvin's doctrines of predestination and election as trifling. For although he thought on justification "just as Mr. Calvin does,"[42] he did not see eye to eye with him on predestination. He reprinted a con-densation of the portions of Propositions V and VI from Bar-clay's *Apology* dealing with that doctrine. Wesley's flair for editing was never better demonstrated. He carefully excised every superfluous word or phrase, eliminated the patristic and contemporary documentation, which was primarily of academic interest, in order to accelerate the flow of Barclay's prose. The interspersed material on the doctrine of the Inward Light of Christ, which was really a separate topic, was also omitted.

The result was a 26-page pamphlet[43] entitled *Serious Con-siderations on Absolute Predestination, extracted from a late author.* Originally published by Farley at Bristol in 1741, it was reissued in at least five other editions through 1816. It gave the significant content in about a fourth of the words of the original, and in most places was so close to the original

[39] *Journal,* Saturday. 11 May 1745 [*Works,* London, 1872, vol 1 (of 14), p 495].

[40] *Works,* X, 187.

[41] loc cit.

[42] Outler, op cit, p 30.

[43] No. 22 in Richard Green, *The Works of John and Charles Wesley, A Bibliography,* London, C. H. Kelly, 1896. Drew University Library very kindly permitted me to refer to their copy of this item.

wording that the differences can be determined only by close comparison.

In a letter to Charles Wesley, John states: "We presented a thousand [copies] of Barclay to Mr. Whitefield's congregation on Sunday. On Sunday next I propose to distribute a thousand more at the Foundery."[44] Whether there was any connection between this and the fact that Whitefield (generally acknowledged as the most skilled of the early Methodist evangelists) for a time became a Quaker and then returned to Methodism is unrecorded.

Wesley also engaged in a three-part dialogue with a Quaker who had quit the Methodist ranks.[45] Wesley conceded that "eight out of fifteen of Barclay's propositions" were "agreeable to scripture" and did not "differ from Christianity" and continued the fundamental doctrines of the Gospel. However, the mistake of one biographer who virtually made a Moravian of Wesley, or of others who have overemphasized the "Enthusiastic" or Anglican elements ought not to be counterbalanced here by an overly Quaker estimate of his doctrine. Just what was his relationship to these formative elements? An unkind critic did say, but unfairly, "that it was his destiny to kick away the three ladders on which he had risen to fame."[46] But a closer and more sympathetic examination of his writings leads to a more accurate judgment.

Outler's excellent synopsis of Wesley's theology[47] states that "the most distinctive single element . . . was the notion of 'Christian perfection'." In Wesley's hands "the Popish doctrine of Perfection, that they can live without sin, or that some of them can" (as Richard Baxter[48] characterized the beliefs of the Ranters "of greater sobriety" along with those of the Quak-

---

[44] *Works*, XII, 109.

[45] *A Letter to a Person Lately Join'd with the People Call'd Quakers, In Answer to a Letter Wrote by Him* (1748); answered by John Helton (1731[2?]-1817) in his *Reasons for Quitting the Methodist Society; Being a Defense of Barclay's Apology. In Answer to a Person Joined with the People Called Quakers*, 3rd ed corr, Dublin; Philadelphia, reprinted by Joseph Cruckshank, 1784.

[46] This is one of the least charitable and less astute judgments of Msgr. Knox's *Enthusiasm*, Oxford, 1962 ed, pp 465-466. However, mysticism rather than Quakerism may have been the third "ladder" that Knox had in mind.

[47] Outler, op cit, pp 27-32.

[48] Richard Baxter (1651-1691), *Practical Works*, vol 2, p 349, as quoted by Umphrey Lee, op cit, p 53.

ers), became "not a state, but a dynamic process." Saving faith was its beginning and sanctification its proper climax. Wesley left more room for "backsliding" than Barclay, holding that there was no level of spiritual achievement from which pride or self-will could not topple a person. But Barclay held a greater perfection possible than did Wesley.

Spiritual and ethical concerns were the primary motivation for Wesley's theologizing. "Opinions," he stated, "do not reach to the marrow of Christian truth." The Christian life is a means to a higher end — holiness, and the fullness of faith with its consecration of the entire self to God and to the neighbor in love. Like the Friends he emphasized that awareness of God's gracious presence was as real and unmistakable a perception as any sensory awareness might be — his theory of "religious knowledge" was a corollary of his view of "revelation."

Such second and deeper looks at Wesley's theology as Outler's have been difficult because Wesley did not systematize, but they have shown him to be a capable and consistent theologian who could assimilate the best elements from other systems.[49] Essentially he synthesized Moravian, Pietistic, and continental mystical elements with an already broad-Anglican background. True to his Anglican heritage he never let go of its Catholic elements. He not only published numerous editions of Thomas à Kempis' *Imitation*, but he was disappointed that few Catholics responded to his evangelization of Ireland.[50]

Certainly Wesley never made the error of lapsing into Quakerism as the still unknown churchman who wrote under the pseudonym of John Smith[51] warned him that he might.

---

[49] Although he had his less weighty moments, as when he delved into science or pharmacology. He published *The Cause and Cure of Earthquakes*, a sermon preached from Psalm 46:8, London, 1750, 24 pp. after the Lisbon disaster of that year.

Richard Green, op cit, comments on item No. 202, *The Desideration; or Electricity Made Plain and Useful* (1760), that he had "strong faith in the efficacy of electricity as a curative agent," and that when asked why he "meddled with electricity," he replied, "to do as much good as I can."

Boiled nettles, bruised garlic, and powdered brimstone mixed with the white of an egg are other prescriptions recorded in Knox, op cit, p 425.

[50] In his *Short Method of Converting All the Roman Catholics in the Kingdom of Ireland* (1752), it was his opinion that only the Apostles were holier and wiser than the Irish Catholic clergy. If the (Anglican) priests of the Church of Ireland, he said, will only "live like the Apostles, preach like the Apostles, and the thing is done."

[51] Outler, op cit, p 4, opens his introduction with an appraisal of Wesley from one of the six letters written between September, 1745, and March, 1748, by this rumored archbishop, who was at least "a responsible

There is a fruitful field for research, however (and it is hoped that the present edition of Barclay's *Apology* might provide one appropriate basis), in comparing early Quakerism and early Methodism in depth. Both grew out of an Anglican environment. Both cherished their Catholic heritage. Both had or later developed a fondness for continental mystics — particularly the Catholic Quietists: Fenelon, Mme. Guyon, and Molinos. Both preferred "perfection" as their term for Christian maturation. Both have been classed as "Enthusiasts."[52] Both stressed everyday application and disparaged theological abstractions.

Yet, Quakerism appeared solemn and uninteresting to most Methodists — although Wesley had great respect for Quaker character[53] — and Methodism appeared overemotional and too verbal for most Quakers. The degree of sophistication or popularization in Methodism or Quakerism varied from doctrine to doctrine and neither one could claim a monopoly of either quality. But perhaps, after all, they are denominational "cousins" who could profit by becoming better acquainted.

THIS EDITION OF THE APOLOGY

Indeed, a hope for closer ecumenical relations and greater depth in unity with all Christians was at the heart of the years of effort which have gone into the preparation of this edition of the *Apology*. It is hoped that the straddle between scholar-

---

churchman and a good theologian." The anonymous correspondent said that the devil's skill was not enough to make Tertullian a profligate, but it did make him a Montanist. He warned Wesley that if he allowed "perceptible inspiration" he ought to be a Quaker, for except for that one false principle he found Barclay's system to be very "consistent and coherent."

[52] Not only by the far from objective Knox opus already cited, but by others trying to cope with the great attention given to spirituality and the experiential side of religion.

[53] In addition to the Wesley compliment already quoted, John Walsh, in "Methodism at the End of the Eighteenth Century," in Davies and Rupp, eds, op cit, vol 1, p 310, notes that if Wesley did not originate the slogan about cleanliness being next to godliness, he certainly popularized it. In enjoining his people to "be cleanly," he told them: "In this let the Methodists take pattern by the Quakers. Avoid all nastiness, dirt, slovenliness, both in your person, clothes, house and all about you... Mend your clothes, or I shall never expect to see you mend your lives. Let none ever see a ragged Methodist."
The article continues: "Like the Quakers before them, Methodists found that the moral virtues of honesty and hard work were also economic virtues, bringing their temporal as well as their spiritual reward. In a rapidly expanding society, strict Methodists were much sought after by employers anxious to find a reliable man for a position of trust."

ship sufficient for the ecumenist and easy readability for the average Friend has not been too great and that both will find the results satisfactory and inviting for their own purposes. The *Apology* was first published in Latin in 1676 and in English in 1678.[54] It provided such a satisfactory interpretation that other comprehensive and formal statements of the Quaker faith on the level of systematic theology have been generally, and somewhat naively, regarded as superfluous.

However, the hardening of the linguistic arteries which overtook the King James Version of the Bible has taken an even greater toll on the English edition of Barclay, since its value lay less in customary and majestic phrases and more in lucid prose. The several new and excellent translations of the Bible have restored it to a place among works classified as "living literature." But, although the English edition of Barclay's *Apology* has been faithfully kept in print since its first appearance, it is a rare person today who has been a "cover-to-cover reader." The many historical, patristic, theological, or biblical references are obscure without a considerable quantity of reference works. The impediments to smooth reading which these handicaps and the language barriers provide give a rather quaint and disconnected effect to what was originally highly skilled writing.

The present volume began merely as an attempt to put the substance of Barclay into briefer compass and modern English — a runner's digest, as it were.[55] But less than 100 pages

[54] The original Latin title was: *Theologiae verè Christianae Apologia.* Pro Jacob Claus. Bibliopola, habitante Amstelodami, veneunt praeterea Londini, apud Benjamin Clark, Roterdami apud Isaacum Naeranum, Francofurti apud Henricum Betkium, 1676, 4to, pp (24), 374, (25).
One of the two English editions of 1678 was: *An Apology For the True Christian Divinity, As the same is held forth, and preached by the People, Called, in Scorn, Quakers:* Being a full Explanation and Vindication of their Principles and Doctrines, by many Arguments, deduced from Scripture and right Reason, and the Testimony of famous Authors, both ancient and modern, with a full answer to the strongest objections usually made against them, Presented to the King. Written and Published in Latine, for the information of Strangers by Robert Barclay. And now put into our own Language, for the benefit of his Country-men. [No publisher or place.] Printed in the Year 1678. 8 in. high, pp (22), 392, (22).
[55] Several attempts have been made to epitomize Barclay's *Apology.* In 1948 Fleanore Price Mather's *Barclay in Brief* appeared as Pendle Hill Pamphlet No. 28. It is a skillful selection which captures much of the message of the original, although it is handicapped by the original wording. It has recently been reprinted.
In 1948 J. Philip Wragge did a very satisfactory analysis of *The Faith of Robert Barclay* which was published in London by the Friends Home

had been dealt with when a deep appreciation developed for the style in which Barclay wrote and the logic that he employed. It began to seem a pity to depart thus far from the original, and a compromise was effected.

It was decided to treat the original as if it were a manuscript submitted to an editor today. Where the pace needed acceleration, abridgement would be used. In the few rare paragraphs where the author's thinking had not been fought through, and he fell back on "academic prose," which is obviously not a new invention, this would be reworded. Where his word order demonstrated some of the German ancestry of the English language, or followed the Latin too closely, it would not be considered criminal to break up the sentences into more fluid current English.[56] Paul's epistles have been disentangled in this way by most of the newer Bible translations, so it did not seem "sacrilegious" to do it to Barclay.

Except where points are drawn rather fine, as in critical doctrinal or theological statements, it has seemed better to be more faithful to Barclay's meaning than to use word-for-word substitution, although this should not be taken to imply a loose paraphrase. The process might better be described as "transphrasing" — something between translation (from an earlier form of English) and what is generally meant by paraphrase.

Barclay is not, and I hope never will be, a Quaker "bible" which will be used as a source of proof-texts for ammunition in disputation. Where a theological doctrine was of greater interest in Barclay's day, or the argument seemed dated — the

Service Committee. Whereas Mather's *Barclay in Brief* uses selected passages without breaks or page references, in the interest of continuous reading, Wragge's study is a scholarly, annotated analysis of Barclay's theology in approximately 100 pages. Again, however, it is handicapped by the original language.

A Little Apology (The Gist of Barclay's) by Charles M. Kelly was published in 1960 (rev 1963) by The Barclay Press, Newberg, Oregon. In the same category as Mather and Wragge, it compresses the major points of the *Apology* into 81 pages. The linguistically difficult passages have been simplified in structure and modernized in vocabulary to provide "a readable synopsis."

Howard Brinton masterfully interwove the essence of Barclay into his *Friends for 300 Years*, published by Harper in 1952 and now available as a Pendle Hill paperback. By careful combination of less antiquated phrases with his own wording he was able to make much of Barclay more readily understandable to modern readers.

[56] Excellent comment on the changes in the English language from 1611 — a mere 65 years before the *Apology* was written — to the present is given in the preface to the Revised Standard Version of the Bible.

latter was surprisingly rare — it seemed advisable to abridge or eliminate. In the many fine pages where Barclay is truly inspirational, the changes have been kept to a minimum and the feel of his prose has been maintained. He had a particular gift for editing biblical quotations into vernacular phrases, which brings them home in a way that no other device can.

Because of the limitations of a single individual, even of one whose scholarly attainments might be considerably greater than mine, it has seemed best in a work which touches on so many different academic disciplines to rely on the value judgments contained in standard works for the footnote comments. This may be unimaginative, and considerably less than "perfect," but at least within the possibility of accomplishment.

There was one exception to this. The notes on Roman Catholic points of doctrine had the benefit of review by a recognized scholar, Father Bowman (see Personal Acknowledgments, p xii). It is hoped that this will compensate for the few remarks about Catholicism which Barclay made which have not lost their sting in three centuries. I hope that readers of all denominations will give me the benefit of their criticisms and corrections, in the event of future editions.

Dean Freiday

November, 1966

NOTE: Two minor corrections were made in the fifth printing. On pages xiv and xix, the Scots College in Paris is no longer described as "a Jesuit institution." Information received in 1970 from Fr. Edmund Lamalle, S.J., in charge of the order's archives in Rome, indicates clearly that it was not, and that the Robert Barclay (1633-1661) who attended the Jesuit Scots College in Rome and died at Reggio di Calabria was a cousin of the Apologist.

On page 38, a garbled citation of Aquinas's *Summa Theologica* now reads correctly.

Because of cost considerations, male-gender references in the text or older version Bible quotations have been allowed to stand. Making these non-sexist would require costly resetting of the entire volume.

Barclay's APOLOGY

IN MODERN ENGLISH

R. B. WISHES SALVATION FOR THE FRIENDLY READER

In confidence that with God's help there is nothing that I cannot do, I have undertaken to declare and defend the truth, to whose service I have devoted myself and all that is mine.

Some time ago, I published certain theological propositions, which gave the chief principles and doctrines of truth in brief form. Since these have apparently been profitable to some and have been far more widely received than I had anticipated, it seems fitting to expand that labor. Although there were some who criticized that work through envy, nevertheless, it has prevailed sufficiently to remove in part the false and monstrous opinions concerning our doctrines which the lies and malice of our adversaries had implanted in the minds of some.

Being actuated by the same Divine Spirit and with the same intention of propagating the truth which motivated the publishing of the propositions themselves, I have felt it appropriate to explain them more fully at this time, and to defend them with certain arguments.

I am not concerned if my method of writing seems different, or even contrary to that which is commonly used by theologians. For, I confess that I am not only no imitator and admirer of the Schoolmen,[1] but that I oppose and despise them. The Christian religion is far from being made better by their labors. In fact, it has been greatly harmed.

Neither have I written this work to accomodate it to "itching ears."[2] It is written for those who wish to embrace the

---

[1] An older term for Scholasticism, "a method of philosophical and theological speculation which aims at a better understanding of revealed truths, that is, as an attempt by intellectual processes, by analogy and by defining, co-ordinating, and systematizing the data of faith, to attain to a deeper penetration into the meaning of Christian doctrine." — *O.D.C.C.*, p 1225.

Nevertheless, according to Henry J. Cadbury's supplemental note, p 685 of the 2nd ed of Wm. C. Braithwaite's *The Second Period of Quakerism*, Cambridge Press, 1961, an editorial in the *Friend* (London) for 10th Month 1846 objected to the scholastic form of Barclay's *Apology*. The editorial proposed a reissue of it with changes, but this met with strong objections.

[2] 2 Tim 4:3.

sublime notions of truth with their hearts, rather than with their heads.

What I have written comes more from what I have heard with the ears of my soul. I have declared what my inward eyes have seen and what my hands have handled of the Word of Life. It is what has been inwardly manifested to me of the things of God. I have been less concerned with eloquence and excellence of speech than I have with demonstrating the efficacy and operation of truth. If I sometimes fail in the niceties of speech, it is unimportant. For I am writing here not as a grammarian, nor as an orator, but as a Christian. Instead of grammatical rules, I have followed the certain rule of the Divine Light and of the Holy Scriptures.

In conclusion, what I have written is written not to satisfy the wisdom and knowledge, or rather, the vanity of this world, but to starve and oppose it. This is obvious from the little preface prefixed to the theological propositions which follow.

R. B.

To the Clergy, of every kind into whose hands these theses may come, but particularly to the Doctors, Professors, and Students of Divinity in the Universities and Schools of Great Britain, whether Episcopal,[1] Presbyterian, or otherwise;

Robert Barclay, a Servant of the Lord God, and one of those who in derision are called Quakers, wishes sincere repentance, leading to the acknowledgment of the Truth.

Friends:

The following propositions are offered so that you may perceive the simple naked truth which man's wisdom has rendered so obscure and mysterious. They should be read and considered in the fear of the Lord to remove some of the burden of those great and voluminous treatises which have been written on this subject; and whose empty quarrelsome comments have rendered truth a hundred times darker and more intricate than it actually is.

Theological schooling, which is considered of such great significance, does not bring a man one whit nearer to God. Even though it requires half a lifetime of study, it does not make a man any less wicked, or any more righteous, than he was.

That is why God has laid aside those of this world who are wise and learned and accustomed to philosophical arguments. Instead, he has chosen a few contemptible and illiterate instruments, as he did with the fishermen of old, to publish his pure and naked truth. He has used them to clear away the mists and fogs with which the clergy have beclouded it, in order to receive admiration and maintenance. According to the grace that has been given me as one of several whom God has chosen to be dispensers of this Gospel, it seemed good, and appropriately my duty, to offer you these propositions.

Although they are short, yet they are weighty and comprehend a great deal. They declare what the true foundation of knowledge is, especially of that knowledge which leads to Life Eternal. That is what is witnessed to here, and the testimony to it is left to the Light of Christ in your consciences.

Farewell,

                                        R. B.

[1] The original word was "Prelatical."

THEOLOGICAL THESES

PROPOSITION 1 — THE TRUE FOUNDATION OF KNOWLEDGE

Since the height of all happiness is the true knowledge of God ("This is eternal life: to know thee who alone art truly God, and Jesus Christ whom thou hast sent." John 17:3 NEB), it is primary and essential that this foundation of knowledge be properly understood and believed.

PROPOSITION 2 — INWARD AND UNMEDIATED REVELATION

Since "no one knows the Son but the Father, and no one knows the Father but the Son and those to whom the Son may choose to reveal him" (Mat 11:27 NEB), and since the revelation of the Son is in and by the Spirit, therefore it is only through the testimony of the Spirit that the true knowledge of God has been, is, and can be revealed.

It was by the motions of his own Spirit that God converted the chaos of this world into that wonderful order which has existed since the beginning, and created man a living soul, to rule and govern it. It was by the revelation of the same Spirit that he has always manifested himself to the sons of men, whether they were patriarchs, prophets, or apostles.

These revelations of God by the Spirit, whether by outward voices and appearances, dreams, or inward objective manifestations in the heart, were formerly the main purpose of faith. This should continue to be so, since the object of faith is the same in all ages regardless of the variations in form by which it is administered. Moreover, these divine inward revelations are considered by us to be absolutely necessary for the building up of true faith. But, this does not mean that they can, or ever do, contradict the outward testimony of the scriptures, or proper and sound judgment.

Nevertheless, it does not follow that these divine revelations should be subjected either to the outward testimony of the scriptures, or of the natural reason of man, as more positive or more noble rules or touchstones. These divine revelations and

*inward illuminations possess their own clarity and serve as their
own evidence. They force the well-disposed mind to assent and
they inevitably move it in that direction in the same way that
the common principles of natural truths move and incline the
mind toward a natural agreement.*

PROPOSITION 3 — THE SCRIPTURES

*From the revelations of the Spirit of God to the faithful
have come the scriptures of Truth, which contain: (1) a faithful historical account of the behavior of God's people in various ages and of the many unusual and remarkable acts of God
which they experienced, (2) a prophetic account of some things
already past, and of others yet to come, (3) a full and adequate
account of all of the chief principles of the doctrine of Christ
which were spoken, or which were written, by the motions of
God's Spirit at various times in treasured declarations, exhortations, and maxims which were given to certain churches and
their pastors.*

*Nevertheless, because the scriptures are only a declaration
of the source, and not the source itself, they are not to be considered the principal foundation of all truth and knowledge.
They are not even to be considered as the adequate primary
rule of all faith and practice.[2] Yet, because they give a true and
faithful testimony of the source itself, they are and may be
regarded as a secondary rule that is subordinate to the Spirit,
from which they obtain all their excellence and certainty. We
truly know them only by the inward testimony of the Spirit or,
as the scriptures themselves say, the Spirit is the guide by which
the faithful are led into all Truth (John 16:13). Therefore,
according to the scriptures, the Spirit is the first and principal
leader (Rom 8:14). Because we are receptive to the scriptures,
as the product of the Spirit, it is for that very reason that the
Spirit is the primary and principal rule of faith.*

PROPOSITION 4 — THE CONDITION OF MAN IN THE FALL

*All of the descendants of Adam, that is, all of mankind, are
in a fallen, demoralized, and deadened state. They are deprived
of sensing or feeling the inward testimony or seed of God (Rom
5:12, 15). They are subject instead to the seed of the serpent,*

---

[2] Barclay's own word was "manners."

*sown in men's hearts while they remain in this natural and cor-
rupted state. Not only their words and deeds, but their thoughts
are evil in the sight of God while they remain in this state. In
this state man can know nothing correctly. Even his thoughts
of God and spiritual matters are unprofitable to himself and
others until he has been disjoined from this evil seed and has
been united to the Divine Light.*

*In so saying, we reject the Pelagian and Socinian errors
which exalted a natural light....*[3]

*However, we do not impute the evil seed to infants until
they have actually been joined to it by their own transgression.
All of us are by nature "the children of wrath." "We all lived
our lives in sensuality, and obeyed the promptings of our own
instincts and notions. In our natural condition, we, like the
rest, lay under the dreadful judgment of God. But God, rich
in mercy, for the great love he bore us, brought us to life with
Christ even when we were dead in our sins; it is by his grace
you are saved;"* (Eph 2:3-5 NEB).

PROPOSITIONS 5 AND 6 — THE UNIVERSAL REDEMPTION BY CHRIST,
AND ALSO THE SAVING AND SPIRITUAL LIGHT BY WHICH EVERY
MAN IS ENLIGHTENED

PROPOSITION 5:   *God, out of his infinite love, takes "no
pleasure in the death of the wicked man"* (Ezek 18:32, 33:11),
*but God has given his only Son, that whoever "has faith in him
may not die, but have eternal life"* (John 3:16 NEB). *He is
"the real light which enlightens every man"* (John 1:9 NEB).
*And makes visible everything that is exposed to the light. And
teaches all temperance, righteousness, and godliness. And enlightens the hearts of all to prepare them for salvation.*

*It is this light which reproves the sin of every individual,
and if it were not resisted it would effect the salvation of all men.*

*This light is no less universal than the seed of sin, being
purchased by his death who tasted death for everyone: "For as
in Adam all die, so in Christ all will be made to live"* (1 Cor
15:22 Cath-CCD).

---

[3] The statement: *"We also reject the errors of Roman Catholics and
of most Protestants who maintain that the true grace of God is not necessary for a man to be a true minister of the gospel."* has been omitted here,
since it is more appropriately dealt with in PROP. X, 17. — ED.

PROPOSITION 6: *In this hypothesis, all of the objections to the universality of Christ's saving death are easily resolved.* *It is not necessary to fall back on the ministry of the angels, or those other miraculous means which they say God uses to manifest the doctrine and history of Christ's passion to those who live in parts of the world where the outward preaching of the gospel is unknown. Just as many of the ancient philosophers may have been saved, so may some of those today whom providence has placed in the remote parts of the world where the knowledge of the history* [i. e. the historical Jesus] *is lacking, be made partakers of the divine mystery if they do not resist the manifestation of grace which is given to everyone for his benefit* (1 Cor 12:7). *This doctrine is established and confirmed against the objections of all who deny it.* There is an evangelical and saving light and grace in everyone, and the love and mercy of God toward mankind were universal, both in the death of his beloved Son, the Lord Jesus Christ, and in the manifestation of the light in the heart.

Therefore, Christ has tasted death for everyone (Heb 2:9) — not merely for all kinds of men, as some foolishly say, but for everyone of every kind. The benefit of his suffering is extended not only to those who have a well-defined outward knowledge of his death and sufferings, as these are declared in the scriptures, but even to those who by some unavoidable accident were excluded from the benefit of this knowledge.

We willingly admit that this knowledge is very beneficial and inspiring, but not absolutely necessary for those from whom God himself has withheld it. For, if they allow his seed and light to enlighten their hearts, they may become partakers of the mystery of his death, even though they have not heard of it. In this light, which Christ himself affirms is available to all, communion is enjoyed with the Father and with the Son. Wicked men can become holy and lovers of that power by whose inward and hidden touches they feel themselves turned from evil to good. By it they can learn to treat others as they would like to be treated themselves.

It is false and erroneous to teach denial of the fact that Christ died for all men, and yet require outward knowledge of this fact as a prerequisite to salvation. Those who assert universal redemption with this limitation have not taken full account of the scriptures in which our doctrine is very well supported and clearly explained — Gen 6:3; Deut 30:14; John 1: 7-9, 16; Rom 10:8; and Titus 2:11.

PROPOSITION 7 — JUSTIFICATION

*For those who do not resist the light, but receive it, it be-
comes a holy, pure, and spiritual birth in them. It produces
holiness, righteousness, purity, and all those other blessed fruits
that are acceptable to God.
Jesus Christ is formed in us by this holy birth and by it he
does his work in us. By it we are sanctified and we are justified
in the sight of God. Paul has said: "But you have been through
the purifying waters; you have been dedicated to God and justified through the name of the Lord Jesus Christ and the Spirit
of our God." (1 Cor 6:11 NEB).
It is not by works produced by our own wills, or by good
works themselves, but by Christ, who is not only the gift and
the giver, but the cause which produces these effects in us. While
we were still enemies, he saved us and justified us in this way.
Titus 3:5 RSV says: "He saved us, not because of deeds done by
us in righteousness, but in virtue of his own mercy, by the washing of regeneration and renewal in the Holy Spirit."*

PROPOSITION 8 — PERFECTION [OR THE ACHIEVEMENT OF SPIRITUAL
MATURITY]

*He in whom this pure and holy birth occurs in all its full-
ness, finds that death and sin are crucified and removed from
him, and his heart becomes united and obedient to truth. He
is no longer able to obey any suggestions or temptations toward
evil, but is freed from sin and the transgression of the law of
God, and in that respect perfect. Yet there is still room for
spiritual growth, and some possibility of sinning remains if the
mind is not diligently and watchfully applied to heeding the
Lord. (Rom 6:14; 8:13; 6:2, 18; and 1 John 3:6).*

PROPOSITION 9 — PERSEVERANCE IN THE FAITH AND THE POSSI-
BILITY OF FALLING FROM GRACE

*Even though this gift of the inward grace of God is suffi-
cient to bring about salvation, yet for those who resist it, it not
only may become their condemnation, but does. Moreover, by
disobedience, those whose hearts have been partly purified and
sanctified by this grace may fall from that state, turning to licentiousness (Jude 4) making shipwreck of faith (1 Tim 1:19).
They fall away again after they have tasted the heavenly gift*

and have partaken of the Holy Spirit (Heb 6:4-6). *Nevertheless, it is possible to achieve such an increase and stability in the truth in this life that total apostasy is impossible.*

PROPOSITION 10 — THE MINISTRY

It is by the light or gift of God that all true knowledge of things spiritual is received and revealed. It is also by the strength and power of these, as they are made manifest and received in the heart, that every true minister of the gospel is ordained, prepared, and equipped for the work of the ministry.

Every evangelist and every Christian pastor ought to be led and directed in his labor and in the work of the gospel by the leadings, motions, and drawings of God's light. These should govern not only the place where, but the persons to whom he speaks, and the time when he should speak. Those who have this authority ought to preach the gospel even though they are without human commission or are illiterate. If they lack the authority of the divine gift, no matter how learned they may be, or what authorization they may have from men, or how well they may be commissioned by churches, they should be considered deceivers and not true ministers of the gospel.

Those who have received this holy and unspotted gift have received it without cost and should give it without charge (Mat 10:8). They should certainly not use it as a trade to earn money. But, if God has called any of them from their regular employment, or the trade by which they earn their living, they should receive such worldly necessities as food and clothing. It is lawful for them to accept these as far as they feel allowed by the Lord, and as far as they are freely and cordially given by those with whom they have shared spiritual matters.

PROPOSITION 11 — WORSHIP

True and acceptable worship of God stems from the inward and unmediated moving and drawing of his own Spirit. It is not limited by places, times, or persons.[4]

Although we should always maintain a profound reverence for God and in that sense worship him continually, whenever we formally worship him with prayers, praises, or preaching, it

---

[4] This should not be misconstrued as discontinuing set times and places for worship. — ED.

*should not be done of our own volition, or at the place and
time that we wish. But we should be moved by the secret stimulation and inspiration which the Spirit of God provides in
our hearts. God hears our need and accepts this responsibility,
and never fails to move us to worship when it is required. He
alone is the proper judge of this.*

*All other worship, which begins and ends at man's own
pleasure, which can be done or left undone as he himself sees
fit, is merely superstition, self-will, and abominable idolatry in
the sight of God. Whether it be praise, prayer, or preaching;
whether it be a prescribed form, like a liturgy; or extemporaneous prayers conceived with the natural capacities and abilities
of the mind; these should be rejected and done away with in
this time of spiritual emergence.*

*In the past, it may have pleased God to overlook the igno-
rance of the age because of the simplicity and integrity of some.
Because of his own innocent seed which lay buried in the hearts
of men under that mass of superstition, he may have been willing to blow upon the dead and dry bones [Ezek 37:1-14] and to
raise some breath of his own in answer to them. But the day
has dawned more clearly when these empty forms are to be denied and rejected.* (Ezek 13; Mat 10:20; Acts 2:4, 18:5; John
3:6, 4:21; Jude 19; Acts 17:23.)

PROPOSITION 12 — BAPTISM

*Just as there is "one Lord, and one faith," so is there "one
baptism" (Eph 4:5), which is not "a removal of dirt from the
body but ... an appeal to God for a clear conscience, through
the resurrection of Jesus Christ" (1 Pet 3:21 RSV). This
baptism is a pure and spiritual thing (Gal 3:27), namely, the
baptism of the Spirit and of fire, by which we are "buried with
him" (Rom 6:4; Col 2:12) so that being washed and purged
of our sins, we may "walk in newness of life" (Rom 6:4).*

*The baptism of John was figurative, and was commanded
for a time, but it was not to continue forever (John 3:30;
1 Cor 1:17). The baptism of infants, however, is a mere human
tradition, for which neither precept nor practice is to be found
anywhere in scripture.*

PROPOSITION 13 — COMMUNION, OR PARTICIPATION IN THE BODY
AND BLOOD OF CHRIST

*The communion of the body and blood of Christ is inward
and spiritual. It is by participation in his flesh and blood that
the inward man is nourished daily in the hearts of those in
whom Christ dwells. The breaking of bread by Christ with his
disciples was a symbol* (1 Cor 10:16-17; John 6:32-33, 35; 1 Cor
5:8). *For the sake of the weak, it was used in the church for a
time, even by those who had received the substance.*

*Just as abstaining from things strangled and from blood
was practiced for a time* (Acts 15:20); *this, and the washing of
one another's feet* (John 13:14) *and the anointing of the sick
with oil* (James 5:14) *were all commanded with no less authority and solemnity than the breaking of bread. But since they
were but shadows of better things, they are no longer to be
practiced by those who have obtained the substance.*

PROPOSITION 14 — CONCERNING CIVIL POWER IN MATTERS PURELY
RELIGIOUS AND PERTAINING TO THE CONSCIENCE

*The power and dominion of the conscience are the prov-
ince of God, and he alone can properly instruct and govern it.
No one whatsoever may lawfully force the consciences of others
regardless of the authority or office[5] he bears in the government
of this world. Death, banishment, fines, imprisonment and
similar things that are inflicted upon men solely because of the
exercise of their consciences, or differences in worship or opinion, proceed from the spirit of Cain, the murderer, and are
contrary to the Truth. This is, of course, always subject to the
provision that no man, under pretense of conscience, may prejudice the life or property of his neighbor, or do anything that
is destructive to human society or inconsistent with its welfare.
In such cases, the transgressor is subject to the law, and justice
should be administered without respect of persons.* (Luke 9:55-
56; Mat 7:12-13, 29; Titus 3:10.)

[5] The biblical word "principality" was used.

PROPOSITION 15 — VAIN AND EMPTY CUSTOMS AND PURSUITS

The chief purpose of all religion is to redeem men from the spirit and vain pursuits of this world, and to lead them into inward communion with God. All vain and empty customs and habits whether of word or deed, should be rejected by those who have come to fear the Lord.

Taking one's hat off to another person, bowing or cringing, and the other similar foolish and superstitious formalities which accompany them, should be forsaken. All of these were invented to feed man's pride through the vain pomp and glory of this world.

Theatrical productions which are not beneficial, frivolous recreation, sports and games which waste precious time and divert the mind from the witness of God in the heart, should be given up. Christians should have a living sense of reverence for God, and should be leavened with the evangelical[6] Spirit which leads into sobriety, gravity, and godly fear. When we abide in these, the blessing of the Lord is felt to attend us in the necessary occupations by which we gain sustenance for the outward man. (Eph 5:11; 1 Pet 1:14; John 5:44; Jer 10:3; Acts 10:26; Mat 15:13; Col 2:8.)

[6] It is difficult to know what the word evangelical" meant in the original, just as the word has many meanings today which can only be understood in context.

In PROP. VI Barclay speaks of "an evangelical and saving light and grace in everyone." — ED.

THE APOLOGY

Part A—The Faith of the Individual Christian

True Knowledge

PROPOSITION 1 — THE TRUE FOUNDATION OF KNOWLEDGE

Since the height of all happiness is the true knowledge of God ("This is eternal life: to know thee who alone art truly God, and Jesus Christ whom thou hast sent." John 17:3 NEB), it is primary and essential that this foundation of knowledge be properly understood and believed.

Anyone who desires to learn an art or science first looks for the ways in which that knowledge may be obtained. As important as this is for natural and earthly matters, how much more important it is for spiritual matters!

A man first proposes to know God when his conscience brings about a sense of his own unworthiness, and a great weariness of mind is unwittingly affected by the gentle yet real glances of God's light upon him. The earnest desires he has to be redeemed from his present troubles make him tender in heart and ready to receive any impression. He desires to be freed from his disordered passions and lusts and to find quietness and peace in the certain knowledge of God, and in the assurance of God's love and good will toward him. Since he has not yet achieved clear discernment, he is eager to embrace anything that will alleviate his present condition.

THE IMPORTANCE OF FIRST OPINIONS

If he centers himself on certain principles at that stage, it will be very difficult to alter these opinions no matter how wrong they may be. These first opinions are often arrived at through respect for certain persons, or through unconscious compliance with his own natural disposition. Once the first anguish is over, he becomes more hardy, and a false peace and a certain confidence are created. The enemy is near and is strengthened by the unwillingness of the mind to resume its doubts or the anxiety of searching. How much more difficult

Note: Headings for parts, chapters, and subheads were not in the original, but have been added to this edition to make for easier reading. Barclay indicated a tripartite plan for the *Apology*. See the first sentence of the text on page 171.

it is to bring him then to enter the right way, if he has missed his road at the beginning of his journey and was mistaken in his first guideposts.

The Pharisees and Jewish doctors furnish a good example. They resisted Christ principally because they did not wish to be considered ignorant, and this pride in their learning hindered them from receiving the true knowledge. The common people who were not so preoccupied with earlier principles, nor conceited about their own learning, believed easily. The Pharisees upbraided them for this, saying, "Is there a single one of our rulers who has believed in him, or of the Pharisees? As for this rabble, which cares nothing for the Law, a curse is on them;" John 7:48-49 NEB.

WRONG IDEAS CONTRIBUTE TO ATHEISM

There is also plenty of proof from the experience of all of those who applied themselves to false teachers when they were secretly touched by the call of God's grace. The remedy is worse than the disease. Instead of knowing God, or the things which pertain to their salvation in the right way, they drink in wrong opinions. It is then harder to straighten them out than it was while their soul remained a blank, or *Tabula rasa*. For they who consider themselves wise are worse to deal with than those who are aware of their ignorance. Actually it has served the devil's purpose better to convince men of wrong notions of God than it has to prevent them from acknowledging him altogether.

This has constantly led the world to ruin, for there has hardly been a nation that has not had some form of religion. Idolatry and superstition have come not from denying God, but from misapprehensions and mistaken knowledge of him. Indeed, atheism itself has been fostered by these ideas. For the many and varied opinions concerning God and religion have been so intertwined with guesses and the uncertain judgments of men, that they have fostered the idea in many people that there is no God at all.

This, and much more that might be said, demonstrate how dangerous it is to be wrong in this first step. "The man who does not enter the sheepfold by the door, but climbs in some other way, is nothing but a thief or a robber," as it is stated in John 10:1 NEB.

TRUE KNOWLEDGE BRINGS LIFE ETERNAL
How necessary and how desirable the true knowledge which
brings life eternal is, has been said very well by Epictetus (cap
38) *ithi oti to Kyriōtaton,* etc. "Know that the main foundation of piety is this, to have *orthas hypolēpseis,* right opinions
and apprehensions of God."
I doubt if much more explanation or defense of this first
principle is needed. It is generally and universally acknowledged, and in matters of general agreement I love to be brief.
Since this principle so easily commends itself to everyone's
reason and conscience, let us proceed to the next proposition.

Communication

PROPOSITION 2 — INWARD AND UNMEDIATED REVELATION

Since "no one knows the Son but the Father, and no one knows the Father but the Son and those to whom the Son may choose to reveal him" (Mat 11:27 NEB), and since the revelation of the Son is in and by the Spirit, therefore it is only through the testimony of the Spirit that the true knowledge of God has been, is, and can be revealed.

It was by the motions of his own Spirit that God converted the chaos of this world into that wonderful order which has existed since the beginning, and created man a living soul, to rule and govern it. It was by the revelation of the same Spirit that he has always manifested himself to the sons of men, whether they were patriarchs, prophets, or apostles.

These revelations of God by the Spirit, whether by outward voices and appearances, dreams, or inward objective manifestations in the heart, were formerly the main purpose[1] of faith. This should continue to be so, since the object of faith is the same in all ages regardless of the variations in form by which it is administered. Moreover, these divine inward revelations are considered by us to be absolutely necessary for the building up of true faith. But, this does not mean that they can, or ever do, contradict the outward testimony of the scriptures, or proper and sound judgment.

Nevertheless, it does not follow that these divine revelations should be subjected either to the outward testimony of the scriptures, or of the natural reason of man, as more positive or more noble rules or touchstones. These divine revelations and inward illuminations possess their own clarity and serve as their own evidence. They force the well-disposed mind to assent and they inevitably move it in that direction in the same way that the common principles of natural truths move and incline the mind toward a natural agreement.

---

[1] Barclay used the word "object" frequently in PROP. II. Sometimes it meant "objective" or purpose, in other cases the "source," "basis," or "foundation" or that which was the "essence" or the "center" of faith. Sometimes "object" has been allowed to stand; in other cases, substitutions have been made. — ED.

MANY CHRISTIANS CONSIDER
INWARD REVELATION UNNECESSARY

¶I. Many Christians who are wholly unacquainted with the motions and actions of God's Spirit upon their hearts will consider inward and unmediated revelation unnecessary. In fact, some who are still in their natural state are apt to flout and ridicule it. The majority of Christians are so apostatized that even though nothing is more plainly asserted, more seriously recommended, or more certainly attested in all the writings of the holy scriptures, there is nothing that receives so little attention or is more rejected by all kinds of Christians than unmediated and divine revelation. This is so true that it is considered a matter for reproach if one lays claim to it. Formerly it was stated that "anyone who does not have the Spirit of Christ does not belong to him," and ". . . all who are led by the Spirit of God are Sons of God," Rom 8:9, 14 RSV. But, now many boldly assert that they are Christians even though they do not have the Spirit and they laugh at those who say they do, or they proclaim them heretics. They have wholly shut their ears from hearing and their eyes from seeing this inward guide and have become strangers to it.

Even many great doctors, ministers, teachers, and bishops of Christianity have either the shadow of the true knowledge of God or claim that this knowledge can be acquired without direct revelation.

THE DIFFERENCE BETWEEN INTELLECTUAL
AND SPIRITUAL KNOWLEDGE

In order to clarify this proposition, it is necessary to distinguish between the certain knowledge of God and the uncertain, between the spiritual knowledge and the literal, the saving heart knowledge and intellectual knowledge. Lofty, ethereal, and intellectual knowledge of God can be obtained in many ways, but true knowledge can be obtained only by God's Spirit shining in upon the heart, enlightening and opening the understanding.

¶II. The indisputability of this truth has been acknowledged by some of the finest and most famous Christians of all ages. Augustine *(Tract. Ep. Joh. iii)*[2] spoke of an "inward mas-

---

[2] This is apparently Homily IV, sect 1 on the Epistle of St. John; the version is that of *A Select Library of the Nicene and Post-Nicene Fathers*, Philip Schaff, ed, N. Y., 1888, 1st ser, vol 7, p 482. Homily III is in a similar vein and worth adding, loc cit, p 481: " 'Call no man your

ter" and said: "But only He that created and redeemed and called you, He, dwelling in you by faith and the Spirit, must speak to you within else vain is all our noise of words."

Clement of Alexandria says[3] (lib I, *Strom.*): "One speaks in one way of the truth, in another way the truth interprets itself. The guessing at truth is one thing, the thing itself another. And the one results from learning and practice; the other from power and faith. For the teaching of piety is a gift, but faith is grace 'for by doing the will of God, we know the will of God' (John 7:17)." Clement also said: "Truth is neither hard to be arrived at, nor is it impossible to apprehend it; for it is most nigh unto us, even in our houses, as the most wise Moses hath insinuated." *(Paedag.)*

Tertullian states[4]: "The reason why the Lord sent the Paraclete was that since human mediocrity was unable to take in all things at once, discipline should, little by little, be directed, and ordained and carried on to perfection, by that vicar of the Lord, the Holy Spirit."

"For the law is spiritual, and a revelation is needed to enable us to comprehend it," says Jerome *(Ep. Paulin. 103)*.[5] And elsewhere *(Ep. 150 ad Hedibia,* quest 11) he says: "The whole Epistle to the Romans needs 'interpretation', it is involved in

---

master upon earth; One is your Master, even Christ' [Mat 23:8-9]. Let Him therefore Himself speak to you within, when not one of mankind is there; for though there be someone at thy side, there is none in thy heart. Yet let there not be none in thy heart: let Christ be in thine heart: let His unction be in the heart, lest it be a heart thirsting in the wilderness, and having no fountains to be watered withal. There is then, I say, a Master within that teacheth: Christ teacheth; His inspiration teacheth. Where His inspiration and His unction is not, in vain do words make a noise from without."

[3] Clement of Alexandria (c. 150 - c. 215). The work cited is Book I of his *Stromateis* or "Miscellaneous Studies," Chapter VII. The version is that of Alex. Roberts and James Donaldson in the *Ante-Nicene Fathers,* Buffalo, 1885. vol 2, p 308.

The citation following it is from the *Paedagogus* on Christian life and manners, but I have been unable to find the precise location.

4 *Liber de veland. Virginibus,* cap 1.

The version used is that of Roberts and Donaldson, *Ante-Nicene Fathers,* vol 4, p 27. Tertullian (c. 160 - c. 220) was one of the African Church Fathers.

[5] Hierom or Eusebius Hieronymus, better known as St. Jerome (c. 342-420), was a Biblical scholar who spent a great part of his life under eremitic or monastic discipline. His writings "issued from a scholarship unsurpassed in the early Church. His greatest achievement was his translation of the Bible into Latin from the original tongues." This was the

such 'great obscurities', that to understand it we need the help
of the 'Holy Spirit', who 'dictated it' through the apostle."
Athanasius stated *(de Incarn. Verbi Dei):*[6] "Such great
things does our Saviour do daily: he draws us to piety, persuades
us to be virtuous, teaches immortality, excites us to desire of
heavenly things, reveals the knowledge of the Father, inspires
power against death, and shows himself unto every one."

In speaking of the words, "He shall teach you all things,"
Gregory the Great[7] says *(Hom. 30 upon the Gospel):* "Unless the
same Spirit is present in the heart of the hearer, the doctor's
discourse is in vain. Therefore, let no one ascribe to him who
Teaches, what he hears from the mouth of the one who speaks.
For unless he who Teaches is within, the tongue of the doctor,
who is without, labors in vain."

Cyril of Alexandria[8] plainly affirms *(Thesauro,* lib xiii,
c 3) "that men know that Jesus is the Lord by the Holy Spirit,
in the same way that those who taste honey know that it is
sweet, because that is its characteristic quality."

"Therefore," says Bernard[9] (in *Psal. 84),* "we daily exhort

---

famous Vulgate, basic to all later Roman Catholic editions of the Bible.
— *O.D.C.C.,* pp 719 and 1431.

The commentary on the Epistles of Paul cited as 103 is actually 53. The
version used here is that of the *Nicene and Post-Nicene Fathers,* ed by
Schaff and Wace, N. Y., 1893, 2nd ser, vol 6, St. Jerome, p 98.

The *Epistle 150 to Hedibia* is actually 120. See Schaff and Wace, op cit,
p 224. The text is not given but the questions are.

[6] An attempt to locate this text precisely was unsuccessful. The
famous *De Incarnatione* was one of two short treatises written by Saint
Athanasius (c. 296-373) "before c. 318 while still in his twenties." —
O.D.C.C., p 99.

[7] Saint Gregory I (c. 540-604), the fourth and last of the traditional
"Latin Doctors of the Church" (see fn p 43), although in later times the
list has been gradually increased to over 20. It was during his Pontificate
that England was converted by St. Augustine of Canterbury (d. 604 or 605)
whom he had selected. His *Homilies on the Gospels* were sermons preached on texts from the Gospels. They were also much drawn on as lessons
for the third Nocturn in the Breviary. — *O.D.C.C.,* pp 583-584 and 410.

[8] St. Cyril, Patriarch of Alexandria (d. 444). "The most brilliant
representative of the Alexandrian theological tradition, he put into systematic form, on the basis of the teaching of St. Athanasius and the Cappadocian Fathers, the classical Greek doctrines of the Trinity and of the
Person of Christ." — *O.D.C.C.,* p 365.

[9] Bernard of Clairvaux (1090-1153), one of the great builders of the
Cistercian Order, was canonized in 1174 and created a "Doctor of the
Church" (see fn p 43) in 1830. He was possessed of "a faith inspired by
the sublimest mysticism." — *O.D.C.C.,* p 160.

you, brethren, to walk in the ways of the heart, and keep your souls under control so that you may hear what the Lord says in you." And in commenting upon the words of the apostle, "Let him who glories, glory in the Lord,"[10] says: "This is the three-fold vice with which all sorts of religious men are more or less dangerously affected, because they do not listen diligently with the ears of the heart, to what the Spirit of truth, who flatters no one, says inwardly."

This was the very basis and principal foundation upon which the earliest Reformers built. Luther[11] in his book addressed to the nobility of Germany (tom 5, p 76) says: "This is certain, that no man can make himself a teacher of the holy scriptures, but by the Holy Spirit alone." In reference to the Magnificat,[12] he says: "No man can rightly know God, or understand the word of God, unless he receives it immediately from the Holy Spirit. And no one can receive it from the Holy Spirit, unless he finds it in himself by experience. And it is by this experience that the Holy Spirit teaches. That is his proper school. And outside of this school nothing is taught but mere talk."

GOD IS KNOWN BY THE SPIRIT ALONE

Philip Melancthon[13] said (in his annotations upon John 6): "Those who hear only an outward and bodily voice, hear the creature; but God is a Spirit, and is neither discerned, nor known, nor heard, but by the Spirit; and therefore to hear the voice of God, to see God, is to know and hear the Spirit. By the Spirit alone God is known and perceived. This is acknowledged to this day by all who are not satisfied with a superficial religion and who are unwilling to use it as a cover or an art. Indeed,

[10] 1 Cor 1:31 and 2 Cor 10:17 loosely quoting Jer 9:23-24.

[11] The reference is to *An den christlichen Adel deutscher Nation,* one of the three celebrated reforming writings of 1520 by which Martin Luther (1483-1546) completed the break with the medieval Church. — *O.D.C.C.,* p 832.

[12] Luke 1:46-55.

[13] Philip Melancthon (1497-1560), one of the Protestant Reformers, was for a time the leader of the Reformation movement during Luther's confinement in the Wartburg. "The leading figure at the Diet of Augsburg (1530), he was mainly responsible for the Augsburg Confession," still one of the central creedal statements of Lutheranism. "His commentaries on Scripture broke new ground. They discarded the medieval 'four senses', treated the New Testament like the classics, and emphasized the need of history and archeology for their understanding." — *O.D.C.C.,* p 882.

all of those who apply themselves effectively to Christianity, are satisfied only when they have known its work upon their hearts, redeeming them from sin. The knowledge which effectively produces this is the warm influence of God's Spirit upon the heart, and the comfort of his light shining upon their understanding."

This truth has been very well stated by a contemporary author, Dr. Smith of Cambridge,[14] who says in his *Select Discourses:* "To seek our divinity merely in books and writings, is to seek the living among the dead; many times we vainly try to find God in these, where his truth is too often not so much enshrined as entombed. *Intra te quaere Deum,* seek God within your own soul. He is best discerned, *noera epaphe,* as Plotinus phrases it, by an intellectual touch of him. We must see with our eyes, and hear with our ears, and our hands must handle the word of life[15] — to express it in St. John's words, *esti kai psyches aisthesis tis,* etc., the soul itself has its own sense, as well as the body. And that is why David, when he wants us to know what divine goodness is, calls not for speculation, but sensation: 'Taste and see that the Lord is good' (Psalm 30:8). The best and truest knowledge of God is not that which is wrought by the labor and sweat of the brain, but that which is kindled within us, by a heavenly warmth in our hearts."

THE HUMBLE AND LOVING SPIRIT OF JESUS

Elsewhere, he says: "There is knowledge of the truth as it is in Jesus, as it is in a Christ-like nature; as it is in that sweet, mild, humble. and loving Spirit of Jesus, which spreads itself, like a morning sun, upon the souls of good men, full of light and life. There is little profit in the mere knowledge of Christ; instead it is because he gives his Spirit, the Spirit that

[14] John Smith (1618-1652), Cambridge Platonist. His *Select Discourses,* ed. by John Worthington. London, 1660, are also found with a sermon preached at his funeral and a short account of his life and death by Simon Patrick, pp 483-526; 4th ed rev by H. G. Williams, Cambridge, 1859. The Cambridge Platonists "stood between the Puritans and High Anglicans and consistently advocated tolerance and comprehension within the Church, basing their demand on their conception that reason was the arbiter both of natural and revealed religion. They held that it could judge the data of revelation by virtue of the indwelling of God in the mind since 'the Spirit in man is the candle of the Lord (B. Whichcote)'. This mystical view of reason was derived principally from Neoplatonism, though the Cambridge Platonists interpreted it not so much as ecstasy as an abiding direction of will and affection alike ..." — *O.D.C.C.,* pp 222 and 1265.

[15] 1 John 1:1.

searcheth the deep things of God, to good men."[16] And in still
another place, he says: "Only thin airy knowledge is acquired
by mere speculation, by the use of syllogisms and demonstrations; but the kind which springs forth from true goodness,
theioteron ti pasēs hypodeixeōs, as Origen says: 'brings such a
divine light into the soul, that it is clearer and more convincing than any demonstration.' "

A CHRISTIAN IS ONE WHO HAS THE SPIRIT OF CHRIST

¶III. ... Christianity has become, as it were, an art, acquired by human knowledge and industry, like any other art or
science. Men have not only assumed the name of Christians by
certain artificial tricks, but they have even procured the honor
for themselves of being considered masters of Christianity, even
though they are altogether strangers to the spirit and life of
Jesus. But if we make a definition of a Christian which is scriptural, that a Christian is one who has the Spirit of Christ and is
led by it, we will have to divest many Christians and indeed
many of these great masters and doctors of Christianity of that
designation.

When Christians are learned in all other methods of obtain-
·ing knowledge — whether it be the letter of the scriptures, the
traditions of the churches, or the works of creation and providence — and are able to produce strong and undeniable arguments from these sources, but remain altogether ignorant of the
inward and unmediated revelations of God's Spirit in the heart,
they ought not to be considered Christians.

On the other hand, there are those who are altogether ignorant of some of the learned aspects of Christianity and who have
very little skill in other methods of obtaining knowledge, but
who have been brought to salvation by the unmediated revelation of God in the heart.

Who will deny that many illiterate men may be saved and
that many have been saved? Those who would claim that this
is impossible would have to exclude Abel, Seth, Noah, Abraham,
and Job from those who have had true knowledge of God and
who have been brought to salvation.

NOT A QUESTION OF WHAT IS BENEFICIAL, BUT OF WHAT IS ESSENTIAL

¶IV. However, this should not be understood as a claim
that the other means of knowledge of God are useless and of no

---

[16] 1 Cor 2:10.

service to man. This will be clear from what is said of the scriptures in the next proposition. The question is not what may be profitable or helpful, but what is absolutely necessary. Many things may contribute to the furtherance of a work without being the essential thing that makes the work go on.

In summary, what has been said amounts to stating that where true inward knowledge of God exists through the revelation of his Spirit, everything essential is there, and there is no absolute necessity for anything else. But, where the best, highest, and most profound knowledge exists without the revelation of his Spirit, there is nothing, so far as the great object of salvation is concerned. Furthermore:

The only knowledge of the Father is by the Son
The only knowledge of the Son is by the Spirit
God has always revealed himself to his children by
  the Spirit
These revelations were formerly the main purpose
  of faith
That purpose continues to be the object of faith
  to this day.

THE ONLY KNOWLEDGE OF THE FATHER IS BY THE SON

¶V. The words of the scriptures make it very plain that there is no knowledge of the Father except by the Son, therefore this provides a fitting premise from which the other assertions can be deduced.

Jesus said, "No one knows the Father except the Son and anyone to whom the Son chooses to reveal him." Mat 11:27 RSV (Luke 10:22). And again, "Jesus said . . . 'I am the way, and the truth, and the life; no one comes to the Father, but by me'." John 14:6 RSV.

For the infinite and most wise God who is the foundation, root, and spring of all our actions, has wrought all things by his eternal Word and Son. "In the beginning was the Word, and the Word was with God. He was in the beginning with God; all things were made through him, and without him was not anything made that was made," John 1:1-4 RSV. In him, we have "unfathomable riches," Eph 3:9 NEB. "In him everything in heaven and on earth was created, not only things visible, but also the invisible orders of thrones, sovereignties, authorities, and powers," Col 1:16 NEB. Therefore, "He is the image of the invisible God, the firstborn of every creature," Col 1:15 Cath-CCD.

HE IS THE INFINITE AND INCOMPREHENSIBLE SOURCE

He is the infinite and incomprehensible source of life and action which operates in every creature, the eternal word and power by which the creature has access again to his maker. Thus he is fitly called the mediator between God and man; for having been with God through all eternity, being himself God, and also in time partaking of the nature of man, it is through him that the goodness and love of God is conveyed to mankind, and by him that man receives and partakes of God's mercies.

BY HIS SPIRIT WE UNDERSTAND THE GIFTS OF GOD

¶VI. There are many clear scriptural statements that the saving, certain, and necessary knowledge of God can only be acquired by the Spirit. For Jesus Christ, in whom and by whom the Father is revealed, also reveals himself to his disciples and friends in and by his Spirit. Although he is no longer with us in the flesh, he teaches and instructs mankind inwardly by his own Spirit. "Behold, I stand at the door and knock; if anyone hears my voice and opens the door, I will come in;" Rev 3:20 RSV. Paul speaks of this revelation of Christ in[17] him, Gal 1:16, and credits the quality of his ministry and the certitude of his calling to it. Christ's promise to his disciples: "Lo, I am with you alway, even unto the end of the world," (Mat 28:20 KJ; "to the close of the age," RSV; "to the end of time," NEB), is similar confirmation, for this is an inward and spiritual presence. "For what person knows a man's thoughts except the spirit of the man which is in him? So also no one comprehends the thoughts of God except the Spirit of God. Now we have received not the spirit of the world, but the Spirit which is from God, that we might understand the gifts bestowed on us by God," 1 Cor 2:11-12 RSV.

"What no eye has seen, nor ear heard,
  nor the heart of man conceived,
  what God has prepared for those who love him,
  God has revealed to us through the Spirit.
  For the Spirit searches everything, even the depths
      of God;" 1 Cor 2:9-10 RSV.

The comparison of the things of man being known by the spirit of man and the things of God being known only by the Spirit of God is very appropriate. Consider the fact that none of

---

[17] KJ, Cath-CCD have "in me"; RSV, "to me"; and NEB has "to me and through me."

the creatures below man can properly attain or understand the things of man, since these are of a higher and nobler nature. Likewise, the natural man cannot receive or discern the things of God because they are of a higher nature. That which is spiritual can only be known and discerned by the Spirit of God. Since the revelation of Jesus Christ, and the true and saving knowledge of him are spiritual, therefore they can be known and discerned only by the Spirit of God.

BY THE SPIRIT, TOO, JESUS IS LORD
The same apostle says: "No one can say 'Jesus is Lord' except by the Holy Spirit:" 1 Cor 12:3 RSV. In other words, the Holy Spirit is so important to the enlightened understanding of the true Christian that he cannot so much as affirm that Jesus is the Lord without the Spirit's assistance. Thus it is insinuated that even though the things of the gospel are true in themselves, they are as lies if they are not uttered in and by that principle and Spirit which should properly activate and direct the mind in such matters. When they are uttered without the Spirit, they are like the words of actors upon a stage or the prattling of a parrot who has been taught a few words. A parrot can even learn to utter a rational sentence, just as the intellect of man can learn the words or writings of spiritual men. But these words are not true unless they come from the spiritual rather than the rational principle.

BY THE SPIRIT GOD REVEALS HIMSELF
¶VII. It is by the Spirit that God has always revealed himself to his children. In the very first chapter of Genesis, we read that even though "The earth was without form and void, and darkness was upon the face of the deep . . . the Spirit of God was moving over the face of the waters;" Gen 1:2 RSV.

God's converse with man from Adam to Moses was by the unmediated manifestation of his Spirit. Afterwards, during the whole time that the Law was being developed, he spoke to his children in no other way. The writings from Moses to Malachi declare that during all that time God revealed himself to his children by his Spirit. Even when he was revealed only to the High Priest in the Holy of Holies, the revelation was explained to the whole people, so that unmediated speaking never ceased in any age.

Furthermore, none was excluded from this unmediated fellowship who earnestly sought after it and waited for it. Many

besides the High Priest, who were not even of the kindred of
Levi, or of the prophets, received it and spoke from it.

It is recorded in Numbers 11:25 Cath-CCD: "The Lord then
came down in the cloud and spoke to him [Moses]. Taking
some of the spirit that was on Moses, he bestowed it on the seventy elders; and as the spirit came to rest on them, they prophesied." The Spirit even reached two who had been on the list to
attend the meeting, but had not gone to the tent, and they prophesied right where they were, in the camp (v 26). When some
of the elders asked Moses to forbid this (v 27-29), he was happy
that it had happened and he replied that he wished all of the
Lord's people were prophets and that the Lord would put his
Spirit upon them!

Even when the Israelites had committed great blasphemies
God did not forsake them, but gave them his "good Spirit to instruct them," Neh 9:20, and "many years thou didst bear with
them, and didst warn them by thy Spirit through the prophets,"
Neh 9:30 RSV.

Many are the sayings of the Psalmist to the same effect, like
Ps 51:11 RSV, "take not thy holy Spirit from me," and Ps 139:7
RSV, "whither shall I go from thy Spirit?"

Isaiah credited his testimony to the same source, saying:
"Now the Lord God has sent me, and his Spirit;" Isa 48:16 RSV
and Cath-CCD.

Everyone acknowledges that God revealed himself to his
children in the New Testament — to apostles, evangelists, and
the disciples. To what extent this still continues and is to be
expected, will be spoken of later.

THE OBJECT OF FAITH IS TO OBTAIN
THE PROMISE, WORD, OR TESTIMONY OF GOD

¶VIII. It is these revelations which were the main purpose of faith in ancient times. In the plain and positive words
of Paul,[18] faith is described in two ways. "Faith," he says (Heb
11:1 RSV), "is the assurance of things hoped for, the conviction
of things not seen."

The object of this faith is to obtain the promise, word, or
testimony of God, as it is spoken in the mind. He makes this
clear with the numerous examples he cites throughout the chapter. The faith of the persons he refers to was not founded upon

---

[18] Modern scholars do not consider Paul the author of Hebrews, but
there is little agreement on who did write it. — ED.

any outward testimony, nor upon the spoken or written word, but upon God's revelation of his will to them, and in them. In the case of Noah (v 7 NEB), having been "divinely warned about the unseen future, [he] took good heed and built an ark to save his household. Through his faith he put the whole world in the wrong, and made good his own claim to the righteousness which comes of faith." The only thing on which Noah could base his faith was what God had said to him. He had no scripture, or prophecies, or the concurrence of any church or people to strengthen him. Yet, his faith in the word of God contradicted the whole world and saved him and his household.

Abraham is cited for his willingness to leave his father's country, his readiness to sacrifice his only son Isaac, and his belief that his seed would possess the land in which he was merely a pilgrim. The source of Abraham's faith in all of this was nothing other than inward and unmediated revelation. God signified his will to him inwardly and unmediatedly, by his Spirit.

Since it has been stated that God sometimes made himself known by external voices or appearances and sometimes by dreams, it might be said that those who now base their faith on unmediated and objective revelation should have similar experiences.

Let us consider how important these actually were in ancient times. For while such things may be subject to doubt and delusion, there is a part of faith which is not. For the faith of old was not built upon so fallacious a foundation as man's outward and fallible senses. What made them give credence to these visions? Certainly it was nothing else but the secret testimony of God's Spirit in their hearts, assuring them that these voices, dreams, and visions were of and from God.

It is the secret persuasion of God's Spirit in the heart that must be recognized as the principal origin of their faith. Without it there can be no true and certain faith and by it faith is frequently begotten and strengthened without any external or visible helps.

GOD SPEAKS TO OUR SPIRITUAL EAR

This may be observed in many passages of holy scriptures which merely mention that "God said," or "the word of the Lord came." It does not say how God's word was delivered or received. If anyone claims that an outward audible voice is required, he is basing this merely on simple conjecture. For it is said emphatically that "The Spirit witnesseth with our Spirit,"

Rom 8:16 KJ — not to our outward ears. Since the Spirit of
God is within us, and not merely outside us, it speaks to our
spiritual ear, and not to the physical one. There is no reason to
conclude that when the scriptures say, as they often do, that the
Spirit moved or called someone to do something, or caused him
to forbear doing something, that this was done by an outward
voice speaking to a bodily ear, rather than an inward voice
speaking to the ear of the soul.

DIRECT REVELATION IS STILL
THE ESSENTIAL PURPOSE OF FAITH

¶IX. Not only was direct revelation the essential purpose
of faith in ancient times, but it continues to be so today.

Although many have agreed with what has been said up to
this point, they will differ now. Nevertheless, there is a very
firm and a very simple argument which confirms the truth of
this assertion. The purpose of faith is the same in all ages, although the way in which it has been administered or applied
has varied. Paul has clearly asserted in Eph 4:5 that there is
but one Lord and one faith and has implied that it would be as
ridiculous to affirm two faiths as it would be to claim two gods.
If the faith of the ancients did not agree in substance with that
of today, and receive the same definition, it would have been
incongruous for the author of Hebrews 11 to have illustrated
his definition of faith by the example of the ancients. He would
not have expected to move us by appealing to the example of
Abraham if the nature of Abraham's faith differed from our
own. Furthermore, it makes no difference that they believed
that Christ's outward appearance was to take place in the future,
and that for us he has already appeared. As the apostle said,
1 Cor 10:4-5 RSV: "... all ate the same supernatural food and
all drank the same supernatural drink. For they drank from
the supernatural Rock which followed them, and the Rock was
Christ." Nor do we believe that because he appeared in the
past, we cannot also know him to be present with us, and to
feed upon him.

Paul says, 2 Cor 13:5 RSV: "Do you not realize that Jesus
Christ is in you? — unless indeed you fail to meet the test
[whether you are holding to your faith]." How can the ancient
examples which the author of Hebrews cites be pertinent? The
answer is simple. Because, as we have already shown, their faith
was in God, and the object of their faith was an inward and
unmediated revelation!

Paul makes this even clearer by citing his own case, Gal 1:16 Cath-CCD, in which, once it pleased God "to reveal his Son in me . . . without taking counsel with flesh and blood" he believed and obeyed immediately. There is also Heb 13:7-8 KJ: "Jesus Christ the same yesterday and today, and forever."

As to the variety of ways in which faith has been applied or administered, the same apostle says, 1 Cor 12:4-6 NEB: "There are varieties of gifts, but the same Spirit. There are varieties of service, but the same Lord. There are many forms of work, but all of them, in all men, are the work of the same God."

If the objective of faith were not the same for us as it was for those of old, it would follow that we are to know God in some other way than by the Spirit. But this would be absurd. . . .

OTHERS FIND GOD THROUGH THE SCRIPTURES

Those who currently deny this proposition use a distinction. They grant that God is to be known by his Spirit, but they deny that revelation is unmediated or inward. They find it instead in and through the scriptures. They say that the "mind of the spirit" is fully and amply expressed in the scriptures, and that it is by these that we are to know God and to be led in all things.

The converse of this assertion — that is, that the scriptures are not sufficient and never were appointed to be the adequate and only rule — will be examined in the next proposition. What is to be proved here is that Christians are now to be led inwardly and unmediatedly by the Spirit of God, in the same manner as the saints of old, even though it will not happen that many will be led in the same measure.

THE GIFTS OF THE SPIRIT

¶X. This will be proved by a number of arguments. First there is the promise of Christ, who said, John 14:16-17 NEB: ". . . and I will ask the Father, and he will give you another to be your Advocate, who will be with you for ever — the Spirit of truth. The world cannot receive him, because the world neither sees nor knows him; but you know him, because he dwells with you and is in you." Again, in verse 26, ". . . your Advocate, the Holy Spirit whom the Father will send in my name, will teach you everything, and will call to mind all that I have told you."

And in John 16:12-13 NEB: "There is still much that I could say to you, but the burden would be too great for you

now. However, when he comes who is the Spirit of truth, he
will guide you into all the truth..." Actually, the same thing
has been expressed in several ways. Christians are to be led by
the Spirit in the same manner as the early Christians. Some
statements have used the Comforter or Advocate, others the
Spirit of truth, the Holy Spirit, or the Sent of the Father in the
name of Christ. It is by this that the ridiculousness[19] is proven
of the view of the Socinians[20] and others who neither know nor
acknowledge any internal Spirit or powers except those of natural men. By this they declare themselves to be "of the world"
and incapable of receiving the Spirit because they "neither see
him nor know him."

The second proof is the location of this Spirit: "He dwells
with you, and in you." The third is the nature of his workings:
"He will teach you everything, and will call to mind all that I
have told you."

When we come to the question: "Who is this Advocate?"
most people acknowledge that nothing else is to be understood
than what the words of scripture plainly indicate. Blasphemy
cannot be avoided when making any other claim. If "scriptures"
could be truly and properly understood wherever the Spirit is
mentioned, it would soon become apparent what an idiotic
monstrosity this would make of the Christian religion. If we
substitute scripture for Spirit in 1 Cor 12:7 NEB, it becomes
ridiculous: "In each of us the *scripture* is manifested in one particular way, for some useful purpose." Logic and reason are
the core of Socinianism. Would it be logical or reasonable to
affirm that the scripture divides in several ways to give to some

---

[19] Barclay used "sottishness." — ED.

[20] Socinianism, sometimes called Old Unitarianism, was an anti-
Trinitarian religious system initiated in the 16th c. by Laelius Socinus
[latinization of Lelio Sozzini (1525-1562)] and developed by Faustus Socinus
[Fausto Sozzini (1539-1604)]. Containing elements of both humanist ration-
alism and the Reformation, "it combined faith in the goodness and ration-
ality of man with an acceptance of the literal authority of the Scriptures.
...Christ was accepted as a Messiah but his essential deity was denied."
It "achieved its greatest success in Poland where Faustus welded the unitarians into a sect known as the Polish Brethren, which promoted educa-
tional and social institutions until banned by the Catholics in 1638." —
Columbia Encyc., 2nd ed, p 1846.
    It was Faustus Socinus who rejected the natural immortality of man, first
in a letter of 1563 and in a later disputation. It is not surprising that
Barclay was familiar with Socinianism, as the works of Faustus were printed
in Amsterdam in 1668, less than a decade before Barclay's *Apology* first
appeared. — *Encyc. Brit.*, 1958, v 20, p 510.

the gift of healing, to others the working of miracles — as the verses which follow state? This Spirit, a manifestation of which is given to every man, cannot be scripture for there are a hundred more instances where it would be absurd to substitute that word.

To state that this Spirit is inward, needs no interpretation or commentary. The quotation: "He dwells with you and is in you" is self-sufficient. This indwelling of the Spirit is asserted in the scripture as clearly as anything can be. "But you are not in the flesh, you are in the Spirit, if the Spirit of God really dwells in you," Rom 8:9 RSV. "Do you not know that your body is a shrine of the indwelling Holy Spirit, and the Spirit is God's gift to you?" 1 Cor 6:19 NEB. "Surely you know that you are God's temple, where the Spirit of God dwells?" 1 Cor 3:16 NEB.

THE SPIRIT IS THE MAIN TOKEN OF A CHRISTIAN

Without this Paul did not consider a man a Christian — "Any one who does not have the Spirit of Christ does not belong to him," Rom 8:9 RSV. These words immediately follow the quotation: "But you are not in the flesh, you are in the Spirit, if the Spirit of God really dwells in you." The context shows that the apostle considered the Spirit as the main token of a Christian, stating this in both positive and negative ways.

He who acknowledges himself ignorant and a stranger to the inward existence of the Spirit of Christ in his heart, thereby acknowledges that he is still of the "carnal"[21] mind, which is enmity to God; to be yet in the flesh, where God cannot be pleased. In short, whatever he may otherwise know or believe of Christ, or no matter how much he may be skilled in the holy scriptures or acquainted with their letter, he is not yet — notwithstanding all of that — in the least degree a Christian. In fact, he has not even embraced the Christian religion.

[21] The King James version used this word universally for a Pauline concept which meant something like a man's lower nature, referring sometimes but not *universally* to his physical as opposed to his spiritual characteristics. It dealt with the inferior type of behavior or thought which arose out of man's "fallen nature" before the "Spirit of Christ" or "mind of Christ" which he received as a Christian began to remold his character. The concept is variously handled in the newer translations: Rom 8:7 "lower nature" NEB; "of the flesh" Cath-CCD; "set on the flesh" RSV. 1 Cor 3:1 "on the natural plane" NEB. Rom 7:14 "unspiritual" NEB. 2 Cor 10:4 "human" NEB. Heb 7:16 "earthbound" NEB. And they render it variously elsewhere. I have not tried to be consistent either. — ED.

WITHOUT THE SPIRIT CHRISTIANITY IS DEAD

Take away the Spirit and Christianity is no more Christianity than a corpse is a man, once the soul and spirit have departed. And a corpse is a noisome and a useless thing which the living can no longer stand and bury out of sight, no matter how acceptable it was when it was actuated and moved by the soul.

Finally, whatever is excellent, whatever is noble, whatever is worthy, whatever is desirable[22] in the Christian faith is ascribed to the Spirit. Without the Spirit, the Christian faith could no more subsist than this planet could continue to exist without the sun.

All true Christians in all ages have attributed their strength and life to the Spirit. It is by the Spirit that they claim to have been redeemed from the "world", given strength in time of weakness, comfort in affliction, resistance in temptation, endurance in suffering, and triumph in the midst of persecution. The writings of all true Christians are full of great and notable things which they affirm were done by the power and virtue of the Spirit of God working in them.

"The Spirit alone gives life." John 6:63 NEB. It was the Spirit that gave the apostles the power of utterance at Pentecost (Acts 2:4 NEB). When the members of the Synagogue of Freedmen argued with Stephen "they could not withstand the wisdom and the Spirit with which he spoke," Acts 6:10 RSV. Those whose conduct "is directed by the Spirit" receive no condemnation and are made free by "the life-giving law of the Spirit," Rom 8:1, 4 NEB. If "God's Spirit dwells within you," Rom 8:9 NEB, you are "not in the flesh" but "on the spiritual level" (loc. cit., NEB and RSV combined). It is the Spirit of Christ "dwelling within you" that "is life itself," v 10 NEB.

It is through the Spirit that "you put to death all the base pursuits of the body" and "life" is obtained, v 13. It is by the Spirit that we are adopted and cry "Abba! Father!" v 15. "In that cry the Spirit of God joins with our spirit in testifying that we are God's children" and heirs, v 16.

"Likewise the Spirit helps us in our weakness; for we do not know how to pray as we ought, but the Spirit himself intercedes for us with sighs too deep for words," v 26 RSV.

---

[22] Reminiscent of Phil 4:8, although there is no direct tie with the Spirit in that verse.

It is by this Spirit that the glorious things which God hath laid up for us, which neither outward ear hath heard, nor outward eye hath seen, nor the heart of man conceived by all his reasoning, are revealed to us (1 Cor 2:9-10). It is by this Spirit that both wisdom and knowledge, and faith, and miracles, and tongues, and prophecies are obtained (1 Cor 12:8-10). It is by this Spirit that we are "all baptized into one body," v 13.

IN A CHRISTIAN LIFE, WHAT CAN BE OBTAINED OR DONE CORRECTLY WITHOUT THE SPIRIT?

In brief, what is there that is related to the salvation of the soul, or the life of a Christian, that is rightly performed or effectually obtained without it? What else needs to be said? Time would not permit the telling of all the things which the holy men of old, or the saints[23] of this day, have done by the virtue and power of this Spirit dwelling in them.

CALVIN ON THE INDWELLING SPIRIT

Space does not permit a listing of all of the places where this truth is confirmed. In addition to the citations from the Early Church Fathers whom all Christians claim to revere, and those of Luther and Melancthon which have been given al-

---

[23] Barclay was probably using the word "saints" in this instance to mean those who were leading more perfect lives in his own day, although elsewhere he used it in its Biblical sense. As a Biblical concept, "saints" is considerably broader, with widespread usage in both the OT and the NT to mean those who had "sanctified" their lives to the Lord's service. (Although several Hebrew terms are translated "saints" in the KJ OT, all of the NT usage of "saints" is derived from the single Greek term *Hagios*.) In most places "saints" means nothing more than the "believers" or the "faithful," although one usage by Paul (2 Thes 1:10 RSV), in which he refers to "when he comes on that day to be glorified in his saints, and to be marveled at, in all who have believed" suggests that it may have represented a "degree" of admission into the early Christian church.

It may possibly have represented a step above catechumens whose dismissal as well as that of the "fidelium" or "faithful" gave its name to the mass at a later date (Augustine, *Serm.* 49, 8). Only the "initiated" shared in the whole Roman rite whose origins are obscure.

The KJ "saints" is rendered (Deut 33:3) "holy ones" Cath-CCD; "those consecrated to him" RSV. Ps 145:10 "faithful ones" Cath-CCD; "saints" RSV. In Mat 27:52 it was "God's people" NEB ("saints" Cath-CCD and RSV) whose bodies arose on that terrible day when the veil of the temple was torn in two, the earth quaked, and the rocks were rent. In 1 Thes 2:4 NEB, it is "all those who are his own" and in 2 Thes 1:10 "his own" NEB.

Certificated and book-recorded membership never appears in the OT or NT. The term "members" was used only in a spiritual sense. Those who were "members" in Christ were analogous to the physical members of his Body, the Church. They were all united to him and part of him, making up his Body of which he also was the Head. — ED.

ready, a quotation from Calvin[24] will refute those of his followers who refuse to acknowledge the indwelling Spirit and its
ways. Because they have not experienced it themselves, they
deride it as uncertain and dangerous. If neither the testimony
of scriptures, the sayings of others, or correct reasoning can
move them, they may at least be reproved by the words of their
own master who says: "But they contend that it is a matter of
rash presumption for us to claim an undoubted knowledge of
God's will. Now I would concede that point to them only if
we took upon ourselves to subject God's incomprehensible plan
to our slender understanding. But when we simply say with
Paul: 'We have received not the spirit of this world, but the
spirit that is from God...,' by whose teaching 'we know the
gifts bestowed on us by God' [1 Cor 2:12], how can they yelp
against us without abusively assaulting the Holy Spirit? But if
it is a dreadful sacrilege to accuse the revelation given by the
Spirit either of falsehood or uncertainty or ambiguity, how do
we transgress in declaring its certainty?

"But they cry aloud that it is also great temerity on our
part that we thus dare to glory in the Spirit of Christ. Who
would credit such stupidity to those who wish to be regarded
as the schoolmasters of the world, that they so shamefully trip
over the first rudiments of Christianity? Surely, it would not
have been credible to me, if their extant writings did not attest
it. Paul declares that those very ones 'who are led by the Spirit
of God are sons of God...' [Rom 8:14]. And these men would
have it that those who are the children of God are moved by
their own spirit, but empty of God's Spirit. Paul teaches that
God is called 'Father' by us at the bidding of the Spirit, who
alone can 'witness to our spirit that we are children of God'
[Rom 8:16]. Even though these men do not keep us from calling upon God, they withdraw the Spirit, by whose leading we
ought to have been duly called upon. Paul denies that those
who are not moved by the Spirit of Christ are servants of Christ
[cf Rom 8:9]. These men devise a Christianity that does not
require the Spirit of Christ. He holds out no hope of blessed
resurrection unless we feel the Spirit dwelling in us [Rom 8:11].
These men invent a hope devoid of such a feeling.

24 *Institutes*, lib 3, cap 2, s 39.
The translation is that of Ford Lewis Battles, *Library of Christian
Classics*, ed by John T. McNeill, Phila., Westminster, 1960, vol 20, pp 586-7.

"Yet perchance they will answer that they do not deny we ought to be endowed with the Spirit; but that it is a matter of modesty and humility not to be sure of it. What then does he mean when he bids the Corinthians examine themselves whether they are in the faith, to prove themselves whether they have Christ? Unless one knows that Christ dwells in him, he is reprobate [2 Cor 13:5]. 'Now we know,' says John, 'that he abides in us from the Spirit whom he has given us.' [1 John 3:24; 4:13]. And what else do we do but call Christ's promises into question when we wish to be accounted God's servants apart from his Spirit, whom he has declared he would pour out upon all his own people [Isa 44:3; cf Joel 2:28]? What else is it, then, than to do injury to the Holy Spirit if we separate faith which is his peculiar work, from him? Since these are the first beginnings of piety, it is a token of the most miserable blindness to charge with arrogance Christians who dare to glory in the presence of the Holy Spirit, without which glorying Christianity itself does not stand! But, actually, they declare by their own example how truly Christ spoke: 'My Spirit was unknown to the world; he is recognized only by those among whom he abides.' [John 14:17]." That concludes the quotation from Calvin.

If this is so, why should anyone be foolish enough to deny, or unwise enough not to seek, the Spirit which Christ has promised will dwell in his children? Those who maintain that the indwelling and leading of his spirit has ceased must also suppose that Christianity has ceased, since it cannot subsist without him.

WHAT IS THE WORK OF THE SPIRIT?

What is the work of the Spirit? Christ comprises the work of the Spirit, which has already been shown in part, in two or three things. "He will guide you into all the truth," John 16:13 RSV. He "will teach you everything, and will call to mind all that I have told you," John 14:26 NEB. Since Christ has provided such a good instructor, why is it necessary to lean so much on the traditions and declarations with which so many Christians have burdened themselves? Why must we set up our own carnal and corrupt reason as a guide for us in spiritual matters? Is not the Lord's complaint about Israel applicable? "For my people have committed two evils: they have forsaken me, the fountain of living waters, and hewed out cisterns for themselves, broken cisterns, that can hold no water," Jer 2:13 RSV. Have not many forsaken, do not many deride and reject this inward and unmediated guide, this Spirit that leads into all truth? Have they not adopted other ways, broken ways indeed, which do not lead them from the flesh and the world or from their lusts and sinful affections, making truth, which is really only learned by the Spirit, so much a stranger in the earth?

From all that has been said concerning Christ's words and practice, it follows that Christians will always be led inwardly and unmediatedly by the Spirit of God dwelling in them, and that this is a standing and a perpetual ordinance both to the Church in all ages and to every individual member.

Christ has promised that the Comforter, the Holy Spirit, the Spirit of truth, shall abide with his children forever; shall dwell with them, shall be in them, shall lead them into all truth, shall teach them all things, and bring all things to their remembrance.

No man is yet in the Spirit, but is still in the flesh, and cannot please God unless the Spirit of God dwells in him. But every true Christian is partially redeemed from the carnal mind, and from animosity to God, to subjection to the law of God, if the Spirit of God dwells in him. Therefore, every true Christian has the Spirit of God dwelling in him. "Anyone who does not have the Spirit of Christ does not belong to him," Rom 8:9 RSV.

But every true Christian is a child, a friend, a disciple of Christ, therefore every true Christian has the Spirit of Christ. Moreover, whoever is the temple of the Holy Spirit is the dwelling and abiding place of the Spirit of God. But every true Christian is the temple of the Holy Spirit, therefore the Spirit of God dwells and abides in every true Christian.

THE SPIRIT MOVES, ACTUATES, GOVERNS, AND INSTRUCTS

The Spirit of God is not a lazy, dumb, useless thing, but he moves, actuates, governs, instructs, and teaches him in whom he dwells whatever he needs to know. Indeed, the Spirit brings all things to his remembrance. Since the Spirit of God dwells in every true Christian, the Spirit of God leads, instructs, and teaches every true Christian whatever he needs to know.

¶XI. There are some who confess that the Spirit continues to lead and influence the faithful. But they hold that he does it only subjectively, or in a blind manner, by enlightening their understanding of the truth to be found in the scriptures. They deny that he ever presents these truths directly to the mind but insist that he operates in a way of which the individual is insensible, *medium incognitum assentiendi.*

THE SPIRIT IS NOT LIMITED TO ENLIGHTENING OUR UNDERSTANDING

Although this opinion is somewhat more tolerable than the previous one, nevertheless it is not altogether according to truth or comprehensive of the total truth.

Argument 1. There are many truths which are not to be found in scripture even though their knowledge is badly needed for application to particular situations and individuals.

In addition, the arguments that have already been stated prove not only that the Spirit helps us subjectively in discerning truths delivered elsewhere, but also objectively by presenting those truths directly to our minds. For anything which will teach me all things, and is given to me for that purpose, undoubtedly presents to my mind the things that it teaches.

Argument 2. From the nature of the New Covenant and the other points which follow, it will be proved that we are led by the Spirit, both directly and objectively.

The nature of the New Covenant is expressed in several places. One is Isa 59:21 Cath-CCD: "This is the covenant with them which I myself have made, says the Lord: My Spirit which is upon you and my words that I have put into your mouth shall never leave your mouth, nor the mouths of your children nor the mouths of your children's children from now on and forever, says the Lord." The latter part certainly expresses the perpetuity and continuance of the promises that the Spirit of God is upon them and that the words of God will be put in their mouths.

THE SPIRIT PUTS WORDS INTO OUR MOUTHS

This was to be a direct experience. No mention is made of any medium. God does not say that by means of such and such books he will convey such and such words into your mouths, but "my words that I have put into your mouth." He does not say he will enlighten your understanding and assent only to words which you will see written, but: you will have my words which I have put into your mouths.

From which it is argued that the righteous man, upon whom the Spirit will remain forever, is taught by the Spirit — directly, objectively, and continually.

The nature of the New Covenant is even more amply expressed in Jer 31:33 Cath-CCD (it is repeated and reasserted in

Heb 10:11) in these words: "But this is the covenant which I will make with the house of Israel after those days, says the Lord." The objective that is expressed here is God's law placed in the heart, and written in the mind; from which they become God's people, and are truly brought to know him. "I will place my law within them ["into their mind" Heb 8:10], and write it upon their hearts: I will be their God, and they shall be my people. No longer will they have need to teach their friends and kinsmen how to know the Lord. All, from the least to the greatest, shall know me, says the Lord."

This is what distinguishes the gospel from the law. Previously the law was outward, written on stone tablets, but now it is inward, written in the heart. Formerly the people depended upon their priests for their knowledge of God, but now they all have a positive knowledge of him through their own senses. Augustine writes well of this in his book *De Littera et Spiritu*[25] which was referred to by Aquinas.

UNDER THE GOSPEL DISPENSATION
THE LAW IS INWARD AND WRITTEN UPON THE HEART

Based upon this Aquinas seems to have been the first to ask whether the new law was a written law, or an implanted law, *lex scripta, vel lex indita?* He resolves the question with an affirmation that the new law, or gospel, is an implanted law written on the tablet of the heart.

How badly deceived are those who instead of making the gospel preferable to the law have debased the condition of those who are under the gospel! For there is no doubt that it is a far better and more desirable thing to converse with God directly rather than indirectly. Yet these men acknowledge that under the law many men conversed directly with God, but claim that now it has ceased.

Under the law the high priest entered the holy of holies and received the word of the Lord from between the cherubim so that the people could be certain of God's will. But now, according to these men, we are in a much worse condition, having only the outward letter of scripture. We must guess and

---

[25] The Aquinian citation seems to be *Summa Theologica* Pt 1 of II, q 106, art 1, which refers to Augustine's *De Spiritu et Littera*, 24, saying. "It should not disturb us that he said that these do by nature the things contained in the law. For this is wrought by the spirit of grace, to restore within us the image of God in which we were naturally made." — "Nature and Grace," trans and ed by A. M. Fairweather, *Library of Christian Classics*, vol 11, Phila., Westminster, 1954, pp 144-145.

divine from this, even though it is difficult to find two who will agree on the sense or meaning of a single verse.

But Jesus Christ has promised us better things, even though many are unwise enough not to believe him. He removed the veil whereby one and only one can enter once a year and he promised to guide us by his own unerring Spirit. All of us, at all times, have access to him as often as we draw near him with pure hearts. He reveals his will to us by his Spirit, and writes his law in our hearts.

Therefore that which is sought by faith, and the revelation of the knowledge of God, is inward, direct, and objective.

¶XII. The third argument is from the words of 1 John 2:27 RSV: "But the anointing ["initiation" NEB] which you received from him abides in you, and you have no need that anyone should teach you; as his anointing teaches you about everything, and is true, and is no lie, just as it has taught you, abide in him."

THERE IS AN INWARD ANOINTING

This could not be any special or extraordinary privilege. It must have been common to all the faithful, since this was a general epistle addressed to all of the faithful of that era. The apostle suggests that they use this anointing to detect those who would mislead them. He says that it is even a more positive test than his own writings (to which he refers in the previous verse saying "those things I have written you"). The inward anointing which teaches all things is the firmest, most constant, and most positive bulwark there is against anyone who would mislead them.

This anointing is an abiding and lasting thing. It is an inward and immediate teacher. Anyone who has it requires no human teacher, and there are some things which are inwardly and directly revealed to him.

THE SPIRIT IS INFALLIBLE BUT MEN ARE NOT

¶XIII. The most common objection made to this is that these revelations are not reliable. But this represents a failure to distinguish between the divine and human aspects of revelation. For it is one thing to affirm that the true and indubitable revelation of God's Spirit is certain and infallible, and another thing to state that a particular person (or people) speaks or writes infallibly because he claims to be led by the inward and unmediated revelation of the Spirit. Only the first is asserted

by us. The latter may be subject to question. But the question
is not who are or who are not so led, but whether everyone
should be or can be so led.

Merely because some pretend to be led by the Spirit into
things that are not good, it does not follow that the guidance
of the Spirit is uncertain or should not be followed. Does it
mean that the sun does not emit light because a blind man, or
one who willfully shuts his eyes, falls into a ditch at noonday; or
that no words are spoken because a deaf man can't hear them?
Mistakes result from the physical defects or the weakness or the
wickedness of men and not from any defect in the Holy Spirit.
Those who object the most to the certainty and infallible guidance of the Spirit generally use the example of the ancient
Gnostics and the recent monstrous and mischievous behavior of
the Anabaptists of Münster. But the second part of the proposition guards against this.

INWARD REVELATIONS DO NOT CONTRADICT
SCRIPTURE OR REASON

Furthermore, these divine and inward revelations do not
and cannot contradict the testimony of scripture, nor are they
contrary to sound reason. We can boldly assert this, both as a
result of our own experience and because of the intrinsic and
indisputable truth of the assertion. For this Spirit has never
deceived us. He has never urged us to do anything that was
wrong. But his revelations are clear and obvious as they become discernible to us while we wait in the pure and undefiled
light of God which is the proper and suitable instrumentality
for their reception.

Any are misled who reason that because some ungodly or
diabolical men have committed wicked actions no one should
turn to the Spirit of God. It is even worse to fail to seek the
Spirit or his guidance because these wicked men have claimed
that they were led into these actions by the Spirit of God.

It is just as absurd to say that no one should seek the leading of the Spirit because some ungodly men have claimed that
they were led into their evil deeds by him as it is to say that Eve
should not have trusted the promise of God because she was
deceived by the serpent. It would be equally foolish to say that
Noah, or Abraham, or Moses should not have trusted the Spirit
of the Lord because the old world was deluded by evil spirits.
The lying spirit that spoke through the 400 prophets and persuaded Ahab to go up to Ramoth Gilead was not justification

for distrusting and disregarding the testimony of the true Spirit in Micaiah. It is unjustifiable to say that because seductive spirits crept into the ancient church it is not good, or it is unreliable to follow the anointing which taught all things and which is truth and is no lie.

Those who dare to draw this conclusion should beware, for this not only makes the faith of the people of God and his ancient church unreliable, but the faith of all kinds of Christians today is subject to a similar hazard. This applies even to those who seek a foundation for their faith elsewhere than from the Spirit. If the Spirit is not to be followed because some have committed evil while pretending to be led by him, then neither tradition, nor the scriptures, nor reason — which the Roman Catholics, the Protestants, and the Socinians respectively make the rule of their faith — is one bit more certain. The Roman church cites tradition as the basis for her way of celebrating Easter. However, the Greek church which puts equal emphasis on tradition[26] does it another way. Would the Roman church argue from this that tradition should not be followed?

The same difficulty is encountered when it is asserted that the primacy of the Pope is based on tradition, for there are those who assert, also on the basis of tradition, that Peter never saw Rome and therefore the bishop of Rome cannot be his successor. But is this any basis for rejecting all traditions?

As to scripture, Lutherans affirm that their belief in consubstantiation is based on scripture, but the Calvinists say that this is a gross error, according to the same scripture.[27] Is this any justification for saying that scripture is not a good or a positive rule of faith?

[26] Barclay states that tradition was so ineffectual in this case that even though both sides regarded Polycarp, the disciple of John, and Anicetus, the bishop of Rome who directly succeeded him, as the authorities on this matter, they could not agree. His reference was to Euseb., *Hist. Eccles.*, lib 5, c 26. He also uses an example from the Council of Florence (in 1439) during which the Roman and Greek churches' scholars debated for the entire session over a single sentence from the council of Ephesus based on Epiphanius and Basil but could never agree. The reference is to *Conc. Flor.* Sess. 5 decretoquodam *Conc. Eph.* Act. 6, Sess. 11, 12. *Conc. Flor.* Sess. 18, 20, *Conc. Flor.* Sess. 21, pp 480 et seq. — ED.

[27] Barclay also cites "absolute reprobation" which is affirmed by Calvinists but denied by the Arminians who maintain a contrary doctrine which is also based on the scripture.
He also says that the Episcopalians, Presbyterians, Independents, and Anabaptists [actually, Baptists] of Great Britain are "continually buffeting one another with the scripture."

When it comes to reason,[28] very little comment is necessary. Don't nearly all controversies come about because both parties feel that they are following correct reasoning? This was the source of all the ancient arguments between Stoics, Platonists, Peripatetics, Pythagoreans, and Cynics, and more recently between the Aristotelians, Cartesians, and other naturalists.

What of the endless wars, rebellions, and insurrections with which Europe has been plagued in many ages because scripture and reason were used as the pretences? Heretics have been burnt and blood has been shed by those who said that reason persuaded them, tradition allowed them, or the scriptures commanded them to do so.

It is a poor argument indeed to despise and reject any principle because men who have pretended to be led by it have committed evil.

[NOTE: ¶XIV has been omitted except for the incorporation above of some matter from the first and second paragraphs. It is almost entirely historical, and difficult to follow for anyone who is not well versed in the era. — ED.]

THE VALIDITY OF INWARD ILLUMINATION IS SELF-EVIDENT

¶XV. Because the Spirit of God is the source of all truth and sound reason, it has been well said that the Spirit cannot contradict either the testimony of scripture or correct reasoning. But it does not follow that these divine revelations must be subjected either to the outward testimony of scripture, or of sound reason, as though these were more noble and more certain guides. The divine revelation or inward illumination is evident by itself and irresistibly gains assent by its own obviousness and clarity, just as the common principles of natural truths bend the mind toward natural assent.

The scriptures testify that the manifestations of God by his Spirit to the patriarchs, prophets, and apostles were unmediated and objective. They did not examine them by any extrinsic criteria.

It is an unworthy and inappropriate thought to think that the Spirit of God is less self-evident in the mind of man than natural principles. Why does David invite us to taste and see that God is good if this cannot be done? Why was Paul clearly persuaded by the evidence which the Spirit of God gave him that nothing could separate him from the love of God? The

[28] As "authority" and "source of revelation."

apostle John knew very well where the certainty of faith is to be found. He did not consider it a bit absurd to ascribe it to the Spirit. His knowledge and assurance, and that of all the faithful, he expressed very well in the words of 1 John 4:13 RSV: "... we know that we abide in him and he in us, because he has given us of his own Spirit." "There is the Spirit to bear witness, because the Spirit is truth;" (1 John 5:6 NEB).

THE SPIRIT IS BOTH THE PRIMARY AND FINAL RULE OF FAITH

¶XVI. A final argument, it is hoped, will have weight with all Christians of whatever kind, to prove, as we have maintained all along, that this inward, unmediated, objective revelation is the only sure, certain, and immovable foundation of all Christian faith. The argument is that whenever Christians of any kind are pressed to give the ultimate reason that any principle is accepted as the rule of faith and considered worthy of belief, they turn finally to inward, direct, and objective revelation by the Spirit.

The Roman Catholic church emphasizes the judgment of the church and tradition, but if pressed for the reason, the answer is: "Because the church is always led by the infallible Spirit." So here the leading of the Spirit is the final foundation. If asked why tradition should be trusted, the answer is: "Because these traditions were delivered by the Doctors[29] and Fathers of the church. By the revelation of the Holy Spirit these Doctors and Fathers commanded the church to observe them." Here, everything refers ultimately to the revelation of the Spirit.

The Protestants consider the scriptures the foundation and rule of their faith and they believe that they are subjectively influenced to use them by the Spirit of God. Ask them why they trust the scriptures and base their faith on them, and they

---

[29] The early church Fathers were theologians of the first eight centuries who were outstanding for their sanctity and learning. Their unanimous acceptance of a doctrine of faith as divinely revealed was the basis for considering it a part of the "deposit of faith," so important in Catholic theology, and meaning essentially that it was part of the preaching of the apostles.

Apostolic Fathers were Christian writers of the first and second centuries who were known or believed to have had personal contact with the Apostles and whose writings echo genuine apostolic teachings.

The Doctors of the Church, numbering 30, and including many Fathers of the Church, extend over a greater period and are those whose doctrine has been of great advantage to the church. St. Thomas Aquinas (1225-1274) was the last to be so declared, on April 4, 1567. — Ed.

will not say that it is because this or that man wrote them. They
will say instead that it is because the mind of God was inwardly,
directly, and objectively revealed by the Spirit of God to their
authors — that is, that the Spirit of God dictated them.

FELLOWSHIP, REPROOF, AND REBIRTH
ARE ALL THE WORK OF THE SPIRIT

It is strange that on the one hand men should consider the
Spirit responsible for the certain ground and foundation of
their faith, and on the other hand they should consider it too
dangerous and uncertain to follow. In doing so, they shut themselves out of the holy fellowship with God which is enjoyed only
when we walk and live in the Spirit, as we are commanded. If
the reader finds himself moved by the strength of the scriptural
arguments to believe that the revelations of the Spirit are necessary, and yet has never experienced them, it is not strange. For
this is one reason that the possibility is so much gainsaid and
contradicted. It is not because the experience of the Spirit has
ceased to be the privilege of every true Christian, but rather
because Christians now are more so by name than by nature.

Let him know that the secret light which shines in the
heart and reproves unrighteousness is the small beginning of
the revelation of God's Spirit, which was first sent into the
world to reprove it of sin, John 16:7-8.[30]

By forsaking iniquity you first become acquainted with the
heavenly voice in your heart. By the same working of the
Spirit, you will feel the old or natural man put off with his evil
and corrupt affections and lusts. The new man will be raised
in a spiritual birth and will feel, see, taste, handle, and smell
the things of the Spirit. Until then, the knowledge of things
spiritual is merely an historical faith.

The most intelligent blind man, even with the best description, cannot understand the light of the sun or the meaning of
color as well as a sighted child. Neither can a natural man who
receives the best description of the mysteries of God's kingdom,
even if they are the words of scripture, understand them as well
as the least or weakest child who tastes them by having them revealed inwardly and objectively by the Spirit.

---

[30] "If I do not go, your Advocate ["Counselor" RSV; "Comforter"
KJ] will not come, whereas if I go, I will send him to you. When he comes
he will confute the world, and show where right and wrong and judgment
lie," NEB.

Wait then for that small revelation of the pure light which is the primary and the better way for the things of the Spirit to be revealed. By a living experience you will easily refute the ignorance of those who ask: "How do you know you are actuated by the Spirit of God?" The question will appear no less ridiculous than asking one whose eyes are wide open how he knows that the sun shines at noonday.

Inspiration

PROPOSITION 3 — THE SCRIPTURES

From the revelations of the Spirit of God to the faithful have come the scriptures of Truth, which contain: (1) a faithful historical account of the behavior of God's people in various ages and of the many unusual and remarkable acts of God which they experienced, (2) a prophetic account of some things already past, and of others yet to come, (3) a full and adequate account of all of the chief principles of the doctrine of Christ which were spoken, or which were written, by the motions of God's Spirit at various times in treasured declarations, exhortations, and maxims which were given to certain churches and their pastors.

Nevertheless, because the scriptures are only a declaration of the source, and not the source itself, they are not to be considered the principal foundation of all truth and knowledge. They are not even to be considered as the adequate primary rule of all faith and practice.[1] Yet, because they give a true and faithful testimony of the source itself, they are and may be regarded as a secondary rule that is subordinate to the Spirit, from which they obtain all their excellence and certainty. We truly know them only by the inward testimony of the Spirit or, as the scriptures themselves say, the Spirit is the guide by which the faithful are led into all Truth (John 16:13). Therefore, according to the scriptures, the Spirit is the first and principal leader (Rom 8:14). Because we are receptive to the scriptures, as the product of the Spirit, it is for that very reason that the Spirit is the primary and principal rule of faith.

¶I. In spite of what has been said, we consider the scriptures undoubtedly and unequivocally the finest writings in the world. Nothing else that has been written is preferable or even comparable. We agree with the Protestants that the authority of the scriptures does not depend upon the approval or canons of any church or assembly, nor is it subject to the fallen, corrupt, and defiled reason of man. But we cannot go to the length of those Protestants who derive their authority from the

---

[1] Barclay's own word was "manners."

virtue and power that is in the writings themselves. We desire to ascribe everything to the Spirit from which they came.

THE SPIRIT INTERPRETS SCRIPTURE IN A CONSCIENCE-SATISFYING WAY

Indeed, although there is no lack of majesty in style, coherence between parts, or comprehensiveness, yet it is the Spirit of God which must give us the belief in the scriptures which will satisfy our consciences. Some of the principal Protestant theologians have been forced to admit this in their writings and public statements.

Calvin[2] says that if there is a God in heaven, he can prove the scriptures have come from him. Nevertheless, he comes to the conclusion that other knowledge is necessary: "If we desire to provide in the best way for our consciences — that they may not be perpetually beset by the instability of doubt or vacillation, and that they may not also hesitate at the smallest scruples — we ought to seek our conviction in a higher place than human reason, judgment, or conjecture, that is, in the secret testimony of the Spirit." And again: "To those who ask that we prove to them by rational arguments that Moses and the prophets spoke by divine inspiration, I answer, that the testimony of the Holy Spirit is superior to all reason. For as God alone is a fit witness of Himself in His Word, so also the Word will not find acceptance in men's hearts before it is sealed by the inward testimony of the Spirit." And again: "Let it be considered, then, as an undeniable truth, that only those who have been taught inwardly by the Holy Spirit feel entirely satisfied with the scripture." And finally: "A conviction which requires no reasons, but, a knowledge with which the best reason agrees ... can be produced only by a revelation from Heaven."

The first public confession of the French churches, published in the year 1559,[3] makes a similar affirmation in Article

2 *Institutes*, book 1, chap 7, sects 4 [& 5.]

The translations which follow are my own combination of portions of those of John Allen, *Calvin's Institutes*, 7th Amer Ed Rev and Corrected, Phila., Presbyterian Board of Christian Education, 1936, vol 1, pp 88-91; and John T. McNeill and Ford Lewis Battles, *Calvin: Institutes ...*, Library of Christian Classics, vol 20, pp 78-80.

3 Schaff, *Creeds*, vol 3, p 361. The year 1559 was that of the Synod of Paris, when the French Protestant Church (later called "Huguenots") formally organized itself on a Calvinist basis. Lutheranism, in spite of toleration, had gained few adherents in France. Although Calvinists had been ruthlessly persecuted after 1547, there were 2,000 Calvinist churches in France by 1561. — *O.D.C.C.*, pp 519 and 664.

4: "We know these books to be canonical, and the sure rule of
our faith, not so much by the common accord and consent of
the church, as by the testimony and inward illumination of the
Holy Spirit."

The fifth article of the confession of faith of the churches
of Holland, confirmed by the Synod of Dort,[4] states: "We
receive these books as alone holy and canonical not so much
because the church receives and approves them, as because the
Spirit of God doth witness in our hearts that they are of God."

The theologians who were assembled at Westminster were
afraid of the testimony of the Spirit because they sensed a new
dispensation which was beginning to dawn, and which would
eclipse them. Nevertheless, they could not ignore the testimony of the Spirit, although they have not expressed it as
clearly and distinctly, or as honestly, as those who preceded
them. What they said[5] was: "notwithstanding [the testimony
of the Church], our full persuasion and assurance of the infallible truth, and divine authority therof, is from the inward

---

[4] Assembly of the Reformed Church of the Netherlands (1618-1619),
with delegates from England and other countries, convened by the States-
General. It condemned the doctrines of the Arminians or Remonstrants.
(See fn p 108 for explanation of Arminianism.)

5 *The Westminster Confession of Faith,* chap 1, sect 5.
The full text is given in Philip Schaff, *Creeds of Christendom,* N. Y.,
Harper, 1877, vol 3, pp 600-673.
The comment of John H. Leith, ed, *Creeds of the Churches,* Garden
City, N. Y., Anchor, 1963, broadens the base of Barclay's comment. Leith
says: "The Westminster Confession was written ... during the Puritan
Revolution. Representatives of the Church of Scotland met with the
Assembly as commissioners of their government, which had signed the
Solemn League and Covenant.
"... Produced a full century after the Reformation ... [it] represents
the precision and comprehensiveness of a fully developed theology. It is
the product of numerous theological traditions: native British Augustin-
ianism, Puritan Covenant theology, the Reformed theology of the Rhine-
land, and Calvinism. Some members of the Assembly had participated in
the Synod of Dort. The influence of the Irish Articles in the composition
of the Confession is obvious and considerable though other Reformed
Confessions were also used. While members of the Assembly were careful
to keep the Confession in the mainstream of Reformed theology, the Confession did effectively stifle the liberal Calvinism of Saumur, which was
represented in the Assembly, and of Arminius.
"The Confession and Catechisms were adopted by Presbyterians in
Scotland and England and became the dominant standards of Presbyterianism in the English-speaking world. The Westminster Confession
was also adopted by Congregationalists in England and New England, and
it was the basis of the Baptist Creeds, the London Confession, 1677, 1688,
and the Philadelphia Confession of Faith, 1742." - op cit, pp 192-193.

work of the Holy Spirit, bearing witness by and with the Word in our hearts."

From all of these quotations, it is obvious how necessary it is to seek the certitude of the scriptures in the Spirit, and nowhere else. The infinite arguments and endless contention of those who seek their authority elsewhere are the best proof that this is so.

Even in the first centuries of Christianity general agreement was lacking on the scriptural canon. Some books that were rejected then are approved now, and others which they approved are no longer accepted by everyone.[6] There were great arguments[7] concerning the epistles of 2 Peter and James. Many, even very ancient authorities, deny that 2 John and 3 John, as well as Revelation, were written by the beloved disciple who was the brother of James, but believe that they were written by another person of that name.[8]

CHRIST'S SHEEP DISCERN HIS VOICE BY THE SPIRIT

What would have happened to Christians if they had not received the Spirit and those spiritual senses by which we know how to discern the true from the false? It is indeed the privilege of Christ's sheep to hear his voice and refuse that of a stranger. If that privilege were taken away, we would be prey to all manner of false teachers.

[6] The Apocrypha, which are accepted in the Catholic canon, are recommended by Anglicans as books "of good religious instruction," but they do not apply them to establish any doctrine. (*Articles of Religion,* VII.) Protestants, in general, disallow them.

7 Conc. Laod. Can. 58, in *Cod. Ec.* 163. The Council of Laodicea held in the year 364, excluded from the canon Ecclesiasticus, the Wisdom of Solomon, Judith, Tobias, and the Maccabees. These were reinstated by the Council of Carthage in 399.

There is some doubt about the date of the Council of Laodicea, according to the *Cath. Encyc.,* vol 8, p 794, some placing it before Nicaea (325) or at least Constantinople (381), as Barclay's source did. The author of the *Cath. Encyc.* article favors a date after Constantinople. He states: "The canons are, undoubtedly, only a resumé of an older text, and indeed appear to be derived from two distinct collections. They are of great importance in the history of discipline and liturgy."

8 According to the *Interpreter's Bible,* vol 8, p 437, "A common authorship is now generally attributed to the three epistles and the gospel (John, 'the elder', a Christian leader in a group of Churches), while Rev is attributed differently. Some scholars however attribute the first epistle to a disciple of the evangelist."

¶II. We acknowledge that the scriptures are holy writings which possess more than earthly beauty, and whose use imparts strength and hope and is very necessary for the church of Christ. We are grateful and give thanks for the wonderful way in which divine providence has preserved these scriptures in the purity in which we have them. They have been corrupted very little, and, ironically, they continue to be a testimony of God's truth against the very wickedness and abominations of those who were instrumental in preserving them.

In spite of all of this, we can not call the scriptures the principal source of all truth and knowledge, or even the first adequate rule of faith and practice. The principal source of truth must be the Truth itself. When we trace a stream to the place where it gushes from the earth we can go no farther. The wellspring has to be considered the source, for the interior of the earth cannot be plumbed and its ramifications are inscrutable.

THE SPIRIT — NOT SCRIPTURE — IS THE FOUNDATION AND BASIS OF ALL TRUTH AND KNOWLEDGE

In the same way, when we trace what men have said or written to the word of God and find that it agrees with the Eternal Word, we stop. We can go no further, for the wisdom of God is unsearchable, just as what was conceived in the heart of God and caused him to reveal his will and counsel to us is also unsearchable.

In summary, if it is only by the Spirit that we can come to the true knowledge of God, and if it is by the Spirit that we are led into all truth and taught all things, then the Spirit — and not the scriptures — is the foundation and the basis of all truth and knowledge.

Furthermore, the very nature of the gospel itself makes it impossible for the scriptures to be the chief and only rule for Christians. Otherwise, there would be no distinction between the law and the gospel. This has been proved by various scriptural citations for the previous proposition. The law also differs in lacking the power to save. It can bring matters to condemnation but that is all. But the gospel, in addition to declaring what is evil, is an inward powerful thing which also gives the power to obey and delivers us from evil. That is why it is called "*evangelion,* the glad tidings."

The law or letter, which is external, kills; but the gospel, which is the inward spiritual law, gives life, for it consists not so much in words as in virtue. It is for this reason that those who become acquainted with it realize greater power over their iniquities than all outward laws or rules can give them. Hence Paul concludes, Rom 6:14 NEB: "For sin shall no longer be your master, because you are no longer under law, but under the grace of God."

INWARD GRACE IS THE RULE AND GUIDE FOR CHRISTIANS

It is inward grace, then, not an outward law that is to be the rule and guide for Christians. It is to this that the apostle commends the elders of the church, saying, Acts 20:32 NEB: "And now I commend you to God and to his gracious word, which has power to build you up and give you your heritage among all who are dedicated to him." He does not commend outward laws or written words to them, but inward grace! Elsewhere, he speaks of the spiritual law which makes men free, Rom 8:2 RSV: "For the law of the Spirit of life in Christ Jesus has set men free from the law of sin and death." It was this spiritual law which the apostle declares that he preached, and directed people to, distinguishing it further from the law in Rom 10:8 RSV: "The word is near you, on your lips and in your heart (that is, the word of faith which we preach)."

From these statements, it can be argued that the principal rule of Christians under the gospel is not an outward letter, even the letter of scripture, which in itself is a dead thing and a mere declaration of good things, rather than the things themselves. It is an inward spiritual law engraved upon the heart — the law of the Spirit of life.

¶III. Anything which is given to Christians as a rule and guide has to be broad enough to give them clear and distinct guidance in all circumstances. But there are many things with which the individual Christian may be concerned for which there is no particular rule in the scriptures. Several examples will serve to prove this point.

There is no doubt that some men are called for a particular service, and it would constitute a considerable sin of omission if they did not answer their call. This is true even though that service is not a general obligation for all Christians. God is zealous of his glory and every act of disobedience to his demonstrated will is enough not only to greatly hinder the inward peace and comfort of the person who is disobedient, but to condemn him as well.

For example, some are called to the ministry of the word, and as Paul has stated, woe unto him if he doesn't preach the gospel when the necessity has been placed upon him (1 Cor 9:16). Now, as then, some are called more than others to minister unto the Church, but there is nothing in the scriptures that will tell us which persons they are. Even the qualifications of a bishop or minister as given in Timothy and Titus are not confined to those offices but should belong, in some measure, to every true Christian. No one could determine from them whether he was particularly qualified for such service. Even if he could, capability is not necessarily a sufficient call to service. Furthermore, how can the individual judge whether he has even the general qualifications that are given there? How does he know whether he is sober, meek, holy, or harmless? Isn't it the testimony of the Spirit in his conscience that he has to assure him? Suppose he were qualified and called, then what scriptural rule would tell him where it was his duty to preach, whether it was France or England, Holland or Germany? What would tell him whether he should devote his time to confirming the faithful, reclaiming apostates, or converting infidels? How would he even know which churches to write to?

The general rules that are found in scripture can shed no light on this. They give you excellent advice but it is not very specific. They tell you to be diligent in your duty and to do everything for the glory of God and the good of his church. If there are two kinds of advice and I follow one, I may commit a very grievous error, because I was really called for the other purpose.

THE ORDERING OF THE CHURCH

Every member has his own particular place in the Body of Christ as Paul so clearly shows in 1 Cor 12. But if I am a foot and offer to perform the service of a hand, or being a hand, that of the tongue, my service would be troublesome and unacceptable. I would harm rather than help the Body. In effect, something which is good for someone else to do may be sinful for me.

Surely a master with many servants would assign them particular stations. He would not just tell them to do whatever was useful. This would only leave them in doubt and it would undoubtedly end in confusion. How can we dare to ascribe to Christ, in the ordering of his Church and servants, things which would be justifiably considered disorderly and confusing if they were done by ordinary men?

Paul shows the distinction between callings in Rom 12:6-8 NEB: "The gifts we possess differ as they are allotted to us by God's grace, and must be exercised accordingly: the gift of inspired utterance, for example, in proportion to a man's faith; or the gift of administration, in administration. A teacher should employ his gift in teaching, and one who has the gift of stirring speech should use it to stir his hearers." But what rule of scripture shows me that I should speak rather than teach? Or engage in administration? There is none at all! And there are many more difficulties of this kind which occur in the life of a Christian.

Moreover, on the most important point of all — whether or not he is being true to his faith and an heir to salvation — the scriptures can give him no assurance and they cannot provide any rules for him. It is universally agreed that this knowledge is exceedingly desirable and reassuring. What is more, we are especially commanded, 2 Cor 13:5 RSV: "Examine yourselves, to see whether you are holding to your faith. Test yourselves. Do you not realize that Jesus Christ is in you? — unless indeed you fail to meet the test!" And in 2 Pet 1:10 Cath-CCD: "Therefore, brethren, strive even more by good works to make your calling and election sure." What rule of scripture can assure us that we have been true to our faith? That our calling and election[9] are sure?

---

[9] "Election" is a biblical concept often translated "chosen" or "selected." Wm. D. Mackenzie, a former president of the Hartford Seminary Foundation, says in *A New Standard Bible Dictionary*, N. Y., Funk & Wagnalls, 1926, p 206: "It is taken for granted throughout the whole of Scripture that the call of God can be and is rejected by the choices of men. The election is conditioned by its material. . . . The material may be recalcitrant, but it cannot finally defeat that eternal wisdom and power. Thus we are brought face to face with theological attempts to understand the fact of election in its relation to the fact of freedom."

The early Church Fathers and most Jesuits seemed to use the terms "election" and "predestination" without distinction although in some Thomistic interpretations God had to "elect" or "will" salvation before ordaining it, that is, "predestining" it.

"The doctrine of election filled a central place in the *Institutes* of John Calvin, who affirmed that certain persons are elected by God wholly without relation to faith or works. This belief was everywhere held by Calvinist theologians till questioned by the school of Arminius, for whom election was God's choice of those who believe and persevere by grace in faith and works." — *O.D.C.C.*, p 444.

This obviously bears on the composition of the Church. The Ana-

THE MARKS OF TRUE FAITH IN THE SCRIPTURE

Perhaps it will be said that we can compare the scripture marks of true faith with our own. The question then is: "How do we make the comparison?" "How do we know that we are not mistaken?" If it should be said: "By our hearts," it needs only to be pointed out that they are not unbiased when they are judging their own case. They are particularly likely to be biased if they have not been renewed yet. Doesn't scripture say, Jer 17:9 KJ, that "the heart is deceitful above all things"? Both the promises and the threats are to be found in scripture, but who tells us that one belongs to us more than the other?

The scripture says that those who believe shall be saved (1 Pet 1:8-9). We conclude from what it says that we will be saved, but the scriptures merely declare these things, they make no application of them or give us any assurance that they apply to us.

This is indeed such an important point that the best of Protestants, who argue for this assurance, ascribe it to the inward testimony of the Spirit. Even the Westminster Confession of Faith[10] says: "This certainty is not a bare conjectural and probable persuasion, grounded upon a fallible hope; but an infallible assurance of faith, founded upon the divine truth of the promises of salvation, the inward evidence of those graces unto which these promises are made, the testimony of the Spirit of adoption witnessing with our spirits that we are the children of God: which Spirit is the earnest of our inheritance, whereby we are sealed to the day of redemption."

---

baptists, Quakers, and some others tried to incorporate only proven Christians in the Church. "However, in practice, one had to beware of distinguishing the elect from the reprobate, which God alone could do. By virtue of a 'certain judgment in charity' Christians therefore have to ascribe election and membership of the Church to all those who confess faith in God and in Christ, separating themselves only from those who are excommunicated as heretics and from notorious evil livers." — Francois Wendel, *Calvin*, N. Y., Harper & Row, 1963, p 140.

Although the boundaries between the concept of the visible Church composed of the "mixed multitude" and that of the "gathered Church" composed of those who are already members of the invisible Church and come together for fellowship and common effort, are thus blurred in practice, the distinction does have some validity. A greater commitment is, at least theoretically, expected from those who would join a "gathered Church." — ED.

10 Chapter 18, sect 2.
For a comment on the significance of this Confession, see fn p 48.

The scriptures themselves, which urge us so earnestly to seek this assurance, do not claim to be a sufficient rule of faith. They ascribe everything to the Spirit, as in Rom 8:16 NEB: "The Spirit of God joins with our spirit in testifying that we are God's children"; or 1 John 4:13 NEB: "Here is the proof that we dwell in him and he dwells in us: he has imparted his Spirit to us"; and in 1 John 5:7 RSV: "And the Spirit is the witness, because the Spirit is the truth."

EVEN THE HANDICAPPED AND THE ILLITERATE ARE TAUGHT BY GOD

¶IV. Finally, nothing can be the only, the principal, or the chief rule which does not universally reach every individual who needs it. Many who are handicapped by some physical defect, or those who are mentally retarded, or even children are excluded from the benefit of the scriptures in spite of the fact that they are members of the visible church. Should we conclude that they are left without any rule of faith or that they are damned?

This would be inconsistent with both the justice and the mercy of God. No one will deny that they are included in the dispensation under the new covenant. Therefore, there must be some rule and some means of knowledge provided for them. In fact, this is expressly stated in John 6:45 RSV & NEB: "It is written in the prophets: 'And they shall all be taught by God'." "For all shall know me, from the least of them to the greatest;" (Heb 8:11 RSV).

But even if we did not have this difficulty, how many good but illiterate men belong to the church of God. Even though illiteracy is inconvenient, we can hardly consider it sinful. Since these people have no direct knowledge of the scriptures, their faith necessarily depends upon what is read to them or what others tell them. Even the alteration, addition, or omission of a single word could be the beginning of a very dangerous mistake. They might ignorantly continue some iniquity or they might be very confident in believing a lie.

THE UNCERTAINTY OF SCRIPTURE

Even if everyone could read the scriptures in his own language, there would still be only one in a thousand who had a thorough enough knowledge of the original languages in which they were written to get the full benefit of them in that respect. Most readers have to depend upon the honesty and faithfulness of the translators. What an uncertain basis for a

rule of faith this is. Even the latest translations require many
corrections and amendments, as could easily be proved if this
were the proper place.

Even those who are skilled in the original tongues are dependent upon the honesty and faithfulness of the transcribers
since the original copies are no longer extant. Even Jerome,
in his time (340-420 A. D.), complained[11] that the transcribers
wrote not what they found but what they understood. Epiphanius[12] (c. 315-403 A. D.) said that in the good and correct
copies of Luke, it was written that Christ wept, and that Irenaeus cites it that way. However, the Catholics blotted it out
for fear the heretics would abuse it. Other early church fathers
also declared that entire verses had been taken out of Mark
because of the Manichaeans.[13]

There is also the uncertainty about the date of some of
the Hebrew manuscripts. There is the disagreement of various passages from the Old Testament cited by Christ and the
apostles with the originals. There was a great controversy
among the Fathers of the Church about the superiority of the
Greek Septuagint over the Hebrew copy. Some claimed that
the latter was altered and vitiated in many places by the Jews.
Others exalted the Hebrew copy.

All these things and many more give the minds, even
of the learned, infinite doubts and hesitation, and they offer
inextricable difficulties. We may safely conclude that Jesus
Christ, who promised that he would always be with his children, that he would lead them into all truth, that he would
guard them against the devices of the enemy, and that he
would establish their faith on an immovable rock, did not
leave them dependent upon anything which included so many
uncertainties. He gave them his Spirit as their principal guide
and neither moths nor time can wear it out.[14] Neither tran-

---

11 *Epist. 28 ad Lucin.*, p 247.

12 in *Anachor.* [*Anacoratus*], tom 3, oper.

13 A non-Christian sect which originated in Persia in the 3rd c. and
to which St. Augustine belonged in his youth. It taught a syncretistic
religious dualism, based on Zoroastrianism with Buddhist and Gnostic
influences, in which the spirit was released from matter through asceti-
cism. It spread rapidly throughout the Roman Empire and Asia and
continued as a major faith in the Orient for over 1000 years, although it
ceased to be a dynamic faith in the West about 500 A. D.

14 A rather broad allusion to Mat 6:19-20 and Luke 12:33-34.

scribers nor translators can corrupt it. And there is no one so young, or so illiterate, or in such a remote place, that he cannot be reached or properly informed by it.

THE CLARITY OF THE SPIRIT

The clarity of the Spirit is in contrast to the difficulties which occur in connection with the scriptures. I myself have been a witness of the dispensation of Christ's Spirit. I have seen the real and unquestionable experience of the great love of God for his children in these latter days. Some of my friends who profess the same faith as I do, and who are faithful servants of the Most High God, are full of the divine knowledge of his truth. This was directly and inwardly revealed to them by the Spirit in a true and living experience. They are not only ignorant of Greek and Hebrew but some cannot even read their own language. Yet when pressed by some of their adversaries with certain citations from the English translations they have boldly asserted that God never said so. They were sure that the cited passages were wrong because they disagreed with the manifestation of truth in their own hearts. They said they did not believe that any of the holy prophets or apostles had ever written anything like that. When I seriously examined these passages because of their doubts, I found that they were right. These passages contained errors and corruptions by the translators. This seems to agree with what Augustine has said:[15] "That he gives only such honor to those books which are called canonical, as to believe that their authors made no mistakes." He adds: "and if I shall meet with anything in these writings that seems repugnant to truth, I will not hesitate to say, that either the volume is faulty or erroneous, that the expounder has not reached what was said, or that I have not understood it."

In other words, he presumes that there may be errors in the transcription or translation.

¶V. If I should be asked whether I intend by this to render the scriptures completely uncertain or useless, the answer is, not at all. I have already stated at the beginning of the proposition how much the scriptures are esteemed. We plead only for the Spirit from which they were given to receive the place which the scriptures themselves assign to it. I freely concede that the scriptures are entitled to second place regard-

---

15 *Epist. 19, ad Hier.*, tom 2, fol 14.

less of what their words themselves say.   The apostle Paul has mentioned this principally in two places.   In Rom 15:4 RSV, he says: "Whatever was written in former days was written for our instruction, that by steadfastness and by the encouragement of the scriptures we might have hope." The other place is 2 Tim 3:15-17 RSV: "You have been acquainted with the sacred writings which are able to instruct you for salvation through faith in Christ Jesus. All scripture is inspired by God and profitable for teaching, for reproof, for correction, and for training in righteousness, that the man of God may be complete, equipped for every good work."

THOSE WHO ARE LED BY THE SPIRIT CHERISH THE PRODUCT OF THE SPIRIT IN OTHERS

Although God leads us chiefly by his Spirit, sometimes he conveys his comfort and consolation by a word written or spoken at an opportune time.   By it, the faithful are made instruments in the hand of the Lord to strengthen and encourage one another.   This also tends to foster their growth and lead them to salvation. Those who are led by the Spirit naturally love and cherish the things which represent the product of the Spirit in other persons.   They also find that such mutual manifestations of the heavenly life also tend to quicken the mind and to provide the recollection of truth, so necessary for progress in the gospel. Peter declares that the value of this recollection was the principal reason that he wrote, saying in 2 Pet 1:12-13 NEB: "And so I will not hesitate to remind you of this again and again, although you know it and are well grounded in the truth that has already reached you.   Yet I think it right to keep refreshing your memory so long as I still lodge in this body."

GOD TEACHES HIS PEOPLE HIMSELF

God teaches his people himself; and nothing is made more clear than the fact that under the new covenant no human teacher is needed.   In spite of this one of the major results of Christ's ascension was the sending of teachers and pastors for the perfecting of the faithful.   The same work is ascribed to them as to the scriptures.   Both are primarily for the development of greater maturity in the faith of those who believe. But human teachers are by no means to have preference over the teaching of God himself under the new covenant.   Nor is the scripture to rob us of this great privilege which Christ purchased for us by his blood.   ["His blood will cleanse our consciences from the deadness of our former ways and fit us for the service of the living God," Heb 9:14 NEB.]

THE SCRIPTURES OFFER A LOOKING GLASS

In the scriptures God has deemed it proper to give us a looking glass in which we can see the conditions and experiences of ancient believers. There we find that our experience is analogous to theirs. We may thus become more confirmed and comforted and strengthened in our hope of obtaining the same end. Observing the providence that watched over them, and the snares which they encountered, and beholding the ways in which they were delivered, we may find ourselves directed toward salvation, and appropriately reproved, and instructed in righteousness.

THEY FIND A RESPONDENT SPARK IN US

This is the great work of the scriptures, and their usefulness to us. They find a respondent spark in us, and in that way we discern the stamp of God's ways and his Spirit upon them. We know this from the inward acquaintance we have with the same Spirit and with his work in our hearts. The prophecies of the scriptures are also uplifting and of profit to us. For the same Spirit gives us the insight by which we can fulfill them and be fulfilled.

Only the spiritual man can make proper use of the scriptures, not the natural man. They are able to make the man of God perfect, and whatsoever was written in them was written for our enlightenment. We are the faithful [the "saints"] of whom the apostle speaks. As for the others, the apostle Peter plainly declares that the unstable and unlearned wrest them to their own destruction.[16] He was referring to those who were unlearned in the divine and celestial learning of the Spirit, rather than to the illiterate and untutored.

We can safely assume that Peter, himself, had no literary skill since he was a fisherman. And it can certainly be said that he undoubtedly had no knowledge of Aristotelian logic which both Catholics and Protestants now [1675] make the handmaid of theology and require as a foundation for their worldly ministry. It is by the infinite labor of this kind of scholar who intermixes this heathenish stuff that the scriptures are rendered so meaningless for the average person.

---

[16] 2 Pet 3:16.

Jerome[17] complained 1200 [now 1500] years ago, that: "It often happens with the majority of learned men, that it is more difficult to understand their explanations, than the things which they are trying to explain."

What can be said then about those great heaps of commentaries which have been written since then in ages much further removed from primitive Christianity?

WE ARE WILLING FOR ALL OUR DOCTRINES
AND PRACTICES TO BE TRIED BY SCRIPTURE

¶VI. We have already demonstrated how useful the scriptures are to the Church of God when they are administered by the Holy Spirit. And it is for that reason that we consider them a secondary rule. Furthermore, since they are universally regarded as written by the dictates of the Holy Spirit, and the errors which have crept in are not bad enough to obscure their clear testimony to the essentials of the Christian faith, we consider them the only proper outward judge of controversies among Christians. Whatever doctrine is contrary to their testimony may properly be rejected as false. We are very willing for all of our own doctrines and practices to be tried by them. We have never refused to honor them as the judge and test for any disputes we have had on matters of doctrine. We are even willing to allow this to be stated as a positive maxim: Anything which anyone may do while claiming to be led by the Spirit, which is contrary to the scriptures, may be considered as a delusion of the devil. We never claim the Spirit's leading as a cover for anything that is evil. Since every evil contradicts the scriptures, it must also be contrary to the Spirit from which they came. The motions of the Spirit can never contradict one another, although they sometimes appear to do so in the blind eyes of the natural man, just as Paul and James, at first, seem to contradict one another.

THE PRIMACY OF SCRIPTURE

¶VII. For those who insist upon making the scriptures their principal rule, in spite of all arguments, and in spite of the fact that there is no place where the scriptures themselves make this claim, we will briefly examine their objections and endeavor to answer them.

17 *Epist. 134, ad Cypr.*, tom 3 [transphrased from Barclay's quotation].

The first objection is usually based on Isa 8:20 KJ: "To the law and to the testimony: if they speak not according to this word, it is because there is no light in them."[18] They claim that this law, testimony, and word are the scriptures. But this begs the question of their primacy and the reference to scriptures remains to be proved. . . .

Their second objection is from John 5:39-40 Cath-CCD: "You search the Scriptures, because in them you think that you have life everlasting. And it is they that bear witness to me, yet you are not willing to come to me that you may have life."[19]

We do not deny that the scriptures should be searched and we are perfectly willing to have our doctrines tried by them, as we have already stated, but that is not the question. The question is whether they are the one and only rule of faith. Far from proving our opponents' point, this passage actually proves the contrary, for Christ is censuring them for holding the scriptures in too much esteem and neglecting him of whom they testify. While they thought that they had eternal life in the scriptures they were neglecting to come to Christ and to have the life itself of which the scriptures bore witness.

Our adversaries today exalt the scriptures and think that they have life in them. In other words, they look upon them as the only and principal rule and way of life. They refuse to come to the Spirit of which they testify, particularly the inward spiritual law which could give them life. Thus, the cause of this people's ignorance and unbelief is not their lack of respect for the scriptures, for as Christ testifies in the preceding verses, although they knew the scriptures and held them in high esteem, they did not know the Father. "His voice you

[18] As Barclay states, this begs the question of the primacy of scripture. It is further weakened as a proof text by the newer translations. RSV has it: "To the teaching and to the testimony! Surely for this word which they speak *there is no dawn.*" The Cath-CCD finds this an area of transposition and shifts some verses to chap 14, v 25 where the contextual support is better, but this particular verse does not occur at all.

[19] The meaning is so clear in the newer translations that Barclay is fully supported in the points which follow. In the KJ the citation appears to be an injunction to search the scriptures, but the above and NEB make it clear that this is not so. NEB reads: "You study the scriptures diligently, supposing that in having them you have eternal life; yet, although their testimony points to me, you refuse to come to me for that life."

have never heard, his form you have never seen; and you do
not have his word abiding in you, for you do not believe him
whom he has sent," John 5:37 RSV.

THE BEREANS' UNDERSTANDING WAS OPENED BY THE WORD

¶VIII. The third objection that is usually raised is from
Acts 17:11 NEB: "The Jews here were more liberal-minded
than those at Thessalonica: they received the message with
great eagerness, studying the scriptures every day to see whether
it was as they said." It is claimed that the Bereans are commended for searching the scriptures and making them the rule.
However, there is nothing in this passage which makes the
scriptures the primary rule, and we recommend their use for
the same purpose to which they were applied here — for trial
and judgment!

It should also be observed that for the Jews of Berea the
scriptures consisted of the Law and the Prophets. What they
were searching for was to determine whether the birth, life,
works, and sufferings of Christ fulfilled the prophecies concerning him. Since they were Jews, it was most proper for them
to examine these scriptures since he claimed to be the fulfillment of them.

Nevertheless, it is said that first "they received the message
with great eagerness" and then "searched the scriptures"; not
that they searched the scriptures and then received the word.
If this had been the case, they would not have been converted,
because it was the fact that they first hearkened to the word
abiding in them which opened their understanding.

Wasn't it also a fact that the scribes and Pharisees remained in unbelief because they searched the scriptures and exalted
them, but they did not have the word abiding in them?

Lastly, if we were to accept the inference from this
condemnation of the Jewish Bereans that the scriptures are the
only and principal rule to try the apostles' doctrines by, what
would have become of the Gentiles? Since they did not know
the scriptures or believe in them, how would they ever have
received the faith of Christ? At the end of the same chapter,
it is told how the apostle used another method with the Athenians. He directed them to something of God in themselves,
so that they might seek him there. He did not proceed to
proselytize them first to the Jewish faith with its belief in the
law and the prophets and prove the coming of Christ from
that. He took a shorter route.

Certainly there is not one absolute rule for the Jews and another for the Gentiles. The universal rule must reach both. However, secondary and subordinate rules and means may vary according to the purpose and the people for whom they are intended. Thus the apostle referred to one of the Athenian poets. He expected this to have weight for them and no doubt they valued it more than all the sayings of Moses and the prophets, whom they neither knew nor cared for. However, it does not follow that because the apostle used the testimony of an Athenian poet he should be made the principal rule or the only rule by which doctrine could be tried.

THE SCRIPTURES GIVE A FULL AND AMPLE TESTIMONY TO ALL THE PRINCIPAL DOCTRINES OF CHRISTIANITY

¶IX. The last, and what appears at first glance to be the greatest objection, is that if the scriptures are not the adequate, principal, and indeed the only rule, then it would follow that the canon is incomplete and those who are now led and ruled by the Spirit may add new scriptures with equal authority to the old. What assurance would we have that everyone wouldn't bring in a new gospel according to his fancy? As said before, we will freely disclaim all pretended revelations that are contrary to the scripture. If this is not sufficient answer, we can only say that you are not accusing us, but Christ and the apostles who preached these principles. In addition, we have firmly shut the door on such a possibility by affirming that the scriptures give a full and ample testimony to all of the principal doctrines of the Christian faith.

We firmly believe that there is no other doctrine or gospel to be preached other than that which was delivered by the apostles. And we freely subscribe to the saying in Gal 1:8 RSV: "If we, or an angel from heaven, should preach to you a gospel contrary to that which we preached to you, let him be accursed."

NOT A NEW GOSPEL, BUT NEW INSIGHTS

In other words, we distinguish between a revelation of a new gospel and new doctrines, and new insight into the established gospel and doctrines. We plead for the latter, but we utterly deny the former. We firmly believe that there are no new foundations to be laid other than those which have already been laid. But added insight is needed on the matters for which the foundations have already been laid. This dis-

tinction is made to guard against the hazard that has already
been mentioned.

However, I see no need for believing that the scriptures
are a filled canon. Those who are consistent with their own
doctrine of the primacy of scripture will come to the same
conclusion, for it is impossible to prove the canon by the
scriptures themselves. There is no place in any book where it
is stated that these books — these and no others — are canonical. Since everyone acknowledges this, how can they possibly
invite the argument which follows?

That is, anything which cannot be proved by scripture is
not a necessary article of faith. But it cannot be proved by
scripture that precisely so many books, no more and no less,
constitute the canon. Therefore it is not a necessary article
of faith.

If they argue that the admission of any new books written
by the same Spirit might infer the admission of new doctrines,
I deny that consequence. The principal or fundamental doctrines of the Christian religion are contained in only one-tenth
of the scriptures, but it does not follow from this that the rest
are impertinent or useless. If it should please God to deliver
to us any of the books which have been lost by the exigencies
of time and which are mentioned in the scriptures, such as
the Prophecy of Enoch, the Book of Nathan, or the Third Epistle of Paul to the Corinthians, and the others, I do not see
any reason why they should not be placed along with the rest
of the scriptures. What displeases me is to have a man affirm
first that the scriptures are the only and principal rule of faith,
and then make a great article of faith of a matter on which
the scriptures can shed no light.

THE DILEMMA OVER AUTHENTICITY

How can a Protestant prove by scripture to those who
deny it that the Epistle of James is authentic and should be
included in the canon of scripture?

If he says, first because it doesn't contradict the rest, even
though some think that it contradicts Paul in relation to faith
and works, it is still unmentioned elsewhere in the scriptures.
But, even if it were granted that it does not contradict the
other scriptures, does it follow that everything which does not
contradict the scriptures should be included in the canon?
This is a greater absurdity than any that they charge to us because of our doctrine of the primacy of the Spirit. To be con-

sistent they would have to consider the writings of their own sect equal with the scriptures, for I am sure they would not consider their own confession of faith contrary to the scriptures. Does it follow from that, that it should be included for binding with the Bible? Yet there doesn't seem to be any better argument that is consistent with their principles and which would prove that the Epistle of James is authentic.

It is unavoidable to say either that we know it is authentic by the same Spirit from which it was written, or else to step back to Rome, and say that we know it is authentic by tradition, because the church has declared it to be canonical, and the church is infallible.

Let them find a way out of this dilemma if they can! We will consider this objection suitably answered by an unanswerable argument *ad hominem.*

As a final point, on the argument from the words of Rev 22:18 KJ: "If any man shall add unto these things, God shall add unto him the plagues that are written in this book," I wish they would demonstrate how this applies to anything other than this particular prophecy...[20]

Moreover, in effect, the same thing was commanded long before in Prov 30:6 RSV: "Do not add to his words, lest he rebuke you, and you be found a liar." But how many books of the prophets were written after this? Moses said the same thing: "You shall not add to what I command you nor subtract from it," Deut 4:2 Cath-CCD.

Even if we extend the prohibition found in Revelation to other matters than the particular prophecy which is found in that book, it can only be applied to a new gospel or to new doctrines, or to the mixing of human words with the divine. It would not apply to new insights into old truths, as we have said before.

[20] The newer translations make this very clear. RSV reads: "I warn everyone who hears the words of the prophecy of this book: if anyone adds to them, God will add to him the plagues described in this book."

Estrangement

PROPOSITION 4 — THE CONDITION OF MAN IN THE FALL

All of the descendants of Adam, that is, all of mankind, are in a fallen, demoralized, and deadened state. They are deprived of sensing or feeling the inward testimony or seed of God (Rom 5:12, 15). *They are subject instead to the seed of the serpent, sown in men's hearts while they remain in this natural and corrupted state. Not only their words and deeds, but their thoughts are evil in the sight of God while they remain in this state. In this state man can know nothing correctly. Even his thoughts of God and spiritual matters are unprofitable to himself and others until he has been disjoined from this evil seed and has been united to the Divine Light.*

In so saying, we reject the Pelagian[1] *and Socinian errors which exalted a natural light. We also reject the errors of Roman Catholics and of most Protestants who maintain that the true grace of God is not necessary for a man to be a true minister of the gospel.*

However, we do not impute the evil seed to infants until they have actually been joined to it by their own transgression. All of us are by nature "the children of wrath." "We all lived our lives in sensuality, and obeyed the promptings of our own instincts and notions. In our natural condition, we, like the rest, lay under the dreadful judgment of God. But God, rich in mercy, for the great love he bore us, brought us to life with Christ even when we were dead in our sins; it is by his grace you are saved;" (Eph 2:3-5 NEB).

---

[1] **Pelagius** (c. 355 - c. 425), a lay monk and theologian probably born in Britain, fathered an heretical Christian sect which challenged Augustine's conceptions of predestination and freedom of the will. He considered these unduly pessimistic and argued that Christ's admonition, "Be ye perfect," implied that perfection was within the reach of anyone who wholly desired it. Children he considered to be born innocent (as Adam was before the fall), and the subsequent lapse of innocence was due to sin (a personal act of the will). Hence sin was not transmitted and infant baptism was meaningless. — *Col. Encyc.*, p 1506.

His central teaching was that the initial and fundamental steps toward salvation were taken by the individual by his own efforts and apart from the assistance of Divine Grace. — *O.D.C.C.*, p 1040.

Socinianism is outlined in a fn, p 30. — ED.

THE EXTREMES OF EXALTING NATURAL LIGHT OR TEACHING ETERNAL DAMNATION ARE AVOIDED BY OUR DOCTRINE

¶I. There are those who exalt natural light, or the natural capability of man, to such an extent that they consider him capable by his own will of following that which is good and making real progress toward heaven. There are others, including Augustine (although it must be said that it was when he had reached old age and in the context of combatting Pelagian error), who not only consider man prone to evil and incapable of doing good by himself, but contaminated with real guilt and deserving eternal death even before he commits any transgression, in fact while he is still in his mother's womb. They claim that many poor infants are eternally damned and forever endure the torments of hell. Therefore the God of truth has again revealed his truth in his good and unchanging way — by his own Spirit — teaching us to avoid both extremes.

MAN'S FALL EXCLUDED HIM FROM TRUE FELLOWSHIP AND COMMUNION WITH GOD

¶II. It is unnecessary to delve into the many strange and novel ideas about Adam before the fall. As to the condition of man since the fall, everyone agrees that he has suffered great losses by it. His losses were not confined to material things. He also lost the true fellowship and communion he had with God. Since his physical death did not occur for many hundreds of years after he ate the fruit of the forbidden tree, the death which is referred to in Gen 2:17 as the penalty for that act must have been a spiritual one.

In addition to the consequences of his fall which relate to the fruits of the earth, Gen 3:24 RSV reads: "He drove out the man; and at the east of the garden of Eden he placed the cherubim, and a flaming sword which turned every way, to guard the way to the tree of life." Now whatever literal significance that may have, we may safely ascribe a mystical significance to the paradise it describes and consider it to be really the spiritual communion and fellowship which those who have faith obtain with God through Jesus Christ. To them only do the cherubim give way, and to as many as enter by him who calls himself the Door (John 10:7-9).

Thus, even though we do not subscribe one iota to the idea that all men are guilty because of Adam's guilt, neither can we claim any natural good for him. Although he does not share Adam's guilt until he commits his own acts of disobedience, nevertheless he is descended from Adam and derives his nature from him. How can he inherit any good from Adam when Adam had no good to pass on to him?

WHATEVER REAL GOOD A MAN DOES IS A CONSEQUENCE OF THE SEED OF GOD IN HIM

Since Adam did not retain any will or light in his nature that was capable of giving him knowledge of spiritual things, neither can his posterity. Whatever real good any man does proceeds not from the natural man who is descended from Adam, but from the seed of God in him, as the new life with which he is invested to bring him out of his natural condition. The Lord himself observed this as Gen 6:5 RSV says: "The Lord saw that the wickedness of man was great in the earth, and that every imagination of the thought of his heart was only evil continually." These words are not only very definite, but very comprehensive. Notice their emphasis first on every thought and then on continually evil. This excludes the possibility of any good as a result of man's natural thoughts. The Lord expressed this again, a little later, in Gen 8:21 Cath-CCD: "The inclination of man's heart is evil from his youth." Jer 17:9 KJ says: "The heart is deceitful above all things, and desperately wicked: who can know it?" How can anyone with any imagination believe that anything desperately wicked and deceitful can lead a man to righteousness? That is as contrary to logic as it is to state that a stone should fall upward because the law of gravity tends to cause it to fall downward.

Paul describes the condition of the generality of mankind in the fall in Rom 3:10-18 RSV, quoting various Psalms:[2] " 'None is righteous, no, not one; no one understands, no one seeks for God. All have turned aside, together they have gone wrong; no one does good, not even one.' 'Their throat is an open grave, they use their tongues to deceive.' 'The venom of asps is under their lips.' 'Their mouth is full of curses and bitterness.' 'Their feet are swift to shed blood, in their paths are ruin and misery, and the way of peace they do not know.' 'There is no fear of God before their eyes'."

Could anything be more definite? He seems to be particularly careful to avoid ascribing any good to natural man. He shows how polluted he is in all of his ways. He shows how

---

[2] The respective citations are Psalms 14:3 and 53:2; Psalm 5:9; Psalm 140:3; Psalm 10:7; Prov 1:6 and Isa 59:7-8; Psalm 36:1.

void he is of righteousness, of understanding, of the knowledge of God. How lost he is, and in short, useless. Nothing could be said which would more fully confirm our judgment that if this is the condition of natural man, he is incapable of one single correct step toward heaven.

The preceding verses show that it is impossible to claim that this does not refer to man's general condition, but only to certain particulars — or at least that it isn't inclusive of everything. The apostle, in speaking of himself in his natural condition, says (Rom 3:9-10 NEB): "What then? Are we Jews any better off? No, not at all! For we have already formulated the charge that Jews and Greeks alike are all under the power of sin. This has scriptural warrant." Since he follows this with the passages already given, he is clearly speaking of mankind in general.

THE NATURAL MAN IS INCAPABLE OF RECEIVING THE THINGS OF GOD

Some will object that in verse 14 of the preceding chapter he says that some Gentiles do by nature the things contained in the law, and so do by nature what is good and acceptable in the sight of God. But, this was intended to refer to their spiritual nature, which proceeds from the seed of God in man. The following verse refers to conscience, and the law written on the heart, making it clear that this is so. The other interpretation would also be inconsistent with what Paul says elsewhere, positively declaring that the natural man does not and can not receive the things of God. This is clearly stated in 1 Cor 2:14 RSV: "The unspiritual man does not receive the gifts of the Spirit of God, for they are folly to him, and he is not able to understand them because they are spiritually discerned." ...

¶III. These words of the apostle in 1 Cor 2 have already been dealt with, but since there are strenuous objections to this interpretation by some groups, I will deal with them before proceeding. Some object that the Greek word translated "natural" should be translated "animal." If this were not so, they say that a different Greek word would have been used. However, this seems to weaken the argument rather than strengthen it, since the only thing which distinguishes man "the animal" from the other beasts is his rational property. The apostle has deduced his argument in the verses cited from a simile which states that since the thoughts of man can only

be known by the spirit of man, the thoughts of God can only
be comprehended by the Spirit of God. Let us hope that these
men will admit that the thoughts of man are known by his
rational component rather than by his animal portion. It
must be the rational that was intended here. Otherwise his
intent, according to them, would be that: "God knows no man
by his animal spirit, but rather by his rational spirit." But to
say that the Spirit of God spoken of by the apostle is nothing
more than the rational spirit of man borders on blasphemy,
since they are so frequently contrasted and distinguished. Furthermore, he does not go on to say that they are rationally discerned, he says that they are spiritually discerned.

MAN'S WISDOM IS UNFIT TO JUDGE THE THINGS OF GOD

What is more important, throughout this chapter the
apostle shows how the wisdom of man is unfit to judge the
things of God and is ignorant of them. Should a man be called
wise because of his animal property, or because of his rational
quality? The apostle declares that both are part of man's natural state, and in verse 15 (RSV) he distinguishes them from the
spiritual, saying that: "The spiritual man judges all things."

This statement cannot be made about anyone merely because he is rational, for some of the greatest reasoners, like the
ancient Greeks, were often enemies to the kingdom of God.
Paul also said that the preaching of Christ is foolishness to the
wise men of this world, and that the wisdom of the world is
foolishness to God.[3]

Any disinterested rational man can easily judge whether
it is only with respect to their animal property that these men
consider the gospel to be foolishness or whether their rational
quality has something to do with it.

CHILDREN ARE NOT EVIL BY IMPUTATION
BUT ONLY WHEN THEY HAVE ACTUALLY TRANSGRESSED

¶IV. A reason for not imputing the evil and corrupt seed
to infants until they actually transgress is given at the end of
the passage in Eph 2:1 NEB: The children of wrath are described as those who "were dead in your sins and wickedness,
when you followed the evil ways of the present age, when you
obeyed the commander of the spiritual powers of the air, the
spirit now at work among God's rebel subjects." The reasons

---

[3] 1 Cor 3:19.

given for being "children of wrath" are following and obeying, and not anything which does not involve action.

It is strange that men can entertain such an absurd opinion which is so cruel and so contrary to the nature of God's mercy. The scriptures say nothing like that! It is obviously an egotistical opinion which derives from that bitter root which is the source of all errors. Most of the Protestants who hold this view think that they have benefitted from an absolute choice which will guarantee salvation for them and for their children. They have no compunction about sending all others, both young and old, to hell, even though the far greater part of mankind will be involved in these inextricable difficulties. Roman Catholics, on the other hand, use this argument to enhance the esteem of their church and its sacraments. They maintain that original sin is washed away by baptism. They are a little more merciful than the Protestants, for in their doctrine unbaptized children aren't sent to hell, but to a certain limbo. However this interpretation is not derived from scripture either.

No such views are authorized in the scriptures. In fact they are plainly contrary to their express tenor. Rom 4:15 NEB says clearly "where there is no law there can be no breach of law." How can sin be imputed to infants who know no law?[4]

Finally, Ezek 18:20 Cath-CCD says: "Only the one who sins shall die. The son shall not be charged with the guilt of his father, nor shall the father be charged with the guilt of his son. The virtuous man's virtue shall be his own; as the wicked man's wickedness shall be his." That hardly seems to impute wickedness to infants because of Adam's transgressions![5]

---

[4] What is more, the whole point of Rom 5 from which Barclay cites single verses here and later is that even though death held sway from Adam to Moses over those who had not sinned, God's act of grace was out of all proportion to Adam's misdeed.

Verses 16-18 NEB state: "the act of grace, following upon so many misdeeds, issued in a verdict of acquittal. For if by the wrongdoing of that one man death established its reign, through a single sinner, much more shall those who receive in far greater measure God's grace, and his gift of righteousness, live and reign through the one man, Jesus Christ. It follows, then, that as the issue of one misdeed was condemnation for all men, so the issue of one just act is acquittal and life for all men." — ED.

[5] Zwingli's *De Baptismo* is cited as also denying and refuting the eternal damnation of unbaptized infants; and as being anathematized by the Council of Trent, in the fifth session.

Reconciliation

PROPOSITIONS 5 AND 6 — THE UNIVERSAL REDEMPTION BY CHRIST, AND ALSO THE SAVING AND SPIRITUAL LIGHT BY WHICH EVERY MAN IS ENLIGHTENED

PROPOSITION 5: *God, out of his infinite love, takes "no pleasure in the death of the wicked man"* (Ezek 18:32, 33:11), *but God has given his only Son, that whoever "has faith in him may not die but have eternal life"* (John 3:16 NEB). *He is "the real light which enlightens every man"* (John 1:9 NEB). *And makes visible everything that is exposed to the light. And teaches all temperance, righteousness, and godliness. And enlightens the hearts of all to prepare them for salvation.*

It is this light which reproves the sin of every individual, and if it were not resisted it would effect the salvation of all men.

This light is no less universal than the seed of sin, being purchased by his death who tasted death for everyone: "For as in Adam all die, so in Christ all will be made to live" (1 Cor 15:22 Cath-CCD).

PROPOSITION 6: *In this hypothesis, all of the objections to the universality of Christ's saving death are easily resolved. It is not necessary to fall back on the ministry of the angels, or those other miraculous means which they say God uses to manifest the doctrine and history of Christ's passion to those who live in parts of the world where the outward preaching of the gospel is unknown. Just as many of the ancient philosophers may have been saved, so may some of those today whom providence has placed in the remote parts of the world where the knowledge of the history* [i. e. the historical Jesus] *is lacking, be made partakers of the divine mystery if they do not resist the manifestation of grace which is given to everyone for his benefit* (1 Cor 12:7). *This doctrine is established and confirmed against the objections of all who deny it. There is an evangelical and saving light and grace in everyone, and the love and mercy of God toward mankind were universal, both in the death of his beloved Son, the Lord Jesus Christ, and in the manifestation of the light in the heart.*

Therefore, Christ has tasted death for everyone (Heb 2:9) *— not merely for all kinds of men, as some foolishly say, but for*

everyone of every kind. The benefit of his suffering is extended not only to those who have a well-defined outward knowledge of his death and sufferings, as these are declared in the scriptures, but even to those who by some unavoidable accident were excluded from the benefit of this knowledge.

We willingly admit that this knowledge is very beneficial and inspiring, but not absolutely necessary for those from whom God himself has withheld it. For, if they allow his seed and light to enlighten their hearts, they may become partakers of the mystery of his death, even though they have not heard of it. In this light, which Christ himself affirms is available to all, communion is enjoyed with the Father and with the Son. Wicked men can become holy and lovers of that power by whose inward and hidden touches they feel themselves turned from evil to good. By it they can learn to treat others as they would like to be treated themselves.

It is false and erroneous to teach denial of the fact that Christ died for all men, and yet require outward knowledge of this fact as a prerequisite to salvation. Those who assert universal redemption with this limitation have not taken full account of the scriptures in which our doctrine is very well supported and clearly explained — Gen 6:3; Deut 30:14; John 1: 7-9, 16; Rom 10:8; *and* Titus 2:11.

HOW CAN MAN BE FREED FROM HIS DEMORALIZED CONDITION?

We have considered man's fallen, lost, corrupted, and demoralized condition. It is only fitting to inquire by what means he may be freed from this miserable and depraved condition. This is declared and demonstrated in these two propositions which have been combined, since one is really an explanation of the other.

We share this cause in common with many others who have rejected the horrible and blasphemous doctrine of predestination whereby God is supposed to have consigned the greater part of mankind to eternal damnation without any consideration of whether they have been disobedient or sinned. This is supposed to have been done. so that his justice may lay hold of them, yet it is claimed that he has withheld all grace from them by which they could obtain salvation. Although there is little to add to what has already been said, this doctrine is so opposed to our view that it cannot be dropped yet.

THE DOCTRINE OF PREDESTINATION IS A NOVELTY

¶I. This doctrine can safely be called a novelty, for no mention was made of it for the first 400 years after Christ. It is so contrary to the testimony of the scriptures, and to the tenor of the gospel, that all ancient writers, teachers, and Doctors of the Church[1] pass over it in profound silence. The first foundation for it is to be found in the later writings of Augustine, when he was eager to refute Pelagius. Unhappily, some of the expressions he used have been gleaned and embellished to establish this error. The truth of the more numerous expressions of Augustine to the contrary has thus been gainsaid and denied. The doctrine was developed by Dominicus and the monks of his order and was later taken up by John Calvin. It is unfortunate that he did so because this put a great stain on his reputation which was otherwise commendable, and it has slandered both Protestantism and the Christian religion. Although the Synod of Dort confirmed it, it has since lost ground and is beginning to be exploded by most men of learning and piety in all of the Protestant churches.[2]

[handwritten margin note: Protestantism vs Christian religion.]

[1] "Doctors of the Church," see fn p 43.

[2] The following comments give a brief history of the doctrine:
"This side of Augustine's teaching ... found its most extreme formulations in the writings which he issued at the end of his life," after long preoccupation with the Pelagian Controversy which "evoked his teaching upon the Fall, Original Sin, and Predestination." *De Praedestinatione Sanctorum* and *De Dono Perseverantiae* both appeared in 428, two years before Augustine's death. — *O.D.C.C.*, pp 106-108.
According to Wendel (p 264): "Calvin attributed great importance to predestination in both its forms — election and reprobation," although "his earliest writings do not contain any systematic statement of the problem." The frequently reiterated opinion of Alexandre Schweitzer and Ferdinand Christian (stated in 1844 and 1847) "that predestination was the central doctrine of Calvin's theology and that all the originality of his teaching proceeded from it," however, is not warranted.
Calvin "accorded a growing importance to it ... under the sway of ecclesiological and pastoral preoccupations." The 1539 edition of his *Institutes* owes a great debt in this matter to Augustine by way of Martin Bucer [a Dominican who joined the Reformation after release from his monastic vows by Papal dispensation in 1521]. Traces of the latter's 1536 publications are very plain in that and the 1541 edition. — Francois Wendel, *Calvin, The Origins and Development of His Religious Thought*, N. Y., Harper & Row, 1963, pp 263-264 and 140.
"The Calvinist doctrine of Predestination, which was not accepted by the Arminians, was imposed by the Synod of Dort (1618-1619) and by the Westminster Assembly (1647)." — *O.D.C.C.*, p 1099.
Calvin's doctrine found complete expression in the Westminster Confession and in the Westminster Larger Catechism (*Col. Encyc.*, p 1595), compiled by that body, and still in use by English-speaking Presbyterians.

We could overlook the silence of the early Church Fathers and the fewness of its advocates or even the learning of those who oppose it, if it had any basis in the writings and sayings of Christ and the apostles and if it were not a great injustice to God himself, to Jesus Christ our Mediator and Redeemer, and to the power, virtue, nobility and excellence of his blessed gospel, and also to all mankind.

PREDESTINATION MAKES GOD THE AUTHOR OF SIN

¶II. It is grossly unfair to God, because it makes him the author of sin, and of all things this is most contrary to his nature. It is true that those who assert the doctrine deny this consequence, but that is nonsense since it follows as naturally as the fact that one and two make three. For if God has decreed that those foreordained to damnation shall perish without any regard to whether they committed evil deeds, but merely because he wishes it to be; and if he also decreed long before they were born that they were predestined to wicked ways; who was the first author and cause of this, if not God who willed it thus and decreed it so?

INTRICATE EXPLANATIONS CANNOT AVOID THIS CONSEQUENCE

Many who preach this doctrine have developed all sorts of strained and intricate distinctions which would defend their opinion and still avoid this consequence. Yet some of its most eminent advocates have expressed this consequence so clearly that they leave no doubt. The following citations are just a few of the passages of this type.

Calvin:[3] "I say that it was by the ordination and will of God that Adam fell. God wanted man to fall. Man is blinded by the will and the command of God, and we refer the causes of our hardening to God. The highest or remote cause of hardening is the will of God, and it follows that the hidden counsel of God is the cause of hardening."

[3] John Calvin on chapter 3 of *Gen;* Id. 1. *Inst.* c 18, s 1. Id. *lib. de Prov.* Id. *Inst.* c 23, s 1.

Although there seems to be little doubt that Calvin made such a statement, since the gist of it can be found in the *Inst.*, 1 3, c 23, s 7, 8 and elsewhere, I have been unable to locate the precise statement quoted here. Unfortunately these citations from the *Inst.* are incomplete, omitting the book, and giving only chapter and section. — ED.

Beza:[4] "God has predestined whomever he saw fit, not only to damnation, but also to the causes of it." "The decree of God cannot be excluded from the cause of corruption."

Zanchius:[5] "It is certain that God is the first cause of obduration. Reprobates are held so fast under God's almighty decree, that they can do nothing but sin and perish."

Paraeus:[6] "It is the opinion of our doctors, that God inevitably decreed the temptation and fall of man. Thus it was necessary for the creature to sin according to the most just judgment of God. Our men do most rightly affirm that the fall of man was necessary and inevitable, by accident, because of God's decree."

Martyr:[7] "God inclines and forces the wills of wicked men into great sins."

Zwingli:[8] "God moves the robber to kill. He kills because God forces him to. But, you will say, then he is forced to sin; I permit truly that he is forced."

Piscator:[9] "Reprobate persons are absolutely ordained to this twofold end, to undergo everlasting punishment, and necessarily to sin; and therefore to sin, that they may be justly punished."

These quotations not only make God the author of sin but more unjust than the most unjust of men. . . .

¶III. The doctrine also does a great injustice to God because it makes him delight in the death of sinners, indeed, to desire many to die in their sins, contrary to what is written in Ezek 33:11, 1 Tim 2:4, and 2 Pet 3:9. . . .

4 [Theodore Beza (1519-1605), French reformer and Calvinist theologian], lib. de Praed. Id. de Praed. ad Art. 1.

5 [Jerome Zanchius (1516-1590)], de Excaecat. [see Schaff Creeds, v 1, p 305] q 5. Id. lib 5 de Nat. Dei, cap 2 "de Praed."

6 Paraeus, lib 3 de Amis. gratiae, c 2. Id. c 1.

7 [Probably Peter Martyr (1500-1562) who preceded Zanchius as professor of theology at Strasbourg, and who, at Cranmer's invitation, was at one point Regius professor of divinity at Oxford.] in Rom.

8 Ulrich Zwingli (1484-1531), lib. de Prov., c 5.
(For biographical note see pp 335 and 349.)

9 Piscator [Fisher the Jesuit? (1569-1641)], Resp. ad Vorst pa 1, p 120.
He was a contemporary of Vorstius (Konrad von der Vorst, 1569-1622), an Arminian theologian condemned as a heretic by the Synod of Dort.

PREDESTINATION MAKES CHRIST'S MEDIATION INEFFECTIVE

¶IV. It is grossly unfair to Christ our Mediator and to the efficacy and excellence of his gospel. It renders his mediation ineffectual, as if he had not completely broken down the middle wall by his suffering. It is, in effect, as if he had not removed the wrath of God or purchased the love of God for all mankind. What good is it to allege that the death of Christ is capable of saving all mankind if all mankind did not receive the capacity of being saved by his death?

IT MAKES PREACHING THE GOSPEL
A MOCKERY AND A DELUSION

It makes a mockery and a delusion of the preaching of the gospel if any of those to whom it is preached are excluded by an irrevocable decree from deriving any benefit from it. It makes the preaching of faith and repentance wholly useless and it declares that all of the gospel promises and threats are irrelevant. In the face of it, a man can never attain salvation if he belongs to those who are rejected. If he belongs to those who are chosen for salvation he has nothing to do but wait for the inevitable, which will come even if it is only in the last hour of his life.

IT DISTORTS THE COMING OF CHRIST

It distorts the coming of Christ and his propitiatory sacrifice into a testimony of God's wrath to the world. This becomes one of the greatest judgments and severest acts of God's indignation towards mankind. This act was then ordained to save very few and to harden and augment the condemnation of the far greater part of mankind because they do not believe in it. This unbelief, again, would be attributed to the hidden counsel of God by some of the proponents of the doctrine. Certainly, the coming of Christ was never a testimony of God's love in their eyes, but rather of his implacable wrath. According to this doctrine which condemns the major part of the world, God never loved the world, but hated it greatly in sending his Son to be crucified in it.

IT IS HIGHLY UNFAIR TO MANKIND

¶V. It is highly unfair to mankind, for it puts human beings in a far worse condition than the devils in hell. For these suffer only for their own guilt, and a measured time, whereas many millions of men who never knew of Adam's sin and were never accessories to it will be tormented forever. It renders them worse than the beasts of the field whose master requires no more of them than they are capable of. If they are killed, death is the end of their sorrow. But man is forever tormented for something he couldn't do. It is worse than Pharaoh's treatment of the Israelites for they could have obtained the straw that was withheld from them if they went and gathered it for themselves. But by this doctrine not only are all means of salvation withheld from men, but it is made impossible for them to attain it.

Just as Tantalus could not reach the fruit hanging at his very lips, they cannot attain salvation. Their consciences smite the unenlightened enough to convince them of their sin and thus to condemn and judge them, but there is no way that they can be helped to salvation. Because of a secret impotence which they possessed from childhood they are denied the efficacy of the gospel, the sacraments, prayer, and good works even if these engender the hope that they will be effective and they accept the faith. Not only is salvation denied them but their condemnation is made greater and their torments are made more violent and intolerable.

GOD IS PLEASED BY THE CONVERSION OF THE WICKED

This ought to dispose of this false doctrine so that we can proceed to the proposition that God out of his infinite love, who takes "no pleasure in the death of the wicked man, but rather in the wicked man's conversion, that he may live" (Ezek 33:11 Cath-CCD) "gave his only Son, that everyone who has faith in him may not die but have eternal life." (John 3:16 NEB). This is also affirmed in the sixth proposition, which states that Christ tasted death for all men and for every kind of man. Since these truths are stated almost in the exact words of scripture, little proof is needed. We hold these beliefs in common with many others who have pleaded earnestly for them and have based their pleas firmly on scripture. For this reason, we will deal with universal redemption only briefly in order to get on to some of the beliefs which seem to be limited to us.

THE DOCTRINE OF UNIVERSAL REDEMPTION

¶VI. The doctrine of universal redemption — that is, that Christ died for all men — is so evident from the scriptural testimony that there are few other articles of the Christian faith that are so frequently and plainly asserted and with as much conviction. It is universal redemption that makes Christ's preaching truly the gospel, or the annunciation of the glad tidings to all men.

The angel who declared the birth and coming of Christ to the shepherds said not that his news was for a few men, but (Luke 2:10 RSV): "Behold, I bring you good news of a great joy which will come to all the people." If these tidings had just been for a few it would have been more appropriate to consider them bad news of great sorrow to most people. And if most of mankind had been excluded, the angels would have had no reason to sing: "Peace on earth and good will towards men."

A DOOR OF MERCY AND HOPE FOR ALL

The feet of those who bring the glad tidings of the gospel of peace are said to be beautiful,[10] for they offer a door of mercy and hope for all. Through Jesus Christ, who gave himself a ransom for all, those who repent may reach common salvation. Christ most certainly did not intend to delude and deceive the majority of mankind when he issued the invitation: "Come to me, all whose work is hard, whose load is heavy; and I will give you relief. Bend your necks to my yoke, and learn from me, for I am gentle and humble-hearted; and your souls will find relief. For my yoke is good to bear, my load is light;" (Mat 11:28-30 NEB).

God is a God of truth and not a mocker of men, nor does he require anything of anyone which it is impossible for him to do. It is a truth graven in everyone's mind that no man is bound to do the impossible. It would be inconsistent with the mercy and justice of God for him to bid anyone to repent and believe in him if it were impossible for him to do so.

¶VII. As far as I know, there isn't a single passage of scripture which states that Christ did not die for all men. But there are many passages which say in very positive and explicit terms that he did. For example, 1 Tim 2:1, 3-6 NEB says: "First of all, then, I urge that petitions, prayers, intercessions and thanksgivings be offered for all men ... Such prayer is right, and approved by God our Saviour, whose will it is that all men should find salvation and come to know the truth. For there is one God, and also one mediator between God and men, Christ Jesus, himself man, who sacrificed himself to win

[10] Rom 10:15.

freedom for all mankind, so providing, at the fitting time, proof of the divine purpose." Unless we are to completely controvert this statement by the apostle, it is a very plain affirmation of what we have maintained.

¶VIII. It is clearly asserted that our Saviour gave himself a ransom for all men. Heb 2:9 RSV says: "We see Jesus, who for a little while was made lower than the angels, crowned with glory and honor because of the suffering of death, so that by the grace of God he might taste death for every one." There is no one who might not benefit by it, for: "It was not to judge the world that God sent his son into the world, but that through him the world might be saved;" John 3:17 NEB.[11]

The apostle Peter asserts it negatively in 2 Pet 3:9 NEB: "It is not his will for any to be lost." Or, to quote all of that verse: "It is not that the Lord is slow in fulfilling his promise, as some suppose, but that he is very patient with you, because it is not his will for any to be lost, but for all to come to repentance." This corresponds closely to Ezek 33:11 Cath-CCD: "I take no pleasure in the death of the wicked man, but rather in the wicked man's conversion, that he may live. Turn, turn from your evil ways!"

THE SCRIPTURES ARE FILLED WITH EARNEST INVITATIONS

The scriptures are full of such earnest invitations: Why do you not come to me so that you may have life? I have waited to be gracious unto you. I have sought to gather you: I have knocked at the door of your hearts: Are you not responsible for your own destruction? I have been calling all the day long! This doctrine is confirmed frequently, as in 1 John 2:1-2 RSV: "But if anyone does sin, we have an advocate with the Father, Jesus Christ the righteous; and he is the expiation for our sins and not for ours only but also for the sins of the whole world." There are those who rather ridiculously maintain that the phrase here, "the whole world," means only those who believe. If they can, I wish they would show me any place in the scriptures where "the whole world" is taken to mean only those who believe! There are many places that can be cited to the contrary, such as: The world knows me not; the world receives me not; I am not of this world. In

---

[11] John 12:47 NEB is quite similar: "I have not come to judge the world, but to save the world."

addition to these passages there are: Psalm 17:14, Isa 13:11,
Mat 18:7, John 7:7, 8:26, 12:19, 14:17, 15:18-19, 17:14, and
18:20, 1 Cor 1:21, 2:12, and 6:2, Gal 6:14, Jas 1:27, 2 Pet
2:20, 1 John 2:15, 3:1, 4:4-5, and many more.

THE EARLY CHURCH FATHERS BEGGED THE PAGANS TO PARTAKE OF THE BENEFITS OF CHRIST

All the Fathers and Doctors of the church, for the first
four centuries, boldly held forth the gospel of Christ and the
efficacy of his death.   They invited, in fact they begged, the
pagans to come and be partakers of its benefits, showing them
how there was a door opened for them all to be saved through
Jesus Christ.

Prosper[12] (or whoever was author of), *de vocat. gentium,*
says: "There is no reason to doubt that our Lord Jesus Christ
died for sinners and wicked men. And if anyone can be found,
who is not of this number, then Christ has not died for all;
but he, in fact, made himself a redeemer for the whole world."[13]

Chrysostom[14] says: "If he enlightens every man coming
into the world, how does it happen that so many men remain
without light?   For not everyone so much as acknowledges
Christ.   How then does he enlighten every man?   He illumin-
ates as far as it is possible for him to do so.   But if anyone
of his own accord closes the eyes of his mind, and will not
direct his eyes into the beams of this light, the reason he remains in darkness is not from the nature of the light. Instead,
it is the result of his own malignity, which has willfully rendered him unworthy of so great a gift.   But why did they not
believe?   Because they did not want to!   Christ did his part."

The Synod of Arles, held about 490 A. D.,[15] "pronounced
him accursed, who would say that Christ has not died for all,
or that he does not want all men to be saved."

[NOTE: In ¶IX and most of X, which are omitted here
except for the final paragraph below, Barclay further elaborates

---

12 [Prosper of Aquitaine or Prosper Tiro (c. 390-c. 465)],
lib 11, cap 6.

13 Quotations from Augustine *on Psalm 94* and Prosper's *ad Gall.,*
c 9, included in the original, are omitted here.

14 [St. John Chrysostom (c. 347-407), Doctor of the Church,
greatest of the Greek Fathers]   *on John 1.*

15 At least fifteen Synods of Arles were held between 314 and 1275.
I have not attempted to confirm this one. — ED.

on the reactions to Pelagian errors, and the later reformers including the Remonstrants who developed contrary doctrine,
and on how the Dark Ages gradually brought a veil over civi-
lization until the 16th century. He states that God reserved a
more complete discovery of the glorious and evangelical dispensation for the author's own age. — ED.]

A new interpretation of the gospel has been developed by
which all the scruples, doubts, hesitations and objections that
have been mentioned are easily and clearly answered and the
justice and mercy of God are exhibited, established, and confirmed.

We can clearly and confidently affirm the following points
on the basis of this certain light and gospel which has been
manifested to us by the revelation of Jesus Christ in us, rein-
forced by our own perceptible experience, and sealed by the
testimony of the Spirit in our hearts.

GOD HAS GRANTED A DAY OF VISITATION
TO EVERYONE OF EVERY NATION

¶XI. First, God, who out of his infinite love sent his Son,
the Lord Jesus Christ, into the world, and who tasted death
for everyone, has given a certain day or time of visitation to
everyone, whether Jew or Gentile, Turk or Scythian, Indian or
Barbarian, or of whatever nation, country, or place. During
that day or time of visitation, it is possible for them to be
saved, and to partake of the fruit of Christ's death.

GOD HAS GIVEN A MEASURE OF GRACE TO EVERYONE

Secondly, for this purpose God has communicated and
given a measure of the light of his own Son, a measure of
grace, or a measure of the Spirit to every man. The scripture
describes this gift by several names. Sometimes it is the seed
of the kingdom. Mat 13:18-19; the light that makes all things
manifest, Eph 5:13; the word of God, Rom 10:17; a manifestation of the Spirit for some useful purpose, 1 Cor 12:7; a
talent, Mat 25:15; a little leaven, Mat 13:33; or the gospel
preached to every creature, Col 1:23.

BY HIS LIGHT AND SEED GOD STRIVES WITH EVERYONE

Thirdly, God, in and by this light and seed, invites, calls,
exhorts, and strives with every man, in order to save him. If
this light is received and not resisted, it works the salvation
of all, even of those who are ignorant of the death and sufferings of Christ, and of Adam's fall. It does this not only by

bringing them a sense of their own misery, but by allowing them to share inwardly in the sufferings of Christ. They participate in his resurrection by becoming holy, pure, and righteous and by recovering from their sins. Those who have outward knowledge of Christ are also saved by it, since it opens their understanding of the right use and application of things delivered in the scriptures so that they may make saving use of them. But, this light can also be resisted and rejected both by the ignorant and by those who have outward knowledge of Christ. God is then said to be resisted and pressed down and Christ is again crucified and put to shame among men. To those who resist and refuse him, he becomes their condemnation.

THE GRACE OF GOD IS EXALTED ABOVE ALL ELSE

Among other consequences[16] of this doctrine, it exalts above everything else the grace of God, to which it attributes all good, even the least and smallest actions that are so. Thus, not only the first motions and the beginnings of good are ascribed to God's grace, but also the whole conversion and salvation of the soul.

It does not exalt the light of nature or the freedom of the will as some false doctrines have done, but entirely excludes the natural man from any place or part in his own salvation. He can make no act, nor set anything in motion by his own efforts until he has first been stimulated, elevated, and actuated by God's Spirit.

While it makes the salvation of man solely dependent upon God, it makes his condemnation entirely his own doing in every respect. Since he refuses and resists that of God which wrestles and strives in his heart, he is forced to acknowledge the fairness of God's judgment in rejecting and forsaking him.

Not only does this doctrine agree with the whole tenor of the gospel and with the nature of the ministry of Christ, but it magnifies and commends the merits and death of Christ. It not only considers them of sufficient account to save everyone, but declares that they have been brought so close that salvation is near at hand.

It commends the certainty of the Christian faith to the unbeliever, as well as the believer, since it demonstrates its

---

[16] Barclay numbers them from 1 to 12, but the numbering has been omitted, there has been some rearrangement, and those which repeat material just covered have been omitted. — ED.

own truth to everyone. There has never existed a place on earth that was so barbarous that men have not been able to find there reproof in their hearts for some of the evil that they have done. In the same way they have felt threatened with a certain horror if they continued in that evil. If they have given way to the light and have not resisted the seed of God in their hearts they have not only been promised a certain peace but they have also communicated it.

God will be merciful to them if they follow his ways. And he is also merciful to them when he reproves them for evil and encourages them to good.

¶XII. In proving this doctrine, some of its other consequences will become evident. But, in order to avoid arguments based merely on a misunderstanding of the doctrine itself, it is desirable to state the matter more clearly.

DAY OF VISITATION DEFINED

When we speak of the day or time of visitation which God gives to all, we are not referring to the entire lifetime of a person. For some people it may be extended to the very hour of death, as it was to the thief who was converted on the cross. For some it comes early in life and for others later, as God in his wisdom sees fit. However, many men outlive this day, and after it has passed there is no possibility of salvation for them. God then causes them to be hardened for their unbelief, and sometimes he uses them justly as instruments of wrath, causing one to be a scourge against another. To such men we can properly apply those scriptures which are abused to make it appear that God incites and compels men to sin.

This is expressed very well in Rom 1:17-32 and particularly in verse 28 NEB: "Thus, because they have not seen fit to acknowledge God, he has given them up to their own depraved reason. This leads them to break all rules of conduct."

The example of Esau, who lost his birthright, Heb 12:15-17 RSV, shows very well how many may outlive the day of God's gracious visitation to them: "See to it . . . that no one be immoral or irreligious like Esau, who sold his birthright for a single meal. For you know that afterward, when he desired to inherit the blessing, he was rejected, for he found no chance to repent, though he sought it with tears." It is also apparent in Christ's weeping over Jerusalem, Luke 19:42, 44 NEB, where he says: "If only you had known, on this great

day, the way that leads to Peace! But no; it is hidden from
your sight... because you did not recognize God's moment
when it came."

GOD'S ESSENCE IS INDIVISIBLE

¶XIII. When we speak of the seed, grace, word of God,
or the light and say that everyone possesses a measure of it
and is enlightened by it, we do not refer to the proper nature
and essence of God. That is indivisible! The seed or light
in man may be quenched, bruised, wounded, pressed down, or
slain and crucified, but this is not so of God's own nature.
God is a most pure and uncomplicated being, devoid of all
composition or division, who cannot be resisted, hurt, wounded, crucified or slain by all of the efforts and all of the strength
of men.

When we speak of the seed or light we understand a spiritual, celestial, and invisible principle, a principle in which
God dwells as Father, Son, and Spirit. A measure of this divine and glorious principle exists as a seed in all men which
by its nature draws, invites, and inclines the individual toward
God. Some call this the *vehiculum Dei,* or the spiritual body
of Christ, the flesh and blood of Christ, which came down from
heaven, and on which all who have faith are fed and nourished
with eternal life. This light and seed witnesses against and
reproves every unrighteous action. It is hurt, wounded, and
slain by such actions and flees from them, just as the flesh of
man creeps away from anything contrary to human nature.

Because it is never separated from God nor Christ, it is
said that in that respect God is resisted. Where it is borne
down God is said to be pressed down as blades of grass are
pressed down under the wheels of a cart, and Christ is said to
be slain and crucified.

CHRIST IS RESURRECTED AND THE NEW MAN TAKES SHAPE WHERE THE SEED IS RECEIVED

On the other hand, where the seed is received in the heart
and allowed to bring forth its natural and proper effect, Christ
is resurrected and takes shape as the new man which the scriptures so often speak of: Christ within, the hope of glory. This
is the Christ within of which we speak so often. We preach
him up and exhort people to believe in the light, and to obey
it, so they may come to know Christ in them who will deliver
them from all sin.

WE DO NOT EQUATE OURSELVES
WITH THE LORD JESUS CHRIST

By this we do not in any way equate ourselves with that holy man, the Lord Jesus Christ, who was born of the virgin Mary, in whom the fullness of the Godhead dwelt bodily.[17] Nor do we destroy the reality of his present existence as some falsely accuse us. For, although we affirm that Christ dwells in us, it is not without a mediator, but mediated as he is in that seed, which is in us. Whereas in Jesus himself there was no mediator. He was the Eternal Word, which was with God and was God. He is as the head and we are the members. He is the vine and we are the branches. Just as the soul is more immediately present in the heart and the mind than it is in the hands or the legs, and as the sap and life of the vine is present in greater quantity in the stock and root than in the branches, so does God dwell differently in Jesus than in us.

We also reject the heresy of Apollinarius,[18] who denied that Jesus had a soul, but said his body was actuated directly by the Godhead. Likewise, we reject the error of Eutyches, who declared that Christ's manhood was completely absorbed by his divinity.

[17] While Quakers have been wary of Christology in recent years because it has been the root of the majority of their internal schisms, as nearly as a consensus could be framed today, it would come close to these two opening sentences. This can be said in spite of small unitarian, ethically centered, or humanist minorities. These are bound to occur in a religious society which does not require creedal affirmation and which is inherently opposed to creeds. The average Friend, however, tends to give deeper thought to such matters than his, shall we say, "better-regulated" Christian brother. But his conclusions are apt to stop short of the theological definitions which have evolved through the centuries, and may be somewhat naive by comparison. Nonetheless real freshness and beauty characterize many of these. The statement of Yorkshire (England) Quarterly Meeting in 1919 is unusually profound:
"The New Testament clearly sets out Christ as fully human and as fully divine. The writers are conscious of no difficulty or contradiction involved in this position. It seemed to them the most natural thing in the world. Probably the sense of contradiction only arises in our minds through ignorance of what is meant by personality.... It is a pity that we insist on using the terms 'humanity' and 'divinity' as though they imply opposition. May we not rather say that Jesus 'shows us the divine life humanly lived and the human life divinely lived.' But of one thing we can be certain — there are depths beneath depths, and heights above heights in the personality of Jesus, which make rash generalizations or superficial solutions absurd."

[18] Apollinarius (c. 315 - c. 390) was bishop of Laodicea near Antioch. Barclay's synopsis of his views is almost paraphrased by the *Encyc.*

We believe he was truly and really man. We also believe that he continues to be glorified as such in heaven, both in soul and body. By him God will judge the world, in the great and general day of judgment.

THE THINGS OF GOD ARE BEYOND OUR ORDINARY SPIRIT AND SENSES

¶XIV. This seed, light, or grace is not an accident,[19] as most men ignorantly consider it, but a real spiritual substance which the soul of man can feel and apprehend. It is from this substance that the new man arises in the heart of the believer. This seems strange to those who are unacquainted with it, but it is a well-known and thoroughly established experience among us.

It is difficult for a man to comprehend this with his mind until he himself has experienced it, and merely understanding it in the mind would be of little value if that were as far as it went. But we know that it is true, and that our belief is not without solid ground. As the inward and substantial seed in our hearts is nourished and grows we become capable of tasting, smelling, seeing, and handling the things of God, for these things are beyond our ordinary spirit and senses.

We know that it is a substance, because it exists in the hearts of wicked men, even while they are in wickedness. This seed of holy substance often lies in men's hearts like a naked grain in stony ground, or like medicine in an unhealthy body.

Brit. (v 2, p 109), which states: "In his eagerness to combat Arianism he went so far as to deny the existence of a rational human soul in Christ's human nature, this being replaced in Him by a prevailing principle of holiness, to wit. the Logos."

Eutyches (c. 378-454) was the Archimandrite of a large monastery at Constantinople. He "insisted that Christ's humanity was absorbed in his divinity." (*Col. Encyc.*, p 611) "He also maintained that there were 'two natures before, but only one after, the Union' in the Incarnate Christ and was thus the real founder of Monophysitism." (*O.D.C.C.*, p 916) A schism occurred over this at the Council of Chalcedon (451) and survives in a large group known as the non-Chalcedonian Eastern churches — the Coptic, Abyssinian, Syrian Jacobite, Malabar Jacobite, and, to some extent, the Armenian churches.

[19] Classical and Scholastic philosophy made much of the distinction between the inherent nature or "substance" of an object or being, and the "accidents" which were less essential or inherent, but nonetheless distinguished from mere attributes or properties. The distinction was particularly employed in the Roman Catholic doctrine of Transubstantiation, where the bread and the wine were unchanged in appearance (their accidents), but in substance became the body and blood of Christ. — ED.

When the divine medicine begins its work in a man's heart, part of him may become cured and good, and part may remain sick and evil. Many men are referred to as good and holy when the seed has done a good measure of work in them. This is true even though they may still be liable to many spiritual ills and weaknesses, even some iniquities.

But, just as the seed of sin and ground of corruption, and the capacity to yield to them, and sometimes even actually to fall, do not make a good and holy man impious, neither does the seed of righteousness in evil men and their possibility of being transformed by it, of itself make them good or holy.

THE ATONEMENT AND SACRIFICE OF CHRIST ARE EXALTED BY OUR DOCTRINE

¶XV. Our doctrine in no way lessens or detracts from the atonement and sacrifice of Jesus Christ, but on the contrary magnifies and exalts it. We believe that everything which is recorded in the holy scriptures concerning the birth, life, miracles, suffering, resurrection, and ascension of Christ actually happened. Anyone to whom it pleases God to reveal the same and bring a knowledge of these events has the duty to believe them. In fact it is a matter for condemnation if he does not believe these things when they have been declared to him — to resist the holy seed which would incline and lead everyone toward belief as it is offered to him. The seed may not afford outward and explicit knowledge of the life of Christ to everyone, nevertheless wherever such knowledge is declared, *ubi declaratur,* it always assents to it.

We further believe that the remission of sins of which anyone may partake is only by virtue of his complete atonement and nothing else. It was necessary for him to be born in order to offer himself a sacrifice to God for our sins. It was by his death and sufferings that he "carried our sins to the gallows, so that we might cease to live for sin and begin to live for righteousness;" (1 Pet 2:24 NEB). It is by his obedience that the free gift of justification has come to all.

Just as we affirm that even though thousands of thousands are ignorant of Adam's fall, and yet everyone is inclined toward evil because he partook of the forbidden fruit, everyone is equally turned from evil toward good by the influence of this holy and divine seed and light, even though he knew nothing of Christ's coming in the flesh. His obedience and sufferings purchased this grace.

Furthermore, just as we confess that it is absolutely necessary for those who have been brought by God to a knowledge of Christ's outward appearance to believe in it, we willingly state that outward knowledge is very comforting to those who are influenced and led by the inward seed and light. Not only does the knowledge of Christ's love and sufferings tend to humble them, but they are also strengthened in their faith and are encouraged to follow the excellent pattern which he has left us. "Unto this, indeed, you have been called, because Christ also has suffered for you, leaving you an example, that you may follow in his steps," (1 Pet 2:21 Cath-CCD). And many are the gracious sayings of Christ by which we are greatly edified and refreshed.

THE HISTORY PROVIDES PROFIT AND COMFORT IN ASSOCIATION WITH THE MYSTERY

The history, then, provides profit and comfort in association with the mystery, and never without it. But, the mystery is and may be profitable without the explicit and outward knowledge of the history.

CHRIST AS LIGHT AND CHRIST AS THE SOURCE OF LIGHT

This brings us to another question — whether or not Christ is in all men. This question has been raised because in some of our writings, and in our public meetings and declarations, we assert that we want every man to know and be acquainted with Christ in him, and we tell him that Christ is in him. To elaborate, as we have said before, a divine, supernatural light or seed is in all men, and that divine, supernatural light or seed is the *vehiculum Dei* in which God and Christ dwell and from which they are never separated. As this light or seed is received and accepted in the heart, Christ takes form and is brought forth. But that is far from ever saying Christ is formed in this manner in all men, or in the wicked. Far from it! To bring about this acceptance is a great achievement, as can be judged by the way in which the apostle labored to bring it about in the Galatians.

Thus Christ is not in all men by being united with them, nor indeed, strictly speaking, does he dwell within them in the sense of making them his habitation. Because, in the way in which this is generally understood, it would imply union, the manner in which Christ was present in the saints [mystics]. But, it is written: "I will live in them and move among them,

and I will be their God, and they shall be my people," 2 Cor
6:16 RSV. Thus, to the extent that Christ is in all men as a
seed, a holy, pure seed and light from which he cannot be
separated, and which is in all men, it can be said in the larger
sense, he is in all men, as has already been observed.

Is it not analogous to the situation where the scripture
reports, in Amos 2:13 KJ, that God said:[20] "Behold, I am
pressed under you, as a cart is pressed that is full of sheaves"?
In Heb 6:6 it is said that Christ is crucified in the ungodly.
Properly speaking, of course, God cannot be pressed down, and
Christ, as God, cannot be crucified.

It is in this respect — that is, that he is in the seed that
is in all men — that we have preached that he is in all men.
We direct all men to that of Christ in them so they may look
upon him whom they have pierced, who lies crucified in them
by their sins and iniquities, and that they may be led to repent
and be saved. Then he who lies now, as it were, slain and
buried in them may rise and have dominion over all in their
hearts. This is what the apostle Paul preached to the Corinthians and Galatians — Christ crucified in them (1 Cor 2:2 and
Gal 3:1).[21]

It was this Jesus Christ that the apostle desired them to
know in themselves and to make known unto them. Then they
might come to realize how they had been crucifying Christ in
that way, and with this knowledge they might repent and be
saved.

Sometimes Christ, who is in reality the source of light, is
considered synonymous with the light. For Christ is called
the light that enlightens every man, the light of the world,
and since Christ is in that light and is never separated from
it, the light itself is sometimes called Christ.

THE DIVINE PRINCIPLE IS NEITHER INHERENT NOR A RELIC

¶XVI. This should make it clear that we do not consider
the divine principle as being part of man's nature, or a relic
of the good that Adam lost by his fall. It is something sepa-

---

[20] This is an unfortunate choice of quotation to illustrate this point,
since the KJ translation is confused. In the newer versions, for example
Cath-CCD, it reads: "Beware, I will crush you into the ground as a wagon
crushes when laden with sheaves."

[21] This reference is based on the KJ version and is not borne out
by the modern translations of these passages.

rate and distinct from a man's soul and from all of the soul's faculties. We do not deny that reason is a property that is natural to man and an essential one by which he can know and learn many arts and sciences. It enables him to progress far beyond what any other animal can do merely by its animal nature. We do not deny that man can apprehend and know spiritual things with his brain. But, since that is not the proper organ by which we know God, as has been dealt with in the second proposition, it cannot advance him toward salvation, but instead it hinders him.

Indeed, the great cause of the apostasy has been the fact that man tried to fathom the things of God solely by this natural and rational principle. He tried to build a religion with it while he neglected and overlooked the seed of God that was in his heart. It is in this way that in the most universal and catholic sense Anti-Christ has set himself up in every man, and sits in the temple of God as God, and above everything else that is called God. For man is the temple of God, as the apostle has said, 1 Cor 3:16, and when the rational principle sets itself above the seed of God, and reigns and rules as the prince of spiritual things, the holy seed is wounded and bruised. Reason has been exalted above and against Christ.

REASON IS FIT TO ORDER AND RULE MAN IN NATURAL MATTERS

Nevertheless we do not maintain that man was given reason for no purpose or for no use to himself. We look upon reason as fit to order and rule man in the things of nature. God gave two great lights to rule the outward world — the sun and the moon — the greater light to rule the day and the lesser light to rule the night. Similarly he has given man the light of his Son as a spiritual and divine light to rule him in things spiritual, and the light of reason to rule him in things natural. And even as the moon borrows her light from the sun, so should men have their reason enlightened by this divine and pure light if they wish to be correctly and adequately ordered in natural matters. Such enlightened reason may also be useful to men even in spiritual things if it is kept subservient to the Spirit and the true light is followed and obeyed, just as the animal life in man helps him in doing things that are rational if it is regulated and ordered by reason.

CONSCIENCE FOLLOWS JUDGMENT
BUT THE LIGHT OF CHRIST INFORMS IT

This light is further distinguished from man's natural conscience, because conscience arises from the natural faculties of man's soul which may be defiled and corrupted. It is explicitly stated of the impure, Titus 1:15 RSV, that "their very minds and consciences are corrupted." But this light can never be corrupted or defiled. It never consents to evil or wickedness in anyone. Eph 5:13 says that it makes all things manifest that are reprovable and it is thus a faithful witness for God against every bit of unrighteousness in man.

Conscience, on the other hand, is the knowledge that develops in a man's heart from whatever agrees, contradicts, or is contrary to anything that is believed by him. It is the faculty by which he becomes conscious of having trespassed when he does something which he knows is contrary to what he should do. When the mind has been blinded or contaminated by a wrong belief, his conscience will still trouble him when he goes against that belief, even if it is erroneous. The conscience of a Turk will smite him if he drinks wine, but it will allow him to keep many concubines without troubling him, because his judgment has been corrupted with the false notion that it is lawful for him to do so. If a Catholic should eat meat during Lent, this would cause his conscience to smite him, even though a Protestant might not be bothered by the same act.

Conscience follows judgment, rather than informing it. But light, as it is followed, increasingly removes the blindness of judgment, opens the understanding, and corrects the errors of both judgment and conscience. Conscience is a wonderful thing when it is properly informed and enlightenend. It has been compared to a candle holder, and the light of Christ to a candle. When a clean candle burns in the holder it shines brightly and sheds a useful light, but otherwise the holder is useless as illumination. It is to the light of Christ in their consciences that we direct people and not to their natural consciences. We preach up this light as a most certain guide to life eternal.

This light is not a natural faculty of man's mind. A man in good health can stir up and exercise or move the faculties of his mind[22] whenever he pleases. He is absolute master of them

---

[22] Barclay used "soul," but "mind" makes better sense at this point.

unless he has some physical handicap. On the other hand, the light and seed of God in man is uncontrollable. It moves, blossoms, and strives with him as the Lord sees fit. Salvation is possible for anyone during the day of his visitation, but there is no way in which a man can stir up that light and grace at his pleasure or even when he needs it. He must wait for it. There are certain times and seasons when it exerts a powerful influence and makes the soul tender and breaks its bonds. At those times, if a man does not resist it but works with it, he will come to know salvation by it. The pool of Bethesda cured only those who stepped into it immediately after the angel had troubled the waters. Similarly, God moves this seed in the heart of mankind only at particular times. He does it to show a man his sins, and by it seriously invites him to repentance, offering him remission of his sins and salvation. If a man then accepts, he may be saved. This is something which he cannot bring upon himself, no matter how great are his pains or his industry.

This, then, oh men and women, is the day of God's gracious visitation to your soul! If you do not resist, you will be happy forever. This is the day of the Lord! As Christ says, it is like the lightning, which shines from the east to the west (Mat 24:27). It is the wind, or the Spirit which blows upon the heart. No one knows where it comes from or where it is going (John 3:8).

SALVATION IS BY GRACE ALONE

¶XVII. The operation of this seed or light in the heart is sufficient to cause us more than any others to attribute our entire salvation to the mere power, Spirit, and grace of God. He who resists its strivings is the cause of his own condemnation. He will not find his salvation. Its work is one of passiveness and grace, although as it continues to work, it arouses the desire to become a co-worker with it. As Augustine has said: "He who made us without our help will not save us without it." The initial step is not the work of man, but merely seeing that he does not work against it. Until grace has laid hold of him in these particular times, he cannot move a single step away from his natural condition.

Just as iron is a hard and cold metal which can be warmed and softened by fire, the soul of man, even though it is prone to evil, can be worked upon and wrought by the grace of God moving in and upon it. If a man resists or if he departs from the grace of God, his heart can return to its former condition, just as iron rehardens when the fire is removed.

Perhaps two everyday examples will help to clarify what we have said. Who is to blame for a man's failure to recover from illness if he does not follow the advice of his doctor and refuses to rest or insists on eating forbidden foods? Or if men trapped in a pit do not listen when their deliverer comes at certain times to inform them of the great hazard of remaining there, particularly if he takes hold of them and exerts a pull to help them out of their misery.

The grace of God can differ in its effects since its object is to minister mercy and love to those who do not reject it (John 1:12, but to minister wrath and condemnation to those who do (John 3:19). In this respect, it is more like the action of the sun which hardens clay although it melts wax!

The function of the sun is to nourish creation. The living are refreshed by the sun and under its beams the flowers send forth a pleasant aroma and the fruits of the trees are ripened. But cast a lifeless carcass into its beams and the same rays of the sun will cause it to putrefy and have an evil odor. Nonetheless, that does not mean that the sun's real purpose has been frustrated.

When the sun of righteousness shines upon the individual soul it can be melted and influenced to send forth good fruit, and a good savor. But if the individual has continued to sin throughout his day of visitation, the same sun will harden him as it does the clay. His wickedness will be more apparent and its putrefying effect will send forth an evil savor.

A SPECIAL MEASURE OF GRACE WAS GIVEN TO SOME

¶XVIII. God does not wish anyone to perish, and for that reason he has given sufficient grace for salvation to everyone. But he also gives a special measure of his grace to some people so that they must necessarily be saved. It would be ridiculous to say that God had not extended himself in a special way to the Virgin Mary and the apostle Paul that was different from the customary grace extended to others. It would be ludicrous to say that he loved both the traitor Judas and the beloved disciple John to the same degree. Yet it would be inexcusable if they had not desired a measure of grace by which they could be saved. To preclude self-satisfaction and any pre-

sumptuousness on the part of those to whom he gives a prevalence of grace, God does his work in secret. Thus they are
humbled, and the free grace of God is magnified. All credit
accrues to the free gift and nothing is claimed to arise from the
individual's own strength. Those who perish remember the
times of God's visitation and recall how he wrestled with them
by his light and Spirit. They have to confess that there was
a time when the door of mercy was open to them and that
they were justly condemned because they rejected their own
salvation.

In that way, both the mercy and justice of God are established, and the will and strength of man are minimized. The
individual's condemnation is attributable only to himself, while
his salvation depends upon God. These two positions should
be a good answer to the great objections that are often brought
against our doctrine of universal and saving light.

The first of these is that there are certain places in the
scriptures where God seems very precisely to have decreed that
some were predestined for salvation. He also seems to have
ordained certain means which were not available to others.
The calling of Abraham and David are examples, among
others, as well as the conversion of Paul. When these are included among those to whom a prevalence of grace was given,
the basis for the objection is gone.

The other objection is based on the places where God
seems to have ordained certain wicked persons for destruction.
He made them obdurate and forced them to commit great sins.
But if we consider their day of visitation to have passed, this
objection also disappears.

THE DAY OF VISITATION IS LIMITED

¶XIX. The first thing to prove is that God has given every
man a day of visitation in which he might be saved. If it can
be proved that this day and time were given to those who perished and that they might have been saved, the matter is ended,
for no one will deny that those who *have* been saved have had
a day of visitation. The regrets and complaints which the Spirit
of God utters throughout the scriptures in sharp reproof of
those who perished because they did not accept God's visitation
and his offers of mercy make this apparent. The Lord first expressed himself in that manner to Cain, Gen 4:6-7 Cath-CCD:
"The Lord said to Cain, 'Why are you angry and why are you

downcast? If you do well, will you not be accepted: but if you
do not do well, will not sin crouch at the door?' " This was
said to Cain before he slew Abel, and when the evil seed was
beginning to tempt him, and was at work in his heart. God
gave Cain a warning, in time for him to accept his remission if
he acted as God wanted him to. This was his day of visitation.

On the other hand, if God had not given Cain sufficient
strength to enable him to do good, it would have been useless
to propose the doing of good as a condition for salvation. God
offered this day of visitation even to the ancient world, and
this is the interpretation that should be given to Gen 6:3 Cath-
CCD: "My spirit shall not remain in man forever."[23] This
clearly implies that the season in which God strives to save a
man is limited. It is said of this day of visitation that God has
given to everyone, Isa 30:18 Cath-CCD: "Yet the Lord is waiting to show you favor, and he rises to pity you; for the Lord is
a God of justice: blessed are all who wait for him!" He is "a
merciful and gracious God, slow to anger and rich in kindness
and fidelity;" (Exod 34:6 Cath-CCD).[24] In his prayer in Jer
15:15 Cath-CCD, the prophet throws himself on God's "long-
suffering" nature to escape banishment. In verse 18 of the
same chapter, his complaint is: "Why is my pain continuous,
my wound incurable, refusing to be healed? You have indeed become for me a treacherous brook, whose waters do not
abide!" However, in the following verse God says:[25] "If you
repent, so that I restore you ... if you bring forth the precious
without the vile, you shall be my mouthpiece."

There are those of a different doctrine who would say
that the pain and the wound are incurable for most men.

BUT GOD IS LONG-SUFFERING

The long-suffering of God in ancient times is also referred
to in the New Testament. In 1 Pet 3:20 Cath-CCD, there is

*

[23] Barclay's point is weakened by the newer translations, for this
passage continues (RSV) "... for he is flesh, but his days shall be a
hundred and twenty years."

[24] The same idea is repeated in Num 14:18 and Psalm 86:15, both
cited by Barclay, which read respectively (Cath-CCD): "The Lord is slow
to anger and rich in kindness, forgiving wickedness and crime." "But
you, O Lord, are a God merciful and gracious, slow to anger, abounding
in kindness and fidelity." — ED.

[25] RSV: "If you return, I will restore you ... if you utter what is
precious, and not what is worthless, you shall be as my mouth."

reference to the "times past ... when the patience of God waited in the days of Noe [Noah] while the ark was building." If anyone should claim that God's steadfastness, his forebearance and patience were not for the purpose of saving him, the same apostle says explicitly in 2 Pet 3:15 Cath-CCD: "And regard the long-suffering of our Lord as salvation." In verse 9 he says: "he is very patient with you, because it is not his will for any to be lost, but for all to come to repentance." Peter also gives references to the writings of Paul on this matter and proclaims this as universal doctrine. It is noteworthy that he adds (verse 16) that in the epistles of Paul "there are certain things difficult to understand, which the unlearned and the unstable distort ... to their own destruction." He clearly insinuates that he is referring to such expressions in Paul's epistles as those in Rom 9, which some who were unlearned in spiritual things distorted so that they would seem to mean that God was not long-suffering toward everyone and did not wish that all might be saved, or that none should perish. More heed should have been taken of his commentary. The most explicit statement in Paul's writings which Peter seems to be hinting at in particular is Rom 2:4 RSV: "Do you not know that God's kindness is meant to lead you to repentance?"

If God pleads with the wicked to accept the possibility of being saved! If God's Spirit strives for a time, even in those who later perish! If he wants to be gracious to them! If he is steadfast toward them! If his steadfastness means salvation for them as long as it lasts! Then, there is a day of visitation, and in it those who will perish might have been saved if they had repented.

¶XX. Isaiah was highly incensed when his vineyard brought forth only wild grapes, even though it was situated on a very fertile hill, and he had fenced it, removed all of the stones, and planted only the choicest vines. He asked if the men of Judah would judge between him and his vineyard, saying (Isa 5:4-5 Cath-CCD): "What more was there to do for my vineyard that I had not done?" Then he carried the analogy over to those in Israel who had refused God's mercy (verse 7): "The vineyard of the Lord of hosts is the house of Israel, and the men of Judah are his cherished plant."

Jesus used the same analogy — Mat 21:33, Mark 12:1, Luke 20:9 — telling how a master gave his tenants all of the things that were needed for planting a vineyard and having it bear fruit. When they refused to pay him his share of the proceeds, he was very patient and passed over many offenses and the mistreatment of his servants and the murder of his son before he decided to destroy them and cast them out. This cannot be applied to those who already have faith, or who have repented and are saved, for it says explicitly: "He will bring those bad men to a bad end." The parable could not have been used to illustrate his point if these men had not had the capacity to do good. He might have added, as the prophet did: "What more could I have done?"

It is more than clear from this parable, which is repeated by three different evangelists, that Christ is very patient with men and their wickedness, but that nevertheless those who resist the means of salvation that are offered to them do so to their own condemnation. There are other parallel scriptures: Prov 1:24-26, Jer 18:9-10, Mat 18:32-35, and Acts 13:46.

NEVERTHELESS ONCE THEIR DAY OF VISITATION HAS EXPIRED, MEN ARE HARDENED IN THEIR UNBELIEF

It is evident from Christ's lamentations over Jerusalem that the wicked are cut off from salvation once their day of visitation has expired. This is expressed in three different places, Mat 23:37, Luke 13:34, and 19:41-42 NEB: "When he came in sight of the city, he wept over it and said, 'If only you had known, on this great day, the way that leads to peace! But no; it is hidden from your sight.'" Then he goes on to say that it will be completely destroyed "because you did not recognize God's moment when it came" (v 44 NEB). In both of the first two versions he enlarges on that time of visitation in identical words, saying: "How often have I longed to gather your children, as a hen gathers her brood under her wings; but you would not let me."

How significant it is that the offer of salvation was not made for the sake of his vanity, but as naturally and as willingly "as a hen gathers her brood." Christ's desire to gather lost men and women and redeem them from their corrupt and degraded condition was as natural as the love and concern of a hen for her brood. But because they refused, "the way that leads to peace" was hidden from their eyes.

Why was it hidden? Because they just would not see the things that were good for them in the season of God's love toward them. Now that the day has passed, they cannot possibly see them, and as a further judgment, God allows them to be hardened in their unbelief.

It is after these very genuine offers of mercy and salvation have been rejected that men's hearts are hardened and not before. Thus the saying, Mat 25:29 KJ, is verified: To him "that hath, shall be given ... but from him that hath not shall be taken away even that which he hath." This apparent riddle makes sense when this doctrine is applied. He who has not will forfeit even what he has, for the time will pass when he can make use of even that little, so it will become nothing. For Christ used this expression when the talent was taken away from the slothful servant who failed to make use of it, and it was given to the servant who had been trustworthy.

THIS IS THE JUDGMENT OF OBDURATENESS

Once the day of visitation has been rejected, men and women receive the judgment of obdurateness. This is what Christ was saying in the incident described by all four of the evangelists (Mat 13:14, Mark 4:12, Luke 8:10 and John 12:40), taking his text from Isa 6:9 [Mark 4:11-12 NEB]: "To you the secret of the kingdom of God has been given; but to those who are outside everything comes by way of parables, so that (as Scripture says) they may look and look, but see nothing; they may hear and hear, but understand nothing; otherwise they might turn to God and be forgiven."

Paul used the same theme, after he had offered salvation to the Jews at Rome, as described in Acts 28:26-27 NEB: "How well the Holy Spirit spoke to your fathers through the prophet Isaiah when he said, 'Go to this people and say: You will hear and hear, but never understand; you will look and look, but never see. For this people has grown gross at heart; their ears are dull, and their eyes are closed. Otehwise, their eyes might see, their ears hear, and their heart understand, and then they might turn again, and I would heal them.' "

God would have liked them to see, but they closed their eyes, so they were justly hardened.

WALKING IN THE LIGHT

¶XXI. Let us now consider how this comes about. With God's assistance, it will be demonstrated by some simple and clear scriptural testimony that he has given a measure of supernatural light and grace to everyone that is sufficient for his salvation.

John 1:9 RSV says: "The true light that enlightens every man was coming into the world." This passage so clearly favors our assertions that some have called it the Quaker text. No inference or interpretation has to be added. The verse is stated in the very terms of our faith, and it is a logical consequence of the two propositions stated in the preceding verses [4 and 5]: "In him was life, and the life was the light of men. The light shines in the darkness, and the darkness has not overcome it." From these, he infers that he was "the real light which enlightens every man."

The apostle considers the fact that Christ was the light of man as one of his chief attributes, or at least one that was to be given special and particular notice. As we walk with him in the light which he communicates to us, "we share together a common life, and we are being cleansed from every sin by the blood of Jesus his Son," as it is stated in 1 John 1:7 NEB.

Avoiding the hypercriticism of those who claim that the universality of grace under the guidance of God's Spirit is limited, the apostle states that this true light enlightens everyone who comes into the world. Even though this light shines in darkness, the darkness never quenches it. It is quite clear that the light shines in everyone whether his heart is in darkness or not.

The purpose for which this light was given is stated in John 1:7. John the Baptist was sent by God to bear witness to the light. He was "to testify to the light, that all might become believers through him." [Barclay then refers to the original Greek to make it clear that the "him" refers to the nearest antecedent, the light, rather than to John. The latter would make it appear that all were supposed to believe through John. Although there is nothing to contradict this in so many words, this puts a ridiculous strain on the context.]

THIS LIGHT IS THE LIGHT OF JESUS CHRIST

Since this light is the light of Jesus Christ, there is no doubt that it is a supernatural light and that it is sufficient for salvation. If it were not supernatural, how could it be called the light of Jesus? Although all things are his, and are of and from him, we do not usually extend this concept to natural matters in such a way that we would say emphatically that these are from Christ in such a special way. Furthermore, at this particular point, the evangelist is expounding on

Christ's office as mediator and speaking of the particular benefits which we receive from him in that particular capacity.

There are places where Christ is quoted as referring to
himself as the light. There are those who claim that the reference is to his outer person and that that is what he would
have them believe in. "While you have the light," he says in
John 12:36 RSV and Cath-CCD: "believe in the light, that you
may become sons of light." There is no denial of the fact that
they should have believed in Christ as the Messiah who was to
come. But it is difficult to understand why they insist that
that is what Christ meant in this particular instance.

The reference to "while you have the light" cannot be
understood as referring to his person, or else there would have
been no reason for the Jews to believe in him, since the Messiah was supposed to remain with them forever. How could
anyone believe in him today when the outward man, or his
bodily presence, is far removed from them? The light in which
they were commanded to believe has to be the inward spiritual
light which shines in their hearts for a season — that is, during the day of their visitation. While it continues to call, invite and exhort the individual to believe, men can possess it
and can believe in it. But when men refuse to believe in it
and reject it, then it ceases to be a light that will show them
the way. They do retain a sense of having been unfaithful to
it and it is a sting to their consciences. This gives them a
sense of terror and darkness in which they do not know where
to go and cannot achieve any works which will bring about
their salvation. For such rebellious ones, the day of the Lord
is said to be one of darkness and not one of light, Amos 5:18-
19 Cath-CCD: "Woe to those who yearn for the day of the
Lord! What will this day of the Lord mean for you? Darkness and not light! As if a man were to flee from a lion, and
a bear should meet him; or as if on entering his house he
were to rest his hand against the wall, and a snake should
bite him."[26]

THE LIGHT IS THE IMPLANTED WORD
AND THE SEED OF SALVATION

¶XXII. Christ tells us expressly in the parable of the
sower (Mat 13:18ff, Mark 4, and Luke 8:11) that his saving

[26] Two quotations from Cyril of Alexandria's commentary *on John*
have been omitted from sects 20 and 21 above. The first was from l 6,
c 21; the second from l 1, c 2.

light and seed is sown in several kinds of ground and that it
is the word of the kingdom.   This is what the apostle calls
the "word of faith" in Rom 10:8 and "the implanted word,
which is able to save your souls" in Jas 1:21 RSV. The biblical
words themselves declare that it is saving by its very nature,
for in the good ground it fructified abundantly, although in
the stony thorny ground, and by the wayside, it was useless.

As Christ himself interpreted the parable, it was the fear
of persecution and the corrupting power of wealth that prevented the seed from growing in many hearts.   But, nevertheless, it was the same seed which grows up and prospers in the
hearts of those who receive it. Although everyone is not saved
by it, it is the seed of salvation planted in their hearts which
would grow and redeem their souls if not choked and hindered.

Victor Antiochenus is cited by Vossius in his *Pelagian History*[27] as saying of the Mark 4 version of the parable: "That
our Lord Christ has liberally sown the divine seed of the word,
and proposed it to all, without respect of persons; and as he
who sows does not distinguish between various qualities of soil
but simply casts in the seed without distinction, that is the way
that our Saviour has offered the food of the divine word, even
though he was not ignorant of what would become of many.
And he so behaved himself that he could justly say, 'What
should I have done that I have not done?'"

The answer, given in the parable of the talents, Mat 25:
14ff, is that he who had only two talents had acted as acceptably as the one who had five, because he had used them for
his master's profit.   He who had only one might have done the
same, because his talent was of the same kind as the others. It
was just as capable of bringing forth its share of interest as the
rest. In the same way, an equal portion of grace is not given to
everyone.   Some have five talents, some have two, and some
only one. But everyone receives enough and requires no more.

27 book 7.
Gerard Jan Vossius (1577-1649), Dutch philologist and theological historian. His *Historia Pelagiana sive Historiae de controversus quas Pelagius
ejusque reliquia moverant* was published in 1618 while he was director of
the theological college at Leyden.   He was among the first to treat theological dogma and the non-Christian religions from a historical viewpoint.
— *Col. Encyc.* and *Encyc. Brit.*   (See also fn p 167.)
Victor Antiochenus was presumably the 5th C presbyter of Antioch who
made a compilation of earlier exegetical writings on Mark of which no
critical, or even complete, text exists. — *O.D.C.C.*, p 1418.

"Where a man has been given much, much will be expected of him," Luke 12:48 NEB. The four talents returned by the man who had two were equally acceptable with the ten returned by the man who had been given five. Had the man with one returned two, he also would have been accepted.

THE LIGHT IS THE GOSPEL, PREACHING GLAD TIDINGS IN THE HEARTS OF ALL MEN

¶XXIII. This saving spiritual light is the gospel, which the apostle says explicitly has been preached "to every creature under heaven," the same gospel "of which I, Paul, became a minister" Col 1:23 RSV. For the gospel is not merely a declaration of good things, "it is the saving power of God for everyone who has faith," Rom 1:16 NEB.

Although the mere outward declaration of the gospel is sometimes considered to be the gospel, this is actually only a figurative usage, of the nature of a metonymy. Properly speaking, the gospel is the inward power and life which preaches glad tidings in the hearts of all men, offering them salvation, and attempting to redeem them from their iniquities. This is the reason for saying that it has been preached "to every creature under heaven" even though there are many thousands of men and women who have never heard the outward gospel preached.

The apostle Paul, where he says of the gospel, Rom 1:16 NEB, that "it is the saving power of God for everyone who has faith," adds, "because here is revealed God's way of righting wrong. It is based on faith and addressed to faith." That is, it reveals to the soul what is good, just, and righteous. As the soul accepts this and believes, the degree of righteousness becomes greater and faith advances from one stage to another. Even though the verses which follow state that God's everlasting power and deity can be plainly seen by the eye of reason in the things that he has made, yet without the inward principle the invisible things of God could no more be understood from his visible creation than the variety of shapes and colors or the beauty in creation could be discerned by a blind man.

BELIEF ALONE WILL NOT INFORM US OF THE WILL OF GOD FOR US

Even though the belief that there is some eternal power or virtue by which the world was created might be engendered by viewing God's handiwork, nevertheless by itself this would not inform anyone of what is holy, just, or righteous. Nor would it tell me what the will of God is, or how I should do what is acceptable to him. In what way will I be delivered from my temptations and my evil desires if it is not by some inward manifestation in my heart?

The prophet Micah, in speaking of mankind in general, declares in Mic 6:8 RSV: "He has showed you, O man, what is good; and what does the Lord require of you but to do justice, and to love kindness, and to walk humbly with your God?" He does not state what the Lord requires of us, until he has first assured us of the fact that God has shown us what is good.

On the other hand, Paul says in Rom 1:18 RSV that: "The wrath of God is revealed from heaven against all ungodliness and wickedness of men who by their wickedness suppress the truth." They hide their talent in the earth by burying it in the unrighteous part of their hearts. Instead of allowing it to bring forth fruit they choke it with the sensual cares of life, the fear of reproach, or the deceitfulness sometimes bred by wealth, as the parables make clear.

THE WORD HE PREACHED IS NEAR YOU

Paul enlarges further on this in Rom 10:8 NEB, declaring that the word he preached "is near you: it is upon your lips and in your heart." Certainly the word which he preached, and the gospel which he preached (and of which he was a minister) were one and the same. Just as though he were anticipating the objections which our adversaries have raised, he phrases their question for them in verse 14 RSV: "And how are they to believe in him of whom they have never heard? And how are they to hear without a preacher?"

He answers his own question in verse 18 RSV: "But I ask, have they not heard? Indeed they have, for 'Their voice has gone out to all the earth, and their words to the ends of the world.' " The insinuation is that the divine preacher has sounded his message in the ears and the hearts of all men. He was certainly not speaking of the outward preaching of the apostles in his own times, or for hundreds of years later. For even today there may be large areas where Christ has never been heard of.

There is a more complete description of the inward and powerful word of God in the epistle to the Hebrews. In Heb 4:12-13 NEB, we read: "For the word of God is alive and active. It cuts more keenly than any two-edged sword, piercing as far as the place where life and spirit, joints and marrow, divide. It sifts the purposes and thoughts of the heart. There is nothing in creation that can hide from him; everything lies naked and exposed to the eyes of the One with whom we have to reckon."

Although the ultimate reference in that quotation is to God, it is by way of the word or light. For it is in and by this word that God discerns the thoughts of man. This is the faithful witness and the messenger of God that bears witness for God and for his righteousness in the hearts of all men, for he has left no one without a witness, Acts 14:16-17, and he is said to be, like David in Isa 55:4, "a witness to the peoples."

Since the word bears witness to God it is not placed in men merely to condemn them. David was said by the prophet to be given not only for a "witness" but as a leader and a commander. The light is given, as John 1:7 says, so that through it all men may believe. For "faith then depends on hearing, and hearing on the word of Christ" (Rom 10:17 Cath-CCD), which is placed in man's heart, both to be a witness for God, and to be a means to bring man to God through faith and repentance.

It is powerful. It is like a two-edged sword which cuts away iniquity and separates the precious from the vile. Because man's heart is naturally cold and hard like iron, God has placed this word in him which is said to be like a fire and a hammer (Jer 23:29). It is warmed and softened by the heat and by the strength of the hammer. It is shaped according to the mind of the blacksmith. If the heart does not resist, it is warmed and softened by the virtue and power of this word of God and takes on a heavenly impression and a celestial image.

BEING "GATHERED INTO THE ONE ALONE LOVE"

The majority of the early Church Fathers have spoken at some length of this word, seed, light, and saving voice that calls all to salvation and is able to save. Clement of Alexandria says:[28] "Hear, therefore, you who are afar off; hear, you who

28 lib 2, *Stromat.*

The *Stromateis* (or "Miscellaneous Studies") was one of the principal works of Clement of Alexandria (c. 150 - c. 215). [In spite of some search these particular quotations were not specifically located, although book 2 is included in the *Ante-Nicene Fathers*.]

are near; the word is hidden from none, the light is common to all, and shines upon all. There is no darkness in the world; let us hasten to salvation, to the new birth, that we, being many, may be gathered into the one alone love." Elsewhere he refers to the innate witness, "worthy of belief, which by itself plainly chooses that which is most honest." He says to the unbelieving nations: "Receive Christ, receive light, receive sight, to the end that you may rightly know both God and man." "The heavenly Spirit will help you: resist and flee pleasure." In his *Paed.*[29] he says: "There is something lovely and desirable in man which is called the in-breathing of God."

Justin Martyr[30] refers to: "The word which was and is, is in all; even that very same word which, through the prophets, foretold things to come."

AND REBORN BY THE LIGHT OF CHRIST IN THE HEART

¶XXIV. It is by this light, seed, or grace that God brings about the salvation of all men. By them, many come to partake of the salvation purchased through Christ's death. Many pagans who were not descendants of Abraham have partaken in the promises made to him. Many for whom it would be impossible to hear of the historical Jesus have been saved by Christ through the inward and effective operation of grace.

Whether those who are saved have had Christ and the gospel preached to them or whether they have never heard of the gospel and are completely ignorant of the outward history of Christ, it is still by the working of his grace and light in their hearts that they are brought to salvation.

Christ's words to Nicodemus, John 3:3 RSV, speak of spiritual rebirth: "Truly, truly, I say to you, unless one is born

---

29 lib 1, cap 3.
This may be the following quotation from the *Ante-Nicene Fathers*, vol 2, p 211: "If then man is an object desirable for itself, then He who is good loved what is good, and the love charm is within even in man, and is that very thing which is called the inspiration [or breath] of God." A number of other Clementine citations by Barclay have been omitted here, as well as several from the anonymous author of *de Vocatio Gentium* (Prosper of Aquitaine?).

30 in his *First Apology*.
Justin Martyr (c. 100 - c. 165) was born of pagan parents in Samaria. After long search among the pagan philosophies he embraced Christianity about 130 A. D. His *First Apology* was written about 155 and was addressed to the emperor Antoninus Pius and his adopted sons Marcus Aurelius and Lucius Verus. — *O.D.C.C.*, pp 756-757.

anew, he cannot see the kingdom of God." This rebirth does not come from the preaching of the gospel, or knowledge of Christ, or historical faith in him. Many have received these without ever being renewed.

The apostle Paul speaks of this outward knowledge of Christ in 2 Cor 5:16-17 RSV: "From now on, therefore, we regard no one from a human point of view; even though we once regarded Christ from a human point of view, we regard him thus no longer. Therefore, if anyone is in Christ, he is a new creation; the old has passed away, behold, the new has come." He makes it clear that the knowledge of the human Jesus is rudimentary. It is like the basic things which young children learn. These are of less use to them after they have become better scholars, because the very substance of these precepts has by then become ingrained in their minds. All comparisons have their limitations, and so does this one, but it is a valid statement that those who never got beyond the A B C's can hardly be considered learned. Nevertheless when they advance beyond these things they have less use for them. In the same way those who never get beyond the mere outward knowledge of Christ will never inherit the kingdom of heaven.

But those who come to know this new birth, to be truly "in Christ," to be new creations for whom "the old has passed away" and the "new has come," may safely say with Paul, "though we once regarded Christ from a human point of view, we regard him thus no longer." This new creature results from the work of this light and grace in the heart, from the word which is sharp and piercing and able to save the soul.

"THE MANIFESTATION OF THE SPIRIT FOR THE COMMON GOOD"

Christ has purchased for us this holy seed which can bring forth this rebirth in us. For this reason it is also called "the manifestation of the Spirit for the common good;" (1 Cor 12:7 RSV). For it is written, in verse 13, that "by one Spirit we were all baptized into one body."

The apostle Peter also ascribes rebirth to this seed and word of God of which we have been speaking. He says, 1 Pet 1:23 Cath-CCD: "You have been reborn, not from corruptible seed but from incorruptible, through the word of God who lives and abides forever."

Although this seed is small — Christ compared it to the "grain of mustard seed . . . the smallest of all seeds," Mat 13:

31-32 RSV — still, it is in this tiny seed, hidden in the earthly part of a man's heart, that life and salvation are enveloped. In this seed in the hearts of all men is the capacity to produce the kingdom of God if it receives proper nourishment. Christ even said that the kingdom of God was in the Pharisees who opposed and resisted him (Luke 17:20-21). Surely the kingdom of God could have been in them only as a seed like those in the parable of the sower which had the capacity to increase thirtyfold or a hundredfold but which fell on barren ground and produced nothing. Or it was like the mustard seed which had the potential of becoming a great tree in which the birds could nest. The capacity to become a man or woman exists not only in a child but even in the embryo.

THE INCORRUPTIBLE SEED OF THE KINGDOM

In the same way, the kingdom of God is in every man's or woman's heart, in that little incorruptible seed, ready to be brought forth if it is cherished and received in love. Christ himself, Christ within, who is the hope of glory, becomes wisdom, righteousness, sanctification and redemption there. For there can be no worse and unbelieving man than these Pharisees were. Yet the kingdom of God was within them and they were directed to seek it there. So few know Christ brought forth in them because they pay so little attention to this light, seed, and grace which appears in their hearts and is so often overlooked.

Calvinists put such emphasis on the irresistible power of grace that they neglect the eternal seed of the kingdom in their hearts. They look down upon it and consider it of little value and useless for their salvation. Roman Catholics, Arminians and Socinians,[31] on the other hand, emphasize natural power and will, and deny that this small manifestation of the light is the supernatural grace of God given to every man for his salva-

---

[31] The Roman Catholics referred to may be particularly the Jesuits, since they are specifically named two paragraphs later. The world-famous scholarship of this order founded by St. Ignatius Loyola (1491 or 1495-1556) needs no elaboration here. Probably there is also an allusion to the differences between Dominican and Jesuit concepts of efficacious grace.

The Arminians were named for Jacob Arminius (1560-1609), whose opposition to the Calvinistic doctrine of predestination brought about "the greatest doctrinal controversy in the history of the Reformed Church" (Molland, Christendom, p 251). It also set up a tension between the two points of view within Protestantism which persists to this day and which became marked in Methodism in particular, where John Wesley held the

tion. They have given verification to the saying of the Lord Jesus Christ, John 3:19 Cath-CCD: "The light has come into the world, yet men have loved the darkness rather than the light, for their works were evil."

All confess this, but they will not attribute saving power to the seed within. Some want the cause of salvation to be reason, others a natural conscience, and some attribute it to a residual part of God's image that remained in Adam. Christ himself met with all sorts of opposition from religious people, just as his inward manifestation is being resisted now. Many despised Christ because of the ordinary circumstances of his birth and his humbleness, saying: "Is not this the carpenter's son? Is not his mother called Mary? And are not his brothers James and Joseph and Simon and Judas? And are not all his sisters with us?" (Mat 13:55-56 RSV). "Can anything good come from Nazareth?" (John 1:46 NEB). "Has a prophet ever come from Galilee?" [a loose but legitimate paraphrase of John 7:52].

THE MESSIAH OFFERS HUMBLE REPROOF

A prince was expected who would deliver them from their enemies, not the kind of Messiah who would be shamefully crucified, and who would lead them into numerous troubles and afflictions and great sorrow. It is the humbleness of the inward manifestation which makes the wise Jesuits, the rational Socinians, and the learned Arminians overlook it. They are looking for something on which they could exercise their subtleness, their reason, and their learning as well as the freedom of their own wills. Calvinists desire a Christ who will save them without any exertion on their part. They want him to destroy all their outward enemies, but little or none of their inward enemies, that is, themselves, so they can continue to live comfortably with their sins.

Arminian position in contrast to the Calvinistic Methodism of Whitefield. The controversy "turned upon the relation between the sovereignty of God and the responsibility of Man" (loc cit).

In 1610 the Arminian party within the Reformed Church submitted a petition, or "remonstrance," requesting protection against oppression by the orthodox wing of the church. But they were condemned at the Synod of Dort (1618-1619), leading to persecution and banishment. Although greater tolerance was exercised by 1630 the "Remonstrants," as they came to be known, were not officially recognized until 1795. — Molland, op cit, p 251, and O.D.C.C., pp 87-88.

The Socinians are sometimes known as Old Unitarians (see fn p 30).

With one voice, they reject this light "because their deeds are evil," and it would secretly reprove even the wisest and most learned of all. But all of their rationalizing cannot silence it, and the most self-satisfied among them cannot stop its voice from crying out and reproving them from within. All of their confidence in their outward knowledge of Christ and what he suffered for them is of no avail.

BUT THE OLD ADAM DENIES THE INWARD TEACHER

As has been said so often, "in a day it strives with all, wrestles with all;" and it is the old Adam, the unmortified first nature, that denies the inward teacher. To their own condemnation, even the wisest, most learned, and most zealous for outward knowledge of Christ deny his inward manifestation, despising him, and shutting him out. "Bad men all hate the light and avoid it, for fear their practices should be shown up;" John 3:20 NEB. We can say this now, as it was said of old, from true and positive experience — Psalm 118:22, Mat 21:42, Mark 12:10, Luke 20:17, Acts 4:11. The stone that was rejected by all kinds of builders has become the cornerstone for us. Eternal glory be to God, who has chosen us as his first fruits in this day when he has arisen to plead with the nations. To do this, he has sent us forth to preach the everlasting gospel to everyone — Christ is near to all, the light in all, the seed sown in the hearts of all, in order that all may come and apply their minds to it.

We rejoice that those of us who had any wisdom and learning have been required to lay it down in order to learn of Jesus. Let us sit down at the feet of Jesus in our hearts and hear him who makes all things manifest there and who reproves all things by his light, Eph 5:13.

IT WOULD BE BETTER TO CONSIDER LEARNING AS DROSS AND A DRUG

There are many who are wise and learned in both the philosophy and the letter of the scripture, as the Pharisees were. They can say a great deal about Christ and make a strong case against Infidels, Turks, and Jews, and even against some of the heresies, at the same time that they are crucifying Christ in the small appearance of his seed in their hearts. It would be better to be stripped and naked, and to consider learning as dross and a drug, and to become a fool for Christ's sake, in order to know his teaching in your heart. Then you may witness him resurrected there, and say with the apostle, Gal 6:14 Cath-CCD: "God forbid that I should glory save in the cross of our Lord Jesus Christ, through whom the world is crucified to me, and I to the world." This is better than writing thousands of commentaries or preaching many, many sermons.

God has raised us up to preach Christ and to direct people to his pure light in their hearts. It is for this that the wise men of this world consider us fools. Through the operation of the cross of Christ in our hearts we have denied our own wisdom and forfeited our own will in many things. We have forsaken the exaggerated respect shown to officials, the vain fashions, and the empty customs of this world.

THE WORLD FEEDS UPON THE HUSK AND NEGLECTS THE KERNEL

For many centuries the world has had much dry, fruitless, and barren knowledge of Christ. It has fed on the husk and neglected the kernel. It has pursued the shadow without knowing the substance. Evil does not care how abundant that kind of knowledge is as long as it possesses the heart and rules the will. Then Christ will be crucified when he appears there, and the seed of the kingdom will be unable to take root.

It is this that has led men astray and caused them to contend among themselves over this or that outward observance and to seek *Christ* in this or that external thing. They contend at great length over such things as the bread and wine of outword communion. Some consider Christ present in one way, some in another. Some look for him in the scriptures, or books; others in various societies, pilgrimages, or tokens. Some take refuge in an external barren faith, and they think that all will be well if they merely believe firmly enough that he died for their past and future sins.

Meanwhile in the appearance of Christ in their hearts, he lies crucified and slain and is resisted and contradicted daily. Blindness and ignorance have come over Christendom and we are led and moved by the Lord to call frequently for everyone to turn to the light within. We invite them to mind the light in themselves and we request them to believe in Christ as he exists in them.

Many consider us fools and madmen. But we do not ply them with academic and learned arguments, but command them to lay aside their wisdom in the name and the power and the authority of the Lord. We urge them to descend from that proud realm of ethereal brain knowledge. To stop the most eloquent of speeches, however pleasing to the ear. Then, to be silent and quiet, like one who is waiting for the dust to settle. For then they will be able to heed the light of Christ in their own consciences.

If they were to heed it, they would find it like a sharp two-edged sword in their hearts. Like fire and a hammer it would forge away all that belonged to the natural man, and the stoutest of them all would tremble and become Quakers indeed. If they do not feel this now, but harden their hearts and do not embrace the Son while the day lasts, they will learn that this is the most certain of all truths when it is too late. In conclusion, as the apostle says in 2 Cor 13:5 RSV: "Examine yourselves, to see whether you are holding to your faith. Test yourselves. Do you not realize that Jesus Christ is in you? — unless indeed you fail to meet the test!"

THE UNIVERSALITY OF THE SAVING GRACE OF JESUS

¶XXV. What remains to be proved is that some have been saved by the operation of this light and seed who have not known the story of Christ or heard the gospel preached. The excellent statement in Titus 2:11 NEB should be added to the arguments that have already been given for the universality of the saving grace of Jesus. It says: "For the grace of God has dawned upon the world with healing for all mankind; and by it we are disciplined to renounce godless ways and worldly desires, and to live a life of temperance, honesty, and godliness in the present age." This is clearly a two-part statement. First, it says that saving grace, or light, is not a natural principle, but states plainly that it brings salvation. Secondly, it does not say that it brings it to a few, but to all men.

How efficacious this saving grace is can be seen from the fact that it comprehends man's entire duty. First, it leads him to renounce godless ways and worldly desires and then to live a life of temperance, righteousness, and godliness. Living a life of temperance comprehends sobriety, chastity, and humility — the things that pertain to a man's self. A life of righteousness comprehends equity, justice, and honesty — the things which relate to our neighbors. Godliness comprises piety, faithfulness, and devotion — the duties relating to God. There is nothing required from a man or needed by him that is not taught by God's grace.

Nevertheless, there are those who claim that God's grace referred to in the text from Titus is merely of the common variety which provides such things as the heat of fire and the outward light of the sun, even though the text says clearly that it is saving. Others who acknowledge its saving properties say that the "all" does not refer to all mankind but merely to all kinds of men.

The same apostle is his own commentator on the question of universality. In Rom 5:18 RSV, he says: "Then as one man's trespass led to condemnation for all men, so one man's act of righteousness leads to acquittal and life for all men." It is a natural consequence of this comment that salvation extends even to the pagan, for Christ was given, according to the prophecy in Isa 49:6 Cath-CCD, not merely to "raise up the tribes of Jacob and restore the survivors of Israel," but as a light to all nations so that his "salvation may reach to the ends of the earth." Isn't it a bit uncharitable to claim that even though they *could* have been saved — none were? Or that no one in their condition can possibly be saved?

THE NAME OF JESUS SIGNIFIES SALVATION BY THE EXPERIENCE OF HIS POWER

Sometimes an objection is based on the quotation which states that there is no name under heaven by which salvation is known, except by the name *Jesus*. Since many do not know his name, it is claimed that they cannot possibly be saved. It seems only fitting to reply that if they know him inwardly by the virtue and power of his light, they can be saved by such knowledge. Indeed, the name *Jesus* signifies the saviour who will free them from the sin and the iniquity in their hearts.

I confess that there is no other name by which to be saved. But salvation does not lie in the literal knowledge of that name, but in the experience of what it signifies. Those who merely know his name, without any real experience of its meaning, are not saved by it. But those who know the meaning and have experienced his power can be saved without knowing his name.

Certainly, if those who have never heard of Adam are injured by his fall through the seed of evil that lies within them, why can't they be saved by the gift and grace of Christ in them? Although they may not know the way in which this was purchased for them by the death and sufferings of the Jesus who was crucified at Jerusalem, it is he who makes them righteous and holy.

Many men have been killed by a poison that was infused into their flesh without their knowing what poison it was or who gave it to them. And on the other hand, many have been cured by medical remedies without knowing how the medicine was prepared or what the ingredients were, and often without knowing who made it.

This may also be true of spiritual matters.

GOD SHOWS NO PARTIALITY

¶XXVI. If it is absolutely necessary to know the name of Jesus in order to be saved, why do those who maintain this make an exception in the case of deaf-mutes and children? If they maintain that it is because such persons are without sin, I have no doubt that the iniquities of many deaf-mutes could easily be proven. If they maintain that it is because they are within the bosom of the visible church and partake of the sacraments, that does not assure salvation. The Protestants maintain that the mere administration of the sacraments *(ex opere operato)*[32] does not confer grace. But if the means of grace are extended to handicapped persons because they are incapable of knowing the means by which they are saved, why isn't this excuse also valid for the man in China or India who has never heard of Jesus by an accident of geography rather than because of physical infirmity?

Isn't this manifestly what Peter meant when he said in Acts 10:34-35 RSV: "Truly I perceive that God shows no partiality, but in every nation any one who fears him and does what is right is acceptable to him." Previously, Peter had made the same mistake as the rest of the Jews — they considered everyone unclean except themselves, and considered salvation to be reserved only for those who were proselytized to their religion and

---

[32] This was one of the great points of dispute between the churches of the Reformation and the Roman Catholic Church. It is so no longer. *Ex opere operato* emphasizes God, i.e., the Spirit's work through the sacramental action; *ex opere operantis* emphasizes the role of the human person who administers or receives the sacrament. This modern Roman Catholic position is close to the Orthodox one. Florovsky says, for example, "Sacraments must be 'worthily' received indeed; therefore they cannot be separated or divorced from the inner effort and spiritual attitude of believers." — Wilhelm Niesel, *The Gospel and the Churches, a Comparison of Catholicism, Orthodoxy, and Protestantism*, translated by David Lewis, Philadelphia, Westminster, 1962, pp 72-73, 145, and Father Bowman.

circumcised. But in a vision God showed Peter otherwise and taught him to call nothing common or unclean. Peter saw that God accepted Cornelius even though he was a stranger to the law and to the outward knowledge of Jesus Christ. It is said that he feared God before he heard the gospel, and from that Peter concluded that God is impartial and that everyone in every nation who fears him and lives righteously is accepted by him. Peter makes no qualification of this that would require outward knowledge. If they fear God and are righteous, they are saved.

WHO TAUGHT JOB HOW TO BE RIGHTEOUS?

Job was also a righteous man who feared God and eschewed evil. Many consider him a contemporary of Moses. Who taught him to do this? How did he know about Adam's fall? What scriptures did he have to teach him the wonderful faith by which he knew that his redeemer lived? Wasn't it by an inward grace in his heart that Job was taught to eschew evil and fear God? Wasn't it by the work of this inward grace that he became a just and upright man? How does God reprove men for their wickedness? After taking account of their wickedness, doesn't he condemn them for rebelling against the light? (Job 24:13). For not knowing the ways of the light or abiding in its paths?

Apparently, Job must have believed that men did have a light and that because they rebelled against it they did not know its ways or abide in its paths. In a similar way, even though the Pharisees had the scriptures, they did not know them. Although Job's friends did some things wrong, who taught them all of the marvelous things that they said and gave them what knowledge of things they did have? Didn't God give it to them in order to save them? Or was it merely to condemn them? Who taught Elihu that: "The Spirit of God has made me, and the breath of the Almighty gives me life"? (Job 33:4 RSV)

The Lord accepted a sacrifice for them. Who dares to say that they were damned?

The apostle Paul removes this controversy even further from the realm of doubt. He says very plainly in Rom 2:14 RSV that some Gentiles who do not have the law "do by nature what the law requires." Could it be more evident that they do these things because they fear God and live righteously? Another point in our argument is made clear in verse 13, which says: "For it is not the hearers of the law who are righteous before God, but the doers of the law who will be justified."

If any further confirmation is necessary, it can be said that all of chapter 2 resembles an argument for us by the apostle in confirmation of our doctrine. This is particularly true of verses 9-11 RSV: "There will be tribulation and distress for every human being who does evil, the Jew first and also the Greek, but glory and honor and peace for every one who does good, the Jew first and also the Greek. For God shows no partiality." Everyone, then, who is justified can partake of the honor, glory, and peace which everyone who does good receives.

IT IS NOT THE OUTWARD KNOWLEDGE THAT SAVES, BUT THE INWARD

Thus, we see that it is not the outward knowledge that saves, but the inward. Whether they knew it or not, those who were aware of their inclination toward sin and also of the inward power and salvation which come from Christ were saved whether it was before or after his appearance in the flesh.

It is doubtful whether it could be proved that all of the patriarchs before Moses knew the story of the tree of the knowledge of good and evil, or of Adam eating the forbidden fruit. It is much less likely that they knew that Christ would be born of a virgin and crucified and treated in the manner that he was. It seems only reasonable that what Moses wrote about Adam and the first times was written not from tradition, but from revelation.

We also see how in spite of all that had been written by Moses, David, and all of the prophets who prophesied so much about Christ, and in spite of the fact that the Jews were expecting the Messiah and hoping for him, so few were actually able to recognize him when he came. By mistaking the prophecies concerning him, they were able to crucify him as a blasphemer rather than receive him as the Messiah. Peter says explicitly in Acts 3:17 NEB: "I know quite well that you acted in ignorance, and so did your rulers." Paul says in 1 Cor 2 that the powers that rule the world have never known the wisdom of God, or his secret purpose which would bring us to our full glory. "If they had, they would not have crucified the Lord of glory" (1 Cor 2:8 NEB).

Even Mary herself to whom the angel had spoken, and who stored in her heart all of the miraculous things that ac-

companied his birth, did not understand how, when he had his
dispute with the learned doctors in the temple, he was about
his Father's business.   And the apostles who had believed him,
had conversed with him daily, and had seen his miracles, could
not understand the things which related to his death, sufferings, and resurrection.   In fact, they were in certain respects
"a stumbling block" for them.

MANY PAGAN PHILOSOPHERS WERE AWARE OF ADAM'S LOSS

¶XXVII. You can see from this how it is the inward work,
rather than the outward history and scriptural testimony, that
conveys true knowledge.   By this inward light many of the
pagan philosophers were aware of Adam's loss, even though
they had never heard of him.

Plato[33] asserted that "man's soul had fallen into a dark
cave, where it conversed with shadows."

Pythagoras[34] said that "man wanders in this world as a
stranger, banished from the presence of God."

Plotinus[35] compared "man's soul, fallen from God, to a
cinder, or dead coal, from which the fire has been extinguish-

---

[33] Although Barclay gives no location for this quotation, it is the
epitome of one in the Jowett translation of Plato's *Republic*, New York,
Modern Library, n d, chap 7, pars 514, 515, pp 253-254, which reads: "Behold! human beings living in an underground den, . . . and they see only
their own shadows, or the shadows of one another." I am indebted to
Pearl Hall, co-director of Powell House, for this citation. — ED.

[34] The followers of Pythagoras (c. 582 - c. 507 B. C.), who are best
known today for the theorem in Euclidean geometry which bears their
name, were a religious brotherhood which believed in the transmigration
of souls, and whose basic tenet was that the essence of all things was
number, and that all matter was essentially numerical. Pythagoreans held
that all relationships in the universe could be expressed numerically. —
Col. Encyc., p 1625.

[35] Plotinus (c. 205-270) was a Neo-Platonist philosopher and mystic.
"Owing to the difficulty of his style and subject matter Plotinus has been
variously interpreted, and it is disputed whether his thought is fundament-
ally pantheistic or tending towards Theism." His mystical system was
highly developed, with contemplation occupying a central place as the most
perfect activity by which souls can attain union with God. "In order to
reach this its last end the soul has to prepare itself by purity of heart and
ascetical practices turning away from all ,sensible things. It must devote
itself to recollection, in which memory, sensibility, and discursive reasoning
progressively disappear, until it reaches a state in which it 'feels' an in-
effable Presence in an ecstasy of 'joyous stupor' and blissful plenitude."
The main difference between this so-called "natural mysticism" and
"that of the orthodox Christian mystics is that in Plotinus' system, union
is reached by the unaided effort of the soul, whereas in Catholic teaching

ed." Some of them said that "the wings of the soul were clipped or had fallen off, so that they could not flee to God."

SOME OF THE PHILOSOPHERS KNEW THE REMEDY FOR EVIL BUT DID NOT KNOW HIS NAME

All of these expressions and many others which could be gathered from their writings show that they were not unaware of their loss. They also knew and discovered Jesus Christ inwardly, knowing him as a remedy that would deliver them from the evil seed and the evil inclinations which existed in their own hearts, even though they did not know his name.

Some called him a Holy Spirit, as in Seneca's[36] *Epistle 41,* which says: "There is a Holy Spirit in us, that treats us as we treat him." Cicero[37] in his book *De Republica,* called it an "innate light," which he says is "correct in its reason, agrees with nature, is diffused among all men. It is unchanging and everlasting, and calls us to duty by commanding, and deters from wrong by forbidding." He adds, "it cannot be entirely abrogated. Nor, indeed, can we be released from this law, either by the senate or by the people ... but the same law, everlasting and unchangeable, will bind all nations, at all times; and there will be one common Master and Ruler of all, even God, the framer, arbiter, and proposer of this law; and he who

---

it is the work of Divine grace. Despite this fundamental difference Plotinus seems to have exercised indirectly much influence on Christian thought, especially on Saint Augustine and Dionysius the Pseudo-Aereopagite, and through them, on the theologians and mystics of the Middle Ages." *O.D.C.C.,* pp 1084-1085.

[36] Lucius Annaeus Seneca (c. 4 B.C.-65 A.D.) was a Roman moralist, whose brother Gallio, the Proconsul of Achaia, is mentioned in Acts 18:12. His writings include a set of 124 *Epistulae Morales* addressed to Lucilius. There is also an apocryphal correspondence of fourteen letters supposed originally to have been exchanged by Seneca and St. Paul.

"His writings represent Stoicism at its best and have been much studied by Christian apologists for the similarities as well as the contrasts of their moral teaching with the Gospel ethic."

There have been innumerable editions of Seneca's works, beginning with the *editio princeps* of B. Romerus, Naples, 1475, which was probably accessible to Barclay. — *O.D.C.C.,* p 1240.

37 Cited by Lactantius, *6 Inst.*

Lucius Caelius Frimianus Lactantius (c. 260-340), a converted Christian author and apologist, was born in Africa. The *Col. Encyc.* evaluation of him is: "His works, which were influenced by Cicero and Seneca, were sincere, well-written expositions of Christian doctrine, but erroneous in theological details." (2nd ed, p 1080.) The version of the quotation from lib 3 of the *Republic* that is used here is largely that given in Lactantius, *Divine Institute,* book 6, ch 8, p 170 of vol 7 of the *Ante-Nicene Fathers.*

will not obey it will flee from himself, and, despising his own nature, will suffer the greatest punishments through this very thing, even though he shall have escaped the other punishments which are supposed to exist."

Plotinus[38] also calls him light, saying that "as the sun cannot be known but by its own light, so God cannot be known but with his own light; and as the eye cannot see the sun but by receiving its image, so man cannot know God but by receiving his image; and man must come to purity of heart before he can know God." He also calls him Wisdom, a name frequently given to him in scripture. Wisdom is personified in that way in Prov 1:20-33, and in Prov 8:9, 34, where Wisdom is said to call, entreat, and invite all to come to her and learn of her. What is this Wisdom but Christ? Among the pagans, those who forsook evil and clung to righteousness were called philosophers, that is, lovers of wisdom. They knew this wisdom was close at hand, and that "the best knowledge of God, and divine mysteries, was by the inspiration of the wisdom of God." Phocylides[39] affirmed that "the word of the wisdom of God was best, *Tēs de Theopneustēs sophias logos estin aristos.*"

THE APOSTLES AND PRIMITIVE CHRISTIANS CONSIDERED THEM JUSTIFIED

Many other instances could be cited as proof that they knew Christ. They were brought from unrighteousness to righteousness by his work in them and they came to love the power by which they were redeemed. As the apostle says: "They show the work of the law written in their hearts," and did the things contained in the law.[40] They were undoubtedly justified, like all doers of the law, and thus they were saved by the power of Christ in them.

This was not only the judgment of the apostle, but also of the primitive Christians. Hence Justin Martyr[41] did not

---

[38] See p 117.

[39] Phocylides of Miletus was a 6th c. B. C. moralist and Greek gnomic poet. "A few fragments of his 'maxims' have been preserved (chiefly in the *Florilegium* of Stobaeus)." — *Encyc. Brit.,* vol 17, p 763.

[40] Rom 2:15.

[41] The quotation was located in the *First Apology,* ch 46, p 178. There is one somewhat similar in the *Second Apology,* ch 10, p 191: "Christ, who was partially known even by Socrates (for He was and is the Word who is in every man . . .)". Ch 10 is called "Christ compared with Socrates." (Both page references are to the *Ante-Nicene Fathers.*)

hesitate at all to call Socrates a Christian. He said that "we
have been taught that Christ is the first-born of God, and we
have declared above that He is the word of whom every race of
men were partakers; and those who lived with the word are
Christians, even though they have been thought atheists; as
among the Greeks, Socrates and Heraclitus, and men like them."

Clement of Alexandria says[42] that "this wisdom or philosophy was necessary for the Gentiles, and it was their schoolmaster to lead them to Christ, by which of old the Greeks were
justified."

"Nor do I think," says Augustine,[43] "the Jews themselves
dare contend that no one has belonged to God except the Israelites." Upon which Ludovicus Vives[44] comments, that "thus
the Gentiles, not having a law, were a law unto themselves;
and the light of so living is the gift of God, and proceeds from
the Son; of whom it is written, that he 'enlightens every man
who comes into the world.' "

Augustine also testifies[45] that "he had read in the writings
of the Platonists, although not in the very same words, never-

---

[42] Although the precise quotation was not located, much of the
theme of book 1 of the *Stromateis* or *Miscellanies* is summarized here, i.e.:
The philosophers had attained some portion of the truth which was
their "schoolmaster," preparing the Greeks for Christ in the way that the
Jews were prepared for him by the law. As they were faithful to this portion of truth, they were justified.

[43] *City of God*, lib 18, cap 47.
The translation is that of Marcus Dods in *Great Books of the Western
World*, Chicago, 1952, vol 18, p 500.

[44] John Healey's English translation of Augustine's *De Civitate Dei*,
with the earlier commentaries by Joannes Lodovicus Vives, was first published in 1610, followed by a revised edition in 1620.
Juan Luis Vives (1492-1540) was a Spanish scholar who later became
professor of humanities at Louvain. His commentary on *The City of God*
had been published at the insistence of his friend Erasmus. The dedica-
tion to Henry VIII, dated Louvain, July 7, 1522, with a gracious reply to
the effect that the monarch did not know who most to congratulate (Vives
or Augustine), is reprinted in the Everyman's Library ed. of 1950.
Vives' *De Causis corruptarum artium*, "which has been ranked with
Bacon's *Novum Organum*," was his chief work. His *De anima et vita* (1538),
"one of the first modern works on psychology," preceded that of Descartes
and Bacon. — *Encyc. Brit.*, vol 23, p 227.

[45] In chap 9 of *The City of God* he states: "Whatever [i.e. whichever]
philosophers, therefore, thought concerning the supreme God, that He is
both the maker of all created things, the light by which things are known,
and the good in reference to which things are to be done ... we prefer
these to all other philosophers, and confess that they approach nearest to
us." — *The Nicene and Post-Nicene Fathers*, vol 2, p 150.

theless, words which by many and multiplied reasons were persuasive, that in the beginning was the word, and the word was with God; this was in the beginning with God, by which all things were made, and without which nothing was made that was made: in him was life, and the life was the light of men; and the light shined in the darkness, and the darkness did not comprehend it. And although the soul gives testimony concerning the light, yet it is not the light, but the word of God; for 'God is the true Light which enlightens every man who comes into the world:' " and he repeats as far as verse 14 of John 1, adding, "these things have I there read."

There is also a book[46] translated from Arabic which tells how Hai Eben Yokdan reached such profound knowledge of God that he had direct conversations with him. He affirmed: "That the best and most certain knowledge of God is not that which is attained by premises premised, and conclusions deduced; but that which is enjoyed by the conjunction of the mind of man with the supreme intellect, after the mind is purified from its corruptions, and is separated from all bodily images, and is gathered into a profound stillness."

[46] *The Life of Hayy ibn Yakzan* was a fictitious story translated from the original Arabic by Simon Ockley, published at London in 1708 and reprinted by E. A. Van Dyck at Cairo, Egypt, in 1905 "with slight changes" (cross-referenced from *Hai ebn Yokdhan* at Union Theological Seminary Library). Barclay evidently referred to an earlier translation. The preface refers to Edward Pococke's Latin translation, published in 1671, and states that the author died about 1200 A. D.

"The design of the author is to show how human capacity, unaided by any external help, may, by due application, attain to the Knowledge of material things and so by degrees find out its dependence upon a Superior Being, the immortality of the soul, and all things necessary to salvation." The preface goes on to say that he had not been willing to do the translating because it had been done twice already from the Latin, "once by Dr. Ashwell, another time by the Quakers, who imagined that there was something in it that favored their enthusiastic notions."

The 1671 Edition had a preface by the father of the Edward Pococke (1604-1691) who was appointed the first professor of Arabic at Oxford by Archbishop William Laud.

Henry J. Cadbury's Additional Notes to the 2nd ed of Wm. C. Braithwaite's *The Second Period of Quakerism*, Cambridge University Press, 1961, p 686, gives a bibliography of articles and several books on Hai Ibn Yokdan or Hayy Ibn Yaqzan, as it is variously rendered. George Keith (c. 1639-1716), who precipitated the first major Quaker schism and who later became an Anglican priest, made the Quaker translation (already referred to) from a Latin edition (apparently by Edward Pococke) into English in 1674, just before Barclay's *Apology*. — Ed.

WE PROCLAIM THE DAY OF THE LORD

¶XXVIII. It is by this inward gift, grace, and light, that
those who have the gospel preached to them, have Jesus
brought forth in them and receive the saving and sanctified use
of all external aids and advantages. It is also by this same
light that everyone may be saved. God calls, invites, and struggles with everyone for a day and saves many to whom he has
not seen fit to have outward knowledge preached.

It is for these reasons that we who have experienced the
inward and powerful work of this light, which is Jesus revealed
to us in our hearts, cannot stop proclaiming the day of the
Lord that has arisen there. We say with the woman of Samaria:
"Come and see a man who has told me everything I ever did.
Could this be the Messiah?" (John 4:29 NEB).

We proclaim him so that others may come to experience
the same thing themselves. Then they will know that no matter how much they despised and neglected this tiny thing in
their hearts which reproves them, it is nothing less than the gospel preached in them. In and by that seed, Christ, the wisdom
and power of God, is trying to save their souls.

"LATE HAVE I LOVED THEE"

Of this light, Augustine says:[47] "In this beginning, O God:
thou madest the heavens and the earth, in thy word, in thy
Son, in thy virtue, in thy wisdom, wonderfully saying, and wonderfully doing. Who shall comprehend it? Who shall declare
it?* What is that which shines through me, and strikes my
heart without injury, and I both shudder and burn? I shudder
inasmuch as I am unlike it; and I burn inasmuch as I am like
it. It is Wisdom itself that shines through me, clearing my
cloudiness, which again overwhelms me, fainting from it, in the
darkness and amount of my punishment." And again he says:[48]
"It is too late that I have loved thee, O thou beautifulness, so
ancient and so new! late have I loved thee, and behold thou
wast within, and I wast without, and there was seeking thee!
thou didst call, thou didst cry, thou didst break my deafness,

---

[47] *Confessions,* lib 11, cap 9 as given in Barclay up to *; from there
on, the translation is from the *Nicene and Post-Nicene Fathers,* 1st ser,
vol 1, p 166.

[48] *Confessions,* lib 10, cap 27.
[Since the newer translations maintain an antique flavor here, there
seemed to be no point in modernizing this.]

thou didst glance, thou didst shine, thou didst chase away my darkness."

CHRIST WITHIN IS OUR HOPE OF GLORY

George Buchanan, in his book,[49] says: "Truly I understand nothing other than that light which is divinely infused into our souls: for when God formed man, he not only gave him eyes for his body, by which he might shun those things that are harmful for him, and follow those things which are profitable; but he also has set before his mind, as it were, a certain light by which he may discern the things which are vile from the things which are honest. Some call this power 'nature', others the 'law of nature';[50] I truly judge it to be divine, and am persuaded that nature and Wisdom never say different things. Moreover, God has given us a compend of the law, which in a few words comprehends the whole; to wit, that we should love him from our hearts and our neighbors as ourselves. And of this law all the books of the holy scriptures which pertain to practice are nothing more than an explanation."

This is the universal evangelical principle. In it and by it the salvation of Christ is shown to every man, whether Jew or Gentile, Scythian or Barbarian, of whatever country or kindred. This is why God has raised faithful witnesses and evangelists in our age to preach again his everlasting gospel. It is their task to help all become aware of the light within themselves and to know Christ in them. This is equally true whether

---

[49] *De jure regni apud Scotos,* [published in 1579].
George Buchanan (1506-1582), "Scotland's greatest humanist," tutored Mary Queen of Scots in languages and was entrusted with the education of James Stewart, eldest of James V's natural sons. He sat on four occasions in the general assembly of the Scottish kirk; and under Lennox was director of chancery and keeper of the privy seal.
"*De jure regni apud Scotos,* the most important of his political writings, and immensely popular, was a resolute assertion of limited monarchy in dialog form." — *Encyc. Brit.,* vol 4, pp 310-311.

[50] Natural law plays a part, less prominent now, in Roman Catholic theology. Philosophically it is defended "on the ground that men everywhere and at all times have acknowledged some moral code, however imperfect, resting on the fundamental principle that good is to be done and evil avoided." "The chief NT text on which the Christian teaching on the subject rests is Rom 2:14ff, where St. Paul affirms that 'when Gentiles, which have no law, do by nature the things of the law, these, having no law, are a law to themselves; in that they shew the work of the law written in their hearts, their consciences bearing witness therewith.'" — *O.D.C.C.,* p 940.

they are learned divines who know the law and the scriptures or they are infidels and pagans who do not know him in that way. For this is he of whom James 5:6 NEB says: "You have condemned the innocent and murdered him; he offers no resistance." This is he for whom they are bidden to give up their sins, their iniquities, their false faith, professions, and external righteousness.

Then they will be crucified by the power of the cross in them, in order to know that the Christ within is their hope of glory, and they will walk in his light and be saved. For he is the "true light which enlightens every man who comes into the world."

Justification

PROPOSITION 7 – JUSTIFICATION

For those who do not resist the light, but receive it, it becomes a holy, pure, and spiritual birth in them. It produces holiness, righteousness, purity, and all those other blessed fruits that are acceptable to God.

Jesus Christ is formed in us by this holy birth and by it he does his work in us. By it we are sanctified and we are justified in the sight of God. Paul has said: "But you have been through the purifying waters; you have been dedicated to God and justified through the name of the Lord Jesus Christ and the Spirit of our God." (1 Cor 6:11 NEB).

It is not by works produced by our own wills, or by good works themselves, but by Christ, who is not only the gift and the giver, but the cause which produces these effects in us. While we were still enemies, he saved us and justified us in this way. Titus 3:5 RSV says: "He saved us, not because of deeds done by us in righteousness, but in virtue of his own mercy, by the washing of regeneration and renewal in the Holy Spirit."

WHAT IS IT THAT JUSTIFIES?

¶I. It is very appropriate to take up consideration of the doctrine of justification immediately after discussing the extent of the grace which was communicated to us by Christ's death. This is the point on which there have been numerous disputes and on which some of the sharpest controversies have arisen concerning justification. However, if attention had really been paid to what it is that justifies, there would have been less clamor about the varying doctrines of justification.

Before expounding our own view, a brief review will be given of this controversy. Then, if it be the Lord's will, our own understanding of this matter will be proved by the scriptural testimony and by the testimony of some who have truly experienced justification.

THE DOCTRINE OF CONDIGN MERIT

¶II. We do not question the fact that the doctrine of justification has been greatly vitiated by the Roman Catholic Church, although this has not stopped others from charging us with siding with them. *Meritum ex condigno*[1] ("condign merit") was undoubtedly a very common doctrine of the Roman church, especially before Luther. Most modern Catholic writers, however, partially deny this and somewhat qualify it, particularly in their controversies with Protestants. They seem to state it as if they alone pleaded for the good works which others deny. Yet Luther's opposition had considerable grounds if we examine the effects of this doctrine on the majority of their members. If he had not gone to the opposite extreme, his work might have stood up better. In this as in most other things that he dealt with, he can be commended more for what he destroyed of Babylon[2] than for what he built of his own.

Whatever Catholics may pretend, or some of their best men may have thought, experience shows, and the approved practices of their people demonstrate, that they do not consider their justification to be located in works that are truly and morally good, and in being truly renewed and sanctified in the mind. Instead, they locate their justification in things which are neither good nor evil, but which can only be considered good because the pope chooses to call them so.... It is not based on the power, virtue, and grace of Christ which renews the heart [and is revealed there].

This first becomes apparent in Catholic belief considering their sacraments, which they say confer grace *ex opere operato*.[3] If a man merely partakes of them, he thereby obtains remission

---

[1] The term "merit" as a theological expression of man's right to be rewarded for a work done for God, which has both OT and NT roots, seems to have been first applied by Tertullian. The theology of merit was fully developed under Scholasticism into two kinds, *meritum de condigno* and *meritum de congruo*. Condign merit accrues for services rendered which are morally good, freely done, assisted by actual grace, performed by a supernatural motive, in the sphere of this life, and done in a state of grace. God must have promised to reward it. *Meritum de congruo* is conferred on similar conditions, except that a state of grace is not always possible — i.e., the man is still a sinner. — *O.D.C.C.*, p 888.

[2] The Babylonian captivity of the Church was a favorite Reformation figure stemming from Martin Luther's treatise on the *Babylonish Captivity of the Church* (1520), which was "a sustained attack on the 'bondage' in which the Church had been held by the withdrawal of the chalice from the laity, the doctrine of transubstantiation, and the Sacrifice of the Mass." — *O.D.C.C.*, p 117. (See p 206 for a more complete note.)

[3] That is, where they are performed under given conditions that very action conveys grace without reference to the worthiness or unworthiness of the minister, or in spite of the distraction of the recipient. (See also fn p 114.)

of sins, even though he is still a sinner at heart. The virtue that is in the sacraments makes up for the virtue that is lacking in the individual. Thus, he is justified by the act of faith and submission to the laws of the church rather than by any real inward change.

For example, if a man avails himself of the sacrament called penance, and tells his sins to the priest, he procures remission of sins. It does not matter that he does not have true contrition, even though the Lord said that this was absolutely necessary for penitent sinners. It is sufficient for him to have attrition,[4] as they call it. This means that he is sorry that he has sinned, not because of a love of God or for his law which he has transgressed, but because he is afraid of punishment. Being absolved by the priest, he stands accepted and justified in the sight of God.

It can be seen that his justification does not proceed from true penitence and inward change and renewal by the action of God's grace in his heart, but merely from the virtue of the sacrament and the authority of the priest. Justification is from without and not from within.

This is even more important in the matter of indulgences. In these, remission not only of past sins, but of others for years to come, depends upon visiting particular churches or relics and saying particular prayers. The person who does these things is then cleared from the guilt of his sin, and justified and accepted in the sight of God.

THE AUTHORITY OF THE CHURCH AND OF THE POPE

For example, he who goes to Rome for the great jubilee,[5] and presents himself at the gate of Peter and Paul for the papal blessing, receives an indulgence. Or forgiveness of sins is prom-

---

[4] "The sorrow for sin which proceeds [largely] from a sense of fear rather than (as does contrition) [primarily] from the love of God. Even so, it is held by moral theologians to be sufficient to procure God's pardon." — *O.D.C.C.*, p 104. The bracketed insertions suggested by Father Bowman.

[5] Also called the Holy Year, during which the pope grants a special indulgence to all who visit Rome on certain conditions laid down in a special bull on the preceding Feast of the Ascension. When instituted by Boniface VIII in 1300, it was to be celebrated every 100 years. Clement VI, in 1343, changed it to 50; Urban VI, in 1389, to 33 (in honor of the years of our Lord's life); and Paul II, in 1470, settled on the 25-year interval that has been kept since then. The most recent was 1950. — *O.D.C.C.*, pp 650-651.

ised to anyone who makes a pilgrimage to James' sepulchre in Spain,[6] or the shrine of Mary of Loretto.[7] If it is asked how things which are not morally good in themselves can have virtue, they reply "because of the authority of the church and the pope." The pope being the great treasurer of the magazine of Christ's merits, he can dispense them under certain conditions.

Mass is made a chief instrument of justification, for in it Christ is offered daily as a propitiatory sacrifice for the sins of the living and the dead. A man can pay to have Christ offered for him whenever he pleases. By this, he is said to obtain remission of sins, and to stand justified in the sight of God.

From all of this and much more which could be cited it is apparent that Catholics place their justification in the mere performance of certain ceremonies. It is located there rather than in any work of holiness that is brought forth in them, or in any real forsaking of iniquity. A blind belief that the church and the pope are the absolute dispensers of the merits of Christ has been begotten by them in their teachers. These merits are effectual for the remission of sins and the justification of those who will perform these ceremonies. This is the true and the real method of justification for the majority of the members of the church of Rome. I have been an eye and ear witness to its high commendation by public preachers in their sermons to the people, in spite of the extent to which some of their modern writers have labored to qualify it.

PROTESTANTS WENT TO ANOTHER EXTREME

This doctrine offered good reason for the denial and opposition of the Protestants. Many of them, however, went to another extreme. They denied that good works were necessary

---

[6] St. James, "the Great," son of Zebedee and elder brother of St. John, was the first of the Twelve to suffer martyrdom. He was beheaded by Herod Agrippa I in 44 A. D. (Acts 12:2). According to an old Spanish tradition his body was translated to Santiago de Compostela, a city in N.W. Spain. It continues to be a center for pilgrimages from all over Spain and many other parts of the world. — O.D.C.C., pp 710-711 and 322. (See also fn p 186 regarding "translations.")

[7] "Near Ancona in Italy is the site of the Holy House, alleged to have been inhabited by the Blessed Virgin Mary at the time of the Annunciation and to have been miraculously transported by angels from Nazareth to Tersatz in Dalmatia in 1291 and thence by the same agency to Loreto in 1295. The earliest attestation of the legend is an account of the sanctuary written c. 1470. The whole story is now commonly regarded as unhistorical, not least by Roman Catholic writers of unquestioned orthodoxy." — O.D.C.C., pp 821-822.

for justification and they advocated faith alone as sufficient not only for the remission of sins but for justification. Men are justified, according to the doctrine, merely by believing that Christ died for them, and not by being inwardly sanctified and renewed. For them, some are perfectly justified even though they are committing great wickedness. The example of David is given. They say that he was fully and perfectly justified even when he was committing the gross sins of murder and adultery.

In this way the Protestants have left themselves open to the Catholic charge that those who neglect good works are enemies of mortification and holiness if they consider themselves justified even while they are committing great sins. The reformation has been greatly defamed and hindered by such accusations, for which there is much ground in the writing of some rigid Protestants. Unfortunately many souls have also been ensnared.

BOTH ARGUMENTS COME TO THE SAME CONCLUSION

Those who take a close look at both arguments will find that they differ more in particulars than in general principles, since they both come to the same conclusion. It is like two men in a circular enclosure who meet at the same center even though they travel in different ways.

The Catholics maintain that they obtain remission of sins and are justified as the merits of Christ are applied to them in the sacraments, and as these are dispensed in certain ceremonies, pilgrimages, prayers, and performances. Inward renewal of the mind or the inwardly formed knowledge of Christ are not necessary. For them, remission is obtained *ex opere operato* by virtue of the power and authority accompanying the sacraments and those who perform them.

Protestants, on the other hand, say that they obtain remission of sins and are justified in the sight of God by virtue of Christ's merits and sufferings. They obtain remission not by having righteousness infused into them, but by having their sins pardoned. They are considered as righteous and accepted as such because of their faith in him and his righteousness. It is not a matter of being accepted as a faithful believer because they have been righteous.[8]

Hence, neither Catholic nor Protestant bases justification on any inward renewing of the mind, or by virtue of any spir-

8 *Westminster Confession of Faith,* chap 11, sect 1.

itual birth, or formation of Christ in them. The fact that Christ died and suffered is the basis. One view rests its faith on that fact alone, whereas the other considers that Christ's death is made effective by expressing certain prayers and performing particular ceremonies.

These are generalizations, however, for it would be wrong to ignore the fact that some modern Catholics and modern Protestants have tried to strike a balance between the extremes by insisting on the necessity of inward holiness.

However, as far as I know, our interpretation represents the first time since the apostasy that this doctrine has been so clearly and distinctly set forth according to the scriptural testimony. The way in which this view differs from that of those who oppose it will now be explained more fully than it is in the opening thesis.

NO ACT OF OUR OWN WILL OBLIGE GOD TO JUSTIFY US

¶III. First, we repudiate natural power and ability of any kind as capable of bringing us out of our lost and fallen condition and our first nature. We confess that by ourselves we are unable to do anything good.

There is no act of our own that will procure remission of sins for us or oblige God to grant this to us. Justification arises, instead, from the love of God for us, and this is the original and fundamental reason why he accepts us.

THROUGH THE CROSS CHRIST HAS RECONCILED US UNTO HIMSELF

Second, God demonstrated this love for us by sending into the world his beloved Son, the Lord Jesus Christ. He "gave himself up for us, a fragrant offering and sacrifice to God;" (Eph 5:2 RSV). He made peace through the blood of his cross in order to reconcile us to himself. By the Eternal Spirit he offered himself spotless before God, and — as the just one — he suffered for us, the unjust, in order to bring us to God.

HE ALONE IS THE MEDIATOR WHO HAS PROCURED REMISSION OF SIN

Third, since all men except Jesus have sinned if they have reached man's estate, they need this Savior to remove the wrath of God which they have incurred by these offences. In this respect, he truly bore all of our iniquities in his body on the tree. Therefore, he alone is our Mediator who has qualified the wrath of God toward us. Our former sins have been re-

moved and pardoned and no longer stand in our way because
of the complete satisfaction of his sacrifice. There is no other
way whatsoever to seek remission of sins, whether it be works
or sacrifices. It cannot be expected or obtained in any other
way. Nevertheless, those who have never heard his name may
still participate in this remission.

THROUGH CHRIST WE ARE RECONCILED TO GOD

Christ, by his death and sufferings, then, has reconciled us
to God even while we are enemies. That is, he offers reconciliation to us. We are given the capability of being reconciled.
As has been so well expressed in 2 Cor 5:19 NEB, God is willing to forgive our iniquities and accept us: "God was in Christ
reconciling the world to himself, no longer holding men's misdeeds against them, and ... he has entrusted us with the message of reconciliation." Because of this, he entreats us in the
next verse, "in Christ's name, we implore you, be reconciled
to God!"

REDEMPTION IS TWO-FOLD: THE FIRST STATE GIVES US THE POWER TO COUNTERBALANCE EVIL, AND WE ARE REDEEMED AND CONFORMED TO HIM BY THE SECOND

Thus, we consider redemption a two-fold state, each aspect
of which is complete in itself, but when it is applied to us one
is as necessary as the other for redemption to be considered
complete. Man receives the capacity to be saved from the first
aspect and possesses a measure of the power, virtue, spirit, life,
and grace which were in Christ Jesus. It is conveyed to him
by the free gift of God. By that gift, he is able to counterbal-
ance, overcome, and root out the evil seed which occurs naturally in all of us.

By the second aspect, we witness. And by witnessing we
know this pure and perfect redemption within us, purifying,
cleansing, and redeeming us from the power of corruption and
bringing us into unity, favor, and friendship with God.

By the first aspect, God is reconciled unto us in Christ, who
calls and invites us to himself, and it is in this respect that we
apply the following scriptures: "In his own person he put the
enmity to death" (Eph 2:16b NEB). "He loved us first" (1 John
4:10-11). "And when I passed by you, and saw you weltering
in your blood, I said to you in your blood, 'Live,'" (Ezek 16:6

RSV). He who committed no sin and was convicted of no falsehood, "he himself bore our sins in his body on the tree" (1 Pet 2:22, 24 RSV). For Christ "died for [our] sins once for all, the righteous for the unrighteous, that he might bring us to God, being put to death in the flesh but made alive in the spirit;" (1 Pet 3:18 RSV).

By the second aspect, this capacity to be saved is brought into action. By it, if we do not resist the purchase of his death, we come to an awareness of union and friendship with God. By the light, Spirit, and grace of Christ revealed in us, we are inwardly and truly redeemed from the power and prevalence of sin and become justified in the sight of God and genuinely righteous. Thus, he died for us "to redeem us from all iniquity" (Titus 2:14 RSV). Thus we come "to experience the power of his resurrection, and to share his sufferings in growing conformity with his death" (Phil 3:10 NEB).

THE FIRST IS THE PROCURING CAUSE, AND THE SECOND IS THE FORMAL CAUSE

Thus we regard both aspects as the causes of justification. The first is the remote or procuring cause, and the second is the formal cause.

JUSTIFICATION IS THE FORMATION OF CHRIST WITHIN US FROM WHICH GOOD WORKS FOLLOW NATURALLY

Fourth, this justification is not understood merely as good works, even those that are wrought by the Spirit of Christ. As Protestants correctly affirm, these are an effect of justification rather than the cause of it. Justification, according to our understanding, is the formation of Christ within us, from which good works follow as naturally as fruit from a fruitful tree.

THE INWARD BIRTH BRINGS FORTH RIGHTEOUSNESS AND HOLINESS

We are justified by this inward birth in us which brings forth righteousness and holiness. Since it has removed and abolished everything of a contrary nature and spirit, that formerly ruled there and brought condemnation, now it has dominion over everything in our hearts. Those who come to know Jesus thus formed in them, enjoy him wholly. "The Lord is our righteousness" (Jer 23:6 RSV). This is what it means to be clothed with Christ, and to have put him on. God will consider anyone who has done this truly righteous and just.

This is so different from Catholic doctrine that their ordinary member does not understand it, and their learned members, particularly Bellarmine,[9] dispute and oppose it.

To reiterate, the formal cause of justification, properly
speaking, is not works. They are merely an effect of justification. The formal cause is the inward birth which brings Jesus
forth in the heart. He is the well-beloved, whom the Father
cannot help but accept, as he will all who thus are sprinkled
with the blood of Jesus and washed with it. By this, the goodness of Christ is communicated to us, and we "become partakers of the divine nature," as 2 Pet 1:4 RSV (and Cath-CCD)
says. We become as united with him as the branches with the
vine, and we have a title and a right to what he has done and
suffered for us. His obedience becomes ours, his righteousness
ours, his death and suffering ours.

By this nearness, we come to have a sense of his sufferings,
and to suffer with his seed where it still lies weighted down and
crucified in the hearts of the ungodly. So we travail with it
and work for its redemption and for the repentance of the
souls who are still crucifying the "Lord of Glory." Just as the
apostle Paul said of his sufferings: "This is my way of helping
to complete, in my poor human flesh, the full tale of Christ's
afflictions still to be endured, for the sake of his body which is
the church." (Col 1:24 NEB).

Although this is a sealed mystery to all of the wise men
who have yet to learn of this seed in themselves, nevertheless
there are some Protestants who speak of justification in terms
of Christ being inwardly put on, as will be shown farther along.

GOOD WORKS ARE AN INDISPENSABLE PART OF JUSTIFICATION

Finally, we do not exclude works from our concept of justification as some Protestants have done unwarily. This is true,
even though we consider the remote or procuring cause of

[9] Robert Bellarmine (1542-1621). In the polemical theology which
developed in the 16th c., "the leading figure in Lutheran circles was Martin Chemnitz (1522-1586), who wrote an *Examen Concilii Tridentini* in
four large volumes (1565-1573), in which he reviewed critically all the
dogmatic resolutions of the Council of Trent. The principal Roman
Catholic controversialist was Roberto Bellarmino, whose three folio volumes, entitled *Disputationes de controversiis Christianae fidei* (1586-1593),
gave a complete survey of all the differences in doctrine between the
Roman Catholic and Evangelical Churches. His work provoked more than
fifty treatises in reply from his opponents. — Einar Molland, *Christendom*,
London, Mowbray, 1961, pp 1-2. (See also fn p 376.)

remission of sins to be the acts of obedience and righteousness performed by the historic Christ. It is true even though we consider formal justification as resulting from the formation and bringing forth of Christ in us. For although, properly speaking, we are not justified because of our good works, yet we are justified by doing them. They are a *sine qua non* or indispensable part of justification.

It is contrary to the scriptural testimony to deny this. It has brought great scandal upon Protestantism and it has been the source of rebukes by Catholics. Many have been made to feel too secure and have believed that they could be justified without good works. Since good works are rewarded, many of the Fathers have not hesitated to apply the word *merit,* even though it is not safe to say that good works are meritorious. Although some of us have done this in a qualified sense, it has not been in a way that would lead to the Catholic abuses that have been mentioned.

Actually, if we shared the notion of good works which most Protestants possess, we should agree readily that they are not only unnecessary, but actually harmful. For even the best works of the saints are defiled if they proceed only from their own strength and will and represent nothing more than an endeavor to conform to the outward law. But works which proceed naturally from a spiritual rebirth and the inward formation of Christ are as pure and as holy as the root from which they come. Therefore God justifies that kind of good works and he justifies us in doing them, and he rewards us for them of his own free grace.

Having outlined the controversial points, it is now necessary to prove the following points.

AS LONG AS ANYONE REMAINS IMPURE AND UNJUST, JUSTIFICATION IS POTENTIAL AND GRACE IS MERELY OFFERED

¶IV. The obedience, sufferings, and death of Christ are the means by which the soul obtains remission of sins and procures the grace for us by whose inward working Christ comes to be inwardly formed and the soul is made to conform to him and hence becomes just and justified. It is because of the potentiality and the offer of grace that God is said to be reconciled. But he is not actually reconciled, or actually justified, nor does he consider anyone just, so long as he remains sinful and really impure and unjust.

THE SCRIPTURAL USE OF JUSTIFICATION
IS OFTEN THE EQUIVALENT OF SANCTIFICATION

It is by the inward birth of Christ in man that he is justified and so considered by God. As it is most often used in scripture, justification refers to making one just, rather than merely having the reputation for being just. It is the equivalent of sanctification.

GOD CANNOT DO ANYTHING BUT ACCEPT
AND REWARD GOOD WORKS

Good works follow as naturally from this birth as heat from fire. Although they are not the cause of justification, nevertheless they are that in which we are justified, and without which that cannot be so. Although they are not meritorious, and in no way obligate God, he could not possibly do anything but accept and reward them. It is contrary to his nature for him to deny his own, and since they proceed from a pure holy birth and root they share in his perfection.

BECAUSE OF CHRIST'S DEATH
GOD IS FORBEARING TOWARD MANKIND

¶V. The effectiveness of Christ's death for redeeming men from evil needs no other proof than Rom 3:25-26 NEB: "For God designed him to be the means of expiating sin by his sacrificial death, effective through faith. God meant by this to demonstrate his justice, because in his forbearance he had overlooked the sins of the past — to demonstrate his justice now in the present, showing that he is both himself just and justifies any man who puts his faith in Jesus."

The apostle speaks of the extent and efficacy of Christ's death showing that remission of past sins is obtained by it and by faith in it. In that way God exercises forbearance toward mankind. Although men deserve eternal death for the sins they commit daily, and although the wrath of God should take hold of them, the grace and seed of God moves toward them in love, during the day of their visitation. God does not strike against the evil, but redeems men from it so that it is consumed and destroyed.

THROUGH FAITH AND REPENTANCE
WE HAVE THE CAPACITY TO BE RECONCILED

If God were completely reconciled with men and considered them just even when they were actually unjust and continued in their sins, then he would have no controversy with them.[10]

If this were so, why does God complain so frequently throughout the scriptures about those who are said to be justified in this sense? Why does he say of them: "your iniquities have made a separation between you and your God" Isa 59:2 RSV? If there were a full and complete reconciliation, there would be no separation!

It is a necessary consequence of this doctrine that either those for whom Christ died and who were thus reconciled to him never sin, or else they are justified in their sins, and even the greatest of their sins are the same as their good works in the sight of God.

This not only opens the door for every sort of lewd practice and affords great security for it. It makes the practical doctrine of the gospel altogether void. Faith itself is unnecessary.

The whole question hinges on whether we are fully reconciled to God or merely have the capacity to be reconciled when we achieve the attitudes of faith and repentance which are the necessary requirements called for throughout the gospel. . . .

OUR RECONCILIATION AND JUSTIFICATION ARE PERFECTED BY SEEING OUR ERROR AND REPENTING

And, then too, it should also be stressed that these conditions are of such a nature that they cannot be done merely once but must be met throughout life. Otherwise, this would be contrary to a very clear testimony of the scriptures which is acknowledged by all Christians: For "without faith it is impossible to please him [God]." (Heb 11:6 KJ). "He who does not believe is condemned already, because he has not believed in the name of the only Son of God." (John 3:18 RSV). "Unless you repent, you will all perish in the same manner." (Luke 13:3 Cath-CCD). "For if you live according to the flesh you will die." (Rom 8:13 RSV and Cath-CCD). Of those who

---

10 This is said not only of men before their conversion who were later converted and whom the Antinomians would say were justified from the beginning, but of those who were converted in the general sense in which it was used by Protestants. Even though they confess, they continue to do some misdeeds forever, and sometimes they commit such heinous crimes as David's adultery and murder. Yet they claim that they are perfectly and wholly justified.

were converted but had lost their early zeal: "Repent and do the works you did at first. If not, I will come to you and remove your lampstand from its place." (Rev 2:5 RSV).

Over 1600 years ago, Christ said: "It is finished" and gave up the Spirit. If, as the Antinomians[11] say, he perfected redemption then to such an extent that we are reputed just, even before we believe, or after we have given assent to the truth of the historical Christ and are sprinkled with the baptism of water but nevertheless remain unjust, then the whole doctrinal part of the Bible is useless and worthless. The apostles were sent forth to preach repentance and the remission of sins in vain if the historic fact of Christ's death did not merely open the door of mercy for us so that we could repent and obtain the remission of our sins. It is a waste of breath on the part of preachers and they labor in vain and write without purpose if the sacrifice of his body did not communicate a measure of his grace by which we are able to see our error and repent.

CHRIST'S INTERCESSION FOR US IS BASED ON OUR HUMAN EFFORTS

On the other hand, if human efforts are to be ignored as not worth arguing about or as unnecessary for salvation, what happens to that great article of faith in which we affirm that Christ sits at the right hand of God and makes daily intercession for us? Wouldn't it be absurd if Christ were making intercession for those for whom salvation is impossible?

There are those who claim that he does not pray for the world at all. But it would serve no purpose if he merely prays for those who are already reconciled and perfectly justified.

---

[11] Antinomianism, derived from the Greek *anti*, against, and *nomos*, law, was an extreme interpretation of the antithesis between law and gospel. Paul's disparagement of Mosaic Law in favor of that "written in the heart" was interpreted as setting Christians free from the need for observing any moral law. The idea recurs throughout Christian history. "Indications are not wanting that St. Paul's doctrine of justification by faith was, in his own day, mistaken or perverted in the interests of immoral licence." — *Encyc. Brit.*, vol 2, p 69.

This is true even though the great argument against antinomianism is the sixth chapter of Romans. — *Col. Encyc.*, p 80.

Some of the Anabaptist excesses at Münster are attributed to antinomianism, and "During the Commonwealth period Antinomianism was found among the high Calvinists who maintained that an elect person, being predestined to salvation, is absolved from the moral law and is not called upon to repent. In less extreme forms, Antinomianism is a feature of those forms of Christianity which lay stress on justification by faith." — *Encyc. Brit.*, loc cit.

There is even less point in praying for the remission of our sins
if all of our sins of the past, present, and future have been remitted.

The only sound solution to all of this is to acknowledge
that Christ's death removed the wrath of God and obtained
remission of sins for those who will receive the grace and light
which he communicates to them and which he has purchased
for them with his blood. If they truly repent and believe in
him, in time they will have their past sins remitted. If they
apply his grace, they will receive power to save them from sin
and to blot out sin as often as it is committed because of un-
watchfulness or weakness.

WE BECOME CHILDREN OF GOD THROUGH HIS POWER

"But to all who received him, who believed in his name,
he gave power to become children of God." (John 1:12 RSV).
None become his children, none become justified, none become
reconciled until they receive him in that little seed in their
hearts. To those who patiently persist in doing the best of
which they are capable and who seek glory, honor, and immortality in that way, life eternal is offered. But if the righteous
man departs from righteousness, the good that he has done will
be forgotten. None continue to be his children and justified
unless they patiently persist in righteousness and good behavior. That is why Christ continues to make intercession, so that
everyone may be converted[12] during the day of his visitation.

[12] "Converted" is actually the word used by Barclay although some
Friends today more commonly speak of "being *convinced* of truth," a
phrase that is at least as old as 1697 when Richard Claridge wrote: "This
was the way that Friends used with me, when I was convinced of truth,
they came oftentimes to visit me; and sat and waited upon the Lord in
silence with me; and as the Lord opened our understandings and mouths,
so we had very sweet and comfortable seasons together. They did not ask
me questions about this or the other creed, or about this or the other
controversy in religion; but they waited to feel that living Power to quicken
me, which raised up Jesus from the dead. And it pleased God so in his
wisdom to direct, that all the great truths of the Christian religion were
occasionally spoken to. Now this was Friends way with me, a way far
beyond all rules or methods established by the wisdom of this world, which
is foolishness with God: And this is their way with others that are convinced of the truth." [Item #369 in *Christian faith and practice in the
experience of the Society of Friends,* London Yearly Meeting of the Religious Society of Friends, 1961, from his *Lux evangelica attestata,* p 10.]

On the other hand, William Penn stated in his preface to Fox's *Journal*
in 1694: "And when you are converted, as well as convinced, then confirm
your brethren; and be ready to every good word and work, that the Lord
shall call you to." (See also fn p 254.)

And when they have been converted to some extent, he intercedes for them to continue and go on, and not to faint or go back again.

Much more could be said in confirmation of this truth, but it is time to consider the objections that have been raised and the arguments used in support of them.

IN HIS LIFETIME CHRIST BEGAN THE WORK OF RECONCILIATION BUT HE DID NOT COMPLETE IT THEN

¶VI. The first and principal objection is made by citing 2 Cor 5:18-19 NEB to infer that Christ completely perfected his work of reconciliation while he was on earth: "God was in Christ reconciling the world unto himself, no longer holding men's misdeeds against them, and ... he has entrusted us with the message of reconciliation. ..."

Christ actually began this work on behalf of everyone in the days of his flesh and indeed even long before that. For he was the mediator from the very beginning and the lamb who was slain from the foundation of the world. But it was in the flesh, after he had perfectly fulfilled the law and the righteousness which it called for, and had rent the veil, that he made way for the clearer and most universal revelation of the gospel to everyone, Jew and Gentile alike. He gave himself as a most satisfactory sacrifice for sin. This becomes effective for everyone who is willing to receive his inward appearance — his light in the heart.

To reiterate, the cited passage shows that the only form of reconciliation intended is the opening of the door to God's mercy and the removal of his wrath for past sins. In spite of their sins, men receive the capacity to be saved. For the apostle says in the following verse, 2 Cor 5:20 RSV: "So we are ambassadors for Christ, God making his appeal through us. We beseech you, on behalf of Christ, be reconciled to God."

Why would it be necessary to beseech them to be reconciled if this were already completed?

IT IS ARGUED THAT CHRIST'S RIGHTEOUSNESS IS IMPUTED TO US

An argument is also made from the following verse, 2 Cor 5:21 NEB, which says: "Christ was innocent of sin, and yet for our sake God made him one with the sinfulness of men, so that in him we might be made one with the goodness of God himself." The argument that is drawn from this is that if our sin

is imputed to Christ who knew no sin, then Christ's righteousness is imputed to us without our being righteous.

But it is easy to disprove this interpretation. For although
"Christ bore our sins" and "suffered for us," and although men
"accounted him a sinner," and he was "numbered among transgressors," yet there is no proof anywhere that God considered
him a sinner. For it is said (Heb 7:26 NEB) that he was "devout, guileless, undefiled, separated from sinners," nor was any
"guile found on his lips" (1 Pet 2:22 RSV). Under no circumstances did he die so that we could be considered righteous
even though in reality we were no more righteous than he was
sinful. . . .

His "being made sin for us" must be understood as his
suffering for our sins so that we might partake of the grace
which he purchased. By the operation of that grace we are
made the righteousness of God in him.

GENUINE RATHER THAN IMPUTED RIGHTEOUSNESS WAS WHAT THE APOSTLE MEANT

It is clear that in 2 Cor 5:20 the apostle meant being really
made righteous rather than merely reputed as such, for in the
next chapter, 2 Cor 6:14-16 NEB, he is largely arguing against
the supposition of any agreement between light and darkness,
or of righteousness and unrighteousness: "Do not unite yourselves with unbelievers; they are no fit mates for you. What
has righteousness to do with wickedness? Can light consort
with darkness? Can Christ agree with Belial, or a believer
join hands with an unbeliever? Can there be a compact between the temple of God and the idols of the heathen? And
the temple of the living God is what we are."

Yet alliances of this kind would have to be recognized if
we were to accept a completely external and merely imputative
righteousness. It would be necessary to consider men as acceptable and engrafted into Christ and real members of him while
they themselves were still actually unrighteous. It may be
considered strange indeed that some men have made this such
a fundamental article of their faith, since it is so contrary to
the whole strain of the gospel.

Any of Christ's speeches or sermons make it clear that he
never wanted anyone to rely on such a belief. These always
emphasize and recommend works as essential for our justification. Even more to be wondered at is the fact that the imputed

righteousness of Christ is never found in the Bible. It is not necessary to dwell on this, because many who stress justification by bare imputation, nevertheless confess that even the elect are not justified until they have been converted, that is, until this imputative justification has been applied to them by the Holy Spirit.

¶VII. Coming to the second part of the proposition, we are formally justified in the sight of God by the inward birth or Christ formed within. We have probably said enough about how much significance we ascribe to the death and sufferings of Christ. We have said how God's justice was satisfied by these, how sins were remitted, and how grace and the seed from which this birth takes place were purchased by it. It remains to be proved that we are justified or made just by having Christ formed in us. The sense in which justification is used here should be noted.

The first proof is 1 Cor 6:11 RSV: "And such were some of you. But you were washed, you were sanctified, you were justified in the name of the Lord Jesus Christ and in the Spirit of our God." The *justified* must refer to being really made just and not merely reputed as such, or else it would be necessary to consider the *sanctified* and *washed* as merely considered or reputed rather than actual. But if this were done, it would completely upset the whole intent of the context....

It would be absurd to maintain that the Corinthians had not forsaken their wickedness and that they were justified even though they continued in it. This is not only absurd in itself, but it clearly destroys the implications and intent of this passage. The Corinthians would not really have been changed by becoming Christians. They would merely have accepted some barren notions which had no effect whatever on their affections or desires, or their manner of living.

What could be seen, heard, or read that would offer convincing proof that the word *justified* as it is used here should be interpreted in any other way than as meaning a genuine change by which the individual becomes just? ...

Paraeus, a chief Protestant and Calvinist, says:[13] "We never at any time said, or thought, that the righteousness of Christ

---

13 *De Just. cont. Bell.*, lib 2 cap 7, p 469.

David Paraeus (1548-1622) was one of the leaders in the efforts to secure a union of Protestants in the late 16th and early 17th c. A Reformed

was imputed to us, that by him we should be named formally
just, and not be so, as we have already shown many times; for
that would be no more consistent with correct reason, than if
a guilty man should claim that he was formally just because
of the clemency of the judge in granting him his life."

BOTH HOLINESS AND GOOD WORKS ARE NECESSARY

Isn't it strange that men should be so facile on a matter of
such moment? They build their acceptance with God upon a
mere borrowed and metaphorical meaning. They exclude holiness or at least consider it unnecessary, in spite of the fact that
Heb 12:14 Cath-CCD says: "Strive for peace with all men, and
for that holiness without which no man will see God." If holiness is necessary, then good works must also be necessary. Can
anyone show us a holy man who has done no good works?

What is more, *justified* in the figurative sense is used for
approved. However, in most cases in the scripture where *justified* is used it is used in the worst sense, that is, to mean usurp-
ing for oneself something which really does not belong to him.
If the following citations are examined, it will be seen that
they all refer to "justifying the wicked" or to "wicked men
justifying themselves — that is, approving themselves in their
wickedness: Ex 23:7, Job 9:20 and 27:5, Prov 17:15, Isa 5:23,
Jer 3:11, Ezek 16:51, 52, Luke 10:29 and 16:15.[14]

Justification is seldom used in a positive sense, and on the
rare occasions when it is, the context is so obvious that the
meaning is plain and there is no doubt. But the question is
not so much one of occasional usage as it is a matter of what is
said where the doctrine of justification itself is considered. If
we content ourselves with an imaginary justification when God
requires a real one, the consequences are very harmful. As for
the formal discussion of the doctrine of justification there is
nothing absurd about it, when the word is given its proper sig-

---

theologian of Heidelberg, he proposed in his *Irenicum* that Protestants
seek union against the Roman Catholics through "a regular and free
council." — Kenneth Scott Latourette, *A History of Christianity*, N. Y.,
Harper, 1953, p 891.

[14] Although all of these refer specifically to justification in the KJ,
only the passages from Prov and Luke do so in the RSV. God says he will
not *acquit* the wicked in Ex 23:7. *Acquit* is also used in Isa 5:23. Job
refuses to say that someone is *right* (27:5). Faithless Israel is *less guilty*
than false Judah in Jer 3:11. The alternative translations are an interesting commentary on the significance of the concept of justification and its
relation to "guilt." — ED

nificance. This should be considered in relation to the places where Paul handles the theme in Romans, Corinthians, Galatians, and in other places.

BUT FAITH, NOT LAW, SHOULD BE THE BASIS

There is nothing harmful or absurd about believing that a man cannot be made just by the law of Moses or by performing the works which the law prescribes. This is clearly stated in Gal 2:16 and 3:11 as well as in Rom 3:20, and it is in complete agreement with the statement made in Heb 7:19 RSV that "the law made nothing perfect." Where it is said that "we are justified by faith," this can be properly understood as being made just, since it is also said that "faith purifies the heart," and there is no doubt that the pure in heart are just, and that "the just shall live by faith." Where it is said that we are justified by grace, we are justified by Christ, we are justified by the Spirit, it is reasonable to consider this as being made just, since it is by his Spirit and grace that he does make men just.

THE PASSAGE FROM CALLING TO GLORIFICATION IS MADE BY TRUE RIGHTEOUSNESS

But to understand this as universally true in the other sense, that is, as merely providing acceptance and imputation, would lead to ridiculous inferences whose discussion, for the sake of brevity, will be deferred until later. What is more, in the most significant passages in the scriptures where the word *justify* is used with immediate reference to the doctrine of justification, it must be admitted that it is to be understood as genuinely making just rather than a bare legal acceptance. First, as has already been noted, is 1 Cor 6:11 RSV: "But you were washed, you were sanctified, you were justified in the name of the Lord Jesus Christ and in the Spirit of our God." Second is the much observed statement in Rom 8:30 NEB: "And those whom he called he has justified, and to those whom he justified he has also given his splendor." This is commonly called the golden chain which describes the method and sequence of salvation. Certainly if justification did not mean being made just, sanctification would have to be omitted from this chain. It is also noteworthy that in this succinct compendium Paul uses the word *justified* to cover everything between calling and glorifying. The implication is clear that the only way that we can pass from our calling to our glorification is by true righteousness.

Melancthon says:[15] "That to be justified by faith, signifies
in scripture not only to be pronounced just, but that also the
unrighteous are to be made righteous."[16] Some of the other
principal Protestant theologians have also hinted at our doctrine, although not so clearly. But they partly agree with us
in ascribing remission of sins to Christ's death and the work of
justification to the grace of the Spirit acquired by his death.
Martinus Boraeus[17] says in explanation of Rom 4:25: "Who
was given for our sins and rose again for our justification," that
"there are two things beheld in Christ, which are necessary to
our justification; the one is his death, the other is his arising
from the dead. By his death, the sins of the world behoved to
be expiated: by his rising from the dead, it pleased the same
goodness of God to give the Holy Spirit, whereby both the gospel is believed, and the righteousness lost by the fault of the
first Adam is restored." And he later says that the apostle
expressed both parts in the words " 'who was given for our sins'
... In his death is beheld the satisfaction for sin; in his resurrection, the gift of the Holy Spirit, by which our justification
is perfected." And he also says elsewhere:[18] "Both these kinds
of righteousness are therefore contained in justification, neither
can the one be separate from the other. So that in the definition of *justification*, the merit of the blood of Christ is included, both with the remission of sins, and with the gift of the
Holy Spirit of justification and regeneration."[19]

[15] in *Apol. Conf. Aug.*

[16] This would seem to imply more than the mere imputed righteousness conferred by justification which Wendel (op cit, p 236) attributes to
Melancthon.

[17] *On Gen.* cap 15 and in *Credidit Abraham Deo*, p 161.

This may be Martin Borrhaus, generally known as Cellarius and also as
Martin Bellius (1499-1564, b. at Stuttgart, d. at Basel). He published his
first work, *De operibus Dei*, in 1527. He was professor of OT at Basel,
and is referred to in lives of Luther, Melancthon, and Zwingli. — *New
Schaff-Herzog Encyc. of Rel. Knowledge*, N. Y., Funk & Wagnalls, 1908, vol
2, p 236.

[18] ibidem, lib 3, *Reg.* cap 9, vol 4, p 681.

[19] There are also citations by Barclay in the unabridged original
from:

William Forbes (1585-1634), a native of Barclay's Aberdeen, who was
appointed first Bishop of Edinburgh by Charles I in 1634. "He is remembered especially for his erudite *Considerationes modestae et pacificae
Controversarium de Justificatione, Purgatorio, Invocatione Sanctorum,
Christo Mediatore et Eucharistia*, published posthumously in 1658." This

THE "FORMAL CAUSE" OF JUSTIFICATION IS
THE REVELATION AND FORMATION OF CHRIST IN THE SOUL

¶VIII. Having demonstrated that justification should be understood as meaning to be made truly righteous, there remains only the assertion that the "formal cause"[20] of justification is Christ revealed and formed in the soul. This is the way in which we are truly justified and accepted in the sight of God. It is by the revelation of Jesus Christ in the soul, changing, altering and renewing the mind, that this is brought about. As we are covered and clothed with him, in whom the Father is always well pleased, we may draw near to God, and stand with confidence before his throne. We are purged by the blood of Jesus poured into our souls and we are clothed with his life and the righteousness that it revealed. This is the sequence and the method of salvation of which the apostle spoke in Rom 5:10 NEB: "For if, when we were God's enemies, we were reconciled to him through the death of his Son, much more, now that we are reconciled, shall we be saved by his life" — a very clear statement of reconciliation by his death and salvation by his life.

The same apostle says that this is an inward spiritual transformation that is wrought in the soul. By the nature of things the soul has been dead since the fall of Adam, but by this inward spiritual transformation the soul is brought forth from death and quickened and made alive to God. In Eph 2:5 NEB he says that God "brought us to life with Christ even when we were dead in our sins; it is by his grace you are saved." In 2 Cor 4:10-11 NEB he adds: "Wherever we go we carry death with

---

is the work actually cited by Barclay: 1, 2, s 8. It was reissued with an English translation in 1850-1856.—*O.D.C.C.*, p. 513.

Calvin's *Institutes*, 1 3, c 11, s 15; Beza, Bucer, Bullinger and Thysius.

The *Exam. Conc. Trid.* "de Just.," p 129, by Chemnitius [Martin Chemnitz (1522-1586), a Lutheran theologian, see fn p 133].

Zanchius on Eph 2·4 and the "loc. de Just.," Thes 13. [Probably Hieronymus Zanchi (1516-1590). Source : *Realencyklopädie für protestantische Theologie und Kirche*, Leipzig, 1908, vol 15, pp 607-677. Union Theol. Seminary catalog has "Girolamo Zanchi," with the same dates.]

Jerome Zanchius, as his name is also rendered, was a Calvinist theologian born at Alzano, Italy. After entering the Augustinian Order of Canons Regular, he became convinced of the truth of Reformation doctrine. He had to flee Italy but received a call to Strasbourg, where he became professor of OT. "Though he was neither original nor creative, he was one of the most learned of the theologians of the 16th c." — *Schaff-Herzog Encyc. of Religious Knowledge*, N. Y., Funk and Wagnalls, 1912, vol 12, pp 496-497.

20 (if we must condescend to some and use this term)

us in our body, the death that Jesus died, that in this body also life may reveal itself, the life that Jesus lives. For continually, while still alive, we are being surrendered into the hands of death, for Jesus' sake, so that the life of Jesus also may be revealed in this mortal body of ours." It is by this inward life of Jesus that we are saved.

BY THE WASHING OF REGENERATION AND RENEWAL IN THE HOLY SPIRIT WERE WE SAVED

It is also by this revelation of Jesus Christ, and the new creation in us, that we are justified. This is so well stated in Titus 3:5 RSV that the very words have been included in the statement of the proposition on justification. "He saved us, not because of deeds done by us in righteousness, but in virtue of his own mercy, by the washing of regeneration and renewal in the Holy Spirit." Justification and salvation are synonymous so far as the source by which they are obtained is concerned. The apostle clearly ascribes the immediate cause of justification to the inward work of regeneration. It is Jesus Christ revealed in our souls which enables us to be reconciled to God. The washing of regeneration is the inward power and virtue by which the soul is cleansed and then clothed with the righteousness of Christ to make it fit to appear before God.

Paul shows how eager he was to have his hearers know Christ inwardly by the fact that he repeats and restates his question in 2 Cor 13:5 RSV: "Examine yourselves, to see whether you are holding to your faith. Test yourselves. Do you not realize that Jesus Christ is in you? — unless indeed you fail to meet the test!" The inward formation of Christ is referred to in other places. In Gal 4:19-20 Cath-CCD, he states that he wishes he could change his tone and stop scolding those "with whom I am in labor again, until Christ is formed in you!" In Col 1:27 RSV he speaks of: "This mystery, which is Christ in you, the hope of glory."

OUR JUSTIFICATION AND SALVATION ARE AND WERE ACHIEVED IN AND BY CHRIST AND HIS SPIRIT

Our sins were remitted by the love of God manifested in the appearance of Jesus Christ in the flesh. He made a way for our reconciliation by his life, death, sufferings, and obedience. Our birth arises from the seed of grace which he purchased for us. In that birth, Jesus Christ is received inwardly, and he is formed and brought forth in us. We are clothed in him and have put him on, and our souls live according to God's own pure and holy image of righteousness, as Eph 4:23-24[21] and Gal 3:27[22] say. Our justification and salvation are achieved in and by him, and by his Spirit and grace, as is stated in Rom 3:24, 1 Cor 6:11, and Titus 3:7.

As often as we turn to him with genuine repentance we partake of the fullness of his merits. His cleansing blood is near to wash away every sin and infirmity, and all of our backslidings are healed by the renewal of his Spirit. Those who find him raised and ruling in them in that way have a true ground for the hope and belief that they are justified by his blood. But none should deceive themselves and think that they are justified by the death and sufferings of Christ as long as "sin lies at their door" (Gen 4:7 KJ), iniquity prevails, and they are still unrenewed and unregenerate. They hope in vain if they do not have confidence that "I know you not" will not be said to them.

Remember how Christ said: "Not everyone who calls me 'Lord, Lord' will enter the kingdom of Heaven, but only those who do the will of my heavenly Father" (Mat 7:21 NEB). The following passages from 1 John 3:7, 20 NEB should be added to it: "My children, do not be misled: it is the man who does right, who is righteous, as God is righteous; ... This is how we may know that we belong to the realm of truth, and convince ourselves in his sight that even if our conscience condemns us, God is greater than our conscience and knows all."

Many famous Protestants bear witness to this justification by the inwardly formed and revealed Christ in man. M. Boraeus says:[23] "In our justification then Christ is considered, who breathes and lives in us, that is, by his Spirit being put on by us; and it is concerning this kind of putting on that the apostle says, 'Ye have put on Christ.' " ... A little further on he says:[24]

---

[21] Cath-CCD: "Be renewed in the spirit of your mind, and put on the new man, which has been created according to God in justice and holiness of truth."

[22] RSV: "For as many of you as were baptized into Christ have put on Christ."

23 *On Gen.*, p 161. [See p 144 for biographical fn.]

24 p 171.

A brief confirmatory reference to the *Orat. Apodict. Lausaniae Excus.* of Claudius Alberius Inuncunanus, 1587, orat 2, pp 86-87, is omitted here.

Claude Aubery (d. 1596) was a 16th c. French physician, who after em-

"As then blessed Paul would comprehend under the term justification, by saying, 'Whom he justified, then he glorified,' all of the things which pertain to our being reconciled to God the Father, and to being renewed, and to the recovery of righteousness and innocence, which fits us for attaining unto glory: such as faith, righteousness, Christ, and the gift of righteousness exhibited by him, whereby we are regenerated, to the fulfilling of the justification which the law requires; so would we."

Zwingli also says:[25] "That the sanctification of the Spirit is true justification, which alone suffices to justify."

Estius says:[26] "Lest Christian righteousness should be thought to consist in the washing alone, that is, in the remission of sins, he adds the other degree or part, 'but ye are sanctified'; that is, you have attained to purity, so that you are now truly holy before God. Lastly, expressing the sum of the benefit received in one word, which includes both parts, 'But ye are justified,' the apostle adds, 'in the name of the Lord Jesus Christ,' that is, by his merits, 'and in the Spirit of our God,' that is, the Holy Spirit, proceeding from God, and communicated to us by Christ."

Richard Baxter, a famous English preacher, says:[27] "Some ignorant wretches gnash their teeth at this doctrine, as if it

---

bracing the Reformation became a professor of philosophy at Lausanne. *Apodictae Orationes* is numbered among his works in the *Biographie Universelle, Ancienne et Moderne,* Paris, A. Michaud Freres, 1811, vol 3, p 7.

25 [Ulrich Zwingli] in his epistle to the princes of Germany as it is cited by Himelius, cap 8, p 60.

Prof. Barrois suggests that Himelius may have been Enoch Himmel (d. 1666), a doctor of theology of Speyer, who wrote a *Disput. de disciplina ecclesiastica* and *de vera Religione abramitica,* etc.; or Johann Himmel (1581-1642), a voluminous Lutheran theologian, who preached at Speyer, and was later a professor of theology at Jena.

26 Commenting on 1 Cor 6:11.

William Hessels van Est (1542-1613), exegete and hagiographer. A native of Gorcum in S. Holland, he became a chancellor of Douai, then the foremost theological faculty in Europe, in 1595. His principal work, the *Comentarii in Omnes Divi Pauli et Catholicas Epistolas* (1614-1616), "is especially valuable for its careful exegesis of the literal sense and its judicious choice of patristic material. It was frequently reprinted to the end of the 19th cent." — *O.D.C.C.,* p 464.

27 in *Aphorisms of Justification,* p 80.

Baxter (1615-1691) was a largely self-educated Puritan theologian who "so far as possible ignored the differences between Presbyterians, Episcopal-

were flat popery. They do not understand the nature of the righteousness of the new covenant which is all out of Christ in ourselves, though wrought by the power of the Spirit of Christ in us."

"FAITH APART FROM WORKS IS DEAD"

¶IX. Any imputation to us of a Roman Catholic view of justification[28] should be removed by what has already been said of the necessity of good works for justification. The words of the holy scripture speak plainly on this point, James 2:24, 26 RSV: "You see that a man is justified by works and not by faith alone. . . . For as the body apart from the spirit is dead, so faith apart from works is dead." This is a self-evident truth in the scriptures, which is asserted so clearly in a few of these places that they can be quoted without explanatory commentary: Heb 12:14 KJ: "without holiness no man shall see God." John 13: 17 RSV: "If you know these things, blessed are you if you do them." 1 Cor 7:19 NEB: "Circumcision or uncircumcision is neither here nor there; what matters is to keep God's commands." Rev 22:14 alternate phrasing (s) RSV: "Blessed are those who do his commandments, that they may have the right to the tree of life and that they may enter the city by the gates."

---

ian and Independent and secured co-operation among the local ministers in common pastoral work" among a "corrupt and unhealthy population of hand-loom workers" at Kidderminster, 1641 to 1660. — *O.D.C.C.*, p 143.

The Saints Everlasting Rest, still a devotional classic, is the greatest of his nearly 200 writings.

[28] In recent Catholic thought, justification is the event by which man "genuinely and radically passes from the state of sin" to one in which sin and justification do not co-exist dialectically. Although man is still exposed to "the attacks of sin," cannot discover with certainty his condition before God, and still sins, he continues to "flee from his own perdition" to God's grace.

God in his "overflowing grace" is ready to have him share in the divine nature (2 Pet 1:4) through the efficacious indwelling of his own Spirit "in the depths of man's being"; to adopt him as a son (Rom 8:15) with freedom in the Spirit (2 Cor 3:17) and with holiness (Rom 1:4).

Through the self-communication of God. man is divinized and given proof of his new creation. Justice "is not merely imputed in juridical fashion," but man is made truly just (Rom 1:17, 6:20, 8:10; 1 Cor 15:17ff; Gal 5:5; Eph 4:24 and passim).

"Because salvation must be won historically, justification may be preceded by preparatory acts which the grace of God makes possible (faith, imperfect contrition) and man can both preserve and continually increase it (*see* Merit, and Good Works)." — Karl Rahner and Herbert Vorgrimler, *Theol. Dict.*, N. Y., Herder and Herder, 1965, pp 247-248.

If only those who do the will of the Father can enter the Kingdom, if only those who base their actions on the sayings of Christ are considered wise builders and happy, if they are blessed who do the commandments and thereby gain the right to the tree of life and entrance to the city through the gates, then works are absolutely necessary for salvation and justification.

SOME CLAIM THAT WORKS ARE NOT NECESSARY

¶X. The objection that works are not necessary for justification is based on the saying of Christ in Luke 17:10 NEB: "When you have carried out all your orders, you should say, 'We are servants and deserve no credit; we have only done our duty.'" Merely because we deserve no credit does not mean that there is no point in keeping God's commandments. That would not only be absurd but would be completely contradictory to Christ's doctrine. The beatitudes of Mat 5 pronounce men blessed for their purity, their meekness, their peaceableness and similar qualities. In Mat 25:21, 23 Christ declares that those who improved their talents were "good and faithful servants." But when speaking of the servant who hid his gold in the ground, he says (in v 30 NEB): "fling the useless servant out into the dark."

The claim of non-necessity for works is also based on Paul's statements which exclude deeds of the law from justification such as Rom 3:20 NEB: "For (again from Scripture) 'no human being can be justified in the sight of God' for having kept the law: law brings only the consciousness of sin." "For our argument is that a man is justified by faith quite apart from success in keeping the law;" (Rom 3:28 NEB).

THE WORKS OF THE LAW AND THOSE OF GRACE

In answer to this, it can be said that there is a great difference between the works of the law and those of grace or of the gospel. The works of the law are excluded, but those of grace or of the gospel not only are not excluded, but are necessary. Works of the law are performed by man's own will, in his own strength, and in conformity to the letter of the law. They share man's own imperfection, or that of the law which makes nothing perfect.

The works of the Spirit of grace in the heart, on the other hand, are wrought in conformity to the inward and spiritual law. They are not wrought in man's will or by his power and ability, but in and by the power and Spirit of Christ in us. Therefore they are of a pure and perfect kind, and they may be called Christ's works for he is the immediate author of them. We insist that such works are absolutely necessary for justification and that a man cannot be justified without them. As the apostle James says, without them, all faith is dead.

The admissability of this distinction by which only the works of the law are excluded in what the apostle says is supported by the epistle to the Galatians, which treats this matter at some length. It was addressed to a situation in which some of the Jewish proselytes were trying to convince the Gentile faithful that legal ceremonies and observances were necessary for their justification. Paul contrasted the empty formalism of the law and its works with the righteousness engendered by the faith of Christ. He showed how the works of the law had ceased and were no longer required but how those of Christ not only continued but were necessary.

The pervading theme of the first four chapters of the epistle to the Galatians is that it is the works of the law which are excluded by the apostle. After upbraiding the Galatians in chapter 4 for returning to the celebration of days and times, he shows, at the beginning of chapter 5, the folly of adhering to the ceremony of circumcision, and the estrangement from Christ that would result. And then he adds in 5:6 RSV: "For in Christ Jesus neither circumcision nor uncircumcision is of any avail, but faith working through love."

IT IS THE FAITH WHICH WORKS BY LOVE THAT AVAILS

Circumcision, the word which is frequently used to encompass all of the ceremonies and legal performances of the Jews, is shown to be unnecessary and of no avail. This is the type of works by which no one is justified. It is the faith which works by love that avails, and it is the new creature who results that is absolutely necessary. For the faith which produces its effects by love cannot exist without works. For, as Gal 5:22 says, love is part of the harvest of the Spirit, and the new creature who is necessarily formed by it cannot exist without the good works which come about naturally.

This interrelatedness is very clearly stated in Gal 6:7-9 NEB: "Make no mistake about this: God is not to be fooled; a man reaps what he sows. If he sows seed in the field of his lower nature, he will reap from it a harvest of corruption, but if he sows in the field of the Spirit, the Spirit will bring him a harvest of eternal life. So let us never tire of doing good, for if we do not slacken our efforts we shall in due time reap our harvest." It is very apparent that the apostle wanted the Galatians to know how important good works are. Not those of the outward ceremonies and traditions of the law, but those which are the fruits of the Spirit which had been mentioned a little before. It is by the Spirit that he would have them led and by which he would have them walk in good works. In fact, he affirms that life everlasting is to be reaped from that kind of good works. And anything which enables a man to reap so rich a harvest is certainly not useless as far as his justification is concerned.

Another citation which is sometimes misused to prove that good works are not necessary is Titus 3:5 NEB: "Not for any good deeds of our own, but because he was merciful, he saved us through the water of rebirth and the renewing power of the Holy Spirit." It is generally agree that *saved* in this sense is the same as *justified*. And what do we receive renewing power for, if it is not for good works? Although in a sense it is we who do these things, in reality it is Christ alive in us, the worker in us, who is actually responsible. In the same epistle, Gal 2:20 NEB, Paul says: "I have been crucified with Christ: the life I now live is not my life, but the life which Christ lives in me." These works are to be particularly ascribed to the Spirit of Christ and the grace of God in us, by which we are immediately led and act, and are enabled to perform them. This is not a strained figure of speech, but one that was commonly used by the apostles as Gal 2:8 RSV shows: "For he who worked through Peter for the mission to the circumcised worked through me also for the Gentiles." It is even more directly expressed in Phil 2:13 NEB: "For it is God who works in you, inspiring both the will and the deed, for his own chosen purpose."

¶XI. Some say that works of any kind can not have a part in justification because nothing which is impure can be useful. They say that this applies even to the works of Christ in us and they cite Isa 64:6 RSV: "We have all become like one who is unclean, and all our righteous deeds are like a polluted garment." The argument is that since we are impure our works must also be impure. Although these are good in themselves, they receive a tincture of impurity by being performed by us, just as water is defiled by flowing through an unclean pipe.

Harking back to the two types of works — those performed in our own will and those performed in Christ's — the
first would certainly be impure. They are wrought in our
unrenewed or impure state, but those of the second type are a
different matter. If even the righteousness of Christ were included, all of the fruits of the Spirit mentioned in Gal 5 would
be like filthy rags or menstruous garments which ought to be
thrown away.

But, on the contrary, some of the works of the faithful are
said to have "a sweet savor in the nostrils of the Lord" or to be
an "ornament of great price in the sight of God." They are
said to "prevail with him" and to be "acceptable to him."[29]

James Coret, a French minister in the church of Basil,
says:[30] "Nevertheless, according to the counsel of certain good
men, I must admonish the reader that it never came into our
minds to abuse that saying of Isa 64:6[31] against good works,
in which it is said that 'all our righteousnesses are as filthy rags'
as if we would have that which is good in our good works,
and proceeds from the Holy Spirit, to be esteemed as a filthy
and unclean thing."

THE SPIRIT BRINGS FORTH GOOD AND PERFECT WORKS

¶XII. It is begging the other part of the question to claim
that the best of men are imperfect and therefore their works
are too. Even though a man may not be perfect in every respect, that does not prevent good and perfect works from being
brought forth in him by the Spirit of Christ. The example of
water flowing through an unclean pipe and becoming tainted
does not apply, even though it is sometimes cited in this connection. Although water can become tainted, the Spirit of God
cannot, and it is God's Spirit that is the immediate author of

[29] The quotations in this paragraph apparently represent the sense
but not the exact words of KJ scriptural citations, respectively: Eph 5:2;
1 Pet 3:4; unlocated; 2 Cor 5:9 or 1 Pet 2:20.

[30] in his *Apology*, published in Paris in 1597, p 78.

Jacques Couet [not "Coret"] (1546-1608) was born and died at Paris,
but served as pastor of the French Reformed church at Basle, Switzerland,
from 1588 to 1598. The *Apologia de justificatione* ... in the Bibl. Nat.,
however, is dated 1594. Ant. Lescaille [Alescales], with whom he and
Léonard Constant debated Justification, is named in the title of two other
volumes published in 1593. — Haag, *La France protestante*, 1854, vol 7,
pp 80-82, and 2nd ed, vol 4, col 764   I am grateful to M. Jean Bruno,
Conservateur, Bibliotheque Nationale, for tracking down this reference.

[31] As did Calvin and some other Protestants [Musculus, Bertius, and
Alescales, among others] cited by Barclay, but here omitted.

the works which avail in justification. Christ's works in his
children are pure and perfect. He is at work in and through
that which is pure and of his own creation in them. If this
were not so, no one could ever be perfect. Even the miracles
and the works which Christ wrought in the apostles by his
power, Spirit, and grace would also be imperfect and impure.
Even the conversion of the nations to the Christian faith, the
gathering of the churches, and the writing of the scriptures, as
well as the sacrifice of their lives for Jesus, would all be tainted.

But, nevertheless, the idea that man deserves anything
from God because of his works is farthest from our thinking
or beliefs. For all of the gifts of God are of his own free grace.
That is why we have always denied the Roman Catholic idea of
meritum ex condigno.[32] However, we cannot deny that God
does give recompense and reward his children for their good
works out of his own free will. He does this out of the infinite
goodness with which he has loved mankind, and after he communicates his holy grace and Spirit to man. There is no doubt
but what God judges and accepts men according to their works
if the following citations are read and considered seriously:
Mat 16:27, Rom 2:6, 7, and 10, 2 Cor 5:10, Jas 1:25, Heb 10:
35, 1 Pet 1:17, Rev 22:12.

THE HOPE OF THE UNSANCTIFIED AND UNJUSTIFIED IN HEART WILL PROVE TO BE THAT OF THE HYPOCRITE

¶XIII. To conclude this proposition, let no one be so
bold as to mock God and assume that he is justified and accepted in the sight of God by virtue of Christ's death and sufferings if he remains unsanctified and unjustified in his own
heart. His hope will prove to be that of the hypocrite and he
will perish if he continues to be polluted by his sins.

[32] See fn p 126. The correct phrase is *meritum de condigno.*

Maturity

PROPOSITION 8 — PERFECTION [OR THE ACHIEVEMENT OF SPIRITUAL MATURITY]

He in whom this pure and holy birth occurs in all its fullness, finds that death and sin are crucified and removed from him, and his heart becomes united and obedient to truth. He is no longer able to obey any suggestions or temptations toward evil, but is freed from sin and the transgression of the law of God, and in that respect perfect. Yet there is still room for spiritual growth, and some possibility of sinning remains if the mind is not diligently and watchfully applied to heeding the Lord. (Rom 6:14; 8:13; 6:2, 18; *and* 1 John 3:6).

TO WHAT EXTENT CAN CHRIST PREVAIL IN US WHILE WE ARE ALIVE?

¶ I. To what extent can Christ prevail in us while we are alive? Can we overcome the enemies of the soul by his strength?

Those who claim that justification is an external matter, attributable solely to imputative righteousness, deny that there is any need to be clothed with genuine inward righteousness. They say, in the words of the Westminster Larger Catechism:[1] "That it is impossible for a man, even the best of men, to be free of sin in this life, which they say no man ever was; but on the contrary, that none can, neither of himself, nor by any grace received in this life [what a wicked saying against the power of God's grace! — R. B.] can keep the commandments of God perfectly; but that every man doth break the commandments in thought, word and deed." They also maintain from this, as has already been said: "That the very best actions of the saints, their prayers, their worships are impure and polluted."

We freely acknowledge that, whatever his representation or confession, the actions of a man are imperfect as long as he is in his first state and unconverted and unregenerate. But this

---

[1] "In essence a popular restatement of the Westminster Confession," the Larger Catechism was mainly the work of A. Tuckney. The Shorter Catechism, completed with it in 1647 and together approved by Parliament in 1648, has had a more important place, and has been in regular use among Congregationalists and Baptists as well as Presbyterians. — *O.D.C.C.*, p 1451.

is not true of those in whom Christ comes to be formed. In them a new man is brought forth and born of incorruptible seed. Such persons do the will of God naturally, and are consistent enough in their performance, that they are no longer daily transgressors of the law of God.

THOSE IN WHOM CHRIST HAS BEEN FORMED ARE NO LONGER DAILY TRANSGRESSORS

¶II. This is impossible for man in his natural state. As long as he remains the son of fallen Adam, however wise or knowing he may be, whatever conceptions or literal knowledge of Christ he may be endowed with, this is impossible. At best he can only conform outwardly to the letter of the law.

Perfection is attributed only to the reborn man who has been raised by Christ and renewed in his mind. He will know Christ, living, reigning, and ruling in him and revealing the law of the Spirit of life in him. He will be led by the Spirit which not only reproves sin, but provides the power to overcome it.

THIS PERFECTION LEAVES ROOM FOR GROWTH

This is not a perfection that has no room for daily growth. It is by no means a claim to be as pure, holy, and perfect as God. It is a perfection that is proportional to a man's requirements. It is sufficient to keep him from transgressing the law of God and to permit him to do what God requires of him. The person who improved his two talents to make four was just as acceptable to the Lord as a "good and faithful servant" as the one who made ten out of five. A little gold is just as perfect as a large mass, and a child's body is as perfect as a man's although it grows more and more each day. Thus Christ is said (in Luke 2:52 KJ) to have "increased in wisdom and stature, and in favor with God and man," even though he had never sinned and was undoubtedly perfect in a literal sense as well.

Those who have attained a measure of perfection must be diligent in their attention to that of God in their heart. If they are not watchful they may fall into iniquity and lose it. Many good and holy men have had their ups and downs of this kind. For although every sin weakens the spiritual condition of a man, it does not destroy him altogether or make it impossible for him to rise again.

Even though a man may reach the state where he is capable of resisting sin but sins anyhow, nevertheless a state can be attained in this life in which it becomes so natural to act righteously that a condition of stability is achieved in which sin is impossible. Perhaps there are those who can say with certainty that they have attained this state. Personally, I have to be modest and merely say that it *is* attainable, because I confess ingenuously that I have not yet attained it. But that is no reason to deny that there is such a state. One of the apostles has clearly asserted that there is, in 1 John 3:9 NEB: "A child of God does not commit sin, because the divine seed remains in him; he cannot be a sinner because he is God's child."

YET, GOD'S PEOPLE "COME TO SHARE IN THE VERY BEING OF GOD"

¶III. It is inconsistent with the wisdom of God and with his glorious power and majesty to maintain that it is impossible for those who are faithful to be free of sin in this life. For he is "of purer eyes than to behold evil;" (Hab 1:13 RSV). Since it was God's purpose to choose a people who would worship him and be witnesses for him on earth, undoubtedly he will also sanctify and purify them. For God does not delight in evil, but abhors transgression. Although he pities the transgressor and provides a way out of his misdeeds for him, he does not love him or delight in him as long as he continues to transgress. If man were eternally doomed to sin, then God would always be at a distance from him as Isa 59:2 RSV says: "Your iniquities have made a separation between you and your God, and your sins have hid his face from you."

On the contrary, God's people are said, even while here, to "come to share in the very being of God" (2 Pet 1:4 NEB) or to "partake of the divine nature" (RSV), and to be one with Christ spiritually, 1 Cor 6:17. Obviously no unclean thing could be one with him. It is expressly stated in 2 Cor 6:14 that there is no communion between light and darkness. But God is light, and in a measure every sin is darkness. What greater stain could there be upon God's wisdom than a failure to provide a way by which his children could perfectly serve and worship him? Or to provide even an imperfect way in which they could serve him, so that they would be forced to continue to worship evil even more than they worshipped him? For he that sinneth is the servant of sin, Rom 6:16 KJ. Who would not consider a human master foolish if he did not provide a way in which his servants could actually serve him? What are we to think, then, of a doctrine that would imply that the Omnipotent and Only Wise God has committed this folly?

GOD WILL ENABLE THEM TO DO WHAT HE REQUIRES

¶IV. It would also be inconsistent with the justice of God. God would be requiring more than his own enabling power provided if he asked more of a person than he was capable of doing. He does require his children to be pure and he commands them to abstain from every iniquity. It would be very unjust for him to be such a hard master with slothful servants. It is bad enough to ascribe such injustice to God as to have him condemn the wicked by not providing any means for them to be good. It is even more irrational and inconsistent to say that he does not afford the means to please him for those he has chosen to be his own and whom he loves.

What is the purpose of such a strange doctrine? The imperfection of Christians comes either from God or from themselves. If it is of their own doing, it must be because they fall short of using the power of obedience that was given them. In that case, they were capable of achieving God's will with his aid. But our opponents deny this, so they are not to be blamed for continuing in sin since they are incapable of doing otherwise.

They maintain that we should seek power from God to redeem us from sin, and yet they believe they will never receive such power. Their prayers are not made in faith, but in vain! But praise be to God, he does not deal in this way with those who truly trust him. Such faithful ones find that his grace is sufficient for them, and they know how to overcome evil by his power and spirit.

¶V. This doctrine of the impossibility of perfection is highly unjust to Jesus Christ. It greatly derogates the power and virtue of his sacrifice, rendering his coming and ministry ineffectual. For the principal reason for Christ's appearance was the removal of sin and the gathering of a righteous generation that would serve the Lord in purity of mind, and walk before him in fear. Everlasting righteousness would be brought in in this way — the evangelical perfection which the law could not provide. Hence it is said, Titus 2:14 NEB: "He it is who sacrificed himself for us, to set us free from all wickedness and to make us a pure people marked out for his own, eager to do good." This certainly refers to us while we are on earth. And how can we be eager to do good if we continue to commit evil? What is more, 1 John 3:5 NEB says: "Christ appeared, as you know, to do away with sins, and there is no sin in him."

GOD FREES US OF GUILT

If anyone attempts to interpret that passage as if it meant freeing us from the guilt of sin without reference to this life, he would have to consider whether the apostle was not anticipating and answering that kind of objection in the words of the verses which follow: "No man therefore who dwells in him is a sinner; the sinner has not seen him and does not know him." And to clarify exactly what he means, he adds: "My children, do not be misled: it is the man who does right who is righteous, as God is righteous."[2]

Christ came to gather a people out of sin into righteousness! Those who are thus gathered by him are his servants, his children, his brethren, his friends! And they are supposed to be holy, pure, and undefiled, just as he was in this world. Christ still watches over them, stands by them, prays for them, and preserves them by his power and Spirit, dwelling in them and walking among them! It would be gross blasphemy to assert that Christ wants anything for his servants except thorough purity. Many scriptural passages make this assertion. It would be even worse to claim that he lacked the power to protect his children and enable them to serve him. The scriptures declare that he has overcome sin and death, hell and the grave, and that he has triumphed over them openly and that all power in heaven and earth is given to him.

CHRIST PRESENTS HIS CHURCH HOLY AND WITHOUT BLEMISH

"Christ also loved the church and gave himself up for it, to consecrate it, cleansing it by water and word, so that he might present the church to himself all glorious, with no stain or wrinkle, or anything of the sort, but holy and without blemish;" (Eph 5:25-27 NEB). Certainly if Christ's coming served its purpose, the members of his church are not always sinning in thought, word, and deed. There would be no difference then between being sanctified and unsanctified, clean and unclean, holy and unholy, being blemished with sin and being unblemished.

---

[2] 1 John 3:7 NEB.

"NOTHING LESS THAN THE FULL STATURE OF CHRIST"

¶VI. Such a doctrine renders the work of the ministry, the preaching of the word, the writing of scripture, and the prayers of devout men altogether useless and ineffectual. Eph 4:11-13 NEB says that the work of pastors and teachers is "to equip God's people for work in his service" until finally we "attain to the unity inherent in our faith and our knowledge of the Son of God — to mature manhood, measured by nothing less than the full stature of Christ."

"Every inspired scripture has its use for teaching the truth and refuting error, or for reformation of manners and discipline in right living, so that the man who belongs to God may be efficient and equipped for good work of every kind;" (2 Tim 3:16-17 NEB). What good are the scriptures if this cannot be achieved in this life? In the other life we will have no need for them

Prayer is also rendered useless, even though the apostles believed in its efficacy. Paul told the Colossians that Epaphras "prays hard for you all the time, that you may stand fast, ripe in conviction and wholly devoted to doing God's will;" (Col 4:12 NEB). Paul himself pronounces a benediction upon the Thessalonians in which he says: "May he make your hearts firm, so that you may stand before our God and Father holy and faultless when our Lord Jesus comes," (1 Thes 3:13 NEB). It is true that in this and the following passages the reckoning is postponed, but the deeds are not! As if for emphasis, the very next benediction makes almost the same prayerful request, I Thes 5:23-24 NEB: "May God himself, the God of peace, make you holy in every part, and keep you sound in spirit, soul, and body, without fault when our Lord Jesus Christ comes." And then the most positive of all the assertions is made: "He who calls you is to be trusted; he will do it."

REPROBATES OR JUSTIFIED

¶VII. The doctrine that perfection cannot be achieved in this life is also contrary to common sense. For the two opposite principles which rule respectively in children of darkness and children of light are sin and righteousness. Whether they are to be considered reprobates or justified can be determined by which of these principles activates and leavens them. Furthermore,, it is an abomination in the sight of God either to justify the wicked or to condemn the just. To say that men

cannot be so leavened by righteousness as to deliver them from
sin, is — to put it in plainer words — to say that sin and righteousness are compatible. How can a man be called truly righteous even though he sins daily in everything he does? What
difference is there, then, between good and evil? This would
be falling into the nefarious practice of claiming light for
darkness, and calling good evil and evil good! Could anything
be more repugnant to common sense?

When whiteness predominates, a wall is called white, and
when there is considerable blackness it is called black. Certainly when there is more unrighteousness in a man than righteousness, he should be called unrighteous. Surely if every man
sins daily in thought and deed and all of his righteous actions
are polluted and mixed with sin, then everyone is more unrighteous than righteous. In that case no one should be called righteous and no one should be referred to as sanctified or washed.
Then where are the children of God? Where are the purified
ones? Where are those who were sometimes unholy, but now
are holy? That sometimes were darkness, but now are light in
the Lord?

This is the horrid blasphemy of the Ranters[3] and Libertines who claim that there is no difference between good and
evil and that both are one in the sight of God.

THE ACHIEVEMENT OF PERFECTION
IS THE PURPOSE OF THE GOSPEL

¶VIII. If scriptural proof is desired that perfection can
be achieved in this life, there is the imperative command of
Christ and his apostles to keep all the commandments, and to
be perfect in this respect. Since it is a maxim naturally engraved in every man's heart that no one is bound to do any-

---

[3] The Ranters were "a fanatical Antinomian and pantheistic sect of
the mid-17th c. They appealed to their inward experience of Christ and
denied the authority of scripture, creeds, and the ministry. Their revolu-
tionary and immoral doctrines made them the object of deep suspicion.
They were at first popularly associated with the Quakers who suffered
misrepresentation from the confusion." — O.D.C.C., p 1138.

Although "Libertines" was a name given to certain Antinomian sects,
Niesel cautions: "We must remember not to confuse the party of the 'libertines.' of which Perrin, Vandel, and Favre were leaders, with the sect of
'spiritual libertines' against which Calvin launched his treatise *Against the
fantastic sect of the libertines* (1545) ... These spiritual libertines were
mystics, more or less connected with the Reform. (Cf W. Niesel, 'Calvin
und die Libertiner,' in *Zeitschrift für Kirchengeschichte,* 1929, pp 58-74)."
— Wendel, *Calvin,* p 87 n.

thing which is impossible, it must be possible for us to follow
Christ's command. This command was very plain. It was given
without any commentary or qualification in the following passages: Mat 5:48 RSV (NEB) and 7:21 NEB; John 13:17 RSV;
1 Cor 7:19 NEB; 2 Cor 13:11 NEB; 1 John 2:3-6 and 3:2-10
NEB. These make it clear that this was a positive command
and that it was absolutely necessary. As if they had been written to refute the objections of our opponents, they show the
folly of those who regard themselves as children or friends of
God and yet act otherwise.

Even more to the point is the fact that the achievement of
perfection is the purpose for which we receive the gospel. The
possibility of attaining it is expressly promised to us in Rom
6:14 NEB — since we are under grace, we are told: "Sin shall
no longer be your master, because you are no longer under law,
but under the grace of God." Rom 8:3 NEB says: "What the
law could never do, because our lower nature robbed it of all
potency, God has done: by sending his own Son in a form like
that of our own sinful nature, and as a sacrifice for sin, he has
passed judgment against sin within that very nature, so that
the commandment of the law may find fulfillment in us, whose
conduct, no longer under the control of our lower nature, is
directed by the Spirit."

If this condition is not required and also attainable under
the gospel, then there is no difference between the gospel and
the law which makes nothing perfect.

There is no point in bringing in a greater hope. Those
who walk in the life of the gospel and the mere legalists of the
law are one and the same. But throughout the entire sixth
chapter of Romans, the apostle argues not only the possibility,
but the necessity of being free from sin, since those addressed
are under the gospel and under grace, and not under the law.
Verses 2-7 are a statement that he and those to whom he wrote
are in that condition. Therefore he argues in verses 11-13,
17-18 that it is not only possible, but absolutely necessary to be
free from sin. In verse 22 he declares that they have in a measure attained this. He says (NEB): "But now, freed from the
commands of sin, and bound to the service of God, your gains
are such as make for holiness, and the end is eternal life." Perfection is possible where the gospel and the inward law of the
Spirit are received and known. Man in his natural state considers the law to be external and literal. But if he pays atten-

tion to the inward light, or the "law written on the heart," this will not only show him his sins but how to overcome them, and he will no longer be a stranger to the new life and the birth that is born of God. Then he will naturally do God's will and be unable to transgress his commandments. Whereas by the letter of the law he would have been reproved and convicted, he would have been killed, rather than brought to life.

ONLY A NOTION OF CHRISTIANITY MAY BE OBTAINED UNDER THE LAW

Thus, finding himself wounded, he struggles for a conformity to an external law which he can never attain, rather than apply himself inwardly to that which can heal. The more he wrestles, the more he falls short. This is the Jew, still in the first covenant state. "The offerings and sacrifices there prescribed cannot give the worshipper inward perfection" (Heb 9:9 NEB), although he may obtain a notion of Christianity in that way, and an external faith in Christ.

This has made the Jews strain and distort the scriptures to obtain a wholly external imputative righteousness to cover their impurities. This has made them imagine that it is possible to be acceptable to God even though they consider it impossible to ever obey Christ's commands.

But unfortunately for the souls who are thus deceived this will be of no avail in the day when God judges whether every man's work was good or bad. It will not save you to say that it was necessary for you to sin daily in thought, word, and deed. For those who do have been unrighteous. And what is in store for them other than tribulation and anguish, indignation and wrath? But glory, honor, peace, and immortality await those who have not only done good but continued patiently at it.

BUT PERFECTION AND FREEDOM FROM SIN ARE POSSIBLE IF YOU ALLOW THE REPROOFS OF THE LIGHT OF CHRIST

If you wish to know the perfection and freedom from sin that are possible for you, turn your mind to the light of Christ and his spiritual law in your heart and allow its reproofs. Bear the judgment and indignation of God upon the unrighteous part in you as it is revealed there, and which Christ has made it tolerable for you to do. Allow this judgment in you to become victorious, and thus come to partake of the fellowship of Christ's sufferings. Be made conformable to his death so that with him you may feel yourself crucified to the world by the power of the cross within you. Then that life that was once alive in you to this world and its love and lusts will die and a new life will be raised. Henceforth you will live for God and not for yourself. Then you can say with the apostle, Gal 2:20 NEB: "I have been crucified with Christ: the life I now live is not my life, but the life which Christ lives in me."

"CHRIST'S YOKE IS EASY"

Then you will be a Christian indeed, and not in name only, as too many are. Then you will know what it is to have "put off the old man with his deeds," who does indeed sin daily in thought, word and deed. You will have put on the new man who is renewed in holiness, after the image of him who created him (Eph 4:24). And you will not sin continually but will give witness of being God's workmanship, created in Jesus Christ for good works. To this new man "Christ's yoke is easy, and his burden is light" [roughly Mat 11:30 and the meaning of 1 John 5:3], although it is heavy for the old Adam. The commandments of God are not oppressive for the new man, because it is his meat and drink to be found fulfilling the will of God.

Perfection of freedom from sin is possible. The scriptures testify that many have achieved it — some before the law, some under the law, and many more under the gospel. Gen 5:22, 24 records that Enoch walked with God, which no one who sins could do, and no failings are attributed to him in the scriptures. "Noah was a righteous man (RSV), blameless among the men of his day" (Cath-CCD) (Gen 6:9). The Lord said of Job: "there is no one on earth like him, blameless and upright, fearing God and avoiding evil," (Job 1:8 Cath-CCD). In the case of Zechariah and Elizabeth (Luke 1:6 NEB): "Both of them were upright and devout, blamelessly observing all the commandments and ordinances of the Lord."

Eph 2:4-6 NEB says of the faithful in general: "But God, rich in mercy, for the great love he bore us, brought us to life with Christ even when we were dead in our sins; it is by his grace you are saved. And in union with Christ Jesus he raised us up and enthroned us with him in the heavenly realms, so that he might display in the ages to come how immense are the resources of his grace, and how great his kindness to us in Christ Jesus." It is doubtful if he intended us to sin daily while we are sitting enthroned in the heavenly realms!

Heb 12:23-24 NEB speaks of "the spirits of good men made perfect." Among the qualifications for the 144,000 "who alone from the whole world had been ransomed" in the final vision of Rev 14:1-5 NEB is the fact that "no lie was found in their lips" and that, in the summing up, "they are faultless."

[¶ IX and X in the original are rather tedious refutations of the arguments of those who maintain that perfection is unattainable. They are omitted here. — Ed.]

BLESSED ARE THEY WHO BELIEVE IN HIM

¶XI. Blessed are they who believe in him who is both able and willing to deliver from all sin whoever comes to him through true repentance. They who, in abandoning unrighteousness, and forgetting those things that are behind, "press toward the goal to win the prize which is God's call to the life above, in Christ Jesus," (Phil 3:14 NEB). Their faith and confidence will not be in vain. In due time they will conquer through him in whom they have believed, and they shall be established as pillars in the temple of God, and nevermore shall they go outside (Rev 3:12 Cath-CCD).

Stability

PROPOSITION 9 — PERSEVERANCE IN THE FAITH AND THE POSSIBILITY OF FALLING FROM GRACE

Even though this gift of the inward grace of God is sufficient to bring about salvation, yet for those who resist it, it not only may become their condemnation, but does. Moreover, by disobedience, those whose hearts have been partly purified and sanctified by this grace may fall from that state, turning to licentiousness (Jude 4) making shipwreck of faith (1 Tim 1:19). They fall away again after they have tasted the heavenly gift and have partaken of the Holy Spirit (Heb 6:4-6). Nevertheless, it is possible to achieve such an increase and stability in the truth in this life that total apostasy is impossible.

¶I. It has already been shown in the fifth and sixth propositions that the same light which is given for life and salvation becomes the condemnation of those who refuse it. This is so obvious from the scriptures that it cannot be denied by those who will seriously consider Prov 1:24-26, John 3:18-19, 2 Thes 2:11-12, Acts 7:51 and 13:46, and Rom 1:18.

The rest of this proposition can largely be proved by the citations included in its statement. Since "our cause is common with many other Protestants"[1] in this there is need for only enough detail to make our position clear.

THE DOCTRINE OF ELECTION AND REPROBATION IS BUILT UPON A FALSE PREMISE

¶II. The doctrine of election and reprobation[2] is built upon a false premise. It states that the grace necessary for sal-

---

[1] It seems strange to have Barclay (the quoted portion is in his exact words) class Quakers with "other Protestants." This is the only place in the *Apology* that he does this. Although some Quaker historians have classed them as "radical Protestants" or extreme Puritans or even Congregationalists, these are over-simplifications. It is more accurate to describe them (as Howard Brinton has done) as a third form of Christianity, *neither* Catholic nor Protestant, but with elements of *both*.

[2] The reference is to Calvin's doctrine of predestination which, according to some, was one of the cornerstones of his system of theology. "Rejecting the universal saving will of God, he maintained that Christ's atoning death was offered for the elect alone. He added to the gratuitous predestination of the elect the equally gratuitous reprobation of the

vation is not given to everyone, but only to an elect few who cannot lose it. All the rest of mankind is barred from grace and salvation. This is wholly inconsistent with the exhortations to believe and be saved which are preached by some people. Obviously those who have been decreed reprobate cannot be saved, whether they believe or not, and whether or not they remain faithful.

It is equally erroneous to maintain the impossibility of falling from grace, as the Anabaptists did when they claimed that those who have once been justified cannot lose the Holy Spirit. Similar statements are commonplace in the writings of Philip Melancthon and Vossius. The latter states[3] that this was the common opinion of the early church Fathers.

MAKING SHIPWRECK OF THE FAITH

¶III. Those who maintain this point of view allege that where making shipwreck of faith is mentioned it is meant to apply only to apparent faith and not true faith. But this is a very weak argument and apparently contrary to 1 Tim 1:19 NEB where "a good conscience" is coupled with faith. Certainly one can not attain a truly good conscience without the operation of God's saving grace. Far less can a good conscience exist side by side with an apparently false and hypocritical faith. Furthermore, the apostle was speaking with regret of those who had fallen from good and real attainments, and not those who were false and deceitful. If this were not so, why would he have said in the same letter, 1 Tim 1:5 NEB, that: "The aim and object of this command is the love which springs from a clean heart, from a good conscience, and from faith that is genuine"?

---

damned, to whom salvation is denied from all eternity without any fault on their part." — *O.D.C.C.*, p 1099 s.v. "predestination," also "election" and "reprobation." (For another view of predestination's place in Calvin's theology see Wendel's comment, fn p 74.)

3 in his *Pelagian History*, lib 6, thesis 12, p 587.

Gerhard Jan Voss (1577-1649) was a Dutch humanist theologian. Born in Germany, he was educated at Leyden where he formed a lifelong friendship with Grotius. His *Historia Pelagiana* was published in 1618. The following year he was suspected of Remonstrant leanings and had to resign his post as regent of the College of the States-General in Leyden. He became a professor of "rhetoric and chronology" at Leyden University in 1622. He was one of the first scholars to apply the historical method to Christian dogmatics. — *O.D.C.C.*, p 1429-1430.

They also cite Phil 1:6 NEB: "The One who started the good work in you will bring it to completion by the Day of Christ Jesus;" and 1 Pet 1:5 NEB which says that you "are under the protection of his power until salvation comes." But these are neither here nor there, since they do not argue any more for the impossibility of erring than they do for it. Both statements are premised on certain obligations which we must fulfill.

Rom 8:13 NEB affirms that: "If by the Spirit you put to death all the base pursuits of the body, then you will live." Heb 3:14 RSV says: "For we share in Christ, if only we hold our first confidence firm to the end." It would do violence to the rest of scripture if we maintained that the citations from Philippians and Peter could be accepted at face value and without regard for good deeds and firmness in the faith.

But it is better not to labor these points which have been well refuted by others. Instead we will get to the testimony of the truth which is especially ours in this matter. It is contained in the latter part of the proposition in the words: "Nevertheless it is possible to achieve such an increase and stability in the truth in this life that total apostasy is impossible."

STABILITY IN THE TRUTH ALLOWS A FALL FROM GRACE BUT PREVENTS TOTAL APOSTASY

¶IV. This is really a matter of extremes. It is equally as erroneous to maintain that it is impossible to fall from grace in the slightest degree as it is to deny the possibility of achieving sufficient increase and stability in the truth to make total and final apostasy impossible. The truth lies somewhere between these extremes. This has been made clear in the scriptures whose meaning God has revealed to us by the testimony of his Spirit, and of which we have been made aware by our own experience.

¶V. It is good for everyone to be humble and not overconfident. For diligence and watchfulness are indispensable for all mortal men as long as they breathe. God wants this to be the constant practice of a Christian so he will be more fit to serve him, and better armed against all of the temptations of the enemy. Since the wages of sin is death no one can lawfully consider himself immune from perishing if he persists in sinning.

The apostle Paul said of himself, 1 Cor 9:27 NEB: "I bruise my own body and make it know its master, for fear that after preaching to others I should find myself rejected." He said this in spite of the fact that he was far more advanced in the inward work of regeneration than our contemporaries who maintain that it is impossible to fall from grace. His supposition that he might become a castaway himself was his inducement for being watchful.

And yet the same apostle has no hesitation in asserting elsewhere that he had conquered sin and the enemies of the soul by sensing and feeling God's holy power and being under its domain. In Rom 8:38-39 NEB he says: "I am convinced that there is nothing in death or life, in the realm of spirits or superhuman powers, in the world as it is or the world as it shall be, in the forces of the universe, in heights or depths — nothing in all creation that can separate us from the love of God in Christ Jesus our Lord." Certainly he must have attained a condition from which he knew that he would not fall away.

It is clear that such a condition can be attained, because we are exhorted to it. And, as has been proved, the scripture never proposes things that are impossible for us. We have an exhortation of this kind in 2 Pet 1:10 NEB: "My friends, exert yourselves to clinch God's choice and calling of you. If you behave so, you will never come to grief." If this assurance were not granted and there was still room for doubt and despair, there would never be a place in this world where one could have freedom from them. Yet this is not only absurd in itself, but it is contrary to the manifest experience of thousands.

GOD'S COMPLETE AND POSITIVE ASSURANCE IS READY FOR EVERYONE

God has given many of his people the assurance that they are his, and that no power whatever will be able to pluck them from his hand. He is ready to give all of them this complete and positive assurance. But what good would this be if those who received it were not established and confirmed beyond all doubt and hesitation? Once that has been done, there is no possibility of missing what God has assured.

The scriptures abound with declarations that such assurance is attainable in this life, both for everyone in general, and for particular individuals. In addition to the general promise to everyone contained in Rev 3:12 NEB: "He who is victorious — I will make him a pillar in the temple of my God; he shall never leave it," there is the apostle's statement that some are sealed, 2 Cor 1:22 NEB: "It is God also who has set his seal upon us, and as a pledge of what is to come has given the Spirit to dwell in our hearts." Eph 1:13 NEB says that when you heard the good news of your salvation and believed it, you "became incorporate in Christ and received the seal of the promised Holy Spirit; and that Spirit is the pledge that we shall enter upon our heritage."

Paul declared that he had attained that condition, not only in the passage cited from Romans, but also in 2 Tim 4:7 RSV, where he affirms: "I have fought the good fight, I have finished the race, I have kept the faith."

Both of old and of late there have been those who have turned the grace of God into wantonness, and have fallen from their faith and integrity. Thus we can conclude that such falling away is possible. We have also seen that there have been those, both of old and of late, who have received assurance that they would inherit eternal life. They received this assurance before they departed, and it was the Spirit of God that testified that they were saved. Since it was none other than the Spirit of God which gave this testimony, obviously such an estate is attainable in this life. For he who cannot lie gave this witness.

Part B—Joint Fellowship and Communion

Ministry

PROPOSITION 10 — THE MINISTRY

It is by the light or gift of God that all true knowledge of things spiritual is received and revealed. It is also by the strength and power of these, as they are made manifest and received in the heart, that every true minister of the gospel is ordained, prepared, and equipped for the work of the ministry.

Every evangelist and every Christian pastor ought to be led and directed in his labor and in the work of the gospel by the leadings, motions, and drawings of God's light. These should govern not only the place where, but the persons to whom he speaks, and the time when he should speak. Those who have this authority ought to preach the gospel even though they are without human commission or are illiterate. If they lack the authority of the divine gift, no matter how learned they may be, or what authorization they may have from men, or how well they may be commissioned by churches, they should be considered deceivers and not true ministers of the gospel.

Those who have received this holy and unspotted gift have received it without cost and should give it without charge (Mat 10:8). They should certainly not use it as a trade to earn money. But, if God has called any of them from their regular employment, or the trade by which they earn their living, they should receive such worldly necessities as food and clothing. It is lawful for them to accept these as far as they feel allowed by the Lord, and as far as they are freely and cordially given by those with whom they have shared spiritual matters.

¶I. Previously, only the matters of the Christian faith which pertain to the individual Christian have been dealt with. It is now time to speak of the things that relate to the joint fellowship and communion of Christians as they come under an outward and visible society, the society called the Church of God and compared to a body in the scriptures and therefore called the body of Christ. As in a physical body there are many members, all contributing to the preservation and composition of the whole, there are also many members in this spiritual and mystical body possessing different gifts of grace and of the Spirit. From this diversity arises the distinction between indi-

viduals in the visible society of Christians whereby some are
apostles, some pastors, evangelists, ministers, and so forth.

What makes or constitutes anyone a minister of the church?
What should his qualifications be? How should he conduct
himself? It would seem a little odd to speak of the various
offices of the church without first saying something about the
church in general, even though it isn't mentioned in the proposition. For that reason, certain premises will be established
concerning the church, before going further concerning the
particular members.

THE NATURE OF THE CHURCH INVISIBLE

¶ II. There is no need to meddle in the numerous and
tedious controversies between Catholics and Protestants over
the nature of the Church.[1] But a brief introduction to our beliefs concerning the Church will be given as a necessary preface
to the matters of ministry and worship which follow. This will
be according to the truth manifested to me and revealed in me
by the testimony of the Spirit and according to the share of
wisdom given me.

The Church, according to the grammatical significance of
that word, as it is used in the holy scriptures, signifies an assembly or gathering of many into one place. The substantive
ekklēsia comes from the word *ekkaleō*, meaning *I call out of*,
and originally from *kaleō*, *I call*. And this is also the real and
proper significance of the Church. It is nothing other than the
society, gathering, or company of those whom God has called
out of the world and the worldly spirit, to walk in his light

---

[1] A decade ago J. S. Whale (*The Protestant Tradition*, Cambridge
1955, pp 168-170) contrasted the "indivisible impersonal Magnitude, endowed with immutable attributes" of the Catholic view of the church, as
he saw it then, with Protestant emphasis on community. Vatican II, "On
the Church," however, de-emphasized the juridical and hierarchical, seeing (sect 8) "one complex reality which coalesces from a divine and a
human element ... [and which] inseparably united to him, serves the
divine Word as a living instrument of salvation;" a people [according to
Avery Dulles, S. J.] who are in constant need of renewal and purification
"to whom God communicates himself in love."

The concepts of the "Church visible" and "Church invisible" to which
Barclay alludes are used in most considerations. Catholics consider them
one and the same, whereas most Protestants consider those who truly belong to the invisible Church to be known only to God; and to include
those of past ages as well as the living. Barclay might be said to picture
a church at the opposite end of the institutional spectrum from the Catholic, composed only of those "called and truly gathered by God" and in
that sense indistinguishable from the earthly and living members of the
Church invisible. — ED.

and life. The Church as thus defined is to be considered as comprising all of those who are thus called and truly gathered by God. It includes both those who are still in this inferior world and those who, having already laid down the earthly tabernacle, have passed into their heavenly mansions. Together they make up the one catholic Church about which there is so much controversy.

Aside from this Church there can be no salvation, because this Church and its denomination[2] comprehend all, regardless of what nation, kindred, tongue or people they may be, who have become obedient to the holy light and testimony of God in their hearts. Although they may be outwardly unknown to and distant from those who profess Christ and Christianity in words and have the benefit of the scriptures, yet they have become sanctified by their obedience and cleansed from the evil of their ways. For this is the universal or catholic Spirit, by which many are called from all the four corners of the earth, and they shall sit down with Abraham, Isaac, and Jacob. By it, the secret life and virtue of Jesus is conveyed to many who are far away, just as life is conveyed from the head and heart to the extremities of the physical body by the blood running in the veins and arteries. There may be members of this catholic Church not only among all the several sorts of Christians, but also among pagans, Turks, and Jews. They are men and women of integrity and simplicity of heart. They may be blind in their understanding of some things, and perhaps burdened with the superstitions and ceremonies of the sects in which they have been collected. Yet they are upright in their hearts before the Lord, aiming and endeavoring to be delivered from iniquity, and loving to follow righteousness.

THE CHURCH INVISIBLE HAS EXISTED IN ALL GENERATIONS

In this respect, the Church has existed in all generations. For although there have been many times when God has been slighted and little observed by this world, and the Church has often been, as it were, "invisible," he has never lacked faithful witnesses. Even when Israel was faithless the Lord reminded his children to acknowledge their guilt and return to him. He

---

[2] This is the only place in the *Apology* where this word is used and it is difficult to determine precisely what is meant unless the phrase be translated "this Church and those who bear its name."

An obsolete usage of the word equated it with "parishes" but that would not make sense here. — ED.

assured them that he was master and would bring to Zion
"One from a city and two from a family" (Jer 3:14 RSV).

Yet, in spite of that fact, there are times when the Church
may be hidden from wicked men and may not appear to be
gathered into a visible fellowship, even to some who are members of it; nevertheless there are many who belong even then.
When Elijah (Elias) complained that he was left alone, 3 Kings
19:18 Cath-Douay (1 Kings 19:18 in the Protestant canon)
quoted in Rom 11:4, God replied that he would leave "seven
thousand men in Israel, whose knees have not bowed before
Baal." It is from this that Paul argued in Rom 11:5 NEB: "In
just the same way at the present time a 'remnant' has come
into being, selected by the grace of God."

THE CHURCH VISIBLE

¶III. "The church" also signifies a certain number of persons who have been gathered by God's Spirit and by the testimony of some of his servants who were provided for that purpose. This visible fellowship has been brought to a belief in
the true principles and doctrines of the Christian faith. With
their hearts united by the same love, and their understandings
informed of the same truths, they gather, meet, and assemble
together to wait upon God, to worship him, and to bear a joint
testimony for the truth against error and to suffer for this truth.
Through this fellowship they become in many respects like one
family and household. They watch over, instruct, and care for
one another according to their several abilities and attainments. Such were the churches of the primitive times which
were gathered by the apostles. A number of them were mentioned in the holy scriptures. There has been a great interruption of the visibility of the Church in this respect because
of the apostasy since the apostles' days.

MEMBERSHIP IN THE UNIVERSAL CHURCH

¶IV. The inward calling of God by his light in the heart
is necessary for membership in the Church catholic. One must
be leavened into the nature and spirit of it so that he will forsake unrighteousness and turn toward righteousness. In inwardness of mind he must be cut out of the wild olive tree[3] of his

___

[3] The allusion is to Rom 11:17 where Paul refers to the Gentiles as
the wild olive branches that were grafted onto the people of God to take
the place of the Jews whose branches were lopped off because of their
unbelief.

own first fallen nature, and engrafted into Christ by his word
and Spirit in the heart. And this may be done even when God
has not seen fit to have him hear the story of Jesus, as was
proved in the fifth and sixth propositions.

MEMBERSHIP IN A PARTICULAR CHURCH

However, to be a member of a particular church of Christ,
not only is this inward work indispensably necessary, but also
profession of belief in Jesus Christ and in the holy truths
delivered by his Spirit in the scriptures. And the testimony
of the Spirit as recorded in the scriptures answers the testimony
of the same Spirit in the heart, just as face answers face in a
looking-glass. Hence it follows that the inward work of holiness and the forsaking of iniquity are necessary in every respect
for becoming a member of the Church of Christ. The outward
profession is necessary for membership in a particular gathered
church, but not for membership in the Church catholic. But
this does not do away with the absolute necessity for believing
the outward testimony where God has afforded the opportunity of knowing it.

MEMBERSHIP IN THE TRUE CHURCH

¶V. It is substituting light for darkness and darkness for
light to claim that no one, however holy, can be a member of
the Church of Christ who has not made the outward profession
and been initiated into it by some outward ceremonies. Or on
the other hand, it is equally fallacious to claim that those who
have made this outward profession may be members of the
true Church of Christ even though they are inwardly unholy.
Let it be said that Antichrist has built his Babylon-like structure upon this false and rotten foundation. In the apostasy,
the Antichristian church has attained such height and grandeur
as to exalt herself above all that is called God, and to sit in
the temple of God as God.

Soon after they had been gathered in the apostles' days,
the inward life of the particular churches of Christ began to
decay. They became overgrown with several errors and the
hearts of the professors of Christianity became leavened with
the old spirit and conduct of the world's people. Nevertheless
it pleased God to preserve the inward life in many persons for
some centuries. He emboldened them with the zeal to stand

and suffer for his name through the ten persecutions.[4] But when these were over, the meekness, gentleness, love, long-suffering goodness and temperance of Christianity began to be lost. For after the princes of the earth took up the profession of Christianity, it was no longer a reproach to be called a Christian but instead became a means to preferment. Men no longer became Christians by the conversion and renovation of the Spirit but by birth and education. There was no one so vile, so wicked, or so profane that he did not become a member of the church.

When the teachers and pastors of the church became the companions of princes they were enriched with vast treasures and estates by their benevolence. They became puffed up and, as it were, drunk with the vain pomp and glory of this world. They marshalled themselves into many orders and degrees and there were innumerable contests and altercations over who should have precedence (as between the bishop of Rome and the bishop of Constantinople).

Thus the virtue, the life, the substance, and the essence of the Christian religion came to be lost, and nothing remained but a shadow and an image. To make it more acceptable to the superstitious multitudes of pagans, the carcass was decked with many outward and visible orders, and it was beautified with gold, silver, precious stones and the other ornaments of this dying world. The pagans who had been taken into the church in such great numbers were admitted not because of any inward conversion of their hearts or any decrease in their wickedness or superstition, but by a slight change in the object of their superstition. This was no more the Christian religion, or the Christian Church, than a dead body can be considered living. No matter how cunningly it may be embalmed, how much gold, silver, or precious stones may adorn it, or how much sweet ointment may be applied, it is still a dead body and without intelligence, life, or motion.

The apostate church of Rome introduced as many ceremonies and superstitions into Christianity as there had been among the Jews or pagans. And there was as much or more

---

[4] Orosius (early 5th c.) popularized the notion of ten Early Christian persecutions which still persists, even though the truth is less simple. The list is given in full in *O.D.C.C.*, p 1047, and begins with Nero's use of the Christians as scapegoats for the burning of Rome in 64 A.D. and concludes with Diocletian's order for the churches to be destroyed and the scriptures burnt in 303 A.D.

pride, covetousness, uncleanness, luxury, fornication, profane-
ness, and atheism among her teachers and chief bishops as had
ever existed among any people. Her own authors, particularly
Platina[5] and others, have recorded this truthfully.

Although the Protestants have reformed her on some of
the grossest points and on the absurd doctrines relating to the
church and the ministry, it is regrettable that they have only
lopped off the branches. They retain the same root from which
these abuses have sprung and they plead earnestly on its behalf.
Although the whole mass of superstition, ceremonies, and hierarchical orders has not been re-established, nevertheless the
same pride, covetousness, and sensuality have spread through
their churches and ministry. The life, power, and virtue of true
religion are lost among them, and the same lifelessness, barrenness, dryness, and emptiness are found in their ministry.

In effect there is little difference between them and Roman
Catholics except in certain forms and ceremonies. They too
have become apostatized from the life and power that were to
be found in the true primitive church and among her pastors.
It can be truly said of both, without a breach of charity, that
they have denied the power of God and have been enemies to
it, since they have only the form of godliness, if they have that
much. This is said not merely because they do not live up to
their own principles, but because the additional principles
which they have defined and to which they adhere are like an
accursed root from which these bitter fruits are brought forth
naturally.

MEMBERSHIP IN THE NATIONAL CHURCHES

Actually, the Protestants do not differ from the Roman
Catholics in the nature and constitution or the practices of their
national churches, although they are always questioning the
invariable visibility, infallibility, and primacy of the church of
Rome. They include entire nations within their compass, bringing infants into membership by sprinkling a little water upon
them. Thus no one is so wicked or profane that he is excluded

---

[5] Bartolomeo Platina (1421-1481) was an Italian humanist who upon
return to favor with the church was made Vatican librarian in 1475. During his term of office he compiled his *Lives of the Popes*. In the 19th c.
a fable that the pope had excommunicated Halley's comet arose from
mention in Platina's *Lives* "of the prayers and curses of Callistus III in
1456 against the Turks, followed by a reference in the same context to the
appearance of Halley's comet." — *O.D.C.C.*, p 1081.

from being a fellow member, and no evidence of holiness is required to become a member of the church. In fact, there is no observable difference in the lives of the bulk of the people in a Protestant nation and those in a Catholic one. He who rules in the children of disobedience reigns in both. Although the Reformation reduced some of the grossest errors of doctrine, it did not renew and reform the hearts of the individuals within the church, although this is the main purpose of Christianity.

ROMAN CATHOLIC ERRORS CONCERNING THE MINISTRY HAVE BEEN RETAINED BY THE PROTESTANTS

¶VI. Most regrettable of all is the fact that the Roman Catholic errors concerning the ministry have been retained by Protestants. The life and power of Christianity are shut out from among them and they remain in lifelessness, barrenness, and dryness. Nothing is more harmful than an error of this kind. Where a false and corrupt ministry enter, all manner of other evils follow from it. As Hosea 4:4, 7-9 Cath-CCD says: "With you is my grievance, O priests! ... One and all they sin against me, exchanging their glory for shame. They feed on the sin of my people, and are greedy for their guilt. The priests shall fare no better than the people: I will punish them for their ways, and repay them for their deeds." All of the backsliding of the ancient Jewish congregations is ascribed to the fact that the leaders of the people caused them to err. All of the prophetic books are full of such complaints.

That is why we are warned so often in the New Testament to beware of false prophets and false teachers. What conclusion can we come to, however, when everything concerning these matters is wrong? Not only are the foundations, calling, qualifications, and maintenance of the ministry different from those of the primitive church, but the whole discipline of that ministry is contrary to it. Of necessity, this tends to shut out a spiritual ministry and to introduce and establish a worldy one. This will become apparent from the different parts of this ministry that are to be questioned.

HOW IS A MAN CALLED TO BE A MINISTER?

¶VII. The first part to be questioned concerns the call of a minister. What makes a man a minister, pastor, or teacher in the Church of Christ? How does he come to be one? We answer: "By the inward power and virtue of the Spirit of God which will not only call him but will in some measure purify

and sanctify him." Since the things of the spirit can only be
truly known by the aid of the Spirit of God, it is by this same
Spirit that a man is called and moved to minister to others.
Thus he is able to speak from a living experience of the things
to which he is a witness. Knowing the terror of the Lord, he
is fit to persuade men and to "have something to say to those
whose pride is all in outward show and not in inward worth;"
2 Cor 5:11-12 NEB.

His words and ministry come from the inward power and
virtue of the Spirit of God. By the same power they reach the
hearts of his hearers and persuade them to approve of him and
to be subject to him. Our opponents are forced to admit that
this is indeed desirable and that this would be best, but they
will not admit that it is absolutely necessary.

But, certainly, anything that is necessary to make a man a
Christian, and without which he cannot truly be one, is even
more essential for making a man a minister of Christianity.
One is not only a degree above the other in attainment but it
is inclusive as well, just as the schoolmaster must first attain the
knowledge and stature of a pupil.

But the inward call, power, and virtue of the Spirit of God
are necessary for making a man a Christian. This has been
proved by numerous scriptural citations in the second proposition. Therefore, how much more essential they are for making
a man a minister. "Such qualification as we have comes from
God; it is he who has qualified us to dispense his new covenant — a covenant expressed not in a written document, but in
a spiritual bond;" (2 Cor 3:6 NEB). These qualifications should
be of the Spirit and not of the letter, for, as the passage continues: "the written code kills, but the Spirit gives life" (RSV).

But how can a man be a minister of the Spirit if he has
not been inwardly called, and if he does not consider this operation and testimony essential to his call? One cannot instruct
in letters without knowing them; how can anyone be a minister of the Spirit if the Spirit is unknown to him? If he is
unacquainted with the motions of the Spirit how can they
draw, activate, and move him and go before him in the work
of the ministry? How do those who make the ministry of the
gospel a mere outward vocation differ from ministers of the
letter? If they are unaware of any work of the Spirit or of
any inward call, how can they satisfy themselves or others that
they are ministers of the Spirit?

WITHOUT THE INWARD CALL, NEW TESTAMENT MINISTRY
IS NO BETTER THAN MINISTRY UNDER THE LAW

If this inward call or testimony of the Spirit were inessential or unnecessary for a minister, then the ministry of the New Testament would be no better, and in many ways far worse, than that of the law. For under the law, a certain tribe was allotted for the ministry, and of that tribe certain families were set apart for the priesthood and other offices by the immediate command of God to Moses.[6] There was no need for the people to have any doubt about who should be priests and ministers of holy things. And in addition, at various times God called forth Samuel, Nathan, Elijah, Elisha, Jeremiah, Amos, and many other prophets. He called them by the immediate testimony of his Spirit so that they might teach, instruct, and reprove his people.

Under the new covenant the ministry ought to be more spiritual, the way more certain, and the access to the Lord more easy. But our opponents make it something altogether different by denying this inward and spiritual vocation. Without the limitation of the ministry to a certain tribe or family we are left in doubt and must venture to choose pastors without any guarantee of assent from the will of God. Since the scriptures cannot supply a rule for this, as was shown in the third proposition, there is no certainty in this matter.

Christ proclaimed that all are thieves and robbers who do not enter the sheepfold by him — the door — but who come in some other way (John 10:1-9). Neither should the sheep hear false prophets who come in without the call, motions, or leading of Christ's Spirit. For if they have not come in by Christ

---

[6] In Num 1:50 the Lord told Moses to exempt the Levites from the census for military service and to give them "charge of the Dwelling of the Commandments" and to "be its ministers," (Cath-CCD). They had previously had the somewhat bloodier assignment of slaying about 3,000 of their own kinsmen, friends, and neighbors (Ex 32:27-28) who had participated in the idolatrous practice of worshipping the golden calf while Moses was receiving the Ten Commandments.
The assignment of the duties of the Levitical Clans is related in ch 3 of Numbers and further defined in ch 4. Aaron the Levite, who was already known to the Lord as "an eloquent speaker" (Ex 4:14), was made Moses' assistant, and in Ex 28:1-5, he and his four sons were set apart for service as priests, and this was made a "perpetual ordinance for him and his descendants." Ex 28:43. Slaughter continued to be a Levitical function, for in discharging the obligations of the sanctuary for the Israelites it was mandatory that "any layman who comes near it shall be put to death" (Num 1:51 Cath-CCD).

they are not true shepherds and are not led by the Spirit by which he leads his children into all truth.

THE SUCCESSION OF THE CHURCH

¶VIII. They say that the answer to all of this is the succession of the church.[7] It is alleged that since Christ gave a call to his apostles and disciples, they in their turn have conveyed that call to their successors who have the power to ordain pastors and teachers. These have successively conveyed the authority for the ordination and making of ministers down to our time. Thus they say that those who are ordained and called by the pastors of the church are true and lawful ministers, and others who are not called in this way should be considered intruders. To this, some Protestants do add that everyone called should have the inward call of the Spirit. But they say that this choice by the inclination of the Spirit is necessary but not essential, and they say that it is subjective rather than objective. Since they consider the inward call of the Spirit unessential for a true call, but rather a sort of supererogation, it shows how little store they set by it. They do not even ask those who are trying out for the ministry whether they have it or not.

Yet the treatises of the earliest Protestants mentioned this so frequently that it is evident that they were unwittingly convinced that the inward call of the Spirit was the best and most preferable of all. They laid claims to it for all of the great and heroic acts of the Reformation. Many of the first Protestants had no scruples whatever about disowning and despising the call by succession when the Roman Catholics chided them with not having it. But now Protestants have departed so far from the testimony of the Spirit that they claim the same succession. When faced with the example of their forefathers' practice

---

[7] The "apostolic succession," or derivation of the ministry of the Christian church from the Apostles by an unbroken succession. Spiritual authority is transmitted by the laying on of hands in ordination. Not only Eastern Orthodox and Roman Catholics but Anglicans and some others consider it important. The reality and validity of the English succession has been the subject of "a definite attack" since 1604 by Roman Catholics. It was opened by Kellison and followed by the Jesuits Holywood (1604), Fitzherbert (1613), and Fitzsimons (1614). — Ollard, Crosse, and Bond, *Dict. of Engl. Church Hist.*, 3rd ed rev, N. Y., Morehouse-Gorman, 1948, pp 433-437.

The issue has been modified in recent years, and the matter of the apostolic succession is being studied anew from both sides. Some change seems likely in the near future. — Father Bowman

against Rome (by those whom God now raises by his Spirit to
reform the abuses that are to be found among them) they un-
abashedly and utterly deny that their forefathers were called to
their work by the inward and unmediated summons of the
Spirit. In fact, they clothe themselves with the successional call
which they say their forefathers had as pastors of the Roman
church.[8]

MANY ABSURD PITFALLS WHEN PROTESTANTS DERIVE THEIR MINISTRY THROUGH ROME

¶IX. Deriving their ministry through Rome has led the
Protestants into many absurd pitfalls. First, they have to acknowledge the Roman church as being a true church of Christ
that was only erroneous in certain matters. But this quite contradicts their forefathers who so frequently, and indeed truly,
called her Antichrist. Second, they have to acknowledge that
the priests and bishops of the Roman church are essentially true
ministers and pastors of the Church of Christ. Otherwise, how
could they be fit subjects in which the authority and power to
ordain could reside? Or how could they have been vessels capable of receiving that power and transmitting it to their successors? In the third place, it would follow from this that the
priests and bishops of the Roman church are still true pastors
and teachers. Since the church of Rome is unchanged in doctrine and customs from what she was at the time of the Reformation, it can easily be seen how really absurd this position is.
How can this be made to fit in with Luther's doctrine that every good Christian (whether a man or a woman) is a preacher?[9]

8 *A Theological Exercitation,* sect 40, by Nicolaus Arnoldus, who styles himself Doctor and Professor of Sacred Theology
at Franequer, [is cited as source. See biographical fn p 221.]

9 The reference is undoubtedly to the "priesthood of all believers"
which Luther made a "touchstone" for the true Church and a mark of
the Reformation's faithfulness to "an original Christianity long subverted."
It was based on the "chosen race," "royal priesthood" and "holy nation"
of 1 Pet 2:9.

Although this was one of the few areas of Lutheran doctrine with which
the Quakers agreed, they alone based their vocal ministry on it and
opened it to everyone. Lewis Benson says that as far as he knows, Fox
never used the term "priesthood of all believers" (and it was avoided by
Barclay here); but he did say: "Christ ... maketh priests of all his church"
(Headley MS, p 379) and "Christ makes all his believers priests" (*Works,*
vol 6, 1831 ed, p 41).

It is interesting that Gill, quoted in the first paragraph, continues,
"Looking back across the centuries in which the Church had come to dis-

THE MINISTRY IS NOT ENTAILED TO A SUCCESSION

¶X. Those who plead for this absolutely worthless succession declare how ignorant they are of the nature of Christianity, and how much they are strangers to the life and power of Christian ministry. This ministry is not entailed to succession like an inheritance. Jesus Christ did not set apart any particular family or nation in gathering his children. He selected those who were joined to his own pure and righteous seed, and he hasn't the slightest regard for any merely external succession which lacks his pure, immaculate, and righteous life. To avoid approving them in their erroneous ways or allowing them to fall into their ancient ways he did not take the Jewish nations into the new covenant. Instead he gathered himself a people who were free from moral fault or guilt from throughout the earth.

The great error of the Jews was that they thought they were the Church and the People of God because they could trace their descent from Abraham, who was the Father of the Faithful. But the scriptures severely rebuke this vain and frivolous pretense! They say that God is able to raise children of Abraham from stones (Mat 3:9 and Luke 3:8). The true children of the faithful Abraham are not his outward seed but those who are found faithful to his beliefs.

This pretense has even less validity for Christians since Christ rejected all external relationships of that kind. He said that those who do the will of his father who is in heaven are his mother, brethren, and sisters (Mat 12:48-50, Mark 3:33-35). Thus, those who do not follow Christ's commands, and who are not clothed with his righteousness, are not his disciples. And a man cannot give someone else something he does not possess. It is equally clear that no man or church, even though it has been truly called by God, can retain its power and authority any longer than it retains the power, the life, and the righteousness of Christianity. For the form is inherited with the power and

tinguish sharply between clergy and laity, between religious and secular vocations, the Reformers could find no scriptural ground for the development. Certainly in the little company of Jesus and His friends there was no division into clergy and laity. In manner, speech and mood Jesus identified Himself as what today would be called a layman. And the disciples, who might look from here like laymen, were really the preachers who were sent out." — Theodore A. Gill, "Priesthood of Believers," in *A Handbook of Christian Theology,* ed by Martin Halverson, Cleveland, World Publishing Co., 1961 (6th printing), p 281.

substance, and not the substance with the form. When a man
ceases to be a Christian in his heart, he is no more a Christian
than a statue or a picture is a man. It doesn't make any difference how faithfully it resembles the original. The lifeless
images of men cannot produce living men or convey their life
and spirit. God alone, who first made man, can revive him,
and only the living are capable of succeeding one another. In
the same way, a lifeless institution cannot produce a living
succession.

THE SPIRITUAL THINGS THAT TAKE PLACE IN THE INDIVIDUAL HEART ARE THE LIFE OF CHRISTIANITY

To summarize, it is the spiritual things that take place in
the individual heart that are the life of Christianity. These are
what make a person a Christian. And a number of Christians
— alive and joined together in the life of Christianity — make
a Church of Christ. When this life no longer exists in a person
he ceases to be a Christian, and all the power, virtue, and authority which he had as a Christian also ceases. If he was a
minister or a teacher, he is no longer one. Even if he retains
the title, and refuses to give up his written authority, these
have no more significance and no more real virtue or authority
than the mere likeness of a deceased person.

This conclusion not only agrees with our sense of reason,
but agrees with similar testimony from the scriptures. Acts 1:25
Cath-CCD says that it was necessary to find someone "to take
the place in this ministry and apostleship from which Judas
fell away." His transgression brought his apostleship to an end.
If the apostleship had merely been entailed to his person, the
transgression of betraying Christ would not have caused him
to lose it until he had been formally degraded by the church
(and Judas never was, as long as he lived).

NOTHING BUT THE GATHERING OF SEVERAL TRUE CHRISTIANS INTO ONE BODY MAKES A CHURCH

Nothing except the gathering of several true Christians
into one body makes a church. When all of the members of
a church lose the life of Christianity and it no longer rules in
their hearts, the Church ceases to exist in that place. For they
cease to be a church when they have lost the quality which
made them a church. It was for this reason, that is, because
of her lukewarmness, that the Spirit threatened to spew the
church of Laodicea out of his mouth (Rev 3:16). A church
which continued to be lukewarm would lose any authority

which she and her pastors and teachers had ever had, even if it came directly from the apostles. Certainly this would be true where succession was claimed through the Roman Catholic Church, since the majority of her bishops and priests became wicked during the apostasy. If it should be protested that even then there were some good men among them, what of it? The Protestants do not claim their ministry through a line of good men separate and clearly distinguished from the rest of the bishops and clergy of the Roman church. They derive it from an authority which is supposed to have resided in the Church as a whole. In fact, they consider it heresy to judge the quality or condition of an administrator in any way that would invalidate or prejudice his work.

This empty and feigned succession not only militates against Christ's manifest purpose and intention in the gathering and calling of his Church, but makes him, so to speak, even blinder and less prudent than ordinary men are in conveying and establishing their worldly inheritances. For where an estate is entailed to a certain name or family and that family dies out, the title to the estate returns to the prince or lord, as the *ultima Haeres*, so that he can give it to anyone he wishes.

WHEN THE HEAVENLY INHERITANCE IS LOST THE TITLE RETURNS TO CHRIST

Where the right to the heavenly inheritance is lost by extinguishing the inner righteousness and holiness which redeem men from the vanities, evil desires, and wickedness of this world, the title returns to Christ. For he is the righteous heir of life, and it is he who gives the title and true right again to whomever he pleases by turning them to his pure light in their consciences. They walk again in his righteous and innocent life, and so become true members of his body, the Church. Thus the authority, power, and inheritance are not attached to persons who merely bear the name or retain the form — the mere shell or shadow of Christianity. The promised inheritance belongs to Christ and as many as are united to him by purity and holiness. And the bond is the seed in which the authority is inherent and by which the inward renovation and regeneration of their minds takes place.

SUCCESSION IS CONTRARY TO THE SCRIPTURAL DEFINITIONS OF THE CHURCH

This pretended succession is also contrary to the scriptural definitions of the nature of the Church of Christ and of the true members of the Church. First, the Church is the household of the living God, the pillar and bulwark of truth, 1 Tim 3:15. Those who pretend to be Jews, but are not, are styled a synagogue of Satan, Rev 2:9. Thus the scripture looks upon hypocrisy and deceit as an aggravation of guilt and calls it blasphemy. Certainly, of two wicked men, the one who covers his wickedness with a false pretence of God and righteousness is more abhorrent than the other.

It is made very clear in Jer 7:4 Cath-CCD that outward respectability is not regarded more highly by the Lord than inward holiness: "Put not your trust in the deceitful words: 'This is the temple of the Lord!' The temple of the Lord! The temple of the Lord! Only if you thoroughly reform your ways and your deeds; if each of you deals justly with his neighbor; if you no longer oppress the resident alien, the orphan, and the widow; if you no longer shed innocent blood in this place, or follow strange gods to your own harm, will I remain with you in this place."

Second, the Church is defined as the kingdom of the beloved Son of God, into which the people of God are translated,[10] being delivered from the power of darkness. It is called the body of Christ, who is the "Head, from whom the whole body, nourished and knit together through its joints and ligaments, grows with a growth that is from God" (Col 2:19 RSV).

Let us "cleanse ourselves from all that can defile flesh or spirit, and in the fear of God complete our consecration" (2 Cor 7:1 NEB). "For what has justice in common with iniquity? Or what fellowship has light with darkness? What harmony is there between Christ and Belial? Or what part has the believer with the unbeliever? And what agreement has the temple of God with idols? For you are the temple of the living God," (2 Cor 6:14-16 Cath-CCD). No one can be called the temple of God, or of the Holy Spirit, until his vessel has been purified and prepared in that way as a dwelling for God.

---

[10] In ecclesiastical terminology, "translation" has a number of special usages. Here Barclay is using it according to one of *Webster's Third International* senses: "to convey to heaven or to a nontemporal condition without death." It is also used when speaking of the transfer of a bishop from one jurisdiction to another, or of a saint's day to another date to avoid conflict. In the medieval era it often referred to the inexplicable and mysterious methods of heavenly transportation whereby a shrine or saint's relics landed in a place remote from its origins. (See the notes on James' sepulchre and the shrine of Mary of Loretto, p 128.)

Many who have thus been made suitable by Christ become his body, in and among whom he dwells and walks as the citation from 2 Cor continues: "I will dwell and move among them, I will be their God and they shall be my people" (Cath-CCD). "And therefore, 'come away and leave them, separate yourselves, says the Lord; I do not touch what is unclean. Then I will accept you, says the Lord, the Ruler of all being; I will be a father to you, and you shall be my sons and daughters.' Such are the promises which have been made to us, dear friends." (2 Cor 6:17 - 7:1 NEB).

MERE OUTWARD PROFESSION AND NAME ARE NOT ENOUGH TO CONSTITUTE A TRUE CHURCH

What was the reason for this exhortation? Why would we need to separate ourselves from the unclean if the mere outward profession and the name were enough to constitute a true Church? It would not be necessary if the unclean and the impure could be both the Church and the lawful successors of the apostles, inheriting their authority and transmitting it to others. If those who compose the kingdom and power of darkness are genuine members of the true Church of Christ, how can the Church be the kingdom of the Son of God as distinguished from the kingdom and power of darkness? If those who compose the kingdom and power of darkness are not only members but the very pastors and teachers of the true Church of Christ, how can they grow with the growth that comes from God? How can they receive spiritual nourishment from Christ, the head, if in their hearts and in their wicked deeds they are his enemies? Frivolous and trumped up distinctions will not please or delude the Lord God, nor will they satisfy truly tender and Christian consciences. We may very well object to such fine metaphysical distinctions! There is the story of the poor man who chided a proud prelate for his vanity and his sumptuous display of wealth. In answer, the prelate said that it was not as a bishop, but as a prince that he acquired such splendor. The poor rustic gave what may have been a wise reply: "When the prince goes to hell, what will become of the prelate?"

Christ himself stated in John 15:1-9 NEB: "I am the real vine, and my Father is the gardener. Every barren branch of mine he cuts away; and every fruiting branch he cleans, to make it more fruitful still. You have already been cleansed by the word that I spoke to you. Dwell in me, as I in you. No branch can bear fruit by itself, but only if it remains united

with the vine; no more can you bear fruit, unless you remain
united with me.... He who does not dwell in me is thrown
away like a withered branch.... If you dwell in me, and my
words dwell in you, ask what you will, and you shall have it.
This is my Father's glory, that you may bear fruit in plenty
and so be my disciples."[11]

MOST PROTESTANTS ALLOW FOR THE CALL OF THE SPIRIT IN A TIME OF GREAT APOSTASY

¶XI. Although most Protestants now dissent from this succession of the church, even those who do not are beginning to
make a special distinction for a great apostasy. They say that
in a case like that of the pre-Reformation Church of Rome,
God may act in a special way. Solely by his Spirit, he may
cause some to arise who will perceive from the testimony of the
scriptures the errors into which those who bear the name of
Christians have fallen. They will have only such authorization
as the people give by joining with them and accepting their
ministry as they teach and instruct them. Most of those who
hold this view will also affirm that in so doing, the Spirit is
subjective rather than objective.[12]

However, they say that when a church has been reformed,
as they claim the Protestant churches have been, only an ordinary orderly call is necessary. The call of the Spirit, being
extraordinary, is not to be looked for. They base this on a
claim that there is a difference between the constituting of a
church and one that is already constituted.[13] But this claim is
meaningless as far as we are concerned, since we accuse the
Protestants of being as guilty of gross errors as the Roman
Catholics were and as much in need of reformation. We are
ready to prove this from the scriptures. Therefore, if we
wanted to, we could claim the same extraordinary call of the

[11] Additional vituperative and polemical material, based upon Platina and "Onuphrius" is eliminated here as impertinent. (The latter is
probably Onufrio Pauvinio, an Italian Augustinian of the 16th c. who did
a general history of the Popes and Cardinals.) — Encyc. Universal Illus-
trada, Bilbao, Spain, 1920, vol 39, p 1328 (with bibl).

[12] The objectivity of God's action on the human soul in sacramental
theology is generally expressed by an outward rite. "The reception of
God's gifts [through the sacrament] is normally dependent not on changing subjective feelings, but on obedience to the Divine will." — O.D.C.C.,
p 1198, s v "Sacrament."

[13] Res aliter se habet in ecclesia constituenda, quam in
ecclesia constituta.

Spirit. We have the same reason as they do and just as good evidence to prove our case against them as they had to prove theirs against the Catholics.

BUT THE SAME UNMEDIATED ASSISTANCE OF THE SPIRIT THAT IS PRESENT IN A GATHERING CHURCH IS NECESSARY FOR MINISTERS IN A GATHERED ONE

We do not deny that a greater measure of power may be required for the constituting of a church than is necessary once it has been set up. God in his wisdom distributes power as he sees fit. However, there is no real reason to maintain that the same unmediated assistance of the Spirit that is present in gathering one is not necessary for ministers in a gathered church. Surely Christ's promise was that he would be with his children until the end of the world, and they need him no less for guarding and preserving his Church and children than they did when he begot and gathered them.

It was by the inward and unmediated operation of his Spirit that Christ promised to lead his children into all truth and to teach them all things. By his Spirit Christians are to be led in their last steps as well as in their first, when these relate to God's glory and their own salvation. It is truly a device of Satan to maintain that the direct leading and guidance of God's Spirit is an extraordinary thing which their forefathers had, but which they are no longer to wait for or expect. This is a major cause of the growing apostasy in many of the gathered churches.

It is the greatest single reason for the abundance of dry, sterile, lifeless, and spiritless ministry which leavens people into the same lifelessness, and which is spreading over even the Protestant nations. Their preaching, their worship, indeed all of their conduct is indistinguishable from that of the Roman Catholics. It lacks any fresh living zeal or any accompanying power of the Spirit. The two are distinguishable merely by their differences in some ideas and opinions.

NO NEW MIRACLES ARE NEEDED

¶XII. Some rash and unwise Protestants have sometimes said that if we really have the direct call that we lay claim to, we ought to confirm it by miracles. But since the same thing was said about the first Protestants, all that ought to be required of us is the same answer that they gave the Roman Catholics.

We do not need miracles, because we preach no new gospel, but only what has already been confirmed by the numerous

miracles of Christ and his apostles. We offer nothing which we
are not ready and able to confirm with the testimony of the
same scriptures which are already acknowledged to be true by
both Catholics and Protestants.   John the Baptist and many of
the prophets performed no miracles that we know of and yet
they were not only directly but extraordinarily sent. This common Protestant answer suffices, even though more could be said
if we were not trying to be brief.

CONGREGATIONALISTS AUTHORIZE THEIR OWN MINISTERS AND GIFTED BRETHREN

¶XIII. Another type of Protestants, the English Independents,[14] differ from the Calvinistic Presbyterians.   They deny
that there is any need for the succession of the church, or for
the authority of any national church.   They take another way.
They say that any group of people who agree on the principles
of truth as they find them declared in the scriptures may constitute a church among themselves without any outside authority.
They may choose their own pastor, who is authorized by the
consent of the church that has thus been constituted.   If there
are any neighboring churches [of the same type] this requires
their assistance and concurrence, not so much because it is absolutely necessary for authorization as for the sake of good order.
They also go as far as to affirm that in a church so constituted
any "gifted brother," as they call him, may instruct, exhort, and
preach in the church.   But, since he does not have the pastoral
office, he cannot administer what they call their sacraments.

Of this it can be said that it was a good step out of the
Babylonian darkness.   It no doubt came from a real discovery
of truth and from the sense of a great abuse by the heterogene-
ous national gatherings.   At first, too, the preaching of the
gifted brethren was the result of definite vigorous touches and
movements of the Spirit of God upon many.   But alas, because
these did not continue, this has considerably decayed among
them.   They are now beginning to deny and reject the motions
of God's Spirit as much as others do.

As to their pretense of being called by the scriptures, it can
be said that the scriptures merely declare what things are true·
but they do not call particular persons.   Even though, as an

---

[14] A name generally used in Britain until the end of the 18th c. for
the Congregationalists, because of their upholding of the independence or
autonomy of each local congregation.

individual, I believe that the things that are written there are true, and I deny the errors that are testified against, yet I still have to seek the will of God to find my particular duty. The scriptures do not say by name that I or anyone else ought to be a minister. To resolve this question it is necessary to have recourse to the inward and direct testimony of the Spirit.

HE WHO GATHERS CHRISTIANS ALSO PROVIDES MINISTERS AND TEACHERS AMONG THEM

¶XIV. From all of this we firmly conclude that it is necessary for men to be extraordinarily called and awakened by the Spirit of God whenever individual assemblies or churches are gathered by his power. This is true not only in a general apostasy when it is necessary to deny errors and heresies, but whenever people need to be brought into the life, power, and spirit of Christianity, so that they may truly become the body and household of Christ and a fit spouse for him.

He who gathers Christians also provides ministers and teachers among them by the inward unmediated operation of his own Spirit, to watch over and instruct them and maintain them in an animated, refreshed, and powerful condition. Their call is verified in the hearts of their brethren, and the seals of their apostleship are the awareness of the life and power passing through them which daily and inwardly reinforces them in the most holy faith. As Paul says, 2 Cor 13:3 NEB: "Then you will have the proof you seek of the Christ who speaks through me, the Christ who, far from being weak with you, makes his power felt among you."

It is this which constitutes the true substance of a call to the ministry. It is by this that a minister genuinely succeeds to the virtue, life, and power which the apostles had, and not merely to the bare name. For such ministers the outward ceremony of ordination, or the laying on of hands, is unnecessary. We cannot see what purpose it serves, since those who employ this ceremony admit that the power of conveying the Holy Spirit by these means has ceased. Isn't it a bit ridiculous to keep up the shadow by ape-like imitation if the substance is lacking? If it is possible to bring the Holy Spirit to them in that way, by the same rule they ought to be able to bid the blind to see and the lame to walk, in imitation of Christ and the apostles. They mock both God and men when they put their hands on men and tell them to receive the Holy Spirit

when they believe that it is impossible and that the ceremony
has no real affect.

THE QUALIFICATIONS AND DUTIES OF A MINISTER

¶XV. So far, we have been speaking of the way in which a
minister is called. What are the qualifications and duties of a
minister? Just as the true call of a minister is by the motion
of the Holy Spirit, the principal and required qualifications are
the power, life, and virtue of the Spirit, and the pure grace of
God which comes from it. Without these a minister cannot
perform his duties in a way that will be acceptable to God, or
of benefit to men.

Those who do not agree with us maintain that there are
three requirements for a minister: (a) He must not be a fool
by nature; (b) he must be schooled in languages, philosophy,
and theology; (c) he must be favored by the grace of God. They
say that a man cannot be a minister without the first two, and
that the third is only necessary if he is going to be a "good"
minister. They say that a man can lawfully and truly be a minister without God's grace, and that he should be accepted and
received as such. On the other hand, we take natural ability
and lack of idiocy for granted, but we consider the grace of God
absolutely indispensable for a minister regardless of whether he
is to be a "good" minister or merely a lawful one. Scholarly
learning is not as necessary for good ministry, although there
are occasions where the two accidentally concur in certain respects. However scholarly learning is more frequently harmful than helpful. Taulerus[15] is a good example. Although he
was a learned man and an eloquent preacher, nevertheless it
was a poor layman who instructed him properly in the way of
the Lord.[16]

[15] Johann Tauler (c. 1300-1361), German Dominican mystic. His
teaching, which was "firmly grounded in Thomist doctrine, is eminently
practical. He emphasized the indwelling of God in the human soul, and
describes in detail the Mystic Way, which he conceives as consisting chiefly
in the practice of the virtues, especially humility and abandonment to the
will of God. Union is to be desired not so much for its own sake as for
the results it produces in the soul, which are an increase of charity and the
strength to lead a life of suffering and self-sacrifice." — O.D.C.C., pp 1323-
1324.

[16] The Encyc Brit. (in this particular instance, the 11th ed is cited),
vol 26, p 452, says that the well-known story of Tauler's conversion and
discipline by "the Friend of God of the Upland" cannot be regarded as
historical, and the Cath. Encyc., vol 14, p 465, says that Denifle has produced strong proofs against attributing the authorship of the "Meister-

THE GRACE OF GOD IS AN IMPORTANT QUALIFICATION

Certainly if the grace of God is necessary to make one a true Christian, it is an even more important qualification for a true minister of Christ. No one will question the necessity of grace to make a true Christian. "For it is by his grace you are saved," (Eph 2:8 NEB). "By it we are disciplined to renounce godless ways and worldly desires, and to live a life of temperance, honesty, and godliness." (Titus 2:12 NEB). Christ says explicitly in John 15:5 NEB: "Apart from me you can do nothing," and the way in which Christ helps, assists, and works with us, is by his grace. Hence he said to Paul, 2 Cor 12:9 RSV: "My grace is sufficient for you, for my power is made perfect in weakness."

A Christian without grace is not a Christian at all, but a hypocrite and a pretender. But certainly if grace is necessary for the individual Christian, it is far more necessary for a teacher among Christians. This dignity is bestowed upon those who have attained a greater measure than their brethren and they must be fathers and instructors to others. It is only common sense that a teacher must know more than those who are taught. In whatever art or science he teaches others, the master must be above and ahead of his pupil. If Christianity cannot be truly enjoyed and no one can be called a Christian without the true grace of God, neither can anyone be a true or lawful teacher of Christianity without it.

Furthermore, no one can be a true member — and ministers are considered to be the most eminent of members — unless he receives nourishment, virtue, and life from the head of the body. For members of the body who do not receive life and nourishment wither and decay, and are cut off. For Eph 4:16 NEB says of Christ: "He is the head and on him the whole body depends," and it is (Eph 4:16 RSV) "Christ from whom the whole body, joined and knit together by every joint with

---

buch," from which the story comes, to Tauler. Nonetheless it gives the story to which Barclay probably alludes: An account is given of a master of the Scriptures "who attracted great attention in 1346 by his preaching. One day a layman accused the master of seemingly seeking his own honor rather than that of God, saying also that probably he had not himself borne the burdens he had laid upon others. Without making any stipulations the master allowed himself to be guided by the layman and learned from him to forget the world and himself, to turn all his thoughts upon God and to lead a life of the Spirit."

which it is supplied, when each part is working properly, makes bodily growth and upbuilds itself in love."

That which is thus communicated and which thus unites the whole is none other than the grace of God. In the seventh verse of the same chapter, the apostle says (Cath-CCD): "But to each one of us grace was given according to the measure of Christ's bestowal." Verse 11 shows how by that grace apostles, prophets, evangelists, pastors, and teachers are given for the work of the ministry and for the edification of the body of Christ.

Since all who are called by Christ are qualified by grace, no one destitute of grace is fit for this work. Those who are not so qualified are not given or sent by Christ, and they should not be heard, received, or acknowledged as ministers of the gospel. His sheep should not and will not hear the voice of a stranger.

This is also clear from the whole of 1 Cor 12 which speaks of the variety of gifts and uses the analogy of the members of the human body, showing how all contribute to the total function of the body. Then it is stated in verse 13 NEB that "we were all brought into one body by baptism, in the one Spirit." "And each of you a limb or organ of it," (verse 27). The whole chapter emphasizes and re-emphasizes that it is from the Spirit that the power comes for each of these gifts or services "distributing them separately to each individual at will."

It is by the Spirit that we are baptized into the body and without which we cannot be true members, and if we cannot do any of the work of edification without the Spirit, then certainly no one should be allowed to work or labor in the body without the Spirit. The work would be ineffectual without this grace and Spirit.

THOSE WHO MINISTER MUST DO SO ACCORDING TO THE GRACE AND GIFT RECEIVED

¶XVI. It is clear that this grace and gift is a necessary qualification for the ministry; 1 Pet 4:10-11 NEB says: "Whatever gift each of you may have received, use it in service to one another, like good stewards dispensing the grace of God in its varied forms. Are you a speaker? Speak as if you uttered oracles of God. Do you give service? Give it as in the strength which God supplies. In all things so act that the glory may be

God's through Jesus Christ; to him belong glory and power for ever and ever. Amen."

It is apparent that those who minister must do so according to the grace and gift received. Those who do not have this gift cannot minister. How could a man be a good steward of something he hadn't received? This cannot be understood as referring to mere natural ability, because man in his natural state is said "not to know the things of God," and so cannot minister them to others. The words which follow in this quotation are further demonstration, adding "that God in all things may be glorified." Most assuredly God would not be glorified but would be greatly dishonored if natural men were to meddle in spiritual things which they neither knew nor understood.

It is apparent from the qualifications which the apostle specifies for a minister that grace is most necessary. In 1 Tim 3:2-3 NEB these are stated thus: "Our leader, therefore, or bishop, must be above reproach, faithful to his one wife, sober, temperate, courteous, hospitable, and a good teacher; he must not be given to drink, or a brawler, but of a forbearing disposition, avoiding quarrels, and no lover of money." Essentially the same qualifications are repeated in Titus 1. How can a man have all of these virtues, and be free of all those evils, without the grace of God? If grace is required to produce these virtues which are necessary for a true minister of Christ, surely grace must also be necessary independently of these qualities.

... Francis Lambertus Avenionensis wrote, about the time of the Reformation:[17] "Therefore never by tongues or learning can anyone make a sound judgment concerning the holy scriptures, and the truth of God. Finally, one of Christ's sheep seeks nothing but the voice of Christ, which he knows by the Holy Spirit, with which he is filled: he does not regard learning, tongues, or any outward thing as the voice of Christ, his true shepherd: he knows that nothing else is needed but the testimony of the Spirit of God."

[17] In his book concerning prophecy, learning, tongues, and the Spirit of prophecy, *Argent. excus.,* anno 1516 *"de prov.,"* cap 24.

Francis Lambert (1486-1530). The "Avignonensis" and the date would indicate that the work referred to was written while he was still a member of the Franciscan Order at Avignon. In 1522 he established relations with Zwingli, left his order and traveled to Wittenberg where Martin Luther obtained a pension for him. — *O.D.C.C.,* p 780.

A MINISTER MUST HAVE GRACE IN FULL MEASURE

¶XVII. There are those who say that if all ministers had the saving grace of God, then all ministers would be saved since no one can fall away from or lose saving grace. They also claim that since we affirm that every man has a measure of true and saving grace, neither a Christian nor a minister requires any special qualification — and since every man has this grace, no one is kept from becoming a minister for lack of it.

But this is a misunderstanding of what we have said, for we have already shown that a special and particular call from God is necessary for the making of a minister. As Heb 5:4 RSV says: "One does not take the honor upon himself, but he is called by God, just as Aaron was." The degree of grace which we consider a qualification for a minister is not merely sufficient light to reprove him and call him to righteousness. But we mean the grace which has converted the soul and is the power at work in it. In other words we do not regard them as having grace in embryo. All men have this to some degree. But we understand them to be gracious, leavened by grace into its very nature. By it they will bring forth those good fruits of blameless conversation, justice, holiness, patience, and temperance — the qualities which the apostle regards as necessary for a true Christian bishop and minister.[18]

... We cannot use the Pharisees and priests under the law as an example for times governed by the gospel. For them, God set apart a particular tribe for the priesthood, and particular families to whom it belonged by lineal descent.[19] Their service and work was not purely spiritual but merely the performance of outward observances and ceremonies which were but a shadow of the substance to come. That is why their work did not provide their followers with a perfect conscience, since they were appointed only in accord with the law and commandments and not in accordance with the power of eternal life. Nevertheless they were supposed to be without physical blemish and in performing their duties they were to be washed and freed from outward contamination. In the same way ministers

---

[16] A reference to Nicolaus Arnoldus, *Exe cit. Theolog.*, sect 32, on [Barclay's] Thesis IV is omitted here; and another pertaining to the lack of necessity of grace for the proper administration of the sacraments is also omitted from this section.

[19] Aaron and his sons were constituted "a perpetual priesthood throughout all future generations," Ex 40:15, Num 25:13. (See fn p 180.) — Ed.

of the gospel must be inwardly free of blemishes in their souls and spirits; or as the apostle would say, "blameless!" In their work and service they must be pure and undefiled, clean and holy, in order to "offer spiritual sacrifices acceptable to God through Jesus Christ," (1 Pet 2:5 RSV, NEB, Cath-CCD).

As for Judas, his ministry was partly under the law and not wholly evangelical, since it was performed before Christ's work was finished. Christ himself and his disciples were still subject to Jewish observances and constitutions. Christ's commission and the one which the others received with him was — at that time — "only to the house of Israel" (Mat 10:5-6). It was not enough of a commission to permit the remaining apostles to go forth and preach after the resurrection until they had waited at Jerusalem for the pouring forth of the Spirit. This demonstrates how apparent it is that Judas' ministry was more legal than evangelical.

Furthermore, Judas' case was extraordinary. He had been called directly by Christ himself and accordingly equipped by him to preach and perform miracles. Those who argue with us do not have this direct commissioning and they thus fall short of Judas who trusted in Christ's words and went forth to preach without gold, silver, or purse for his journey. He gave as freely as he had received. This our opponents will not do. What is more, no proof has been given that Judas did not have the least measure of God's grace at that time.

But isn't it sad that even Protestants lay aside the eleven good and faithful apostles, and all the rest of the holy disciples and ministers of Christ, to take Judas for their example? Why should they take the one who was said to be a devil as the pattern and example for their ministry?

INWARD INSTRUCTION OF THE SPIRIT IS NECESSARY FOR THE MINISTRY

¶XVIII. Although we do not consider human learning necessary for the ministry, we by no means exclude the true learning which is the result of the inward instruction of the Spirit. For by the Spirit, the soul learns the secret ways of the Lord and becomes aware of the many torments and vexations of the mind. We learn through living experience how to overcome evil and its temptations by following the Lord, walking in his light, and waiting daily for the direct revelation of wisdom and knowledge. Thus we store these heavenly and divine lessons among the good treasures of the heart, as the virtuous

Mary did the things she observed and the sayings which she heard. The good scribe brings things both new and old out of this treasure in the truest liberty, that is, as the Spirit moves and as the glory of God requires. For his glory the soul, which is the temple of God, learns to do all things. This is the good learning which we think is necessary for a true minister. At the proper time, a man can instruct, teach, and admonish very well with this learning. He can testify for God from positive experience just as did David, Solomon, the holy prophets of old, and the blessed apostles of our Lord Jesus Christ. They testified of what they had seen, heard, and touched of the word of life (1 John 1:1), and as good stewards of the manifold grace of God they ministered as they had received. They did not preach the uncertain rumors which men receive by hearsay; telling of what they had heard and yet remaining ignorant of its experience in themselves. They did not teach people how to believe even though they did not believe themselves, or how to overcome sin even though they were slaves to it, as all who are without grace are. Nor did they teach them to believe in and hope for an eternal reward which they themselves had not yet attained.

LANGUAGES CONSIDERED NECESSARY
IN THE TRADITIONAL TRAINING OF A MINISTER

¶XIX. Let's look at the literate type of learning which others consider so necessary for a minister. First there are languages: at least Latin, Greek, and Hebrew. They regard these as important so that the scriptures, which are their only rule of faith, can be read in the original languages to enable them to interpret them better and comment upon them. That kind of knowledge was even more greatly prized by the first Protestants because of the dark barabarity that hung over the world in the centuries immediately preceding the Reformation. Until it was restored by Erasmus and some others such knowledge had become almost extinct. This was particularly disgraceful because the entire worship and the prayers of the people were in Latin. Yet barely one priest, monk, or friar in a thousand understood his breviary or the mass which he read and repeated daily. The scriptures were like a sealed book not only for the people, but for the greater part of the clergy. Can the zeal of the first reformers for eliminating this Babylonian darkness be condemned? Or their pious efforts to translate the holy scriptures? They did this candidly and within the limits of their knowledge in an effort to answer the just desires of those who wished to read them. There were other good reasons such as maintaining interchange and promoting understanding among many nations through these common languages. For that purpose, public schools for teaching youth who are gifted linguistically are necessary and commendable.

But such knowledge is not the true basis of reformation, for through their emulation of the Protestants the Catholics have paid more attention to literature, and it now flourishes more than ever before in their universities and cloisters. But the Jesuits in particular, who excel in this area, are as far as ever from true reformation and more hardened than ever in their pernicious doctrines.

But all of this does not make knowledge of languages a necessary qualification for a minister. It is far less necessary than the grace of God, and his Spirit can compensate for a lack of linguistic knowledge in even the most rustic and ignorant. Linguistic knowledge, on the other hand, cannot make up for a lack of the Spirit in even the most learned and eloquent. And all that a man can interpret from the scriptures through his own industry, learning, and knowledge of languages is nothing without the Spirit. Without that, he cannot be sure that he will not miss the sense of it. Whereas, by the Spirit, a poor illiterate person can say when he hears the scriptures read: "This is true." And by the same Spirit he can understand, "open," and interpret it, if necessary. When his "condition"[20] answers the condition and experience of the faithful of old, he knows and possesses the truths that are expressed there, because they are sealed and witnessed in his own heart by the same Spirit.

We have considerable experience of this in many of the illiterate men whom God has elevated to the ministry in his

[20] These were favorite usages among the early Friends. The "openings" of George Fox were his explanations of certain passages of scripture. He also used the word in the passive sense: "it was opened to me." Although such usage is now obsolete or archaic, it was common from c. 1200 to the 18th c. In the sense of "being made manifest to the mental or spiritual view," its vogue was even longer, from c. 900 to the early 19th c. — O.E.D.

"It speaks to my condition" is a phrase still used by Quakers to describe a work which has personal relevance and meaning, particularly an uplifting spiritual meaning.

This is similar to sense 11 of the O.E.D. for "condition," which is now obsolete in general usage and is defined as "mental disposition, cast of mind; character, moral nature; disposition, temper."

Church in this day. By his Spirit some have even corrected the errors of translators. This was mentioned in the third proposition, which deals with the scriptures. I personally know a poor shoemaker, still living, who cannot read a word, but who maintained that a highly esteemed and learned man was mistaken when he constantly asserted that what he was saying was a quotation from scripture. He stated before a magistrate that although he could not read the scriptures, he knew from the positive evidence of the Spirit in himself that the professor of divinity was mistaken. He knew that the Spirit of God had never said any such thing. And when the Bible was brought, it was found that it was just as the shoemaker had said.

LOGIC AND PHILOSOPHY ARE ALSO CONSIDERED NECESSARY

¶XX. The second part of the literate education of a traditional minister is logic and philosophy. Not only is this little needed by a true minister, but if a true minister has had it, it would be safest if he forgot and lost it. For it is the root and ground of all contentiousness and debate, and instead of making things clearer it provides the means of making them a great deal darker. Although it pretends to afford rules and order for the regulation of man's reason by which he may determine the truth, it leads into such a labyrinth of contention that it is far more likely to make a skeptic than a Christian, let alone a minister of Christ. In fact it often hinders a man from obtaining a clear understanding of the things that his own reason could tell him. Through its numerous and varied rules and concepts it often provides the excuse for a foolish person to speak a great deal without purpose, since a man of little wisdom may nevertheless be a perfect logician. If you want to make a man a useless fool, teach him logic and philosophy. Before that, he may have been fit for something, but after it he will be good for nothing but speaking nonsense. For these notions will swim about in his head and make him extremely busy about nothing. Wise and sound minds see the emptiness of it, and one has said that it is an art of contention and darkness by which all the other sciences are made more obscure and harder to understand.

Some will urge, nevertheless, that truth may be maintained and confirmed by logic and philosophy. However, persons who are truly rational do not require its help, and obstinate persons will not be convinced by it.

Truth proceeds from an honest heart. When it is forthrightly spoken by the virtue and Spirit of God it will have more influence and take effect sooner and more forcefully than a thousand demonstrations of logic. It was a few words spoken by a simple unsophisticated person that converted a pagan philosopher to Christianity[21] when all his subtle disputations with the Christian bishops at the Council of Nicaea could not do it. When he was asked how it happened, he said that the bishops contended with him in his own way and he could still trade words for words, but the virtue demonstrated by the old man could not be resisted. This secret virtue and power are the things which ought to be the logic and philosophy of a true Christian minister, and he will not need to be obligated to Aristotle for them. We do not deny the propriety of using natural logic to deduce particular conclusions from true propositions without the use of artificial rules and sophistry. Nearly any man of reasonable intelligence possesses this kind of logic and it has sometimes been used in this treatise to carry conviction without resort to the use of the dialectic art.

ETHICS IS NOT NECESSARY FOR CHRISTIANS

The other part of philosophy, which is called ethics, is not necessary for Christians who have the rules of the holy scriptures and the gift of the Holy Spirit to provide better instruction. The physical and metaphysical part can be reduced to medicine and mathematics, and these contain nothing essential for a Christian minister.

It is for these reasons that the apostle Paul, who understood very well what was good for Christian ministers and what was harmful, warned the Colossians, Col 2:8 Cath-CCD: "See

21 Lucae Osiandrae, *Epit. Hist. Eccles.* lib 2, cap 5, cent 4.
The work cited is *Epitomes historiae ecclesiasticae, centuria i-xvi* (1592 1604), published by Lucan Osiander the Elder (1534-1604), one of a family of German Lutheran scholars and theologians. His *Institutio* (1576-1586) was an exposition of the Evangelical Lutheran doctrinal system in opposition to Calvin's *Institutes*. The *Epitomes* cited by Barclay was "at the same time a digest and a continuation of the *Magdeburg Centuries*" (*Schaff Herzog Encyc..* vol 8, p 281).
The *Magdeburg Centuries,* conceived by Matthias Flacius, was "a church history from the original sources showing that the Church of Christ since the time of the apostles had deviated from the right course, a documentary history of anti-Christianity in the Church of Christ from its beginnings to its highest development up to the restoration of true religion in its purity by Luther."
It represented "immense progress in ecclesiastical historiography, not only by the tracing of the sources and the completeness with which the material was collected," but because the pragmatic method of historical development was applied (op cit, vol 7, pp 123-124).

to it that no one deceives you by philosophy and vain deceit."
And to his beloved disciple Timothy he wrote, 1 Tim 6:20
RSV: "O Timothy, guard what has been entrusted to you.
Avoid the godless chatter and contradictions of what is falsely
called knowledge, for by professing it some have missed the
mark as regards the faith."

SCHOLASTIC THEOLOGY

¶XXI. The third and principal part of the traditional
training of a minister is scholastic theology — a monster
composed of some scriptural notions of truth intermixed with
pagan terms and maxims. It is pagan philosophy Christian-
ized, or rather a paganization of the literal external knowledge
of Christ. It is man in his fallen state, who because he thinks
simple truth is beneath him, devilishly pleases himself with
some notions of truth and adorns them with the wisdom of the
senses and of the world. He so despises simplicity that wherever it is found he sets up and exalts himself, by puffing it up
with this monstrous device, darkening, obscuring, and veiling
the knowledge of God with serpentine and worldly wisdom.
He makes the truth, as it is interpreted, despicable and hard to
know and understand. He multiplies a thousand difficult and
unnecessary questions through endless contentions and debates. Those who are most skilled in it wear out their days and
spend their precious time considering the innumerable questions they have devised.

A certain learned man has called it a twofold discipline
combining unlikely halves like the race of centaurs. Part of it
comes from divine sayings and part from philosophical reasoning. The theologians themselves admit that a thousand of their
questions are unnecessary for salvation. There are many others
on which they never could agree and they will continue to have
endless quarrels over them. The numerous volumes that have
been written about theology could hardly be read in a single
lifetime even if the person lived to be very old. Even if he
could read all of them, they would probably give a great deal
of vexation and produce a more troubled spirit than he had
before. These are certainly the "words of ignorance" by which
divine plans are obscured, Job 38:2 Cath-CCD.

They use the scripture as the text for all of this mass of
words, and it is the subject of voluminous debates concerning
its meaning. But a good man of upright heart may learn more

in half an hour, and be more certain of it, by waiting upon God, and his Spirit in the heart, than by reading a thousand volumes. These can only fill the head with many unnecessary notions which may well deliver a staggering blow to faith, but will never confirm it.

In fact, those most given to the study of theology are the ones most likely to fall into error. Origen is a good example. Because of his learning, he was one of the first to interpret the scriptures in this way. But he wrote so many volumes with so many errors in them that he caused the church a great deal of trouble. Arius is another example. Led by curiosity and the urge for human scrutiny, and despising the simplicity of the gospel, he fell into his error. This was the cause of that horrible heresy[22] which was the source of so much trouble for the church.

The simplicity, plainness, and brevity of the scriptures themselves ought to be sufficient reproof for this kind of study. The apostles, who were plain, honest, illiterate men, can be better understood by that type of person today than with all that mass of scholastic stuff of which neither Peter, nor Paul, nor John ever thought.

IT WAS SCHOLASTIC THEOLOGY THAT STARTED THE APOSTASY

¶XXII. This type of theology was the invention of the devil which started the apostasy and it has had dangerous consequences. For in addition to spoiling the simplicity of truth by perpetuating pagan learning, it has caused such uncertainty among even those called Fathers of the Church[23] that because of this admixture they not only frequently contradict one

[22] Arianism, which denied the true Divinity of Jesus Christ. Arius' teaching, that the Son was not eternal but created by the Father from nothing as an instrument for the creation of the world, was condemned by St. Alexander (d. 328), bishop of Alexandria, at a council of his clergy c. 321 A.D., in which he also excommunicated Arius. By extension, the Son of God was not God by nature, but a changeable creature, his dignity as Son of God having been bestowed on him by the Father on account of his foreseen abiding righteousness. In spite of the condemnation of Arius his doctrine lingered on in modified form in the Roman Empire until 381 and among the Teutonic tribes until 496 and after. — O.D.C.C., pp 80-81.

[23] Since the 4th c. applied to a more or less clearly defined group of ecclesiastical authors whose consensus on doctrinal matters carried special weight. The patristic period is generally held to have closed in the 8th c. with St. Isidore of Seville in the West and St. John of Damascus in the East. Actually it is a popular and unconferred title rather than an exact one like Doctor of the Church. — O.D.C.C., pp 495-496. (See also fn p 43.)

another, but even themselves. As the apostasy grew greater, truth became buried in a vale of darkness, and people were completely shut off from true knowledge. Those who were considered learned busied themselves with idle curiosity and unnecessary questions while the weighty truths of God were neglected and in disuse.

Although the grossest of these abuses have been swept away by the Protestants, the evil root still remains and is nourished and supported. Theology is continued under the guise of being necessary for a minister. While the pure learning of the Spirit of truth is despised and neglected or made ineffectual, the earthly wisdom of fallen man is upheld. Theologians labor over and interpret the scriptures in earthly wisdom rather than in the life and Spirit which belonged to those who wrote them, and which are the only way in which they can be properly understood.

MERCHANDISING WITH THE SCRIPTURES

Hence, one who is going to be a minister must learn this art or trade of merchandising with the scriptures. And he must be what the apostle refused to be, a trader in them; 2 Cor 2:17 RSV: "For we are not, like so many, peddlers of God's word; but as men of sincerity, as commissioned by God, in the sight of God we speak in Christ." [After it is stated in 2 Pet 1:20 that "no one can interpret any prophecy of Scripture by himself," 2 Pet 2:1-3 NEB adds a warning about false prophets (and "lying teachers," Cath-CCD) and says: "In their greed for money they will trade on your credulity with sheer fabrications."]

All of this is done so that the trained minister can acquire a knack of taking a verse of scripture and adding his own barren notions and conceptions to it. He also adds what he has stolen from books, and for this purpose he has to have a great many. Then on each Sabbath-day,[24] as they call it, or oftener,

---

[24] The identification of Sunday with the Jewish sabbath was largely the result in England of Nicholas Bound's *True Doctrine of the Sabbath*, published in 1595. This development was unknown on the Continent, even among Calvinists. The book advocated strict enforcement along Old Testament lines. James I attempted modification with his *Book of Sports* (1618), enjoining cessation of work but allowing lawful recreation. The book was burned by Parliament in 1643 and the Puritan Sabbath was imposed by successive acts of legislation in 1644, 1650, and 1655 which prohibited

he makes an hour-long discourse. This is called "preaching the word."

THE GIFT, GRACE, AND SPIRIT OF GOD, WHICH TEACHES, OPENS, AND INSTRUCTS, IS NEGLECTED

But the gift, grace, and Spirit of God which teaches, opens, and instructs is neglected and its outcome, which is to preach a word at the time when it is appropriate, is in disuse. Thus man's arts and talents and the knowledge and wisdom which are from below are set up and established in the temple of God, and indeed they are given a place above that of the little seed. This in effect is Antichrist, working in the mystery.

The devil can be as good and able a minister as the best of them for he has better skill in languages, and more logic, philosophy, and scholarly theology than any of them. He knows conceptual truth better than all of them, and can talk more eloquently than the best of preachers. But of what avail is all of this? Is not everything like death or a painted sepulchre or a dead carcass without the power, life, and spirit of Christianity which is the very marrow and substance of a Christian ministry?

THE RESTORATION OF THE ANCIENT SIMPLICITY OF TRUTH

¶XXIII. If there has ever been a time since the days of the apostles when God proposed to show his power by using weak instruments to batter down earthly and pagan wisdom, and to restore again the ancient simplicity of truth, this is it! For in our day God has reared many witnesses for himself just as he gathered the fishermen of old. Many, in fact most of them, are laborers and the manually skilled who are completely

---

any kind of recreation on Sunday, even going for a walk. — *O.D.C.C.*, pp 1196 and 1304, s v "Sabbath" and "Sunday."

Sunday had begun to replace the Jewish Sabbath, or Saturday, in New Testament times.

Paul and the Christians at Troas assembled "to break bread" on the first day of the week (Acts 20:7), and he bid his Corinthian converts set aside their alms on that day (1 Cor 16:2).

In strict Quaker usage, now largely confined to minutes and some other official documents, the days of the week are still First-day, Second-day, etc., and the months First-month, Second-month, etc., following biblical usage and as a protest against the pagan names which the days and most of the months have acquired.

The awkwardness of this usage becomes apparent when it is said that Philadelphia Yearly Meeting convenes on the first Sixth-day before the last Second-day in Third-month (the Friday preceding the last Monday in March).

without formal training.   But they have struck at the very root
and ground of Babylon[25] by the power and Spirit of God.

In the strength and might of this power they have gathered
thousands by reaching their consciences.   They have been able
to bring those who have been far better educated into the same
power and life because they could not resist the virtue that
emanated from them.   Of this, I myself am a true witness — I
can declare from actual experience that my heart has often
been filled with contrition and tenderness by the virtuous life
that develops from the powerful ministry of these unschooled
men.   By their very countenance, as well as their words, I have
felt the evil in me often chained down and the good reached
to and raised.

What, then, shall I say to you who are lovers of learning
and admirers of knowledge?   Was I not also a lover and admirer of it, who sought after it as far as my age and capacity
would allow?   But it pleased God in his inexpressible love to
withstand my vain endeavors at an early age. While I was still
only 18 years old, he made me seriously consider (as I hope he
will others) the fact that no man can see God without holiness
and regeneration.   It is said in Job 28:28 Cath-CCD: "Behold,
the fear of the Lord is wisdom; and avoiding evil is understanding."   But how much knowledge is vanity and leads away
from that inward quietness, stillness, and humility of mind in
which the Lord appears, and his heavenly wisdom is revealed.

NATURAL WISDOM AND KNOWLEDGE ARE DROSS
AND WORTHLESS COMPARED WITH THE CROSS OF CHRIST

If you will ponder these things, then you will say with me
that all the learning, wisdom, and knowledge that are gathered

---

[25] The metaphorical usage of the Babylonian Captivity (the original
was under Nebuchadnezzar, 604-562 B.C., and is described in 2 Kings
24:14-16 and 25:11) dates from Petrarch who applied it to the exile of the
Popes at Avignon from 1309 to 1377. Barclay's reference is undoubtedly in
the vein of Martin Luther's usage in his treatise, the *Babylonish Captivity
of the Church* (1520).   Luther referred to the "bondage" in which the
church was held by the withdrawal of the chalice from the laity, the doctrine of transubstantiation, and the Sacrifice of the Mass (*O.D.C.C.*, p 117).
This type of usage is still common among Protestants.
   A clearer idea of the specific application of the term by early Friends is
contained in the following quotation from George Fox (Bicentenary ed of
his *Journal*, vol 2, p 420), contributed by Lewis Benson: "And they that
forsake Christ, the new and living Way, and the worship of God in Spirit
and in truth, which Christ set up in his New Testament, go into captivity
in spiritual Babylon."

by the aid of man's own nature are but as dross and worthless compared with the cross of Christ. This is particularly true if they are destitute of that power, life, and virtue which I perceived that these excellent witnesses of God were filled with (even though they were despised because of their lack of learning). Since I and many others have found the heavenly food that gives contentment in and among them, let my soul seek this learning and wait on it forever.

EPISCOPAL ORDERING OF THE CHURCH

¶XXIV. Having thus spoken of the call and qualifications of a minister of the gospel, it is in order to consider next what his vocation properly is and in what way and by what rules he is to be governed. Our opponents always insist upon external things and therefore they have prescribed certain rules and methods which they have contrived from their human and earthly wisdom.

We, on the contrary, still abide with the original foundation and always lean upon the unmediated assistance and influence of that Holy Spirit which God has given his children to teach them all things[26] and to lead them in all things.[27] This Spirit, being the Spirit of order, and not of confusion,[28] leads us and as many as follow it into such a becoming and decent order as is appropriate for the church of God. Paradoxically, much confusion and disorder resulted when our opponents, in attempting to establish order in this matter, cut themselves off from the immediate counsel and influence of the Spirit.

Some want a chief bishop or pope to be first in the church and to rule and be an over-all prince. Under him and by degrees they have cardinals, patriarchs, archbishops, priests, deacons, sub-deacons,[29] and also Acoluthi, Tonsorati, Ostiarii,[30] etc.

[26] John 14:26 NEB: "your Advocate, the Holy Spirit ... will teach you everything; and will call to mind all that I have told you."

[27] John 16:13 KJ, RSV, NEB: "he will guide you into all truth."

[28] 1 Cor 14:33-40.

[29] The list could be considerably extended: metropolitans, bishops, suffragan-, auxiliary-, coadjutor-, and assistant-bishops, archpriests, and archdeacons have not been mentioned; nor has primate.

[30] The acolyte is the highest of the four Minor Orders (porters, lectors, exorcists are the others), which were first mentioned in a letter of Pope Cornelius to Fabius of Antioch in 252 A.D. They are now only transitory stages to the priesthood in the Roman Catholic Church, and all four are often conferred on seminarians on a single day. In the East, of five Minor Orders only lectors and cantors have survived since 692 A.D. The

And in their theology (as they call it)[31] they have professors, bachelors, doctors etc.

Others would have every nation independent of the others with its own metropolitan or patriarch and the rest subject to him in the order just given.[32]

ORDERING BY SUBORDINATION OF POWERS

Still others are opposed to all precedence among pastors and constitute their subordination not in persons but in powers. First they have the consistory or session, then the classis or presbytery, then the provincial, and then the national synod or assembly.[33] There has been as much contention over the ordering, distinguishing, and making of the several orders and offices as there has been over the conquering, overthrow, or establishment of kingdoms. These have consisted not only of verbal battles but even of wars and bloodshed.

---

other three (porters, exorcists, and acolytes) have been merged in the subdiaconate. — *O.D.C.C.*, p 904.

"Tonsorati": literally, those whose hair has been cut. Shaving of part or all of the head is prescribed in Roman Catholic canon law for all clerics except in England and the U. S. The ceremonial cutting was part of the admission into the clerical state as distinct from Minor Orders. — *O.D.C.C.*, p 1366.

"Ostiarii": the doorkeeper, or porter, of the Minor Orders.

[31] Barclay's original usage was "theology" rather than "divinity" at this point, although he generally favored the latter.

[32] This is, of course, Eastern Orthodox polity. Modern Anglicanism also uses it with some modifications, recognizing the Archbishop of Canterbury as spiritual head of the Anglican communion, although he is without authority beyond the limits of the Church of England. As Primate of All England he enjoys special deference as head of the "mother church."

The 40-million-member Anglican Communion is a loose federation of national churches on the basis of the four points of faith outlined in the Lambeth Quadrilateral. All of these churches are episcopal in polity, but with variations in title, function, and the method of selection of the top office.

The Protestant Episcopal Church in the United States is headed by an elective Presiding Bishop. The Anglican Church of Canada is headed by the Archbishop of the Province of Rupert Land whose further title is Primate of All Canada. The Scottish Episcopal Church has a Primus without metropolitical power, whose principal function is to convene and preside at meetings of the Episcopal Synod. — ED.

[33] Except for a slight variation in the last two "courts" described by Barclay in the pyramidal hierarchy, this is modern Presbyterian polity. The term "synods" is generally used to designate Barclay's provincial assemblies, and the national assembly is called a General Assembly and consists usually of equal numbers of ministers and elders commissioned by the presbyteries. "These courts are representative bodies based ultimately upon popular election." — *O.D.C.C.*, p 1101.

Recent history is as full of the tragedies resulting from this spiritual and ecclesiastical monarchy and commonwealth, as ancient history is of the wars that took place in the Assyrian, Persian, Greek, and Roman empires. The most recent of these[34] were just as bloody and cruel in the way that they were conducted and in their conquest as any that took place among the pagans, even though they were fought among people called Christians.

All of this strife among both Catholics and Protestants obtains because they seek to uphold a form and shadow of the things which they imitate, even though these lack the power, virtue and substance of the originals. Many of the orders and forms which they use are not even mentioned in the scripture.

THE SUBSTANCE OF ORDER RESIDES IN THE POWER, VIRTUE, AND SPIRIT

In opposition to all this mass of formality and the innumerable, orders, rules, and forms of church government, we maintain that the substance is the principal thing to be sought. It is the power, virtue, and Spirit that are to be known and waited for. These are the things which bring unity to all of the different names and offices used in the scripture.

As 1 Cor 12:4 (RSV, NEB, and Cath-CCD), so frequently cited, states: "There are varieties of gifts, but the same Spirit." After devoting the entire chapter to showing how one and the self-same Spirit is at work in each member and brings him to the life, the apostle shows in verse 28 how God provided the Church with first apostles, then prophets, teachers and so forth, by the work of the Spirit. Eph 4:11 serves the same purpose, showing that by these gifts some were to be "apostles, some prophets, some evangelists, some pastors and teachers, to equip God's people for work in his service, to the building up of the body of Christ" (NEB).

[34] The reference is probably to two proximate events in United Kingdom history. The Bishops' Wars of 1639-40 resulted from the attempt of Charles I to strengthen episcopacy in Scotland by imposing the English *Book of Common Prayer*. The Scots countered by pledging themselves to restore Presbyterianism.

This was part of the long development of Puritanism which began under Queen Elizabeth and culminated in the Puritan Revolution. "The early Puritans felt that the Elizabethan ecclesiastical establishment was too compromising, too broad and liberal, and too Catholic in its liturgy, vestments, and episcopal hierarchy. They believed that the Scriptures did not sanction the setting up of bishops and churches by the state." — *Col. Encyc.*, 2nd ed, p 1620.

Christ and the apostles never intended to set up orders which had only shadow and form and were without this Spirit and heavenly gift. It was not their intention to make several ranks and degrees and to establish a man-made ministry without the life, power, and Spirit of Christ. This is the work of Antichrist and the "mystery of iniquity"[35] and the inexplicable development that took place in the dark night of apostasy.

In a true church of Christ, gathered together by God, not only into belief in the principles of truth but also into the power and life and Spirit of Christ, it is the Spirit of God that is the orderer, ruler, and governor, not only in general, but in each particular matter. Whenever the believers are assembled together to wait upon God, and for adoration and worship, those whom the Spirit sets apart for the ministry are thus ordained by God and admitted to the ministry. Their mouths are opened by the divine power and influence of the Spirit and words are given to them by which they exhort, reprove, and instruct with virtue and with power. Their brethren cannot do otherwise than hear them, receive them, and also give them honor for the sake of their work.

THE MINISTRY IS NOT MONOPOLIZED BY THE CLERGY

The ministry is not monopolized by a certain kind of men, set aside as clergy (who are educated and brought up for that purpose like people in any other profession), while the rest are despised as laymen. Instead, it is left to the free gift of God to choose anyone he may deem appropriate, whether rich or poor, servant or master, young or old, yes, even male or female. Those who have this call verify the gospel by preaching not only in words, but in power, and in the Holy Spirit, and in full conviction (1 Thes 1:5),[36] and cannot be other than received and heard by the sheep of Christ.

¶XXV. The objection is raised that no distinction at all is made between ministers and others and that this is contrary to 1 Cor 12:29 KJ which asks: "Are all apostles? Are all prophets? Are all teachers? Are all workers of miracles?" etc. From this it is also insinuated that we contradict the comparison, in that chapter, of the church of Christ with a human· body, particularly verse 17 (NEB): "If the body were all eye,

---

[35] 2 Thes 2:7 KJ, or "secret power of wickedness," NEB.

[36] RSV: "for our gospel came to you not only in word, but also in power and in the Holy Spirit and with full conviction."

how could it hear? If the body were all ear, how could it smell?..." The apostle further distinguishes not only the ministers from the rest of the members of the church, but also among themselves, naming them distinctly and separately as apostles, prophets, evangelists, pastors, teachers, and so forth.

To answer the latter part of the objection first, it is apparent that this diversity of names is not to distinguish separate offices, but to denote the various and different ways in which the Spirit functions. This is a frequent manner of speaking with the apostle Paul which he sometimes uses to glorify and praise God's grace.

Rom 12:6-8 RSV is a good example: "Having gifts that differ according to the grace given to us, let us use them: if prophecy, in proportion to our faith; if service, in our serving; he who teaches, in his teaching; he who exhorts, in his exhortation; he who contributes, in liberality; he who gives aid, with zeal; he who does acts of mercy, with cheerfulness." No one would say from all this that these are distinct offices, or that they do not or may not coincide in one person, as well as the things that are mentioned in the subsequent verses, namely loving, being kindly, having a fervent spirit, being hospitable, diligent, beneficent, rejoicing, which he again enumerates as different gifts. It would be most absurd to claim that these should be considered separate and distinct offices.

SEPARATE OFFICES WERE NOT INTENDED BY THE SPIRITUAL GIFTS DESCRIBED IN 1 CORINTHIANS

What is more, in the places previously cited it is clear that no real distinction as separate offices is intended. Everyone is willing to acknowledge that pastors and teachers, which are separated and distinguished there, are not separate offices any more than pastors and prophets or apostles are distinct and cannot coincide in the same person or office. Therefore this can be said to be true of the rest. For prophecy in the sense of foretelling things to come is indeed a distinct gift but not a distinct office. For this reason our opponents do not give it a place among their several orders. On the other hand, they will not deny that it can be and has been given by God not only to some who were pastors and teachers, but that it has also been bestowed on some of the laity. By their own confession, then, it has been found outside the limits of the clergy.

ANY OF THE FAITHFUL MAY BE MOVED TO SPEAK BY THE SPIRIT

Prophecy in the other sense[37] — that is, speaking from the Spirit of truth — is not only the particular responsibility of pastors and teachers, but it is also a common privilege of all believers. Some acts belong to all, but more particularly to a few. That is the way it is with instructing, teaching, and exhorting, which are the special responsibility of those who have been particularly called to the work of the ministry. Yet the privilege is not exclusively theirs, but is common to the others. Whenever the faithful meet together, any of them may be moved to speak by the Spirit.

It is somewhat analogous to sight, which is highly developed in man, and the act of seeing is also a proper one for a man. Yet this capability, and its companion hearing, are not confined to man alone but are common to other creatures as well. In the same way, although prophecy may be properly said to be the work of ministers and teachers, it is also common to the rest of the faithful. It is permissible to them when they are so moved, even though it is not their particular prerogative. Even though they are not particularly called to the work of the ministry, they may be moved to it on particular occasions.

In 1 Cor 14:30-31 Cath-CCD, where Paul is speaking in general of the order and ordinary method of the Church, it can be seen that no one was excluded from prophesying: "But if anything is revealed to another sitting by, let the first keep silence. For you all can prophesy one by one, so that all may learn and all may be encouraged." Nevertheless, there is a subordination, based on the measure of the gift that has been received, as the next verse shows: "the spirits of prophets are

---

[37] The first meaning of "prophesy" is "to utter by divine inspiration"; the second, "to predict" *(Webster's Third New International Dict.).*

The latter usage has been so overshadowing in modern common parlance that the first is frequently forgotten. "Prophecy" in that sense, and strictly applied, is said to have ended early in the history of the Christian church, although there are numerous NT references and Paul regarded it as the highest of the gifts of the Spirit (1 Cor 14:1-6, 39).

By extension, some regard all preaching as prophecy, while other modern usage interprets it as speaking with particular reference to the relevance of religion for the social and political issues of the day (since this was the subject matter of much of OT prophecy).

Friends revived the ancient practice described by the word in its first sense. They consider the role of the spoken ministry as being "to utter by divine inspiration" when moved by the Spirit, or the light of Christ within the soul.

subject to prophets" (RSV). [Or as NEB has it: "It is for prophets to control prophetic inspiration, for the God who inspires them is not a God of disorder but of peace."]

Further evidence that prophesying in this sense may be common to all of the faithful is given in verse 39, set in a general context (Cath-CCD): "So then, brethren, desire earnestly the gift of prophesying," which is really a reiteration of verse 1 (RSV): "Make love your aim, and earnestly desire the spiritual gifts, especially that you may prophesy."

WHOEVER PREACHES THE GOSPEL IS IN REALITY AN EVANGELIST

The same may be said about evangelists, for whoever preaches the gospel is really an evangelist. Consequently, every true minister of the gospel is one. What other particular function can be assigned to it? And would anyone be so foolish as to state that only Matthew, Mark, Luke and John — who wrote the account of Christ's life and sufferings — were evangelists? Even if that were so it would not be a particular office. John and Matthew were also apostles, and Mark and Luke were pastors and teachers as well as evangelists. So several offices coincided.

In fact it is ridiculous to think that the word "evangelist" was used merely to designate those who wrote the scriptures. Calvin acknowledged as true evangelists those who preach the gospel in purity after a time of apostasy and says therefore that there were apostles in his day. For similar reasons, the Protestants called themselves *evangelici,* or evangelicals, at the time when they first emerged.

EVERY TRUE MINISTER SENT BY GOD IS AN APOSTLE

Finally, according to the etymology of the word *apostle,* he is "one who is sent." To the extent that every true minister is sent by God, it can also be said that he is an apostle. Although the twelve who were especially sent by Christ can be called apostles *per eminentiam,* or because of their pre-eminence, there was no limitation to that number. The apostle Paul, for example, was called later. For that reason we do not consider these titles as offices, but as names used to designate the more pronounced shining forth of God's grace.

If any minister of Christ were now to proselyte a whole nation, I have no doubt that both Catholics and Protestants would be willing to call him an apostle or evangelist, even though he had no distinct office as such.   In fact, the Jesuits refer to some of their sect as apostles of India and Japan. And the Calvinists have often called John Knox the apostle of Scotland.

MINISTERS, PASTORS, AND TEACHERS CONSTITUTE A SINGLE OFFICE OF ALL THE FAITHFUL

That is the reason we consider everyone to be ministers, pastors, and teachers, and to constitute a single office.   That is the reason we do not believe that there should be any precedence among them.   It is unnecessary to prove this point here, because it has already been done at length by those who deny the Diocesan Episcopacy,[38] as it is called.

THE WORK OF THE SPECIAL MINISTRY

¶XXVI.   To those who claim that we make no distinction between the minister and the people, that is true if they are referring only to the liberty to speak or prophesy when moved by the Spirit.   However, we do believe that some have a more particular call to the work of the ministry and that therefore

---

[38] Barclay may have had the Scoto-Pictish Church particularly in mind in coupling the word "diocesan" with episcopacy.   During the 9th and 10th c. it was a united body under a national bishop whose seat was at Dunkeld and later St. Andrews.   The local units were monastic and missionary communities whose heads were presbyter-abbots, not bishops, until the diocesan episcopacy was introduced during the reign of David I (1124-1153).   Scotland seesawed between presbytery and episcopacy until 1690 when the Presbyterians finally triumphed over the Scottish Episcopalians.

Luther, however, was the first to question the doctrine of the origin and nature of the episcopacy.   The word *episkopos* means "overseer" or "superintendent" and may have been exercised over a single congregation in NT times.

"Calvin, however, considered episcopacy one of the worst corruptions which had crept into the church.   According to him the churches had originally been governed by colleges of presbyters or elders, and the monarchical episcopate which had prevailed for so many centuries was a usurpation of authority which it was the duty of Christians to destroy." (*Encyc. Brit.*, 1958 ed, vol 8, p 659)

By act of Parliament in 1643 the episcopacy was removed and Presbyterianism was the legal form of church government in England until 1663 when the Act of Uniformity (1662) ejected about 2,000 ministers who had not been episcopally ordained or refused to conform.   In 1673, three years before Barclay's *Apology* was first issued, the Test Act was passed.   This required reception of the holy communion and a denial of transubstantiation as necessary qualifications for public office, thereby excluding both nonconformists and Roman Catholics and establishing the Church of England as the norm (op cit, vol 8, p 470).

they are especially equipped for that work by the Lord.[39] We affirm that their work is to instruct, exhort, admonish, oversee and watch over their brethren more frequently and more particularly than the others. Something more is incumbent upon them in that respect than upon every common believer.

And in that relationship, such obedience and subjection are due them from the flock as are mentioned in Heb 13:17 NEB: "Obey your leaders and defer to them; for they are tireless in their concern for you, as men who must render an account. Let it be a happy task for them, and not pain and grief, for that would bring you no advantage."

There is also 1 Thes 5:12-13 NEB: "We beg you, brothers, to acknowledge those who are working so hard among you, and in the Lord's fellowship are your leaders and counsellors. Hold them in the highest possible esteem and affection for the work they do." And in 1 Tim 5:17 RSV: "Let the elders who rule well be considered worthy of double honor, especially those who labor in preaching or teaching." And finally, 1 Pet 5:5 NEB: "In the same way you younger men must be subordinate to your elders. Indeed, all of you should wrap yourselves in the garment of humility towards each other, because God sets his face against the arrogant but favors the humble."

ELDERS WATCH OVER, CARE FOR, AND ADMONISH THE FAITHFUL

In addition to those who are particularly called to the ministry, and to constant labor in the word and doctrine, there are also elders. Although the elders are not those who are moved to frequent testimony by declaration in words, they are mature

---

[39] From the beginning, the Quakers most accustomed to speak in meeting met together at regular intervals to advise and help one another and to consider ways of strengthening the spiritual life of the meeting. After 1714, to include criticism from their hearers, as well as from themselves, "elders" were added to these meetings, which were then called "meetings for ministers and elders." The "ministers" admitted to these meetings were those who were "approved," "recommended," or "recorded," which meant that their local congregation, acting in its business session, had expressly stated unity with their ministry. While these Friends sometimes devoted their entire time to itinerant ministry and received such food, clothing, and travel expense as were freely tendered by their hosts and hearers, they were not in the usual sense "professional," i.e., "paid" and "trained" ministers. All had a farm, shop, or some other means of support of their own and they frequently paid their own expenses while traveling. — Drawn in part from ch 5 of Howard Brinton's *Friends for 300 Years*, N. Y., Harper, 1952.

in the experience of the blessed work of truth in their hearts. Their work is to watch over and privately admonish the young, and to take care of widows, the poor, and the fatherless and to see that they lack nothing. They see to it that peace, love, unity, harmony, and sound doctrine are preserved in the church of Christ. This also applies to the deacons mentioned in Acts 6.

CLERICAL DISTINCTIONS ARE NOT ADMITTED

What we are opposed to is the distinction between clergy and laity which allows only those who have been educated at schools for that purpose to be admitted to the ministry. This distinction is not found in the scripture. By it, preaching becomes an art and a trade learned by an apprenticeship that includes instruction in logic, philosophy, and so forth. Manually skilled and virtuous persons who do not have this heathenish art are excluded from preaching. Furthermore the scholar who is trained in the ministry is not allowed to have an honest trade by which he can gain a livelihood. Once he shows that he intends to enter the ministry he must go about locating a place for himself and then he will receive set hire for his livelihood. He must also be distinguished from others by the color of his clothes, for he can wear only black. He must also have a master of arts degree.

SUCCESSION IS A SHADOW AND AN EMPTY IMAGE WITHOUT THE NATURE, VIRTUE, AND LIFE OF THE APOSTLES

¶XXVII. This manner of separating men for the ministry was not the practice of the church in the apostles' days. It has led to a number of evils. Because of the honor and profit which accompany the positions of clergy, parents sometimes allot their children to it from infancy and deliberately train them to be clergymen. Others who have the natural talents decide upon the same trade when they come of age and then proceed to acquire the other qualifications that are considered necessary for a minister. Once they have been admitted, they become accustomed to idleness and pleasure and consider it a disgrace to work with their hands. They study a little in their books to make a discourse once or twice a week during the running of an hourglass. The gift, grace, and Spirit of God as qualifications for their ministry are neglected and overlooked. Many covetous, corrupt, worldly wise and ignoble men follow the prescribed forms and put on a good show, but are strangers to and completely ignorant of the inward work of grace upon their hearts.   Death, barrenness, and darkness have followed their intrusion and as a result superstition, error, and idolatry have entered and leavened[40] the church.   And those who examine closely will find that it was thus that the apostasy came about.   Although many examples could be cited, they are omitted for the sake of brevity.

The office and the respect and·reverence that were due to it were annexed to the mere name.   Once a man had been ordained as a bishop or a priest he was listened to and believed even though he had none of the Spirit, power, and life that belonged to the true ministers and apostles.   In a short while the succession, instead of being to the nature, virtue, and life of the apostles, was merely one of name and title, with the office annexed.   In effect they were no longer the ministry and ministers of Christ but merely a shadow and an empty image. Even this decayed and became so metamorphosed that in some ages not only the substance but even the mere forms became wholly vitiated and were altered and marred.   It could more properly be asked of the Christian church, than of Theseus' boat, if it did not have so many pieces of new timber added to it that it was questionable whether it was the original structure.

CLERICAL DISTINCTIONS FREQUENTLY QUENCH THE PURE BREATHINGS OF GOD'S SPIRIT

The distinction which has been made between laity and clergy automatically leads to the abuse that good, virtuous, manually skilled men and others who have not learned the art and trade of preaching are excluded from the ministry.   They cannot be licensed under the rules which the clergy prescribe for themselves.   In fact the clergy have the erroneous opinion that it is unlawful for others to meddle with the ministry and that they are unfit for it.   Because of this attitude and their lack of the prescribed literary qualifications of the ministry, many neglect the gift that they have and frequently quench the pure breathings of the Spirit of God in their hearts.   But if this were yielded to, it might contribute much more to the edification of the church than many of the studied sermons of the learned.

The apostle Paul's advice is slighted by limiting the ministry to the professionally trained.   For he exhorts us (1 Thes 5:19-22 NEB): "Do not stifle inspiration, and do not despise

---

[40] That is, "permeated."

prophetic utterances, but bring them all to the test and then keep what is good in them and avoid the bad of whatever kind." Ironically, that is just what is done by men who pretend to be Christians. They do it even though they glory in the fact that the first preachers and propagators of their faith were just such plain laborers and unlettered men. The Protestants are no less guilty of this than the Catholics, even though their founders originally asserted their opposition to the Catholics on this point. Their own histories demonstrate how by the Spirit of God that type of person contributed greatly to the Reformation in various places.

THE MINISTRY OF WOMEN

From all of this it is apparent that we believe that the knowledge of the Spirit of God should not be confined to the calling and qualifying of a true minister. But the virtue and life of the Spirit should assist him in preaching and praying and in all of the other particulars of the ministry. Because this relates to worship, it will be developed at greater length in the next proposition.

Since male and female are one in Christ Jesus,[41] and he gives his Spirit no less to one than to the other, we do not consider it in any way unlawful for a woman to preach in the assemblies of God's people when God so moves her by his Spirit. Nor do we consider Paul's reproof of the inconsiderate and talkative women who caused trouble in the church at Corinth with their inappropriate questions, 1 Cor 14:34, to be in any way contrary to this doctrine. The same applies to 1 Tim 2:11-12 NEB: "A woman must be a learner, listening quietly and with due submission. I do not permit a woman to be a teacher, nor must woman domineer over man." It is clear that women prophesied and preached in the early Church, or else it would not have been appropriate for Peter to quote Joel (Acts 2:17) to the effect that "your sons and daughters shall prophesy."

In fact, in the same epistle to the Corinthians already referred to, Paul gives rules on how women should conduct themselves when preaching or praying publicly.[42] This would obviously be contradictory if the other citation were construed

---

[41] Gal 3:28.
[42] 1 Cor 14:34.

in a larger sense than its context. Paul also speaks of a woman who labored with him in the work of the gospel.[43]

Acts 21:8-9 speaks of Philip the evangelist, who was one of the Seven [a sort of "Board of Almoners" representing the first formal organization in the Church, and set up to relieve the apostles of "waiting on tables" — Acts 6]. He had "four unmarried daughters, who possessed the gift of prophecy."

Finally, it has been observed how God in this day has effected the conversion of many souls through the ministry of women. He has also used them frequently to comfort the souls of his children. Certainly this demonstration of actual practice should place the question beyond controversy.

COMPULSORY TITHING

¶XXVIII. The obligation of those among whom God calls a minister, or to whom he sends one, to provide for his worldly necessities is freely acknowledged in the summary statement at the beginning of this proposition. Conversely, it is lawful for him to receive whatever is necessary or convenient. It is not necessary to prove this, as this is one point on which all agree.

However, we affirm that that is all that the scriptural testimonies on this subject grant: Gal 6:6, 1 Cor 9:11-14, and 1 Tim 5:18. What we are opposed to is, first, that compensation should be fixed and compulsory. Second, that such recompense should be granted when it is superfluous and unnecessary, that it should be chargeable against a county or parish, or that it should involve large outlay or lavish expenditure.

On the first point, our opponents fall back on the example under the law. This is the refuge they use to defend most of their errors and superstitions which are contrary to the nature and purity of the gospel. They say that since God appointed

---

[43] Rom 16:1-2.

[44] The assignment to the Levites is found in Num 18:21-32. Tithing is described somewhat differently in Deut 14:22-29 Cath-CCD: "Each year you shall tithe all the produce that grows in the field you have sown; then in the place which the Lord, your God, chooses as the dwelling place of his name you shall *eat in his presence* your tithe of the grain, wine and oil, as well as the firstlings of your herd and flock, that you may learn always to fear the Lord, your God . . . you shall partake of it and make merry with your family. But do not neglect the Levite who belongs to your community, for he has no share in the heritage with you. At the end of every third year . . . deposit them in community stores, that the Levite . . . the alien, the orphan and the widow . . . may come and eat their fill; so that the Lord, your God, may bless you in all that you undertake."

tithes for the Levites[44] these also belong to those who minister in holy things under the gospel. However the only generalization that can be applied to both groups is that both are entitled to maintenance, because there is no gospel command on this subject by either Christ or his apostles.[45] What is more, the situation of the Levites under the law and preachers under the gospel are not comparable. The Levites were one of the tribes of Israel and they had a right to part of the inheritance of the land along with the rest of the brethren. But since they had no land, this was allotted to them in lieu of it. Furthermore, only a tenth of the tithes was allowed to the priests who served at the altar.[46] The rest was for the Levites, or to be put in storage for the use of widows and visitors.[47]

But, in spite of the fact that preachers inherit what belongs to their parents just like other men, they still claim the entire tithes, allowing nothing for widows or aliens. It is unnecessary to dwell on tithes for there have been many lucid and learned treatises on the subject and various Protestants confess that they are not of *jure divino*.

The maintenance which is obligatory for those who hear ministers should be neither stinted nor forced, and they are remiss in their duty if they fail to give. This can be proved from Mat 10:8 NEB. After instructing the Twelve on the ministry they were to perform, Christ said: "You received without cost; give without charge. Provide no gold, silver, or copper to fill your purse, no pack for the road, no second coat, no shoes, no stick; the worker earns his keep." The following verse adds that meat and drink could be accepted from those who offered them. If any town were stinting, or would not listen to what they said, they were to "shake the dust of it" off their feet. But that hardly allows for making a bargain beforehand as both Protestant and Catholic preachers do these days. They will not preach to anyone until they are assured of so much a year. The apos-

---

[45] It is true that there is no command in the gospels to this effect. However 1 Cor 9:14-15 states that "the Lord gave instructions" (NEB); or "the Lord directed" (Cath-CCD); or "the Lord commanded" (RSV); or "the Lord ordained" (KJ) "that those who preach the gospel should have their living from the gospel" (Cath-CCD). Paul adds, however, verse 15 NEB: "But I have never taken advantage of any such right, nor do I intend to claim it in this letter. I had rather die!"

[46] Num 18:27.

[47] Barclay seems to be intertwining the Deut and Numbers versions.

tles, on the contrary, were supposed to do their duty, and freely communicate what they had received from the Lord without seeking or expecting a reward.

NIKOLAUS ARNOLD'S MAXIM

The statement on this that was made by Nicolaus Arnoldus[48] should not be forgotten and should serve as a perpetual memorial to him and his brethren. For he frankly states: "We have not freely received, and therefore are not bound to give freely." The statement is ingenious and clever. For if those who receive freely are to give freely, by the rule of opposites those who do not receive freely do not need to give freely. But they must also grant that unless they preach according to the gift and grace that they have received from God they cannot be good stewards of the manifold grace of God, as every true minister should be.

If this is not so then Simon Magus'[49] construction of it would apply. But, to be fair, I believe that to which Arnoldus was referring was not what they were going to preach from the gift or grace of God, but from the acquired arts and studies at the university which had cost them considerable labor and some money. Just as the person who puts his money in a public bank expects interest, these scholars who have spent money in learning the art of preaching think that they may boldly say that they expect both money and leisure in repayment of their labor and expense. Arnoldus received money for teaching his young students the art and trade of preaching, therefore he expected them to be paid before they gave to others.

There is an old saying: *"Omnia venalia Romae";* that is, "all things are put on sale at Rome." But the same proverb

---

48 *Exercit. Theolog.,* sect 42-43.
Nikolaus Arnold (1618-1680), Reformed theologian. Maccovius and Cocceius were his teachers at Franeker, Holland, where he became professor of theology in 1651 and remained until his death. — Schaff-Herzog *Encyc. of Rel. Knowledge,* N. Y., Funk and Wagnalls, 1908, vol 1, p 303.

49 "Simony," the term for the purchase or sale of spiritual things, is derived from Simon Magus, the Samaritan sorcerer of the 1st c. A.D., who professed Christianity and was baptized. When he saw that the Holy Spirit was conveyed by the apostles by the laying on of hands, he offered to buy that power. But Peter rebuked him sternly, saying: "You and your money may come to a bad end, for thinking God's gift is for sale!" (Acts 8:9 NEB)

can now be applied to Franequer.[50] For that reason, when
Arnold's students seek a preaching position they may safely expect and demand money by using their master's maxim: *"Nos
gratis non accepimus, ergo neque gratis dare tenemur."*

But of course their hearers could reply that they did not
find them or their master to be one of the ministers of him
who sent forth his disciples with the command (RSV):[51] "You
have received without pay, give without pay." ["Freely you
have received, freely give." — Cath-CCD.] Hence we will have
none of your teaching, because we perceive that you are one
of those who each "goes his own way, every one of them to his
own gain," Isa 56:12 Cath-CCD.

THE FREE MINISTRY

¶XXIX. The scriptural testimonies which urge the free
ministry are in the same vein as those which urge charity and
generosity toward the poor, and command hospitality and deal
with other similar matters. But these things cannot be reduced
to fixed and proper quantities. The obedience to the command lies in the cheerful consent of the giver, and not in the
matter of what is given. This is what Christ illustrated with
his example of the widow's mite. Although there is an obligation for Christians to give material things to their ministers,
still there can be no definition of the quantity except by the
giver's own consent. A little from one person may fulfill the
obligation more truly than a great deal from another one. Just
as acts of charity or hospitality can neither be limited nor required, neither can this.

Some will object that it is the duty of ministers to earnestly press Christians into greater endeavors when they are de-

---

[50] The University of Franeker, Holland, where Arnold taught.
Arnold, with whom Barclay is in dialogue on a number of points, particularly the ministry (see Author index), wrote several tracts against the
Socinians, "particularly *A Refutation of the Catechism of the Socinians, A
Commentary on the Epistle to the Hebrews,* and *Lux in Tenebris* . . . con-
taining an explanation of passages of scripture brought by the Socinians in
support of their system." — Smith's *Bibliotheca Anti-Quakeriana,* p 50.
Arnold's *Exercit. Theolog.* is apparently lost, as a diligent search of American, United Kingdom, and Netherlands libraries (the latter by Prof. H.
Berkhof of the University of Leyden, to whom I am indebted) has failed
to uncover a copy, although Arnold's other works are relatively common.
Barclay's Latin reply, printed at Rotterdam in 1675, is represented by several copies at Friends House in London and at Haverford. — ED.

[51] Mat 10:8.

fective in acts of charity. Similarly, they say this could apply to the act of giving maintenance, even though there is not a single solid argument for a fixed and forced maintenance to be drawn from scripture. I agree that ministers may use exhortation for this purpose, as much as for any other, just as the apostle did in showing the Corinthians their duty. But it would be well for ministers who do (so their testimony may have more weight and be freer of suspicion of covetousness and self-interest) if they are able to say truly, in the sight of God, what the same apostle added on that particular occasion, 1 Cor 9:12-18 NEB: "But I have availed myself of no such right. On the contrary, I put up with all that comes my way rather than offer any hindrance to the gospel of Christ. You know (do you not?) that those who perform the temple service eat the temple offerings, and those who wait upon the altar claim their share of the sacrifice. In the same way the Lord gave instructions that those who preach the Gospel should earn their living by the Gospel. But I have never taken advantage of any such right, nor do I intend to claim it in this letter. I had rather die! No one shall make my boast an empty boast. Even if I preach the Gospel, I can claim no credit for it; I cannot help myself; it would be misery to me not to preach. If I did it of my own choice, I should be earning my pay; but since I do it apart from my own choice, I am simply discharging a trust. Then what is my pay? The satisfaction of preaching the Gospel without expense to anyone; in other words, of waiving the rights which my preaching gives me."

It is not only that there is no precept or example for a fixed and enforced maintenance to be found in scripture, but in his solemn farewell to the pastors and elders of the church of Ephesus, he warned them against it, Acts 20:33-35 Cath-CCD: "I have coveted no one's silver or gold or apparel. You yourselves know that these hands of mine have provided for my needs and those of my companions. In all things I have shown you that by so toiling you ought to help the weak and remember the word of the Lord Jesus, that he himself said, 'It is more blessed to give than to receive'."

PAUL DID NOT SAY: "BE CONTENT WITH YOUR SALARY"

It is certain that if fixed remuneration had been either lawful or practiced, he would have exhorted them to be content with their salary and not to want more. But what he does

show them, primarily by his own example, is that, first, they
are not to covet or expect any man's silver or gold. Then, next,
that they should work for an honest living by their own hands,
just as he had done. And, finally, by way of exhorting them to
it, he adds the words of Christ, "because it is more blessed to
give than to receive." Thus he shows that fixed remuneration
is far from being something which a true minister should aim
for or expect, but rather that being reduced to such a necessity
that he desires it is a cross and a burden for him to bear.

BEWARE OF FALSE PROPHETS

¶XXX. When a forced and fixed maintenance are presumed, ministers of Christ are one with the hirelings the
prophets cried out against. Certainly if a man bargains to
preach for so much a year and refuses to preach unless he gets
it, and violently tries to force people to give it, it cannot be
denied that he preaches for hire. Thus he looks "for his gain
from his quarter" (Isa 56:11 KJ) and indeed is like those false
prophets who "cry 'Peace' when they have something to eat,
but declare war against him who puts nothing in their mouths"
(Mic 3:5 RSV). The context indicates that this is precisely the
special mark of a false prophet and a hireling and therefore
cannot belong to a true minister of Christ.

Little proof is needed of the fact that maintenance in excess of what is necessary is not to be received by Christian ministers. The more moderate and the more earnest among both
Catholics and Protestants readily confess that this is so. With
a single voice, they protest vehemently against the excessive
revenues of the clergy. But just so this will not lack scriptural
proof, what could be more plain than 1 Tim 6:7-11 Cath-CCD:
"For we brought nothing into the world, and certainly we can
take nothing out; but having food and sufficient clothing, with
these let us be content. But those who seek to become rich
fall into temptation and a snare and into many useless and
harmful desires, which plunge men into destruction and damnation. For covetousness is the root of all evils, and some in
their eagerness to get rich have strayed from the faith and have
involved themselves in many troubles."

To bring this to a head on the matter under discussion,
the following verse says (NEB): "But you, man of God, must
shun all this, and pursue justice, piety, fidelity, love, fortitude,
and gentleness."

RICH BENEFICES, PLEASURE, AND HONOR

¶XXXI. There is now great excess and abuse among Christians on this point. This is attested by the vast revenues which both Catholic and Protestant bishops and priests possess. It can probably be said without exaggeration that some particular persons are paid more per year than Christ and his apostles made use of in their entire lives. Yet they did not lack the necessary material requirements and undoubtedly they deserved them far more than those who enjoy such fullness. It is apparent that these bishops and priests love their rich benefices, and the pleasure and honor which accompany them, so well that there is no proposal to follow the example or advice of either Christ or his apostles on this matter.

It is usually objected that Christians have become so hard-hearted, and in general pay so little attention to spiritual things, that if their ministers did not have a settled and fixed maintenance guaranteed them by law, they and their families might starve for lack of bread. This might have some weight for a secular ministry, made up of earthly men, who have no life, power, or virtue, and hence need maintenance for such a ministry. But it says nothing to those who are called and sent by God, who sends no one wayfaring at his own expense. They go forth with the authority and power of God in order to turn people from darkness to light. They can trust him who sends them and believe that he will provide for them, knowing that he will require nothing of anyone for which he does not provide the ability to perform. When they return, if he should inquire, they can say that they lacked nothing.

This is also true of those who remain in one place. Since their requirements are furnished directly by God, and for preaching they do not have to spend their time borrowing and stealing from books, they are free to work at their lawful employments and labor with their hands as Paul did, when he gathered the church at Corinth. Indeed, if the objection had any weight, the apostles and primitive pastors would never have gone forth to convert the nations, because of the fear of poverty. Does not the doctrine of Christ teach us to venture everything and part with everything to serve God? Can those who are afraid to preach Christ because they may not get money for it be considered ministers of Christ? Or those who will not do it until they are assured of payment? What is the purpose of ministry if it is not the perfection of the people of God and their conversion from such hard-heartedness?

If you should answer, I have labored and preached to them and they are still hard-hearted and will not give me anything, then surely you have not been sent by God, and your ministry among them has not been in the power, virtue, and life of Christ. So you deserve nothing. Or else they have rejected your testimony and are unworthy and you should not expect or receive anything even if they wanted to give it to you. Instead, you should "shake off the dust from your feet" (Mat 10:14 RSV) and leave them.

RICHEST REWARDS WERE LEAST DESERVED

How little weight this objection has becomes apparent when it is remembered that the priests' revenues increased most in the darkest and most superstitious times. They were the most richly rewarded when they least deserved it. He who is truly sent by God will neither suffer nor be afraid of want as long as he serves so good a master. Neither will he ever shun his work for that reason.

¶XXXII. Finally, if we wanted to cite all of the abuses that stem from this kind of maintenance, they are so numerous that we could fill a huge volume even though we barely touched upon them. These abuses, like others, crept in with the apostasy, for they did not exist in primitive times. Ministers then claimed no tithes and sought no fixed or forced maintenance. Those who were in need had their necessities supplied by the church and others worked with their hands. When the persecutions were over and emperors and princes came under the name of Christians, the zeal of those great men was quickly abused by the covetousness of the clergy. These soon learned to trade their cottages for the palaces of princes and did not rest until by degrees some became princes themselves and were in no way inferior to them in splendor, luxury, and magnificence. It was a method of living, however, that the scrupulous Peter and John the fishermen, and Paul the tent-maker[52] never

---

[52] The nature and function of the ministry and its relationship to the whole people of God are in the process of being completely reconsidered in both ecumenical and denominational contexts. *A Tent-Making Ministry*, subtitled "towards a more flexible form of ministry" has been issued (1963) in pamphlet form (16 pp) by the Division of World Mission and Evangelism of the World Council of Churches. The same division is also responsible for *Where in the World*, by Colin W. Williams, a study guide

coveted. And perhaps they little realized that men who pretended to be their successors would ever come to such things. As soon as bishops were seated and constituted in that way, they forgot the life and work of a Christian. They put their heads together over precedence and revenues, and each one coveted the principal and fattest benefice.

PROTESTANTS, TOO, CLAMORED FOR THE CHURCH PATRIMONY

It is also to be regretted how soon this mischief crept in among Protestants. They had scarcely appeared when the clergy among them began to speak in a familiar manner and to show that although they had forsaken the bishops of Rome they had not resolved to part with their former benefices. So as soon as any princes or states shook off papal authority and demolished the abbeys, nunneries,[53] and other monuments of superstition, the reformed clergy immediately began a clamor for the magistrates to beware of meddling with the church's patrimony.[54] A fat benefice always has many anticipants. The

---

on the changing forms of the Church's witness, and has been responsible for a special study on the missionary structure of the congregation.

Montreal's view (4th World Conference on Faith and Order) that ministry is the responsibility of the whole people of God, but that there has always been a "specialized ministry" whose boundaries and functions are far from agreed upon, has been accepted in principle by the Second Vatican Council as a basis of giving the laity a larger role in that church. The ready acceptance of this view at Montreal was principally due to the preliminary studies made by the Department on the Laity and on the Co-operation of Men and Women in Church, Family and Society of the WCC; especially the semi-annual publication (since 1956) of *Laity*, the departmental bulletin devoted to various aspects of this subject. — ED.

[53] Barclay may refer to the continent. However at the start of the visitation and despoliation and dissolution of the monasteries in England (1536-1539) a popular uprising took place. Known as the Pilgrimage of Grace, it was led by attorney Robert Aske who assembled between 30,000 and 40,000 men. It was successful enough that negotiations on equal terms were opened with the Duke of Norfolk and Earl of Shrewsbury who had been sent to suppress it. Treachery, however, ensued and Aske was executed. — *O.D.C.C.*, p 1073.

[54] A patrimony is an estate or endowment belonging to a church by ancient right. The patrimony of St. Peter consisted of the estates belonging to the Church of Rome. "Although the Church of Rome had long been wealthy, persecutions had prevented the acquisition of permanent property until an edict of Constantine (*Cod. Theod.* XVI, 2, 4) made it legal to leave property to the Church. In the following period, up to 600, economic conditions encouraged large donations of land and commendations... By gifts and inheritance the patrimony came to include lands in Sicily (confiscated by Emperor Leo II in 730), Illyria, Gaul, Corsica, Sardinia, around Hippo in Africa, as well as vast estates in Italy. They were

bribing, the courting, the industry and the shameful actions
that are used to acquire these things are too openly known to
require proof.

THE SCANDAL OF GREED AND IDLENESS

The scandal which this has caused among Christians is so
obvious that it has become proverbial that the kirk is always
greedy. The gift and grace of God are so neglected that for the
most part in applying for a pastorate, the only motive or rule
that governs is which has the greater benefice. It is hypocritic-
ally pretended when a church is accepted that there was no
other consideration than the glory of God and the salvation of
souls. But if a richer benefice presents itself it is soon found
more to God's glory to leave the first one and go there. Thus
the clergy have no difficulty in changing frequently and in not
being tied to one place.

To this charge they reply that Quakers allow a minister to
go from place to place. However we do not allow this as a
way of gaining money, but because God requires it. For if a
minister is called to minister in a particular place, he should
not leave unless God calls him away. Then he should obey, for
we consider the basic reason for moving to be the will of God
inwardly revealed, rather than the love of money and greater
gain.

To the great scandal of Christianity, the luxury and idleness in which the majority of Catholic and Protestant clergy
dwell has come from this abuse. Since they do not work at lawful trades with their hands, and they have such sumptuous and
superfluous provision, they live in idleness and luxury. More
vanity, pride, and worldly glory are found among their wives
and children than among those of other people. This is apparent to everyone. They become so glued to the love of money
that no one can equal them in malice, rage, or cruelty. If they
are denied their hire, they rage like drunken men. They fret,

---

governed by a centralized administration which facilitated the extension of
Papal influence. The revenues were employed not only for administrative
purposes, but widely for relief of the poor, redemption of captives, and
later for defence." The papal states, independent of any temporal power,
derived from them; and the term is sometimes loosely used for them. —
O.D.C.C., p 1026.

Those in France were lost in 1791 and in Italy in 1861, except for Rome
itself which was lost in 1870, when only the Lateran and Vatican and the
country seat of Castel Gondolfo were declared extraterritorial. The Popes
finally acquiesced to this in 1929. — *O.D.C.C.*, p 1287.

fume, and, as it were, go mad. A man can more easily satisfy his severest creditor.

The general voice of the poor confirms these statements. For they are far more exact about taking tithes[55] of sheep, geese, swine, eggs, and other produce and look after it more closely than they do the members of their flock. They will not overlook the least mite. The poorest widow cannot escape their avarice. They will hear twenty lies without offering reproof, and a man may swear many times in their hearing without offending them. Even greater evils than these can be overlooked, but not anything that is owing to them. If payment is refused, they will fight over it with thunderous abuse. They will stigmatize the debtor with the horrible charge of sacrilege. They will send him to hell without mercy, as if he had committed a sin against the Holy Spirit.

SUFFERINGS FOR THE SAKE OF CONSCIENCE

Of all people, we can best bear witness to this. God has shown us the corruptness and unchristian character of this ministry and called us from it. He has gathered us into his own power and life to be a people apart. We dare not join with or hear these anti-Christian hirelings or put food in their mouths. Oh, what malice, envy, and fury this has raised in their hearts against us. Although we get none of their wares, in fact refuse to buy them, knowing they are worthless, they force us to give them money. Because we cannot do it for the sake of conscience, our sufferings have been unutterable. To give an account

---

[55] The payment of a tenth part of the produce of all land in England began at an early date. At first the owner was allowed to pay this to whatever clergyman he pleased, usually the bishop who distributed it among his clergy. Later, tithes were allocated to the parson of the parish where they were collected, and in time this allocation became general law. Payment was strongly enjoined by a synod in 786 A.D. and enforced by law in 900.

Tithes were of three sorts: praedial, or from the fruits of the ground; personal, or from the profits of labor; mixed, or partly from the ground and partly from labor. They were divided into: great, originating in the major crops — wheat, oats, etc.; and small, originating in minor produce — lambs, chickens, etc.

In time many lands were discharged from payment, often by substitution of a fixed annual sum of money. Acts in 1918, 1925, and 1936 provided for the abolition of tithes in England by payments of land taxes into a sinking fund for a period of 60 years. "Thus there is now in England no such thing as tithe." — O.D.C.C., pp 1361-1362.

of their cruelty and the various types of inhumanity which they have applied against us would make quite a history.[56]

These greedy hirelings have reached such a state of malice and rage that several poor workingmen have been taken hundreds of miles from their homes and shut up in prison for two, three, or even seven years in a row for the value of one pound sterling or less. I personally know a poor widow who was kept in a prison 30 miles from her home for about four years for the tithes on her geese, which amounted to less than five shillings.

They have violently plundered men's goods that were worth 100 times the tithes[57] and have damaged even more. Hundreds have spilt innocent blood for this cause by dying in filthy, unhealthy, smelling holes and prisons. Some of the priests have been so enraged that the goods which were ravished were not enough to satisfy them. To satisfy their fury by their own hands they beat, knocked together, and wounded innocent men and women who refused for the sake of conscience to put food into their mouths.

ALL FIXED AND FORCED MAINTENANCE AND STIPENDS SHOULD BE ABOLISHED

The only sound way to reform and remove all of these abuses is to take away the basis and the opportunity for them. That is, to remove all fixed and forced maintenance and stipends. Since these things were given by the people, long ago, they should be returned to the public treasury. In that way,

[56] It did just that. Joseph Besse of Colchester (c. 1683-1757) undertook the work of digesting some 224 printed pieces published between 1660 and 1689, and the pages and pages of records of particular sufferings for various causes including tithes, refusal to take oaths, attending Quaker meeting, etc. It "records the sufferings and some of the adventures of 12,000 Friends in the period prior to the Toleration Act in 1689. It is a record without parallel in religious history." (Brinton, *Friends for 300 Years*, p 178)

Fox himself estimated that in a single year, 1656, not less than 1,000 Quakers were in English prisons. In 1657 Fox advised each meeting to keep a careful record of the fines, imprisonments, and other abuses of its members. (Jessamyn West, *The Quaker Reader*, N. Y., Viking, 1962, pp 114-115)

In the 25 years of Charles II's reign 321 died in prison, and another 79 in Cromwell's time. (John Stephenson Rowntree, *His Life and Work*, London, Headley, 1908, pp 129-130)

For further details on Besse and his *Sufferings* see *Journal of the Friends Hist. Assoc.*, vol 23, pp 1-11.

[57] "Three quarters of a million pounds being distrained between 1730 and 1830." — Harold Loukes, *The Quaker Contribution*, London, SCM Press Ltd., 1965, p 70.

the people would benefit greatly to the extent that they would be relieved of the public taxes and impositions which these funds would replace.

Whoever would call or appoint teachers for themselves, let them maintain them accordingly. Undoubtedly those who receive and sample the goodness of their ministry will provide what they need. No law will be required to compel their hire. For he who sends them will take care of them, and they who are sent will be content with food and clothing.

CONTRAST WITH THE APOSTOLIC MINISTRY

¶XXXIII. To summarize, the ministry that we plead for, and the Lord has raised up among us, in all of its constituent parts is like the true ministry of the apostles and the primitive church. Whereas the ministry which our opponents seek to uphold and plead for differs from them in every respect. It resembles the false prophets and teachers who are testified against and condemned in the scripture. To illustrate briefly:

THE CALL OF CHRIST AND HIS SPIRIT

I. The ministry and ministers we plead for are the kind that are unmediatedly called and sent forth by Christ and his Spirit. That this was also true of the holy apostles and prophets is apparent from Mat 10:1 Cath-CCD: "Then having summoned his twelve disciples, he gave them power over unclean spirits, to cast them out, and to cure every kind of disease and infirmity," and verses 5 and 6 RSV: "These twelve Jesus sent out, charging them, 'Go nowhere among the Gentiles, and enter no town of the Samaritans, but go rather to the lost sheep of the house of Israel. . . .' "

Also Eph 4:11 RSV: "And his gifts were that some should be apostles, some prophets, some evangelists, some pastors and teachers."

And Heb 5:4 RSV: "And one does not take the honor upon himself, but he is called by God, just as Aaron was."

1. But the ministry and ministers our opponents plead for have no immediate call from Christ and they consider the leading and moving of the Spirit to be unnecessary. Just as the false prophets and teachers were in ancient times, they are called by wicked and ungodly men. This is apparent in the following scriptural citations:

Jer 14:14-15 RSV: "And the Lord said to me: 'The prophets are prophesying lies in my name; I did not send them, nor did I command them or speak to them. They are prophesying to you a lying vision, worthless divination, and the deceit of their own minds. Therefore thus says the Lord concerning the prophets who prophesy in my name although I did not send them, and who say, "Sword and famine shall not come on this land": By sword and famine those prophets shall be consumed.' "

Jer 23:21 Cath-CCD: "I did not send these prophets, yet they ran; I did not speak to them, yet they prophesied."

Jer 27:15 RSV: "I have not sent them, says the Lord, but they are prophesying falsely in my name, with the result that I will drive you out and you will perish, you and the prophets who are prophesying to you."

MINISTERS WHO ARE GOOD, HOLY, AND FILLED WITH GRACE

II. The ministers we plead for are those who are actuated and led by God's Spirit. By the power and operation of his grace in their hearts they are in some measure converted and spiritually reborn and so are good, holy, and filled with grace. Such were the holy prophets and apostles as is apparent from:

1 Tim 3:2-5 NEB: "Our leader, therefore, or bishop, must be above reproach, faithful to his one wife, sober, temperate, courteous, hospitable, and a good teacher; he must not be given to drink, or a brawler, but of a forbearing disposition, avoiding quarrels, and no lover of money. He must be one who manages his own household well and wins obedience from his children, and a man of the highest principles. If a man does not know how to control his own family, how can he look after a congregation of God's people?" Verse 6 (RSV): "He must not be a recent convert, or he may be puffed up with conceit and fall into the condemnation of the devil."

Titus 1:7-9 RSV: "For a bishop, as God's steward, must be blameless; he must not be arrogant or quick-tempered or a drunkard or violent or greedy for gain, but hospitable, a lover of goodness, master of himself, upright, holy, and self-controlled; he must hold firm to the sure word as taught, so that he may be able to give instruction in sound doctrine and also to confute those who contradict it."

2. But the ministers our opponents plead for are those for whom the grace of God is not considered an essential qualification. These may be true ministers, according to them, even

though they are ungodly, unholy, and profligate men.   Such were the false prophets.   This is apparent from:

Micah 3:5, already quoted.

1 Tim 6:5-8 RSV: "Men who are depraved in mind and bereft of the truth, imagining that godliness is a means of gain. There is great gain in godliness with contentment; for we brought nothing into the world, and we cannot take anything out of the world; but if we have food and clothing, with these we shall be content."

2 Tim 3:2 NEB: "Men will love nothing but money and self; they will be arrogant, boastful, and abusive; with no respect for parents, no gratitude, no piety, no natural affection."

2 Pet 2:1-3 NEB: "But Israel had false prophets as well as true; and you likewise will have false teachers among you. They will import disastrous heresies, disowning the very Master who bought them, and bringing swift disaster on their own heads. They will gain many adherents to their dissolute practices, through whom the true way will be brought into disrepute. In their greed for money they will trade on your credulity with sheer fabrications."

WHO MINISTER ACCORDING TO THE GIFT
THEY HAVE RECEIVED

III.   The ministers we plead for are those who act, move, and labor in the work of the ministry as they are moved, supported, assisted, and influenced by the Spirit of God.   Their ministry does not spring from their own strength and ability, but according to the gift that they have received, and as good stewards of the manifold grace of God.   Such were the holy prophets and apostles, as the scriptures testify:

1 Pet 4:10-11 NEB: "Whatever gift each of you may have received, use it in the service of one another, like good stewards dispensing the grace of God in its varied forms.   Are you a speaker?   Speak as if you uttered oracles of God.   Do you give service?   Give it as in the strength which God supplies.   In all things so act that the glory may be God's through Jesus Christ; to him belong glory and power for ever and ever.   Amen."

1 Cor 1:17, 2:3-5, 13 RSV: "For Christ did not send me to baptize but to preach the gospel.... And I was with you in weakness and in much fear and trembling; and my speech and my message were not in plausible words of wisdom, but in demonstration of the Spirit and power, that your faith might

not rest in the wisdom of men but in the power of God.....
And we impart this in words not taught by human wisdom but
taught by the Spirit, interpreting spiritual truths to those who
possess the Spirit."

Acts 2:4 Cath-CCD: "And they were all filled with the
Holy Spirit and began to speak in foreign tongues, even as the
Holy Spirit prompted them to speak."

Mat 10:20 Cath-CCD: "For it is not you who are speaking,
but the Spirit of your Father who speaks through you."

Mark 13:11 RSV: "And when they bring you to a trial and
deliver you up, do not be anxious beforehand what you are to
say; but say whatever is given you in that hour, for it is not
you who speak, but the Holy Spirit."

Luke 12:12 Cath-CCD and RSV: "For the Holy Spirit will
teach you in that very hour what you ought to say."

1 Cor 13:2 NEB: "I may have the gift of prophecy, and
know every hidden truth; I may have faith strong enough to
move mountains; but if I have no love, I am nothing."

3. But the ministers our opponents plead for do not wait
for, or expect, or need the Spirit of God to set them in motion
in the work of the ministry. What they do, they do out of
their own natural strength and ability. In the strength of their
own wisdom and eloquence they preach what they have gathered and stolen from the letter of the scripture and from other
books. This is done without the evidence and demonstration
of the Spirit and power. Such were the false prophets and
apostles. This can be seen from:

Jer 23:30-32 Cath-CCD [also 34ff]: "Therefore I am against
the prophets, says the Lord, who steal my words from each
other. Yes, I am against the prophets, says the Lord, who borrow speeches to pronounce oracles. Yes, I am against the
prophets who prophesy lying dreams, says the Lord, and who
lead my people astray by recounting their lies and by their
empty boasting. From me they have no mission or command,
and they do this people no good at all, says the Lord."

1 Cor 4:18 RSV: "Some are arrogant, as though I were not
coming to you."

Jude 16 RSV: "These are grumblers, malcontents, following their own passions, loud-mouthed boasters, flattering people
to gain advantage."

WHO GIVE PREFERENCE TO OTHERS AND SERVE IN LOVE

IV. The ministers we plead for are holy and humble and do not contend for precedence and priority. Instead, they give preference to others and to serving one another in love. They do not desire to be distinguished from others by their garments and "large phylacteries,"[58] or seek greetings of honor in the marketplace, the uppermost rooms at feasts, or the chief seats in the synagogues. They do not wish to be addressed as master by other men. Such were the holy prophets and apostles, as is evident from:

Mat 23:8-10 RSV: "But you are not to be called rabbi, for you have one teacher, and you are all brethren. And call no man your father on earth, for you have one Father, who is in heaven. Neither be called masters, for you have one master, the Christ."

Mat 20:25-27 NEB: "You know that in the world, rulers lord it over their subjects, and their great men make them feel the weight of authority; but it shall not be so with you. Among you, whoever wants to be great must be your servant, and whoever would be first must be the willing slave of all."

4. But the ministers our opponents plead for strive and contend for superiority and claim precedence over one another. By affectation and ambition they seek such things. Such were the false prophets and apostles in times past:

Mat 23:5-7 has already been quoted on broad phylacteries, deep fringes, chief seats, and titles.

WHO ARE CONCERNED FOR EVERYONE'S SALVATION

V. The ministers we plead for have received freely and give freely. They covet no one's silver, gold, or garments. They

---

[58] The reference is to the scribes and Pharisees in Mat 23:5-6 Cath-CCD: "In fact, all their works they do in order to be seen by men; for they widen their phylacteries, and enlarge their tassels, and love the first places at suppers and the front seats in the synagogues, and greetings in the market place, and to be called by men 'Rabbi' ["master" or "teacher"]."

The phylacteries were based on a literal interpretation of four passages of the Law (Ex 13:9, 16, Deut 6:8, 11:18) which could be interpreted to mean preserve the Law in the memory, but were taken as meaning to wear the Law on the arm and forehead. They consisted of two leather cases containing vellum strips inscribed with the passages already referred to. One was worn on the forehead, the other on the inside of the left arm, to bring it close to the heart.

The custom, which originated in the 2nd c. B.C., continues among Orthodox Jews. Some conception of them as charms which would protect the wearer from harm is also involved — Jacobus, Nourse, Zenos, *New Standard Bible Dictionary*, N. Y., Funk and Wagnalls, 1926, p 712.

seek no man's possessions but only his welfare and the salvation of his soul. Their hands supply their own necessities. They work honestly for bread for themselves and for their families. If at any time they are called from their trades to do God's work, they accept what is freely given them by those to whom they have been of spiritual help. They are content with food and clothing. Such were the holy prophets and apostles. This is apparent from:

Mat 10:8 RSV: "Heal the sick, raise the dead, cleanse lepers, cast out demons. You have received without pay, give without pay."

Acts 20:33-35 NEB: "I have not wanted anyone's money or clothes for myself; you all know that these hands of mine earned enough for the needs of me and my companions. I showed you that it is our duty to help the weak in this way, by hard work, and that we should keep in mind the words of the Lord Jesus, who himself said, 'Happiness lies more in giving than in receiving.' "

1 Tim 6:8 Cath-CCD: "Having food and sufficient clothing, with these let us be content."

5. But the ministers our opponents plead for have not received freely and will not give freely. They are covetous and do things they should not for the sake of filthy lucre.[59] They are belligerent against those who will not put food in their mouths.[60] They preach for hire and prophesy for money, and they have no understanding; each one has turned to his own way, looking to that quarter for his gain. They are greedy dogs who never have enough.[61] They are shepherds who feed themselves rather than their flock. They eat the fat and clothe themselves with the wool.[62] They make merchandise out of

[59] Among the qualifications for a bishop given in 1 Tim 3:3 KJ are that he shall be "not given to wine, no striker, not greedy of filthy lucre ...not covetous."

[60] The reference is to Micah 3:5, 11 quoted in the following citations.

[61] After the opening phrase, these two sentences paraphrase Isa 56:11 KJ: "Yea, they are greedy dogs, which can never have enough, and they are shepherds that cannot understand: they all look to their own way, every one for his gain, from his quarter."

[62] This is a particularly rich reference, applying directly to Ezek 34: 2-5, included in the following citations, and also to instructions on fat and wool. Fat belonged to Jehovah and was to be burnt at the altar "with the other oblations of the Lord" (Lev 4:8-9, 26, 35). Among the regulations applying to priests Ezek 44:17 Cath-CCD stipulates: "Whenever they enter the gates of the inner court, they shall wear linen garments; they shall

souls.[63] They follow the way of Balaam who loved the ways of unrighteousness.[64] Such were the false prophets and apostles:

Isa 56:11 RSV [the KJ has already been given in a footnote]: "The dogs have a mighty appetite; they never have enough. The shepherds also have no understanding; they have all turned to their own way, each to his own gain, one and all."

WOE TO THE SHEPHERDS
WHO HAVE BEEN PASTURING THEMSELVES

Ezek 34:2-5 Cath-CCD: "Son of man, prophesy against the shepherds of Israel, in these words prophesy to them (to the shepherds): Thus says the Lord God: Woe to the shepherds of Israel who have been pasturing themselves! Should not shepherds, rather, pasture sheep? You have fed off their milk, worn their wool, and slaughtered their fatlings, but the sheep you have not pastured. You did not strengthen the weak nor heal the sick nor bind up the injured. You did not bring back the strayed nor seek the lost, but you lorded it over them harshly and brutally. So they were scattered for lack of a shepherd, and became food for all the wild beasts. My sheep were scattered."

Micah 3:5, 11 Cath-CCD: "Thus says the Lord regarding the prophets who lead my people astray; who, when their teeth have something to bite, announce peace, but when one fails to put something in their mouth, proclaim war against him.

"Her leaders render judgment for a bribe, her priests give decisions for a salary, her prophets divine for money, while they rely on the Lord, saying, 'Is not the Lord in the midst of us? No evil can come upon us!' "

Titus 1:10-11 RSV: "For there are many insubordinate men, empty talkers and deceivers, especially the circumcision party; they must be silenced, since they are upsetting whole families by teaching for base gain what they have no right to teach."

---

not put on anything woolen when they minister at the gates of the inner court or within the temple."

[63] 2 Pet 2:3 KJ: "And through covetousness shall they with feigned words make merchandise of you."

[64] 2 Pet 2:15-16 RSV: "They have followed the way of Balaam, the son of Beor, who loved gain from wrongdoing, but was rebuked for his own transgression; a dumb ass spoke with human voice and restrained the prophet's madness."

2 Pet 2:1-3 NEB, 14-15 Cath-CCD: "But Israel had false prophets as well as true; and you likewise will have false teachers among you.   They will import disastrous heresies, disowning the very Master who bought them, and bringing swift disaster on their heads.   They will gain many adherents to their dissolute practices, through whom the true way will be brought into disrepute.   In their greed for money they will trade on your credulity with sheer fabrications.

"They have eyes full of adultery, and turned unceasingly towards sin. They entice unstable souls; they have their hearts exercised in covetousness; they are children of a curse.   They have forsaken the right way and have gone astray; they have followed the way of Balaam, the son of Bosor, who loved the wages of wrongdoing."

A MINISTRY CALLED, QUALIFIED, ORDERED, AND ACTUATED BY THE SPIRIT

And in a word, we are for a holy, spiritual, pure, and living ministry actuated and influenced by the Spirit of God in every step. By the Spirit they are called, qualified, and ordered as ministers, and without it they cease to be ministers of Christ.

But our opponents do not consider the life, grace, and Spirit an essential part of their ministry.   They uphold a human, worldly, dry, barren, fruitless, and dead ministry.   And, alas, we have seen the fruits of it in a majority of their churches, of which the saying of the Lord is certainly apropos, Jer 23:32 Cath-CCD: "From me they have no mission or command, and they do this people no good at all, says the Lord."

Holy Expectancy

PROPOSITION 11 — WORSHIP

True and acceptable worship of God stems from the inward and unmediated moving and drawing of his own Spirit. It is not limited by places, times, or persons.[1]

Although we should always maintain a profound reverence for God, and in that sense worship him continually, whenever we formally worship him with prayers, praises, or preaching, it should not be done of our own volition, or at the place and time that we wish. But we should be moved by the secret stimulation and inspiration which the Spirit of God provides in our hearts. God hears our need and accepts this responsibility, and never fails to move us to worship when it is required. He alone is the proper judge of this.

All other worship, which begins and ends at man's own pleasure, which can be done or left undone as he himself sees fit, is merely superstition, self-will, and abominable idolatry in the sight of God. Whether it be praise, prayer, or preaching; whether it be a prescribed form, like a liturgy; or extemporaneous prayers conceived with the natural capacities and abilities of the mind; these should be rejected and done away with in this time of spiritual emergence.

In the past, it may have pleased God to overlook the ignorance of the age because of the simplicity and integrity of some. Because of his own innocent seed which lay buried in the hearts of men under that mass of superstition, he may have been willing to blow upon the dead and dry bones [Ezek 37:1-14][2] and to raise some breath of his own in answer to them. But the day has dawned more clearly when these empty forms are to be denied and rejected. (Ezek 13; Mat 10:20; Acts 2:4, 18:5; John 3:6, 4:21; Jude 19; Acts 17:23.)

---

[1] This should not be misunderstood as discontinuing set times and places for worship. — ED.

[2] The reference is to the vision of the valley of dry bones in Ezek 37:1-14 Cath-CCD, a metaphor for the whole house of Israel, to whom the prophet was ordered to preach on God's promise that he would put breath into them and they would live. "And even as I was prophesying I heard a noise; it was a rattling as the bones came together, bone joining bone. I saw the sinews and the flesh come upon them ... and the spirit came into them; they came alive and stood upright, a vast army."

¶I. In general, the duty of man toward God consists chiefly of two things: (1) Holy conformity to the pure law and light of God, in such a way that evil is forsaken and the eternal moral precepts of righteousness and equity are practiced; and (2) rendering the reverence, honor, and adoration of God that he requires and demands of us — the things that are included under worship.

We have already considered the first duty. We have also considered the way in which Christians are related to each other by the several measures of grace that are received by them as distinguished from those that are given to all. These furnish the basis for the various offices which they have in the body of Christ which is the church.

WORSHIP IS WHERE CHRISTIANS HAVE DEFECTED THE MOST

It is now in order to consider worship, or those acts whereby man renders to God the part of his duty which relates directly to him. Both private and public worship, and the general and particular acts of which it consists, will be considered. Obedience is better than sacrifice, and the only sacrifice that is acceptable is that which is made according to the will of him to whom it is offered. But men find it easier to make sacrifices according to their own wills than they do to obey God's will. They have heaped up sacrifices without obedience. By giving a show of reverence, honor, and worship they think they can deceive God, as they do one another. But they are inwardly alienated from his holy and righteous life. They are complete strangers to the pure breathings of his Spirit. Yet it is only in the purity of such breathings that acceptable sacrifice and worship are offered.

Thus, there is nothing relating to man's duty toward God that has been more vitiated by people of all kinds. There is no way in which the devil has been more prevalent than in the way he has abused man's mind concerning this. As some Catholics and all Protestants have acknowledged, nothing has been more corrupted among Christians. Since the reforms that Protestants have made in Catholic ways, in this regard, have my approbation, I won't meddle in their controversies over it at this point.

Suffice it to say that I join them in denying any place in the true worship of God for that abominable superstition and

idolatry, the Roman Catholic mass.[3] The same can be said of
the adoration of saints and angels, the veneration of relics, the
visitation of sepulchres, and all those other superstitious ceremonies, confraternities, and endless pilgrimages of the Roman
"synagogue."

This generally suffices to convince Protestants that Antichrist has wrought more here than in any other part of the
Christian religion. However, they should look closely and see
if they have really made a clear and perfect reformation. That
is where the controversy arises between them and us. For we
find that they have lopped off many of the branches but the
roots still remain.

Essentially their worship is one which is performed by and
from the human will and spirit, rather than from the Spirit of
God. The worship of God in the true Christian spirit was lost so
early that getting at the evil root of the defection was most difficult. Man's will and wisdom had been mixed in so thoroughly
and so quickly that this was the area of greatest apostasy.

We trust that the reader will not feel suddenly perplexed
by our statement of the proposition on worship, but that he will
be patient and hear our explanation. With the assistance of
God, I hope that it will become apparent that although our
manner of speaking and doctrine seem most singular and different from those of all other Christians, they are most in accord
with the purest Christian religion, and indeed it is most neces-
essary for them to be observed and followed. In order that
there may be no reason for misunderstanding, it would probably be best to declare and explain what we mean and clarify
the status of the controversy. (Because of the need for brevity
it was necessary to state the proposition rather obscurely and
ambiguously.)

WORSHIP UNDER THE GOSPEL IS NOT THAT OF THE LAW

¶II. First, let it be said that the worship of God referred
to is that of the gospel times and not that under or before the
Law. For the particular commands which God gave men then

---

[3] Nonetheless modern Quakers emphasize the analogy between the
moment when the host is elevated in the Mass (when the Spirit becomes
truly present) and the doctrine of the Presence in the midst which is at
the heart of Quaker "unprogrammed" worship. This is held on a basis
of silent waiting in an attitude of Holy Expectancy, and is described by
Barclay later in this Proposition. — ED.

are insufficient authorization for doing the same things now. Otherwise we could offer sacrifice as acceptably now as they did then. But everyone acknowledges that sacrifice is no longer to be practiced. What may have been commendable and acceptable under the Law may now justly be charged with superstition, in fact, idolatry.

Arnoldus' angry tirade[4] against this proposition says that I deny all public worship and those who in Enoch's time began to call upon the name of the Lord in public. His charge is misplaced! Also his claim that in consequence I deny those who at the command of God went three times to Jerusalem to worship.[5] He would even extend this to Anna, Simeon, Mary[6] and

---

4 *Exercit. Theolog.* sect 44.

5 The reference is to the 489th of the 613 biblical commandments of Orthodox Judaism. It was based on Deut 16:16, which is interpreted to mean that every male who had the strength to do so was to appear in the Temple in Jerusalem at three set times in the year. These were the Feast of Unleavened Bread, the Feast of Weeks, and the Feast of Tabernacles. — Herbert S. Goldstein, *Between the Lines of the Bible, A Modern Commentary on the 613 Commandments,* New York, Crown, 1959, p 288.

6 The ceremony of purification after childbirth, described in Luke 2:22-39. Anna was the 84-year-old widowed prophetess who spent her entire time in the temple, worshipping day and night, fasting and praying. After the pair of pigeons or turtle-doves had been offered as prescribed in the Law, she confirmed the prophecy of Simeon that this was the child to whom Israel looked for the liberation of Jerusalem.
The comment on Simeon by Sir Robert A. Falconer, then president of the University of Toronto, in the *New Standard Bible Dict.,* ed by Jacobus, Nourse, and Zenos, N. Y.. Funk & Wagnalls, 1926, p 848, is of interest. He describes him as a spiritually-minded man who "was supernaturally illumined ['This man was upright and devout, one who watched and waited for the restoration of Israel, and the Holy Spirit was upon him. It had been disclosed to him by the Holy Spirit that he would not see death until he had seen the Lord's Messiah' (Luke 2:25-26 NEB)]; and thus empowered to recognize in the child Jesus the expected redeemer of Israel. His conception of the true work of the Messiah was clearly molded by the picture of the servant of Jahweh in Isa 42:7 and 52:12 - 53:13. This he embodies in the poetic address known in liturgical lore as the *Nunc Dimittis,* and in the supplementary words to Mary (v 34). Simeon was one of the 'Pious' who were 'looking for the consolation of Israel'. They also constituted a party at this time, though, unlike the Zealots, they were without political aims, and, submissive to the will of Jehovah (and they were spoken of frequently as 'the meek,' 'the humble'), they waited for his salvation. This devout element had persisted in Israel from the time of the earlier prophets (Amos 2:6), although it finds recognition especially in the Psalms and later prophets (Psalms 22:26, 35:10, 68:10, Isa 41:17), where the 'poor' — i.e., the godly poor — though grievously oppressed by a cruel aristocracy or a foreign enemy and forming only a small minority, represent the ideal Israel, and hope for speedy deliverance by Jehovah."

others who used the form of public worship of their day. Such
an extension is most impertinent and no less absurd than if
I should infer from Paul's condemnation of the Galatians for
returning to Jewish ceremonies that he thereby condemned
Moses and all the prophets as foolish for using such things.
Arnoldus becomes impertinent in his extreme arguments because he ignores the different dispensations of the times.

CEREMONIAL WORSHIP WAS A CONCESSION TO THOSE INCLINED TOWARD IDOLATRY

Although spiritual worship may have been, and no doubt
was, practiced in great simplicity by many under the law, it
does not follow that all of these ceremonies that were used were
without superstition. Even though they were a dispensation of
God to the Jews, this is still true. For they were not given because they were essential for true worship. Neither were they
given as necessary in themselves for the transmission and maintenance of a holy fellowship between him and his people. On
the contrary, they were a concession to those who were inclined
toward idolatry.

Then, in this as in other things, the substance was enjoyed
under the law by those who were truly spiritual. But it was
veiled, and surrounded with many rites and ceremonies which
are by no means lawful for us under the gospel.

A JOINT AND VISIBLE FELLOWSHIP IS NECESSARY

¶III. Even though the proposition says that true worship
is not limited to times, places, or persons, this should not be
misunderstood as meaning the discontinuance of all set times
and places for worship. God forbid that I should entertain
such an opinion.

Furthermore, we are not of those who forsake assembling
altogether. We have certain times and places in which we diligently meet together to wait upon God and worship him. What
is more, we cannot be driven from this practice by the threats
or persecutions of men. We consider it necessary for the people
of God to meet together as long as they are clothed with this
outward tabernacle. We concur with our persons, as well as
our spirits, in believing that the maintenance of a joint and visible fellowship, the bearing of an outward testimony for God,
and the sight of the faces of one another are necessary. When
these are accompanied by inward love and unity of spirit, they
tend greatly to encourage and refresh the faithful.

THE SPIRIT OF GOD SHOULD MOTIVATE
PARTICULAR ACTS OF WORSHIP DIRECTLY

The limitation that we condemn is the setting up of a particular man to preach and pray merely by human motivation. When the people of God meet together, it is the Spirit of God which should be the direct activator, mover, persuader, and influencer in particular acts of worship. The Spirit is limited in his operations when everyone except a single person is excluded from even so much as believing that he should wait for God's Spirit to move him in such matters. Thus the very thing which should quicken them is neglected. Instead of waiting to feel the pure breathings of God's Spirit in order to obey them, they are led merely to depend on the preacher and to listen to what he will say.

[These professional preachers say that worship is over when they have said their sermon and offered their humanly inspired prayers.] Their people do not come together to wait for the inward motions or operations of his Spirit. Nor do they pray as they feel the Spirit breathing through and in them, or as the present condition and state of their hearts may require. They do not preach as God's Spirit gives utterance and in such a way as to refresh weary souls. They do not allow God to prepare people's hearts by his Spirit, or wait for the preacher to be given what may be fit and seasonable for them.

THE UNFRUITFULNESS OF CUSTOMARY WORSHIP

Instead, the preacher fills the space of an hour with what he has hammered together in his study. It is done in the strength of his own will and from his own human wisdom and learning. He steals words of truth from the letter of the scriptures, and patches these together with quotations or thoughts from other men's writings until he has enough to keep him speaking for the full hour. This he declaims haphazardly without any consideration for the condition of the people. When he has concluded his sermon, he also says a prayer of his own and then the business is at an end. The present condition of the nations offers sufficient proof of the unfruitfulness of such customary worship. It is thoroughly unacceptable to God and unprofitable to those who participate.

ALL DAYS ARE ALIKE HOLY IN THE SIGHT OF GOD

It should be quite apparent, then, that what we are opposed to is not set times for worship even though that is what

Arnoldus nevertheless alleges in Sect. 45. He unnecessarily offers to prove what is not denied. However, since these times
are merely approved for convenience, we cannot agree with the
Catholics that these days are holy and urge people to a superstitious observance of them as such. We are persuaded that all
days are alike holy in the sight of God.[7] And although it is
not my present purpose to undertake a long digression over the
debate among Protestants about the first day of the week, commonly called the Lord's day, nevertheless, since it is appropriate
at this point, I will briefly interpret our understanding of it.

THE FIRST DAY OF THE WEEK

¶IV. Since there is no basis for it in scripture, we cannot
be so superstitious as to believe either that the Jewish sabbath
continues now or that the first day of the week is its antitype,
or the true Christian sabbath. We believe with Calvin that a
spiritual interpretation is more important.[8] For that reason
we do not feel morally obligated by the fourth Commandment,
or otherwise, to keep the first day of the week any more than
any other day, or that there is any holiness inherent in it.

However, it is necessary for some particular time to be set
apart for the faithful to meet together and wait upon God. It
is also fitting for them to be freed from their outward affairs at
certain times. Both reason and equity recognize the right and
privilege of servants and even beasts to have a time of ease al-

---

[7] The Quaker "testimony against the keeping of days" was an abolition of the new moons, sabbaths, and festivals instituted in Num 10:10,
which the Lord was so tired of in Isa 1:13-14, and elsewhere in the OT.
Paul states in Col 2:16-17 RSV: "Let no one pass judgment on you . . .
with regard to [the observance of] a festival or a new moon or a sabbath.
These are only a shadow of what is to come; but the substance belongs to
Christ." Also pertinent are Rom 14:5-6, Gal 4:10-11, and Heb 8:5-13.

One day was emphasized by the Quakers no more than another, that
all might be, as Barclay's statement says, "holy in the sight of God." Anyone who has ever stopped to ponder the significance of "Christmas and
Easter Christians" (i.e., those who attend only on those occasions) realizes
that the emphasis of these great festivals does become a substitute for day-
by-day holiness and service to God.

Even now a few Quakers still refer to the day "which some call Christmas" and simply say, as the Bible does, First-day [of the week] for the
assigned day of worship. — ED.

[8] Calvin says, *Inst.* II, 8, 28: "The early fathers customarily called
this commandment [the Fourth] a foreshadowing because it contains the
outward keeping of a day which, upon Christ's coming, was abolished with
the other figures [refers to Augustine]." — *Library of Christian Classics*,
Philadelphia, Westminster, 1960, vol 20, pp 394ff.

lowed them from their continual labor. The apostles and primitive Christians used the first day of the week for these purposes. We find these reasons to be sufficient for us without superstitiously straining the scriptures to find others. Many Protestants, including Calvin himself, have given evidence that nothing is to be found there. And although we meet and abstain from work on that day, it does not hinder us from also having meetings for worship at other times.

PURE AND SPIRITUAL WORSHIP

¶V. According to the knowledge of God which has been revealed to us by his Spirit, we consider it our duty to demonstrate the pure and spiritual worship which the Lord has brought about in this day through a greater dispensation of light. This is the worship that is acceptable to God and faithful to the testimony of Christ and his apostles. It is also our duty to testify against manifest superstition and to deny not only idolatry but all formal will-worship[9] which does not stem from the power of God. Nevertheless, we do not deny the entire worship of all who have borne the name of Christians even in the apostasy. God forbid that we should be so devoid of charity as to maintain that God had never heard their prayers or accepted any of them. The latter part of the proposition shows the contrary.

Nevertheless, this is not justification for continuing in this darkness and error. Merely because God pitied some who were in Babylon is no reason to refuse to come out of Babylon when God reveals how. The Roman Catholic Mass and Vespers[10] I

[9] Col 2:23 KJ: "Which things have indeed a show of wisdom in will-worship, and humility, and neglecting of the body; not in any honor to the satisfying of the flesh."
Or as NEB has it: "That is to follow merely human injunctions and teaching. True, it has an air of wisdom, with its forced piety, its self-mortification, and its severity to the body; but it is of no use at all in combating sensuality."

[10] It is difficult to understand why Barclay coupled the Mass and Vespers. Roman Catholic worship has become so Mass-centered that we are apt to forget the Divine Office, which was the obligatory vocal prayer of the Western Church, recited by priests, religious, and clerics, probably as Eucharistic preparation before great feasts. By the end of the 5th c., it consisted in monastic usage of the "Night Office (Matins)" and the seven "Day Hours" — Lauds, Prime, Terce, Sext, Nones, Vespers, and Compline.
At the Reformation, their place was taken in the Church of England by the two offices of Morning and Evening Prayer (Matins and Evensong). — O.D.C.C., pp 978-979. See also fn p 241 for a less polemical view.

believe are abominable idolatry and superstition as far as their content is concerned. So do the Protestants. Yet neither I nor they will affirm that men of upright heart have not been heard by God or accepted by him because they were zealous in the practice of these.

THE ROMAN CATHOLIC MYSTICS KNEW THE LOVE OF GOD

Who can deny that Bernard, Bonaventure, Tauler, Thomas a Kempis[11] and many others have both known and tasted the love of God and have felt the power and virtue of God's Spirit working with them for their salvation? But this is no reason not to forsake and deny the superstitions they practice.

COMMON PRAYER IS SOMETIMES ACCOMPANIED BY GOD'S POWER AND PRESENCE

The Calvinistic Presbyterians considerably upbraid the formality and deadness of the Episcopalian and Lutheran liturgies, and, I would add, not without reason. Yet they will not deny that there have been some good men among them. And they wouldn't dare to refuse to say what a good step it represented to translate the public prayers into the vernacular.[12] This was

---

[11] Bernard of Clairvaux (1090-1153), an abbot of the Cistercian Order whose "saintliness and personality rather than the force of his intellect made him so powerful in the Europe of his day." Above all, his faith was "inspired by the sublimest mysticism." He believed that "prayer, preaching, and the life of self-denial and worship should be the *militia* of Church and state, monk and layman, alike." — *O.D.C.C.*, pp 160-161.

Bonaventure (1221-1274), a theologian of the Franciscan Order, "emphasized that all human wisdom was folly when compared with the mystical illumination which God sheds on the faithful ..." — *O.D.C.C.*, p 184.

Johann Tauler (c. 1300-1361), a German Dominican mystic who probably came under the influence of Meister Eckhart and Henry Suso at Strasbourg, where he entered the Order of Preachers in 1315. He was also closely associated with the Friends of God at Basle. (See biog fn p 192.)

Thomas à Kempis (c. 1380-1471), best known as the author of the *Imitation of Christ* (although, according to *Col. Encyc.*, Gerard Groote may have written it). A widely-sought spiritual advisor, his writings are all pervaded by the devotional spirit which finds its classical expression in the *Imitation*. — *O.D.C.C.*, p 1354.

[12] The Anglican *Book of Common Prayer* issued in 1549 owed much to Thomas Cranmer who wanted to simplify and condense the Latin services of the medieval church and produce a single volume in English as a convenient, comprehensive, and authoritative guide for priest and people. The way had been paved by the (Latin) Sarum Breviary (1543), the Litany in English (1544), and the Order of the Communion (1548), which was an English supplement to the Latin Mass.

The American Book of Common Prayer, ratified in 1789 and still in use in 1965, has been changed only in minor details, other than the substitution of the KJ version of Gospel and Epistle texts. — *O.D.C.C.*, p 318.

acceptable to God even though they continued to use the liturgy, and it was sometimes accompanied by his power and presence. However, the Presbyterians do not conclude from this that common prayers should still continue.

Likewise, although we confess that there have been those who were upright in heart among both Catholics and Protestants, through the mercy and wonderful condescension of God, in general, we cannot approve of their way for that reason. And it does not constitute a reason for not progressing to approval and support of the spiritual worship to which the Lord is calling everyone, and to testifying against whatever stands in its way.

ASSEMBLY FOR PUBLIC WORSHIP IS EVERYONE'S DUTY

¶VI. Coming to the controversial part, we consider it everyone's duty to be diligent in assembling together for public worship. What we have stood for and continue to stand for in this matter even our enemies in Great Britain can bear witness, although they have used every means at their disposal to hinder us from assembling together to worship God.[13]

IT IS A TIME FOR WAITING UPON GOD

When assembled, it should be the common task of one and all to wait upon God. It should be a time for turning away from one's own thoughts and for suspending the imagination in order to feel the Presence of the Lord in the midst and to know a true gathering in his name according to his promise. Then, when everyone is thus gathered, and all meet together inwardly in their spirits, as well as outwardly in their persons, the secret power and the virtue of life are known to refresh the soul. It is there that the pure motions and breathings of God's Spirit are felt to arise.

As words of declaration, prayers, or praises arise from these promptings of the Spirit, the acceptable worship is known which edifies the church and is pleasing to God. No one limits the Spirit of God in such worship or brings forth his own laboriously assembled ideas. But everyone will state whatever the Lord has placed in his heart. And it will not be uttered from man's own will or wisdom, but in the evidence and demonstration of the Spirit and of power.

Yes, even when a word has not been spoken, true spiritual worship has been performed and the body of Christ has been

13 See p 270-272.

edified. Indeed it can and often does happen that many of our meetings take place without the utterance of a single word. Yet our souls have been greatly edified and refreshed, and our hearts wonderfully overcome with the secret sense of God's power and Spirit, which has been ministered without words from one vessel to another.

This seems truly strange and incredible to the person who thinks only in physical rather than spiritual terms. He will be apt to consider the time lost when nothing happens that is obvious to the outward senses. Therefore I shall dwell a little on this subject, as one who can speak from his own experience rather than hearsay. This wonderful and glorious dispensation has so much more of the wisdom and glory of God in it because it is contrary to the nature of man's spirit, will, and wisdom.

SILENT WAITING IS CONTRARY TO
NATURAL WILL AND WISDOM

¶VII. Nothing could be more unlike the natural will and wisdom of human beings than this silent waiting upon God. It can only be attained and correctly understood when man is able to set aside his own wisdom and will and is content to be completely subject to God.

IT IS ONLY PRACTICED BY THOSE
UNSATISFIED BY CEREMONIES AND OBSERVANCES

It is only preached and practiced by those who are unable to find satisfaction for their weary and afflicted souls in outward ceremonies and observances. They are those for whom words, the best and purest words, even the words of scripture, may not offer such solace. For the life, power, and virtue which make such things effective, may be lacking. They are those who, of necessity, had to give up all externals and be silent before the Lord.

"The Lord will give you the bread you need and the water for which you thirst."

"No longer will your Teacher hide himself, but with your own eyes you shall see your Teacher, while from behind, a voice shall sound in your ears: 'This is the way; walk in it,' when you would turn to the right or to the left;" (Isa 30:20-21 Cath-CCD). Being directed to that inward principle of light and life in yourself, as your most excellent Teacher who will not "hide himself," you will become taught thereby to wait upon God in the measure of life and grace received from him. You will cease being forward, and acting and speaking from your own natural will and understanding, and will wait to feel this inward seed of life. As it moves, you will move with it, and be actuated by its power, and you will be influenced by it, whether it is to pray, preach, or sing.

EACH WORSHIPPER RETIRES INWARDLY TO THE MEASURE OF GRACE IN HIMSELF

From this principle of being silent and not doing God's work until actuated by God's light and grace in the heart, the manner of sitting together and waiting upon the Lord together came about naturally. For many who followed these principles and who met together in the pure fear of the Lord, did not immediately apply themselves to speaking, praying, or singing for fear of acting beyond their leading and from their own wills. Each one made it his work to retire inwardly to the measure of grace in himself, not only being silent in words but even abstaining from all of his own thoughts, mental images, and desires. Thus watching in holy dependence upon the Lord, and meeting together not only outwardly in the one place, but inwardly in the one Spirit, and in the one name of Jesus, it is his power and virtue that they thereby come to enjoy.

As it prevails in every individual, it becomes like a flood of refreshment and extends over the whole meeting. Since man, the human element, and human wisdom are denied and chained down in every individual, God is exalted. His grace has dominion in each heart. His name[14] comes to be one in all, and his

[14] Reverence for the Name of Jesus has been largely lost in Quakerism as well as in Protestantism, although the special place for such devotions in Roman Catholicism is illustrated by the prominence of Holy Name Societies. Devotion to the Holy Name was popularized in the 15th c. by Bernardino of Sienna and Giovanni Capistrano.

The Name of Jesus is used in the NT as a synonym for Jesus himself, to denote his character and authority. — ED. and *O.D.C.C.*, p 397.

George Fox used it in the NT sense in numerous references to the fact "that there is no salvation in any other name under heaven" (*Works*, 1837 ed, vol 5, p 87); see also his *Letter to the Governor of Barbadoes.* "The place of your meeting is in the Name of Jesus" and there is "no safety out of his name, their strong tower" (Kent MS ii, 8, 53F and 8, 54F, from Henry Cadbury's *Annual Catalogue of George Fox's Papers*, Philadelphia, Friends Book Store, 1939, p 105). "Holy is the Lord's name above every other name, and his name is an ointment and a strong tower, and precious." (Headley MSS, p 42). — The Fox quotations were contributed by Lewis Benson.

glory breaks forth and covers all. There is such holy awe and reverence upon every soul that anything which is not in accord with the life would disappear under this subtle judging. If man's natural part, or his wisdom, should arise in anyone it would soon be chained down. When, because of a breaking forth of this power, anyone is constrained to utter a sentence of exhortation or praise, or to breathe to the Lord in prayer, all are alive[15] to it. For the same life in them answers to it "as in water face answers to face" (Prov 27:19 RSV).

THE WORLD NEITHER KNOWS NOR UNDERSTANDS THIS DIVINE AND SPIRITUAL WORSHIP

This is the divine and spiritual worship which the world neither knows nor understands and the vulture's eye cannot see.[16] Yet many and great are its advantages. My soul and many others have tasted of them,[17] and others who seriously

---

[15] Barclay used "sensible," implying a sixth sense.

[16] "There is a path which no fowl knoweth, and which the vulture's eye hath not seen ... But where shall wisdom be found? And where is the place of understanding? ... God understandeth the way thereof, and he knoweth the place thereof ... and unto man he said, Behold, the fear of the Lord, that is wisdom; and to depart from evil is understanding." (Job 28:7, 12, 23, 28 KJ).

[17] Descriptions of the meeting for worship are numerous in Quaker literature. Probably most of the more than 1,000 Quaker Journals, recounting the religious experiences of average men and women, contain some material on it, and numerous other attempts have been made to express the inexpressible. Barclay has done extraordinarily well here. Another example may be of interest:
"Whilst waiting upon the Lord in silence, as we often did for many hours together, with our hearts toward him, being stayed in the light of Christ from all fleshly motions and desires, we often received the pouring down of his Spirit upon us, and our hearts were made glad, and our tongues loosened, and our mouths opened, and we spoke with new tongues, as the Lord gave us utterance, and his Spirit led us, which was poured upon sons and daughters. Thereby things unutterable were made manifest, and the glory of the Father was revealed. Then we began to sing praises to the Lord God Almighty, and to the Lamb, who had redeemed us to God, and brought us out of [the] bondage of the world, and put an end to sin and death ... and mighty and wonderful things hath the Lord wrought for us, and by us, by his own outstretched arm ... Being prepared of the Lord, and having received power from on high, we went forth as commanded of the Lord ... We sounded the word of the Lord, and did not spare; and caused the deaf to hear, the blind to see, and the heart that was hardened to be awakened; and the dread of the Lord went before us and behind us, and took hold of our enemies." — I am indebted to Edmund Goerke for this "Epistle to the Reader," by Edward Burrough (1633-1663), prefixed to George Fox's *The Great Mystery* ... (1659).

apply themselves could also. For when people are thus gathered together, they do not merely meet to hear men, or depend upon them, but they are inwardly taught to dwell with their minds on the Lord and to wait for his appearance in their hearts (Isa 10:20 and 26:3 RSV).[18] Thus the forwardness of the spirit of man is prevented from mixing itself with the worship of God. The form of this worship is completely naked and devoid of all outward and worldly splendor. Any occasion for the superstitious or idolatrous exercise of man's wisdom has no place here.

In the inward quietness and withdrawal of the mind, the witness of God arises in the heart, and the light of Christ so shines that the soul becomes aware of its own condition. Many share in this common effort and there is inward travail and wrestling. To the extent that there is an abiding in grace, there is an overcoming of the power and spirit of darkness. Often we are greatly strengthened and renewed in mind and spirit without a word being spoken. We enjoy and possess the holy fellowship and communion of the body and blood of Christ by which the inward man is nourished and fed (and by which you will "be renewed in the spirit of your minds, and put on the new nature, created after the likeness of God in true righteousness and holiness" (Eph 4:23-24 RSV). And this is the reason we do not dote upon outward water, and bread, and wine in our spiritual things.

AS TRUTH BECOMES DOMINANT IN THEIR SOULS THEY SPEAK UNFALTERINGLY

When many are thus gathered together they grow in the strength, power, and virtue of truth. As truth becomes victorious and dominant in their souls, they receive an utterance and speak unfalteringly for the edification of their brethren. The pure life has a free passage through them and what is spoken in that manner truly edifies the body.

The divine strength that is communicated by meeting together in that fashion and by waiting in silence upon God is very evident. Sometimes a person will come in who has not been vigilant and whose mind is restless, or who comes in suddenly from the rush of worldly business and therefore is not gathered with the rest. As soon as he retires inwardly, the

---

[18] "In that day the remnant of Israel and the survivors of the house of Jacob will no more lean upon him that smote them, but will lean upon the Lord, the Holy One of Israel, in truth." And: "Thou dost keep him in perfect peace, whose mind is stayed on thee, because he trusts in thee."

power which has already been raised in good measure by the whole meeting will suddenly lay hold upon his spirit. In a wonderful way it will help to raise up the good in him and will give birth to a sense of the same power. It will melt and warm his heart in the same way that a man who is cold feels warmth when he approaches a stove, or a flame takes hold in some small combustible material that is nearby.

SOMETIMES LIFE IS MINISTERED WITHOUT WORDS

If it should happen that several of those who are meeting together should begin to stray in mind and depart from the grace that is in them, even though they are outwardly silent, and someone comes in, or is present, who is watchful and in whom the life has been raised to a great measure, he will feel a secret travail for the others. It will be a sympathetic response to the seed which is oppressed in them and kept from rising by their meandering thoughts. If he remains faithful and waits in the light, continuing this divine work, God often answers this hidden travail and works through the breathings of his own seed in such persons. Then the rest find themselves secretly smitten without words. The faithful person becomes like a midwife whose inward travail brings forth the life in them. He is like a pump which brings up water by the bucketful when it has been primed with a cup or two. The useless wandering of the imagination is discontinued and the life becomes raised in all. Those who have been helped are aware that such a person has ministered life to them without words.

THE POWER OF DARKNESS MAY BE CHAINED DOWN
BY THE SECRET STRENGTH OF THE GATHERING

Occasionally someone rude or wicked will come into a silent meeting with the intention of being mocking or of doing mischief. If the meeting is gathered into the life and raised to a good measure, it will strike terror in such a person and he will feel unable to resist. By the secret strength and virtue of the gathering, the power of darkness in him will be chained down. If his day of visitation has not expired, the measure of grace in him may be reached to and lifted up for the redemption of his soul. We have frequently witnessed this since God gathered us as a people, in such a way that many believe it renews the story told in 1 Sam 10:11 RSV: "And when all who knew him before saw how he prophesied with the prophets, the people said to one another, 'What has come over the son of

Kish? Is Saul also among the prophets?'" Many have become
convinced of the truth[19] in this fashion.

IT WAS "BY BEING MYSTERIOUSLY REACHED BY THIS LIFE THAT I WAS CONVINCED"

In part, this is how I came to be a true witness. For it was
not by the strength of arguments, or by the formal discussion
of each doctrine in order to convince my understanding, that I
came to receive and bear witness to the truth. Rather it was
by being mysteriously reached by this life. For when I came
into the silent assemblies of God's people, I felt a secret power
among them, which touched my heart. And as I gave way to
it, I found the evil in me weakening, and the good lifted up.
Thus it was that I was knit into them and united with them.
And I hungered more and more for the increase of this power
and life until I could feel myself perfectly redeemed.

---

[19] "Convincement" preceded repentance (or "self-conviction") in the
early Friends' consideration of the way in which one became a follower
of Christ.

In a sense, it was a matter of being convinced, not only intellectually
but also in the heart and by the power of the Spirit, of the truth of
Christianity.

"Conversion," which involved a conscious turning toward God, sometimes followed, but for others it did not. Fox refers to "some ... that
had been formerly convinced of truth, but were not come into obedience
to it" (The 8th [Bi-Centenary] ed of *The Journal of George Fox*, London,
1902, vol 2, p 282). Elsewhere he refers to "such as have been convinced
of God's truth, but have not lived in it."

The terms translation, regeneration, redemption, and remission of sins
also occur in Fox (the last term only once). They do not appear sharply
defined, but intermixed, and the following (op cit, vol 1, p 346) is representative: "The way ... is Christ ... in and through whose power, light,
and life, conversion, regeneration, and translation are known from death
to life, from darkness to light, and from the power of Satan to God
again. These are members of the True Church."

Another from the Headley Mss, p 318 (8, 98F), is also of interest: "Conversion is from darkness to the light, and from death to life, and from
vice to virtue, and from ungodliness to godliness, and from unrighteousness to righteousness, and from the power of Satan to God; and of all
false ways, worships, and teachers to the true way and teacher and church
which Christ is the head of. So conversion is a work of the power and
Spirit of Christ."

Some modern Quaker usage has oversimplified this, referring only to
"convincement" and disdaining the use of "conversion," which some other
religious groups have abused into a sort of "catching" of instant religion.
The Friends refer instead to "convincement" as the initial step on the
long road to Christian perfection. — Lewis Benson is my source for much
of this note and the references to Fox.

THIS IS THE SUREST WAY TO BECOME A CHRISTIAN

Indeed, this is the surest way to become a Christian. Later, the knowledge and understanding of principles will not be lacking. That will grow as it is needed. It will be the natural fruit of this good root, and such knowledge will not be barren or sterile. This is the way in which we would like all who come among us to be proselyted. Even if thousands were to be convinced intellectually of the truths that we maintain, if they could not feel this inward life, and their souls did not turn away from unrighteousness, they would add nothing to us. For this is the bond by which we become "one spirit with him" (1 Cor 6:17 Cath-CCD) and so with one another. Without this no one can worship with us.

In fact, if anyone should come among us and speak ever so true things and say them with ever so excellent words, it would not edify us if it were not said purely from such understanding and convincement of the truth as he might have. If this life were lacking, he would merely be as "sounding brass, or a tinkling cymbal;" (1 Cor 13:1).

JOINT FELLOWSHIP AND COMMUNION

¶VIII. When we meet together, our purpose and our form of worship is to watch and wait for God to draw us inward and away from all visible things. And when everyone has arrived at that state, he finds that the good has risen over the evil and the pure over the impure. God not only reveals himself and draws near to each individual but is in the midst of the group as well. Each one partakes not only of the particular strength and refreshment which comes from the good in himself, but shares with that of the whole body. Being a living member of the body, he has joint fellowship and communion with all. If this form of worship is continued faithfully, it becomes easy, although it is very difficult at first. Man's roving imagination and unceasing worldly desires are not easily silenced.

THE GOOD SEED HAS A CATHARTIC EFFECT UPON THE SOUL

But often, when the desire to wait upon him is truly present, the Lord shows compassion. In spite of any difficulty with unsteadiness of mind, he causes his power to break forth with great strength in those who turn toward him. When the conscious mind sinks down, it waits for the appearance of life, which the power of darkness in the soul wrestles and works against; then as the good seed arises it will be found to have a

cathartic effect on the soul.[20] This will be especially true if the
weak person is in the company of many others in whom the life
has achieved greater dominion. There will be an inward striving in the soul that will be as mysterious as the striving of Esau
and Jacob in Rebecca's womb.

FROM THIS INWARD TRAVAIL
THE LIGHT WILL ALWAYS BREAK THROUGH

From this internal travail the light will always break
through, unless the soul yields its strength to the darkness. The
agony of the soul may be so painful that it will even have its
external effect. Frequently, the body is greatly shaken, and
there are many groans, sighs, and tears. Sometimes even the
pangs of a woman in labor will lay hold upon it.

Sometimes the enemy works strongly against a whole meeting, spreading and propagating his dark power and drawing
the minds of those who are met away from the life that is in
them. But as they begin to sense this power that works against
them, and wrestle with it in the armor of light, the power of
God sometimes breaks forth in the whole meeting. Then the
inward struggle is like the onset of two contrary tides. Every

---

[20] This psychological analysis of what takes place seems surprisingly
modern. There has been no interpolation in this sentence, other than the
word "conscious" before mind, which was thoroughly justified by the context. The original words were: "And when the mind sinks down, and
waits for the appearance of life, and that the power of darkness in the
soul wrestles and works against it, then the good seed, as it ariseth, will
be found to work as physic in the soul" (1906 ed, p 341).

A psychological study of the interpersonal relationships in a Quaker
meeting for worship is appended to *Democracy and the Quaker Method*,
by Francis E., Beatrice E., and Robert S. W. Pollard, N. Y., Philosophical
Library, 1950. In addition to the analogy to the therapeutic groups organized by psychiatrists it continues (pp 148-149): "The deliberate and effective use by Friends of group experience at other than primitive levels
suggests that the help it gives in moral development is in promoting the
integration of personality. . . . It seems that Quaker Meetings more fully
than most groups accept individuals as they are, without foregoing their
right to judge conduct as such. Under this sort of handling, the disabling
tension of guilty feelings is relaxed. Recent study of group therapy suggests that this attitude on the part of a group is even more effective than
on the part of an individual, for example a priest or a parson. Groups
even faster than individual therapists can often help people to achieve a
reasonable balance of personality. Not until this is achieved on the level
where a person is (and not where you would like him to be) is the way
open for advance to an equilibrium at a higher level. It is these parts of
the psychological mechanism which Friends have probably always been
using."

More on this is also to be found in section 10 of Proposition XI.

individual is strongly exercised as in a day of battle. Most, if not all, of those present will tremble and their bodies will move, but as the power of truth prevails, their pangs and groans will end with a sweet sound of thanksgiving and praise.

It was from this that the name of Quakers,[21] that is, 'Tremblers', was first reproachfully applied to us. Although it was not of our choosing we are not ashamed of it, but on the contrary have cause for rejoicing because we know this power. For there have been many times when it has laid hold of our opponents and made them yield and join with us in confessing the truth. This often happens before they have any clear or coherent knowledge of our doctrines. Many have sometimes been convinced in this way at a single meeting. And sometimes this power also reaches little children, performing a wonderful work in them, which causes many to ponder and be astonished.

MANY EXPERIENCES HAVE BEEN TRULY BLESSED

¶IX. There are many experiences that have been truly blessed that have occurred in this silence and in this manner of worship which I could relate. But I do not want to commend silence so much that we appear to have bound ourselves to a law that would exclude praying or preaching. Not at all. Our worship consists neither in words nor in silence as such, but in a holy dependence of the mind upon God. For such dependence, it is necessary to begin with silence until the words can

---

[21] This is a matter on which there has been some difference of opinion, although Braithwaite seems to support Barclay. Previously Friends had been chiefly referred to as Children of the Light.

Referring to the 1651 imprisonment of the founder of Quakerism, for violation of the Blasphemy Act of 1650, he says: "Before leaving the Derby imprisonment there is one last point to note. When examined before the magistrates Fox and his followers were called Quakers by Gervase Bennett, and the derisive name at once came into vogue... Fox says that Justice Bennett gave the nickname because Fox had bidden them tremble at the name of the Lord. Barclay, on the other hand, tells us that the name came from the trembling of Friends under the powerful working of the Holy Spirit. There is no real inconsistency between the two accounts. Fox gives the words of his own which led to Bennett's retort, but Barclay correctly states... what must have been in Bennett's mind when he applied the scornful epithet to Fox. The name almost at once found its way into print in a tract published in London early in 1652 called 'The Pulpit Guarded with XVII Arguments.' "

The tract refers to the many sects "now abroad" and on p 29 enumerates: "Enthusiasts, Seekers, Shakers, Quakers, Ranters, etc." — William C. Braithwaite, *The Beginnings of Quakerism*, 2nd ed rev by Henry J. Cadbury, Cambridge University Press, 1961, pp 57-58.

be brought forth which arise from God's Spirit. God does not fail to move his children to bring forth words of exhortation or prayer when they are needed. As a consequence, very few of the numerous gatherings and meetings of those who are convinced of truth take place without someone or other being raised by God to minister to his brethren. There are few meetings that are completely silent. When many are met together in this one life and name they are very naturally and frequently stimulated to prayer and the praise of God, and they quicken one another by mutual exhortation and instruction.

However, we consider a beginning period of silence to be necessary. During this time, everyone may be inwardly gathered[22] to the word and gift of grace, from which he who ministers may receive strength to bring forth what he ministers. It is also necessary so that those who listen may develop a sense of discernment between the precious and the base. It is necessary for all, so they will not rush into the exercise of such things as soon as the bell rings, the way other Christians do.

A MEETING MAY BE GOOD AND REFRESHING ALTHOUGH NOT A WORD HAS BEEN AUDIBLY SPOKEN

Yes, and we do not doubt, but know with assurance, that a meeting may be good and refreshing although not a word has been audibly spoken from the time of sitting down until the rising. Still, each one may feel life in abundance and have a

[22] A gathered meeting in Quaker parlance means (in Barclay's own words from p 253 supra: "gathered into the life and raised to a good measure." It is a meeting of high spiritual quality or the portion of a meeting in which that state has been achieved.

"In the united stillness of a truly 'gathered' meeting there is a power known only by experience, and mysterious even when most familiar." (Caroline E. Stephen, 1908)

"In the gathered meeting the sense is present that a new Life and Power has entered our midst... We are in communication with one another because we are being communicated to, and through, by the Divine Presence... We may not issue from a gathered meeting with a single crisp sentence or judgment of capsuled knowledge, yet we are infinitely more certain of the dynamic, living, working Life, for we have experienced a touch of that persuading Power that disquiets us until we find our home in Him... When one rises to speak in such a meeting one has a sense of *being used*, of being played upon, of being spoken through." (Thomas R. Kelly, 1940) — Both quotations are from *Christian Faith and Practice*, part of the *Discipline* of London Yearly Meeting, London, Headley Bros., 1960, sel .246 and 249. The Kelly quotation is originally from "The Gathered Meeting." It first appeared in *The Friend* (Philadelphia), and has just been reprinted in *The Eternal Promise*, N. Y., Harper and Row, 1966, pp 75-77.

sense of inwardly growing up into it and by it. It might be such an occasion that words could have been acceptably spoken, and spoken from the life. Yet no absolute necessity to do so is laid upon anyone. Instead, everyone may choose to possess and enjoy the Lord rather quietly and silently. This is very sweet and comforting to the soul that has learned to be gathered in this way out of all of its own thoughts and workings, and to feel the Lord bring forth both the will and the deed.

Many can declare that they have had such a blessed experience, although it is difficult for those who have not known it to receive or believe this doctrine. The proof is to be found in a perceptible experience of it, rather than by arguments. What is more, seeing is not believing, unless there has also been an enjoyment and possession of it. But for the benefit of those who might be more willing to apply themselves to its practice and experience if they were first convinced by understanding it, I will add some considerations for that purpose. In addition to what has already been said about our experience, the confirmation to be added has its foundations in both scripture and reason.

WATCHING AND WAITING ARE FREQUENTLY ENJOINED IN THE SCRIPTURES

¶X. I doubt if anyone will deny that waiting upon God and watching before him are duties incumbent upon all. They will probably also grant without question that these are a part of worship. In fact, there are hardly any other forms of worship that are commanded as frequently in the holy scriptures:

Psalm 27:14 Cath-CCD: "Wait for the Lord with courage; be stout-hearted, and wait for the Lord."

Psalm 37:7, 34 RSV: "Be still before the Lord, and wait patiently for him.... Wait for the Lord, and keep to his way."

Prov 20:22 RSV: "Wait for the Lord, and he will help you."

Isa 30:18 Cath-CCD: "Yet the Lord is waiting to show you favor, and he rises to pity you; for the Lord is a God of justice: blessed are all who wait for him!"

Hosea 12:6 RSV: "So you, by the help of your God, return, hold fast to love and justice, and wait continually for your God."

Zeph (Sophonia) 3:8 Cath-CCD: "Therefore, wait for me, says the Lord, against the day when I arise as accuser."

Mat 24:42 RSV: "Watch therefore, for you do not know on what day your Lord is coming." Mat 25:13 RSV and Cath-CCD: "Watch therefore, for you know neither the day nor the hour."

Mat 26:41 RSV and Cath-CCD: "Watch and pray that you may not enter into temptation; the spirit indeed is willing, but the flesh is weak."

Mark 13:33, 35, 37 Cath-CCD: "Take heed, watch and pray.... Watch therefore, for you do not know when the master of the house is coming ... And what I say to you, I say to all, 'Watch.'"

Luke 21:36 Cath-CCD: "Watch,[23] then, praying at all times, that you may be accounted worthy to escape all these things that are to be, and to stand before the Son of Man."

Acts 1:4-5 RSV: "And while staying with them he charged them not to depart from Jerusalem, but to wait for the promise of the Father, which, he said, 'you heard from me, for John baptized with water, but before many days you shall be baptized with the Holy Spirit.'"

Acts 20:31 NEB: "So be on the alert; remember how for three years, night and day, I never ceased to counsel each of you, and how I wept over you."

1 Cor 16:13 Cath-CCD: "Watch, stand fast in the faith, act like men, be strong."

Col 4:2 RSV: "Continue steadfastly in prayer, being watchful in it with thanksgiving."

1 Thes 5:5-6 NEB: "You are all children of light, children of day. We do not belong to night or darkness, and we must not sleep like the rest, but keep awake and sober."

2 Tim 4:5 NEB: "But you yourself must keep calm and sane at all times; face hardship, work to spread the Gospel, and do all the duties of your calling."

1 Pet 4:7 NEB: "The end of all things is upon us, so you must lead an ordered and sober life, given to prayer."

The duty of watching and waiting is often recommended with very great and very precious promises as in:

Psalm 25:3 Cath-CCD: "No one who waits for you shall be put to shame; those shall be put to shame who heedlessly break faith." Psalm 37:9 Cath-CCD: "For evildoers shall be cut off, but those who wait for the Lord shall possess the land." Psalm 69:6 Cath-CCD: "O God, you know my folly, and my faults are not hid from you. Let not those who wait for you be put to shame through me, O Lord, God of hosts. Let not those who seek you blush for me, O God of Israel."

[23] "Watch" is generally "keep awake" or "be alert" in the NEB.

Isa 42:23 RSV: "Who among you will give ear to this, will attend and listen for the time to come?"

Lam 3:25-26 Cath-CCD: "Good is the Lord to one who waits for him, to the soul that seeks him; it is good to hope in silence for the saving help of the Lord."

Isa 40:31 RSV: "They who wait for the Lord shall renew their strength, they shall mount up with wings like eagles, they shall run and not be weary, they shall walk and not faint."

How else can anyone wait upon God or watch before him than in this silence of which we have spoken? Since this is a major duty in its own right, it naturally has precedence both in kind and in time over all other forms of worship.

THE TWO NATURES OF MAN

Since this worship is not only an outward silence of the body but also an inward silence of both the imaginative and thinking portions of the mind, let us weigh this in relation to truth and to the principles and doctrines which have been previously affirmed and proved. Let us consider the two natures of man — his natural, unregenerate, and fallen state, and his spiritual and renewed condition. It is from these that the distinction between the natural or "carnal" man and the spiritual man, which the apostle Paul uses so much, is derived. The two births of the mind also result from the two seeds in man — the seeds of good and of evil.

All sorts of great and loathsome wickedness and profanity as well as hypocrisy are derived from the evil seed. Hypocrisy is what the scriptures call spiritual wickedness because it produces evil things which have the appearance of being good and hence are even more dangerous. The serpent works on the natural man and Satan transforms himself into an angel of light. That is why the scriptures so frequently and so forcefully exclude the natural man from meddling with the things of God. He is denied from taking part in such activities even though his endeavors may bring into action the most eminent of his talents and they may be performed with wisdom and eloquence.

SPIRITUAL WICKEDNESS IS OF TWO SORTS

Spiritual wickedness is of two sorts. Although both are of the same kind, and proceed from the same root, they differ in degree and are sometimes different in their subject matter. One is the contrivance of superstitions, ceremonies, observances and rites of worship which are derived from man's own ideas or insights. It is this meddling by the natural man that has been the source of all the heresies and superstitions that have developed among Christians.   The other variety of spiritual wickedness is prayer or preaching which is developed merely by the natural convictions and understanding of man.   Such action is a product of man's own strength and lacks the influence and leading of God's Spirit.

Both the substance and form of true Christianity are lacking from the first.   The second retains the form without either the life or the substance.   The Christian religion does not consist merely of belief in true doctrines.   Nor is it merely the performance of acts that are good in themselves.   If it were, the barest letter of scripture pronounced by a drunkard or a devil could be said to be Spirit and life.   I doubt if anyone would make such an absurd affirmation.   It would also follow that the power of godliness is to be found wherever the form exists. But this is exactly contrary to the words of the apostle.   For wherever the acts that are performed are evil or wicked, godliness cannot be attributed.   But more will be said about this with particular reference to preaching and prayer.

ERRONEOUS NOTIONS AND EMPTY FORMS PAVE THE WAY FOR WICKED ACTIONS

Although erroneous notions or empty forms are not as bad as wicked acts, nevertheless they pave the way for them.   For men first depart from the life and substance of true religion by perpetuating empty forms.   Having left the inward power and virtue of the Spirit as the basis for all of their actions, they retain only the semblance of the true words and these soon decay and become vitiated.

This is what has happened.   The restless and busy spirit of man could not confine itself to the simplicity and plainness of truth.   Under the pressure of the numerous ideas and creations which he introduced, there was a gradual loss of both the power and the form of godliness.   This kind of idolatry is very apt to happen again and again. Man's love of his own concepts and of the products of his own brain will prevail as long as his own natural spirit is the first author and activator of his deeds.   If he allows these to be his only guides in the worship of God, and does not wait first for another to guide and direct him, he will never perform pure spiritual worship.   He will bear, instead, the fruit of his first, fallen, natural, and corrupt root.

THE TIME HAS COME FOR THE RESTORATION
OF TRUE SPIRITUAL WORSHIP

The time that was appointed by God for the restoration of true spiritual worship through Jesus Christ has now come.[24] The outward form of worship which God decreed for the Jews was appointed for a particular time which has now come to an end. However, no set form of worship under the purer administration of the new covenant is prescribed for his children by Jesus Christ, the author of the Christian religion.[25] He merely tells them that the worship which is now to be performed is spiritual, and in the Spirit. It should be especially observed that the only order or command pertaining to worship in the entire New Testament, other than the injunction to follow the Spirit, is the general instruction to meet together. This instruction is one of our most precious possessions and it is diligently practiced by us.

[24] John 4:23 KJ: "The hour cometh, and now is, when the true worshippers shall worship the Father in spirit and in truth." The full meaning emerges better in the NEB, John 4:20-24, where Jesus is speaking to the Samaritan woman about "living water." She says: "'Our fathers worshipped on this mountain, but you Jews say that the temple where God should be worshipped is in Jerusalem.' 'Believe me,' said Jesus, 'the time is coming when you will worship the Father neither on this mountain, nor in Jerusalem. You Samaritans worship without knowing what you worship, while we worship what we know. It is from the Jews that salvation comes. But the time approaches, indeed it is already here, when those who are real worshippers will worship the Father in spirit and in truth. Such are the worshippers whom the Father wants. God is spirit, and those who worship him must worship in spirit and in truth."

[25] Barclay also stated as follows: "Those who might object that the Lord's Prayer is a prescribed form of prayer, and hence a form of worship given by Christ, should bear in mind the fact that there are no Christians who use this as their only prayer.

"Then too, it was recommended to the disciples before they had achieved any real strength, or received the gospel dispensation. He gave it to them as an example of the short prayers they should use in place of the long ones like those of the Pharisees. He did not intend it to be their sole prayer.

"It becomes obvious that this is so from the number of other prayers which the scripture mentions as being used by various members of the Church. None of them used the Lord's Prayer, nor was it used repetitively. Other words were used as the occasion required and as the Spirit gave utterance.

"The correctness of this interpretation is substantiated by Rom 8:26 NEB: 'In the same way the Spirit comes to the aid of our weakness. We do not even know how we ought to pray, but through our inarticulate groans the Spirit himself is pleading for us.'"

PRAYER, PREACHING, AND SINGING
WITH THE ASSISTANCE OF GOD'S SPIRIT

It is true that the duties of praying, preaching, and singing
are mentioned. However not a single word says in what order
to take them up. Nor does anything require them to be started
the minute Christians gather. Whenever these duties are mentioned, they are coupled with reference to the assistance, leadings, and motions of God's Spirit. Obviously this is to exclude
man from acting or moving in things spiritual by his natural
state. How, or in what way, can he exercise his first and prior
duty of waiting upon God, unless it is in silence and by bringing the natural part of himself to silence?

THE ROVING IMAGINATION MUST BE QUIETED

There is no other way to do this than to abstain from one's
own thoughts and to quiet the imagination. All of the mind's
own labors and the roving of the imagination on things that are
essentially good as well as things that are evil must be brought
to a halt. Then, when the self has been silenced, God may
speak, and the good seed may arise. Although this is difficult
for the natural man, it is so reasonable and demonstrable from
experience in other matters that it cannot be denied.

He who goes to a master for instruction will neither hear
him nor be taught by him if he does all of the talking himself.
The master would have to reprove him as untoward and intract-
able even if he were eager to learn. Instead of speaking perpetually, he would have to wait patiently in the silence and not
speak until he was commanded to do so by his master.

Wouldn't a king's servant be thought impertinent and
lacking in discretion if he didn't wait patiently and willingly
in order to answer the great prince when he speaks? Instead,
he should be watching him to determine the least motions and
inclinations of his will. Then he should be ready to act accordingly instead of deafening him with his discourse, even if that
were one of praise for him. Wouldn't it be rather ridiculous if
he ran around doing things which might be good in themselves,
but for which he had no direct order; things that other people
had been told to do at other times?

THE STILL SMALL VOICE OF THE SPIRIT

Waiting upon God can be achieved only by silencing or
discontinuing the natural part of our actions. God does not
manifest himself to the outward man or his senses as much as

he does to the inward person, that is, the soul and the spirit. If the soul is busy with its own work, and if thought and imagination stem from self-will, even though the matters they may be occupied with are good in themselves and may even be about God, the soul is thus incapacitated from discerning the still, small voice of the Spirit. Since the soul's chief function is to wait upon the Lord, it suffers greatly by this. This is no less than I would be doing if I were to cry out, and if I insisted on speaking of a concern while someone was quietly whispering into my ear the very things I needed to know the most to fulfill that concern.

The most important thing for a Christian is to crucify the natural inclinations of the human will in order to allow God to govern both his actions and his desires. That is why the Lord values profound subjection and self-denial most highly.

Some men gratify their sensual desires with lofty and exquisite speculations on religion. They often aspire to the achievement of a name or reputation in that way, or for conventional, or other non-religious reasons. Although, in time, these speculations may become pleasant and habitual, actually they may not be one bit more regenerated or inwardly sanctified in their spirits than others who gratify their lusts with acts of sensuality. Both are harmful to other persons, and sinful in the sight of God. Both demonstrate the effect of man's natural and unrenewed will and spirit.

SOME FRIGHTEN THEMSELVES AWAY FROM SIN

Some seek to frighten themselves away from sin because of the fear of punishment. Either they magnify their thoughts on death, hell, and judgment, or they dwell on the joys of heaven and multiply their prayers and other religious acts. But without the secret and inward power of God's Spirit and grace these cannot deliver them from a single iniquity. They have no more significance than the fig-leaves with which Adam attempted to hide his nakedness.

Since this is only the product of man's natural will and proceeds from self-love it is rejected by God. It is unacceptable to him since man is trying to save himself in a way other than purely by the divine seed of righteousness which God gives everyone for his grace and salvation. While he remains in that natural state, he is rejected with all of his artifices, skills, and actions. The great duty of waiting upon God has to be exercised in both inward and outward self-denial. A tranquil and unqualified dependence upon God is required. There must be a withdrawal from all of the active speculation and imagination of man's own mind. When he has been completely emptied of self, and the natural products of self-will have been thoroughly crucified, he will be fit to receive the Lord, who will brook no co-partners in power and no co-rivals for his glory.

A HOLY BIRTH TAKES PLACE

When man reaches that state, the little seed of righteousness which God has planted in his soul has a place to arise. The measure of grace and life which Christ purchased for him is freed from its burden. It is no longer crucified by the natural thoughts and figments of his imagination, but becomes a holy birth in him. It is the divine air by which man's soul and spirit become leavened. By waiting in that measure of grace and life he becomes accepted in the sight of God. He stands in his presence, hears his voice, and complies with the movings of his Holy Spirit. If any concepts are presented to his mind concerning God, or pertaining to religion, his soul may be exercised in them without impairment and with great profit both for himself and for others. These will originate with God's Spirit rather than his own self-will. This should also be the basis for the more obvious acts of preaching and praying.

WE ARE NOT OPPOSED TO MEDITATION

We are not opposed to meditation, as some have falsely concluded from our doctrine. What we are opposed to is all of the thoughts and fictions of man's will, which have been responsible for the numerous errors and heresies of the Christian religion throughout the world. It is a wonderful thing, too, when it pleases God not to exercise the thoughts or imaginations which spring from the Spirit, but to simply keep us in his holy dependence. As we persist in this, he causes his secret refreshment and the pure influx of his holy life to flow in upon us. Then we have good reason to be content, for we know from good and blessed experience that the soul is better strengthened, renewed, and confirmed in the love of God in this way than in any other. And it is better armed against the power of sin.

This is a foretaste of the real and perceptible enjoyment of God which the saints in heaven experience daily. God frequently provides it to comfort and encourage his children on

earth, particularly when they are assembled together to wait
upon him.

TWO CONTRARY POWERS EXIST

¶XI. Two contrary powers or spirits exist. There is the
power and spirit of this world, and the prince of darkness is the
ruler of all who are motivated by. this power and base their
actions upon it. There is the power and Spirit of God, and
God is the ruler of all who are motivated by this power and
base their actions upon it. Whatever thoughts a man may have,
no matter how spiritual or religious in nature they may be, as
long as his actions are motivated by his own will, in its natural
and corrupt state, rather than by the power of God, everything
he does is sinful and unacceptable to God. Both the ploughing
and the praying of the wicked are sinful (Prov 21:4 KJ).

On the other hand, it does not matter whether his acts are
of a religious or a civil kind, or even natural acts, if they are
done in the Spirit and with the power of God. Then the doer
is accepted in the sight of God and is "blessed in his deed." (Jas
1:25 Cath-CCD)

WATCHING AND WAITING SHOULD PRECEDE
PRAYER AND PREACHING

From what has been said, it is clear how foolish and impertinent it is to claim that those who preach and pray are
necessarily waiting upon God. Waiting, in itself, implies a
passive dependence, rather than activity. Some proof has already been given that prayer and preaching without the Spirit
are an offense to God, and further evidence will be offered.
Prayer and preaching by the Spirit necessarily presuppose silent
waiting, in order to feel the influence and moving of the Spirit
that lead to such actions. Furthermore, in several of the places
where there is a command to pray, watching is a specific prerequisite in preparation for it:

Mat 26:41 RSV and Cath-CCD: "Watch and pray that you
may not enter into temptation. The spirit indeed is willing,
but the flesh is weak."

Mark 13:33 RSV [Cath-CCD]: "Take heed, watch [and
pray], for you do not know when the time will [is] come."

Luke 21:36 NEB: "Be on the alert, praying at all times for
strength to pass safely through all these imminent troubles and
to stand in the presence of the Son of Man."

1 Pet 4:7 NEB: "The end of all things is upon us, so you must lead an ordered and sober life, given to prayer."

We may well conclude with considerable certainty that watching and waiting are a necessary part of the worship of God, since they are particularly commanded and recommended. Since they can only be performed properly in the inward silence when men's own thoughts and imaginative faculties have ceased, silence has to be not only a special part, but the principal part of the worship of God.

THE ENEMY CANNOT COUNTERFEIT SILENT WAITING UPON GOD

¶XII. One of the best things about this silent waiting upon God is that it is impossible for the enemy to counterfeit it. The devil cannot delude or deceive any soul in the exercise of it. In all other matters, he can mix himself with the natural mind of man and transform himself in a way that will deceive the soul. He keeps men busy with things which are probably innocent in themselves, but which prevent them from beholding the pure light of Christ, and hence from knowing distinctly what their duty is and doing it. That envious spirit knows very well how to accommodate himself in his opposition to man's eternal happiness. He fits his snares for the various dispositions and inclinations of men. He may find one who is not apt to succumb to gross sins or worldly lusts, but is in fact averse to them and religiously inclined; he can adapt himself to beguile such a person. He will allow the person's thoughts to dwell on spiritual matters. He allows his imagination to run and rushes him into working, acting, and meditating out of his own will. For he well knows that as long as the self rules, and the Spirit of God is not the principal or chief activator, man is not beyond his reach.

He can accompany the priest to the altar, the preacher to the pulpit, the zealot to his prayers. Yes, he can even accompany the doctor of divinity to his study and cheerfully allow him to work among his books. He even helps him to discover and invent subtle distinctions and cavilling questions. With these, his mind, and the minds of others through him, can be kept from heeding God's light in the conscience and from waiting upon the Lord. There is no exercise whatever that he cannot enter and secure the chief place. Many times the only way the soul can discern this is to stand still and be silent, for then he too must stand still.

Therefore, when the soul comes to this silence, and, as it were, is brought to nothingness, the devil is shut out. For he cannot abide the pure presence of God and the resplendence of his light. As long as a man's thinking or meditation is his own, he cannot be certain that the devil is not influencing him. But when he becomes wholly silent, as the pure light of God shines in upon him, then he can be positive that the devil is shut out. He cannot go beyond the imagination, as we have often perceived by experience. For he who is said to have come to the gathering together of the children of God in ancient times is not absent from our assemblies. Indeed, he can very well enter a meeting that is only silent as far as words are concerned. He can do his work either by busying minds with various thoughts and inventions or by stupefying them in such a way that he overwhelms them with a spirit of heaviness and slothfulness. But when we retire from all mental activity and turn inward, we feel that we are out of his reach. By being diligent and watchful on the one hand, yet silent and retired from all thought on the other, we abide in that sure place that is beyond him.

THE POWER AND GLORY OF GOD WILL BREAK FORTH

Sometimes the power of darkness can be sensed as it seeks to cloud and darken the mind and to completely obstruct it from pure waiting upon God. But then the power and glory of God will break forth and appear, just as the bright sun breaks through the clouds or dispels a mist.

¶XIII. Another way in which this form of worship excels is that it can neither be stopped nor interrupted by the malice of men or of devils as all other forms can. Of course the interruption and stopping of worship can be interpreted in two ways. One is to be hindered from meeting by being violently separated from one another. The other is the malicious use of tumult, noise, or confusion to distract and molest those who have been permitted to meet together. In both respects this worship surpasses all others. No matter how much people may be physically separated, when everyone is inwardly gathered to the measure of life in himself, secret unity and fellowship are enjoyed. The devil and all of his instruments can never break or hinder this.

WE HAVE SUFFERED A THOUSAND INTERRUPTIONS AND ABUSES

The statement is no less true for the other type of hindrance. We have suffered a thousand interruptions and abuses, any one of which would have been sufficient to stop any other form of Christian worship. Yet we have been able to maintain our worship uninterrupted toward God. At the same time we have afforded an example of Christian patience toward everyone. Often this has even reached and convinced those who opposed us.

There is no other form of worship which can even subsist unless it is authorized and protected by the magistrate, or the worshippers defend themselves physically. At the same time that we engage in the worship of God, we also bear the reproaches and the ignominy which, as Christ prophesied, are apt to occur to Christians frequently....

When the magistrates have been stirred up by the malice and envy of those who are against us, they have used every possible means to deter us from meeting together openly and publicly in our own houses that were rented for that purpose. Yet all of this has been in vain. For death, banishment, imprisonment, fines, beatings, whippings, and other such devilish inventions have been ineffectual. They could not terrify us into staying away from our holy assemblies.

WE HAVE BEEN JEERED, MOCKED, AND SCOFFED AT

When we have frequently purchased our liberty to meet through deep suffering, our opponents have sometimes tried another tack. They have turned loose upon us the worst and wickedest of men, the very offscourings of humankind. These have tried to provoke, weary, or molest us by every kind of inhumanity and by beastly and brutish behavior. But it has been in vain. The things they have done have been almost incredible. Indeed it is even shameful to have to speak of them among men who claim to be Christians. I, among others, have shared in the suffering. They have beaten us. They have thrown dirt and water at us. They have danced, leaped, and sung. They have said all kinds of profane and ungodly words. Dignified women and virgins have suffered violence and shameful behavior. We have been jeered, mocked, and scoffed at, and have been asked whether the Spirit had arrived yet. Many other things have happened which it would be tedious to relate.

BUT OUR SPIRITUAL FELLOWSHIP HAS NOT BEEN HINDERED

All of this has happened while we have been sitting together seriously and silently and waiting upon the Lord. But our inward and spiritual fellowship with God and with one another in the pure life of righteousness has not been hindered. On the contrary, the Lord has known of our sufferings and reproaches for his testimony's sake. He has caused his power and glory to be all the more abundant among us. He has greatly refreshed us by filling our souls with the sense of his love. We have found how true it is that: "The name of the Lord is a strong tower; the just man runs to it and is safe;" (Prov 18:10 Cath-CCD). In it, we were sheltered from receiving any spiritual harm through their malice. And we also felt that he had delivered us from the emptiness of a profession of Christianity which could bring forth such bitter and accursed fruits.

Sometimes, in the midst of that tumult and opposition, God would move one or another of us by his Spirit. He would testify of the joy we had experienced in spite of their malice, and would make a powerful declaration against their folly and wickedness. As evidence and demonstration of the Spirit, the power of truth has brought them to some degree of quietness and stillness and has stopped their impetuous streams of fury and madness. Just as Moses divided the waves of the Red Sea with his rod, so that the Israelites could pass, God has made way for us. In the midst of this raging wickedness he has allowed us to enjoy and possess him peaceably and to accomplish our worship of him. On several of these occasions, those who opposed or interrupted us have been convinced by these occurrences, and they have been gathered from persecuting us to suffer along with us.

THE YOUNG FRY OF THE CLERGY HAVE BEEN THE WORST

In order for it not to be forgotten, let it be inscribed as a reminder, that none have been busier with the beastly and brutish pranks that were used to molest us in our spiritual meetings than the young university students who were studying philosophy and the so-called divinity. Many of them were preparing themselves for the ministry. If we were to commit to writing all of the abominable things of this type that these young fry of the clergy have done, it would not be a small volume. The churches of Christ that gathered into his pure worship[26] at Oxford and Cambridge in England, and at Edinburgh

---

[26] That is, the Quaker meetings at those places. The first time that Quakers were flogged for their faith was in December, 1653, when two women, Mary Fisher, a 30-year-old "convinced" household serving maid (who was later to walk five or six hundred miles to visit the Sultan of

and Aberdeen in Scotland, where the universities are, can well bear witness.

¶XIV. Moreover, we know that in this worship we are partakers of the new covenant dispensation. We are true disciples of Christ, sharing with him in that spiritual worship which is performed in the Spirit and in truth. As he was, so are we in this world. For the worship under the old covenant had an outward glory. The temple and its ceremonies were full of outward splendor and majesty. There was an outward tabernacle, and an altar that was beautified with gold, silver, and precious stones. The sacrifices were confined to a specific place, the outward Mount Zion. Those who prayed had to pray with their faces toward the outward temple, and all of this had to be protected by an outward arm. The Jews could enjoy it only in the times of peace when they were free from the violence of their physical enemies. Whenever their enemies prevailed over them their glory was darkened, their sacrifice stopped, and the appearance of their worship was marred. That is why they complained about the destruction of the temple. It was a cause for wailing and lament and the loss was irreparable.

But Jesus Christ, who is the author of new covenant worship and who instituted it, testifies that God is not to be worshipped in this or that place, but in the Spirit and in truth. For

---

Turkey), and Elizabeth Williams, a woman of 50, decided to visit the English universities. Fox had already been pamphleteering in that direction and the women began their evangelization by addressing the undergraduates of Sidney Sussex College, Cambridge (undoubtedly along the lines of the inappropriateness of divinity training for true ministers of Christ). The students were at first content to mock and perplex their unlearned visitors with foolish questions. "The women, observing the froth and levity of their behavior, told them they were Antichrists, and that their college was a cage of unclean birds, and the Synagogue of Satan" [Rev 18:2, 2:9 and 3:9].

When they had thus been beaten off the field by their plain-spoken adversaries, the cowardly youths summoned the law to their aid. The mayor slanted his questions in an effort to bring them under the recently revived Medieval Act for the "Punishment of Rogues, Vagabonds, and Sturdy Beggars" and demanded their husbands' names. The women answered that they had no husband but Jesus Christ, and that he had sent them. "Upon this the mayor grew angry, called them whores and issued his warrant to the constable to whip them at the market-cross till the blood ran down their bodies." To their credit, the justices in the town repudiated all part in the mayor's action. — Mabel R. Brailsford, *Quaker Women 1650-1690*, London, Duckworth, 1915, pp 96-97.

inasmuch as his kingdom is not of this world, it does not consist of the wisdom, glory, or riches of this world; nor does it need them for beautification or adornment. It does not require physical power or a fleshly arm to maintain, uphold, or protect it. But it can be and is performed by those who are spiritually minded in spite of all the opposition, violence, and malice of men. Because it is purely spiritual, it is out of reach of the men who would interrupt or obstruct it, just as Jesus Christ, the author of it, enjoyed and possessed his spiritual kingdom while he was oppressed, persecuted, and rejected by men.

In spite of the malice and rage of the devil, "on that cross he discarded the cosmic powers and authorities like a garment; he made a public spectacle of them and led them as captives in his triumphal procession" (Col 2:15 NEB).

"The children of a family share the same flesh and blood; and so he too shared ours, so that through death he might break the power of him who had death at his command" (Heb 2:14 NEB).

Thus his followers are able to worship him not only without a physical arm to protect them, but they are able to do so even when they are oppressed. Since this worship is spiritual, it is defended and maintained by the power of the Spirit.

OTHER FORMS OF WORSHIP REQUIRE CIVIL PROTECTION

But where worship consists of carnal and outward ceremonies and observances, a carnal and outward arm is needed to protect it, or else it cannot exist. It is apparent that the several forms of worship of both Catholics and Protestants are of this type, rather than the true spiritual and new covenant worship of Christ. It has already been observed that they require the protection and favor of the civil power and they cannot be performed if there is the least opposition. Those worshippers do not have the patience of Jesus which would require them to serve him and worship him with suffering, ignominy, calumny, and reproach. From this have sprung all those holy wars and all of the bloodshed among Christians over their various forms of worship, as well as the monstrous approval of persecution.

THE WORSHIP ESTABLISHED BY CHRIST

¶XV. This type of worship, which is performed by the operation of the Spirit while the natural man is silent, was established by Christ, who said, John 4:23-24 NEB: "But the time approaches, indeed it is already here, when those who are real worshippers will worship the Father in spirit and in truth. Such are the worshippers whom the Father wants. God is spirit, and those who worship him must worship him in spirit and in truth." This testimony should be all the more closely observed because it is the first, the principal, and the most complete testimony that Christ gives us of the way in which his Christian worship differs from that under the law.

First he shows that the time has come when worship must be in Spirit and in truth, for the Father is seeking those who will worship him in this way. It is no longer to be a worship which consists of outward observances which man can perform at set times out of his own will and with his own power. Otherwise it would differ only in minor details from the worship performed under the law. The reason which Christ gives is the best possible justification for this type of worship. It is impossible to give any better reason than the one Christ gives, and that ought to be enough to satisfy every Christian. I refer to his statement that "*God is Spirit,* and those who worship him must worship in Spirit and in truth." This should be accepted because it is in Christ's own words. It is also so clearly reasonable that that too should be sufficient evidence of reality. For Christ gives an excellent argument by using the analogy of what should be between the object of worship and the worship directed toward it.

God is Spirit.

Therefore he must be worshipped in Spirit.

This is so obvious that it is impossible to argue with it. Indeed, it is necessary to bear in mind this analogy. For when God instituted ceremonial worship for the Jews, because that worship was outward, he saw that to have an analogous situation, it was necessary for him to condescend to them in a special manner. He dwelt between the cherubim within the tabernacle. Later, when the temple was built at Jerusalem, he made it, in a way, his habitation. He caused something to appear there as an outward manifestation of his glory and majesty. Fire from heaven consumed the sacrifices and the temple was filled with a cloud. Through these media which were visible to the physical eye, he gave a manifestation of himself which was of the same proportion as the outward worship which he had commanded them to perform.

Under the new covenant, he saw meet in his heavenly wisdom to lead his children in a path that was more heavenly and spiritual. And, in a way, it was easier and more familiar. His purpose was to disestablish outward and carnal observances in order for his worship to have an eye more for an inward glory and kingdom than an outward one. He has given us the appearance of his beloved Son, the Lord Jesus Christ, who did and does deliver us by suffering and by dying at the hands of his enemies (just as Moses delivered the Israelites out of their outward bondage by outwardly destroying their enemies). By doing so he triumphed over the devil and delivered us from him and from our inward enemies. He has also instituted an inward and spiritual worship so that God no longer tethers his people to the temple at Jerusalem or to outward ceremonies and observances. Instead, he dwells in the heart of every Christian. There, he will appear without any mediator and give directions on how to serve him with outward acts.

THE HEART OF MAN IS THE TEMPLE OF GOD

Since, as Christ argues, God is a Spirit, he will now be worshipped in the Spirit, where he reveals himself and dwells with the contrite in heart. The heart of man has become the temple of God and the place where he is to be worshipped. He will no longer dwell or be worshipped in specified outward temples. As the blessed Stephen said in Acts 7:48 Cath-CCD: "Yet not in houses made by hands does the Most High dwell."

Before the glory of the Lord descended to fill the outward temple, it was very appropriately cleaned and emptied of all polluted things. In fact, the place where the tabernacle rested was overlaid with gold, the most precious and the cleanest of metals. Before God can be worshipped in the inward temple of the heart, it must be purged of its own filth and of all of its own thoughts, and have the imagination quieted. Then it will be fit to receive the Spirit of God and to be actuated by him. Does this not lead directly to that inward silence of which we have spoken? This worship must be in truth, intimating that spiritual worship, carried out in this manner, is the only true worship, since it cannot be counterfeited or performed by a hypocrite.

CHRISTIAN MYSTICISM

¶XVI. This worship is very different from the various contrived forms that are to be found among Christians, and it may seem strange to many of them. However, it has been written about, commended, and practiced by the most pious Chris-

tians of all kinds in all ages. This can be proved by many
clear declarations of profession and practice. The name mystics has been applied to a certain group whose writings abound
with explanation and commendation of this type of worship.[27]
There are many assertions of this inward introversion and abstraction of the mind, as they speak of it, from all images and
thoughts and the prayer of the will. Indeed, they look upon
this as the height of Christian perfection.

AUGUSTINE BAKER'S *HOLY WISDOM*

Some of them, although they are professed Roman Catholics, do not hesitate to affirm:[28] "That such as have attained

[27] Although, as Anglican Dean W. R. Inge pointed out in the
Preface to the 7th ed of his *Christian Mysticism* (1932): "The great mystics are well aware that language was not made to describe these revelations, which are often formless and incapable of being reproduced; but
that God has spoken to them they know, and in general their accounts of
their journey up the hill of the Lord agree very closely. 'Seek as we have
sought, and you will see what we have seen.' "
However, he says later in the same Preface: "But we cannot insist too
strongly that the essence of mysticism — the mystical state in its purest
form — is just *prayer*, 'the elevation of the mind to God.' Let anyone who
has felt God near him when on his knees think what a perfect prayer
would be like. It need not be vocal; it is probably not petitional; it is
an act of worship, receptiveness, and self-surrender, to the Author of our
being. This is the only way to approach the subject."
But many have approached it in other ways and would define mysticism differently. The *Col. Encyc.* article is an excellent treatment in brief
compass. Fortunately there is more agreement on who the mystics are
and were. Inge says (loc cit): "The Quakers, of course, were always mystics, and made valuable contributions to the literature of mysticism; but
this sect, though its influence has been very much greater than its numbers, was and is very small. In the Roman Church, the study of mysticism
has always been encouraged."
Baron Friedrich von Hügel (1852-1925) was the great expositor of Catholic mysticism in the earlier part of this century. Although he has been
somewhat neglected recently, his *Spiritual Counsels and Letters*, ed with
an Introductory Essay by Douglas V. Steere, was published in both British
and American editions in 1964. Another article on mysticism by Douglas
Steere, a leading Quaker authority along with Howard Brinton and Rufus
Jones, is to be found in the *Handbook of Christian Theology*, Cleveland,
World Publishing, 1958. David Knowles, *The English Mystical Tradition*,
London, Burns and Oates, 1961 and 1964, is a significant Catholic study.

28 in a book called *Sancta Sophia*, published by the English Benedictines and printed at Douay in 1657, tract 1, sec 2,
cap 5, [par 10].
This is the content, but not the exact words of the original, in spite of
the quotation marks. However, it is taken out of context if the implication is drawn that these duties may be given up altogether.
F. Augustine Baker (1575-1641), who wrote it, was the author of more

this method of worship, or are aiming at it, need not, nor ought to trouble or busy themselves with frequent and unnecessary confessions, with exercising corporal labors and austerities, the using of voluntary prayers, the hearing of a number of masses, or set devotions, or exercises to saints, or prayers for the dead, or having solicitous and distracting cares to gain indulgences, by going to such and such churches, or adjoining themselves to confraternities, or entangling themselves with vows and promises; because such kinds of things hinder the soul from observing the operations of the Divine Spirit in it, and from having liberty to follow the Spirit whither it would draw her." And yet who is not aware that it is just such observances that are the very substance of the Roman Catholic religion?

Yet nevertheless it appears from this, and from many other passages which could be cited from the Catholic mystics, that they regard this worship as better than all others. They believe that those who have arrived at this form of worship do not require any other. In fact it is readily confessed[29] that all other forms and ceremonies become useless for them. They

---

than 40 treatises on the Prayer of Contemplation. A monk of the exiled English Congregation of the Order of St. Benedict, his work was methodically digested by R. F. Serenus Cressy of the same order. A new edition from the posthumous work published at Douay in 1657 was prepared by the Rt. Rev. Abbot Sweeney of the same congregation and published at London by Burns, Oates and Washbourne in 1950 and 1964.

29 in the chapter on the "Life of Baltazar Alvares," in the same *Sancta Sophia* [or *Holy Wisdom*], tract 3, sec 1, cap 7.

This chapter, correctly cited as to location, is entitled "The Doctrine of Fr. Baltazar Alvarez S. J. Defended" in the 1950 ed. Barclay probably refers to the statement: "After he had with great diligence spent about 15 years in meditation and the spiritual exercises (peculiar to his Order), and yet received but little profit to his spirit by them, being, on the contrary, tormented with extreme doubtfulness and unsatisfaction, was at last guided powerfully, by God's Holy Spirit, to give up meditation and to betake himself to a serious practice of prayer immediately in the will, by corresponding to which divine motion he presently received abundance of light, and a prefect remedy against all his anguishes and perplexities." — op cit, 1950 ed, p 384.

In fairness to the English Benedictines it should be said that Barclay's assertions are broader than those of *Sancta Sophia*, since long discipline "in the inferior degree of discoursive prayer" (p 390) is generally required "except it be when God presents souls extraordinarily by a special invitation and ennoblement; and those, likewise, that from meditation do ascend to this quiet prayer, do it by the guidance of a supernatural light, and being in it, they exercise themselves therein not by desiring or expecting revelations, but by acknowledging the divine presence in the soul and producing the foresaid holy affections to Him."

no longer perform them because they are necessary, but for the
sake of order or example.

BERNARD OF CLAIRVAUX

Therefore, although some of them shared the common
darkness of their profession, they could nevertheless state that
this spiritual worship should be retained and sought after, even
at the expense of outward ceremonies.   Hence Bernard says in
his *Epistle to William*,[30] abbot of the same order, as well as in
numerous other places in his writings: "Take heed to the rule
of God; the kingdom of God is within you." Later, while stating that the outward orders and rules of their church should
be followed, he adds: "But otherwise, when it shall happen
that one of these two must be omitted, in such a case these are
much rather to be omitted than those former: for how much
the spirit is more excellent and noble than the body, by so
much are spiritual exercises more profitable than corporal."

Is this, then, not the best form of worship?   This is the
one which the best of men in all ages and of all sects have
recommended.   It is also the most suitable for the doctrine of
Christ.   Therefore, I ask, is not this the worship which should
be followed and performed?   How much more so since God
has raised a people to testify for it, and preach it, and who are

---

[30] Bernard of Clairvaux (1090-1153), already cited twice by Barclay
(pp 19 and 247), a saint and Doctor of the Church, remained abbot of
Clairvaux all his life in spite of efforts to promote him.   His fame and
influence greatly benefitted his order, the Cistercians.   "In his lifetime
68 houses were founded out of Clairvaux alone.   He was tireless in jour-
neys to make peace, and he would undertake any mission of charity, however arduous or apparently trivial."

His works, which have had wide influence, "consist of about 330 sermons, some 500 known letters, and thirteen other prose works, or 'treatises,' some of which were originally letters or sermons.   His style, strong
and eloquent, full of biblical allusions, intensely personal and direct, has
gained him the name Mellifluous Doctor." — *Col. Encyc.*, p 191.

Etienne Gilson's *The Mystical Theology of St. Bernard* was translated
into English in 1940.   There is also a modern English translation of his
letters by B. S. James (London, 1953).

This citation may be one of the epistles addressed to William, Abbot
of St. Thierry, a close friend who inspired Bernard to write his *Apology*.
It is not 85 or 86.   On the other hand it might be the treatise *Concerning
Grace and Free Will*, which is addressed to him.   (An ed by Watkin W.
Williams was published by the SPCK in 1920.)

Bernard also wrote several epistles to William, Abbot of Rievaulx, although this is such a well-known English abbey that Barclay would certainly have referred to William's abbacy there rather than merely to his
being "of the same order."

greatly refreshed and strengthened in the very sight of the world and in spite of great opposition. They do not consider it a mystery which can be attained only by a few cloistered men and women as the mystics do. Nor do they make the mistake which the mystics do of considering it the consequence of many outward ceremonies and observances and attained only when they have become weary from· these.

THE UNRESTRICTED LOVE OF GOD

On the contrary, this worship is offered in the unrestricted love of God who is no respecter of persons. A God who was near to hear and to reveal himself as much for Cornelius the centurion and Roman, as for Simeon and Anna. A God who disclosed his glory to Mary, a poor handmaid, and to the poor shepherds, rather than to the high priests and the devout proselytes among the Jews.

In the wideness of his love, God is revealing and establishing this form of worship. He is making many poor tradespeople, even young boys and girls, witnesses of it. We beseech everyone to lay aside worship in their own wills, and the voluntary acts that are performed from their own wills and by their mere natural strength and power. We entreat them to retire from their vain thought and imagination so that they may feel the pure Spirit of God move and stir in them, and in order for them to become practicers of this acceptable worship, which is in Spirit and in truth.

SOME PREFER PRAYER OR MEDITATION

¶XVII. Some people object to this type of worship. They consider it a waste of time for someone to be doing or thinking nothing. They say that one would be better employed either in meditation upon some good subject, or else in prayer or the praise of God.

But this is not a waste of time. In fact it is absolutely necessary to wait in silence before any other duty can be acceptably performed. What is more, it is a mistake of our lower natures to imagine that God is pleased with works and acts which men perform from their own wills. The first step for a man in fearing God is to cease doing his own thinking and imagining, and to allow God's Spirit to do its work in him. For we must "cease doing evil" before we can "learn to do good" (Isa 1:16-17 Cath-CCD). One of the greatest and most dangerous evils to which men are subject is this meddling in spiritual matters with their own natural understanding. It was this that was responsible for our first parents' fall. In their desire for knowledge they were forward and meddled with things in which they not only did not have God's permission, but they acted contrary to his command.

Others ask why it is necessary to have public meetings at all if our worship consists of retiring inwardly to the Lord and feeling his Spirit arise, and then doing such outward acts as we are led to. Why can't these things be done just as well at home?

AN OUTWARD VISIBLE TESTIMONY

The answer is that God has seen fit, as long as his children are in this world, to make use of the outward senses not only for such visible acts of worship as speaking, praying, and expressing praise, but to maintain an outward, visible testimony for his name. He also causes the inward life to be more abundant when his children are diligent in assembling together to wait upon him. "As iron sharpens iron, so man sharpens his fellow man," (Prov 27:17 Cath-CCD). The mere sight of each other's faces when two persons are gathered inwardly into the life gives occasion for that life to rise secretly and pass from vessel to vessel. Many lighted candles, when gathered together in a single place, greatly augment each other's light and make it shine more brilliantly. In the same way, when many are gathered together into the same life, there is more of the glory of God. Each individual receives greater refreshment, because he partakes not only of the light and life that has been raised in him, but in the others as well.

It is for this reason that Christ has particularly promised his blessing on those who assemble together in his name, saying that "where two or three have met together" he is "there among them;" (Mat 18:20 NEB).

The author of Hebrews prohibits the neglect of this particular duty, saying that there are very dangerous and dreadful consequences for doing so. He begins by saying, Heb 10:24-26 NEB, that: "We ought to see how each of us may best arouse others to love and active goodness, not staying away from our meetings, as some do, but rather encouraging one another, all the more because you see the Day drawing near. For if we persist in sin after receiving the knowledge of truth, no sacrifice for sins remains."

THE EARLY CHRISTIANS PREACHED AND PRAYED BY THE SPIRIT

...Some claim that our manner of worshipping in silence is not to be found anywhere in the scriptures. Before answering, it should be stated that we do not make silence the only substance of our worship. Not very many meetings are completely silent. Someone is usually moved to preach, pray, or offer praise. So in this respect, our meetings must be very much like the meetings of the primitive churches that are recorded in scripture [Col 3:16, 1 Cor 14: particularly 26-40, Acts 2:42 and elsewhere — ED.]. Even our opponents admit that the early Christians preached and prayed by the Spirit. Would it be absurd to presume that at times the Spirit did not move them to perform outward acts and that at such times they were silent? Since we may conclude that they did not speak until they were moved by the Spirit, there must have been silence at some time.

In speaking of them before they received the gift of the Holy Spirit, Acts 2:1 NEB says: "While the day of Pentecost was running its course they were all together in one place." After they were "all filled with the Holy Spirit," they "began to talk in other tongues, as the Spirit gave the power of utterance." Would anyone suggest that we were inferring too much if we presumed that they were silent until they had been filled with the Holy Spirit?

For those who might urge that a silent meeting cannot be found in scripture, I would answer that even if this were so, it would not necessarily follow that it was unlawful, particularly since it is a natural presumption from other scriptural citations. The scripture does command us to meet together, and when so met, the scripture prohibits prayer or preaching except as the Spirit moves. From this, it must follow that we are to be silent when the Spirit does not impel us to such acts. Furthermore, there may have been many silent occasions among the faithful of old which were not recorded. As it was, we have enough scriptural examples to indicate that such things did exist.

For Job sat together in silence with his friends for seven days. That was really a long silent meeting! There is also Ezra 9:4, Ezek 14:1, and Ezek 20:1.[31]

_____

[31] Ezra 9:4 says that Ezra sat "appalled" RSV, "astonied" KJ, "sor-

PREPARED SERMONS CONTRASTED WITH
THE IMMEDIATE INCLINATIONS OF THE SPIRIT

¶XVIII. Preaching, as it is practiced by both Catholics and Protestants, consists of one man taking a particular section or verse of scripture and speaking about it for an hour or two. His sermon will consist of what he has studied or previously meditated upon in the privacy of his study, and what he has gathered together of his own creation or from the writings and observations of others. Then, having memorized it as a school-boy does his lesson, he brings it forth and repeats it in front of his people. The more fertile his imagination, the more industrious he is in collecting observations, the more he will be considered an able and excellent preacher if he delivers his findings with sufficient eloquence.

Against this, we say that true preaching is by the Spirit. When the faithful meet together, and are gathered to the gift and grace of God in themselves, he who ministers will be actuated by the grace which arises in himself. He should speak what the Spirit of God furnishes without paying attention to eloquence and words of wisdom. What he says should be in demonstration of the Spirit and of the power of God. If the Spirit, which recalls good things to memory, should suggest some portion of scripture, that would be appropriate. Perhaps he will be led to offer words of exhortation, advice, reproof, or instruction. Or he may be called to explain the meaning of some spiritual experience. All of this will be in agreement with the scripture, although it may not relate to, or be based upon, any particular chapter, verse, or text.

CHRIST'S PREACHING AND OURS

Let us consider which of these two types of preaching is most in accord with the precepts and practices of Christ and his apostles, or of the primitive Church as recorded in scripture. We would find preaching on a text appropriate, if it were done because of the immediate inclinations of the Spirit, rather than because it was customary or planned. There is no prece-

---

rowful" Cath-Douay, until the evening sacrifice, after hearing of the transgressions of the people.

In Ezek 14:1 the elders "sat (down) before me" KJ, RSV, (Cath-CCD), until the word of the Lord came to them.

In Ezek 20:1, on the tenth day of the fifth month, some of the elders of Israel "came to consult the Lord and sat down before me" Cath-CCD; "came to inquire of the Lord and sat before me" RSV, KJ.

dent for doing it in planned fashion that I could ever find in the worship that is described in the New Testament.

Of course the objection can be raised that Christ read from the book of Isaiah and used it as a text for speaking. It can also be said that Peter preached on a sentence recorded by the prophet Joel. But both Christ and Peter did this in an unpremeditated way, and when they had been urged to do it by the Spirit of God. I doubt if anyone will deny this and we heartily approve of this type of ministry. But this is not our opponents' customary studied method of making their scriptural observations. They do it without either waiting for or expecting any guidance from the Spirit. Furthermore, neither Christ nor Peter regularly followed this method of preaching from a text, or established it as a method which should be constantly practiced by all ministers of the Church.

CHRIST AND THE APOSTLES PREACHED WITHOUT CITATIONS

Nearly all of the sermons of Christ and his apostles that are recorded in scripture are without particular citations. That is apparent from Christ's sermon on the mount (Mat 5:1ff), and at the shore (Mark 4:1ff), and from Paul's preaching to the Athenians, Jews, and others. Not only is there no scriptural precept for this method of preaching, but the very nature of it is contrary to the preaching which Christ recommends as appropriate under the new covenant. Christ says explicitly when sending forth his disciples that they are not to speak their own words or plan in advance what they will say. Instead, they are to say what the Spirit will teach them to say in their hour of trial. This is particularly mentioned by the three evangelists:

Mat 10:20 RSV: "For it is not you who speak, but the Spirit of your Father speaking through you."

Mark 13:11 Cath-CCD: "For it is not you who are speaking, but the Holy Spirit."

Luke 12:12 RSV: "For the Holy Spirit will teach you in that very hour what you ought to say."

THE PROMPTINGS OF THE PARACLETE

If Christ gave this order to his disciples before he departed from them and by way of instruction on what they were to do while he was outwardly with them, by inference, how much more were they supposed to practice it after he had departed. Then they were to have an even greater dispensation of the

Spirit, which would "teach you all things," and "bring to your remembrance all that I have said to you" (John 14:26 RSV).

If they were supposed to do this when they appeared before the magistrates and princes of this earth, shouldn't it be even more of an obligation in worship, when they stand before God in an especial way? Particularly since it has been shown that he is to be worshipped in Spirit. Therefore, after they received the Holy Spirit, it is said in Acts 2:4 RSV that they "began to speak ... as the Spirit gave them utterance." This certainly was not done in a premeditated way nor based upon the things which they had studied and gathered from books.[32]

NULLIFYING THE EFFECT OF THE CROSS

¶XIX. Since the customary method of preaching can be and often is performed by men who are wicked or devoid of true grace, it cannot edify the church or nourish true faith. Instead it is destructive to faith and directly contrary to the nature of the Christian and apostolic ministry that is mentioned in the scriptures. For the apostle Paul preached the gospel "without relying on the language of worldly wisdom, so that the fact of Christ on his cross might have its full weight" (1 Cor 1:17 NEB) ["not with eloquent wisdom, lest the cross of Christ be emptied of its power" RSV]. For preaching which is done with eloquence and from man's own will and wisdom is but the wisdom of words and it nullifies the effect of the cross of Christ.

The apostle's own preaching was done "not in the persuasive words of wisdom" ["did not sway you with subtle arguments," NEB], "but in the demonstration of the Spirit and of power, that your faith might rest, not on the wisdom of men, but on the power of God" (1 Cor 2:4-5 Cath-CCD). But both those who preach and those who hear the customary form of preaching confess that they do not wait for the Spirit, and that they are speaking words which their own natural wisdom or their education has taught them.

THE ORDER OF WORSHIP IN THE PRIMITIVE CHURCH

This is contrary to the method and order of worship in the primitive church. In 1 Cor 14:30ff Cath-CCD, all are to "keep silence" in the church unless they are given a revelation

---

[32] Two rather lengthy and uninformative confirmatory quotations from "Franciscus Lambertus (1486-1530), tract 5 of *Prophecy*, chap 3," have been omitted here.

for the edification of others. Can the customary form of preaching be described as waiting for revelation, when it consists entirely of premeditated material that has been thoroughly prepared beforehand?

What good is excellent speech if it lacks the power of the Spirit to touch the conscience?

¶XX. Some will say that many have benefitted by such ministry. They will ask if many have not been both converted and edified by it. And they will ask if the Spirit hasn't often concurred by adding his influence to such premeditated preaching in a way that bears it powerfully in upon the souls of the listeners?

Just because this is true, it does not make that type of preaching good in itself. Paul's persecution of the followers of Christ did not receive any merit from the fact that he was on his way to Damascus to engage in further persecution when he was met by Christ for the conversion of his soul. The degree of God's condescension in times of ignorance is no measure of the value of an individual's actions or even those of whole congregations. Furthermore, God has often entered the heart of a preacher out of consideration for his simplicity and integrity, and with his power and holy influence he has led him to say things that were not included in his premeditated discourse. These might even be things he had never thought of before. And often these passing exclamations and unplanned but living exhortations prove more beneficial and refreshing to both the preacher and his listeners than all of his prepared sermons.

Nevertheless, this does not condone the things which are contrary to the practice of the apostles. Nor does it permit them to be continued when God is raising up a people who will serve him in primitive purity and spirituality. Indeed, such acts of condescension on the part of God in times of darkness and ignorance should win over more and more who will follow him in the most perfect and spiritual way which he reveals.

LITURGICAL AND EXTEMPORANEOUS PRAYER

¶XXI. Now that we have disposed of the subject of preaching, it is appropriate to speak of prayer, since there is a similar controversy over that. Our opponents pray as they preach. Since their religion is largely external and composed of acts which are the product of man's natural will and abilities, they pray whenever they please and with particular set prayers. I do not intend to engage in their own controversies over whether prayers should be liturgical or extemporaneous. Suffice it to say that they all agree that it is not necessary for their prayers to be preceded by the motions and the influence of the Spirit of God. That is why they have set times in their public worship for prayers. In their private devotions they say their prayers both morning and evening and before and after meals and on similar occasions.

At these times, they speak their words to God, whether they feel moved or influenced by the Spirit or not. Even though some of their principal people consider it a sin to pray without the assistance of the Spirit, they say that they consider it their duty to do so.

We readily agree that prayer is very beneficial and that it is an essential duty for all Christians to pray frequently, as they were commanded. But since we can do nothing without Christ, we cannot pray without the concurrence and assistance of his Spirit. In order to state the reason for this difference more clearly, let us first consider the twofold nature of prayer — its inward and outward aspects.

THE TWOFOLD NATURE OF PRAYER

Inward prayer is the secret turning of the mind toward God, where it looks up to him and constantly breathes some of its secret hopes and aspirations toward him. The hidden touches of the light of Christ awaken the conscience and it becomes bowed down under the sense of its iniquities, unworthiness, and misery until it can humbly join with the mysterious radiance from the seed of God to breathe toward him. It is in this sense that we are so frequently commanded by the scriptures to pray continually:

Luke 18:1 RSV: "And he told them a parable, to the effect that they ought always to pray and not lose heart."

1 Thes 5:17 RSV: "Pray constantly" ["without ceasing," Cath-CCD; "continually," NEB].

Eph 6:18 NEB: "Give yourselves wholly to prayer and entreaty; pray on every occasion in the power of the Spirit."

Luke 21:36 NEB: "Be on the alert, praying at all times for strength to pass safely through all these imminent troubles and to stand in the presence of the Son of Man."

These cannot be applied to outward prayer. It would be impossible for men to be continually on their knees expressing

words of prayer, and they would be kept from doing other
things which are no less positively commanded.

OUTWARD PRAYER DEPENDS UPON INWARD PRAYER

Outward prayer is something which arises when the necessary strength and permission for it are granted by the motion
and influence of the Spirit to a degree over and above that
which is required for inward retirement. The breathing of the
Spirit of God arises in the soul so powerfully that audible sighs,
groans, or words are brought forth. This can occur either in
public assemblies, or in private, or at mealtimes.

Inward prayer is necessary at all times. As long as his day
of visitation lasts, man is never without some influence toward
it, although this is greater at some times than others. He no
sooner retires his mind and considers himself in God's presence than he finds himself practicing it.

Since the outward exercise of prayer requires a greater and
additional influence and movement of the Spirit, it cannot be
practiced continually. For outward prayer to be done spon-
taneously and effectively, the mind must have a long acquaintance with inward prayer. Those who are diligent and watchful in mind, and who can withdraw their minds to a great
extent from active business, are the most capable of the frequent use of outward prayer. They receive more constant attention from this holy influence. And since they are better
acquainted with the motions of God's Spirit, they are more
accustomed to them and can easily perceive and discern them.
In fact, those who are most diligent have a near access to God.
He takes great delight in drawing them by his Spirit to approach and call upon him.

When many are gathered together in alertness of mind,
God frequently pours forth the spirit of prayer among them.
They become stirred to its practice and it has an edifying
effect, building up one another in love.

Since this type of outward prayer depends upon inward
prayer and must develop out of it, we cannot predetermine
the times for its practice. The influence and motion of the
Spirit must accompany it and be superimposed on it. We cannot lay a necessity upon someone to speak words at such and
such a time, whether he feels the heavenly influence or not.
For we would consider that to be tempting God and coming
before him without due preparation.

DEPENDENCE UPON THE LORD MUST BE FIRM AND CONSTANT

We think that it is proper for us to present ourselves before him by this inward retirement of mind and then to proceed further as his Spirit helps us and draws us. The Lord finds this acceptable. In fact there are times when he deems it proper to exercise us in this silent place. He tries our patience, not allowing us to speak, so that he may teach us not to rely on outward performances. He does not want us to be satisfied, as too many are, with the mere saying of our prayers. Indeed, he wants our dependence upon him to be more firm and constant. We are to wait for the holding out of his sceptre, as permission to draw near to him and experience the greater freedom that comes with the enlargement of the Spirit upon us as we turn our hearts toward him.

However, we do not deny that there are some particular occasions when God very suddenly, in fact when the mind is first turned toward him, gives the power and the liberty to bring forth words or acts of outward prayer. At such times, the soul can scarcely detect any previous preparation by the Spirit, but the influence and the bringing forth can be said to occur at one and the same time. In spite of this, Bernard's statement[33] remains true that all prayer that is not preceded by inspiration remains lukewarm.

THOSE WHO NEGLECT PRAYER SIN

Although we affirm that no one should pray without the leading of the Spirit nevertheless we agree that those who neglect prayer sin. But the sin is that they do not attain a state in which they might feel led to pray. We do not question the fact that there are many who neglect inward watchfulness and retiredness of mind and thereby miss numerous precious opportunities to pray, and thus become guilty in the sight of God. Yet they would also sin if they began to pray before they felt the primary influence from which prayer should stem.

He who lies in bed and sleeps when he should be busy with his master's business renders a great offense to his master. But if he were suddenly to get up without putting on his clothes, or forget to take along the required tools and instru-

---

[33] Presumably Bernard of Clairvaux. The difficulty of locating it on the basis of a mere allusion and in view of the great quantity of his writings is indicated in the biographical fn, p 278.

ments, he would really be incurring new censure, instead of making amends.

One who is careless and otherwise busy may not hear someone speak to him, or he may not hear the striking of a clock, even though the bell is close to him. Through negligence, many frequently do not hear the call of God which would give them access to his presence and the opportunity to pray to him. However, that is no excuse for going to work in their own wills and without his permission.

Although this alone is the true and proper method of prayer and the only one which has God's approval, we do not deny that he has often answered the prayers of those who have been greatly in error in this matter. Particularly in times of darkness, even though they have been very wrong in the manner in which they prayed and in the content of their prayers, he has concurred with their desires. Even though they have prayed without the assistance or influence of God's Spirit, he has found occasion to break in upon their souls and make them wonderfully tender and refreshed. But, as we have said in connection with preaching, this does not constitute approval of such practices. Furthermore this should not be considered as justification for hindering anyone from practicing pure, spiritual, and acceptable prayer. For God is again leading his people away from superstition and mere empty formalities into true prayer.

INWARD RETIREMENT A PRELUDE TO PRAYER IN THE SCRIPTURES

¶XXII. The necessity for inward retirement of the mind before the Spirit can draw the worshipper into such prayer is apparent from the scriptures. In most of the places where prayer is commanded, watching is prefixed as a necessary prelude. [The citations, Mat 24:42, Mark 13:33, 14:38, Luke 21:36 are in part repetition of those quoted in full in ¶X. — ED.]

Now what is the purpose of this watching? Or what is it, if it is not waiting to feel God's Spirit draw one into prayer so that it may be done acceptably? Eph 6:18-19 NEB tells us: "Give yourselves wholly to prayer and entreaty; pray on every occasion in the power of the Spirit. To this end keep watch and persevere, always interceding for all God's people; and pray for me, that I may be granted the right words when I open my mouth."

The need for the moving and concurrence of the Spirit is
abundantly clear from Rom 8:26-28 NEB: "In the same way
the Spirit comes to the aid of our weakness. We do not even
know how we ought to pray, but through our inarticulate
groans the Spirit himself is pleading for us, and God who
searches our inmost being knows what the Spirit means, because he pleads for God's own people in God's own way; and
in everything, as we know, he cooperates for good with those
who love God and are called according to his purpose."

This quotation first points out that men cannot pray or
call upon God out of their own wills. Even if they have received the faith of Christ and are, in a measure, sanctified by
it — just as the Church of Rome to whom the apostle was
writing had been — they are still incapable of it. It then
points out that the only help and assistance which men can
have in prayer is that of the Spirit. Without the Spirit they
cannot pray acceptably to God, nor in a way that will benefit
their own souls. The Spirit uses our inarticulate sighs and
groans to intercede for us. God receives graciously the prayers
that are offered by the Spirit because he knows that they are
in accord with his will. It is inconceivable that the kind of
prayer which the apostles describe would be inconsistent with
the other testimonies of the scripture which recommend the
use of prayer to us.

USELESS TO PRAY WITHOUT THE SPIRIT

From this, I would argue that if no one knows how to
pray, and prayer cannot be offered without the aid of the Spirit,
then it is completely useless to pray without the Spirit. The
fact that the Spirit is needed for true prayer is apparent from
Eph 6:18 NEB: "pray on every occasion in the power of the
Spirit. To this end, keep watch and persevere." This practic-
ally says that we are never to pray without the Spirit or without watching for it. In Jude 20 NEB, it says: "But you, my
friends, must fortify yourselves in your most sacred faith. Continue to pray in the power of the Holy Spirit."

The apostle Paul says expressly in 1 Cor 12:3 RSV: "No
one can say 'Jesus is Lord' except by the Holy Spirit" [unless
he is "under the influence of the Holy Spirit" NEB]. If Jesus
cannot be acknowledged as Lord, except with the aid of the
Spirit, it must be even less acceptable to call upon him without
the Spirit. Indeed, the same apostle says, 1 Cor 14:15 RSV and

Cath-CCD: "I will pray with the Spirit." This is clear evidence that he was not accustomed to pray without it.

In Prov 28:9, all prayer without the Spirit is declared to be an abomination, and like the prayers of those who do not obey the law. The faithful are assured that God will hear them if they "ask anything according to his will;" (1 John 5:14 RSV). So if the prayer is not according to his will, there is no reason to be confident that he will hear. Even our opponents will agree that prayers without the Spirit are not according to the will of God and that those who pray that way will have no ground for expecting an answer.

LIKE SEEING WITHOUT EYES OR WALKING WITHOUT FEET

Bidding a man to pray without the Spirit is like asking him to see without his eyes, to work without his hands, or to walk without using his feet. And expecting a man to pray before the Spirit in some measure moves him to it is like wanting him to see before he opens his eyes, or to work with his hands before he begins to move them.

VAIN OBLATIONS AND PRAYERS THAT GOD DOES NOT KNOW

¶XXIII. All of the superstition and idolatry that exists among Christians comes from the false idea that one can pray without the Spirit. The Lord is provoked and his Spirit is aggrieved by the number of people who think that it is not necessary to wait for the Spirit. They deceive themselves, as the Jews did in ancient times, by thinking that it is enough if they pay their daily sacrifices and offer their customary oblations. Because, like the whore in Proverbs,[34] they have offered up their sacrifices of morning and evening prayers, they create a false peace for themselves. It is obvious that their constant use of these things hasn't the least bit of influence on their lives and conversations. By and large, they remain as bad as ever.

It is common among both Catholics and Protestants to leap, as it were, from light and profane conversation to their customary devotions at certain fixed times and seasons. These are scarcely finished, and the words to God have barely been uttered, when profane talk begins again. Thus it is the same wicked and profane spirit of this world which actuates them during both pursuits. Certainly, if there are any such things

[34] Prov 23:27.

as vain oblations or prayers that God does not recognize, they
are those that are actuated by man's own strength and by his
own will and without God's Spirit. The scripture definitely
testifies to the fact that there are such prayers, as in:

Isa 66:3-4 RSV where they chose "their own ways" and
"when I spoke they did not listen."

Jer 14:12 RSV is in the same vein, when it says: "Though
they fast, I will not hear their cry, and though they offer burnt
offering and cereal offering, I will not accept them."

Let this be sufficient proof.

JOINING OTHERS IN PRAYER

¶XXIV. There is also the matter of joining in the prayers
of others by concurrence of our spirits and the gestures of our
bodies. We gladly approve of this, because it is appropriate
for those who come before God to pray to do so on bended
knee and with their heads uncovered. This is also our practice.[35] But the matter becomes controversial when it is a question of joining others who do not pray in the heart, but who
pray formally and without waiting for the motion of the Spirit,
which they consider unnecessary.

We have suffered quite a bit for our testimony against
this. We have been not only rebuked but cruelly beaten. When
we have not knelt, either accidentally, or because, as a witness
against their form of worship, we did not feel that it was lawful for us to do so when we have been present, we have received many strokes of the lash. They have accused us of pride,
profanity, and madness, saying that we had no respect or reverence for the worship of God and that we considered ourselves
the only ones who could pray, or who were heard by God. In
answer to this and many other reproaches of this kind, we simply say in all modesty that we have not acted from the motives
they claim, but because we would injure our consciences if we
did otherwise. How, in good conscience, could we join them,
since we are obliged to believe by our principles and doctrines
that the prayers of those who confess that they are not actuated by the Spirit are an abomination?

[35] There has been considerable variation in Quaker practice on this
matter. In some few remaining conservative areas where men customarily
wear their hats at worship, the person praying will remove his hat and
kneel, and very often the whole congregation will rise and remain standing until the prayer is completed. Elsewhere heads are merely bowed.
— ED.

They say that this is the height of uncharitableness and arrogance and that we set ourselves up as judges. They claim that we consider ourselves as always praying with the Spirit while they never do. It is as if we were never deceived into praying without the motions of the Spirit, and as if they were never actuated by it. However, they consider it very beneficial and comforting to pray with the Spirit and they claim that they often feel it influencing them even if they do not consider the motion of the Spirit to be always necessary.

We cannot deny that this is sometimes true. However, now that worship in the Spirit has been openly proclaimed and all are invited to practice it, the situation is somewhat different than it was in the former times of darkness and apostasy. We do not deny that it would be appropriate for us to join with them on the occasions when it is quite apparent that the Spirit is obviously present. However, these occasions are rare, and we hesitate to join with them even then, because it might confirm them in their false principle. Although this is a difficult part of our profession, nevertheless there is so much scriptural confirmation and it is so reasonable that many have been convinced of this before they have accepted other truths which were easier to understand and which some have considered more clearly demonstrated.

ALEXANDER SKENE'S QUERIES

Among the most memorable of recent years was Alexander Skein,[36] a magistrate of the city of Aberdeen, who was very

---

[36] Alexander Skene was converted from "a zealous opposer" to the Christian principles of Friends about the same time as Thomas Mercer, "late dean of the guild." Skene had also been a delegate to a religious assembly in Edinburgh (1651) to inquire into Scotland's religious troubles.

The withdrawal of such influential and highly reputed persons from the "national church" heightened the alarm and indignation of the local ministers. Two of them, Meldrum and Menzies, complained to the visiting circuit judges and the bishops that they had been unable to suppress the Quakers in spite of breaking up their meetings, imprisoning, fining, and even banishing some. The judges were so shocked by a cruel proposal they made that no Quakers were sentenced in the 1671 sittings.

The Quakers were saved from further indignities and disbarment from municipal public office at the action of the town council the following year by the *King's Declaration of Indulgence to all Nonconformists* in 1672. — John Barclay's *Memoirs of the Rise, Progress and Persecutions of the People Called Quakers in the North of Scotland* (added to the *Diary of Alexander Jaffray*), 2nd ed, London, Darton & Harvey, 1834, pp 285-289. Alexander Skene's questions to the public preachers are also reprinted from this present work, pp 555-558, with additional comments.

modest and disliked giving offense to others but nevertheless
was overcome by the power of truth in this matter and for that
reason left the public assemblies and prayers to join us. He
also stated his reason for doing this rather succinctly and in a
way which covered the controversy over worship in a few brief
questions which he posed to the public preachers of the city.
I think it is appropriate to insert them here:

1. Should any act in the worship of God be undertaken
without the motions, leadings, and actuation of the Holy Spirit?

2. If the motions of the Spirit are necessary for each part
of our duty, ought we not to wait in all of our acts of worship
for the assistance of the Spirit so that our words will be according to the utterances he gives?

3. Does anyone who bears the name Christian, or professes to be a Protestant, have such an uninterrupted measure
of God's grace that he does not have to wait for it and can
begin his duties immediately?

4. If such exercises are inappropriate at certain times, or
one does not feel disposed to perform them with life and spirit, should they be performed at all at that time?

5. Can God be expected to accept in good faith any duty
which is undertaken in response to an external command
and which lacks the necessary spiritual life and movement?
Wouldn't this be considered as bringing strange (i.e., "unholy"
or "profane") fire before the Lord (Lev 10:1-2)? At best it
would be performed only with natural and acquired skills. It
would not be done with the strength and assistance of the Holy
Spirit, which was typified by the fire that came down from heav-
en[37] and which alone was appropriate to consume the sacrifice.

6. Although it is not as immediately apparent to the ob-
server, aren't duties which are performed merely with natural
and acquired strength just as much a human creation as Roman
Catholic worship? Isn't is just as superstitious to approve of
worship of this type as it is to approve of Catholic worship,
even though there may be a difference in degree?

7. Is it offensive or scandalous to favor the worship whose
professed principle is not to speak for edification or to pray
unless the Holy Spirit is pleased to assist in some measure, or
to choose to be silent rather than speak without this influence?

---

[37] 2 Kings 1:10-14.

Alexander Skein has long since refuted the cold and rather
weak answers which they gave.

CONFORMITY FOR POLITICAL EXPEDIENCY

We do not dare to hinder or retard the Spirit by any act
of our own, even if it means losing not only worldly honor,
but our lives. Many Protestants have, in fact, weakened the
Reformation and scandalized their profession by complying
with Catholic abominations for political reasons. Take for
example the Elector of Saxony who was commanded by the
Emperor Charles V to be present at the Mass celebrated at the
convention of Augsburg in 1530, so he could be the emperor's
swordbearer. When he developed scruples against this, his
preachers persuaded him with more consideration for his honor
than his conscience that it would be lawful for him to do so.
This was not only a very bad example, and a great scandal to
the Reformation, but it displeased many people, as the author
of the *History of the Council of Trent*[38] so well observes in his
first book.

NEVER A TIME THAT GOD IS NOT NEAR

¶XXV. I come immediately to the objections to this
method of praying that are raised by our opponents. They say
that if it is necessary to have such individual influences of the
Spirit for outward acts of worship, they should be required
before undertaking inward acts like waiting for, wanting, or
loving God. But this is absurd. While the day of a man's
visitation lasts there is never a time that God is not near him,
and his Spirit is not wrestling with him to turn inward. If he
will merely stand still, and forego his evil thoughts, the Lord
will be near to help him. But outward acts of prayer require
a greater influence and a more special motion of the Spirit, as
has already been proved.

They say that it could also be claimed that one should
only perform such moral duties as obeying parents or treating
neighbors properly when moved by the Spirit. The answer is

---

[38] Probably the one by Paolo Sarpi (1522-1623), first published in
English at London in 1619 (1620?) under an anagram of the author's
name, Pietro Soave Polan [trans by Nathaniel Brent, Warden of Merton
College, Oxford, 1620? — *O.D.C.C.* is not clear on this]. See F. A. Yates,
"Paolo Sarpi's 'History of the Council of Trent' " in *Journal of the War-
burg and Courtauld Institutes*, vol 7 (1944), pp 123-144. — *O.D.C.C.*, pp
1216-1217.

that there is a great difference between the general duties of
man to man and the specific individual acts of worship toward
God.   One is spiritual and God has commanded it to be performed by his Spirit.   The other is based on a mere natural
principle of self-love and must be done for that reason.   Even
beasts have natural affections for each other.   This does not
mean that these acts are unacceptable to God or without value
for the soul, if they are done in the fear of God and with
his blessing.   In fact, if his children do everything under such
circumstances, they will be accepted and blessed in whatever
they do.

They object that if a wicked man desists from praying
without the motion of the Spirit because his prayer would be
sinful, he shouldn't plough either, because it is stated in Prov
21:4 Cath-CCD: "Haughty eyes and a proud heart — the tillage
of the wicked is sin."   But this objection is of the same kind
as the preceding one. There is a great difference between such
natural acts as eating, drinking and sleeping — the things
which men have in common with beasts — and spiritual acts.
There is no denial that the natural acts of the wicked and
unregenerate are sinful.   But they are not sinful in themselves,
but only as far as man in that state is a reprobate in all things
in the sight of God.

THE SIN IS NOT IN ABSTAINING FROM PRAYER
BUT IN NOT BEING PREPARED TO PRAY IF MOVED

The objection is raised that wicked men would forbear
praying for years on end with the allegation that they did so
because they lacked the Spirit.   But the false pretenses of
wicked men do not invalidate the truth of this doctrine.   If
that were so, there wouldn't be any Christian doctrines which
men couldn't set aside.   It is granted that they should not pray
without the Spirit.   What they should do, however, is to try to
achieve the state where they might be enabled to feel the
motions of the Spirit.   They sin not in abstaining from praying but in not preparing themselves to be moved to pray. Perhaps they will understand our argument better if I refer to
one of theirs. They say that it is a duty incumbent upon Christians to resort frequently to the sacrament of the Lord's Supper, as they call it.   Nevertheless, they say that no one who is
unworthy should partake of it.   Indeed, they state that those
who find themselves unprepared must abstain and they usually
excommunicate them from the table.   Those who are going to

partake must first examine themselves or else they will eat and
drink to their own condemnation. Although they consider it
sinful to forbear, they consider it even more sinful to participate without examination.

They cite Peter's command to Simon Magus, the wicked
sorcerer, to pray (Acts 8:22) and infer from it that wicked men
should pray. But in citing this passage, as I have often
observed, they overlook the most important part of the verse
(NEB): "Repent of this wickedness and pray the Lord to forgive you for imagining such a thing." He is first told to repent.
Now the least measure of true repentance cannot be achieved
without some of the inward retirement of the mind, of which
we have spoken. Indeed, where true repentance has taken
place, we do not doubt that the Spirit of God will be on hand
to concur with the repentant one and to influence him to pray
and to call upon God.

Their final objection is that many prayers which have
begun without the Spirit have proved effectual, and that the
prayers of wicked men have been heard and have been found
acceptable, as Ahab's was. But as we have already said, the
acts of God's compassion and indulgence at certain times and
to some people on special and unique occasions should not be
considered a general rule for our actions. If that were the
measure of our obedience a great many inconsistencies would
necessarily follow. We do not deny that wicked men often
are aware of the motions and operations of God's Spirit at some
time in their lives. At such times they may pray acceptably.
But their prayer is acceptable not because they remain completely wicked, but because they become pious for a time, even
though they fall away afterwards.

THE SINGING OF PSALMS

¶XXVI. There will be no need for a long discourse on
the subject of the singing of psalms. For the case is the same
as that for preaching and for prayer. This is part of God's
worship, and it is very sweet and refreshing when it proceeds
from a true sense of God's love in the heart. If it arises from
the divine influence of the Spirit, that can just as suitably lead
souls to breathe forth sweet harmony as to provide words suitable for the occasion. It doesn't make any difference whether
these are words which were formerly used by the people of
God and recorded in scripture, such as the Psalms of David,

or whether they were the hymns and songs which occurred to Zacharias, Simeon, and the blessed Virgin Mary.

But the formal and customary way of singing has no foundation in scripture and no basis in true Christianity. And there is no precept or example for artificial music either by organs or other instruments in the New Testament. Indeed, in addition to all of the abuses that are incident to prayer and preaching, singing has its own. There are all kinds of great and horrible lies that are said in the sight of God when all sorts of wicked and profane persons take it upon themselves to impersonate the experiences and attitudes of the blessed David. What they say is not only false as far as they are personally concerned, but also as far as persons who are accustomed to more moderate speech are concerned. For example, take Psalm 22:14-15 Cath-CCD [actually 21:15-16 in Cath-CCD]: "My heart has become like wax melting away within my bosom. My throat is dried up like baked clay, my tongue cleaves to my jaws; to the dust of death you have brought me down." Or Psalm 6:6 Cath-CCD [actually 6:7]: "Every night I flood my bed with weeping; I drench my couch with tears." There are many others which seem just as false to those who utter them.

There is also the inconsistency of those who will confess in their prayers that they are guilty of the very vices with which they have just asserted that they were not endowed. Who can presume that God accepts such juggling? And it is certain that such singing pleases the earthly ears of men more than the pure ears of the Lord, for he abhors all lying and hypocrisy.

The singing which pleases God must be a consequence of that which is pure in the heart, and that which is truly the Word of Life there. It is by that Word which dwells so richly in us that spiritual songs and hymns are returned to the Lord, as Paul says in Col 3:16-17 NEB: "Let the message of Christ dwell among you in all its richness. Instruct and admonish each other with the utmost wisdom. Sing thankfully in your hearts to God, with psalms, and hymns, and spiritual songs. Whatever you are doing, whether you speak or act, do everything in the name of the Lord Jesus, giving thanks to God the Father through him."

¶XXVII. The greatest advantage of this true worship of God which we profess and practice is that it does not consist of man's wisdom, arts, or skills. Nor does it require the glory, pomp, riches, or splendor of the world to beautify it. Being of a spiritual and celestial nature it is too simple and despicable for the natural mind and will of man. He does not like to abide in it because he finds no room there for his imaginative creations or fabrications. There is no opportunity to gratify his outward and worldly senses.

If this form of worship is observed, it is not likely to be kept pure unless it is accompanied by the power of God. For it is so naked in itself that there is little to tempt men to become excessively fond of its mere form, once the Spirit has departed....

CONCLUDING SUMMARY

¶XXVIII. To conclude: the worship, preaching, praying, and singing which we advocate are those which are a consequence of the Spirit of God. They are always accompanied by the influence of the Spirit. They begin when the Spirit moves and are continued by its power and strength. Thus they are purely spiritual forms of worship such as the scriptures preach at length in John 4:23-24, 1 Cor 14:15, Eph 6:18 and elsewhere.

But the worship of our adversaries, to which we are opposed, begins, is carried on, and ends with man's own natural will and strength. It lacks the motion or influence of God's Spirit because they have decided that they do not need to wait for it. It can just as easily be performed in the correct manner and with the proper content by the wickedest of men. It is the type of worship and vain oblations which God has always rejected. This is apparent from:

Isa 66:1-3 RSV, where God asks what kind of dwelling place men can build for him when heaven is his throne, earth is his footstool, and he has made all of this himself. The man he approves of is humble and contrite in spirit and trembles at his word, whereas the man "who slaughters an ox is like him who kills a man; he who sacrifices a lamb, like him who breaks a dog's neck; he who presents a cereal offering, like him who offers swine's blood; he who makes a memorial offering of frankincense, like him who blesses an idol."

Verse 4 Cath-CCD: "Since these have chosen their own ways and taken pleasure in their own abominations, I in turn will choose ruthless treatment for them and bring upon them what they fear."

Jer 14:12ff RSV continues in the same vein: "Though they
fast, I will not hear their cry, and though they offer burnt offering and cereal offering, I will not accept them; but I will consume them by the sword, by famine, and by pestilence." God
goes on to say that those who say there will be no famine, and
that peace is assured, "are prophesying to you a lying vision,
worthless divination, and the deceit of their own minds...
for both prophet and priest ply their trade through the land,
and have no knowledge."

Isa 1:11-20 Cath-CCD: "What care I for the number of
your sacrifices? says the Lord. I have had enough of whole-
burnt rams and fat of fatlings; in the blood of calves, lambs,
and goats I find no pleasure.

"When you come in to visit me, who asks these things of
you?

"Trample my courts no more! Bring no more worthless
offerings; your incense is loathsome to me.

"New moon and sabbath, calling of assemblies, octaves
with wickedness: these I cannot bear.

"Your new moons and festivals I detest; they weigh me
down, I tire of the load.

"When you spread out your hands, I close my eyes to you;
though you pray the more I will not listen.

"Your hands are full of blood! Wash yourselves clean!

"Put away your misdeeds from before my eyes; cease doing evil; learn to do good.

"Make justice your aim: redress the wronged, hear the
orphan's plea, defend the widow.

"Come now, let us set things right, says the Lord: though
your sins be like scarlet, they may become white as snow;
though they be crimson red, they may become white as wool.

"If you are willing, and obey, you shall eat the good
things of the land; but if you refuse and resist, the sword shall
consume you: for the mouth of the Lord has spoken!"

Prov 15:29 Cath-CCD: "The Lord is far from the wicked,
but the prayer of the just he hears."

John 9:31 RSV: "We know that God does not listen to
sinners, but if anyone is a worshipper of God and does his
will, God listens to him."

Baptism

Just as there is "one Lord, and one faith," so is there "one baptism" (Eph 4:5), which is not "a removal of dirt from the body but . . . an appeal to God for a clear conscience, through the resurrection of Jesus Christ" (1 Pet 3:21 RSV). This baptism is a pure and spiritual thing (Gal 3:27), namely, the baptism of the Spirit and of fire, by which we are "buried with him" (Rom 6:4; Col 2:12) so that being washed and purged of our sins, we may "walk in newness of life" (Rom 6:4).

The baptism of John was figurative, and was commanded for a time, but it was not to continue forever (John 3:30; 1 Cor 1:17). The baptism of infants, however, is a mere human tradition, for which neither precept nor practice is to be found anywhere in scripture.

PROTOTYPES AND SHADOWS

¶I. The numerous ceremonies and observances which God prescribed through his servant Moses for his chosen people the Jews, represented condescension on his part. These things were merely to be the prototypes and shadows of the true substance which was to be revealed in due time. For the most part, they consisted of washing, external purifying, and cleansing which were to continue until spiritual worship was set up in the time of reformation. God would then lead his children into all truth and teach them to worship in a more spiritual way which would be acceptable to him. At that time his Spirit would be poured forth more plentifully, and he would guide the anointing, even though it would be less agreeable to the outward and earthly senses.

But in spite of God's condescension to the Jews in providing all these observances, the part of man which delights in following his own imagination was not satisfied. The Jews often slipped into Gentile superstitions or added some new observances or ceremonies of their own. They became so devoted to these that under mistaken notions of zeal or piety they were apt to prefer them to God's own commands.

Examples of this abound among the Pharisees, the principal sect among the Jews, who were reproved so often by Christ
for voiding the commandments of God with their own traditions. Mat 15:6-9 NEB is a good example: "You have made
God's law null and void out of respect for your tradition. What
hypocrisy! Isaiah was right when he prophesied about you:
'This people pays me lip-service, but their heart is far from
me; their worship of me is in vain, for they teach as doctrines
the commandments of men.'"

INNOVATIONS
Today, the complaint can justly be made that many bearing the name of Christians have introduced many things of this
kind. Some were borrowed from the Jews. Largely out of self-
love and self-will, they cling more tenaciously to these and
plead more earnestly for them than they do for the more significant aspects of Christianity. If there is the slightest basis
for stretching any scriptural practice, or there is a conditional
approval which would give some color of authorization for
these innovations, they seize upon it. Then they cling to these
practices so tenaciously, and are so obstinate and obstreperous
in their arguments for them, that they do not have the patience
to hear even the most solid of Christian arguments against
them. If they would only examine their zeal seriously, they
would find that it consisted of nothing more than inherited
prejudices[1] and self-love. These weigh more heavily than that
which comes from God, or his pure worship.
This is certainly verified in considering the things that are
called sacraments. There is a great deal of ignorance about
these, and it is little realized how numerous the debates and
quarrels over them have been among Christians. It is safe to
say that there has been more controversy, contention, and petty
strife over these than over any of the other doctrines of Christ.
There have been arguments over their number, their virtue,
efficacy, administration, and many other aspects — not only between Roman Catholics and Protestants, but among Protestants themselves. It is obvious what great prejudice there has
been among Christians on these points. But for the most part,
the things over which they contend are mere shadows and external manifestations of the true substance.

[1] Barclay's phrase was actually "the prejudice of education." The
more modern idiom does not seem to violate the sense.

ORIGIN OF THE TERM "SACRAMENT"

¶II. The first thing to be considered is the name "sacraments" itself. How strange it is that Christians should cling to
that name and make such strong arguments for it when it does
not occur anywhere in scripture. It was borrowed from the
military oaths used by pagans.[2] As such, it was one of the many
superstitious terms and observances which Christians incorpor-
ated into their faith at the beginning of the apostasy. This
was done to ingratiate themselves with the heathens so they
would be easier to convert. Unfortunately, the practice was the
fruit of human policy rather than of God's wisdom. And
although it was intended to be in the best interests of the
Church, it has had very pernicious consequences. I fail to see
how any of the people of God, whether Catholics or Protestants but particularly the latter, can have any reasonable quarrel
with us for refusing to accept this term, which the Spirit of God
did not see fit to have his penmen incorporate in scripture.

If they will but grant this point, and set aside the traditional term "sacrament," they will see immediately what is to
be gained by following the simple words of scripture without
the complications of extraneous matter. Immediately the great
dispute over the number of sacraments vanishes. Substitute the
term institutions, ordinances, precepts, commandments, appointments, laws, or any other appropriate word, and the debate disappears. Roman Catholics no longer affirm that there are seven
of them, nor Protestants that there are two, when any of these
other terms is used.

VARYING DEFINITIONS OF SACRAMENTS

If it should be said that the controversy arises over the
definition as well as the term that is used, that is not true ei-

[2] The Latin *sacramentum* originally meant an oath, especially the
soldier's oath of allegiance, and traces of this meaning survive in early
Christian literature (for example, Tertullian, *Ad Martyres* 3). But the
main factor in determining Christian usage was its employment in the
Latin New Testament to render the Greek *mysterion* ('mystery')." —
O.D.C.C., p 1198.

It was also "used in classical Latin literature of the pledge deposited
in a temple by the parties to a lawsuit and also of the soldier's oath . . .
and neither of the senses has been without influence on its employment
by Christian theologians." Aquinian usage may have been in accord with
its general etymological signification. He uses the analogy that anything
may be called a sacrament whereby something is made sacred, just as an
ornament is that by which anything is adorned or a medicament that by
which medication is applied. — *Encyc. Brit.*, 1958, vol 19, p 799.

ther. For whether we accept the definition of a sacrament as the outward visible sign of the conferral of an inward grace, or as merely symbolic, there are many things to which these definitions could be applied which neither Catholics nor Protestants would acknowledge as "sacraments." If the expression "sealing ordinances" is used, it is no more appropriate for these ceremonies than it is for many other Christian religious performances. For, correctly speaking, a "sealing ordinance" is anything which makes it infallibly certain to the recipient that the promise which has been sealed will be fulfilled.

If it be said that it serves as a seal for those who are faithful, the answer is, so do praying and preaching, and the performance of every good work. The partaking or the performing of one or the other does not give a greater title to heaven. In fact, in some respects, not as much of a one, since there is no better reason to consider the "sacraments" as seals than any other religious acts.

SCRIPTURALLY, THE SPIRIT OF GOD IS THE ONLY SEAL OF OUR INHERITANCE

Furthermore, nothing except the Spirit of God is called the seal and pledge of our inheritance in the scriptures. Eph 1:13-14 NEB says: "In him you also, who have heard the word of truth, the gospel of your salvation, and have believed in him, were sealed with the promised Holy Spirit, which is the guarantee of our inheritance until we acquire possession of it, to the praise of his glory."

This is reiterated in 4:30 NEB of the same epistle: "And do not grieve the Holy Spirit of God, for that Spirit is the seal with which you were marked for the day of our final liberation."

There is also 2 Cor 1:21-22 RSV, where Paul says: "It is God who establishes us with you in Christ, and has commissioned us; he has put his seal upon us and given us his Spirit in our hearts as a guarantee."

It is the Spirit that is the earnest of our inheritance and not outward water, or eating and drinking. Even the wickedest of men may partake of these, and many do, but nevertheless they are consigned to perdition. For it is not outward washing with water that makes the heart clean. It is not this which fits men for heaven. A man is defiled not by what goes into him but by the things which come out of him.[3] And what a man eats can neither purify him nor fit him for heaven. Obviously, what has been said applies not only to baptism, but equally to Prop. 13 concerning the supper. Of these so-called "sacraments," baptism is always considered first.

THE "ONE BAPTISM" IS A BAPTISM OF THE SPIRIT

¶III. The "one baptism" in Eph 4:5 which acknowledges "one Lord," "one faith," and so forth, is the baptism of Christ. It is not a washing or a dipping in water, but a baptism by the Spirit. The baptism of John was merely figurative of this, and as a figure it was intended to give way to the substance. Although baptism by the Spirit was to be continued, John's baptism was to cease.

It is frequently alleged in explanation of this text that the baptism of water and the Spirit together make up one baptism, by virtue of the sacramental union. But the origin of this exposition is not in scripture, but instead is an attempt to wrest the scripture to suit the principle of water baptism. The only reply necessary is to deny its validity since it is clearly incompatible with the words of the text, which does not say that there are two baptisms — one of water and one of Spirit — which together comprise one baptism. It says very plainly that there is one baptism, just as there is one faith and one God. There are not two faiths, or two Gods, or two Spirits. Nor are there two bodies — one outward and elementary, the other spiritual and pure — which contribute to the making of the one faith, the one God, the one body, and the one Spirit. By the same reasoning there should not be two baptisms to make up the one baptism.

Another argument says that there is only one baptism, but that it has two parts. The water is one part — the symbol — and the Spirit is the other — the thing symbolized. This merely confirms our own doctrine. If water is the symbol, it cannot be the substance of the "one baptism." And it must not be forgotten that we are supposed to consider the "one baptism" as the true substance, and not to accept the prototype or figurative baptism as this substance, but merely as the forerunner.

It is similar to the reference to the one Christ in the scripture. He was prefigured by many sacrifices and signs under the law. But nevertheless the reference is to be understood as mean-

[3] Mark 7:15-16.

ing his offering himself on the cross. The symbols foreshadowed what was to come, but we do not say that together with the actual offering of Christ himself on the cross they make up the one offering. It doesn't follow any better that water baptism, which is clearly described as foreshadowing Christ's baptism, should now be considered as also an integral part of that "one baptism," the baptism of Christ.

IT IS DEFINITELY NOT OF WATER

If anyone should be so foolish as to claim that the baptism of water, rather than that of the Spirit, is the "one baptism" referred to, he would very clearly be contradicting the positive testimony of the scripture. We have John's own testimony that water baptism is not properly and distinctively the baptism of Christ. Mat 3:11 NEB says very definitely: "I baptize you with water, for repentance; but the one who comes after me is mightier than I, and I am not fit to take off his shoes; he will baptize you with the Holy Spirit and with fire."

John has mentioned here two methods of baptizing, and two different baptisms — the one with water, and the other with the Spirit. He was minister of one and Christ was the minister of the other. Those who received the first baptism did not also receive the second, or why would he refer to what he does *now* and what Christ *will* do? Any other construction of this would make John's words devoid of good sense. If the baptisms which he distinguishes so sharply were both one, why would it be necessary for him to say that those he had already baptized should still receive another baptism?

Those who urge the interpretation that the baptism of the Spirit was merely an effect of the baptism with water contradict the manifest intent of the text. He does not say that "I baptize you with water but the one who comes after me will produce the same effects as this baptism only he will bring them about in you by the Spirit." Instead, he says that the baptism that is to follow is a different kind of baptism.

CHRIST HIMSELF MADE THIS CLEAR

This is further confirmed by the statement of Christ himself, Acts 1:4-5 NEB: " 'You must wait,' he said, 'for the promise made by my Father, about which you have heard me speak: John, as you know, baptized with water, but you will be baptized with the Holy Spirit, and within the next few days.' " There can hardly be two other places in scripture where the agreement is as close as between this and Mat 3:11. For Christ concedes altogether that John's baptism was complete, both in regard to its manner and to its substance. "John," he says in effect, "truly baptized with water," which is as much as saying that he truly[4] and fully administered the baptism of water. But although they have received this, they have not yet received Christ's baptism which is still to come.

Peter observes the same distinction, Acts 11:16 NEB: "Then I recalled what the Lord had said: 'John baptized with water, but you will be baptized with the Holy Spirit.'"[5] The apostle is recalling how the Holy Spirit fell upon them on this occasion, as it had at the time called "Pentecost." From it he infers that this was the baptism of the Spirit. The fact that he asked for water after it will be dealt with later.

CORROBORATED BY PETER AND JOHN

From the interrelationship of these three sentences — that of John, that of Christ, and that of Peter — it certainly follows that those who were truly and genuinely baptized with the baptism of water were nevertheless not baptized with the baptism of the Spirit, which is that of Christ. Those who truly and genuinely administered the baptism of water did not, in so doing, administer the baptism of Christ.

So, if there is now but a single baptism, as has already been proved, we may safely conclude that it is the baptism of the Spirit and not of water. Otherwise it is necessary to conclude that the "one baptism" which continues is the baptism of water, that is, John's baptism, and not the baptism of the Spirit, that is, Christ's. This is obviously most absurd. . . .

This is where the controversy between us comes to a head. There are those who consider persons who have been baptized with water to be truly baptized with the "one baptism" although they are not baptized with the Spirit. Yet it is the

---

[4] Barclay's explanation hangs on the word "truly" in the KJ version. I suspect he did not check the Greek, for in the NEB version, quoted here, it comes out "as you know." The RSV omits any interjectory word or phrase, while the Cath-CCD renders it "indeed." The evidence would seem to be against using the passage as "proof" of the validity of John's baptism. — ED.

[5] Here the various translations are differently aligned, but none of them makes use of "truly." KJ and RSV use "indeed" interjected between "John" and "baptized," whereas NEB and Cath-CCD omit it.

These comments do not affect the validity of Barclay's basic argument on the interrelationship of these texts, which follows in the next paragraph.

baptism of the Spirit which is specifically called the baptism of
Christ in the scripture. And these same people do not consider
those who have had the baptism of the Spirit to have been baptized unless they have also been sprinkled or dipped in water.

This is where the controversy between us and our opponents is so frequently drawn. They often prefer the form and
the shadow to the power and the substance. They consider
people to have inherited and possessed the truth if they have
the form and shadow, even though in reality they lack the
power and the substance.

We, on the contrary, always prefer the power to the form,
the substance to the shadow. Where the substance and the
power are, we do not hesitate to say that there has been a baptism even though the form has not been observed.

BAPTISM IS AN APPEAL TO GOD FOR A CLEAR CONSCIENCE

¶IV. It is apparent from 1 Pet 3:21 RSV that the one baptism of Christ is not a cleansing with water. After speaking of
the water which saved eight persons on Noah's ark, the apostle
says: "Baptism, which corresponds to this, now saves you, not
as a removal of dirt from the body but as an appeal[6] to God
for a clear conscience, through the resurrection of Jesus Christ."

This is the plainest definition in the whole Bible and is
greatly to be preferred over all the definitions that have been
devised by the Schoolmen.[7] The apostle first tells us what baptism is not. It is not, he says, a removal of dirt from the body.
Obviously then one is not cleansed by the water. The apostle
then says what it is. It is, he says, "an appeal to God for a
clear conscience, through the resurrection of Jesus Christ."

BAPTISM OF THE SPIRIT AND OF FIRE

How can this be achieved if it is not through the purifying
action of the Holy Spirit on the soul, and the cauterizing of our
unrighteous nature by the fire of his judgment? Those in whom
this has been done can truly be said to have been baptized with
the baptism of Christ — the baptism of the Spirit and of fire.

---

[6] Barclay used the KJ: "answer of a clear conscience towards God,"
and also pointed out that "answer" was rendered "confession" in the
Syriac version.

[7] "The teachers of philosophy and theology at the medieval European universities, then usually called 'schools,' of which Paris and Oxford
were pre-eminent." "Scholasticism" is the term more generally used today. — *O.D.C.C.*, p 1227.

Whatever way we take this definition of Christ's baptism it comes out the same. If we consider the negative part which says it is not a removal of dirt, then it cannot be a water baptism, because water removes dirt. And certainly if we consider the second part first, it cannot be a water baptism, because water has nothing to do with the conscience, and water baptism does not necessarily bring about a clear conscience, as even our adversaries will admit.

If it were not for the way in which it is explicitly made clear that we are not saved by water baptism, the passage could be interpreted as meaning that there was an analogy between water baptism and the eight who were saved by water in Noah's ark. But he does not say that the water puts away the filth of the flesh when it is accompanied by the answer of a good conscience. In other words, he does not say that water is the sacramental element administered by the minister and that the grace conferred by Christ is the thing signified. Instead, he clearly says, in a way which could not be more obvious to those who are judicious and unprejudiced, that it is not any such removal of dirt, or putting away of the filth of the flesh.

Moreover, Peter's declaration of the ark incident as the *antitypon* (the antitype, or that which was prefigured), is usually translated, as in the NEB: "This water prefigured the water of baptism through which you are now brought to safety." But this is contrary to the sense of the rest of the statement, as we have just demonstrated.

It would also contradict the opinion of everyone who opposes our view. For Protestants deny that water baptism is necessary for salvation, while Catholics say that no one can be saved without it, unless he has been martyred or has had some other exceptional reason. But neither Catholics nor Protestants say that all who have been baptized are saved by water baptism. But this is what they should say if they are to interpret the apostle as meaning water baptism in this statement. For, if we are saved by this baptism, as those who were in the ark were saved, it must mean that all who have this baptism are saved by it. But this can be said about the baptism of the Spirit, because all who receive an answer to their appeal for a good conscience, and continue to have it, are saved.

PAUL MAKES IT CLEAR THAT THE "ONE BAPTISM" IS NOT A WASHING WITH WATER

It is apparent from the effects of baptism that are described by Paul that the one baptism of Christ is not being washed with water. There are three particular references to this subject.

Rom 6:3-4 NEB: "Have you forgotten that when we were baptized into union with Christ Jesus we were baptized into his death? By baptism we were buried with him, and lay dead, in order that, as Christ was raised from the dead in the splendor of the Father, so also we might set our feet upon the new path of life."

Gal 3:27 NEB: "Baptized into union with him, you have all put on Christ as a garment."

Col 2:12 RSV: "You were buried with him in baptism, in which you were also raised with him through faith in the working of God, who raised him from the dead."

It would be most absurd to interpret these passages as referring to anything except a baptism of the Spirit. Otherwise you have to say that anyone who has been washed with a water baptism has risen with Christ. This is obviously rather far-fetched.

Suppose that all of the visible members of the churches of Rome, Galatia, and Colossae had been outwardly baptized with water. I do not say that they were, although this is something that our opposers not only take for granted, but on which they base their arguments. However, they do not say that all of these had put on Christ, since there are various expressions to the contrary in these epistles. Then it follows that in spite of their water baptism they had not been baptized into Christ, or with the "one baptism" of Christ.

JOHN'S BAPTISM MERELY A FORESHADOWING

¶V. John's baptism was merely a foreshadowing of the substance that was to come and which was to be the true baptism of Christ. With the one baptism of Christ, John's baptism was to cease. If anyone should doubt this, it can easily be proved by the words of John 3:30 RSV and Cath-CCD: "He must increase, but I must decrease."

It clearly follows that Christ's baptism was to increase or take the place of John's baptism which was to decrease or be abolished. Since water baptism was one of the specific parts of John's ministry and is not part of Christ's baptism, as we

have already proved, it is only a natural consequence for water
baptism to be discontinued.

CHRIST NEVER BAPTIZED WITH WATER

If water baptism was to be continued as a perpetual ordinance of Christ for his Church, he would certainly have practiced it himself, or commanded his disciples to do so. Yet it
is clearly stated parenthetically in John 4:2 RSV that he did
not practice it: "(although Jesus himself did not baptize, but
only his disciples)" [or NEB: "although in fact it was only the
disciples who were baptizing and not Jesus himself."]. There
is no place where the scriptures say he commanded his disciples
to baptize with water. It is begging the issue to claim that
Mat 28:19 RSV refers to water baptism: "Go therefore and
make disciples of all nations, baptizing them in the name of
the Father and of the Son and of the Holy Spirit."[8]

IN ALL OF CHRIST'S COMMANDS IN MAT 5 AND 6
THERE IS NO MENTION OF STANDING ORDINANCES

It is also strange that in all of the commands of Christ contained in the fifth and sixth chapters of Matthew there is no
mention of standing ordinances and appointments. Elsewhere
he says that it is our duty to worship and he exhorts us to meet,
adding the promise of his presence. He commands us to pray,
preach, and watch. Although he issues precepts for some temporary things, such as the washing of one another's feet, and
the breaking of bread, Christ does not give us a single precept
for the one thing that is so earnestly contended for — baptizing.

¶VI. It is derogatory to the new covenant dispensation to
make water baptism a required institution of the Christian religion. Christianity is pure and spiritual and not earthly and
ceremonial. The gospel brings to an end such rites and ceremonies as baptism, or washing with water, that were prescribed

---

[8] It is interesting to note that the comparable passages in Mark
16:9-19 are relegated to a footnote in the RSV; the NEB prints them after
a break in spacing with a note that "at this point, some of the most ancient witnesses bring the book to a close."
  The American Catholic Bible (1961 Benziger ed) includes them without comment, however Gerard S. Sloyan (Catholic Univ. of America) says
in his introduction to the Gospel of Mark in the *New Testament Reading
Guide*, No. 2, The Liturgical Press, Collegeville, Minn., 1960: "although
the non-Markan authorship of these verses seems evident, at no time has
the Church viewed them as non-canonical or non-inspired" (pp 13-14).
  Verse 18's guarantee of immunity from snake-bite and deadly poisons
echoes Luke 10:19 and Acts 28:3-6.

under the law. Heb 9:9-10 NEB says: "(All this is symbolic,
pointing to the present time.) The offerings and sacrifices there
prescribed cannot give the worshipper inward perfection. It is
only a matter of food and drink and various rites of cleansing
— outward ordinances in force until the time of reformation."
If the time of reformation, that is, the dispensation of the gospel, has come, then such baptisms and outward ordinances are
not to be imposed any longer. . . .

It will be said that God confers inward grace upon some
who are baptized. But he undoubtedly did this to some who
were baptized among the Jews. This does not mean that outward ordinances are considered more spiritual at one time than
another. Wasn't God the author of the purifications and baptisms that were used under the law? Wasn't water the constituent then, just as it is now? Wasn't the purpose then, as it is
now, to signify an inward purification by an outward rite? Isn't
this still alleged to be the purpose? Does is make them any
more clean inwardly now than it did under the law? If some
were inwardly purified by the grace of God under the law and
some may be purified that way now, does that necessarily make
it a consequence or effect of water baptism? . . .

Let our opponents show us — if they can — without begging the question, or using one or more of their own principles
which are not recognized by us, where Christ ever appointed or
ordained any institution or observance. Let them show how
this belonged to the new covenant, or was part of its nature,
or was to continue perpetually as a required part of new testament worship. Let them demonstrate how this formerly carnal
ordinance, commanded by God under the law, was the same in
substance and effects (that is, necessary consequences and not
merely accidental effects) as the one which has become the
spiritual ordinance of Christ under the gospel, merely by these
minor alterations in form or circumstances. . . .

OUR OPPONENTS ARE JUDAIZING

In this as in most other things, as we have often observed,
our opponents judaize and renounce the glorious and spiritual
privileges of the new covenant. They cling to the rudimentary
doctrine and worship of the old covenant, finding it better
suited to their worldly apprehensions and physical senses. But
we, on the contrary, struggle to grasp and cling to the light of
the glorious gospel that has been revealed to us. The harmony

of the truth we profess in this matter will become apparent if we make a few brief observations of the way in which we follow the spiritual gospel of Christ in all of these matters, as distinguished from the earthliness, or worldliness, of the legal dispensation. . . .

For the law and rule of the old covenant were outward and written on tablets of stone and parchment. So are those of the Christians who oppose us. But the law of the new covenant is inward and perpetual. It is written in the heart. That is our law!

The worship of the Jews was outward and appealed to the physical senses. It was limited to set times, places, and persons, and it was performed according to prescribed rituals and observances. So is the worship of the Christians who oppose us. But the worship of the new covenant is not limited as to time, place, or person, but it is performed in the Spirit and in truth. It is not acted out according to established forms and prescribed ritual, but as the unmediated Spirit of God actuates, impels, and leads, whether it be to preach, pray, or sing. This is also true of our worship.

Similarly, the baptism of the Jews under the law was an outward washing with outward water. It merely typified an inward purification of the soul which did not necessarily take place in those who were baptized in that manner. But the baptism of Christ under the gospel is the baptism of the Spirit and of fire. It is not the putting away of the filth of the flesh, but the answer of a good conscience before God. This is the baptism that we strive to be baptized with and contend for.

PAUL'S COMMISSION WAS NOT TO BAPTIZE

¶VII. If water baptism was an ordinance of the gospel, surely the apostle Paul would have been sent to administer it. But he says, 1 Cor 1:17 RSV, Cath-CCD, [NEB]: "Christ did not send me to baptize, but to preach [proclaim] the gospel." Paul's commission was as broad as that of any of the apostles. In fact he was in a special way the apostle of Christ to the Gentiles, and if water baptism was intended to be the badge of a Christian, in the way in which circumcision is the badge of a Jew, he would have had more use for it than the rest of the apostles. He would have been especially commissioned to baptize them with water in order to mark his Gentile converts with that Christian sign.

But doesn't it make better sense to consider it another way? To hold that since he was the apostle to the Gentiles he was endeavoring to wean them from the former Jewish ceremonies and observances? That seems to be apparent from his epistles and throughout his ministry. In fact he was sometimes criticized undeservedly by those of his brethren who were unwilling to do away with those ceremonies. That is why his commission did not require him to lead his converts into such Jewish observances and baptisms, even though it was as complete as that of the other apostles in regard to the preaching of the gospel and the new covenant dispensation. However, the practice was indulged by the other apostles among their Jewish proselytes. That is the reason he thanks God (1 Cor 1:14) that he baptized so few. He is intimating that it was not done by virtue of his apostolic commission, but rather out of condescension for their weakness, just as at another time he circumcised Timothy.

In order to avoid the truth of this testimony, others usually allege that he is to be understood as meaning that baptism was not a primary part of his commission, rather than meaning that he was not supposed to baptize at all. But the only foundation for this interpretation is the opinion of those who hold it, and it is rejected for lack of proof.

Paul did not say: "I was not sent primarily to baptize," but: "I was not sent to baptize." To confirm the rejected interpretation, its proponents generally cite other places in the scripture where *not* means *not primarily,* as in Mat 9:13 RSV, Cath-CCD, which says: "I desire mercy, and not sacrifice" ["I require mercy, not sacrifice." NEB]. But the quotation in Hos 6:6 RSV, from which Christ took the statement, is: "For I desire steadfast love and not sacrifice, the knowledge of God, rather than burnt offerings." It is clear from the latter part that burnt offerings, which are the same as sacrifices, are not excluded. However, Paul's statement has no such qualifying phrase and the analogy remains undemonstrated.

For if we accepted this interpretation and applied the same principle to other sections of the scripture, what would become of 1 Cor 2:5 RSV? Here Paul says: "That your faith might not rest in the wisdom of men but in the power of God." This would have to be interpreted as meaning that your faith does not owe its principal duty to God. The gospel would certainly be perverted by such liberty of interpretation.

PAUL WAS NOT ANSWERING AN ABUSE

If it should be said that the apostle was writing because baptism had been abused by the Corinthians, but that such abuse would not be justification for abolishing it, I will say that that would be true if the matter that was abused was lawful and necessary. However, let it first be borne in mind that the apostle exlcudes baptizing but not preaching, but that the abuse stemmed equally from both. For the Corinthians were dividing into groups named for the persons by whose preaching and baptizing they had been converted. This is apparent from 1 Cor 1:16, as well as from 1 Cor 3:3-9 NEB, which says:

"Can you not see that while there is jealousy and strife among you, you are living on the purely human level of your lower nature? When one says, 'I am Paul's man,' and another, 'I am for Apollos,' are you not all too human?

"After all, what is Apollos? What is Paul? We are simply God's agents in bringing you to the faith. Each of us performed the task which the Lord allotted to him: I planted the seed, and Apollos watered it; but God made it grow. Thus it is not the gardeners with their planting and watering who count, but God, who makes it grow. Whether they plant or water, they work as a team, though each will get his own pay for his own labor. We are God's fellow-workers; and you are God's garden."

CHRIST RECEIVED BAPTISM WITH WATER, BUT HE WAS ALSO CIRCUMCISED

¶VIII. Some will ask why it was that Christ, who had the Spirit beyond measure (John 3:34), was nevertheless baptized with water. Nicholas Arnoldus raises a question concerning this thesis in Sec 46 of his *Theological Exercitation.*[9]

Christ was also circumcised, but that does not mean that circumcision is to continue! It behooved Christ to fulfill all righteousness, not only of John's ministry, but that of the law also! That is why he observed Jewish feasts and rites and kept the Passover. But it does not follow that because he did so Christians must do so now. And it is pertinent to remember that when John tried to dissuade Jesus from being baptized, he replied, Mat 3:15 NEB: "Let it be so for the present." That

---

[9] Nikolaus Arnold (1618-1680). See pp 221 and 222 for biog notes, and the Author Index for several other references to this work.

ought to be sufficient intimation that he did not intend to
perpetuate it as an ordinance for his disciples.

The greatest objection that is usually raised is based on
Mat 28:19 NEB: "Go forth therefore and make all nations my
disciples; baptize men everywhere in the name of the Father
and the Son and the Holy Spirit." The only sound answer is
that we grant the entire command but feel that those who base
their objection on this passage should prove that it refers to
water baptism, since it is not specifically mentioned. In fact
we deny that water baptism was meant. The baptism that was
referred to was the "one baptism" and of such a nature that
those who received it "put on Christ."

THE DIFFERENCE BETWEEN JOHN'S AND CHRIST'S BAPTISMS

There are also those who allege that Christ's baptism differed from John's, but that it too was a water baptism. This
view holds that John baptized only into repentance but Christ
commanded his disciples to baptize in the name of the Father,
Son, and Holy Spirit. They say that the distinction between
the two lay in the form. But this is not where the difference
lies, for Christ's baptism was also one of repentance. However,
the opposition is not united, for Calvin considers Christ's baptism and John's to be one and the same.[10] But they do differ,
and the difference is that one is with water, and one is not.

Those who claim that the distinction lies in what Christ
said, that is, to baptize in the name of the Father, Son, and
Spirit, have stated the difference, but it is a great one. For the
distinction does not consist of making something different of
water baptism by varying a few words. The text says no such
thing and I do not see how that can be inferred. For the
Greek is *eios to onoma,* meaning *into the name.* It must be
remembered, however, that the name of the Lord is frequently
used in scripture to signify more than it literally expresses, in
other words, as a connotation of the virtue and power belonging to the one named (as in Psalm 54:1, Song of Sol 1:3, Prov
18:10, and many others).

BAPTISM "INTO THE NAME" OF CHRIST

It is evident from Paul's testimony that the apostles were
supposed to baptize the nations into his name, virtue, and
power, and that they did so. That is what the statement (Gal

[10] *Inst.,* lib 4, cap 15, sect 7-8.

3:27 KJ): that as many of them as were "baptized into Christ, have put on Christ," must have meant — a baptism "into the name" — or in other words into the power and virtue. It was not merely a set form of words to be added to water baptism.

Those who wish their faith to be founded on nothing other than the testimony of God's Spirit and the truth of the scriptures should consider this thoroughly. They should ask themselves if it is not merely the prejudice of the way in which they have been taught to think, and the influence of tradition, which support this allegation. This may be a stumbling block for the uncritical and unthinking reader, because it seems to abolish the very foundation of Christianity. He is startled at being told flatly that this passage of scripture should not be interpreted as referring to water, and that that kind of formal baptizing in the name of the Father, Son, and Spirit is not warranted by Mat 28.

However, just for the sake of argument, let it be assumed that Christ *was* instituting a particular form of water baptism that was to be accompanied by the words "in the name of the Father, Son, and Spirit." Unfortunately for this hypothesis, although there are numerous references in Acts to who was baptized and how (as in Acts 2:41; 8:12, 13, 38; 9:18; 10:48; 16:15; and 18:8), there is not a word about this particular form. In two places, Acts 8:16 [NEB: "For until then the Spirit had not come upon any of them. They had been baptized into the name of the Lord Jesus, that and nothing more"] and Acts 19:5 [NEB: "On hearing this they were baptized into the name of the Lord Jesus"] they were baptized into the name of Jesus only. Either the author was very careless (which is a rather serious accusation since Luke wrote under the guidance of the Holy Spirit) or else the apostles did not understand that they had been enjoined by Christ in Mat 28 to use a particular form of water baptism. I imagine that our opponents would consider it a great heresy to administer water baptism without mentioning the Father and Spirit. Yet it expressly says that this was done in the two places that have been cited.

TEACHING IS DISTINCT FROM BAPTIZING WITH THE SPIRIT

But, they say, if this were not understood to refer to water baptism it would be tautological and there would be no distinction between baptism and teaching. However, baptizing with the Spirit goes beyond teaching or informing the understanding. Its real significance is in reaching the heart and melting it so that a change of heart is brought about as well as an increase in understanding. *Teaching* and *instructing* are often used together in the scriptures in such a way that they are not ridiculous or needlessly redundant. And yet they are more nearly alike in meaning than *teaching* and *baptizing with the Spirit*.

THE APOSTLES WERE THE INSTRUMENTS OF CHRIST IN BAPTIZING WITH THE SPIRIT

Another claim is that baptism in this citation must mean with water, because it is performed by the apostles. It is reasoned that this cannot be the baptism of the Spirit since that is the work of Christ and his grace and not of man! Now, while it is true that baptism of the Spirit cannot be wrought without Christ and his grace, nonetheless men who have been equipped by God for that purpose are his instruments. Therefore, it is not far-fetched to speak of baptism of the Spirit as an act of the apostles.

Although it is Christ who gives spiritual gifts by his grace, nevertheless, the apostle says in Rom 1:11 RSV: "I long to see you, that I may impart to you some spiritual gift ["spiritual grace" Cath-CCD] to strengthen you."

In 1 Cor 4:15 NEB: "In Christ Jesus, you are my offspring, and mine alone, through the preaching of the gospel." And yet, winning people to the faith is the work of Christ and his grace, not of men. Converting the heart is properly the work of Christ, and yet the scriptures often refer to men as the instruments of conversion. Paul was commissioned to turn people from darkness to light, although he could not have done it without the assistance of the grace of Christ. Similarly, man may be the instrument in baptizing with the Spirit, although it is necessary to have the concurring work of Christ's grace. So it is not too far-fetched to say that the apostles administered the baptism of the Spirit.

WATER BAPTISM CLAIMED TO EXTEND UNTIL THE END OF THE WORLD

Others claim that since Christ says he will be with his disciples until the end of the world, water baptism must continue till then. If he had been speaking of water baptism this might be so. But this is denied and has been proved to be false. He is speaking of baptism of the Spirit and we gladly confess that this is to remain until the end of the world.   Indeed, it will remain as long as Christ's presence abides with his children.

THE APOSTOLIC PRACTICE WAS NOT CONSTANT

¶IX. The constant administration of water baptism by the apostles in the primitive church to those converted to the faith of Christ is claimed by our opponents. They say that the apostles understood the baptism referred to in Mat 28 as one of water. Otherwise they would have had no commission to baptize.

However, it should be pointed out that this was not the constant practice of the apostles, as Paul's example has shown. It would be absurd to maintain that he had converted only those few in the Church of Corinth that he says he baptized. It is no less absurd to believe that this was a constant apostolic practice, if he who was in no way inferior to the best of the apostles rejoiced that he had done so little of it.

THE APOSTLES MAY HAVE MISUNDERSTOOD

There is another possibility. It is that their later use of water for baptism led them to misunderstand Christ's commission in Mat 28 as authorization for them to baptize with water. Although I do not see the need for this interpretation, I do not see any harm in it.   Certainly they misunderstood their commission to "teach all nations" for a while and considered it unlawful to teach Gentiles.   Even Peter developed misgivings about teaching Gentiles until he was compelled to change his mind by a vision.[11]   The education of the apostles as Jews and their natural inclination to adhere to the Jewish faith influenced them to such an extent that for a time they could not receive Gentiles, even after Christ's resurrection.

Although Christ had included them in his commission to teach all nations, they would not do it even after the pouring forth of the Spirit.

It could also be reasonably assumed that since many of the principal disciples had also been disciples of John they mistakenly considered Jesus' baptism to be the same as John's. After all, his baptism had been so prized by the Jews that they may well have considered the baptism which Christ intended to be one of the Spirit, to have been one of water. Accordingly, they could have practiced it for a time. Obviously they did not continue it, or Peter would not have said that baptism "is not

---

[11] Acts 10:28-29.

a putting away of the filth of the flesh," which would be a good description of washing with water.

A great deal is also made of the baptism of Cornelius by Peter and two things are claimed from it. As recorded in Acts 10:47-48, Peter not only used water baptism for those who had already received the Spirit, but it says that "he commanded them to be baptized" (KJ, RSV). It is claimed not only that he used water but that he was instituting a standing ordinance for the Church.[12] At the time that Peter baptized Cornelius it had not yet been decided whether Gentiles were required to undergo circumcision, although it was the consensus of the Church's practice, at that time, that they should.

THE MEANING OF "BAPTISM" IS FIGURATIVE

¶X. Still another objection that is raised is based on the derivation of the word "baptize." Since it means "to dip in water," it is alleged that the very word means water baptism. But this is a very weak argument. As Paulus Riccius[13] has shown, baptizing with water was a Jewish rite even before the coming of John. The ceremony received its name from the way in which it was practiced by both the Jews and John. But Christ and his apostles frequently made figurative references to this and other Jewish rites to give them a more spiritual significance. Circumcision was commonly understood[14] among the Jews to be performed in the flesh. However, Paul speaks of a circumcision of the heart and spirit, made without hands (Phil 3:3 and Col 2:11). Even though the word baptism was used among the Jews to signify only washing with water, nevertheless John, Christ, and his apostles all speak of being "baptized with the Spirit and with fire." And it is this latter type of bap-

---

[12] It seems more likely that he was giving acceptance to them as Jews in this fashion, for verse 47 RSV reads: "Can any one forbid water for baptizing these people who have received the Holy Spirit just as we have?" — ED.

[13] Paul Ricci (fl 16th c.) "was a convert from Judaism in the 16th cent. For a time he was professor in Padua, in Italy, when the Emperor Maximilian I appointed him his physician." Especially famous as a cabalist, he translated a large part of Gikatilla's *The Gates of Light*, which Reuchlin used very largely. Erasmus was his special friend and he engaged in dialogue with von Eck. — McClintock and Strong, *Cyclopedia of Biblical, Theological, and Ecclesiastical Literature*, N. Y., Harper, 1880, vol 9, p 9.

[14] Barclay says "only understood" — although there are Deut 10:16 and 30:6. — ED.

tism which they speak of as Christ's baptism as distinguished from John's, which was with water. The spiritual substance was given to that which had been foreshadowed.

Another example of this was Christ's figurative reference to his body and the resurrection which the Jews misunderstood when he said: "Destroy this temple, and in three days I will raise it up." There are many others which could be given.

THE LITERAL MEANING IS IMMERSION

Even if the etymology of the word were closely adhered to, it would tend to disprove the views of other Christians as well as our own. For the Greek "baptism" signifies *immergo,* that is, to "plunge" and "dip in." That is the way in which water baptism was performed among the Jews by John, and also by whatever primitive Christians used it. Sprinkling a little water on the forehead is not at all consistent with the original meaning of the word baptism. Sprinkling was first introduced to prevent harm to those with weak constitutions. However, those who had been sprinkled rather than dipped were not allowed to hold any office in the church. They were not considered sufficiently baptized![15] If those who base their argument on etymology want to be consistent, they will have to alter their method of baptizing.

John 3:5 is often cited as inferring the necessity for water baptism as well as that of the Spirit. It says (RSV): "Truly, truly, I say to you, unless one is born of water and the Spirit, he cannot enter the kingdom of God."

PROTESTANTS ARE INCONSISTENT

If this proved anything, it would prove that water baptism is absolutely necessary, just as Roman Catholics maintain. But

---

[15] Except for sprinkling this would appear to be the Clinical Baptism described in the *O.D.C.C.* (p 125) which "was conferred without ceremonies, but regarded as inferior to regular Baptism and constituted a canonical impediment debarring the persons thus baptized, who were called 'clinici' (Greek *kline,* 'bed'), from ordination to the priesthood. Clinical Baptism gradually fell into desuetude owing especially to the increasing practice of Infant Baptism and the development of the penitential system."

The *O.D.C.C.* account is inconsistent in its logic, however, stating that Clinical Baptism was the result of delaying Baptism until death was believed imminent, in order to avoid the Christian responsibilities implied. If this type of baptism was primarily a death-bed matter, it would hardly have acquired a priesthood-disbarment feature. Barclay would probably be borne out by further investigation, as I have not found him wrong on any major point. — ED.

when this argument is used with Protestants, they maintain correctly that outward *water* is not meant here, but rather a mystical[16] inward cleansing and washing. Just as when Christ speaks of being baptized with fire, he is not referring to outward material fire. It is a metonymical reference to purification. Purification, as in cauterizing, is just as distinctive of fire as washing or making clean are of water. The scripture alludes to water in this way in such passages as Titus 3:5 with its reference to being saved "by the washing of regeneration" ["and renewal in the Holy Spirit"].

Calvin[17] has well observed that there is frequent citation of the place where Peter says very clearly, 1 Pet 3:21 NEB: "Baptism is not the washing away of bodily pollution, but the appeal made to God by a good conscience." Since this is not a reference to outward *water,* it can hardly be called upon to support water baptism.

BAPTISM AS THE VISIBLE BADGE OF CHRISTIANS

There are some who maintain that baptism with water is the visible sign or badge which distinguishes Christians from infidels just as circumcision served for the Jews. But this does not mean a thing unless it can be proved that it was part of the new covenant dispensation. It is hardly legitimate for us to devise some outward ceremonies and rites and then claim that they will distinguish us from infidels merely because we say so. This was not the case with circumcision, which was an absolute command and was called the seal of the first covenant. But, as we have already proved, there is no similar command for baptism. There is not a single word in all of the New Testament that would serve as a basis for calling it a badge of Christianity or the seal of the new covenant.

The profession of faith in Christ and the answer of a holy life is a far better badge of Christianity than any external ritual washing. Although many of the Fathers of the Church spoke of water baptism as *Characterem Christianitatis,* they also said this of the sign of the cross and other similar things which have been properly rejected by Protestants. The simplicity and purity of Christian worship were soon spoiled by a mysterious and iniquitous tendency which began even in the apostles' days.

---

[16] Barclay's own word.

[17] *Institutes,* lib 4, chap 15.

Not only were many Jewish rites retained, but many pagan customs and ceremonies crept into Christian worship. In fact this is the origin of the word "sacrament" and it is folly for a Protestant, in particular, to claim any support from tradition or antiquity for their practices. Neither Catholics nor Protestants perform these rites exactly as the ancients did. For they became very uncertain about such matters since they did not walk according to that most certain rule; which is God's Spirit, but instead placed a foolish emphasis on externals.

CHANGES FROM EARLY CHURCH PRACTICE

In primitive times, the majority completely immersed and dipped those they baptized, but neither Catholics nor the majority of Protestants do this now. In fact some of the principles which Protestants have now adopted were condemned as heretical by several of the early Fathers of the Church. Augustine condemned the Pelagians[18] for saying that infants who died unbaptized might be saved. The Manichaeans[19] were condemned for denying that grace is universally conferred by baptism. Julian, the Pelagian,[20] was condemned by Augustine for denying

[18] The main tenets of Pelagianism are given in a note on page 66. Pelagius also maintained that new-born children are in the state Adam was in before the fall.
Pelagianism was vigorously attacked by Augustine in *De Peccatorum Meritis* and *De Spiritu et Littera* written in 412 and again in *De Natura et Gratia* (415). After all but a small circle of the Church had rejected Pelagianism, Julian of Eclanum (c. 386-454) conducted a violent polemic against Augustine who countered with *Contra Duas Epistolas Pelagianorum* (420) and *Contra Julianum* (421). Nevertheless Pelagianism survived, chiefly in Gaul and Britain, for at least another century. — *O.D.C.C.*, p 1040.

[19] Manichaeanism owes some of its fame to the fact that Augustine was a member for nine years before his conversion to Christianity. The sect's beliefs were "a hotch-potch of many long-dead heresies. It was based on a supposed primeval conflict between light and darkness" and "the object of the practice of religion was to release the particles of light which Satan had stolen from the world of Light and imprisoned in man's brain." Jesus, Buddha, the Prophets, and Manichaeus had been sent to help with the task. The sect survived in Chinese Turkestan until the 13th c. and a collection of Manichaean documents was discovered there in 1904 and 1905. Others, either by Manes (as he is also known) himself or one of his earliest disciples, were found in Egypt in 1933. — *O.D.C.C.*, pp 848-849.

[20] Presumably the Bishop of Eclanum, referred to directly above. His writings are preserved only fragmentarily in Augustine's quotations. "He seems to have possessed keen dialectical ability, as well as philosophical insight. His account of the worth and powers of human nature is coherent, and his indictment of Augustine's doctrine of the total depravity of

exorcism and insufflation[21] in the use of baptism. All of these things are also denied by Protestants. Isn't it rather ridiculous for them to upbraid us for denying water baptism because none of the ancients took a similar view? Certainly they cannot show us any who used it who were not heretical on several other points. Or else they used it together with the sign of the cross and other things which Protestants deny.

"HERETICS" WERE BURNT FOR DENYING THE SACRAMENTS

Nevertheless, there were some who testified against water baptism even in the darkest days of the popes. Alanus[22] refers to some of his contemporaries who were burned at the stake for denying it. They claimed that baptism had no efficacy for either children or adults and hence it was not required for that reason. Ten so-called canons were burned for that crime by

---

fallen man (which he held to be a consequence of the Manichaean errors of Augustine's youth), although couched in rather scurrilous terms, is powerful; but his conception of human self-sufficiency is not easily reconciled with the Christian doctrine of man's sinfulness." — *O.D.C.C.*, p 753.

[21] Exorcism, or the casting out of devils, played a major part in the Church, and the Exorcist was one of the Minor Orders (see p 207) in the Roman Church.

Insufflation is the act of blowing or breathing upon a person to symbolize the influence of the Holy Spirit.

In the Orthodox Church, "the baptism itself is preceded by exorcism, in which the priest breathes thrice on the candidate, and signs him with the sign of the Cross. The Devil is exorcised, partly through direct evocations, 'Satan, the Lord exorcises thee, get thee hence!' and partly through prayers that God would drive out the evil spirit.'" — Einar Molland, *Christendom, The Christian Churches, Their Doctrine, Constitutional Forms and Ways of Worship*, London, Mowbray, 1961, pp 24-25.

22 pp 103, 104, 107.

Probably Alain de l'Isle, "Alanus ab Insulis" (c. 1128-1203), a theologian and eclectic philosopher, sometimes known as "doctor universalis." He took part in the Third Lateran Council (1179) and eventually entered the monastery at Citeaux.

"He held a rationalist-mystical view of the relation of philosophy and religion, maintaining that all the truths of religion are discoverable by unaided reason. His mysticism was based on his philosophy, chiefly a mixture of Pythagoreanism and Neoplatonism, in which a curious feature is his belief in 'Nature' as a mediator in creation between God and matter.... The *Ars Fidei Catholicae*, an attempt to confute non-Christians on rational grounds alone, which until recently was attributed to him [possibly the work to which Barclay alludes], has been shown by M. Grabmann to be the work of Nicholas of Amiens." — *O.D.C.C.*, p 28.

The citation of *De fide catholica contra haereticos sui temporis* (Antwerp, 1654) by Alanus in Ronald Knox's *Enthusiasm*, Oxford, 1962, as a source of information on Waldensian origins suggests an edition of particular interest in Barclay's time. — ED.

order of King Robert of France.[23]   P. Pithaeus mentions it in
his fragments of the history of Guienne.[24] It is also confirmed
by Johannes Floracensis,[25] a famous monk of that time, in his
epistle to Oliva, abbot of the Ausonian church. "I will give
you some understanding," he says, "concerning the heresy that
took place in the city of Orleans on Childermas-day;[26] for it
was true, as you have probably heard, that King Robert caused
about fourteen from that city to be burned alive. They were
some of their chief clergymen, and the more noble of their
laics, who were hateful to God, and abominable to heaven and
earth, for they stiffly denied the grace of holy baptism, and also
the consecration of the Lord's body and blood." The time
when it happened is noted by Papir. Masson in his *Annals of
France,*[27] book 3, and in Hugh and Robert.[28]

   We have only the testimony of their accusers for calling
them heretics and Manichaeans,[29] and this does not invalidate

   [23] The reference to Hugh and Robert, below, identifies him as King
Robert II, or Robert the Pious (c. 970-1031), the son of Hugh Capet, with
whom he ruled jointly after 987, becoming sole king in 996, but later
establishing a duumvirate with his son Hugh, the eldest of four sons by
his third wife, from 1017-1025. His marital irregularities had gotten him
excommunicated and he was "worsted" in war by his younger sons.

   [24] Probably Pierre Pithou (1539-1598), a lawyer of the French Parliament and disciple of Cujas. In 1578 he rejected Calvinism and became
attorney-general of Guyenne. — *Grand Larousse encyclopedique,* Paris, 1963,
vol 8, p 522.

   [25] The epistle referred to is included in M. Bouquet, *Rerum Galli-
carum et Francicarum scriptores* (24 vols, Paris, 1738-1904), a compendium
of Gallican and French historical documents extending up to 1328 A.D.
   It is indexed in August Pothast, *Wegweiser durch die Geschichtswerke
des Europäischen Mitelalters bis 1500,* p 671, as: Johannes Monachus Flori-
acensis. "Epistola ad Olibam abbatem, S. Ausonensis ecclesiae episcopum
anno 1022." — I am indebted to Prof. Geo. Barrois of Princeton Theological Seminary for locating this very elusive reference.

   [26] An old English name for the Feast of the Holy Innocents, Dec. 28.

   [27] Jean (called Papire) Masson (1544-1618), humanist lawyer of the
French Parliament, author of a variety of extended works, written in
Latin. The best of these was *Annales Francorum* in 4 vols, cited here. —
Grand Larousse, Paris, 1963, vol 7, p 152.

   28 *Actum Aureliae publice anno Incarnacionis Domini
1022; Regni Roberti Regis 28; Indictione 5, quando Stephanus
Haeresiarcha et Complices ejus damnati sunt et exusti Aureliae.*
   The citation is, of course, the official acts of the realm for 1022 A.D.,
the 28th year of Robert II's reign and the fifth of his joint rule with his
son Hugh.

   [29] See note on p 323.

their testimony for this truth against the use of water baptism. It is no more ground for calling us Manichaeans than it is for calling Protestants that because they share some other points of doctrine with them.

PAEDOBAPTISM

As for infant baptism, certainly if water baptism was to be discontinued under the new covenant, the baptism of infants is unwarranted. But the converse is not true. Even if it were proved that water baptism is to continue, it would not necessarily follow, without other arguments, that infant baptism is necessary. Nicolaus Arnoldus'[30] statement is a pitiful subterfuge. It characterizes the denial of infant baptism as part of the "gangrene" of Anabaptism,[31] but it doesn't provide any further proof.

[30] Consult the Author Index for various references and biog note.

[31] "Anabaptist" meant "rebaptizer," but they claimed that as Infant Baptism was null and void, there could be no question of repeating the sacrament. Although they are best known for their stand on baptism, their doctrines of the Church, the relationship of Church and State, their pacifism, and their emphasis on 'the voice of conscience' were also distinctive.

In 1523 a group of their priests and laymen declared that "believers should break away from the Church and form 'a pure community' . . . wholly independent of the State. . . .

"The Anabaptist movement soon spread to Switzerland and Germany . . . It flourished between 1525 and 1535, but sustained a severe blow through the disaster at Münster" (see page 364), "but continued in Holland under new forms, influenced by Menno Simons (1496-1561), and becoming known as Mennonites after this early leader. — Molland, *Christendom*, pp 289-290.

"The Anabaptists were vigorously denounced by M. Luther, H. Zwingli, and J. Calvin and severely persecuted by both Roman Catholics and Protestants. Those put to death probably ran into tens of thousands. Down to modern times they have suffered from too hostile criticism; and Anabaptist hymnology and martyrology are only now receiving sympathetic and scholarly study." — *O.D.C.C.*, p 46.

Communion

The communion of the body and blood of Christ is inward and spiritual. It is by participation in his flesh and blood that the inward man is nourished daily in the hearts of those in whom Christ dwells. The breaking of bread by Christ with his disciples was a symbol (1 Cor 10:16-17; John 6:32-33, 35; 1 Cor 5:8). For the sake of the weak, it was used in the church for a time, even by those who had received the substance.

Just as abstaining from things strangled and from blood was practiced for a time (Acts 15:20); this, and the washing of one another's feet (John 13:14) and the anointing of the sick with oil (James 5:14) were all commanded with no less authority and solemnity than the breaking of bread. But since they were but shadows of better things, they are no longer to be practiced by those who have obtained the substance.

THE COMMUNION OF THE BODY AND BLOOD OF CHRIST IS A MYSTERY

¶I. The communion of the body and blood of Christ is a mystery which is hidden from men who are still in their natural state. In this first fallen and corrupt condition they cannot understand it. Nor can they achieve or comprehend it while they still remain in that state. They cannot partake of Christ's body then, since they are not yet able to discern it. Since most of the Christian world have been endeavoring, with their own natural and unrenewed understanding, to conceive of and imagine the things of God and religion, this has been a mystery which has been greatly hidden and well concealed from them. While they have been quarrelling or fighting with one another over the shadow and the external form, they have been strangers to the substance, the life, and the power of it.

¶II. The body of Christ of which the believers partake is one of the Spirit and not of the flesh. His blood which they drink is pure and celestial and is not composed of human and earthly elements. Augustine also makes this affirmation,[1] say-

[1] *Tractat., Psalm 98.*

ing: "Except a man eat my flesh, he hath not in him life eternal;" and he adds: "The words which I speak unto you are Spirit and life; understand spiritually what I have spoken. You shall not eat of this body which you see, and drink this blood which they shall spill, which crucify me — I am the living bread, who descended from heaven. He calls himself the bread, who descended from heaven, exhorting that we might believe in him..."

CHRIST COMMUNICATES LIFE AND SALVATION

If it should be asked: "What is that body, what is that flesh and blood?" the answer is that it is the heavenly seed, the divine, spiritual, celestial substance of which we have already spoken in the fifth and sixth propositions. It is the spiritual body of Christ by which and through which he communicates life to men and salvation to those who believe in him and receive him. It is also the means by which man has fellowship and communion with God.

This can be proved by John 6:32-71 where Christ speaks at greater length on this matter than at any other place. In fact, the evangelist and beloved disciple gives a more complete account of the spiritual sayings and doctrine of Christ than anyone else. With this in mind one should consider the fact that he says nothing either in his gospel or in his epistles of the ceremony used by Christ in breaking bread with his disciples. Nevertheless in this particular account he has more to say about participation in the body, flesh, and blood of Christ than there is anywhere else in the scripture.

THE FOOD OF ETERNAL LIFE

Knowing that the Jews have followed him out of love for the loaves of bread, Christ urges them in verse 27 NEB: "You must work, not for this perishable food, but for the food that lasts, the food of eternal life." But they understood neither the spiritual language nor the doctrine of Christ. They thought that the food which Moses gave their fathers was the finest bread there was, since it came from heaven. To correct their ideas and better inform them, Christ says (v 32 and 48) that it is not Moses who gives the true bread from heaven, but their Father. What is more, he says (v 35) "I am the bread of life" and (v 51) the "living bread which has come down from heaven." He declares (v 51) that "the bread which I will give is my own flesh," for (v 55) "My flesh is real food; my blood is real drink."

As to the necessity for partaking of his flesh and blood, he says (v 53): "unless you eat the flesh of the Son of Man and drink his blood you can have no life in you." And finally, as to the blessed fruits and the necessary effects of this communion of the body and blood of Christ (v 33): "The bread that God gives... brings life to the world," and he who eats it will "never die" (v 58). He will possess "eternal life" (v 54). He "dwells continually in me and I dwell in him" (v 56), and "he who eats me shall live because of me" (v 57).

From this broad description of the origin, nature, and effects of this body, flesh, and blood of Christ, it is apparent that the flesh and blood were spiritual and that it was a spiritual body that was referred to. This was not the body or temple of Jesus Christ who was born of the Virgin Mary. It was not the body in which he walked, lived, and suffered in the land of Judea. It was clearly stated that it came down from heaven. But all Christians agree at the present time that the outward body was not the part of Christ which came down from heaven. Just to put this matter beyond any doubt, since the Jews might still interpret his statements as referring to the flesh and blood of his body, he says (v 63): "The Spirit alone gives life; the flesh is of no avail." This is also based on the soundest of solid reasoning. For it is the soul, not the body, that is to be nourished by this flesh and blood. But there is no relationship between outward flesh and blood and the soul, and there is no similarity that would allow the soul to be fed by them.

LIKE THE COMMUNION OF THE SAINTS

It is like the communion of the saints with God which is also a uniting and mutual participation not of the flesh, but of the Spirit. "He who is united to the Lord becomes one Spirit with him" (1 Cor 6:17 RSV), not one flesh. For flesh can only partake of flesh (and now I refer to physical flesh, and am not using a metaphor which is to be understood spiritually). The body cannot feed upon spirit, nor can the spirit feed upon flesh. It is further apparent that the flesh of which Christ spoke is to be understood spiritually, from the statement that whoever feeds upon it shall never die. But the bodies of all men die once. In fact it was even necessary for the body of Christ himself to die.

It is also apparent that Christ meant the divine and heavenly seed, to which we have already referred, judging from the nature of this body, the spiritual flesh and blood of Christ, and the fruits of it. It is described as that which came down from heaven and which gives light to the world. This certainly corresponds to the light and seed which John 1 testifies is the light of the world and the life of men. For when the spiritual light and seed receives a place in men's souls and room to develop there, it is like bread to a hungry and fainting soul: a soul that was, as it were, dead and buried among the lusts of the world. When it tastes and partakes of this heavenly bread, it receives life again and revives. Those who partake of it are said to come to Christ, for the only way in which they can have this bread is by coming to him and believing in the appearance of his light in their hearts. It is by receiving this light and believing in it that participation is known in this body and bread.

It becomes apparent that what Christ meant here by his body, flesh, and blood is the same thing that is to be understood from John 1 about the "light enlightening every man." For the light of life spoken of in John 1 is Christ. "He is the true light," and the bread and flesh that are spoken of in John 6, which are also called Christ. "I am the bread of life," he says. And similarly, those who received that light and life, John 1:12, obtained power to become the sons of God, by believing in his name. In John 6:35 those who come to this bread of life shall not hunger, and he who believes in him who is the bread shall never thirst.

So then, just as there was the outward visible body and temple of Jesus Christ, which took its origin from the Virgin Mary, there is also the spiritual body of Christ. By it and through it, he who was the "Word in the beginning with God," who was and is God, revealed himself to the sons of men in all ages. By it, men in all ages have come to partake of eternal life and to have communion and fellowship with God and Christ. If Adam, and Seth, and Enoch, and Abraham, and Moses, and David, and all the prophets and holy men of God had not eaten of the flesh and blood of Christ they would not have had life. Nor would their inward man have been nourished. Just as the outward body and temple was called Christ, it is no less proper to call his spiritual body Christ. That existed long before the outward body was created.

From this, the apostle says, 1 Cor 10:3-4 NEB: "They all ate the same supernatural food, and all drank the same supernatural drink; I mean, they all drank from the supernatural rock that accompanied their travels — and that rock was Christ." It is impossible to take this as referring to anything other than the spiritual body of Christ. This is the spiritual body of Christ that was the saving food of the righteous both before the law and under the law. Even so, under the law it was veiled and obscured under various characters, ceremonies, and observances. What is more, it was veiled and hidden in some respects under the outward temple and body of Christ while it existed. Thus the Jews could not understand Christ's preaching about it while he was on earth. Not only the Jews, but even some of his disciples considered it "more than we can stomach" (v 60 of John 6:60-66 NEB) and murmured at it, and many of them left him and were with him no more.

RESURRECTION FROM DEATH AND DARKNESS BY THE POURING FORTH OF CHRIST IN ALL MEN'S CONSCIENCES

There are undoubtedly many today who profess to be disciples of Christ, but who have as little understanding of this matter as his own disciples did. They look upon and follow the outward body of Christ, but they are as apt to be offended and to find a stumbling block over that by which the faithful are daily fed and nourished. In his obedience to the will of the Father and by the eternal Spirit, Jesus Christ offered up his earthly body as a propitiation for the remission of sins. He finished his testimony on earth with a most perfect example of patience, resignation, and holiness so that all might partake of the fruit of that sacrifice. He also poured forth into the hearts of all men a measure of the divine light and seed with which he is clothed. In that way, he reaches into the consciences of all men in order to raise them up out of death and darkness by his life and light. In that way they may partake of his body and have fellowship with the Father and with the Son.

¶III. It will be asked how we are fed by his body and in what way we partake of it. We have the answer in the clear and explicit words of Christ, John 6:35, 55 RSV: "I am the bread of life; he who comes to me shall not hunger, and he who believes in me shall never thirst." "For my flesh is food indeed, and my blood is drink indeed."

Whoever you are who asks this question, or reads these lines, whether you consider yourself a believer or feel through sad experience that you do not yet believe, you may find that you cannot reach or feed upon the outward body and flesh of

Christ. You may often have taken what the Roman Catholics persuaded you was the real flesh and blood of Christ. You may have believed that it was so although your physical senses persuaded you otherwise. Or, being a Lutheran, you may have taken that bread in, with, and under that which the Lutherans assured you was the flesh and blood of Christ, although you never knew how or in what way.

In spite of all this you may find that your soul is still barren, indeed hungry and ready to starve for lack of something that you long for. Then, know that the light which discloses your iniquity to you, which shows your barrenness, nakedness, and emptiness — that is the body that you must partake of and feed upon. Your hunger cannot be satisfied until, forsaking iniquity, you turn toward the light, come unto it, and receive it. For the light has no communion with darkness (2 Cor 6:14) and "You cannot drink the cup of the Lord and the cup of devils; you cannot be partakers of the table of the Lord and of the table of devils;" (1 Cor 10:21 Cath-CCD).

ALLOW THE SEED OF RIGHTEOUSNESS TO ARISE IN YOU

But allow the small seed of righteousness to arise in you and to be formed into a rebirth. That new substantial birth that is brought forth in the soul will naturally feed upon and be nourished by the spiritual body of Christ. In our natural birth, the body does not live until we draw breath from the outward elementary air. In our spiritual birth the soul does not live until it draws in and breathes spiritual air. The animal body cannot subsist without the flesh of animals or without drink. The spirit cannot subsist unless it is fed by the inward flesh and blood of Christ which is analogous in the same manner.

This is very much in agreement with the doctrine of Christ on this matter. For as the natural body has no life without food, Christ says, John 6:53 NEB: "Unless you eat the flesh of the Son of Man and drink his blood you can have no life in you." And as the outward body, eating outward food, lives by so doing, Christ says, John 6:57 NEB, "he who eats me shall live because of me." Thus it is the inward participation of the inward man in this inward and spiritual body by which man is united to God and has fellowship and communion with him. "Whoever eats my flesh and drinks my blood dwells continually in me and I dwell in him."[2]

[2] John 6:56.

Since by this the soul has fellowship with God, as far as all of the faithful partake of this one body and one blood, they also come to have a joint communion. It is in this connection that Paul says, 1 Cor 10:17 Cath-CCD: "Because the bread is one, we, though many, are one body, all of us who partake of the one bread." ["Because there is one loaf, we who are many are one body, for we all partake of the same loaf." RSV.] And to the wise among the Corinthians, he says, v 16 RSV, "The bread which we break, is it not a participation in the body of Christ?" This is the true and spiritual supper of the Lord, of which men partake when they hear the voice of Christ and open the door of their hearts to let him in. This is plainly stated in Rev 3:20 RSV: "Behold, I stand at the door and knock; if anyone hears my voice and opens the door, I will come in to him and eat with him, and he with me."

THE SUPPER OF THE LORD IS NOT LIMITED
TO THE BREAKING OF BREAD AND DRINKING OF WINE

Thus, the supper of the Lord, and eating with him, and partaking of his flesh and blood, is by no means limited to the ceremony of breaking bread and drinking wine at certain times. It is truly and really enjoyed as often as the soul withdraws into the light of the Lord and feels and partakes of that divine life by which the inward man is nourished. This may be witnessed at any time by the faithful, although it is especially so when they are assembled together to wait upon the Lord.

THE SUPPER OF THE LORD AND THE CEREMONY
CHRIST USED BEFORE HIS DEATH

¶IV. The confusion which those who profess to be Christians have created over this is more than obvious. As in most other cases where this has been so, it has been because of a lack of true spiritual understanding. They have tried to connect this supper of the Lord with the ceremony which Christ used before his death when he broke bread and drank wine with his disciples. Although they agree on this point for the most part, how they do contend over others! And to what pains they go, to make the spiritual mystery agree with the ceremony, even though they find it strangely distressing and embarrassing. What monstrous conceptions and wild ideas they have invented to encompass the body of Christ in their bread and wine. This has not only led to great strife among Protestants in particular, but has had such blasphemous, absurd, and irrational consequences that Christianity has become obnoxious to Jews, Turks, and pagans.

TRANSUBSTANTIATION, CONSUBSTANTIATION, AND VIRTUALISM

Christians are divided into three principal opinions on this matter. The first of these is transubstantiation,[3] which means that the bread and wine become the very same substance as the body, flesh, and blood of Christ, who was born of the Virgin Mary and crucified by the Jews. After what they call "words of consecration" it is no longer bread but the body of Christ.

The second opinion is that the substance of the bread remains, but that the body is also in, with, and under the bread. Thus both the substance of the bread, and of the body, flesh, and blood of Christ are there.[4]

The third denies both of these, and states that the body of Christ is not there corporally or substantially, but nevertheless

---

[3] There has been little change in the doctrine of Transubstantiation since Barclay's day. The basis of the devotional life associated with the Blessed Sacrament is the doctrine of the Real Presence of Christ in the sacramental elements after consecration. By God's power the bread and wine are transformed into the Body and Blood of Christ "truly, really, and substantially" *(vere, realiter et substantialiter)*. Both his natures, human and divine, are present in the Sacrament which can therefore be called *totus Christus.* Accordingly the consecrated elements on the altar are treated as Christ Himself, and the Host, when exposed or carried in procession, is venerated by the faithful who genuflect before it.

The "transformation is technically described as a *transubstantiatio* ["reality"]. Scholastic logic distinguished the accidents, material properties, or incidental characteristics of a thing from its substance or inner unity ["entity"] as an object. Its substance constituted it an individual entity, its accidents clothed it with a recognizable description. As applied to the doctrine of the Eucharist this meant that, while the inner unity ["entity"] of consecrated Bread and Wine became the Body and Blood of our Lord, no change was effected after [i.e., "by"] consecration in the external attributes of Bread and Wine." — Molland, *Christendom,* pp 64-65. [Bracketed insertions suggested by Father Bowman.]

Pope Paul VI reaffirmed transubstantiation as basic to the Roman Catholic understanding of the Real Presence in the Mass, and the Adoration of the Blessed Sacrament, in the encyclical *Mysterium Fidei,* issued just prior to session 4 of Vatican Council II in 1965.

[4] This is the Consubstantiation of Martin Luther, which holds that "after the consecration, the substances both of the Body and Blood of Christ and of the bread and wine coexist in union with each other. Luther illustrated it by the analogy of the iron put into the fire, whereby both fire and iron are united in the red-hot iron and yet each continues unchanged." — *O.D.C.C.,* p 337.

St. Irenaeus is regarded as the precursor of the Lutheran view, which is also related to Christology. "To the question whether Christ is present

it is truly and sacramentally received by the faithful when they use the bread and wine. How or why it is there is unexplainable. Still we are to believe that it is there, even though, more properly, it is in heaven.[5]

---

in the Eucharist according to both his natures or only in one, the Formula of Concord replies that . . . both . . . natures of Christ are involved.

"Such a view naturally involves the corollary that both natures are omnipresent. Controversy arose on the matter with the Reformed Church, which maintained that after the Ascension, Christ's human nature was on the right hand of the Father, and that therefore only His divine nature could be present at the Eucharist. Against this objection, the Formula of Concord rejoined that at the Incarnation the two natures became inseparably united. Christ has promised to be present in the Eucharist with His Body and Blood. His human nature must therefore share the omnipresence which is one of the attributes of the Divine Nature." — Molland, *Christendom*, p 214.

[5] This is the Virtualism of John Calvin. Both Lutheran and Calvinist statements on the Eucharist or Lord's Supper are voluminous and diffuse. This was one of the major areas of polemics between Luther, Calvin, Zwingli and Westphal, with others involved in varying degrees. Succinct statements that are not oversimplifications are difficult to come by. Be it said that Barclay has caught a number of the major points in surprisingly few words. The following statements enlarge on the points at issue to some extent but they are not synoptic of the total doctrine. — Ed.

"There are three points to be considered in the sacrament besides the outward sign, which is not at present in question: namely the signification; then the matter of substance; and thirdly the *virtue* or the effect which proceeds from the one to the other.

"The meaning is in the promises, which are imprinted upon the sign. I call Jesus Christ, with his death and resurrection, the matter or substance. By the effect I mean redemption, righteousness, sanctification, the life everlasting and all the benefits brought to us by Jesus Christ." — *Inst.*, lib 4, cap 17, sect 11.

Calvin is somewhat contradictory on the matter of whether or not the elements are changed. The preceding section of the *Institutes* states: "Truly, there is nothing here but some bread and wine . . . the substance is also given us in reality . . . in taking the sign of the body we are likewise taking the body.

"For seeing that it is a thing incomprehensible not only to the eye but to our natural judgment that we should have communion with the body of Jesus Christ, it is here shown to us visibly." — *Opp.*, 5, 438f. The preceding four paragraphs are from Wendel, *Calvin*, pp 335-339.

However, the Belgic Confession of 1561, which was adopted by the Synod of Antwerp in 1566 and readopted by the Synod of Dort in 1619, and which is supposed to summarize Calvinistic principles, states: "But the manner of our *partaking* of the same is *not by the mouth* but *by the Spirit through faith.*" — The quotation and the italicizing are from Wilhelm Niesel. *The Gospel and the Churches*, Philadelphia, Westminster, 1962, p 274. The comment is my own. — Ed.

There was also the Memorial interpretation of the Eucharist by Ulrich Zwingli, which rejected any form of Bodily presence and held that the Lord's Supper was primarily a memorial rite unaccompanied by changes in the elements. See also fn p 349.

NONE OF THESE INTERPRETATIONS HAS ATTAINED
THE TRUTH AND SUBSTANCE OF THE MYSTERY

It is unnecessary to refute these several opinions since each
of their authors has sufficiently refuted the others. Each of them
is also as strong in using scripture and reason to refute contrary
opinion as he is weak in using it to establish his own. No doubt
others have noticed this too. It must be concluded that none
of them has attained the truth and substance of this mystery.

Calvin is a good example. After he has refuted the first
two opinions,[6] he is not very successful with his assertions on
behalf of the truth of his own opinion. In fact, he simply confesses that he does not know what to affirm in place of them.
After he has dealt with the matter at some length, he concludes
"that the body of Christ is there and it is necessary for the faithful to partake of it," and finally says, sect 32:[7] "Now, if anyone should ask me how this takes place, I shall not be ashamed
to confess that it is a secret too lofty for either my mind to
comprehend or my words to declare." This is very ingenuous.
Who would have thought that such a man would have been
brought to this strait in confirming his opinion? It is shortly
before this, in the same chapter, sect 15, that he accuses the
Catholic scholars, and I think his accusation is justified, of
being unable to explain to others how Christ is present in the
Eucharist.[8] It is shortly afterwards that he confesses that he
cannot do it himself.

ATTEMPTS TO RECONCILE THESE CONFLICTING VIEWS
ARE OF NO AVAIL

If neither group understands this and neither can explain
it to others, there is little certitude to be had from either of
them. The great attempts to reconcile this matter between
Roman Catholics and Lutherans, Lutherans and Calvinists, and
even Calvinists and Roman Catholics have been of no avail. It
has all been in vain in spite of the various forms of statement

---

6 In his *Inst.*, lib 4, cap 17.

[7] The translation is that of Ford Lewis Battles, *Institutes*, in *The
Library of Christian Classics*, vol 21, p 1403.

[8] "The Schoolmen, having a horror of such barbarous impiety [the
recantation statement which Pope Nicholas required of Berengarius], speak
more modestly. Yet they also do nothing but indulge in deceitful subtle-
ties. They grant that Christ is not there contained in any circumspective
or bodily fashion. But they then devise a mode which they neither understand themselves nor can explain to others." — *Inst.*, lib 4, cap 17, sect 13.
ibid, vol 21, pp 1373-1374.

and different manners of expression that have been used in an
effort to find something to which all might concede. In the
end, everyone interpreted them in his own way and understood
them differently. Thus they merely equivocated and deceived
one another. All of this contention took place because they did
not have a clear understanding of this mystery and because they
were overly fond of externals and preferred shadows to substance. Both the basis and the content of their struggle concerned extraneous rather than central matters. . . .

Those who are acquainted with the state of Protestant
affairs know that the contention over the body and blood of
Christ has been more harmful to the Reformation than all of
the opposition from common adversaries. If all of these dubi-
ous and absurd opinions were only denied, there would be an
easy path to reconciliation and we would all come together on
one spiritual and true understanding of this mystery.

TWO ERRORS ARE COMMON TO THESE MISINTERPRETATIONS

There are two general errors which are common to all of
these misinterpretations. The first is that of trying to relate
communion, or participation in the body, flesh, and blood of
Christ, to the outward body, vessel, or temple that was born of
the Virgin Mary and that walked and suffered in Judea. It
should be related instead to the spiritual body, flesh, and blood
of Christ, the divine and celestial light and life, which in all
ages has been the food and nourishment of those who have
been reborn.

The second error is in connecting participation in the
body and blood of Christ to the ceremony that was used by him
with his disciples. It is as though this participation could
only be enjoyed in relation to his breaking of the bread with
them and his sharing of the wine. It has no such relation or
exclusiveness. For the bread which Christ teaches us to ask for
in his prayer is the "supersubstantial bread," *tòn arton tòn e-
piousion,* as the Greek has it, of which the soul partakes. Further along, it will be proved at some length that it has no reference or relation to the ceremony used with the disciples.

THERE ARE TWO VALID CENTRAL PRINCIPLES

If these two errors are laid aside, and the arguments over
them are buried, then all will agree on the central principles,
which are: (1) The body, flesh, and blood of Christ are necessary for the nourishment of the soul; (2) The souls of believ-

ers in reality and in truth partake of and feed upon the body, flesh, and blood of Christ.

Is it any wonder that there is confusion because men are not content with the spirituality of this mystery? They go their own way rather than God's, and in the strength of their own inventions they strain and wrest the scriptures in an effort to connect this spiritual communion of the flesh and blood of Christ to outward bread and wine and similar carnal ordinances.

COMMUNION OF THE BODY AND BLOOD OF CHRIST HAS NO SPECIAL RELATIONSHIP TO THE CEREMONY

¶V. Since it has generally been assumed that the communion of the body and blood of Christ had some special relationship to the ceremony of breaking bread, that opinion will be refuted first. We will then proceed to consider the nature and purpose of that ceremony and whether it should be continued now. The reasoning and the objections of those who argue that it must be continued as a standing ordinance of Jesus Christ will then be answered. It must be understood that reference is being made to an obligatory and exclusive relationship to the ceremony of breaking bread, rather than to any general relationship.

Since communion with Christ is our greatest duty and ought to be our most significant work, everything that we do should be done out of respect for God and to further our fellowship with him. But this is different from a special relationship where two things are so closely interrelated and united, either by their very nature or by the command of God, that one cannot be enjoyed wihout the other, except perhaps under very unusual circumstances. Thus salvation has a necessary relationship to holiness, because "without holiness no man shall see God."[9] Eating the flesh and blood of Christ has a necessary relationship to life, because if we do not eat his flesh and drink his blood we cannot have life. Our perception of God's presence is necessarily related to whether we meet in his name by divine precept, because he has promised us that wherever two or three are gathered together in his name, he will be in the midst of them.[10] Similarly the receipt of benefits and blessings from God has a necessary relationship to prayer, because he has promised us that if we ask we shall receive.

[9] An approximate quotation of Heb 12:14.
[10] Mat 18:20.

But the communion or participation in the flesh and blood of Christ has no such necessary relationship to the breaking of bread and drinking of wine. If it had, it would derive either from the very nature of it, or from some divine precept. It is certainly not of an inherent nature because partaking of the flesh and blood of Christ is a spiritual exercise. Everyone agrees that it is by the soul and spirit that we truly partake of communion, for it is the soul and not the body that is nourished by it. But eating bread and drinking wine are physical acts which of themselves add nothing to the soul and there is nothing spiritual about them. The most worldly of men can just as easily eat the bread and drink the wine and do it just as well as the most spiritual of men. The relationship of communion and the breaking of bread is not determined by their nature, or one would infer the other. But everyone acknowledges that many who eat the bread and drink the wine nevertheless do not have life eternal. Even though they say that the elements are consecrated and transubstantiated into the very body of Christ, they do not have Christ dwelling in them. Nor do they live by him as all of those do who truly partake of the flesh and blood of Christ even though they do not use this ceremony.

That is the way the patriarchs and prophets did before the institution of this "ordinance," as it is now considered. There was nothing under the law which had any direct or necessary relationship to this ordinance, although in all ages it was indispensably necessary for salvation to partake of the flesh and blood of Christ. The whole purpose of the paschal lamb was to remind the Jews of their deliverance from Egypt (Ex 13:8, 9).

THE ORDINANCE HAS NO RELATIONSHIP TO DIVINE PRECEPT

This "ordinance" has no relation to divine precept. If it had, it would be possible to give an account of its institution, or else to tell of its practice by the people of God as recorded in scripture. But this is not so. The narration of Christ's practice in this matter is recorded by the evangelists Matthew, Mark, and Luke (Mat 26:26, Mark 14:22, Luke 22:19). The first two are purely factual, recording that Christ broke bread and gave it to his disciples to eat, saying: "This is my body." Blessing the cup, he gave it to them to drink and said: "This is my blood." There is no mention of any desire for them to do it. In the conclusion, after the bread (but before he blessed the

wine and gave it to them) he bid them to do it in remembrance
of him.   Postponing a consideration of the meaning of these
acts and statements of Christ for a while, let us consider what
necessary relationship all of this has to believers partaking of
the flesh and blood of Christ.   The purpose of doing this, if
they were to do it at all, was to remember Christ.   The apostle
expresses this more clearly in 1 Cor 11:26 as to "proclaim the
death of the Lord until he comes" (NEB, Cath-CCD; the RSV
says "Lord's death" but is otherwise the same).

But to remember the Lord, or declare his death — the particular reasons that are annexed to the use of the ceremony —
is not to partake of the flesh and blood of Christ.   Nor is there
any more of a necessary relationship between them than there
is to any other case of two distinctive spiritual duties.   For although those who partake of the flesh and blood of Christ cannot do otherwise than remember him, it is perfectly possible
to remember him without partaking of his flesh and blood.

CHRIST DREW SPIRITUAL LESSONS FROM EVERYDAY OBJECTS

It may be said by some that a special relationship to his
disciples can be inferred from the fact that Jesus Christ refers
here to the bread as his body and the wine as his blood, of
which they would be partaking.   But no such thing is implied
by his calling the bread his body and the wine his blood.
Whatever Jesus did, he always took the occasion to raise the
minds of his disciples and those who heard him to spiritual
matters.   He did the same thing with whatever natural things
he used.   When the woman of Samaria was drawing water, he
used the occasion to tell her of the living water and that whoever drinks of it "will never suffer thirst any more," John 4:14
NEB.   Christ's statement about his blood was also a metaphor,
but it does not follow that there was any necessary relationship
to the well, or to well water.

Christ used the opportunity provided by the Jews who
were following him to be fed with loaves, to tell them of the
spiritual bread or flesh of his body which it was more important
for them to feed upon.   It does not follow that this had any
necessary relationship to following him for loaves.

That is just the way it was here.   Christ was at supper with
his disciples and used the occasion to draw a spiritual lesson
from the bread and wine which were before them.   Just as the
bread which he broke and the wine which he blessed would

contribute to the nourishment of their bodies, his body was to be given and his blood shed for the salvation of their souls. That is why it is proposed that those who observe this ceremony should do it as a memorial of his death.

But, it will be said, in 1 Cor 10:16 the apostle calls the bread which he broke the communion of the body of Christ, and the cup the communion of his blood.[11]

This is very true, but it does not pertain to outward bread, nor can it be evinced that it does. In fact the opposite is manifest from the context. In the entire chapter, not a word is said about that ceremony. At the beginning of the chapter, Paul shows how the ancient Jews were made partakers of the spiritual food and water which was Christ. He recounts how, through disobedience and idolatry, a number of them fell from that good condition. He uses the example of the ancient Jews who were destroyed by God for their defection in order to exhort them to flee from evil. He shows them how the Corinthians themselves also partake of the body and blood of Christ, and how, if they did evil, they would rob themselves of communion, because: "You cannot drink the cup of the Lord and the cup of demons. You cannot partake of the Lord's table and the table of demons" (v 21 NEB). This shows that he is not referring to outward bread and wine, because the wickedest of men, those who do indeed drink the cup of devils and eat from the devils' table, may partake of the outward bread and the outward wine.

THERE IS ONE LOAF

This is the place (v 17) where the apostle calls the bread one, and says (RSV): "Because there is one loaf, we who are many are one body, for we all partake of the same loaf." If the bread is one, it cannot be the outward bread or that would exclude the inward spiritual bread. But on the other hand, it cannot be denied that where they partake of the inward bread the followers of Christ become truly one body and one bread. Those who affirm that by virtue of the sacramental union the one bread spoken of here includes both the outward and the

[11] The passage reads, NEB: "When we bless 'the cup of blessing,' is it not a means of sharing in the blood of Christ?" RSV asks if it is not "participation," with a footnote reading "or communion." The Cath-CCD says: "The cup of blessing that we bless, is it not the sharing of the blood of Christ? And the bread that we break, is it not the partaking of the body of the Lord?"

inward, express an opinion but do not offer proof. Because there is no such thing as that figment of the imagination, the sacramental union, anywhere in scripture, let alone in the New Testament.

Actually there is nothing in this chapter which could give rise to such a thing. The apostle is not giving a treatise on that ceremony at all but is hortatory instead. He advises those who have the privilege, which the Corinthians had as believing Christians, of partaking of the flesh and blood of Christ, to avoid idolatry and abstain from the partaking of sacrifices offered to idols. For by such participation they might offend or hurt their weaker brethren.

DISCERNING THE LORD'S BODY

But the chapter which those who favor the outward ceremony cite the most and are always urging on their behalf is 1 Cor 11. In it, they say, the apostle is especially concerned with communion, and some of the words appear to support their assertion. An example is verse 27 where he calls the cup the "cup of the Lord" and says (NEB): "It follows that anyone who eats the bread and drinks the cup of the Lord unworthily will be guilty of desecrating the body and blood of the Lord." In verse 29 he adds, NEB: "For he who eats and drinks, eats and drinks judgment on himself if he does not discern the body."

At first glance this may trap the unwary reader, but upon greater consideration it in no way tends to prove the matter in question. It will be considered later whether the Corinthians used this ceremony, why, and in what way that constitutes an obligation for Christians to do the same now. It suffices for the present: (1) To consider it as meaning that they did use it; (2) that in the use of it they committed many abuses; (3) that the apostle is here giving directions on the proper way to do it, and showing them the proper use and purpose of it.

A COMMON AND MEMORIAL RELATIONSHIP TO THE BODY AND DEATH OF CHRIST UPON THE CROSS

Having established these premises, let it be observed that the specific use of it is clearly expressed by the apostle in verse 26. He says, RSV: "As often as you eat this bread and drink this cup, you proclaim the Lord's death until he comes." Thus it is acknowledged that this ceremony, for those who practice it, has a direct relationship to being a memorial for the outward body and death of Christ upon the cross. But it does not follow from that that there is any inward or immediate relation to the communication to believers, or the partaking of the spiritual body and blood of Christ. It is not the spiritual supper that is spoken of in Rev 3:20 ["Behold, I stand at the door and knock; if anyone hears my voice and opens the door, I will come in to him and eat with him, and he with me." RSV].

Since every religious action has a common relation, in a general way, to the spiritual communion of the people of God with their Lord, we will not deny this relationship here. As to his reference to this as the cup of the Lord and his statement that they are guilty of desecrating the body and blood of the Lord if they drink unworthily, and eat to their own condemnation if they do not discern the Lord's body, that is a different matter. This does not imply that the ceremony which they practice is intended to be an obligatory religious act for others. But since they do it as a religious act, they should do it worthily. In Rom 14:6 RSV, the apostle says: "He who observes the day, observes it in honor of the Lord." But that does not mean that the days which some observe and hold in high regard constitute an obligation for others to do the same.

Nevertheless, he who esteems a day and regards it as a matter of conscience to keep it, does so "in honor of the Lord." Having dedicated it to the Lord he must keep it worthily or else it will be his own condemnation.

THOSE WHO OBSERVE THE CEREMONY REQUIRE PREPARATION AND SELF-EXAMINATION

In a similar manner, for those who observe the ceremony of the bread and wine, it is the bread of the Lord and the cup of the Lord for them because it is used as a religious act. Their purpose is to re-enact symbolically the Lord's death and to remember that his body was crucified for them and his blood was shed for them. If, in spite of the fact that they believe it is their duty to do it and they consider it an offence of conscience to forbear, they do it without the due preparation and self-examination which ought to be the prerequisites for every religious act, then instead of truly remembering the Lord's death and his body and blood they become just as guilty, and of the same spirit, as those who crucified him and shed his blood. This is true, even though they pretend to remember it with thanksgiving and with joy.

It is the same fashion in which the ancient scribes and Pharisees are said by Christ to be guilty of the prophets' blood even though they garnished their sepulchres in their memory.[12] It is apparent from another statement of the same apostle that this is the only proper conclusion. He says in Rom 14:23 RSV: "But he who has doubts is condemned, if he eats, because he does not act from faith; for whatever does not proceed from faith is sin." The statement was made with reference to those who considered it unlawful to eat meat. If they eat it doubtingly they eat to their own condemnation. It was made clear that this was a matter of no moment for one who regarded neither doing nor forbearing as a matter of conscience. That is why I say that whoever eats what his own conscience tells him is wrong for him, does so to his own damnation. Conversely, he who does eat bread and wine as a religious act and as a matter of conscience eats and drinks to his own damnation if he does it without regard for the way in which such acts should be performed. He must "discern the Lord's body," that is, have a special respect for the Lord in the way he does it, and remember it is a special commemoration of Christ's death.

NATURE AND CONSTITUTION OF COMMUNION CEREMONY

¶VI. Having given sufficient indication of what the true communion of the body and blood of Christ is; having indicated the way in which it is partaken of; having shown that it has no necessary relationship to the ceremony of bread and wine which Christ used with his disciples; it is now appropriate to consider the nature and constitution of that ceremony. (We have already spoken of its proper use.) Let us now consider whether or not it is a standing ordinance in the Church of Christ that is obligatory for all Christians. Is it a necessary part of worship under the new covenant dispensation? Has it any better or more binding foundation than several other ceremonies which were appointed and practiced at about the same time? This is particularly important, since most of those who oppose our view consider these to have ceased and believe that they are no longer binding upon Christians in any way.

MENTIONED ONLY FOUR PLACES IN SCRIPTURE

There are only four places in scripture where this ceremony is mentioned — Mat 26:26, Mark 14:22, Luke 22:19, and in Paul's first epistle to the Corinthians, 1 Cor 11:23ff. If any inference is to be drawn from the frequency with which it is

---

[12] Mat 23:29-30.

mentioned, that gets us nowhere, because other less memorable things are mentioned more frequently. As has already been stated, Matthew and Mark give very matter-of-fact accounts which do not include any precept stating that it should be repeated. They simply declare that at that time Jesus desired them to eat of the bread and drink of the cup. Luke adds the words: "Do this in remembrance of me."[13]

Carefully weighing this act of Christ with his apostles, there is apparently nothing special in it which would serve as a foundation for the strange superstructure which many have tried to fashion from the thin air of their own imaginations. Both Matthew and Mark report that it was an act which Jesus did while he was eating, "during supper," according to both in the NEB. This was not a special act or solemn institution of a gospel ordinance, but rather a common custom among the Jews. Paulus Riccius[14] observes at some length in his *Celestial Agriculture* that when Passover was eaten, the head of the family took the bread, blessed it and broke it and gave it to the rest of the people at the table. His actions with the wine were similar.

Thus, the most that can be drawn from these scriptural accounts is the fact that Jesus Christ, who fulfilled all righteousness and who also observed Jewish feasts and customs, used this for an illustration, just as he had done with other things. As on other occasions he tried to draw their minds out to a spiritual conclusion, here he was using the opportunity to remind them of his death and sufferings which would soon take place. Since they were averse to believing it, his efforts to inculcate it were more frequent. As for Luke's "Do this in remembrance of me," it amounts to no more than pointing out a way in which his disciples could be reminded of him and thus be stirred to follow him more diligently through suffering and death. It was particularly appropriate then, since it was the last time that he would eat with his disciples.

[13] RSV omits this in the body of the text but has a footnote saying that other ancient authorities add after "this is my body": " 'which is given for you. Do this in remembrance of me.' And likewise the cup after supper, saying, 'This cup which is poured out for you is the new covenant in my blood.' " NEB says that "some witnesses add, in whole or in part, and with various arrangements the following: [the words are essentially the same as those of RSV]. — Ed.

[14] See fn p 320 for biographical note. The *British Museum Catalog* shows the title as *De coloesti agricultura libri 4*, 1587.

But what person who has laid aside the prejudices he has learned and the influence of tradition will logically say that the matter-of-fact accounts in Matthew and Mark, or even Luke's "do this in remembrance of me," are justification for the conclusions which most Christians have sought to draw from it? They call it *Augustissimum Eucharistiae Sacramentum; venerabile altaris Sacramentum;* the principal seal of the covenant of grace, by which all of the benefits of Christ's death are guaranteed to believers, and similar things.

THE FOOT-WASHING CEREMONY

To give further evidence that these conclusions have no basis in Christ's practice of that ceremony, or in the following words "do this...", let us consider another situation of a similar nature that is described in John 13:4-5, 8, 12, 14-15 NEB: Jesus "rose from the table, laid aside his garments, and taking a towel, tied it round him. Then he poured water into a basin and began to wash his disciples' feet and to wipe them with the towel.... Peter said, 'I will never let you wash my feet.' 'If I do not wash you,' Jesus replied, 'you are not in fellowship with me.'... After washing their feet and taking his garments again, he sat down. 'Do you understand,' he asked, 'what I have done for you?... if I, your Lord and Master, have washed your feet, you also ought to wash one another's feet. I have set you an example: you are to do as I have done for you.' "

Let it be observed that John says that this was done at the same time as the other ceremony, the breaking of bread. Both were done during the supper on the night of the Passover. Consider how much more solemnity accompanied this and how much more detail is given in describing this than the other ceremony. The other starts simply and casually "during supper he took bread," so that it would seem relatively inconsequential. But here, he rose up, laid his garments aside, girded himself, poured water, washed their feet, and wiped them with a towel. He did this for all of them.

The first was a common practice among the Jews that was used by all heads of families on that occasion. But this was more unusual, not only in the way in which it was performed, and as to the person who performed it, but particularly notable for the fact that a master got up and washed the feet of his servants and disciples. Nothing is said about the breaking of bread and giving of wine that would indicate that he personally put these into everyone's hands. But breaking it, and blessing it, he gave it to the nearest person and then it was passed from hand to hand. But here it is mentioned that he did not wash the feet merely of two, but of many.

JESUS DID MAKE A POSITIVE EXAMPLE OF THAT

There is nothing said about incurring any prejudice against them if they did not partake of the bread or wine. But in regard to the foot washing, Jesus very definitely says to Peter, if you do not allow it "you are not in fellowship with me."

In the first ceremony, he says almost as though in passing: "Do this in remembrance of me." But here, he sits down, asks them to consider what he has done, and then states positively: "I have set you an example: you are to do as I have done for you." He not only tells them that they are to do it, but reinforces that precept by saying that he has given them an example.

Certainly as far as the nature of it is concerned there is as much in the foot washing ceremony as there is in either baptism or the breaking of bread. It is an outward element of a cleansing nature that is applied to the outward man by the command and example of Christ, to signify an inward purification.

In all seriousness, I ask you to use the reason and understanding which God has given you to ponder a question without being influenced by the custom and tradition of others. Doesn't this ceremony have as much to recommend it as a standing ordinance of the gospel as either water baptism or bread and wine, or any other "ordinance" for that matter? Consider either the time when it was performed, or the circumstances, or the command enjoining the use of it. Why haven't the Roman Catholics included it among their sacraments, instead of merely considering it *Voluntas Ecclesiae* and *Traditio Patrum?*

They will answer that it is used by them. The pope and some others do it once a year for some of the poor.[15] But why

---

[15] This is done on Maundy Thursday, the Thursday before Easter which commemorates the Last Supper. "The chief ceremony, as kept from the early middle ages onwards — the washing of the feet of twelve or more poor men or beggars — was in the early Church almost unknown. From the 4th c. ceremonial footwashing became yearly more common, till it was regarded as a necessary rite, to be performed by the pope, all Catholic sovereigns, prelates, priests, and nobles.

"In England the king washed the feet of as many poor men as he was years old ... At Peterborough Abbey, in 1530, Wolsey made 'his maund in Our Lady's Chapel, having 59 poor men whose feet he washed and

shouldn't it be extended to a daily or weekly practice like the Eucharist? How can they conclude that Christ's command applies only to the pope and a few others and that it is to be done only once a year? There is nothing in the text to support this.

And what about the Protestants who do not use this ceremony at all?[16] If they will merely open their eyes they will see how they were mistaken on this matter just as their fathers were about various Roman Catholic traditions. If we consider the unadorned scripture, what can be inferred from it that would urge the acceptance of one and not the other? Or what would argue for laying aside one and not the other? If they say that washing feet was merely a ceremony, how can they demonstrate any more for the breaking of bread? How can one be said to exemplify humility and purification any more than the other? If they say that one was to be practiced only for a time and was not an evangelical ordinance, how can they say that that is not true of the other?

Since the washing of feet has justly been laid aside, the breaking of bread and drinking of wine should also be discontinued.

FEW PERFORM THE COMMUNION CEREMONY IN THE WAY CHRIST DID

¶VII. It is also strange that those who clamor so loudly for this ceremony and who stick so closely to it take the liberty

---

kissed, and after he had wiped them he gave every of the said poor men 12 pence in money, three ells of good canvas to make them shirts, a pair of new shoes, a cast of red herrings and three white herrings.'

"Queen Elizabeth performed the ceremony, the paupers' feet, however, being first washed by the yeomen of the laundry with warm water and sweet herbs. James II was the last English monarch to perform the rite." — *Encyc. Brit.*, 1958, vol 15, pp 101-102.

[16] Several non-Roman churches have, however, used the footwashing ceremony. The early Moravians used it, but the practice has long since been discontinued.

Among the Adventists, "the two sacraments of Baptism (restricted to adults) and Holy Communion are observed. Before the Holy Communion the congregation wash one another's feet, two by two, the men in one hall, the women in another." — Molland, *Christendom*, p 320.

"The Lord's Supper is observed twice a year in almost all Mennonite congregations, and in most of them baptism is by pouring. Most of them observe the footwashing ordinance in connection with the Supper, after which they salute each other with the 'kiss of peace.' The sexes are separated in the last two ceremonies." — Frank S. Mead, *Handbook of Denominations in the United States*, N. Y., Abingdon, 1956, p 143.

The Brethren (Dunkers) also have the footwashing ceremony. — ibid, p 46.

of dispensing with the manner in which Christ did it. Some
Baptists[17] are the only ones I have ever heard of who now do
it in the same way that he did. Christ did it at supper, while
they were eating. Most Protestants do it in the morning and
separately. On what do they base this change?

WHAT TYPE OF BREAD?

Some will say that these are only surrounding circumstances rather than the heart of the matter. If the core is kept,
they say that alteration of the surrounding circumstances is of
little moment. Well, why not say that the entire matter was
circumstantial, and that it occurred only when Christ ate the
Passover? Since it was only an accidental practice of a Jewish
ceremony and the drinking of wine was included only because
it was a natural product of that country, perhaps it would be
better to use ale or beer in countries where grapes do not
grow. Or perhaps the bread should be barley. Certainly those
who practice this sacrament would consider such changes im-
proper and abusive. In fact such scruples have been the cause
of great strife, like that between the Greek and Latin churches
concerning bread.[18] One uses it unleavened. The other uses

[17] Barclay undoubtedly refers to the Zwinglian or Memorial view of
Communion. "In 1522 he [Zwingli] still accepted the traditional view of
the Eucharist but in a letter to Matthäus Alber of Reutlingen (16 Nov.
1524) he upheld a purely symbolic interpretation, which he developed
further in *Commentarius de Vera et Falsa Religione* (1525). . . . Every
form of the carnal presence of Christ in the Eucharist, whether by transubstantiation, consubstantiation, or impanation, was rejected as 'Capernaitic'
(John 6:51-53, 59)." — *O.D.C.C.*, p 1491.
  While Molland (*Christendom*, p 296) quotes a Swedish Baptist authority to the effect that "the majority of English and Scandinavian Baptists
hold a Zwinglian view," this is somewhat modified in a footnote added by
Canon H. E. W. Turner, who acted as the English editor of the work. He
quotes Dr. E. A. Payne, General Secretary of the Baptist Union of Great
Britain and Ireland, as saying: "From the beginnings of the Baptist witness in the 17th c., there have been many Baptists who have been staunch
Calvinists in their interpretation of the Supper, but there have been many
others who have favoured Zwinglian views. It is doubtful if either one or
the other can claim to be the dominant tradition."

[18] "Leavened bread is used in the Orthodox Liturgy in contrast to
the Western use of unleavened bread. Western churchmen were accused
by the Orthodox of being Judaizers and still under the Law." — Molland,
Christendom, p 27.
  "Transformation" is the term generally used for the Orthodox interpretation of the change in the elements which takes place only after the Invo-
cation of the Holy Spirit (the Epiclesis) and not merely from the Words
of Institution as in the Latin rite. Although the elements (the laity re-

it leavened. Since the Jews used unleavened bread in the Passover, that must have been the kind that Christ broke with his
disciples. Therefore the Lutherans used unleavened bread. However, the Calvinists used leavened. This controversy was so
heated when the Reformation was beginning at Geneva that
Calvin and Farellus[19] were forced to flee because of it.

WHAT PERMITS ONLY CLERGY TO BLESS THE BREAD?

But aren't Protestants, by these practices, opening the door
to the Roman Catholic idea of excluding the people from the
cup? Will not "do this" imply that this should be done absolutely in the same manner and at the same time as Christ did
it? Shouldn't they use the cup too and not merely the bread?
What strange and absurd inconveniences Christians have
brought upon themselves by superstitiously sticking to that
ceremony! The difficulties are so great that they cannot extri-
cate themselves by laying it aside, as they have done with other
similar ones. For in addition to what is mentioned above, I
would like to know how it can be understood that "do this"
allows the clergy to take, bless, and break the bread and give
it to others; but allows the laity only to take it and eat it, but
not to bless it.

If it should be said that only clergy were present, that
opens the door for the Roman Catholic argument against giv-

---

ceives Communion of both kinds) retain their character after the conclusion of the Liturgy and are "reserved" they are not exposed on the altar
for adoration, as in the Roman church. There are a number of other
significant differences. — ibid, pp 26-27.

[19] Guillaume Farel (1489-1565). In 1535 he and Pierre Viret led a
triumphant struggle which established the Reformation at Geneva. The
following year the close lifelong friendship with Calvin began when the
latter was passing through Geneva and Farel persuaded him to stay.
Although the restrained account of Wendel is a little difficult to reconcile with Barclay's statement, the reference is undoubtedly to 1538. "A
conflict seemed imminent, and in fact broke out at the first opportunity,
which arose over the liturgical question. In that domain, the Bernese had
for some time been leaning towards conceptions that were more Lutheran,
and to the minds of the Genevans more traditionalist. In particular,
Berne had retained the use of baptismal fonts, and still used the host in
celebrations of the Eucharist...." As relations deteriorated, the Magistracy forbade Calvin and his colleagues to preach on Easter Day. After
further steps in official adoption of the Bernese ceremonies, Calvin, Farel,
and another minister were deprived of their functions and ordered to leave
the town within three days. The banished ministers betook themselves to
Berne to appeal and were at first well received. In the ultimate outcome,
they were not allowed to re-enter Genevan territory. — Wendel, Calvin,
pp 55-57.

ing the cup to the people. Why not infer that participation in
the ceremony should be limited to the clergy since only apostles
were present when it was said: "Do this"? But, if "do this!" is
to be extended to everyone, why is it that everyone does not
participate in the blessing, breaking, and distributing of the
bread, as well as eating it?

In addition to all of these points of difference, even the
Calvinist Protestants[20] of Great Britain could never agree on
whether the elements should be taken sitting, standing, or
kneeling. Nor could they decide whether they should be given
to the sick and to those who are ready to die. Although these
controversies may be considered of little moment, yet they have
contributed — among other things — not only to a great deal of
contention but also to bloodshed and destruction. In this last
matter, the Prelatic Calvinists have called the Presbyterians
schismatical and obstinate. They in their turn refer to the
others as superstitious, idolatrous, and papistical. If anyone
will just open his eyes, he will see that this is the work of the
devil. Men are kept busy with things of small moment while
more important matters are neglected.

WE DO NOT FIND THE CEREMONY OBLIGATORY

¶VIII. Do we not have good reason to avoid this confusion
since we do not find this practice any more obligatory for us

---

[20] It would require a specialist in the history of this era to pin
down precisely the denominational references in this paragraph. Barclay
would seem to be dealing with a dispute between those within the Anglican establishment and those without, and is using "Protestants" loosely to
include Anglicans ("non-Romans," we would say). The "inside" Calvinists
would be the "Prelatic" ones. The word, according to the O.E.D., is a
hostile one, like "papist" for Roman Catholic.

The comments of J. N. Figgis on "inside" Calvinism are of interest: "In
England, at least, Calvinism is by no means necessarily connected with
Calvin's system of church government. It is tenable with or without a
belief in episcopacy, and indicates no more than a belief in the rigid doctrines of predestination and reprobation, and a dislike of all ceremonial in
religion. coupled with the denial of any final authority outside the Bible . . .
Few were the minds in the English Church in the mid-16th c. whom it
did not dominate, and its power in the other reformed communions was
little short of tyrannical. Fortunately for England, it failed of complete
expression. The Thirty-nine Articles [still the basic Articles of Religion
for Anglicanism] are almost certainly patient of a purely Calvinist interpretation; but they are so adroitly framed that it can be eluded, and despite the ruling influences in the church of Elizabeth, sheer Calvinism
never became authoritative." — Ollard, Crosse, Bond, A Dict. of English
Church Hist., 3rd ed rev, London, Mowbray, 1948. pp 81-83.

than the ceremonies which they have set aside? This is particularly true since they will never agree on the nature, efficacy, or manner of administering it. And the reason for this is because they are not content to follow what is plainly set forth in the scriptures, but insist on intermixing their own inventions.

If they were to follow what is stated, it would mean only that Jesus Christ at that time symbolized the fact that his body and blood were to be offered for them. It was his desire that whenever they ate or drank it might be done in remembrance of him whose blood was shed for them. This is the way the primitive church understood it when they were gathered together immediately after his ascension. That is apparent from the places in Acts where the breaking of bread is said to have this relationship:

Acts 2:42 NEB: "They met constantly to hear the apostles teach, and to share the common life, to break bread, and to pray," cannot be interpreted to refer to anything other than ordinary eating. The text itself says no more and the context makes it even plainer (v 46): "With one mind they kept up their daily attendance at the temple, and, breaking bread in private houses, shared their meals with unaffected joy." In doing this they undoubtedly remembered their Lord whom they had followed with such zeal and resignation.

CEREMONY MAY HAVE BEEN RELATED TO
THE GIVING UP OF ALL THINGS COMMON

Acts 6:2 RSV lends further support. When the business of the church became burdensome, the apostles said: "It is not right that we should give up preaching the word of God to serve tables," and they asked the brethren to appoint deacons for that work. Certainly the reference is not to any sacramental eating or religious act of worship since our opponents consider that properly the function of ministers, not deacons!

Just as the increase in the number of disciples made it impossible for the apostles to manage this, it is probable that their further increase in number and wider dispersal made it difficult to continue the practice of having all things in common. Because this seems to have been the significance of the breaking of bread which they did together from house to house. When it was necessary to discontinue this they met occasionally to break bread together so they might at least remember or have some experience of that ancient community.

Thus Acts 20:7 NEB says that at Troas "on the Saturday night, in our assembly for the breaking of bread, Paul, who was to leave next day, addressed them, and went on speaking until midnight." There is no mention of any sacramental eating. Since Paul was leaving the next day, he used the occasion for preaching to them. The eleventh verse makes it even clearer. After they had determined that Eutychus, the boy who fell out of the window, was not dead, they went upstairs for a midnight snack and went on talking until Paul departed at dawn. This was merely a matter of bodily refreshment. The fact that they met in the fear of God [or in a sense of awe of him] and with singleness of heart (Acts 2:42) does not make it any different from the eating that is done by profane persons.

CALLED A LOVE FEAST BY SOME

Some call this a Love Feast[21] to imply something more than merely filling the stomach and to emphasize that it is done out of respect for the Lord and in his presence as his people. This, we will not condemn. However, let it be observed that there is no further mention of this matter in all of Acts. Isn't it strange, if that ceremony was a solemn sacrifice as some would have it, or such a special sacrament as others claim, that this history is so silent on these matters when so many lesser things have been described in detail?

Undoubtedly as the early Christians departed gradually from their primitive purity and simplicity they accumulated superstitious traditions and they vitiated the innocent practices of their predecessors by intermixing Jewish or pagan rites. That happened in this matter, too, and that is the reason for Paul's lengthy rebuke in 1 Cor 11:17-34 NEB. Let us examine this section carefully, because this is the chief place on which the opposition bases its claims. Then we shall see whether anything further than that which we have already granted is implied.

[The following has been abbreviated considerably. — ED.]

The first reason Paul rebuked the Corinthians was that they were in such a hurry to eat that they took away any spiritual significance from their common meal or Lord's Supper (v 22): "Have you no homes of your own to eat and drink in?" This follows a statement that "while one goes hungry another has too much to eat." The citation continues: "Or are you so

---

[21] Moravians and Brethren (German Baptists), for example.

contemptuous of the church of God that you shame its poorer members?"

COMMON MEAL HARDLY A SACRAMENT

This common meal could hardly have been what Roman Catholics, Lutherans, or Calvinists would call a "sacrament." It is impossible to make any such sense of this part of scripture if it is considered without prejudice. In v 23 he makes it clear that the former custom of eating and drinking together had its origin in Christ's act with the apostles, the night he was betrayed: "For the tradition which I handed on to you came to me from the Lord himself: that the Lord Jesus, on the night of his arrest, took bread and, after giving thanks to God, broke it and said . . ."

Those who understand the difference between narration and a command can see, if they will, that there is no command here. This is merely a matter-of-fact statement. He does not say that it came to him from the Lord himself and that he should command them to do likewise. There is nothing of that sort here. On the contrary, in v 25, where he repeats Christ's statements to the apostles, he puts them in such a context that no such command is implied. For he says: "Whenever you drink it, do this as a memorial of me," and then adds "for every time you eat this bread and drink the cup, you proclaim the death of the Lord, until he comes." The word *whenever* no more implies a command, than the statement "whenever you are in Rome see the Capitol" should be interpreted as a command to go there!

CHRIST'S RETURN, OR APPEARANCE IN THE SPIRIT?

Whether you interpret proclaiming "the death of the Lord, until he comes" as requiring continuance of the ceremony until Christ comes at the end of the world, depends upon your interpretation of the reference to Christ's coming. It remains to be proved that this should be understood as referring to his final outward return, rather than his inward and spiritual visitation. Perhaps some of these weak and sensual ["carnal"] Corinthians had not yet known Christ's appearance in Spirit, and they were permitted the use of these outward things to remind them of Christ's death, until he did indeed arise in them.

For although those who are weak, like the Corinthians, need such outward things to remind them of Christ's death, others do not.

Those who are dead with Christ, and not only dead with Christ, but buried and also risen with him, need no such symbol to remember him. It was to them that the apostle says, Col 3:1 NEB: "Were you not raised to life with Christ? Then aspire to the realm above, where Christ is, seated at the right hand of God." But bread and wine are not the things that are above, they are products of this earth. The whole matter was merely an act of indulgence and condescension which Paul made to the weak and "carnal" Corinthians. The Syriac copy[22] (and other Oriental versions like the Arabic and Ethiopic[23]) begins v 17 with: "In that concerning which I am about to command you (or instruct you) I commend you not, because ye have not gone forward, but are descended unto that which is less, or of less consequence." He was clearly grieved that he had to instruct them in the outward things on which they doted. He would rather have them go forward in the life of Christianity than stick to the beggarly elements. The same version renders v 20 as: "When ye meet together, ye do not do it, as it is just ye should do in the day of the Lord, ye eat and drink it," showing that meeting to eat bread and drink wine was not the proper activity for that day of the Lord.

FAR MORE POSITIVE COMMANDS ARE NOT OBSERVED

Since those who are so zealous for the use of this ceremony make so much of its use by the church of Corinth, even though there is little ground for doing so, how does it happen that they pass over far more positive commands of the apostles as matters of no moment?

---

[22] "The Syriac Versions of the Bible are of exceptional value to the textual critic of the Scriptures on account of their very early date." — *O.D.C.C.*, p 1315.

[23] The Ethiopic version was probably translated from the Greek in the 4th or 5th c. although the surviving texts are all late (oldest 13th c.) and "show strong influence of the Coptic and medieval Arabic versions." Although there is no satisfactory complete edition, the entire NT was available to Barclay. It had been edited and published at Rome in 1548 and 1549 by P. Gaulterius and M. Victorius.
Although several Arabic versions of the NT are known, none seems to antedate the age of Mohammed (6th and 7th c.). Some were made directly from the Greek, others by way of the Syriac and Coptic (Bohairic) versions. The NT was edited by T. Erpenius at Leyden in 1616, preceded by the Gospels alone, with a Latin translation, at Rome in 1590. — *O.D.C.C.*, pp 467-468, 77.

First, there is Acts 15:29, where the apostles peremptorily command the Gentiles, following the statement (NEB) that "it is the decision of the Holy Spirit, and our decision," that "you are to abstain from meat that has been offered to idols, from blood, from anything that has been strangled..." In James 5:14 there is an explicit command to anoint the sick with oil in the name of the Lord.

If it should be claimed that these were only temporary things which were not supposed to continue, what grounds are there for this? If they say that repeal was implied in the apostle's statement that we ought not to be judged in meats and drinks, I will allow their answer. But why doesn't this apply to the other practice as well?

ANOINTING OF THE SICK NEGLECTED BY MANY

With reference to James' injunction to anoint the sick, they say that miraculous recovery of the sick no longer occurs, so the ceremony ought to be discontinued too. Of course, if you are going to be consistent in that logic you could say that praying should be discontinued too, since that was part of the anointing ceremony. And if this is the basic principle, that a ceremony should be given up when its efficacy fails, they should also forego the laying on of hands. Since the gift of the Holy Spirit does not follow, this has become merely an imitation of the practice of the apostles.

EXTERNAL RITES NOT PART OF THE
NEW COVENANT DISPENSATION

¶IX. Several scriptural testimonies are sufficient evidence that such external rites are not a necessary part of the new covenant dispensation. There is no reason to continue them just because they were practiced at one time. If several of these are given, it may make it apparent that the ceremony of the bread and wine has ceased in the same way as the other things for which our adversaries claim this. The first citation is Rom 14:17 NEB: "For the kingdom of God is not eating and drinking, but justice, peace, and joy, inspired by the Holy Spirit." If that is true, the eating of outward bread and wine can hardly be a required part of gospel worship, or a perpetual ordinance of it.

Col 2:16 is even clearer. Throughout the entire second chapter, the apostle clearly pleads against the formality and superstition of outward rites. He wants them to have "all the

riches of complete understanding" which Christians have by
Christ when they have indeed come to the life of Christianity.
In v 6 he says (Cath-CCD): "Therefore, as you have received
Jesus Christ our Lord, so walk in him; be rooted in him; and
built up on him; and strengthened in the faith." Then in
v 8: "See to it that no one deceives you by philosophy and vain
deceit, according to human traditions, according to the elements
of the world and not according to Christ." "In him, also,"
v 11-12 NEB, "you were circumcised, not in a physical sense,
but by being divested of the lower nature; this is Christ's way
of circumcision. For in baptism ... also you were raised to life
with him through your faith in the active power of God."

"ONLY A SHADOW OF WHAT IS TO COME"

Here also they partook of the true baptism of Christ and
since they had risen with him, let us see whether he thought
they needed bread and wine to remind them of Christ's death
or whether they would be subject to judgment if they did not.
Verse 16 RSV says: "Therefore let no one pass judgment on
you in questions of food and drink." Why? Verse 17 RSV says:
"These are only a shadow of what is to come; but the substance belongs to Christ." Since our opponents admit that
bread and wine are a sign and shadow, therefore, according to
the apostle's doctrine, we should not be judged if we do not
observe them. But shouldn't those who are dead with Christ
be subject to such ordinances?

What could be plainer than v 20-23 NEB: "Did you not
die with Christ and pass beyond reach of the elemental spirits
of the world? ... Why let people dictate to you?: 'Do not
handle this, do not taste that, do not touch the other' — all of
them things that must perish as soon as they are used? That is
to follow merely human injunctions and teaching. True, it
has an air of wisdom, with its forced piety, its self-mortification,
and its severity to the body; but it is of no use at all in combatting sensuality."

HOW DOES THE NEW COVENANT DIFFER FROM THE OLD?

If the use of water, bread, and wine were the very seals of
the new covenant and pertained to the chief sacraments of the
gospel and the so-called evangelical ordinances, then the gospel
would not differ from the law or be preferable to it.

But Heb 9:10 NEB clearly distinguishes the new covenant
from what is found in the law: "The offerings and sacrifices

there prescribed cannot give the worshipper inward perfection.
It is only a matter of food and drink and various rites of
cleansing — outward ordinances in force until the time of reformation."

The use of water, bread, and wine as required parts of
gospel worship destroy the very nature of it. They make it
appear as if the gospel were a dispensation of shadows, and
not of the substance! Not only does Colossians argue against
these things, but the same argument runs through the whole
epistle to the Hebrews. It is an attempt to wean the Jews
from their former worship. The reason is that this was figurative and an antitype. Would it make any more sense to provide them with another form of worship of the same type?

WHAT EVIDENCE IS THERE FOR SUBSTITUTING ONE SHADOW FOR ANOTHER?

What evidence can be produced from scripture or reason
that would substitute another shadow or figure rather than the
substance? Yet the claim is made that circumcision points to
water baptism, and the paschal lamb to bread and wine. Even
if it were true that one figure was the antitype of another, what
would be gained, since the Protestants do not claim any more
virtue or efficacy for the antitypes than they do for the types?
For they say, and this is true, that their sacraments do not
confer grace, but that grace is conferred according to the faith
of the recipient. However, it cannot be denied that the faithful among the Jews also received grace in the use of their figurative worship. And although Roman Catholics boast that
their sacraments confer grace *ex opere operato,* experience offers
abundant proof to the contrary.

BY WHAT AUTHORITY DO THEY ADMINISTER THEIR SACRAMENTS?

¶X. But even if water baptism and bread and wine were
used in the primitive church, there was also "abstaining from
things strangled and from blood." There was the use of legal
purification (Acts 21:23-25). The sick were anointed with oil
for the reason already mentioned. But it remains for our opposition to show how they receive the power or the authority
to administer these. They cannot claim it by the letter of the
scripture, or else they would have to do the other things which
the letter states that the primitive church did, and which have
just as much foundation in the letter. Their power must be

derived from the apostles, either mediately or unmediatedly. But we have shown before, in the tenth proposition, that they have no mediate power, because of the interruption made by the apostasy. And none of our opposition pretend that they have unmediated power, or have been commended by the Spirit of God to administer these things. In these as in other things they create an atmosphere out of the constant consent of the church, and of Christians in all ages. However, tradition[24] is not a sufficient basis for faith, so it should have small weight in this matter in particular. As far as ceremonies and superstitious observances were concerned, the apostasy began very early. That is apparent in the epistles of Paul to the Galatians and Colossians. What sense does it make to imitate them in matters which the apostle considered so regrettable? He not only reproved them sharply for these things but withstood their entrance into the church.

THERE HAS BEEN GREAT CHANGE

Furthermore, if we look to antiquity, we find a great deal of uncertainty and changeability on the matter of observances and traditions. Neither Protestants nor Catholics continue to observe this ceremony as they did. They used to give the supper to young boys and little children, and yet, as far as can be learned, this practice and that of infant baptism are of similar age. However, both Catholics and Protestants have laid aside children's communion[25] and yet they stick to infant baptism.

---

[24] Barclay seems to be saying that *sola traditione,* tradition alone, is no more of a sound basis for authority than *sola scriptura,* the Scriptures alone, into which Reformation doctrine was narrowed in opposition to the Catholic emphasis on tradition. — ED.

However, "the Council of Trent (Sess IV, 8 Apr, 1546) laid down that Scripture and tradition were to be received by the Church as of equal authority *(pari pietatis affectu ac reverentia)."* — O.D.C.C., p 1370.

Elsewhere, Barclay deals at some length with the question of authority. See index.

[25] Some opinion credits St. Cyprian (d. 258) with reference to Infant Communion, although Wall (below) maintains they were "four or five years of age" (op cit, vol 4, p 437, and vol 1, p 147). He further states that until the year 400 children were not admitted to the Church at all. It certainly was practiced in the time of Innocent 1. But by about 1000 A.D., coeval with the rise of the doctrine of transubstantiation, administration of the wine was confined to allowing the infant to suck the priest's finger after it had been dipped. Even this was soon discontinued, however, probably because of the "excessive regard" for the outward elements

What is more, we cannot put much stress on antiquity because there is no church now, Catholic or Protestant, which does not differ widely in its worship and ceremonies from those of the early church, as Dalleus[26] has demonstrated in his treatise on the *Use of the Fathers*. Why they should try to force this on us as justification for their usage in this case, when they do not follow ancient practice in other matters is not clear.

Nevertheless, I do not doubt that there have been many who have had some secret sense of their mystery even though their understanding was veiled by sticking to such outward things. It is probably the working of this secret sense which led them to such earthly comprehension as imagining the substance of the bread to be changed, or that the body was there even though it was not changed.

CALVIN'S INGENUOUS ADMISSION

Indeed I am inclined to look very favorably on Calvin's ingenuous admission[27] that although he can neither understand nor express it in words, he knows by having experienced it that the Lord is spiritually Present. No doubt Calvin sometimes had a sense of his Presence without the use of this ceremony. It is probable that the understanding of God that was given, him then made him justifiably reject the false notions of transubstantiation and consubstantiation.[28] But he did not know what to put in their place.

If he had waited entirely in the light that makes all things manifest (Eph 5:13), rather than using his own imagination, he

---

which the new doctrine imbued. — William Wall, *The History of Infant Baptism*, Oxford, 1844, in 4 vols.

The author may have been wearying in his monumental task by p 137 of vol 1, when he says: "So my book written now [1705] in answer to the reasonings of the Quakers, etc., will in the next age seem to be the work of a man that had little to do." Be it said that among Anglicans, at least, his work is still regarded as the classic defense in English of paedobaptism. — ED.

[26] Jean Daillé (1594-1670), a French Reformed theologian. The work referred to is probably his *Traicté de l'employ des saincts Peres* — *Lexikon für Theologie und Kirche*, Verlag Herder, Freiburg, 1959, vol 3, p 123. The *Encyc. Brit.*, 1955, vol 6, p 979, gives the title as *Dunrai emploi des Pères* (1631), translated into English by Thomas Smith under the title, *A Treatise Concerning the Right Use of the Fathers, in the Decision of the Controversies that are at this Day in Religion, etc.* (1651).

[27] See p 336.

[28] See fn p 334 for discussions of transubstantiation and consubstantiation.

might have come closer to understanding this mystery than those who went before him. If that had been the case, he would not have decided that the external ceremony is the chief or principal place where the spiritual presence is to be found. It is not the only place, as he well knew from experience.

THOSE WHO PRACTICE THIS CEREMONY
IN GOOD CONSCIENCE SHOULD BE INDULGED

¶XI. Finally, if there are any in this day who practice this ceremony with a true tenderness of spirit, and with real conscience toward God, and in the manner of the primitive Christians, as recognized in scripture, that is another matter. I do not doubt but that they may be indulged in it. The Lord may take these facts into consideration and appear to them for a time when they use these things. Many of us have known him to do this for us in our own times of ignorance. But there is always the provision that they must not try to force these things upon others, or to be critical of those who have been delivered from these things and who do not cling to them with pertinacity.

For we are certain that the day has dawned in which God has risen and has dismissed all those ceremonies and rites. He is to be worshipped only in Spirit. He appears to those who wait upon him. To seek God in these things is, like Mary at the sepulchre, seeking the living among the dead. For we know that he has risen and has been revealed in Spirit. He is leading his children out of these rudiments, that they may walk with him in his light, to whom be glory forever. Amen.

Religious Freedom

PROPOSITION 14 — CONCERNING CIVIL POWER[1] IN MATTERS PURELY RELIGIOUS AND PERTAINING TO THE CONSCIENCE

The power and dominion of the conscience are the province of God, and he alone can properly instruct and govern it. No one whatsoever may lawfully force the consciences of others regardless of the authority or office he bears in the government of this world. Death, banishment, fines, imprisonment, and similar things that are inflicted upon men solely because of the exercise of their consciences, or differences in worship or opinion, proceed from the spirit of Cain, the murderer, and are contrary to the Truth. This is, of course, always subject to the provision that no man, under pretense of conscience, may prejudice the life or property of his neighbor, or do anything that is destructive to human society or inconsistent with its welfare. In such cases, the transgressor is subject to the law, and justice should be administered without respect of persons. (Luke 9:55-56; Mat 7:12-13, 29; Titus 3:10).

¶I. The subject of the liberty of conscience in respect to civil power has been so thoroughly and learnedly handled in recent years that only a brief treatment is needed here.[2] Never-

---

[1] The Proposition was originally headed "Concerning the power of the Civil Magistrate, in matters purely religious, and pertaining to the conscience." The term "Magistracy" has been retained by Wendel and others in dealing with Calvin's theology; however, contextual evidence and present application to civil liberties, the conflict between military and civil as well as religious authority, and similar contemporary usages seem to justify the substitution of the term "civil power." — ED.

[2] This is a tantalizing reference which makes one wish that Barclay had dropped in a name or two. The relationship of church and state occupied the attention of each of the major reformers, and although Zwingli is accused of confusing the roles, Calvin and Luther sharply differentiated them.

Casuistry, in its best sense — the practical application of conscience to concrete situations — was also in its heyday at Barclay's time among both Anglicans and Nonconformists. The statement may indicate some of the impatience with the volume and academic character of much of the disputation, which were soon to put the subject in disfavor.

"The Calvinists William Perkins (1558-1602) and his disciple William Ames (1576-1633), the Anglicans Joseph Hall (1574-1656), Robert Sanderson (1587-1663), Jeremy Taylor (1613-1667) and John Sharp (1645-1714),

theless, it is lamentable that few have walked in accord with this principle. Each person pleads it for himself, but barely allows it for others, as there will be occasion to observe at greater length. In order to prevent any misunderstandings, it will be well first to summarize the present state of this controversy so that what follows may be more clearly understood.

EVEN AN ERRING CONSCIENCE BINDS

As explained in propositions five and six, when we speak of conscience we mean the persuasion of the mind which arises from a belief in the truth or falsity of anything. Even though his conscience may err, or even be evil in a particular matter, still a man would commit a sin if he acted contrary to his persuasion or his conscience. Because, what a man does that is contrary to his faith, even though his faith may be wrong, is absolutely unacceptable to God. That is why, when he is referring to food offered to idols, the apostle says in Rom 14:23 RSV: "But he who has doubts is condemned, if he eats, because he does not act from faith; for whatever does not proceed from faith is sin." Although this might have been lawful for someone else, if it would bring about any doubts, it would be better to abstain and not raise them. This is true even if the doubts were mere superstitions, as in the case of the kinds of meats that could rightfully be eaten. Or at least it was weakness of faith (since all of God's creatures are good and if they are received with thanksgiving they are useful for a man). Hence Ames' *de Cas. Cons.*[3] says: "Although the conscience may err, it is always binding, and he who acts contrary to his conscience (i.e., as he supposes it to be), sins, because he acts contrary to the will of God. Even though this is not materially and truly so, yet, it is formally and interpretatively so."

---

and Richard Baxter (1615-1691)" were of sufficient stature to be noted today in the *Encyc. Brit.* article on "Casuistry," 1958 ed, vol 5, p 13.

It may be significant that Ames is indeed cited by Barclay a few paragraphs later. (See the next footnote.)

[3] The work cited is *De Conscientia, eius Jure et Casibus,* published in 1632 by William Ames (1576-1633), a Calvinist moral theologian who was educated at Christ's College, Cambridge, but who moved to Holland after becoming an extreme Puritan.

In Holland, Ames "took a prominent part in the Remonstrant controversies and became recognized by the Calvinists as one of their best theologians. In 1622 he became professor of theology at Franeker, where he attracted hearers from all parts of Protestant Europe.... His most important work [here cited] is one of the few Protestant treatises on casuistry and was long held in high repute for its incisive decisions." — *O.D.C.C.,* p 43.

CIVIL AUTHORITIES HAVE NO RIGHT TO FORCE
ACTION CONTRARY TO CONSCIENCE

Thus the question is, first, whether the civil authorities
have the right to force men to act contrary to their consciences
in religious matters. Then, if they will not be coerced, is it
proper for the civil authorities to punish them by depriving
them of their goods, their liberty, or their lives? We claim that
it is not!

On the other hand, we are a long way from siding with or
supporting those libertines who distort liberty of conscience to
include matters which would prejudice the rights of their neighbors or ruin human society. *Thus we understand matters of
conscience to be those which are of immediate relevance for the
relationship between God and men or between men and other
men of the same persuasion.* They should be free to meet together and worship God in the way which they consider most
acceptable to him. But they should not encroach upon their
neighbors or seek to force their ways upon them. Only reason
and such other means as Christ and his apostles used are legitimate, like preaching and instructing those who wish to hear
and receive it.

THIS DOES NOT APPLY TO MATTERS CONTRARY TO MORALS

We do not consider it at all legitimate for men, under the
conception of conscience, to do anything that is contrary to the
moral and eternal statutes that are generally acknowledged by
all Christians. In such cases it is most lawful to impose civil
authority. This would certainly apply to those who, under the
pretext of conscience, consider it a matter of principle to murder and destroy all who are wicked; that is, all who differ from
them, in order to preserve the ruling power of the believers.
This applies also to those who seek to make all things common
and who would force their neighbors to share their estates with
them, and many similar wild notions that are attributed to the
Anabaptists of Münster.[4] It is quite evident that these things

---

[4] A group calling themselves Anabaptists captured Münster, the cap-
ital city of Westphalia, and held it by force from January, 1534, to June,
1535. They were led by a few extremists among the Dutch followers of
Melchior Hoffman, an Anabaptist chiliast. Hoffman himself neither promoted nor condoned the acts of violence which led to the establishment of
the "New Jerusalem" at Münster. Chiliasm was a feature of Dutch Anabaptism for about five years but was rejected after 1535. (See fn p 326
for other points of Anabaptist belief.)

For four hundred years the Münsterites were presented as representative
of Anabaptism as a whole. Today, most church historians take the view

are the result of pride and covetousness, rather than any purity or conscience. The latter part of the statement of the proposition was phrased to guard against that.

FREEDOM OF CONSCIENCE TOWARD GOD
AND AMONG THEMSELVES

The liberty we claim is that which the primitive church justifiably sought under the pagan emperors. It is the liberty of men of sobriety, honesty, and peaceable conduct to enjoy the freedom and exercise of their conscience toward God and among themselves. It is the right to be unmolested by the civil authorities for receiving among them those who come to be convinced of the same truth by their persuasion and influence.

THE CHURCH CENSURES THOSE IN ERROR

We would not have men robbed of their privileges as men and members of the commonwealth because of their inward persuasion. Nor would we have their political privileges suffer. Nevertheless, we are far from holding that the church of God should not exercise censure against those who fall into error, or who commit obvious evils. We believe that this is a very lawful thing for a Christian church to do. If, after due admonition and instruction according to the gospel order, the church finds any of her members pertinacious in error, she should cut them off from her fellowship by the sword of the Spirit. They should be deprived of those privileges which they had as fellow members.

BUT THIS SHOULD NOT ROB THEM
OF THEIR PRIVILEGES AS MEN

But this is not the same as cutting them off from the world by the temporal sword, or robbing them of their ordinary privileges as men. They do not enjoy these privileges because they are Christians and members of such a fellowship, but because they are men and members of the creation. Hence

---

that the Münster episode was atypical of true Anabaptism and contrary to its spirit. Mennonites, themselves, are seeking to recover the Anabaptist vision as it pertained to the Church and spirituality. An extensive literature has accumulated, capped by *The Mennonite Encyclopedia* and the *Mennonite Quarterly*, whose fine standards of scholarship have earned these works a good reputation.

A group of Mennonite theologians with the very best and soundest of European training offers an objective in that field for the other Historic Peace Churches, including the Quakers, who have been strong on history, but weak on theology. — ED.

Chrysostom says well, *de Anath.*: "We must condemn and reprove the evil doctrines that are proclaimed by heretics; but spare the men and pray for their salvation."

GOVERNMENTS HAVE NO JURISDICTION OVER CONSCIENCE

¶II. No man has jurisdiction over the consciences of men by virtue of any power or authority he has in the governments of this world. This should be evident, because the conscience of man is the seat and throne of God in him. And God alone is the proper and infallible judge, who alone can rectify the mistakes of conscience by his power and Spirit. He has reserved to himself the power of punishing errors of conscience as he sees fit. Civil authority meddles in the things which are beyond the compass of its jurisdiction when it assumes this privilege. And the capacity to make such a judgment does not belong to a public official. Even our adversaries will not deny that, inherently, an official is not a proper judge of such matters.

CERTAINLY PAGANS WERE NO JUDGES
OF CHRISTIAN CONSCIENCES

When we consider the pagan officials of early Christian times, it is obvious either that they lacked something essential to their office — which would be contrary to Paul's statement in Rom 13 — or that matters of conscience were not rightfully within their jurisdiction. If that is not so, it must be maintained, and this is even more absurd, that these pagan officials were proper judges on matters of Christian conscience.

It is certainly an evasion of the question to maintain that civil officials should mete out punishment in accordance with the censure and determination of the church. Indeed, this is nothing less than making the civil official the church's hangman. More will be said about this.

Although the chief members of the church are ordained to inform, instruct, and reprove, they do not have dominion over the faith and consciences of the faithful. Paul says this explicitly in 2 Cor 1:24 NEB: "Do not think we are dictating the terms of your faith ... We are working with you for your own happiness." Certainly they have far less right to usurp the power of life and death or to instigate the magistrate to persecute and murder those who cannot yield to them on matters of conscience.

The pretensions of civil authority are inconsistent with the nature of the gospel and contrary to its precepts. Those matters are altogether extrinsic to the ruling and governing of political states. Christ expressly signified that his kingdom was not of this world. If the propagation of the gospel had any inseparable relationship to worldly kingdoms, Christ did not say so. His example furnishes abundant evidence of how we are to act in such matters. He showed us that the gospel is to be propagated by persuasion and by the power of God. It will not be spread by the use of whips, imprisonment, banishment, and murder.

FORCE AND VIOLENCE ARE NOT FOR
MATTERS OF FAITH AND DOCTRINE

Those who truly propagate the faith will often suffer at the hands of the wicked, nevertheless they are not supposed to bring suffering onto the wicked. When Christ sent forth his disciples, he told them, Mat 10:16 RSV: "Behold, I send you out as sheep in the midst of wolves; so be wise as serpents and innocent as doves." He goes on to say, v 17-18 NEB: "And be on your guard, for men will hand you over to their courts, they will flog you in the synagogues, and you will be brought before governors and kings, for my sake, to testify before them and the heathen." He never says that they should whip, imprison, or kill. Indeed, Christians are frequently referred to by Christ as sheep, and sheep certainly do not devour or destroy.

It is a false assumption that Christ could not exercise worldly power because the civil authorities in his time were pagans and unbelievers. As the Son of God, Christ undeniably had a valid right to all kingdoms and was the rightful heir of the earth. Mat 28:18 RSV says: "All authority [Cath-CCD, "power"] in heaven and on earth has been given to me." [NEB has: "Full authority in heaven and on earth has been committed to me."]

If he had thought it proper, he could have summoned legions of angels to defend him and he could have forced the princes and potentates of earth to be subject to him (Mat 26:53).[5] It was contrary to the nature of Christ's gospel to use force or violence for gathering souls. When James and John, the sons of Zebedee, were irked at the Samaritan village for refusing them hospitality and asked: "Lord, may we call down fire from heaven to burn them up?" he rebuked them (Luke 9:54-55 NEB).

---

[5] But he rebuked the disciple who cut off the ear of the High Priest's servant, telling him to put up his sword. — ED.

Is there any reason to doubt that it was just as great a crime then as now to be in error on matters of faith and doctrine? Certainly the power to punish those who refused Christ was not lacking. Those who could perform other miracles could do this one too! There was even the precedent of Elias, one who was considered holy under the legal dispensation. But as some of the ancient authorities add in v 55-56 NEB: "You do not know," he said, "to what spirit you belong; for the Son of Man did not come to destroy men's lives, but to save them."

Christ clearly showed that he did not approve of this kind of zeal. Those who would make way for Christ or his gospel by this means, do not understand what spirit they are of. If it was not lawful to call down fire from heaven to destroy those who refused to receive Christ, it is certainly far less lawful to kindle fire on the earth to destroy those who believe in Christ because — for the sake of conscience — they will not or cannot believe as the civil authorities do. If it was not lawful for the apostles to force other men to obey their judgment, it is far less lawful for men to do so now. The apostles had such a large measure of the Spirit that they were not likely to make mistakes. But experience shows that many are often mistaken now. These men admit that they are fallible when they kill or destroy those whose convictions will not allow them to come to the same conclusions or beliefs in matters of conscience as they do.

CHRIST DID NOT CONSTRAIN OTHERS TO BELIEVE

How can they constrain others to believe in Christ or use force to make them receive him when he did not consider it wise? He was King of Kings, but nevertheless he considered it inconsistent with the nature of his ministry and spiritual government. How can they do anything but grossly offend him when they think that they are wiser than he was and try to force men to conform to their doctrine and worship him contrary to their own persuasion?

"Not by an army, nor by might, but by my spirit, says the Lord of Hosts;" (Zach 4:6 Cath-CCD). But they would say: "Not by the Spirit of the Lord, but by might and earthly power." Yet the apostle says plainly, 2 Cor 10:4 RSV: "For the weapons of our warfare are not worldly but have divine power to destroy strongholds. We destroy arguments and every proud obstacle to the knowledge of God and take every thought captive to obey Christ."

But there are those who find it necessary to wrestle with flesh and blood when they cannot prevail with the Spirit and with the understanding. Not having spiritual weapons, they go about with earthly weapons to establish Christ's kingdom, which they can never do. When their motives have been well sifted it is found that self-love and the desire for others to bow to them outweigh the love of God.

CHRIST'S METHOD TRULY OF ANOTHER KIND
Christ's method is truly of another kind for he says that his people shall be a willing people in the day of his power (Psalm 110:3). But these men struggle against the wills and consciences of men not by the power of Christ, but by the outward sword. They want to force men to become the people of Christ, even though this can never be done.

Christ gives his judgment on this matter in the parable of the tares, Mat 13:25. His own interpretation in v 38-41 says that the weeds are the sons of the evil one. Yet he does not want the servants to uproot them, because they might pull up the wheat too. Heretics are certainly included in the parable. But the intimation is that man's ability to be mistaken should serve as a bridle on him and cause him to be wary in such matters. Thus, those who pull up what they consider tares, declare publicly that they do not have any scruples about breaking Christ's commands.

It is a miserable evasion to maintain that the tares referred to in the parable are hypocrites rather than heretics. Since hypocrites and heretics are both children of the wicked one, it doesn't make much difference, and those who make this distinction find themselves left with a very empty affirmation. It doesn't strengthen their case any to say that hypocrites cannot be discerned. For both hypocrites and heretics can be discovered by those who are spiritually discerning, while those who lack this cannot discover either. Actually, both arguments are of no consequence, for the servants were able to discern the tares, but they were liable to injure the wheat if they pulled them up.

FALSE PROPHETS OFFER NO PARALLEL
¶III. The condemning to death of the false prophets in Deut 13:5[6] is often cited in opposition to liberty of conscience.

[6] RSV: "But that prophet or that dreamer of dreams shall be put to death, because he has taught rebellion against the Lord your God. . . ."

However, there is no parallel which would furnish a rule for
Christians, any more that it would be lawful for Christians to
invade their neighbors' kingdoms and kill them without mercy,
merely because the Jews did that to the Canaanites...

It is said that commands which are not repealed in the
gospel should stand. The answer to that is that the precepts
and practices of Christ and his apostles are sufficient repeal.
Each command that was given to the Jews does not require a
specific repeal to keep it from being binding upon us. If it did,
it would still be lawful for the Jews to revenge the murder of a
Jew without any consideration for the law. The nearest of kin
would simply kill the murderer.

There is also the command in Deut 13:7-10 Cath-CCD: "If
your own full brother, or your son or daughter, or your intimate
friend, entices you secretly to serve other gods... do not yield
to him or listen to him, nor look with pity upon him, to spare
or shield him, but kill him. Your hand shall be the first raised
to slay him..." If this command were followed there would be
no need for any inquisition or local magistrate to do the job.

CHRIST DELIVERS HIS CHOSEN ONES FROM A MYSTICAL EGYPT

Still, is there any reason why we should hurry past this part
of scripture, but on the other hand claim that the other part is
still in effect? In fact, if this type of argument which uses the
practice among the Jews as a precedent were accepted, it would
overturn the very gospel. It establishes the worldly ordinances
of the Jews and pulls down the spiritual ones of the gospel.

We can argue far better when we distinguish between the
figurative and temporal state of the Jews and the real and spiritual one under the gospel. Moses delivered the Jews from outward Egypt by an outward force, and he established them in an
outward kingdom by destroying their outward enemies for
them. Christ does not deliver his chosen ones — those who are
inwardly Jews — by killing others in an outward struggle. Instead, he delivers his chosen ones from a mystical Egypt by suffering and being killed. He destroys their spiritual enemies
before them and establishes his spiritual kingdom (which is
not of this world) among them.

Those who departed from the fellowship of outward Israel
were to be cut off by the outward sword. Those who depart
from an inward Israel are to be cut off by the sword of the
Spirit. In fact, isn't it the essence of the matter to interpret

Jewish matters outwardly and Christian matters inwardly? Just as the Jews intended to cut off their enemies outwardly, in order to establish their kingdom and their outward (that is, ritualistic) worship, they were to uphold them in the same way. But the kingdom and gospel of Christ were not to be established or propagated by cutting off or destroying the Gentiles, but rather by persuading them.

SCRIPTURES CITED AS JUSTIFICATION FOR PERSECUTION

Rom 13 is cited, particularly v 4, to uphold the power of the authorities to execute wrath upon those who do evil, NEB: "It is not for nothing that they hold the power of the sword, for they are God's agents of punishment, for retribution on the offender." They maintain that heresy is evil, therefore . . . But so is hypocrisy, but they do not claim that the authorities should punish that. Therefore, this must be understood to refer to moral evils and to be pertinent to affairs between man and man, and not to matters of judgment or worship. Otherwise, the implications become ridiculous and absurd, when one remembers that Paul was writing to the church of Rome, which was under the government of Nero, an impious pagan, and a persecutor of the church. If heresy was included in the power to punish, it must follow that Nero had this power, indeed he had obtained it from God! It was because of the derivation of their power from God that the apostle urged them to obey the supreme authorities. Could anything be more absurd than maintaining that Nero had the power to judge in such matters? If he did have such power it had to be exercised according to his own judgment and conscience, and this would be enough to justify his persecution of the apostles and murdering of the Christians.

Another passage that is cited to justify persecution is Gal 5:12 KJ: "I would they were even cut off which trouble you."[7]

A similar argument is drawn from Rev 2:20 NEB: "Yet I have this against you: you tolerate that Jezebel, the woman who claims to be a prophetess, who by her teaching lures my servants

---

[7] Barclay, with others, interpreted this to refer to excommunication and quotes Beza: "We cannot understand this otherwise than of excommunication . . ." etc. However, Paul was using a little more irony than that, as the RSV has it: "I wish those who unsettle you [i.e., over whether it was necessary for a Christian to be circumcised] would mutilate themselves." NEB carries it a step further: "As for these agitators, they had better go the whole way and make eunuchs of themselves!" — ED.

into fornication and into eating food sacrificed to idols." The
church at Thyatira is reproved for allowing her to continue,
which can only be interpreted as meaning that they did not
excommunicate or censure her. As for corporal punishment,
it is known that at that time Christians did not have the power
to punish heretics, even if they wanted to.

It is also stated that heresies include the evil works of the
flesh enumerated in Gal 5:20-21 which concludes, NEB: "I warn
you, as I warned you before, that those who behave in such
ways will never inherit the kingdom of God." However, who
has proved that the civil authorities have the power to punish
all evil works of the flesh? Actually, every evil is a work of the
flesh, but not all evils come under the cognizance of the authorities. Hypocrisy, hatred, envy are evils which do not. In fact,
the list in Gal 5 specifically includes "quarrels, a contentious
temper, envy, fits of rage, selfish ambitions, party intrigues, and
jealousies." Civil authority exercises no punishment for these.
In summary, as long as heresy does not commit any act that is
destructive to human society, but confines itself to such matters
as doctrine or the forms of worship, matters which are between
a man and his God, it is not within civil jurisdiction.

IT IS CONTRARY TO BOTH REASON AND THE LAWS OF NATURE TO FORCE MEN'S CONSCIENCES

¶IV. To force men's consciences is contrary to sound reason and the laws of nature. One man cannot inflict enough
bodily suffering on another to make him change his views, especially in matters that are spiritual and supernatural. It is argument and the self-evident demonstrations of reason, together
with the power of God reaching the heart, that can make a man
alter his opinions. Knocks, blows, and similar treatment may
destroy the body, but they can never inform the soul. The soul
is a free agent and it must be influenced by something which
has a nature similar to its own. To attempt to change minds
in any other fashion is to deal with men as if they were brutes.
In that fashion men may be made hypocrites, but they can
never be made Christians. The products of such compulsion
cannot be acceptable to God. It may be possible to achieve an
outward assent in doctrine or worship, but the only sacrifice
which God desires is one which comes thoroughly and completely from the heart. He does not desire any constrained
sacrifices. Instead of making members of the church by such
constraint, men are made ten times greater servants of Satan,

for in addition to their heresy, hypocrisy is added. That is the worst of evils in religious matters, and one which the Lord's soul abhors above all others.

HYPOCRITES ADD NOTHING TO THE CHURCH

Those who maintain that, nevertheless, error is suppressed by such acts and scandal is removed, should remember that Christ does not allow this method. The church is not improved in any way by the addition of hypocrites, but instead it is greatly corrupted and endangered. On the other hand, when heresies are open, men become aware of them and they can shun those whom the church separates by her censures. But secret hypocrites may cause the body to putrefy and the poison to spread before men become aware of it.

DISSENSION IS NOT ELIMINATED BY CREATING MARTYRS

If the dissenters prove resolute and suffer boldly for the opinions which they cherish and consider right, experience shows that such suffering redounds to their benefit and never to that of their persecutors. Such suffering ordinarily breeds compassion and curiosity. Men want to know what it is that permits others to suffer such great losses so boldly, and inquire all the more diligently about the things which are believed. They know that it is not likely that men will venture everything, merely to acquire fame. A better argument than a hangman's noose or a faggot is needed to detract from the reputation of martyrs.

For the sake of argument, however, let us assume that the civil authorities have the power to force the consciences of their subjects; that they can punish them if they will not comply. Great embarrassment and ridiculous conclusions follow, even things which are inconsistent with the nature of the Christian religion. First, if the magistrate has this power, it is his duty to use it, and he commits a sin of omission if he does not. An inference from this is that Christ was defective as far as his Church was concerned when he did not use his power to summon legions of angels to force men to join. In a sense, he was leaving his Church at the mercy of the wicked when he neglected such a necessary bulwark!

Furthermore, this justifies the persecution of Christians by all of the pagan emperors. It justifies the Spanish Inquisition, which is still odious not only to Protestants, but to the many tolerant Roman Catholics as well. How can Protestants con-

demn Catholics for persecuting them when they are only exercising a lawful power? They are acting according to their
consciences and to the best of their understanding. They have
done no more to the sufferers than the persecuted admit that
they would do if they were in a similar position.

This removes all grounds for commiserating with the sufferers. But that used to be the basis on which the Christians of
antiquity gained their reputation. They suffered rather than
be guilty of hurting anyone. It was against their principles to.
do so. But you can't pity anyone who is merely being dealt
with as he would deal with others. It seems to beg the question
rather miserably to say that they have no reason for persecuting
us since they are wrong and we are right.

Such a doctrine strengthens the hands of persecutors everywhere, for, very rationally, they can add the principle of self-
preservation. Who can blame me for destroying someone that
I know is lying in wait for an occasion to destroy me? It makes
all suffering for religion, which used to be the glory of Christianity, purely a necessity. Martyrs are no longer lambs led to
the slaughter, as the captain of their salvation was, but wolves
who cannot bite because they are caught in a snare.

WHAT BECOMES OF FAITH AND PATIENCE?

What becomes of the faith and patience of the saints? It
is small glory, indeed, to suffer merely because it cannot be
helped. Every thief and murderer becomes a martyr at that
rate. Experience has abundantly proved this in the past three
centuries. It also puts a premium on getting the upper hand,
so that each party struggles to gain control in order to enforce
its opinions.

What a tool the pope used to make of his pretended
power in this matter. On the slightest pretext of dislike for
any prince or state he would depose the prince and turn his
subjects against him. Even for the most minor of heresies he
would give their dominions to other princes who served his
interests better. No one can be ignorant of this who has read
the life of Hildebrand.[8]

---

[8] Hildebrand, St. Gregory VII (c. 1021-1085), forbade lay investiture
in 1075, after he had become pope. This "had made the Church dependent on the secular power and led to the bestowal of ecclesiastical offices
on entirely unqualified persons."
Papal legates deposed simoniacal and immoral clerics, and the measure
met with violent opposition, especially in Germany, France, and England.

Protestants too have vindicated the liberty of their consciences in the same manner. They suffered a great deal in France to very good effect since it led to a great increase in their numbers. But as soon as they found that they were numerous enough and had some princes on their side they began to let the king know that either they would have freedom of conscience or else they would purchase it — not by suffering, but by fighting. If Henry IV[9] had not relinquished his religion to obtain the crown more peaceably by conciliating the Roman Catholics, the Protestants would have prevailed with the sword and taught the Roman Catholics with the faggot and stake.

PERSECUTION IS THE ROOT OF MISERY AND STRIFE

It is this principle of persecution, regardless of who administers it, that is at the root of all of this misery and strife. As long as any party is persuaded that while it is in power it is not only its right but its duty to destroy those who differ, every possible means will be used to obtain that power. If the Roman Catholics consider it lawful to compel the civil authorities to do this when they are in power, experience has shown that they

---

"In Germany, Henry IV, threatened with ban and deposition, held two Synods at Worms and Piacenza (1076) which declared the Pope deposed. Gregory replied by deposing and banning Henry and freeing his subjects from their oath of allegiance at the Lenten Synod of 1076. The Emperor, whose situation soon became desperate, submitted to the Pope at Canossa in 1077, did penance, and was absolved from his censures."

Other instances of the exercise of papal authority over civil rulers by Gregory could be cited. "Though Gregory was once regarded as an ambitious tyrant, most modern historians have revised this judgment and are agreed on his purity of intention and his desire for justice." — *O.D.C.C.*, pp 584-585.

[9] This is Henry IV of France (1553-1610), not the Henry IV of Germany (1050-1106) referred to in the previous footnote. "Brought up as a Protestant, he became King of Navarre in 1572. He took part in the wars of religion on the Protestant side and, on the assassination of Henry III in 1589, inherited the crown of France. But his Protestantism made him unacceptable to the Catholic League, which was supported by Philip II of Spain and the Pope; and though he defeated the Guise party in the field he was not recognized as King until his conversion to Catholicism in 1593. "Opinion is now decidedly against the popular legend that this was merely a political move. His lengthy discussions with theologians previous to his submission, together with his protestations that 'Religion is not changed as easily as a shirt,' are considered sufficient proof of his sincerity. It was not until 1595, however, after many difficulties, that the Pope solemnly absolved Henry from the crime of heresy. In 1598 the King promulgated the Edict of Nantes which gave freedom of worship to the Protestants in recognized places and permitted them to garrison certain towns as a security for its maintenance." — *O.D.C.C.*, pp 622-623.

will depose those who do not act accordingly and absolve their subjects from their oath of fidelity. Not only has the pope done so on numerous occasions but Bellarmine has defended this doctrine against Barclay.[10] Protestants, too, have no scruples about deposing or killing wicked kings or magistrates. Scotch Presbyterians are just as arbitrary as Jesuits. They would not permit Charles II to become king, even though he was a Protestant, until he swore to renounce episcopacy. Although this matter was of little moment to him, it was contrary to his conscience.[11]

FREEDOM OF CONSCIENCE IS AN INNATE PART OF THE CHRISTIAN RELIGION

Yet how disproportionate these things are to the acts of the early Christians and the faith propagated by Christ and his apostles is so obvious that it hardly needs to be demonstrated. Even though many superstitions crept into the early church, persecution was so inconsistent with the nature of the gospel that almost all of the Christian writers of the first 300 years pleaded earnestly for freedom of conscience. This was such an innate and natural part of the Christian religion that any opinion which held otherwise was condemned.

[10] William Barclay of Aberdeen (c. 1547-1608) denied the temporal power of the pope, while Bellarmine held that he had an indirect power. Bellarmine was not canonized until 1930 or declared a Doctor of the Church until 1931, to some extent because of this minimizing of papal authority, in spite of the fact that he was "one of the greatest and most saintly figures in the Roman Catholic Church in the latter years of the Counter-Reformation." — *O.D.C.C.*, pp 150-151.

William Barclay's *De Potestate Papae; an, et quatenus, in Reges et Principes seculares jus et imperium habeat* was published in 1609 with place unindicated, probably at London, and the same year at Mussiponti (Pont-a-Mousson) with a preface by his son John Barclay (1582-1621), and in English translation in 1611. It has been reprinted frequently. "It was directed against the claims of the pope to exercise authority in temporal matters over sovereigns" and brought about Cardinal Bellarmine's assertion that "the pope, by virtue of his spiritual supremacy, possesses a power in regard to temporal matters which all are bound to acknowledge as supreme." — *Dict. Nat. Biog.*, N. Y. and London, 1885, vol 3, pp 173-174.

[11] He adopted Presbyterianism in 1650 to obtain Scottish help, but abandoned it in 1651 on the failure of the attempt at restoration. Although his religious indifference inclined him to tolerance, he was at odds with Parliament during most of his reign, in which the Conventicle Act (1664), the Test Act (1673), and other restrictive measures were passed. On his deathbed, the king made formal profession of the Roman Catholic faith. — *O.D.C.C.*, pp 266-267.

"NOT WITH SWORDS... BUT WITH PERSUASION AND COUNSEL"

¶V. Athanasius[12] stated: "It is the essence of piety not to force, but to persuade, in imitation of our Lord, who forced no-one, but left it to the will of the individual to follow him ... But the devil, because he has nothing of truth, uses knocks and axes, to break up the doors of such as receive him. But our Savior is meek, teaching the truth ... and enters when he is opened to,[13] and retires if they delay, and will not open unto him; because it is not with swords, nor darts, nor soldiers, nor armor, that truth is to be declared, but with persuasion and counsel."

It should be observed that it was the impious Arians who first made it a matter of doctrine to persecute other Christians. Athanasius offers further reproof to both their Catholic and Protestant successors when he says:[14] "Where have they learned to persecute? Certainly they cannot say that they have learned it from the saints; but this has been given them, and taught to them, by the devil. The Lord sometimes commanded people to flee, and the saints sometimes fled; but persecution is the invention and means of persuasion which the devil tries to use against everyone." He says further on: "In so far as the Arians banish those who will not subscribe to their decrees, they show that they are opposed to Christianity and friends of the devil."

"But now, lamentably," says Hilary,[15] "it is the privileged ones of the earth who recommend the religion of God, and

---

[12] St. Athanasius, Bishop of Alexandria (c. 296-373), to whom the so-called "Athanasian Creed" was originally attributed, although the research of G. J. Voss (1642) showed that it contains later doctrinal expressions. — O.D.C.C., pp 99-100.

Barclay gives *Epist. ad solit. Vit. ag.* as the source. The full citation may be *Epistola ad omnes ubique solitariam vitam agentes* — Migne, *Patrologiae, Graecae*, vol 28, p 1646.

[13] Rev 3:20.

[14] In *Apol. 1, "de Fuga sua,"* tomo 1.

[15] *contra Aux.*

This is Hilary of Poitiers (c. 315-367), and the work cited is probably *Contra Arianos, vel Auxentium Mediolanensem liber,* published in connection with the controversy over his impeachment of Auxentius, bishop of Milan, in 364. (See also fn p 378.)

Hilary himself had suffered banishment to Phrygia and was involved with the Oriental bishops in the Nicene controversy and over the Trinity.

A convert from paganism, he is known as the "Athanasius of the West." "He became the leading and most respected Latin theologian of his age." He was proclaimed a Doctor of the Church (see fn p 43) in the year 1851 by Pius IX. — *Encyc. Brit.,* vol 11, p 552, and *O.D.C.C.,* p 638.

Christ is found naked of his virtue, while ambition must give credit to his name. The church reproves and fights with banishment and imprisonment, and requires people to believe her, whereas at one time she was believed because of the imprisonments and banishments she herself suffered. She who was once consecrated by the terrors of her persecutors, now depends upon the dignity of those who are in her communion. She who was once propagated by her banished priests, now banishes the priests. And she who now boasts that she is loved by the world, would not have been Christ's if she had not been hated by the world."

THE CHURCH WAS CROWNED BY MARTYRDOM

"The church," says Jerome,[16] "was founded by the shedding of blood, and by suffering, and not by doing harm to others. The church increased by being persecuted, and was crowned by martyrdom."

Ambrose, speaking of Auxentius, says:[17] "Whoever he could not deceive with his discourses, he thought should be killed with the sword. He made bloody laws with his mouth, writing them with his own hands, and imagining that an edict could command faith." He also says (in *Epist. 27*) that when he went into Gaul he would not communicate with the bishops who required heretics to be put to death.

---

16 In *Epist. 62 ad The.*

St. Jerome (c. 342-420), was not only the translator of the Vulgate Bible, but one of the first Christian Fathers to understand the relation of the Apocrypha to the books in the Hebrew canon. In addition to his biblical translations and commentaries he did a bibliography of ecclesiastical writers and possessed a "scholarship unsurpassed in the early Church." — *O.D.C.C.*, pp 719-720.

17 *Epist. 32*, tomo 3.

St. Ambrose, Bishop of Milan (c. 339-397). One of the four traditional Doctors of the Latin Church, he was the son of the Praetorian Prefect of Gaul.

Upon the death of Auxentius, the Arian Bishop of Milan, the Catholic laity demanded that Ambrose should succeed him. Since he was then only a catechumen, i.e., an unbaptized believer, it was necessary for him to be baptized before he could be ordained. He then devoted himself to studying theology.

He was famous as a preacher and a jealous upholder of orthodoxy, and was partly responsible for the conversion of St. Augustine. He maintained the independence of the church against the civil power and protested against the execution of the Priscillianist heretics under Maximus. — *O.D.C.C.*, pp 41-42.

The emperor Martianus, who assembled the Council of Chalcedon, stated[18] that he would not force or constrain anyone to subscribe to the Council of Chalcedon against his will.

Hosius, Bishop of Cordova, testifies[19] that the emperor Constantine would not force anyone to be orthodox.

Hilary says further[20] that God does not require obedience, but teaches knowledge of himself and lends authority to his commands by the miracles of his heavenly works. He does not want anyone to be forced to confess him as Lord. He is the God of the whole universe and does not need a constrained obedience or require a forced confession.

THE DOCTRINE OF HUMILITY

Ambrose also says[21] that: "Christ sent his apostles to sow faith; not to constrain, but to teach; not to exercise coercive power, but to extol the doctrine of humility."

Cyprian,[22] comparing the old covenant with the new, says: "Then they were put to death with the outward sword; but

18 [The Emperor Marcian (396-457), whose] *Epist. ad archimand. etc. Mon. Eg.* [Barclay is citing from] *Acta Concil. Chalced.,* tomo 2, conc. gen.

He did use arms, however, to enforce the decrees of this council, whose sixth session (451) he attended personally.

He is not to be confused with Marcion, the heretic of Pontus, the wealthy shipowner who died about 160, and whose NT canon, consisting only of part of the gospel of St. Luke and ten Pauline epistles, hastened the formation of the Catholic canon.

19 In *Epist. ad Constit. apud Ath. in Eph. ad solit. Vit.,* tomo 1.

In addition to his distinction of living to be 100 years old, Hosius (c. 257-357) served as ecclesiastical adviser to the Emperor Constantine, for whom he made the investigation of the dispute between Alexander and Arius which led to the summoning of the Nicene Council. "There are some grounds for believing that here he presided and also introduced the *Homoousian;*" ("of one substance" — said of the Son in relation to the Father). — *O.D.C.C.,* p 657.

20 *Lib.* 1, *ad Const.*

The full citation is *Ad Constantium Augustum.* — *Encyc. Brit.,* vol 11, p 552.

21 *Comm. in Luc.,* lib 7.

Ambrose, whose sermons helped convert Augustine. His chief literary productions were "homiletic commentaries on the early OT narratives, e.g., of the Hexaëmeron and of Abraham, some of the Psalms, and the Gospel according to Luke [cited here]." — *Encyc. Brit.,* vol 1, p 743.

22 *Epist.* 62.

St. Cyprian, Bishop of Carthage, who died 258 A.D. A pagan rhetorician,

now the proud and contumacious are cut off with the spiritual
sword, by being cast out of the church." This is a good commentary on the question of using Jewish practice under the
law as a precedent for Christian action.

Tertullian says to the pagans:[23] "Consider whether attempts to take away religious liberty and to restrict men's choice
of God do not cause the spread of irreligion. If I am not allowed to worship whom I wish, I will have to be forced to
worship someone else. And no one wishes to be worshipped
by force."

And again, he says:[24] "It is very evident that it is unjust
to constrain and force men to sacrifice against their wills, since
the service of God requires a willing heart." Also:[25] "It is a
human right and natural power for everyone to worship whatever he esteems; and one man's religion does not benefit nor
hurt another. Nor is it any part of religion to enforce religion.
Religion must be undertaken by consent, and not by violence,
since sacrifices cannot be required, but must come from a willing mind."

THE UNANIMITY OF THE EARLY CHURCH FATHERS

How either Catholics or Protestants who boast of the ancient basis of their faith can ignore these very clear testimonies
is a matter which any rational man can judge for himself. I
doubt if there is any other single point in dispute between us
on which all of the Early Fathers and writers are so absolutely

---

he was converted to Christianity c. 246. His profound knowledge of the
scriptures and the writings of Tertullian led to his being elected a bishop
within two years of his conversion.

His writings enjoyed great popularity from the first. They were principally letters and short treatises in the practical rather than the dogmatic
realm.

23 *Apol.*, cap 24.

The African Church Father Quintus Septimus Florens Tertullian (c. 160-
c. 220) was a pagan lawyer who was converted to Christianity in 195 or
196 when he returned to his native Carthage, where he became a catechist
and, according to St. Jerome, a priest.

He was the first Christian theologian to write in Latin and is credited
with creating "the language of Western theology, which owes its characteristic precision to his legally trained mind." His celebrated defense of
Christianity, the *Apologeticum*, cited by Barclay, "is addressed to the pre-
fects of the Roman provinces and deals chiefly with the absurdity of the
accusations brought against the Christians." — *O.D.C.C.*, p 1334.

24 *Apol.*, cap 28.

25 *Ad. Scapul.*, cap 2.

unanimous. This unanimity shows how contrary to the nature of Christianity all of them considered this to be.

In fact, it was on the matter of persecution that no small part of the apostasy hinged. From small beginnings it enlarged until the pope excommunicated princes on the slightest displeasure. Now if Protestants abhor these things among those who acknowledge the pope, as it is only proper that they should, isn't it sad that they act similarly themselves? At first they did not even consider doing such things. In his early innocence Luther said:[26] "Neither pope nor bishop, nor any other man, has power to oblige a Christian to one syllable, except it be by his own consent." And again: "I call boldly upon all Christians, that neither man nor angel can impose any law upon them, any further than they are willing: for we are free of all."[27]

LUTHER'S TESTIMONY AT THE DIET OF SPEYER

When Luther appeared at the diet of Spiers[28] before the emperor, the archbishop of Triers, and Joachim, elector of Brandenburg, there seemed to be no possibility of reconciliation with his opposition. They asked him what remedy seemed

26 In De Captivitate Babylonica [Ecclesiae].
This was one of the three celebrated reforming writings of the year 1520 that completed the break with the medieval Church. It was published in both Latin and German. Martin Luther stated that the Babylonian Captivity of the Church (see fn p 206) consisted in the denial of communion under both kinds to the laity, and in the doctrines of transubstantiation and the sacrifice of the Mass (see fn p 334). Only baptism and the Eucharist were held to be sacraments. Other issues in the separation of 1520 were tributes to Rome, celibacy of the clergy, the authority of the priesthood to mediate between the individual and his God, Masses for the dead, pilgrimages, religious orders, and justification by faith, which freed the Christian of the obligation to perform good works. Luther presented a new ideal of piety in which conscience prompted proper conduct in a Christian brotherhood. — O.D.C.C., p 832, and Col. Encyc., pp 1173-1174.

27 "In his tract On the Civil Power (1523), Luther, in contrast to his attitude to the State in the Address to the German Nobility [one of the three major treatises of 1520], ... sharply distinguished between the political and spiritual spheres, and whilst denouncing the misgovernment of princes, inculcated anew the duty of the subject to submit to the civil power and the established order in the State and to suffer, not actively repel, injustice." — Encyc. Brit., 1958, vol 14, p 495, s v "Luther" by Jas. MacKinnon, professor of ecclesiastical history at Edinburgh, 1908 to 1930.

28 "Several imperial diets were held at Speyer, notably the diet of 1529, which gave complete toleration to Catholics in Lutheran states, denied toleration to Lutherans in Catholic states, and refused toleration to Zwinglians and Anabaptists altogether." — Col. Encyc., p 1871.

most appropriate. He answered, according to the *History of the Council of Trent:*[29] "The counsel that Gamaliel proposed to the Jews, to wit, that if this counsel was of God, it would stand; if not, it would vanish; which he said ought to content the pope." He did not say that because he was in the right he ought to be spared. For such counsel would presuppose that those who were tolerated might be wrong. Yet the same Luther, as soon as he was secure, urged the elector of Saxony to banish poor Carlstadt because he could not submit to Luther's judgment in all matters![30] There is probably good basis for the report that Luther took it so much to heart that he required comforting when Carlstadt styled himself, in his letter to his congregation, as "a man banished for conscience by the procurement of Martin Luther."

Since neither Lutherans nor Calvinists allow one another to worship in their respective domains, they are little better than Catholics or Arians in this particular. Yet Calvin says[31] that the conscience "is exempt from all human authority." If that is true, why did he cause Castellio[32] to be banished? Was it not because his conscience would not allow him to believe that God had ordained men to be damned? If Calvin's own report is to be believed, he had Servetus[33] burned for denying

[29] Probably the one by Paolo Sarpi (1552-1623), a Venetian of the Servite Order, published in English, at London, in 1619, under the name of "Pietro Soave Polan," an anagram of "Paolo Sarpi Veneto." — *O.D.C.C.*, pp 1217 and 1374. (See also fn p 295.)
A limited examination of a 1640 English edition at General Theological Seminary failed to locate the reference and make a positive identification. The index, however, was by no means complete.

[30] Luther attacked him in 1524 with his tract *Wider die himmlischen Propheten*, in which he called him the new "Judas." Carlstadt was forced to renounce his professorship at Wittenburg and flee. Although he was allowed to return in 1525 if he would not lecture, he had to leave again in 1528-9. He spent the rest of his life in Switzerland. — *O.D.C.C.*, p 237.

[31] *Institutes,* lib 3, cap 19, sect 14.
The version is that of the Allen translation. See fn p 47 for full citation.

[32] Sebastian Castellio (1515-1563), whose differences with Calvin arose from humanist influences, and in 1544 such theological differences as rejection of the Song of Solomon from the biblical canon and an unorthodox view of the descent of Christ into hell. — *O.D.C.C.*, p 244.

[33] Michael Servetus (1511-1553). "He denied the Trinity and the true Divinity of Christ, whose humanity he regarded as a compound of three elements, viz (1) the Logos, conceived as the model of all created things, though not really Divine, (2) the soul, and (3) the human body." When Servetus was denounced to the Catholic Inquisition he was imprisoned but escaped to Geneva where he probably counted on the support of an anti-

the divinity of Christ. Although his opinion was an abominable one, it was no more so than Calvin's action in having him burned and maintaining that this was lawful treatment for heretics. It only encouraged the Catholics to greater confidence in leading Calvinists to the stake. What better warrant could they have than the doctrines of the leader of their own sect? Indeed, they did not neglect twitting them with this, and their criticism was unanswerable. The observations of the judicious author of the *History of the Council of Trent* were most sagacious on this matter. In his fifth book,[34] while giving an account of several Protestants who had been burned for their religion, he professes astonishment that the new reformation used punishment in the case of religion. Further along he takes notice of the fact that Calvin justified the punishment of heretics, adding: "But since the charge of heresy may be more or less restricted, or, on the other hand, widely applied, this doctrine may likewise be taken in various ways, and may at one time hurt those, who at another time it might have benefitted."

This doctrine of persecution cannot be maintained by Protestants without strengthening the hands of the Catholic Inquisition. Indeed, in the end it leads directly to popery. If I cannot profess and preach the religion which my own conscience persuades me is true, there is no point in searching the scriptures! What good does it do to try to choose my own faith from convictions that are derived in that way? Whatever I observe there will be subject to the interpretation of the magistrate and of the church at the place where I live. My only choice is to resolve to move or be ready to die!

MOHAMMED PROHIBITED ALL THOUGHT OR DISCOURSE ON THE SUBJECT OF RELIGION

Indeed, this heretical and unchristian doctrine of both Catholics and Protestants ultimately leads to the accursed policy of Mohammed, who prohibited all thought or discourse on the subject of religion because it led to factions and divisions. Those who persecute and prohibit liberty of conscience demonstrate in that way that they are more nearly disciples of Mohammed than of Christ. They certainly do not follow the doctrine of the apostle, who told the Thessalonians: "Do not stifle inspi-

Calvinist party. Calvin had him burned as a heretic Oct. 27, 1553. — *O.D.C.C.*, p 1244.

[31] See fn p 382.

ration, and do not despise prophetic utterances, but bring them
all to the test and then keep what is good in them and avoid
the bad of whatever kind" (1 Thes 5:19-22 NEB). He also says,
Phil 3:15 NEB: "If there is any point on which you think differently, this also God will make plain to you." This does not
mean that it will be knocked into them by being beaten, or that
they should be banished to make it clear.

THE BASIS OF PERSECUTION IS UNWILLINGNESS TO SUFFER

¶VI. As has already been shown, the basis of persecution
is an unwillingness to suffer. No man who persecutes another
for the sake of conscience would suffer for his own if he could
avoid it. He is obliged by principle to establish by force what
he considers to be truth, and to force others to accept it if it is
within his power.

To provide informed opinion for the nations, it seems
proper to add a brief account of some true Christian sufferings.
By them, a very faithful testimony has been given by the witnesses whom God has raised in this age. It is beyond anything
that has been generally known or practiced for many generations, in fact, since the apostasy took place. This is not meant
to minimize in any way the sufferings of the Protestant martyrs.
I believe they have walked in faithfulness toward God according
to the dispensation of light which was given in that day. Many
of them were also absolute enemies of persecution. This could
be shown very well from their verbal testimony.

But true, faithful, and Christian suffering consists in men
professing what they believe is right. Having done this, they
will practice the worship of God in the way that is rightfully
theirs. The outward encouragement of men will make them do
no more, and they will do not one whit less out of fear of the
laws that are passed and the acts that are taken against them.
If a Christian vindicates his just liberty by being both so bold
and so innocent, in due time he will purchase peace, although
it will be through blood. This age has in some measure experienced this, and many are witnesses of it. But it will be even
more apparent as truth takes its rightful place on earth.

IT IS A SIN TO TRY TO ESTABLISH LIBERTY
BY DENYING IT TO OTHERS

It is a great sin against this excellent principle to profess
one's own faith less in a time of persecution than one ordinarily would. It is even more of a sin to try to stretch one's own

liberty to the utmost once civil authority is on that side, or to seek to establish such liberty by denying it to others.

The witnesses of God, who are called "Quakers" in scorn, have given manifest proof of this principle by their distinguished patience and suffering. As soon as God revealed his truth among them they began to travel throughout the land, preaching and propagating the truth in the marketplaces, the highways, the streets, and public temples. They did it without the slightest regard for the opposition they would meet, even though they were beaten, whipped, or bruised daily, and were haled into court and thrown into prison for it.

Wherever and whenever a church or assembly gathered, they kept their meetings openly. They did not shut the door or meet stealthily. They wanted everyone to know about it, and anyone who wished to enter was free to do so. All just occasion for fear that they were plotting against the government was removed in this way. The malice of their adversaries was wearied out by their courage and faithfulness in openly meeting together. What is even more important is that the Presence and glory of God was apparent in their meetings. It was terrible in its effects on the consciences of their persecutors and they often found that they were forced to leave their work undone.

When they came to break up a meeting, they were obliged to remove every individual bodily. Those who had been gathered were not free to give up their right of assembly and dissolve at a mere command. When they were hauled out, unless they were kept out by violence, they soon returned peaceably to their places.

WHEN MEETING HOUSES HAVE BEEN TORN DOWN, QUAKERS HAVE MET ON THE RUBBLE

Sometimes when the magistrates have pulled down their meeting houses they have openly met the next day on the rubble. By doing so and maintaining their innocence they have kept what is properly their own. They have also sustained the right and the basis on which anyone may meet and worship God. When armed men have come to dissolve them, they found it impossible unless they killed every one of them. For they stood so close together that no force could make any of them stir until they were pulled apart violently. When the malice of their opponents was aroused to such an extent that they took shovels and heaped rubbish on them, they stood unmoved. If the Lord wished to permit it, they were willing to be buried alive as they witnessed there for him.

This patient but courageous way of suffering made the work of their persecutors very hard and wearisome. Sufferers who offered no resistance, brought no weapons to defend themselves, and sought no revenge, secretly smote the hearts of their persecutors and made their chariot wheels turn heavily.[35] Much suffering of many kinds was patiently endured. There were, in fact, so many kinds that it would require a whole volume merely to rehearse them. In due time we may publish this to the nations (for we have them on record).[36] A kind of negative liberty has now been obtained in this way. For the most part, we meet at present without being disturbed by the magistrates.

Most Protestants, on the other hand, meet in secret and hide their testimony when they do not have the permission or toleration of the magistrates. If there is any probability that they can escape by force when they are discovered (or by cutting off those who seek them out) they will use it. By doing so, they lose the glory of their sufferings. Instead of appearing as innocent followers of Christ, or leaving a testimony of their harmlessness in the hearts of their pursuers, their resistance kindles greater fury against them. They cannot claim any precept from Christ for resisting those who persecute them, or give any example of the approval of him or his apostles.

To justify fleeing and meeting secretly instead of openly for the truth, they usually cite Mat 10:23 RSV: "When they persecute you in one town, flee to the next." But the following sentence indicates that this was because of the urgency in that particular situation, and that it was not intended to become a general precedent. It says: "For truly, I say to you, you will not have gone through all the towns of Israel, before the Son of Man comes."

John 20:19 NEB, when the disciples met "behind locked doors, for fear of the Jews," is also cited; and finally Acts 9:25, where Paul was let down over the wall of Damascus in a basket. But it must be understood that these are to be used as prece-

---

[35] Probably reminiscent of Exod 14:25, where the Lord helped fight the Egyptians and "so clogged their chariot wheels that they could hardly drive" (Cath-CCD).

[36] They were later published in digest as Besse's *Sufferings* (see fn p 230).

dent only when the Spirit gives the liberty, or else no man who could flee would ever suffer persecution. Or else, why was it that the apostles John and Peter did not flee when they were first persecuted at Jerusalem? Instead, they went the next day, after they had been discharged by the council, and preached boldly to the people.

Indeed, there are many who are far too capable of stretching such statements as these in the interest of their own self-preservation. They have considerable ground for fearing that when they interpret them in that way they are shunning an opportunity to witness for Christ.

The only evidence for a closed meeting of the disciples is an account of the fact that they did it. But that is hardly enough evidence to make it a precedent for us. The fact that men are always ready to imitate the disciples in that (which for all we know may have been an act of weakness), but not in other things of a contrary nature, demonstrates that they are more interested in self-preservation than in following the example of the disciples.

Paul was undoubtedly conveyed out of Damascus under a special dispensation of God. Since he had designed Paul as a principal minister of the gospel, he saw fit in his own wisdom to disappoint the wicked counsel of the Jews. But the Protestants do not have a similar pretext for fleeing. It is not a matter of immediate revelation but is based on self-preservation. This was no consideration for Paul, as is apparent from the time when, in spite of the advice of his friends and the prophecies of suffering, he could not be dissuaded from going to Jerusalem.

WHAT LIBERTY WE POSSESS WE OWN BY HIS MERCY

In conclusion, it can be said — glory be to God and to our Lord Jesus Christ — that in the 25 years that we have been known as a distinct and separate people, we have faithfully suffered for his name without shrinking or fleeing from the cross. What liberty we now possess we own by his mercy and cannot claim that we have procured it ourselves. It is the work which he has wrought in the hearts of our oppressors. It was not any outward testimony which procured it for us, but the testimony of our harmlessness in the hearts of those in power. There are few Christians who can say — as we do — that we have been patient in our suffering as Jesus was, and we have not betrayed our cause by persecuting others, even though our enemies have claimed that we would if we had the power. But this is unreasonably malicious and a claim to being able to predict things to come — even though they say they do not possess unmediated revelation. When those who have no ground for such judgment, on the basis of previous practice, make such claims, they are only judging others by themselves.

Such conjecture will not militate against us, as long as we are innocent.

If we should ever prove guilty of trying to force other men to do things our way by corporal punishment, then we should be considered the greatest of hypocrites and no one should refrain from persecuting us.

Amen, says my soul.

Integrity

Proposition 15 — Vain and Empty Customs and Pursuits[a]

The chief purpose of all religion is to redeem men from the spirit and vain pursuits of this world, and to lead them into inward communion with God. All vain and empty customs and habits, whether of word or deed, should be rejected by those who have come to fear the Lord.

Taking one's hat off to another person, bowing or cringing, and the other similar foolish and superstitious formalities which accompany them, should be forsaken. All of these were invented to feed man's pride through the vain pomp and glory of this world.

Theatrical productions which are not beneficial, frivolous recreation, sports and games which waste precious time and divert the mind from the witness of God in the heart, should be given up. Christians should have a living sense of reverence for God, and should be leavened with the evangelical Spirit which leads into sobriety, gravity, and godly fear. When we abide in these, the blessing of the Lord is felt to attend us in the necessary occupations by which we gain sustenance for the outward man. (Eph 5:11; 1 Pet 1:14; John 5:44; Jer 10:3; Acts 10:26; Mat 15:13; Col 2:8.)

¶ I. Previously we have discussed the principles of religion which relate to doctrine and worship. It is in order, now, to speak of some of the products of these principles which have become the practice of the witnesses that God has raised up in this day to testify for his truth. By way of commendation, even those who oppose them admit that they are free of many of the abominations which are common among those of other professions. Serious-minded and judicious men will approve of the fact that they are free from swearing, drunkenness, whoring, riotousness, and similar offenses. The very act of becoming one of our people often works great change. Many vicious and profane persons have been known to become sober and virtuous. Many light, vain, and unruly persons become grave and serious.

It is necessary for those who would detract from our principles to distort our deeds and call our gravity sullenness, our

---

[a] Prop. 15 was originally entitled "Salutations and Recreations."

seriousness sadness, and our silence stupidity. They distort the fact that those who were profane and dissolute among them have become frugal and diligent with us. They say that we are covetous, hypocritical, or spiritually proud. They call our boldness and Christian suffering mere obstinacy and pertinacity, although they would consider these as Christian courage and nobleness if they had half as much themselves. They misinterpret anything which relates to us, and they consider those acts vices which they would extol as virtues if they were theirs. Nevertheless, the power of truth has extorted the confession from them that we are, in general, a pure and clean-living people in our outward deportment. But they say we act this way in order to commend our heresy.

THE CHARACTER OF A QUAKER

However, I say that Christ and his apostles made use of such a policy, and all Christians should. Indeed, truth has prevailed to such an extent concerning the purity of one of its followers, that if one is called a Quaker he is not expected to do the things which others commonly do. If he laughs [derisively],[1] or is unruly, exaggerates in his speech, or is not punctilious in keeping his word, or becomes impatient or angry, they will say that he is acting contrary to his profession. If they can find a

---

[1] This obvious discouragement of humor is puzzling because Friends traditionally differed from their Puritan contemporaries in being more tolerant and enjoying life. Somewhere along the way they acquired a reputation for a special sense of humor which they have cherished and which is very well described in Dorothy Canfield Fisher's introduction to the volume of *Friendly Anecdotes* collected and arranged by Irvin C. and Ruth Verlenden Poley; New York: Harper & Bros., 1946 and 1950.

She states: "The Quakers are fervent in their faith. But in many ways they are different from other fervently religious men and women. Perhaps an analytic mind might say that these differences stem from one quality: a consciously cultivated sense of the true proportion of things. . . .

"One of the certainly not-planned-for results of this constant Quaker effort to see things in their real proportion is that there is often among these sincerely earnest and deeply spiritual people, the liveliest kind of what Meredith calls 'the Comic Spirit.' No other faith has — has it? — a tradition of sheer fun, derived from its own practices. Are there comic Presbyterian stories based on the Presbyterian way of life? There were, in the Middle Ages, of course, many satires, usually harshly savage attacks on those who failed to live up to the creed of their Church. These satiric comments on medieval religious life are sometimes spoken of as 'humorous.' It is to be supposed that people laughed over them. We do, ourselves, sometimes. But the taste they leave in our mouths is bitter. They have none of the quality of the Quaker jokes which give that rare blessing, a hearty laugh which leaves behind no sting, no shame, no resentment, no blame." — op cit, pp 7-8.

single Quaker who does any of the evil things which they commonly do themselves (and who would not expect to find some
chaff among so many thousands when there was one devil
among twelve apostles?), how insulting they become. They
make more noise about the escapades of one Quaker, than they
do about one hundred of their own people.

THINGS THAT ARE INCONSISTENT WITH
THE CHRISTIAN RELIGION

¶II. However, there are certain things which we have
found unlawful for us even though they do not consider them
inconsistent with the Christian religion. This has caused us no
little suffering and buffeting about, but nevertheless the Lord
has commanded us to lay these practices aside in spite of the
hatred and malice of the world. Because these things were very
obvious by their very nature, our trials and exertions have been
the greater. The mere sight of them distinguishes us from
others and makes us known so that we cannot hide from anyone
without being unfaithful to our testimony. I have attempted
to compress these into the statement of our proposition, however it is better to expand them into six sub-propositions:

1. It is not lawful to give men such flattering titles as
Your Holiness, Your Majesty, Your Eminence, Your Excellency,
Your Grace, Your Lordship, Your Honor, and others of a like
nature, or to use those flattering words commonly called compliments.

2. It is not lawful for Christians to kneel before or prostrate themselves to any man, or to bow the body or uncover
the head.

3. It is not lawful for a Christian to have superfluous details in apparel which serve only as ornaments or are a matter
of vanity.

4. It is not lawful for Christians to use games, sports, plays,
comedies, or other recreations which are inconsistent with
Christian silence, gravity, or sobriety. Laughter, sports, games,
mockery, or jests, useless conversation, and similar matters are
neither Christian liberty nor harmless mirth.

5. Under the gospel it is not legal for Christians to swear
in any fashion, either profanely as in common speech, which
was also forbidden by Mosaic law, or when appearing in judgment before a court.

6. It is not lawful for Christians to resist evil, make war,
or fight under any circumstances.

SOME GENERAL PREMISES

Before beginning a formal inquiry into these matters, some general premises will be made in order to prevent misunderstanding. Then some principles will be stated which apply equally to all of the propositions.

First, we have no intention of destroying the mutual relationship which exists between prince and people, masters and servants, or between parents and children. On the contrary, we will show how these natural relationships become better established by our beliefs, rather than harmed.

Next, let no one conclude that men must have all things in common because of these beliefs, or that any "levelling" will necessarily follow. Our principles allow every man to enjoy peaceably whatever his own industry or that of his parents have purchased for him. His only instruction is that he should use it properly for his own good, for that of his brethren, and to the glory of God. He is in no way constrained, and his acts are to be voluntary. Furthermore, we do not maintain by this that any one man may not use God's creation any more or less than any other. For we know that it has pleased God to dispense it variously, giving more to some and less to others, and that they may use it accordingly. The several conditions under which men are variously stated, together with the appropriateness of their education for these, are sufficient demonstration. The servant is not educated in the same way as his master, nor the tenant in the same way as the landlord, the rich as the poor, nor the prince as the peasant.

MODERATION IN THE USE OF POSSESSIONS

Now although by our principles the use of anything which is merely superfluous is unlawful, this does not deny the enjoyment of luxury for those who are accustomed to it. Those who have abundant possessions, and are accustomed to such things by education, may make better use of them without extravagance or waste than those who are unaccustomed to them or who do not have the capacity to utilize them.

Beyond doubt, whatever creation provides is for the use of man, and use in moderation is lawful. However, *per accidens,* some things may be lawful for some and not for others. For example, whoever is accustomed to eating meat or drinking wine, or clothing himself with the finest woolens, may continue to do so. If he can afford these by his estate in life and is accustomed to them by education, he may use them provided he does not do so immoderately or in excess. If he should attempt to eat or clothe himself as peasants do, he might prejudice the health of his body without advancing his soul. It would be unlawful, however, for a man who was accustomed to coarser food and raiment to exceed these if it was beyond his means and prejudiced his family and children. This would be so, even though he were to eat and be clothed in the same way as someone for whom it was lawful. The other person may have practiced as much denial, and been as mortified in coming down to that, as he was in exceeding his abilities and customary acts in aspiring to it.

MORTIFICATION AND ABSTRACTION
FROM THE PURSUITS OF THIS WORLD

It is safest, then, for those who have an abundance to be on their guard and see that they use it moderately and without excess. They should also be willing as far as possible to help those who are in need because Providence has given them a smaller allotment. Let the brother of high degree rejoice in being abased. Let those whom God calls in a lower degree be content with their condition. They should not envy their brethren who have a greater abundance of worldly goods, knowing that they have received an abundance of the things which belong to the inward man. That is the important point! They should beware of the temptation to use their calling as an agency for becoming richer. They have an advantage over the rich and noble who are called, in that truth in no way abases them in the esteem of the world. On the contrary, they are exalted by truth. In the inward and spiritual fellowship of the people of God, they become the brethren and companions of the greatest and richest. In this respect, let him of low degree rejoice that he is exalted.

Having established these premises I seriously propose that all who wish to be Christians truly, and not merely in name, should consider them. Would it not contribute greatly to the commendation of Christianity and to the life and virtue of Christ if they were observed? Wouldn't those who lay aside superfluous titles of honor, excesses and extravagances in food and clothing, gaming, gay pastimes, and diversions walk more in the way of Christ and his apostles? Wouldn't they be closer to their example than those who do use such things? Would putting them aside prevent anyone from being a good Christian? Or would Christians be better without them than with them?

Since the sober and serious among all sorts of Christians will say yes, surely those who lay these things aside as unsuitable for a Christian should be commended rather than blamed. For in so doing, they in effect advance what others acknowledge as desirable but will never make effective as long as they allow them to be used lawfully.

God has made it manifest in this age that there are many in whom he has effectively produced a mortification and abstraction from the love and pursuits of this world. By discovering the evil in such things and leading his witnesses away from them and to testify against them, he has inwardly redeemed them from the world. Even though they have daily commerce with the world, are married, and lawfully employed, this redemption has been as complete as that which used to be considered possible only for those who were cloistered or in monasteries.

FLATTERING TITLES UNLAWFUL FOR CHRISTIANS

¶III. So much for the general premises. As for sub-proposition 1, we positively affirm that it is not lawful for Christians either to give or to receive such titles of honor as Your Holiness, Your Majesty, Your Excellency, Your Eminence, and the like.

In the first place, these titles are not part of the obedience that is due administrators or superiors. The use of them does not add or detract from the subjection owed to these leaders. This consists of obeying their just and lawful commands and has nothing to do with titles or designations. Such titles are not used either under the law or the gospel. Only a simple compellation like "O King!" was used in addressing kings, princes, or nobles. There was no further designation except perhaps the name of the person, as in "O King Agrippa."

These titles also make it necessary for Christians to lie frequently. Since the titles are hereditary or obtained by election they often fail to correspond with the character of those who bear them. There is no excellence in many to whom Your Excellency is said. He who is called Your Grace is often an enemy to grace. He who is called Your Honor is often base and ignoble. What man-made law or what charter requires me to lie and obliges me to call evil good and good evil? What law of man can protect me from the just judgment of God when he makes me account for every word? Lying is even worse, and every

Christian will most certainly be ashamed of any law which requires this and is obviously contrary to the law of God.

If anyone should suggest that we ought to attribute these virtues to him because the king has bestowed his title, or because he is descended form those who earned them, I will answer that charity does not destroy knowledge. Charity neither obliges me to speak nor to believe a lie. It is obvious that many people who bear such titles do not possess the virtues which their titles claim. On the other hand, one is not allowed to address those who actually merit such titles in that way unless they have been granted to them by the princes of this world.

Jesus commanded his disciples not to allow themselves to be called Master. He said that those who receive such honors from one another cannot be true believers. They should seek only the honors which come from God. This is so obvious to those who wish to be truly Christians that no explanation is required.

SUCH TITLES ARE BLASPHEMOUS FOR PROTESTANTS

Furthermore, it is a most blasphemous usurpation for Protestants to use such titles of honor as Grace, Lordship, and Worship in the way in which Holiness, Eminence, and Excellence are used among Catholics for the pope, cardinals, and other members of the hierarchy. How can they claim such peculiarities for themselves when every Christian should have holiness and grace? Every Christian could be called Your Holiness or Your Grace, but would it be reasonable to claim more titles than those which were given or received by the apostles and early Christians? After all, they claim that they are the successors of the apostles (and will have it no other way) and would be entitled to any honor due them by this succession. But if the apostles neither sought nor allowed such titles, how do they come by them? If there is anything in scripture which says otherwise, let them prove it, for we can find nothing.

The early Christians spoke to the apostles without using any special titles. There is no record that they said: "If it please Your Grace, Your Holiness, Your Lordship, or Your Worship." They are not called My Lord Peter or My Lord Paul or even Master Peter or Master Paul. It is not Doctor Peter or Doctor Paul, but simply Peter or Paul. This was not only true in scripture, but for several hundred years afterward. Thus this is obviously another fruit of the apostasy. If those titles had their origin in the worth of the persons so called, it would be impossible to deny that the apostles were more justly entitled to them than any of those who are now addressed in that way.

But the evidence is plain. Because the apostles were truly holy, excellent, and gracious it was unnecessary to label them as such. Only hypocrites want titles to satisfy their ambitious and ostentatious minds!

MAJESTY ASCRIBED ONLY TO GOD

As for the title Your Majesty, which is usually ascribed to princes, it is not given to any princes or kings in the holy scripture. It is an especial ascription of God alone (1 Chron 29:11; Job 37:22; Psalms 21:5, 29:4, 45:3, and 96:6; Isa 2:10, 24:14, and 26:10; Heb 1:3; 2 Pet 1:16; and many others). Jude 25 Cath-CCD says: "to the only God our Savior, through Jesus Christ our Lord, belong glory and majesty." Jude does not ascribe these qualities to men. When the proud king, Nebuchadnezzar, assumed this title for himself, Dan 4:30 Cath-CCD, he received a sufficient reproof from the sudden judgment which fell upon him [he was "cast out from among men, he ate grass like an ox, and his body was bathed with the dew of heaven, until his hair grew like the feathers of an eagle, and his nails like the claws of a bird"]. Therefore, it can be said that it is not found among the compellations used for princes in either the Old or New Testaments. Paul was very civil to Agrippa, but he gave him no such title, and it was not used among Christians in the primitive times.

The *Ecclesiastical History of the Reformation of France*[2] says of the speech which Lord Rochefort gave at the assembly of the estates of France under Charles IX in 1560 that his harangue was remarkable for the fact that the word Majesty, which had been invented by flatterers in recent years, was not used. Yet Calvin used this flattering title to Francis I, King of France, and also called him Most Christian King in the introductory epistle to his *Institutes,* even though it is apparent that in Calvin's own esteem he was far from this, since he persecuted the reformers daily. The use of these vain titles introduced and imposed by anti-Christ was most certainly a stain on the Reformation and rendered it defective in many ways. The final rea-

2 Lib 4, p 445.
Probably Theodore Beza (1519-1605), *Histoire ecclesiastique des Eglises reformees au royaume de France,* 1580. — *O.D.C.C.,* pp 164-165.

son for Christians to reject all of these titles and styles of honor is that they are to seek the honor that comes from above, and not the honor that is from below. For we all know how worldly are the efforts and industry to which men go to acquire these honors. We also know what part of them motivates them to seek these. It is a proud, haughty, insolent, and aspiring mind which loves titles. It is certainly not the meek and innocent Spirit of Christ which covets such honors!

DOES THE SPIRIT LOVE WORLDLY HONOR?

Can we ask instead if "our citizenship is in heaven" (Phil 3:20 Cath-CCD)? Are our minds free of preoccupation with earthly things, so that we may come to have fellowship with the sons of God? Does the Spirit love worldly honor, plead for it to be upheld, or fret and rage and fume if it is denied? Isn't that more appropriate for Lucifer, the prince of this world? He has long affected such honors and sought after them. He does not love to abide in lowly submission. All of his children are of the same proud ambitious mind and seek and covet the titles of honor which do not truly belong to them.

Let us examine who they are who are truly honorable.[3] Is it not the righteous man? Is it not the holy man? Is it not the humble of heart and the meek in spirit? Poor men, laborers, and simple fishermen may be among them, but are such titles of honor bestowed on them? Who is it who generally looks for and receives such honors? Isn't it apt to be the rich? Those who have an abundance of earthly goods and who are apt to be gluttonous with pride and ambition? Isn't it apt to be those who oppress the poor, or who swell with lust, vanity, and wickedness who are the very abomination and plague of the nations? Are they not proud Hamans (Esther ch 3 ff)? Is this the honor that comes from God or from below? Does God honor those who daily dishonor and disobey him?

If it is worldly honor, how can Christians give or receive such honors without being reproved by Christ? For he says that

---

[3] Jerome, in his *Epistle to Celant,* tells her that she should not expect to be preferred above anyone because of her nobility, because the Christian religion is not a respecter of persons. Men are to be esteemed for the noble dispositions of their minds. He who does not obey sin is free. He who is strong in virtue is noble.

See also 1 Sam 2:30 and the Epistle of James.

those who do, cannot believe. What is more, not one in a thous-
and persons receives these honors because of any Christian virtues. They are usually conferred for things which Christians
should not commend, such as procuring favor with princes by
flattery or even worse means. In fact, the most frequent and
most highly regarded reason is a battle or some great military
exploit, and this certainly adds nothing to a Christian's worth.
It would be much more desirable if there could be no battles
among Christians at all. For as far as they do exist, they demonstrate that the participants are not true Christians. James tells
us that fighting proceeds from lusts. It would be far more
appropriate for Christians to use the sword of God's Spirit to
war against their lusts, than to use the prevalence of lust to
destroy one another.

Whatever honor men formerly attained in this way under
the law, we find that under the gospel Christians are commended
for suffering, not for fighting. Only one of Christ's disciples
ever offered outward violence by the sword. That was when
Peter cut off Malchus' ear in the Garden of Gethsemane, and
he did not receive a title of honor, but merely a reproof.

Finally, if we examine either the nature of an honor, its
cause, the way in which it is conveyed, or the terms on which
it is delivered, those who earnestly desire to be good Christians
will find it impossible to use such things.

THOSE FLATTERING WORDS CALLED COMPLIMENTS

¶IV. In addition to these titles of honor, what great abuses
have crept into the use of compliments among those who are
called Christians. Those who are not related as slaves to a
master write at every turn "Your humble servant" or "Your
most obedient servant." Christians become accustomed to lying
by such wicked customs, and in fact the lie has been taken
for granted as a customary civility. What a horrible apostasy!
Obviously the use of such compliments carries no obligation for
service and no one is foolish enough to think that it does. If
he were to ask for any he would find only a feeling of abuse,
for the words were merely given because they were required by
custom, and meant no more.

It is strange that those who pretend to use scripture as
their rule are not ashamed of such things. Even Elihu, who
did not have any scriptures to go by, could say by the light
within him (which these men consider insufficient), Job 32:21-22
Cath-CCD: "I would not be partial to anyone, nor give flatter-

ing titles to any. For I know nought of flattery; if I did, my Maker would soon take me away."

There is also the case of the devout person who in the early days of Christianity signed himself as "your humble servant" when he wrote to a bishop. Even though he was probably more sincere than most of those who compliment us, he was reproved sharply for it. It was Sulpitius Severus[4] who received the censure of Paulinus, bishop of Nola,[5] who said:[6] "Beware that you do not subscribe yourself his Servant, when he is your Brother: for flattery is sinful, and it is not a testimony of humility to give those honors to men, which are due only to the One Lord, Master, and God."

LUKE'S USE OF TITLES

To defend themselves for using titles, they say that Luke addressed Theophilus as "most excellent" (Luke 1:3) and that Paul called Festus "excellent" (Acts 26:25). Since Luke wrote by the infallible dictates of the Spirit of God, I do not doubt that Theophilus deserved the title, and that he really was endowed with that virtue. In such cases, we will not condemn those who do it for the same reasons. But there is no evidence that Theophilus had inherited that title, or that it had been granted by any earthly princes, or that Luke would have called him so if he had not been truly excellent.

Similarly, Festus would not have been called excellent unless he was truly noble. And this he most certainly was, for he

---

[4] Historian and hagiographer (c. 363 - c. 420/5). His *Chronicle* "is a summary of sacred history from the creation of the world to A. D. 400, intended as a textbook for educated Christian readers. It shows remarkable critical sense and is an important source."
His *Life of St. Martin.* on the other hand, "which is inspired by deep devotion to its hero, suffers from credulousness and inordinate prevalence of the miraculous element. It became at once extremely popular and a much-imitated model of medieval hagiography." — *O.D.C.C.*, p 1303.

[5] The son of a noble and wealthy family at Bordeaux (353/4-431), he was ordained a priest at Barcelona, while on a journey to Spain, at the insistence of the people. He corresponded with several famous Christians of his time such as St. Martin of Tours, St. Ambrose, St. Augustine, and Pope Anastasius I. He and Prudentius were also the foremost Christian Latin poets of the patristic period. — *O.D.C.C.*, p 1035-1036.

[6] The story is told in the book of *Manners and Customs* by Casaubonus, p 160.
Probably *A Treatise of Use and Custome* by Meric Casaubon (1599-1671) [*O.D.C.C.*], printed by I. L. [i.e., John Legate], London, 1638, 4to. — *Brit. Museum Cat.*

insisted on hearing Paul in his own right, instead of giving way to the fury of the Jews against him. If it had been because of any outward title, Paul would have used the same appellation for Felix, his predeccessor in office, but since he was a covetous man Paul gave him no such title.

HOW "THOU" BECAME "YOU"

¶V. This is also an appropriate place to say something about the use of the singular number when speaking to one person. There is no controversy on this point in Latin. When we speak to one, the pronoun is *tu*. Any other usage would be a breach of the rules of grammar. Does a boy exist who has learned the rudiments of Latin grammar who does not know that it is incongruous to say *vos amos* or *vos legis,* that is, you love, or you read, when speaking to only one person? But man's pride has corrupted many things, so that he refuses to use such simplicity of speech in the vulgar languages. Being puffed up with a vain opinion of himself, he wants others to address him in the plural as if the singular number were insufficient for him. Luther reproves and mocks this manner of speaking. He says in one of his plays:[7] *"Magister, vos es iratus."* Erasmus[8] refutes this corruption in his book of literary epistles. James Howel[9] speaks of this in his epistle to the nobility of England even before the *French and English Dictionary* took notice: "That both in France and other nations, the word *thou* was used in speaking to one. But in the course of time, when the Roman Commonwealth grew into an empire, the courtiers began to magnify the emperor (as being furnished with power to confer dignities and offices), using the word *you,* in fact, even deifying him with more remarkable titles. In his epistles to the emperors Theodosius and Valentinianus, Symachus addressed them as: '*Vestra Aeternitas,* Your Eternity; *Vestrum Numen,* Your Godhead; *Vestra Serenitas,* Your Serenity; *Vestra Clementia,* Your

---

[7] That is, one of his plays on words, since he was not the author of any dramatic works, religious or secular.

[8] Desiderius Erasmus (c. 1466-1536), who was the most famous scholar in Europe during his lifetime, and one of those who paved the way for the Reformation. He wrote over 2200 letters, available in full. — *O.D.C.C.,* pp 459-460.

[9] James Howell (c. 1594-1666), author of the *Epistolae Ho-elianae,* imbued his writings "with a certain simplicity and quaintness" which led Thackeray to say that they were one of his bedside books and that he scarcely ever tired of "the artless prattle" of the "priggish little clerk of King Charles' council." — *Encyc. Brit.,* 1958, vol 11, p 850.

Clemency.' Thus the word *you* in the plural number, and the other titles and compellations of honor, seem to have taken their rise from monarchical government. Later, by degrees, they were applied to private persons."

John Maresius[10] of the French Academy makes a similar observation in the preface to his *Clovis,* saying: "There should be no astonishment because the word *thou* is applied in this work to Princes and Princesses; for we do the same with God: and formerly the same practice was used for Alexanders, Caesars, Queens, and Empresses. The use of the word *you,* when one person is spoken to, was introduced in later ages by base flatterers of men, to whom it seemed good to use the plural number to one person. In that way he could imagine that by himself he was equal to many others in dignity and worth. Eventually this usage was extended to persons of lower quality."

HOW GOD BECAME "THOU"

M [onsieur?]. Godeau[11] also addresses the same point in his preface to his New Testament translation, saying: "I would rather be faithful to the express words of Paul, than follow exactly the polished style of our tongue. That is why I always address God in the singular number, rather than in the plural. It is for that reason that I say *thou* rather than *you.* I admit, indeed, that civility and custom require that kind of honor for him. But the contrary is equally true. The original tongue of the New Testament had nothing in common with such manners and civility. None of the numerous old versions that we have does so, and no one should believe that we do not give enough respect to God when we call him by the word *thou.* Instead, it seems to me (perhaps because of the effect of custom) that I do more to honor his Divine Majesty in addressing him in that fashion than I would if I were to follow the customs of men, who are so delicate in their forms of speech." ...

[10] Jean Desmarets (1595-1676). *Clovis, ou la France chretienne,* was an epic national poem by him. — *Nouvelle Biographie Generale,* Paris, Didot Freres, 1855, vol 13, p 847.
He was a member of the circle which met at the house of Valentine Conrart and later developed into the Academie Francaise, of which he became the first chancellor. He was also one of a band who carried out Cardinal Richelieu's literary ideas. — *Encyc. Brit.,* in this case the 11th ed, vol 8, p 97.

[11] Probably Antoine · Godeau (1605-1672). Although *Larousse du XX Siecle,* vol 3, p 812, does not credit him with a NT translation, it does show *Paraphrase des epitres de saint Paul* (1641).

QUAKERS USED THE SINGULAR TO ALL PERSONS EQUALLY

Since it is very clear that this form of speaking in the plural to one person results from pride, and is in itself a lie, we testify against this corruption by using the singular to all persons equally.[12] And although this seems a strange thing to be persecuted for, we have been. Christians who claim that they follow the rule of scripture ignore the fact that this *is* scriptural usage. It would seem incredible if I were to relate how much we have suffered for this very thing. You probably wouldn't believe how much these proud ones have fumed, fretted, and gnashed their teeth when we have spoken to them in the singular. They frequently strike us. But it only serves to confirm our belief that God has given us the responsibility of bearing testimony to the truth in all matters when we know that it vexes the serpentine nature of the children of darkness so severely.

KNEELING, BOWING, AND REMOVING THE HAT

¶VI. Second only to the use of titles among Christians is the other type of honor — the kneeling, bowing, and uncovering of the head[13] to one another. The only basis that those who do it have offered is a few instances from the Old Testament and the custom of the country. Abraham is cited as bowing to the children of Heth and Lot and to the three angels (Gen 23 and 18:2). However, the practice of these patriarchs is told merely as a matter of fact and not as a rule which should be followed by Christians now. We are not to follow them in every practice for which a reproof has not been added. If we followed all of their practices, the consequent inconvenience would be considerable. We do not find Abraham reproved for taking Hagar; and the national customs they observed furnish very little argument for adopting them as Christian practice. We ought to have a better rule to follow than the mere customs of unbelievers. Paul desired us not to be "conformed to this

---

[12] This evolved into a variety of usages based upon *thee* and *thou* and their possessives *thy* and *thine*. In the Philadelphia area *thee* and *thy* were used to the exclusion of *thou* and *thine*, and ungrammatically took the third person singular as their verb form, as "What is it thee wishes?" "Thee speaks only truth."

[13] "When the Lord sent me forth into the world, he forbade me to put off my hat to any, high or low ... neither might I bow or scrape with my leg to any one." -- George Fox, *Journal*, Bi-Centenary Edition, London, Headley, 1902, vol 1, p 38.

world" (Rom 12:2). Since there is so little to be said for observing these customs, why not consider our reasons for doing away with them and decide whether they are strong enough to uphold us?

First, we say that God, the creator of man, and to whom both soul and body should be dedicated, even more importantly deserves to be worshipped and adored not only in spirit but also by the prostration of the body. But since the only outward sign of our adoration of God is kneeling, bowing, or uncovering the head, this should not be done for men. What more can be done for God if we prostrate ourselves before men? The apostle tells us that we are to uncover our heads when we worship him, 1 Cor 11:4. But if we do the same thing before men, what has been reserved for the Creator? The only difference is one of intention, rather than of outward signification, and this leaves the door open for the Catholic veneration of images![14]

ALL MEN ARE CREATED ALIKE

In the second place, the fact that all men are created alike, even though they have various stations in life, requires mutual services from them. However, they do not owe worship to one another. But everyone is supposed to give that equally to God. It is to him and his name alone that every knee should bow and before whose throne the four-and-twenty elders prostrate themselves. Men who accept such honors from one another rob God of his glory. All of the duties which one person owes another may be performed without the bowing which is essential for God. But it is clear that bowing to other men resulted from a servile nature which some possessed. This led them to set up others as gods. And then an ambitious and proud spirit induced those others to usurp the supremacy of God over their brethren.

Thirdly, Peter refused to accept such flattering honor from Cornelius, saying that he was a man like other men. Are the popes any better than Peter? Yet they allow men daily to fall at their feet and to kiss them. This reproof which Peter gave Cornelius demonstrates clearly that such manners were not to

---

[14] Presumably he refers to the Tridentine ruling that due honor should be paid to images of the Lord, the Virgin Mary, and the saints "on the ground not of any virtue inherent in the image, but because in it the person represented is venerated." — O.D.C.C., p 680.

be allowed among Christians. Even the angel in Rev 19:10 and 22:9 refused this kind of bowing from John and gave as his reason (NEB): "I am but a fellow-servant with you and your brothers, the prophets and those who heed the words of this book. It is God you must worship."

If it should be claimed that John was offering religious worship, rather than civil, this is a gratuitous statement for which there is no proof. It hardly seems right to suppose that at that time John was so poorly instructed that he did not know that it was unlawful to worship angels. It seems more likely that he was willing to give the angel a greater sign of respect than usual because of the great and mysterious things which he had revealed to him, and that he was reproved for doing so.

NOT A MATTER OF GOOD BREEDING

Having considered all of these things we are willing to leave it to the judgment of all who really want to be true Christians whether we deserve censure for waiving such honors for men. Let those who are inclined to blame us consider whether they could not equally accuse Mordecai of incivility, since he was just as unique in this matter as we are. So far as we are accused of rudeness and pride, consider whether the testimony of our consciences in the sight of God is not a sufficient protection against such calumnies. The number of men of good education among us who nevertheless forbear doing these things proves that it is not a matter of good breeding.

Since the exercise of conscience in this matter has been purchased very dearly it would hardly make sense to do them solely as a matter of pride. Many of us have been badly beaten and buffeted about, and we have even been imprisoned for several months for no other reason except that we would not uncover our heads or bow our bodies to satisfy the proud and unreasonable whims of egotistical men. Certainly the innocent practice of standing still and erect without taking off our hats any more than our shoes does not show as much rudeness as the beatings and knocking about we have had because of our practice.

Assume that we really were mistaken in this matter. Suppose that we really were acting from human frailty rather than on the basis of any Christian precept. Shouldn't we be given as much tolerance as the apostle asked for those who thought it was wrong to eat meat? Don't those who persecute and revile us for this reason show that they are more like proud Haman than disciples or followers of the meek, self-denying Jesus?

SOME WOULD RATHER HAVE DIED THAN FOREGO THESE "CIVILITIES" BUT NOW THE REVERSE IS TRUE

I can say boldly and in the sight of God both from my own experience and that of many thousands more that however foolish we may seem, we have chosen to die rather than concede. Even though these things seem like small or foolish matters they have been abandoned for the sake of conscience. Oddly, it was so contrary to the natural spirits of many of us to forsake this bowing and ceremony that it seemed like death itself. We certainly would not have stopped these practices if we could have continued to do them and still enjoyed our peace with God.

Far be it from us to judge all those to whom God has not shown under similar hazards the evil in these things. Nevertheless, we do not doubt that God will also do it to those who want to prove faithful witnesses to Christ's divine light in their consciences.

VANITY IN APPAREL

¶VII. Vain display and superfluous uses in apparel are the third thing to be considered. But first, the social position and the country in which the person lives must be taken into consideration. Neither the needs of their bodies, nor the requirements of their estates in life would be satisfied if we maintained that all people should dress alike. If a man dresses quietly and without unnecessary trimmings, we will not criticize him if he dresses better than his servants. For it is probably a greater act of mortification for him to abstain from fine clothes than it would be for his servant. His worldly estate and education have accustomed him to things which the servant has never known.

The natural products of a country also have a great influence on clothing which does not necessarily imply any vain display. Where silk is abundant it may be worn just as properly as wool. If there were countries where gold and silver were as common as iron and brass, one might expect them to be used just as frequently. The iniquity lies in not being content with what one can afford or his country can provide naturally. It exists when vain desires for personal adornment breed such discontent that people overreach themselves. They demand rare things. Because of the price of these, they seem even more

precious, and in that way feed their desire even more. Serious-
minded persons will readily grant the evil in this.

PROPER USE OF THE CREATION

When men are not content to make proper use of the
creation, trouble begins.   They become dissatisfied with the
requirements of necessity and convenience and disregard the
refinement or coarseness of their wants.   They add such superfluous things as ribbons and lace.   They begin painting their
faces and braiding their hair, and everyone will acknowledge
that such acts are the fruits of our fallen, lustful, and corrupt
natures, rather than those of the new creation.

Even though serious-minded men of all kinds will say that
it would be better if such things did not exist, nevertheless they
do not consider them unlawful and they permit the members
of their churches to use them.   However, for several good reasons we consider these things unlawful and altogether unsuitable for Christians.

In the first place, the use of clothes originally came from
the fall of Adam, and otherwise man would apparently have
had no use for them.   But his miserable state made them necessary to cover his nakedness and keep him from becoming cold.
Both are good and sufficient reasons for wearing clothes, and
the principal reasons why we do.   But it can in no way be lawful for a man to delight himself with the fruit of his iniquity
and the consequences of his sin.   Any superfluous additions or
extensions beyond their real use are clear abuses of the creation
and therefore they are not lawful for Christians.   Those who
love gaudy and ostentatious clothing demonstrate little concern
for mortification or self-denial.   They apply themselves more
to beautifying their bodies than to improving their souls.
Those who have so little regard for their mortal condition are
more nominal than real Christians.

THE HAUGHTY DAUGHTERS OF SION

The numerous severe scriptural reproofs for such practices
not only commend but command the contrary.   In Isa 3:16-23
Cath-CCD, the Lord said: "Because the daughters of Sion are
haughty, and walk with necks outstretched, ogling and mincing
as they go, their anklets tinkling with every step, the Lord shall
cover the scalps of Sion's daughters with scabs, and the Lord
shall bare their heads.   On that day the Lord will do away with
the finery of the anklets, sunbursts, and crescents; the pendants,

bracelets, and veils; the headdresses, bangles, cinctures, perfume boxes, and amulets; the signet rings, and the nose rings; the court dresses, wraps, cloaks, and purses; the mirrors, linen tunics, turbans, and shawls."

Yet Christians, from whom even more exemplary conduct is required, allow these practices!

Christ did not want us to be anxious about our clothing, telling those who were (Mat 6:25ff) that even Solomon in all of his glory was not to be compared with the lilies of the field, which flourish today, but are thrown into the oven tomorrow. The apostle Paul was very positive in this respect, 1 Tim 2:9-10 Cath-CCD: "I wish women to be decently dressed, adorning themselves with modesty and dignity, not with braided hair or gold or pearls or expensive clothing, but with good works such as become women professing godliness."

1 Peter 3:3-4 Cath-CCD speaks to the same purpose: "Let not theirs be the outward adornment of braiding the hair, or of wearing gold, or of putting on robes; but let it be the inner life of the heart, in the imperishableness of a quiet and gentle spirit, which is of great price in the sight of God."

THE LYING VANITIES OF A PERISHING WORLD

Isn't it a pity that most of those who want to be considered Christians are so offended by those who love to follow Christ and his apostles in denying and departing from the lying vanities of a perishing world? In so doing, they give evidence of their affinity with those who hate to be reproved, and yet they will not correct themselves or allow those who wish to, to do so.

INCONSISTENT RECREATION

¶VIII. Let us consider the use of gambling, sports, amusing plays, and other similar things. These are a matter of indifference for all sorts of Christians, and are commonly used by them as diversion and recreation. But let us see if they are consistent with the seriousness, gravity, and godly fear which the gospel calls for. Let us review the ideas of those who call themselves Christians, whether they are Catholics or Protestants, and let us see if there are any differences in this regard from the practice of pagans. Are not the same folly, the same vanity, and the same abuse of precious and irrecoverable time found in abundance? The same gambling, pastimes, and frolicking? And from these, quarreling, fighting, swearing, ranting, and revelling?

How can these things be remedied as long as preachers and professing Christians — those who are the leaders of the people — not only allow these things, but do not find them inconsistent with the profession of Christianity? It is strange that these things are universally tolerated. They are allowed in spite of the fact that all sorts of obscenity, folly, and even atheism masquerade in them. The Inquisition does not suppress them in Rome or Spain in spite of the great scandal they bring to the Christian name.

If anyone reproves Christians for this and forsakes these superstitions in an attempt to serve God and worship him in the Spirit, he becomes their prey and is immediately exposed to cruel suffering. Does this have any relationship to Christianity? Do these activities bear any resemblance to the practices of the early Christians? None whatsoever! Let's look at a few scriptural testimonies which offer very positive precepts to Christians. Let's see if any who obey them can practice any of these things.

Paul commands us, 1 Cor 10:31 RSV: "Whether you eat or drink, or whatever you do, do all to the glory of God." Certainly gambling does not glorify God. Men pay more attention to satisfying their own fleshly lusts, desires, and appetites when they follow these practices than they do to glorifying God.

In 1 Cor 7:29-35 Cath-CCD, Paul reminds the Corinthians that "the time is short" and that they should make the most of it. The married person ought to give more consideration to the ways in which he can please God than he does to pleasing his wife. He concludes by saying that he offers his advice not from a negative desire to stop them from doing anything, "but to promote what is proper."

The apostle Peter desires us, in our relation to God, 1 Pet 1:17 NEB, to "stand in awe of him while you live out your time on earth." [KJ, Cath-CCD, RSV use "fear" rather than "awe."]

WALK AS IF YOU WERE IN HIS PRESENCE

Will anyone claim that dancing, entertaining plays, or the use of cards or dice is heeding this precept? There is nothing to be seen in these except frivolity, vanity, lewdness, and obscenity. They are contrived to draw men from the fear of God and are undoubtedly calculated for the service of the devil. No duty is more frequently commanded, or more properly that of a Christian, than fearing the Lord and so standing before him that we walk as if we were in his presence.

Such fear is forgotten by those who gamble or indulge in sporting, as all who speak from their consciences could declare from their own experiences. And when God secretly touches them by his light, they try to shut it out. When he reminds them of their vanity, they use their games as a device to get away from their troublesome guest. They make merry over the Just One whom they have slain and crucified in their hearts. If we would only heed Christ's advice, we would find that he says, Mat 12:35-36 NEB: "A good man produces good from the store of good within himself; and an evil man from evil within produces evil. I tell you this: there is not a thoughtless word that comes from men's lips but they will have to account for it on the day of judgment."

Where do these inventions come from? How many idle words do they bring about? Indeed, what are comedies except a studied complex of idle and lying words? If Christians believe in a day of judgment, how can they condone such things or even make them their trade and employment?

What about the dancing-masters and comedians whose hellish conversations give sufficient evidence of which master they serve and the purpose of these things? Those who are the masters of these occupations or take the most delight in them make religion their least important business, if they are not openly profligate or atheists.

If Christians would discountenance these things, a great scandal and stumbling block would be removed from the Christian name. These wretches would have to find themselves some kind of honest living if they were not fed and supported. It would also take away some of the things which provoke the Lord to withhold his blessing. It is the existence of such things which chains the minds of many, so that they remain in darkness, drowned in lust, sensuality, and worldly pleasures without any sense of the fear of God or any desire for the salvation of their souls.

Many of the early Fathers of the Church and other serious persons have indicated regret that such things exist. There are many citations which could be given to show their desire for a remedy for this situation.

¶IX. You will hear the objection that men's spirits could not stand always being intent upon serious and spiritual matters. They say that some diversion is needed to recreate the mind and refresh it a little so that it can apply itself to serious matters with greater vigor. Even if all this were granted, it would not militate against us in any way, or argue for those things which we would like to have laid completely aside. We do not claim that men should have the same intentness of mind at all times. We know how impossible that is so long as we are clothed with this tabernacle of clay. But this does not allow us to forget God and our soul's chief concern, and to lose a certain sense of fear. The fear of God is the best recreation in the world and much more refreshing than any of these things which we condemn. The necessary occupations which all have to follow, to provide for and sustain the physical man, constitute a letting down of the mind from more serious matters.

A MIND LEAVENED WITH THE LOVE OF GOD

When the mind is leavened with the love of God, and the sense of his presence, these daily tasks are done in another spirit. These acts of eating, drinking, sleeping, and working, which even the wicked perform, are done with his blessing; and the soul carries with it the divine influence and the spiritual habit. In doing them, we please the Lord, serve him, and fulfill our purpose in creation.

The wicked and profane who have not arrived at this holy place are accursed in whatever they do. Their ploughing as well as their prayer is sin.[15]

I am not inclined to argue much with those who contend that a certain amount of liberty is given those who require a little letdown in their mental activities because of their intense use in their particular occupation. That is provided that these activities are not completely superfluous, or of a type that would lead the mind into lust, vanity, or other excesses. They are not proper relaxation if they produce such effects in general, or if they are the vehicle for feeding those qualities in others and thereby propagate wickedness and spread their poison.

There are plenty of other forms of innocent recreation available which relax the mind sufficiently. Friends may visit

---

[15] Prov 21:4.

one another. There is the reading of history, or serious conversation about present or past transactions. One can follow
gardening, or use geometrical or mathematical experiments or
other things of that nature.

"GOD, IN WHOM WE LIVE AND MOVE AND HAVE OUR BEING"

In all of these things we are not to neglect God, in whom
we live, and move, and have our being (Acts 17:28). There
should always be some secret reserve for him and a sense of
awe and his presence. This should also assert itself frequently
with some short prayer of aspiration or a breathing toward
God in the midst of these things.

THE GREAT DESIGN, WHICH IS HIS CHIEF CONCERN

To clear this principle of any strangeness or troublesome
quality, a simple analogy with which all men are familiar will
be used. No one will deny that men should have more love for
God than for anything else, for we should love God above all
else. To get to the familiar situation, it is obvious that when
a man falls in love, if it has taken a deep enough possession of
his heart and mind, it is hard for him to forget it. Even in his
eating, drinking, or sleeping his mind has a tendency to turn
toward his loved one. However intent he may be on his business or recreation, only a short time will be permitted to pass
without some sudden or impulsive thought of his beloved.
Even though he must continue the daily acts which the care of
his body and such things call for, he will avoid like death itself
the things which might offend the beloved, or which are contrary to his design for obtaining what he so earnestly desires.
Even though these things might be useful in themselves, the
great design which is his chief concern will serve as a balance
so that he can survey and dispense with such petty necessities
rather than endanger the loss of the greater thing.

Men should be in love with God in this way and give
thought to the life to come. Mat 6:20-21 reminds us to "store
up treasure in heaven ..." (NEB). "For where your treasure
is, there will your heart be also." (RSV).

Col 3:2 Cath-CCD puts it: "Mind the things that are
above, not the things that are on earth."

The scriptures also declare that this has actually been experienced and attained by some. Psalm 62 (63):2, 7-9 Cath-
CCD says: "O God, you are my God whom I seek; for you my

flesh pines and my soul thirsts like the earth, parched, lifeless, and without water.... I will remember you upon my couch, and through the nightwatches I will meditate on you: that you are my help, and in the shadow of your wings I shout for joy. My soul clings fast to you; your right hand upholds me."

In 2 Cor 5:5 NEB: "We groan indeed, we who are enclosed within this earthly frame; we are oppressed because we do not want to have the old body stripped off. Rather our desire is to have the new body put on over it, so that our mortal part may be absorbed into life immortal. God himself has shaped us for this very end; and as a pledge of it he has given us the Spirit."

SOLEMN OATHS

¶X. The most holy name of God is blasphemed daily in a horrible manner by the use of swearing, which is so frequently practiced among nearly all Christians. This is true not only of the use of profanity, but also of solemn oaths. In fact, those who defend the use of swearing before magistrates do so with great zeal. They even display their piety by stirring up the authorities to persecute those who judge, from obedience to Christ, their Lord and master, that it is unlawful to swear. Many have suffered imprisonment and despoilment of their goods for this belief.

But consider the explicit words of our Savior, Mat 5:33-37 NEB: "Again, you have learned that they were told, 'Do not break your oath,' and 'Oaths sworn to the Lord must be kept.' But what I tell you is this: You are not to swear at all — not by heaven, for it is God's throne, nor by earth, for it is his footstool, nor by Jerusalem, for it is the city of the great King, nor by your own head, because you cannot turn one hair of it white or black. Plain 'Yes' or 'No' is all you need to say; anything beyond that comes from the devil."

There are also the words of the apostle, James 5:12 Cath-CCD: "But above all things, my brethren, do not swear, either by heaven or by the earth, or any other oath; but let your yes be yes, your no, no; that you may not fall under judgment."

Considering the clarity of these words, it is really remarkable that anyone who professes the name of Christ can pronounce an oath with a quiet conscience. It is even more remarkable that he can persecute other Christians who do not dare to swear because of the authority of their master, Christ. If anyone had tried to frame a blanket prohibition of anything, could he make it more embracing than these strictures against swearing under any circumstance? And James adds to this the possibility that you will be judged or condemned if you do persist.

CHRIST MADE NO EXCEPTIONS

How can men counterfeit any exceptions to this? Some say that because there are exceptions to other things prohibited in the fifth chapter of Matthew there is an exception to this. Christ says that anyone who puts his wife away for any cause other than fornication causes her to commit adultery. But no exception is given to this command not to swear, which is to apply anywhere or to anyone under the new covenant. If Christ had wanted to make an exception of judicial oaths, he would have added "except in judgment before the magistrate" or some such words, just as he made a clear exception when he was speaking about divorce.

FOR THE FIRST 300 YEARS ALL OATHS WERE PROHIBITED

Undoubtedly the most learned scholars of each sect also know that for the first 300 years after Christ all sorts of oaths were prohibited. That is how the early Fathers of the Church understood those words. Is it unreasonable, then, for us to wonder why Catholic professors and priests bind themselves by an oath to interpret the holy scriptures according to the universal exposition of the holy Fathers? They understood these controverted texts in a way that was quite different from the modern interpretation. This is good evidence of the vanity and foolishness of asserting the absolute "certainty" (so to speak) of Roman Catholic tradition. For if the faith of the ages may be demonstrated by the writings of those who are called Fathers of the Church, on this point of swearing Catholics have clearly departed from the faith of the church in the first three centuries.

Since not only Catholics, but also Lutherans, Calvinists, and some others, restrict the words of Christ and James, it seems necessary to make clear the shaky foundation on which these presumptions are built.

¶XI. The objection is usually raised that Christ forbade only creaturely oaths, or oaths that pertained to the creation, but not those made in God's name. It is evident that Christ is forbidding something which was allowed under the law.

. That is true, and the law allowed oaths made in the name of
God, so long as they were not made rashly or falsely, for that
would be taking his name in vain.

But Christ was forbidding all oaths of any kind, and like
many other things which were allowed for a time under the
old covenant, this was forbidden under the new. This was one
of the things which were only a shadow of the good things
which were to exist until Christ, who was the substance, should
arrive. Then all of these "shadows" — the sabbaths, circumcision, and the paschal lamb, for instance — would vanish.

THE SUBSTANCE, ETERNAL WORD, ESSENTIAL OATH, AND AMEN

The sacrifices which were used by men who were in constant controversy with one another and with God were all abrogated with the coming of the Son, who is the Substance, Eternal
Word, and Essential Oath and Amen, and in whom the promises of God are Yea and Amen. He came that men might be
redeemed from strife, and to bring an end to controversy.

OATHS AND TITHES

The objection is raised that oaths are neither ceremonies,
nor in any way part of ceremonial law. But this is irrelevant,
unless it can be shown that oaths are an eternal, immutable,
and moral precept. Oaths are not as old in origin as tithes
and the offering of the first fruits of the ground. Abel and
Cain offered these long before ceremonial law or the use of
oaths existed. Whatever may be alleged against these, there
is no question but that they were ceremonies and therefore it
is undoubtedly illegal to practice them now.

To this, they will say that swearing by the name of God
is a moral precept of continual duration, because it is associated with the essential and moral worship of him. They cite
the nearly identical passages in Deut 6:13 and 10:20 Cath-CCD:
"The Lord, your God, shall you fear; him shall you serve, and
by his name shall you swear."

But this does not prove that it is a moral and eternal
precept. It is not to be found among the precepts and ceremonies which Moses enumerates in several places. Although
Deut 10:12-13 RSV follows the statement of something which
God "swore to their fathers," it reads: "And now, Israel, what
does the Lord your God require of you, but to fear the Lord
your God, to walk in all his ways, to love him, to serve the

Lord your God with all your heart and with all your soul, and to keep the commandments and statutes of the Lord, which I command you this day for your good?"

In Deut 14:23 the use of tithes is coupled with learning to fear the Lord. In Lev 19:2-3, 12 the Israelites are commanded to keep the sabbath, to have regard for their parents, and not to swear falsely.

Some object that Christ had no authority to forbid the solemn oaths which God commanded. Christ said that these came from evil, but that cannot be true, for God never commanded anything that was evil, or originated in evil. But the answer is that some things are good because they are commanded, or evil because they are forbidden. Other things are commanded because they are good, or forbidden because they are evil. Circumcision and oaths were good when, and because, they were commanded, but for no other reason. When they were prohibited, and because they were prohibited under the gospel, they are evil.

SPEAK THE TRUTH IN ALL MATTERS

There was some good in all of the things that were constituted by the Jews, no matter how ceremonial they may have been. In addition to prefiguring greater good, these had some value of their own. Circumcision, the various purifications, and other practices, typified the holiness of God and the fact that the Israelites ought to be holy, just as their God was holy. In a similar way, in this time of shadows and ceremonies, oaths signified the faithfulness, certitude, and truth of God. Therefore, in all matters, we should speak the truth and bear witness to it.

But the witness of truth existed prior to all oaths and it will remain when all oaths have been abolished. This is the morality behind all oaths. As long as men remain truthful, oaths are unnecessary and have no place. Polybius[16] testified to this when he said: "The use of oaths in judgment was rare among the ancients; but with the growth of perfidiousness, the use of oaths also grew." Grotius[17] agreed, saying: "An oath is

[16] Polybius (c. 204-122 B. C.) was a Greek historian. Only five of the 40 books in his history have come down to us in complete form. Presumably Barclay is citing one of these.

[17] Hugo Grotius (1583-1645), Dutch jurist and Arminian theologian. "A very precocious boy, he went to Leyden University at the age of twelve, where he was deeply influenced by humanism." His principal religious

only to be used as a medicine, in case of necessity. A solemn oath merely remedies a defect. It was the superciliousness and inconstancy of men that begot diffidence, and swearing was contrived as a remedy." Basil the Great[18] said that "swearing is the effect of sin." And Ambrose[19] that "oaths are merely a concession to defects." Chrysostom[20] says that "An oath entered when evil grew, when men exercised their frauds, when all foundations were overturned. Oaths began when truth was lacking."

But when something is self-evident, there is no need for testimonies. Who forces someone to swear when he believes that person hates to lie? Then, again, as Chrysostom and others say, what good does it do to force someone to swear if you don't believe he will speak the truth?

SWEARING NOT AN ETERNAL PRECEPT

¶XII. Making an oath in God's name is certainly far from being an eternal moral precept. It did not exist at first, and there was no need for it at first. Instead of beginning with the will of God, it was the work of the devil and resulted from unfaithfulness, lying, and deceit. Men first invented it as a mutual remedy for this evil, in which they called upon the names of their idols.

Jerome, Chrysostom, and others testify that God treated the Israelites like children, and gave them the oath in his name, so that they would be able to abstain from the idolatrous oaths of the heathen. Jer 12:16 Cath-CCD says: "And if they care-

---

work was *De Veritate Religionis Christianae.* His great work, *De Jure Belli ac Pacis,* not only finally severed law from theology, but earned him the title of "Father of International Law." His *Opera Theologica* in 3 vols had been reprinted in London in 1660, only a decade and a half before Barclay wrote the *Apology.* — *O.D.C.C.,* p 593.

[18] St. Basil, the Great (c. 330-379), was one of the three Cappadocian Fathers (his brother, St. Gregory, Bishop of Nyssa, and St. Gregory, Bishop of Nazianzus, were the other two) who were principally responsible for the final defeat of Arianism at the Council of Constantinople of 381. The structure and ethos of Eastern monasticism have retained his impress. In addition to eloquence, learning, and statesmanship, he was possessed of great personal holiness. His monastic rule is still followed by members of the religious orders in the Eastern Church. — *O.D.C.C.,* pp 138-139.

[19] St. Ambrose, Bishop of Milan (c. 339-397). See fn p 378.

[20] St. John Chrysostom, Bishop of Constantinople (c. 347-407). A Doctor of the Church, he was educated for the law under the great pagan orator Libanus at Antioch and studied theology under Diodore of Tarsus, leader of the Antiochene School.

fully learn my people's custom of swearing by my name, 'as the Lord lives,' they who formerly taught my people to swear by Baal shall be built up in the midst of my people." This hardly sounds like an eternal moral precept. What is more, the frequent use of oaths for swearing and forswearing in those times was of quite a different nature than any perpetual duty of a Christian.

It is said that since God swore, swearing is good. Athanasius has the right answer for that:[21] "Since when swearing it is proper to swear by someone else, it follows from this that God, properly speaking, never actually swore, but only improperly. It is figuratively said that in speaking to men, he swore, since what he said can be regarded as an oath, because of the certainty and immutability of his will." Athanasius cites Psalm 110:4, where it is stated that the Lord swore, and did not repent. "And I swore," saith he, "by myself." He goes on to say that this is not an oath, for he did not swear by someone or something else, which is the inherent characteristic of an oath, but by himself. Therefore God does not swear in the same sense that men do, and neither can we be induced to swear by using his act as a precedent. But let us show by our speech and deeds that those who have our word do not need an oath from us, and let our words themselves be our testimony of truth. Then we will be plainly and properly imitating God.

CHRIST DID NOT SWEAR

Still others say that Christ swore, and we should imitate him. But Christ did not swear, and even if he had, it would in no way oblige us to do so, for he was still under the law and we are under the gospel. We are not circumcised. We do not offer the paschal lamb. Jerome[22] has this to say on that point: "All things do not apply to us who are servants, that applied to our Lord.... The Lord swore as Lord, and no man could forbid him to swear. But it is unlawful for us who are servants to swear, because we are forbidden by the law of our Lord. Yet, so we would not suffer scandal by his example, he has not sworn, since he commanded us not to swear."

The objection is made that Paul swore, and swore frequently, Rom 1:9, Phil 1:8 NEB: "God is my witness" and

21 In his *pass. et cruc. Dom.*
See biographical fn p 377.

22 Jerome's *lib. Epist.*, part 3, tract 1, Ep. 2.

"God knows"; 2 Cor 11:10 NEB: "God knows"; 2 Cor 1:23 KJ has: "I call God for a record upon my soul," but NEB has it: "I appeal to God to witness what 1 am going to say." Rom 9:1 KJ has: "I say the truth in Christ, I lie not," which NEB gives as: "I am speaking the truth as a Christian, and my own conscience, enlightened by the Holy Spirit, assures me it is no lie." Gal 1:20 NEB: "Before God, I am not lying."

It is also said that Paul requires oaths of others — 1 Tim 5:21 NEB: "Before God and Christ Jesus and the angels who are his chosen, I solemnly charge you." 1 Thes 5:27 NEB: "I adjure you by the Lord to have this letter read to the whole brotherhood." It is added, that if Christ had forbidden oaths, these would not have been used or called for by Paul.

KISSING THE BOOK AND RAISING THE HAND

But why is it that if they are going to charge Paul with swearing when he speaks in that way, the same people would consider these expressions to be mere figures of speech if they had used them? They do not consider it to be swearing when they say on occasions of great moment: "We speak the truth in the fear of God, and before him, who is our witness, and the searcher of our hearts." We have never refused to add such serious attestations when the matter was of great consequence. But our opponents are not satisfied. They insist that an oath is necessary, including the ceremony of putting one's hands upon the book, kissing it, raising the hand, and uttering the common imprecation: "So help me God" or "So truly let the Lord God Almighty help me."

We would like to remind our adversaries that Paul was not standing in front of a judge, and he was not obliged to make an oath. He never acted as a magistrate compelling someone else to swear. What is more, the question is not what Paul or Peter did, but what our master taught them or us to do. If Paul did swear (which we do not believe), was he sinning against Christ's command? After all, he was not swearing in front of a judge, but in an epistle to his brethren.

Another objection that is raised is based on Isa 65:16 Cath-CCD: "He who takes an oath in the land shall swear by the God of truth; for the hardships of the past shall be forgotten, and hidden from my eyes. Lo, I am about to create new heavens and a new earth." In such times as that, men should swear by the name of the Lord.

EVANGELICAL DUTIES EXPRESSED IN MOSAIC TERMS

The answer is that it was quite customary for the prophets to express the greatest duties of evangelical times in Mosaic terms, like those, among others, expressed in Jer 31:38-40[23] and Ezek 36:25-30.[24]

Isa 45:23 Cath-CCD states: "By myself I swear, uttering my just decree and my unalterable word: To me every knee shall bend; by me every tongue shall swear." Isn't it significant that the apostle Paul edits this quotation when he gives it in Rom 14:11 Cath-CCD: "For it is written, 'As I live, says the Lord, to me every knee shall bend, and every tongue shall give praise to God.' " The words "every tongue shall swear" were altered to "every tongue shall give praise to God." Under the gospel the ceremonial oaths were no longer used. In the righteousness of the new Jerusalem and the purity of the gospel, with its spiritual worship and the professing of the name of Christ, the old forms under the law were abolished. The ritual washing, the ceremonies, the temple services and sacrifices, oaths and similar practices were no longer to be used.

THE TRUTH AND THE AMEN OF GOD

Still another objection is based on Heb 6:16 Cath-CCD: "For men swear by one greater than themselves, and an oath given as a guarantee is the final settlement of all their disagreement." Since there are as many disputes as ever, they claim that oaths are still needed. However, the apostle was merely recording the practices of men who live in disbelief and controversy. That does not mean that this was what they should have

---

[23] Cath-CCD: "The days are coming, says the Lord, when the city [Jerusalem] shall be rebuilt as the Lord's from the Tower of Hananeel to the Corner Gate. The measuring line shall be stretched from there straight to the hill Garbe and then turn to Goa. The whole valley of corpses and ashes, all the slopes toward the Cedron Valley, as far as the corner of the Horse Gate at the east, shall be holy to the Lord. Never again shall the city be rooted up or thrown down."

[24] This is the chapter in which God promises the regeneration of the people. Cath-CCD: "I will sprinkle clean water upon you to cleanse you from all your impurities, and from all your idols I will cleanse you. I will give you a new heart and place a new spirit within you, taking from your bodies your stony hearts and giving you natural hearts. I will put my spirit within you and make you live by my statutes, careful to observe my decrees. You shall live in the land I gave your fathers; you shall be my people, and I will be your God. I will save you from all your impurities; I will order the grain to be abundant, and I will not send famine against you. I will increase the fruit on your trees and the crops in your fields; thus you shall no longer bear among the nations the reproach of famine."

done. Nor does it mean that those who had been redeemed from strife and unbelief, that is, the faithful who had come to Christ who was the Truth and the Amen of God, did it also. Furthermore, he was alluding to a custom that was familiar in order to arouse more confidence in what God had promised them. He was not attempting to get them to swear against the law of God, or to confirm them in that, any more than he was trying to teach Christians to race and destroy their bodies for a perishable prize in 1 Cor 9:25 NEB when he says: "Like them, run to win ... a wreath that never fades." Likewise, Christ was not trying to teach his disciples to fight in Luke 14:31. The Prince of Peace was merely using an illustration of the prudence which is used by those kings who are accustomed to fighting.

Our opponents do not need to remind us of the extent to which competition, treachery, and distrust have grown. Our daily experience teaches us that all kinds of deceitful and malicious practices have increased among men of the world and among false Christians. But it will do no good to insist upon oaths because men cannot trust one another. Nor does it follow that true Christians should swear. Christ has brought them to faithfulness and honesty, not only toward God, but toward one another as well. Therefore he has delivered them from competition and deceitfulness, and as a consequence from oaths. ...

IT IS UNLAWFUL FOR A CHRISTIAN TO SWEAR

It is unlawful for a Christian to swear. Christ has called him to his essential truth which existed before oaths, and he has forbidden him to swear. Indeed, he has commanded him to speak truth in all things for the honor of the Christ who called him, and not to be unfaithful in this matter merely to please others or to avoid harm to himself. For some centuries Christians were faithful, and answered unanimously when they were asked to swear: "I am a Christian; I do not swear."

MANY OF THE PAGANS KEPT THEIR PROMISES

What can be said about the pagans, since some of them had reached the same place? Diodorus Siculus[25] says that among

25 in *lib 16*.
Diodorus Siculus (d. after 21 B. C.) was a Sicilian historian who wrote an uncritical and unreliable world history in 40 books, ending with Caesar's Gallic Wars. "Fully preserved are Books 1-5 and 11-20, which cover Egyptian, Mesopotamian, Indian, Scythian, Arabian, and North African history and parts of Greek and Roman history." — *Col. Encyc.*, p 542.

the Persians "the giving of the right hand was a sign of speaking the truth." The Scythians, as Qu. Curtius[26] relates, said in their conferences with Alexander the Great: "Do not think that the Scythians confirm their friendship by swearing. They swear by keeping their promises."

Stobaeus[27] quotes Solon as saying: "A good man ought to be held in such esteem that an oath would not be required of him because it would be considered a lessening of his honor if he were forced to swear."

Among other things in the *Oration* of Pythagoras[28] is a maxim concerning the administration of the commonwealth: "Let no one call on God to witness by an oath, not even in judgment. But let every man discipline himself to speak in such a way that he is worthy of being trusted even without an oath." Basil the Great[29] commends Clinias, a pagan, by saying that he would rather pay three talents (about three thousand pounds) than swear. Socrates, as Stobaeus records,[30] stated that: "The duty of good men requires them to show the world that their manners and actions are more binding than oaths."

Isocrates[31] reached a similar conclusion. Plato was also[32]

---

[26] Quintus Curtius Rufus, the biographer of Alexander the Great. "Modern authorities regard him as a rhetorician who flourished during the reign of Claudius (41-54 A. D.). His work *(De rebus gestis Alexandri magni)* originally consisted of ten books, of which the first two are entirely lost, and the remaining eight are incomplete. The work is uncritical, and shows ignorance of geography, chronology, and military matters." — *Encyc. Brit.*, vol 6, p 885.

27 *Serm 3.*
Probably Joannes Stobaeus (5th cent), Greek anthologist whose large collection of excerpts from poets and prose writers on a variety of subjects is valuable because it preserves fragments from many lost works of early Greek authors. — *Col. Encyc.*, p 1896.
"In all Stobaeus quotes more than 500 writers, generally beginning with the poets, and then proceeding to the historians, orators, philosophers and physicians.... From his silence in regard to Christian authors, it is inferred that he was not a Christian." Nothing is known of his life. — *Encyc. Brit.*, vol 21, p 415.

[28] For the beliefs of the Pythagoreans see fn p 117.
[29] See biographical fn p 416.
30 *Serm 14.*
[31] Isocrates (436-338 B. C.), an Athenian orator, was the pupil of Socrates and of the Sophists, especially Gorgias. "He was perhaps the greatest teacher in Greek history, and every younger orator of his time studied under him." — *Col. Encyc.*, p 981.
32 In his *judgment de Leg. 12.*

against oaths. Quintilianus[53] recorded: "That it was a kind of infamy in ancient times if any was requested to swear, and that demanding an oath of a nobleman was like examining him by the hangman." The Emperor Marcus Aurelius Antoninus[34] says in his description of a good man: "Such is his integrity, that he doesn't need an oath."

SOME OF THE JEWS BORE TESTIMONY AGAINST OATHS

Some of the Jews also bore testimony on this point. Grotius quotes Maimonides[35] to the effect that: "It is best for a man to abstain from all oaths." The Essenes, as Philo Judaeus[36] says, "regarded their word' as firmer than an oath, and oaths were considered unnecessary among them." Philo himself, in speaking of the third commandment, says: "It is better not to swear at all, but to be accustomed always to speak the truth, so that naked words may have the strength of an oath." Elsewhere, he says: "It is more agreeable to natural reason to abstain from swearing altogether. In that way one becomes convinced that whatever a good man says is the equivalent of an oath."

Is there room for any further doubt that Christ wanted his disciples to attain the highest standard of perfection and that

[33] Marcus Fabius Quintilianus, or Quintilian (c. 35 - c. 95 A. D.), was born in Spain and taught rhetoric at Rome. Pliny the Younger and possibly Tacitus were among his pupils. His *Institutio oratoria* was a complete survey of rhetoric in 12 books, which continued to have great influence throughout antiquity and the Renaissance. — *Col. Encyc.,* p 1630.

[34] Marcus Aurelius (121-180), who is one of the most famous Roman emperors in spite of the earthquakes, plagues, and attacks of Parthians, Germans, and Britons, which marked his reign, was also a Stoic philosopher. His *Meditations* "expresses wiith great beauty and humanity" his philosophical side. Nonetheless he continued Trajan's policy of persecuting the Christians. — *Col. Encyc.,* p 1219.

[35] A biographical note on Grotius is given on p 415. Maimonides (1135-1204), also known as Moses ben Maimon, or acronymically as Rambam, is one of the greatest Hebrew scholars. His "*Moreh Nebukim* has dominated Jewish thought and exerted a profound influence upon Christian thinkers." — *Col. Encyc.,* p 1200.

[36] The Essenes were not, as is sometimes popularly supposed, discovered with the Dead Sea Scrolls. They existed from the 2nd cent B. C. to the 2nd cent A. D. "An outgrowth of extreme Pharisaism," they believed in communal possession, stressed ceremonial purity, including the wearing of only white garments, condemned slavery, and prohibited trading because it led to covetousness and cheating. "They abhorred untruthfulness, forbidding oaths." — *Col. Encyc.,* p 633.

Philo Judaeus (c. 20 B. C. - c. 50 A. D.), was an Alexandrian Jewish philosopher whose "doctrines had an extraordinary influence on both Jewish and Christian religious writings." — *ibid,* p 1537.

he abrogated the use of oaths which he regarded as signifying the beginning of frailty? He established the use of truth, in the place of oaths. Who can maintain any longer that the holy martyrs and the ancient fathers of the first 300 years were opposed only to those oaths which referred to creatures or pagan idols? After all, these were prohibited under Mosaic law. It does not make sense to maintain that they and many others were merely opposed to that particular usage and not to swearing by the true God.

MANY OF THE FATHERS OF THE CHURCH AND THE MARTYRS TESTIFIED AGAINST OATHS

There are many testimonies by the Fathers of the Church and the martyrs against oaths and swearing.[37] Who can read these and still have doubts about their beliefs in this matter? And once it is known that they were opposed to all oaths, how can anyone bring such a great indignity upon the name of Christ by re-subjecting his followers to such a thing? Isn't it about time, instead, that all good men worked together to remove this infamous abuse from Christians?

The objection is always raised that this will result in fraud and confusion. It is said that imposters will assume a counter-

---

[37] The following were all cited by Barclay: Polycarpus. Eusebius. Justin Martyr, *Apologia 2.* Tertullian, *Apol.,* cap 32; *ad Scap.,* cap 1; *of Idolatry,* cap 11. Clement Alexandrinus, *Strom.,* lib 7. Origen, *Tract. 25, on Mat.* Cyprianus, lib 3. Athanasius, *in pass. et cruc., Domini Christi.* Hilarius, *on Mat 5:34.* Basilius Magnus *on Psalm 14.* Gregorius Nyssenus, *Orat. 13, on Cant.* Gregorius Nazianzus in *dialog contra juramenta.* Epiphanius, *adversus heres.,* lib 1. Ambrose, *de Virginibus,* lib 3, and *on Mat 5.* Chrysostom, *homil. 15, on Gen.; homil. on Acts of the Apostles,* chap 3. Hieronimus, *Epistol. lib.,* part 3, Ep 2, *on Zach.,* lib 2, cap 8; *on Mat.,* lib 1, cap 5. Augustinus, *de serm. Dom.,* serm 28. Cyrillus on Jeremiah 4. Theodoretus on Deut 6. Isidorus Pelusiota, *Ep.,* lib 1, Ep 155. Chromatius on Mat 5. Johannes Damascenus, lib 3, cap 16. Cassiodorus on Psalm 94. Isidorus Hispalensis, cap 31. Antiochus, *in Pandect. script.,* hom 62. Beda *on Jac.* [*James*] 5. Haimo on Apoc. Ambrosius Ansbertus *on Apoc.* Theophylactus *on Mat 5.* Paschasius Radbertus *on Mat 5.* Otho Brunsfelsius *on Mat 5.* Druthmaras *on Mat 5.* Euthymius Eugubinus [Zigabenus?], *Bibliotheca vet. pat.* on Mat 5. Ecumenius *on James 5:12.* Anselmus *on Mat 5.* The Waldenses, Wickliffe, Erasmus *on Mat 5* and *on James 5.*

The reference to Eugubinus may be a clue to the source Barclay used for his patristic citations. M. de la Bigne's *Bibliotheca SS. Patrum,* issued in Paris, 1575, had only eight volumes, but a more comprehensive 14-vol new ed was printed at Cologne in 1618 and supplemented in 1672. It was further extended as *Maxima Bibliotaeca Veterum Patrum* and published at Lyons, 1677. Perhaps the 1618 or 1672 editions had the title cited by Barclay.

feit integrity, and that they will lie when given the benefit of
this dispensation without any fear of punishment. But there
are only two things which compel a man to speak truth. The
first is the fear of God, with its counterpart, the love of truth.
No oaths are necessary[38] to compel people to speak the truth
where these prevail. The other compelling force is fear of
punishment decreed by a judge.

PUNISH EQUALLY THOSE WITH OR WITHOUT OATH

Why not impose the same, or greater, punishment on those
who refuse to swear in any way for the sake of conscience, if
they fail to tell the truth?[39] Those who pretend to such great
truthfulness in words and such great simplicity of heart that
they cannot lie could be subjected to even greater punishment
than they now receive. Good order would not only be preserved, but it would be better protected than if oaths were continued. Wicked men would be more terrified and good men
would no longer be oppressed and deprived of both their liberty and their goods. The respect for tender consciences by civil
authorities and the state is a thing that is most acceptable to
God.

THE NETHERLANDS OFFERS A PRECEDENT

If anyone has any further doubts that such practices can
be followed in a commonwealth without creating confusion, he
should look at the good effect they have had in the United
Netherlands. Because there are more merchants there than
anywhere else there is frequent occasion to use what would be
sworn statements elsewhere. Although the number who do not
use oaths there is considerable, and the States have deferred to
them these hundred years, and continue to do so daily, there
have been no consequences which were prejudicial to the commonwealth, the government, or good order. Instead the practice has been of great advantage to commerce and hence to the
commonwealth.

---

[38] Quakers have consistently maintained that oaths imply a dual
standard, that by implication it is all right to lie when one is not under
oath. Truth, however, as one of the attributes of God, is obligatory upon
those who profess to worship him.

[39] This is exactly what was done in the acts permitting an affirmation
in place of an oath. Perjury is just as chargeable against the person who
lies under affirmation as under oath.

REVENGE AND WAR UNWORTHY OF THE PRINCE OF PEACE

¶XIII. Revenge and war are the final topics that will be considered in this work. They constitute an evil which is as opposite and contrary to the Spirit and doctrine of Christ as light is to darkness. We have just considered the way in which the world, through contempt for Christ's law, has become filled with various oaths, curses, blasphemous profanity, and horrible perjury. Through contempt for the same law, the world has become filled with violence, oppression, murder, rape, despoliation, destruction by fire and depredation, as well as all kinds of cruel and lascivious behavior.

It is strange that in war men who are made in the image of God can become so depraved that they resemble animals instead. They become roaring lions, slashing tigers, devouring wolves, and wild boars, rather than creatures who are endowed with the gift of reason. Isn't it even more remarkable that these horrid monsters find a place among those who profess to be disciples of our Lord and master Jesus Christ? Even though he, who is well called the Prince of Peace, has very clearly prohibited the practice of violence of any kind by his children, they are among the fomenters of strife. He commanded them to do just the opposite. By his example, they were to follow the ways of patience, charity, forbearance, and the other virtues that are worthy of a Christian.

Every soul has been commanded to hear what Christ said, upon pain of being cut off in judgment. In Mat 5:38-48 NEB he says: "You have learned that they were told, 'An eye for an eye, and a tooth for a tooth.' But what I tell you is this: Do not set yourself against the man who wrongs you. If someone slaps you on the right cheek, turn and offer him your left. If a man wants to sue you for your shirt, let him have your coat as well. If a man in authority makes you go one mile, go with him two. Give when you are asked to give; and do not turn your back on a man who wants to borrow.

LOVE YOUR ENEMIES

"You have learned that they were told, 'Love your neighbor, hate your enemy.' But what I tell you is this: Love your enemies and pray for your persecutors; only so can you be children of your heavenly Father, who makes his sun rise on good and bad alike, and sends the rain on the honest and the dishonest. If you love only those who love you, what reward can you expect? Surely the tax-gatherers do as much as that. And if you greet only your brothers, what is there extraordinary about that? Even the heathen do as much. You must therefore be all goodness, just as your heavenly Father is all good." These words, like those which pertain to swearing, forbid certain things which were formerly lawful for Jews and which represented a dispensation because of their situation at that time. They represent a command to those who want to be disciples of Christ to be more perfect and exemplary. They should be the complete personifications of Christian love, and provide better examples of patience and suffering than those who were of the time, state, and dispensation provided by the law of Moses. This is not only the judgment of most, if not all, of the so-called ancient Fathers of the Church for the first 300 years after Christ, but also of many others, and in general of all of the very same people who have correctly understood and interpreted the law of Christ in regard to swearing.[40]

PRECEPTS AGAINST SWEARING AND WAR RECEIVED TOGETHER

From these it is apparent that there is a major connection between these two precepts of Christ. He uttered and commanded them at one and the same time. They have been received together by men of all ages, not only by the small group of disciples, but also after the Christians had increased considerably during the first 300 years. Even in the time of the

---

[40] Barclay included all of the following citations: Justin Martyr, in *Dialog cum Tryph.*, his *Apolog.* 2, his *ad Zenam.* Tertullian, *de Corona Militis; Apolog.*, cap 21 and 37; *lib. de Idolol.*, cap 17, 18, 19; *ad Scapulam*, cap 1; *adversus Jud.*, cap 7 and 9; *adv. Gnost.*, cap 13; *adv. Marc.*, cap 4; *lib. de Patientia*, cap 6 and 10. Origen, *cont. Celsum*, lib 3, 5, 8; hom. 12, *on Josuam*, cap 9; *on Mat*, cap 26; *Tract. 35.* Cyprian, *Epist. 56, ad Cornel. Lactant. de just.*, lib 5, c 18; *op cit*, lib 6, c 20. Ambrose, *on Luc.* 22. Chrysostom, *hom. 18* on Mat 5; *hom. 85* on Mat 26; *de Sacerdotio*, lib 2; *on 1 Cor 13.* Chromatius *on Mat 5.* Jerome, *ad Ocean; lib. Epist.*, part 3, tom 1, Ep 2. Athanasius, *de Inc. Verb. Dei.* Cyril of Alexandria, lib 11, on John 25:26.

"Even Augustine, although he was inconsistent on this matter, nevertheless condemned fighting in these places: *Epist.* 158, 159, 160; *ad Judices; Epist. 203; ad Darium*, lib 21; *ad Faustum.*, cap 76, lib 22; *de Civit., ad. Marc.*, cap 6, as Sylburgius relates." Euthymius [Zigabenus] *on Mat 26* "and many others of this age." Erasmus *on Luke 3* and *on Luke 22.* Ludovicus Vives in *Introduc. ad. Sap. J. Ferus*, lib 4; and *Comment.* on Mat 7 and Luke 22.

Sylburgius is probably Friedrich Sylburg (1536-1596) editor of a number of late 16th cent texts. The extant writings of Clement of Alexandria, Dionysius of Halicarnassus, and Justin Martyr are the subjects of separate volumes by him at General Theological Seminary.

apostasy, one was not kept and the other rejected, but both were rejected alike. Now in the time of restitution and the renewed preaching of the eternal gospel, they are acknowledged as eternal and unchangeable laws, which belong properly to the evangelical state and its perfection of a Christian man.

Indeed, the words themselves are so clear that I find no need to illustrate or explain them. It is easier to reconcile the greatest of contradictions, than it is to reconcile these laws of our Lord Jesus Christ with the wicked practice of war. They are plainly inconsistent. Who can reconcile "Do not resist one who is evil" (Mat 5:39 RSV) with the injunction that evil must be resisted by force?

Or, "If someone slaps you on the right cheek, turn and offer him your left" with "strike again"? Or, "Love your enemies" with pursuit of them by fire and sword? Or, "Pray for those who persecute you" with visiting fines, imprisonment, and even death itself upon those who not only do not persecute you, but who are earnestly concerned for your eternal and temporal welfare?

Whoever has found a way to reconcile these things must also have found a way to reconcile God with the devil, Christ with Antichrist, light with darkness, and good with evil. If this is impossible, as indeed it is, it is also impossible to reconcile war and revenge with Christian practice. Men only deceive themselves and others when they try unreservedly to do such an absurd and impossible thing.

WAR TEACHES US TO HATE AND DESTROY

¶XIV. Nevertheless, since there are those who transgress this command of Christ, perhaps inadvertently, I will demonstrate briefly how much war contradicts his precepts. I will also show how such great inconsistency of one with the other has been allowed by the force of custom and tradition.

War is absolutely unlawful for those who would be disciples of Christ. In the first place, Christ says that "we should love our enemies" (Mat 5:44), but war teaches us to hate and destroy them. The apostle Paul says, Eph 6:12 NEB: "Our fight is not against human foes but... against the superhuman forces of evil." And he adds in 2 Cor 10:4 NEB: "The weapons we wield are not merely human, but divinely potent." The weapons of war, however, are the most human of weapons —

cannon, muskets, spears, swords, and other things of that kind.
These are not included in the kind of armor that Paul describes.

James asks the questions, Jas 4:1 NEB: "What causes con-
flicts and quarrels among you? Do they not spring from the
aggressiveness of your bodily desires?" How then can "those
who belong to Christ Jesus [and] have crucified the lower nature
with its passions and desires" (Gal 5:24 NEB), indulge them
by waging war?

The prophets Isaiah and Micah prophesied in identical
words: "They shall beat their swords into ploughshares and
their spears into pruning hooks; one nation shall not raise the
sword against another, nor shall they train for war again" (Isa
2:4 and Micah 4:3 Cath-CCD). The primitive Christians were
thoroughly averse to war and the ancient fathers of the first 300
years after Christ affirmed that Christians would fulfill these
prophecies in their day. Justin Martyr, Tertullian and others
can be consulted. This should not seem strange to anyone,
since Philo Judaeus gave plenty of evidence about the Essenes,
that "there was no one to be found among them who would
make instruments of war." Since this was so, how much more
should the coming of Jesus prevent his followers from fighting
and bring them instead to Christian patience and love?

EVERY SOLDIER WAS DISARMED IN THE DISARMING OF PETER

The prophet foretold the day when there would be no
harm or destruction on his holy mountain, Isa 65:25. Christ
added that "My kingship is not of this world; if my kingship
were of this world, my servants would fight" (John 18:36 RSV).
He reproved Peter for using his sword, saying, Mat 26:52 RSV:
"Put your sword back into its place; for all who take the sword
will perish by the sword." Tertullian's comment on this[41] is
very enlightening: "How can he fight in peace without the
sword, which the Lord took away? ... Christ disarmed every
soldier when he disarmed Peter." In his *de Coron. Mil.*, Tertullian asks: "How can it be lawful to use the sword, when the
Lord said that he who uses the sword shall perish by the sword?"

LEAVE A PLACE FOR DIVINE RETRIBUTION

Paul admonishes Christians, Rom 12:17-21 NEB: "Never
pay back evil for evil. Let your aims be such as all men count

41 *Lib. de Idol.*

honorable. If possible, so far as it lies with you, live at peace with all men. My dear friends, do not seek revenge, but leave a place for divine retribution; for there is a text which reads, 'Justice is mine, says the Lord, I will repay.' But there is another text: 'If your enemy is hungry, feed him; if he is thirsty, give him a drink; by doing this you will heap live coals on his head.' Do not let evil conquer you, but use good to defeat evil."

Christ calls his children to bear his cross, not to crucify or kill others (Mark 8:34). He calls them to patience, not to revenge; to truth and simplicity, not to the fraudulent stratagems of war or the role of sycophant, which John himself forbids too.[42] Christ also urges them to flee the glory of this world, not to acquire it by warlike endeavors. Therefore war is completely contrary to the law and Spirit of Christ.

A SPECIAL MEASURE OF PATIENCE AND THE EXERCISE OF LOVE ARE REQUIRED OF CHRIST'S DISCIPLES

¶XV. It is claimed that it is lawful for Christians to make war because Abraham did so before the law was received, and the Israelites did it after they were given the law. But: (1) Abraham also offered sacrifices and circumcised his male children, neither of which are lawful under the gospel. (2) Neither defensive nor offensive war was waged by the Israelites of their own volition, or by their own counsel or conduct. If they desired success they had to inquire from the oracle of God whether the war would be allowed. (3) The wars against the wicked nations prefigured the inward wars by which true Christians overcome their spiritual enemies — the devil, the world, and the flesh. (4) Some of the things which Christ forbids explicitly in Mat 5:38ff were allowed the Jews in their time because of the hardness of their hearts. But we, on the contrary, are commanded to have a special measure of patience and to exercise love, things which Moses did not command his disciples. From this, Tertullian comments:[43] "Christ truly teaches a new patience. He even forbids revenge for an injury, although this was permitted by the Creator." And he says elsewhere:[44] "The law finds more than it lost, from Christ's saying, Love your enemies."

[42] The reference is obscure, possibly Rev 19:10 and 22:8 are intended. — ED.

43 in *Contra Marc.*

44 in *lib de Patien.*

In the time of Clement of Alexandria Christians were so far from making war that he testified that there were no marks or signs of violence among them, saying:[45] "The faces of idols are not to be painted by those who are forbidden even to look at them. Nor can sword or bow be possessed by those who follow peace, or cups by those who are moderate and temperate."

The objection is made that defense is a natural right and religion does not destroy nature. However, it does not destroy nature to obey God and commend ourselves to him in both faith and patience. On the contrary, our natures are exalted and perfected by such acts. They do this by elevating us from the natural to the supernatural life. Christ's life provides us such fulfillment and such comfort that "in all these things we are more than conquerors through him who loved us" (Rom 8:37 RSV).

WE ARE NOT JOHN'S DISCIPLES

Another objection is that John did not abrogate or condemn war when the soldiers came to him.

What of it? We are not John's disciples, but Christ's, and it is Christ's doctrine rather than John's in which we are interested and which we should follow. And although Christ said, Luke 7:28 NEB: "I tell you, there is not a mother's son greater than John," he adds, "and yet the least in the kingdom of God is greater than he." What was John's answer? Let's see if it would justify soldiers today! He actually says, Luke 3:14 NEB, when they ask how they are to apply their faith to their occupations: "No bullying, no blackmail; make do with your pay!" Yet craft, violence, and injustice are such natural consequences of battle and such inherent properties of the warrior's occupation that the soldiers would have had to give up their employment if they followed his teachings.

Along the same lines, it is said that Cornelius and the centurion who is mentioned in Mat 8:5 were both soldiers and no mention is made of their giving up their employment. But, on the other hand, it doesn't say anywhere that they didn't. It is more likely that if they continued to follow the doctrines of Christ (and we don't read anywhere that they gave up their faith), they did not continue to be soldiers. This seems a rea-

---

45 Sylvius *Disc. de Rev. Belg.*

sonable assumption since two or three centuries later Christians still rejected war completely.

Marcus Aurelius Antoninus wrote, much to his credit, that: "I prayed to my country gods. But when I was neglected by them, and observed that I was pressed by the enemy, and considered the fewness of my forces, I called to one. I also entreated those whom we call Christians, and I found a great number of them. Then I forced them with threats, but this should not have been done, because afterwards I knew the source of their strength. That is why they use neither darts nor trumpets; they abstain on behalf of and in the name of their God, and this they bear in their consciences." This was about 160 years after Christ.

WE DO NOT FIGHT WITH OUR ENEMIES

The answer which Christians gave when asked to do battle, as recorded by Justin Martyr, was *ou polemoumen tois echthrois,* that is, "we do not fight with our enemies." There is also the answer of Martin to Julian the Apostate which is related by Sulpitius Severus:[46] "I am a soldier of Christ, therefore I cannot fight." That answer was given about 300 years after Christ. It does not seem likely that the centurions continued their warlike employment!

WHAT ABOUT THE VINCENTIAN CANON?

How are Vincentius Lyrinensis[47] and the Roman Catholics consistent with their maxim, "that which was always received everywhere and by everyone," if they maintain that war is permissible for Christians? What becomes of the oath in which priests say that they should not and will not interpret the scrip-

---

[46] St. Martin, Bishop of Tours (d. 397), who "served in the Roman army until, after he had given half his cloak to a beggar at Amiens, a vision of Christ impelled him to baptism and the religious life.... His protest against the execution of Priscillian by Maximus in 386 raised important issues in the relations between Church and state.

"He wrote nothing, but his life was recorded by his friend Sulpicius Severus (c. 363 - c. 420/5), the historian and hagiographer ... and became at once extremely popular and a much-imitated model of medieval hagiography." — *O.D.C.C.,* pp 864 and 1303.

[47] The reference is to St. Vincent of· Lerins (d. before 450) and the so-called Vincentian Canon included in his *Commonitorium.* This provided a three-fold test of Catholicity by which the Church could differentiate between true and false traditions: "what has been believed everywhere, always, and by all." — *O.D.C.C.,* pp 1422-1423.

Barclay makes the common error of putting antiquity first rather than universality. This does not destroy the validity of his point, however.

tures otherwise than in accordance with the universal consent
of the so-called Fathers of the Church? It is as easy to hide
the sun at noon as it is to deny that primitive Christians
renounced all revenge and war!

OTHERS BEAR THIS TESTIMONY WITH US

Although this fact is well known, it is equally well known
that nearly all of the modern sects neglect this law of Christ
and are contemptuous of it. They also persecute others who
do not agree with them, but who abstain from participation in
war and revenge for the sake of their consciences toward God.
We have suffered a great deal in our country because we would
not bear arms, send substitutes, or contribute money for the
purchase of drums, standards, or other military trappings. Because we could not conscientiously close our doors, windows,
and shops on the days when fasts and prayers were appointed
on behalf of military victory, we suffered further. We could
not conscientiously request a blessing and pray for the success
of the army of the kingdom or commonwealth under which we
live. We could not give thanks for victories which were acquired by the shedding of much blood.

In forcing our consciences, they would have required our
brethren who live in various kingdoms that are at war with
each other to implore their God to grant contrary and contradictory things — things which were consequently impossible.
For two parties fighting together cannot both be victorious.
Because we could not concur with them in this confusion, we
were subjected to persecution.

Although there are others who also bear testimony with us
that the use of arms is unlawful for Christians,[48] these others
often look askance at some of our interpretations of this testimony. Even though they do not approve of war they comply
with the magistrate's order to close their shops and houses at
certain times or to assemble together to pray that their armies
will prosper. But in doing this, or in giving thanks for a victory, they ally themselves with those who approve of war or
fighting. We cannot take part in these things or we would de-

---

[48] Most notably the Mennonites and Brethren, when considered
denominationally. Today, Jehovah's Witnesses would have to be added,
as well as the fact that there are individual conscientious objectors to war
in every denomination.

stroy by our acts what we have established by our words. We leave it to the prudent person to decide if this is not so.

THE "BUY A SWORD" PASSAGE

In Luke 22:35-36 NEB, Jesus says: " 'When I sent you out barefoot without purse or pack, were you ever short of anything?' 'No,' they answered. 'It is different now,' he said, 'whoever has a purse had better take it with him, and his pack too; and if he has no sword, let him sell his cloak to buy one.' " It is claimed on the basis of this that arms are lawful. Now it is true that some consider this passage to refer to material weapons, but only on this particular occasion. Otherwise, they say that under the gospel Christians are prohibited from participating in war.

Ambrose is one who takes this position, commenting on this passage: "O Lord! why do you command me to buy a sword, when you forbid me to smite with it? Why do you command me to have it, when you prohibit drawing it? Unless perhaps it was to have a defense prepared, but not to be used for revenge; so that I might demonstrate that I was capable of revenge, but would not exercise it. For the law forbids me to smite again, and perhaps that is why he said to Peter, when he offered two swords, 'It is enough.'[49] It may have been lawful until the gospel times, so that equity could be learned in the law, but in the gospel there was to be a perfection of goodness."

Others think that Christ was speaking symbolically and not literally. Origen writes concerning Mat 19: "If anyone who looks to the letter and does not understand the intent of the words, sells his bodily garment and buys a sword, taking the words of Christ contrary to his wishes, he shall perish; but it is not proper to discuss here which sword it is that he speaks of." Certainly Christ's answer that two swords were enough shows that he was not speaking literally, or he would have told everyone to sell his coat and buy a sword.

SOME WOULD LIMIT PROHIBITION TO PRIVATE REVENGE

Another objection that is raised is that the scriptures and early Fathers merely intended to prohibit private revenge, not the use of arms to defend our country, our person, wives, chil-

---

[49] Luke 22:38.

dren, or possessions. They say that when we are commanded
by governmental authority to defend these, we should comply,
since Christians are supposed to obey authority. But, if the
magistrate is truly a Christian, or desires to be one, the first
thing he should do is obey the command of his master: "Love
your enemies." Then it would be impossible for him to command us to kill them. If he is not a true Christian, then both
he and we should obey Jesus Christ our Lord and King. In the
kingdom of Christ everyone should submit to his laws — from
the highest to the lowest, from the king to the beggar, and
from Caesar to the clown.

Unfortunately it is difficult to find such obedience. There
has been a deplorable falling from grace in this respect. Ludovicus Vives writes:[50] "The prince entered the church, not as a
true and plain Christian, which would have been most happy
and desirable. But instead, he brought in with him his nobility, his honors, his *arms*, his ensigns, his triumphs, his haughti-
ness, his pride, his superciliousness. In other words, he came
into the house of Christ accompanied by the devil, and that
was an impossibility. He would have joined two houses and
two cities together — God's and the devil's. That could no
more be done than combining Rome and Constantinople, which
are separated by such a long stretch of both sea and land. 'What
communion is there between Christ and Belial?' Paul asks. The
Christian's zeal cooled by degrees, his faith decreased, his whole
piety degenerated. In its place we now have mere shadows and
images, and, as he says, I wish we could retain even these."

The really clinching argument, however, is that there is
nothing more contrary to human nature than refusing to defend oneself. But since this is so difficult for men, it is one of
the most perfect points of Christian faith. It demands self-
denial, and placing one's entire confidence in God.

50 In *lib. de con. vit. Christ. sub Turc.*, as quoted by Fredericus Sylvius, *Disc. de Revol. Belg.*, p 85.

The Vives work cited is *De conditione vitae Christianorum sub Turca
libellus. Machumetis ... ejusque successorum vitae*, etc., tom 3. [1543]
and 1550 editions. — *Brit. Mus. Cat.*

The author is probably Joannes Ludovicus Vives (1492-1540), who was
born in Valencia and died in Bruges. — *Encyc. Ital.*, 1937, vol 35, p 528.

The Sylvius cited may be Francis Sylvius (1581-1649), a Roman Catholic
theologian of Douay whose reputation was based principally on his commentary on the *Summa Theologica* of Thomas Aquinas.

THE "JUST WAR" IS EQUALLY UNLAWFUL

As far as the present authorities of this world are concerned, even though we do not deny entirely that they are Christians, we say without equivocation that they are far from having perfected their Christianity. As has already been said a number of times, even though they profess to be Christians, they have not come to the pure dispensation of the gospel. For that very reason, we will not say that while they are still in that condition, war — undertaken for just reasons — is altogether unlawful for them. The Jews were permitted to use circumcision and other ceremonies for a time because the Spirit had not yet emerged among them. It was not because these things were necessary of themselves or would be lawful after the resurrection of Christ, but because they had not yet been delivered from such rudimentary practices.

In the same way, today's Christians are still an admixture of the old and the new. They have not yet achieved a patient suffering spirit which would equip them for this form of Christianity. Therefore, they cannot leave themselves undefended until they attain that degree of perfection. But it is unlawful for those whom Christ has already brought to that state to defend themselves with arms. They, of all people, should have complete trust in the Lord.

IN SUMMARY —

¶XVI. In summary: If the giving and receiving of flattering titles, which are not descriptive of the inherent virtues of that person, but for the most part are bestowed by wicked men upon themselves —

HONORS AND COMPLIMENTS

If bowing, scraping, and cringing before one another —

If calling themselves each other's humble servants at every turn, and generally without any idea of real service —

If these are the honors which come from God and not from below, then those who practice them can be said to be true believers, and we can be condemned as proud and stubborn because we deny these things.

But if, with Mordecai, who refused to bow to proud Haman (Esther 3:5), and with Elihu, who would not give flattering titles to men (Job 32:21-22), we were to be approved by our Maker —

If, according to Peter's example and the angel's advice, to bow to God and not to our fellow-servants —

If to call no man lord or master, except under those specific relationships, are according to Christ's command —

I say, if these things are not subject to reproof from God, then we should not be blamed for doing them.

MODEST APPAREL

If to be vain and gaudy in clothing —

If to paint the face and braid the hair —

If to be clothed with gold, silver, and precious stones —

If to be covered with ribbons and lace constitutes being clothed in modest apparel —

If these are the ornaments of Christians —

If these can be considered as being humble, meek, and mortified, then our opponents are good Christians indeed, and we are proud, peculiar, and conceited because we are content to have what we need or what is suitable, and because we condemn anything more as being superfluous — but not otherwise!

FRIVOLOUS DIVERSIONS

If to use gambling, diversions, and frolicsome pleasures —

If to play cards, roll dice, and dance —

If to sing, fiddle, or pipe —

If to use stage-plays and comedies —

If to lie, make false representation, and dissemble —

If doing all these things is to the glory of God —

If that means passing our sojourning on earth in fear —

If that is to use this world as though we did not use it —

If that is not fashioning ourselves according to our former lusts, and is not being conformable to the spirit and empty activities of this world, then our opponents who use these things and argue for them are very good, sober, mortified and self-denying Christians and we should properly be blamed for judging them — but not otherwise!

OATHS

If the profane use of the holy name of God —

If the extracting of oaths from one another on every unimportant occasion —

If calling upon God to be a witness, for things of such nature that no earthly king would consider lawful and honorable for him to witness, are Christian duties, I will confess that our opponents are extremely good Christians and we neglect our duty — but if the contrary is true, our obedience to God in such matters has to be acceptable.

WAR

If to revenge ourselves, or to render evil for evil, wound for wound; or to take eye for eye, tooth for tooth —

If to fight for outward and perishable things, to make war against one another, even against those we have never seen, have never had an argument with, or even anything to do with, being completely ignorant of the cause of war, which the authorities of each nation foment against the other, the causes of which are largely unknown to the soldiers who do the fighting, as well as on which side the right or wrong lies, yet to be so furious and enraged with each other that everything can be despoiled or destroyed in order for one form of worship to be abolished or accepted over another —

ARISING WITH HIM IN NEWNESS OF LIFE

If to do that, and many more things of that kind, is to fulfill the law of Christ, then our opponents are true Christians indeed. We are miserable heretics who allow ourselves to be despoiled, taken prisoner, banished, beaten, and evilly treated without any resistance. We mistakenly place our trust only in God, believing that he will defend us and lead us by way of the cross to his kingdom —

But if it is otherwise, we shall certainly receive the reward which the Lord has promised to those who adhere closely to his ways, and who in denying themselves put their trust in him.

In final summation, if the use of all of these things, and many more which could be cited, is to walk in the straight path that leads to life; if it is taking up the cross of Christ; if it is dying with him to the lusts and perishable vain things of this world, and arising with him in newness of life, and being seated with him in the heavenly places, then our opponents may be considered the truest of Christians. They need have no fear that they are in the broad way that leads to destruction. We must be greatly mistaken in putting aside these things for the sake of Christ. We have erred in crucifying our own lusts and thus procuring the shame, reproach, hatred, and ill-will of the men of this world. Then we must realize that we do not merit heaven for our deeds. Instead, they are contrary to the will of him who redeems his children from the love of this world and its desires, and who leads them in the ways of truth and holiness, in which they find it delightful to walk.

THE CONCLUSION

If, out of the fear of God, impartial reader, you apply yourself to the consideration of the system of religion that has been described here, you will say with me, and with many others, that this is the time of Christ's spiritual appearance. Not only is this faith consistent and harmonious, both within itself and with the scriptures, but you will find that Christ is again revealing the ancient ways of truth and righteousness.

You may observe here a true establishment and complete vindication of the Christian religion in all its parts. It is a living, inward, spiritual, and pure thing of great substance. It is not a mere form or shadow. It is not a display. It is not a collection of notions and opinions.

Too many have held that kind of faith, and the fruits of it declare that they lacked the very nature of him whose name they bore. Yet many are so in love with empty forms and shadows that they never cease to malign us for commending the substance to them and calling them to it. They maintain that we deny and neglect the true form and outward portion of Christianity. As God, the searcher of hearts, knows, this is a very great slander.

Because we have earnestly desired people to sense the presence of God in and near themselves, they have maliciously inferred that we deny God, except that of him that is within us. But what we have really been trying to tell them is that their notion of God as being beyond the clouds will be of little use to them if they cannot also find him near them.

Because we say to people that it is the light and law within, rather than the letter without, that can truly tell them their condition and lead them from all evil, they say that we vilify the scriptures and put our own imaginations above them.

We say that merely talking about the outward life of Christ on earth will not redeem or justify them in the sight of God, any more than it did the Jews who kept crying, this is "the temple of the Lord, the temple of the Lord, the temple of the Lord."[1] They must know Christ resurrected in them. It is

[1] Jer 7:4.

he whom they have crucified. He alone can justify and redeem them from their iniquities. Because of this, they say that we deny the life, death, and sufferings of Christ, the justification by his blood, and the remission of sins through him.

We tell them that they need to know the Just One, rather than argue about the resurrection. They should be sure that they partake of the first resurrection, by having him whom they have slain raised in them. If they do this, they will be better able to judge the second resurrection. From this they say that we deny the resurrection of the body.

When we hear them talk foolishly about heaven and hell and the last judgment, we urge them to depart from the hellish condition they are in. We ask them to come to the judgment of Christ in their hearts, to believe in the Light, and follow it, in order to be able to sit in the heavenly places that are in Christ Jesus. From this, they maliciously say that we deny any heaven or hell except that which is within us, and that we deny any general judgment.

The Lord knows what ugly slanders they cast upon us. For God has raised us for the purpose of confounding the wisdom of the wise, and bringing to naught the understanding of the prudent. He did it so that we might pull down the dead, dark, corrupt image and mere shadow and shell of Christianity with which Antichrist has deceived the nations. He did it in and by his own Spirit in a despised people so that no flesh could glory in his presence.

For this purpose he has called us to be the first fruits of those who serve him and who no longer worship him with the oldness of the letter, but in the newness of the Spirit. Although we are few in number, compared with others, and weak in the outward strength which we reject completely, and foolish when compared with the wise ones of this world, yet God has made us prosper. In spite of great opposition he will provide for us, so that neither the artful wisdom or violence of men or devils will be able to quench the little spark that has appeared. It will grow until it consumes whatever opposes it. The mouth of the Lord has proclaimed it! Indeed, he who has arisen in a small remnant shall arise and go on by the same arm of power, until in his spiritual manifestation he has conquered all his enemies, until all the kingdoms of the earth become the kingdom of Christ Jesus.

Unto him who has begun this work,
        not among the rich or the great ones,
        but among the poor and the insignificant,
        and has revealed it not to the wise and learned,
        but to the lowly, to babes and sucklings;
        to him, indeed, the Only Wise and Omnipotent God,
        be honor, glory, thanksgiving, and renown,
        henceforth and forevermore.
        Amen. Hallelujah.

SCRIPTURAL REFERENCES

OLD TESTAMENT

1 COR. *cont.*	
2:5	314
2:8	116
2:9-10	24, 33
2:10	22
2:11-12	24
2:12	34, 81
2:13	233
2:14	69
2:15	70
3:1	31
3:3-9	315
3:16	31, 91
3:19	71
4:15	318
4:18	234
5:8	11, 327
6:2	81
6:11	8, 125, 141, 143, 147
6:17	157, 255, 329
6:19	31
7:19	149, 162
7:29-35	408
9:11-14	219
9:12-18	223
9:14-15	220
9:16	52
9:25	420
9:27	168
10:3-4	330
10:4-5	28
10:16	333, 341
10:16-17	11, 327
10:17	82, 333, 341
10:21	332, 341
10:31	408
11	342
11:4	403
11:17	355
11:17-34	353
11:20	355
11:22	353
11:23	354
11:23ff	344
11:25	354
11:26	340, 342
11:27	342
11:29	342
12	52, 194
12:3	25, 290
12:4	209
12:4-6	29
12:7	7, 30, 72, 82, 107
12:8-10	33
12:13	33, 107, 194

1 COR. *cont.*	
12:17	210
12:27	194
12:28	209
12:29	210
13:1	255
13:2	234
14:1-6, 39	212
14:15	290, 299
14:26-40	281
14:30ff	284
14:30-31	212
14:32	212
14:33-40	207
14:34	218
14:39	213
15:22	6, 72
16:2	205
16:13	260

2 CORINTHIANS

1:21-22	304
1:22	170
1:23	418
1:24	366
2:17	204
3:6	179
4:10-11	145
5:5	412
5:9	153
5:10	154
5:11-12	179
5:16-17	107
5:18-19	139
5:19	131
5:20	139, 140
5:21	139
6:14	157, 332
6:14-16	140, 186
6:16	90
6:17 - 7:1	187
7:1	186
10:4	31, 368, 427
10:17	20
11:10	418
12:9	193
13:3	191
13:5	28, 35, 53, 112, 146
13:11	162

GALATIANS   151

1:8	63
1:16	24, 29
1:20	418
2:8	152
2:16	143

GALATIANS *cont.*	
2:20	152, 164
3:1	90
3:11	143
3:27	10, 147, 301, 310
3:28	218
4	154
4:10-11	245
4:19-20	146
5	151, 153, 372
5:6	151
5:12	371
5:20-21	372
5:22	151
5:24	428
6:6	219
6:7-9	151
6:14	81, 111

EPHESIANS

1:13	170
1:13-14	304
2:1	70
2:3-5	6, 66
2:4-6	164
2:5	145
2:8	193
2:16b	131
3:9	23
4:5	10, 28, 301, 305
4:7	191, 194
4:11	194, 209, 231
4:11-13	160
4:16	193
4:23-24	147, 252
4:24	164
4:30	304
5:2	130, 153
5:11	12, 389
5:13	82, 92, 110, 360
5:25-27	159
6:12	427
6:18	286, 290, 299
6:18-19	289

PHILIPPIANS

1:6	168
1:8	417
2:13	152
3:3	320
3:10	132
3:14	165
3:15	384
3:20	397

PERSONS AND WORKS CITED

Alain de l'Isle (c. 1128-1203): 324 & n.

Alanus, see Alain de l'Isle.

Alexander, Bishop of Alexandria (d. 328): 379n.

Ambrose, Bishop of Milan, (c. 339-397): *Epist. 32,* tomo 3, 378 & n; *Epist. 27,* 378; *Comm. in Luc.,* lib 7, 379; *De Virginibus,* lib 3, 423; *on Mat 5,* 423; *on Luke 22,* 426, 433; unspecified work, 416.

Ambrosius, Ansbertus [possibly Ambrose, Autpert (d. 778), a French Benedictine monk who wrote commentaries on the Psalms and the Song of Solomon]: *on Apoc.,* 423.

Ames, William (1576-1633): *De Conscientia, eius Jure et Casibus,* 363 & n.

Anicetus: 41n.

Anselm (c. 1033-1109): *on Mat 5,* 423.

Antiochus: *In Pandect Script., Hom. 62,* 423.

Apollinarius (c. 315-c. 390): 86n.

Aquinas, see Thomas Aquinas.

Aristotle, 121.

Arius (c.250-c.336): 203, 379n, 416n.

Arminius, Jacobus (1560-1609): 48n.

Arnold, Nikolaus (1618-1680): *Exercit Theolog.,* s 40, 182 & n; *ibid,* s 32, 197 & n; *ibid,* s 42-43, 221 & n-222 & n; *ibid,* s 44, 242 & n-243 & n; *ibid,* s 45, 245; *ibid,* s 46, 315; *ibid,* 326.

Athanasius, Bishop of Alexandria (c.296-373): *De Incarnatione Verbi Dei,* 19 & n, 426 & n; *Pass. et Cruc. Dom.,* 417 & n, 423 & n; *Epist. ad omnes ubique solitarium vitam agentes,* 377 & n; *Apologia 1,* "de Fuga sua," tom 1, 377.

Aubery, Claude, see Inuncunanus, Claudius Alberius.

Augustine (354-430): *Tract. Ep. Joh. 3* [appears to be actually *Homily IV*], 17 & n; *Homily III,* 17 & n; *Sermon 49,* s 8, 33n; *De Spiritu et Littera,* s 24, 38 & n; *Epist. 19 ad Hier.,* tomo 2, fol 14, 57 & n; *On Psalm 94,* 81n; unspecified works, 93; *City of God,* lib 18, c 47, 120; *ibid,* c 9, 120n; *Confession,* lib 11, c 9, 122; *ibid,* lib 10, c 27, 122; condemnation of Pelagians, 323 & n, 324; *Tractat., Psalm 98,* 327; *De Serm. Dom.,* serm. 28, 423n; *Epists. 158, 159, 160,* 426n; *Ad Judices,* 426n; *Epist. 203,* 426n; *Ad Darium,* lib 21, 426n; *Ad Faustum,* lib 22, c 76, 426n; *De Civit.,* 426n; *Ad Marc.,* c 6, 426n; *De Praedestinatione Sanctorum,* 74n; *De Dono Perseverantiae,* 74n; "later writings," 74.

Auxentius, Arian Bishop of Milan (d. 373 or 374): 378n.

Baker, F. Augustine (1575-1641): *Sancta Sophia,* tract 1, s 2, c 5, 276 & n-277 & n; *ibid,* tract 3, s 1, c 7, 277 & n.

Barclay, William (c. 1547-1608) of Aberdeen: 376 & n.

Basil the Great (c. 330-379): 416 & n, 421; *on Psalm 14,* 423n.

Basilius Magnus, see Basil the Great.

Baxter, Richard (1615-1691): *Aphorisms of Justification,* 149 & n; *The Saints Everlasting Rest,* 149n.

Bede, "The Venerable" (c. 675-735): *On James,* 423n.

Bellarmine, Robert (1542 - 1621): 133 & n, 376.

Bellius, see Borrhaus, Martin.

Bernard of Clairvaux (1090-1153): *Commentary on Psalm 84,* 19&n; *Epistle to William,* 278 & n; unspecified works, 247 & n, 288 & n.

Beza, Theodore (1519-1605): *lib. de Praed.,* 76n; *de Pread. ad Art.,*

Eutyches (c.378-454): 86, 87n.

Ferus, J.: lib 4, 426n; *Comment. on Mat 7 and Luke 22?*, 426n.
Fisher the Jesuit (1569-1641)?: *Resp. ad Vorst*, 76 & n.
Flacius, Matthias (1520-1575): *Magdeburg Centuries*, 201n.
Forbes, William (1585-1634): *Considerationes Modestae·... de Justificatione*, lib 2, s 8, 144n-145n.

Gikatilla, Joseph [Spanish Talmudist and Cabalist (1248 - 1305)]: *Gates of Light*, 320n.
Godeau, Antoine (1605-1672): *Paraphrase des Epitres de Saint Paul* (1641), 401n.
Gregorius, Nyssenus, see Gregory, Bishop of Nyssa.
Gregory, Bishop of Nyssa (c. 330-c. 395): 416n; *Orat. 13*, "on Cant.," 423n.
Gregory of Nazianzus (329 - 389): 416n; *Dialog contra Juramenta*, 423n.
Gregory the Great (c. 540 - 604): *Homilies on the Gospels*, 19 & n.
Grotius, Hugo (1583-1645): *De Veritate Religionis Christianae de Jure Belli ac Pacis*, and *Opera Theologica*, 416n; quotes Maimonides, 422 & n.

Haimo [Haymon Halberstatensis (c. 778-853)?]: *on Apoc.*, 423n.
Hierom, see Jerome.
Hieronymus, see Jerome.
Hilarius, see Hilary of Poitiers.
Hilary of Poitiers (c.315-367): *Contra Arianos vel Auxentium Mediolanensem Liber*, 377&n; *Ad Constantium Augustum*, 379; *on Mat 5:34*, 423n.
Himelius, 148n.
Himmel, Enoch (d. 1666)?, *see* Himelius.
Himmel, Johann (1581-1642)?, *see* Himelius.
Hosius, Bishop of Cordova (c.257-357): *Epist. ad Constit. apud ath. in Eph. ad Solit. Vit.*, tomo 1, 379 & n.
Howell, James (c. 1594-1666): *Epistolae Ho-Elianae*, 400 & n.

Inuncunanus, Claudius Alberius (d. 1596): *Orat. Apodict. Lausaniae Excus.* (1587), *Orat. 2*, 148 & n.
Irenaeus (c.130-c.200): 56.
Isidore "Hispalensis" (c. 560-636): [*Etymologiae*?], c 31, 423n.
Isidore of Pelusium (d. c. 450): *Epist. 1, Epist. 155*, 423n.
Isocrates (436-338 B. C.): 421 & n.

Jerome (c.342-420): *Commentary on the Epistles of Paul*, 19 & n; *Ep. 120 to Hedibia*, 19 & n; *Epist. 28 to Lucin.*, 56 & n; *Epist. 134 ad Cypr.*, 60; *Ep. 62 ad The.*, 378 & n; *Epist. to Celant*, 397 & n; general refs., 416-417; *Lib. de Epistol.*, part 3, Ep. 2, 417 & n; *on Zach.*, 423n; *ibid*, lib 2, c 8, 423n; *on Mat*, lib 1, c 5, 423n; *Ad Ocean* [sic], 426n; *Lib. Epist.*, part 3, tomo 1, Ep. 2, 426n.
Johannes Damascenus, see John of Damascus.
John of Damascus (c. 675 - c. 749): [*Fount of Wisdom*?], lib 3, c 16, 423n.
Johannes Floracensis [a monk (fl c. 1022)]: *Epistle to Oliva, Abbot of the Ausonian Church*, 325 & n.
Justin Martyr (c.100-c.165): *First Apology*, 106 & n, 119 & n; *Second Apology*, 119 & n, 423, 426n; *Dialog cum Trypho*, 426n; *Ad Zenam*, 426n; "we do not fight," 431; unspecified work, 428.

Lactantius, Lucius Caelius Frimianus (c.260-340): *Divine Institute*, lib 6, c 8, 118n.
Lambert, Francis (1486-1530): *Prophecy*, tract 5, c 3, 195 & n; 284n.
Luther, Martin (1483-1546): *An den Christlichen Adel Deutscher Nation* [*Address to the German Nobility*], 20 & n, 381n; priesthood of all believers, 182 & n; *De Captivitate Babylonica*, 381 & n; *On the Civil Power*, 381n; Carlstadt, 382 & n; *Wider die Himmlischen Propheten*, 382n; mocks plural "you," 400.

Magdeburg Centuries, see Flacius, Matthias.
Maimonides (1135 - 1204): *Moreh Nebukim*, 422 & n.

Marcian, Emperor (396-457): *Epist. ad Archimand, etc. mon. eg.,* 379 & n; his NT canon, 379n.

Marcus Aurelius (121-180): *Meditations,* 422n, 431.

Maresius, John, *see* Desmarets, Jean.

Martin, Bishop of Tours (d. 397): 431 & n.

Martinus, Boraeus, *see* Borrhaus, Martin.

Martyr, *see* Peter Martyr.

Masson, Papir, *see* Masson, Jean.

Masson, Jean (1544-1618): 325 & n.

Melancthon, Philipp (1497-1560): *Commentaries on Scripture,* 20&n; *Apol. Conf. Aug.,* 144 & n; unspecified work, 167.

Oecumenius, *see* Ecumenius.

Onuphrius [Onufrio Pauvinio (16th c.)?]: 188 & n.

Origen (c.185-c.254): 22, 203; *Tract 25,* "on Mat" 423n; *Cont. Celsum,* lib 3, 5, and 8, 426n; *Hom. 12,* c 9, 426n; *On Mat,* c 26, 426n; *Tract. 35,* 426n; *On Mat 19,* 433.

Orosius (early 5th c.): 176n.

Osiander, Lucas, the Elder (1534-1604): *Epitomes Historicae Ecclesiasticae,* lib 2, c 5, Cent. 4, 201n.

Otho Brunsfelsius [possibly Otto Brunfels (1488-1534), a Carthusian who turned Protestant, then became a physician. His *Historia Plantarum* is the first descriptive botany of Germany]: *on Mat 5,* 423n.

Paraeus, David (1548 - 1622): *De Amis. Gratiae* lib 3, c 2 and c 1, 76 & n; *Just. cont. Bell.,* lib 2, c 7, 141n-142n.

Paschasius, Radbertus (c.785-c.860): *On Mat 5,* 423n.

Paulinus, Bishop of Nola (353/4-431): 399 & n.

Pauvinio, Onufrio ?, *see* Onuphrius.

Peter Martyr (1500-1562)?: *on Rom,* 76 & n.

Philo (c.20 B.C.-50 A.D.): on the third Commandment, 422 & n; on the Essenes, 422 & n, 428.

Phocylides (6th c. B. C.): 119 & n.

Piscator, *see* Fisher the Jesuit ?.

Pithaeus, Pierre (1539-1598)?: *Fragments of the History of Guienne,* 325 & n.

Platina, Bartolomeo (1421-1481): 177.

Plato (427? - 347? B. C.): 117 & n; *Judgment de Leg. 12,* 422 & n.

Plotinus (c.205-270): 21, 117 & n.

Polybius (c.204-122 B. C.): 415.

Polycarp (c.69-c.155): 41n, 423n.

Prosper of Aquitaine (c.390-c.465):: *De Vocat. Gentium,* lib 11, cap 6, 81 & n; *Ad Gall.,* 81 & n.

Pythagoras (c.582-c.507 B. C.): *Oration,* 421 & n; unspecified work, 117 & n.

Quintilian (c.35-c.95): 422 & n; *Institutio Oratoria,* 422n.

Reuchlin, Johannes (1455 - 1522): 320n.

Ricci, Paul [convert from Judaism (fl 16th c.)]: 320 & n; *Celestial Agriculture,* 345; translator, Gikatilla's *The Gates of Light,* 320n.

Sarpi, Paolo (1552-1623): *History of the Council of Trent,* 295 & n, 381 & n, 382 & n.

Seneca, Lucius Annaeus (c.4 B.C.-65 A. D.): *Epistles,* 118 & n.

Servetus, Michael (1511-53): 382&n.

Siculus, Didorus (d. after 21 B. C.): world history by, 420 & n.

Skene, Alexander [Barclay's contemporary in Aberdeen]: 293 & n-295.

Smith, John (1618-1652): *Select Discourses,* 21 & n.

Socrates (469-399 B. C.): *Serm. 14,* 421.

Stobaeus, Joannes (5th c.) ?: *Serm. 3,* 421 & n; *Serm. 14,* 421 & n.

Sulpicius Severus (c.363 - c. 420/5): 399 & n; *Chronicle,* 399n; *Life of St. Martin,* 399n, 431n.

Sylburgius [probably Friedrich Sylburg (1536-1596)] 426n.

Sylvius, Fredericus [possibly Francis Sylvius (1581-1649), a R. C. theologian of Douay]): *Disc. de Rev. Belg.,* 430n, 434n.

Tauler, Johann (c.1300-61): 247&n.

Tertullian, Quintus Septimus Florens (c.160-c.220): *Liber de veland Virginibus,* 18 & n; *Apologeticum,* c 24, 380 & n; *ibid,* c 28, 380 & n; *ibid,* c 32, 423n; *Ad Scapul.,* 423n; *ibid,* c 2, 380 & n; *ibid,* c 1, 426n;

SUBJECT INDEX

Believers, 210, 364.
Benedictines, English, 276-277 & n.
Benefices, 225-228.
Bereans, 62.
Bible (see also Scriptures), 141, 200.
Bishop, 52, 182, 185, 187, 196, 201, 207, 217, 225, 227; Ambrose as catechumen had to be baptized before he could be ordained, 378n.
Blessing of God, 296.
Boldness, 390.
Bond, 255.
Bowing to people, 402-405, 435.
Brandenburgh, Joachim, Elector of, 381 & n.
Breathings, of the Spirit, 240, 244, 248; to the Lord in prayer, 251; toward God, 253, 286-287, 411.
Breviary, 198.
Brevity of the scriptures, 203.
Brook, the Lord will brook no co-partners and no co-rivals for his glory, 266.
Buried with Christ, 355.
Burned at stake, 383.

Calling, 53, 143, 174, 178-182, 188-191, 197, 225.
Calvinist Protestants of Great Britain, 351 & n.
Calvinists, 41, 48n, 108, 109, 214, 247, 336, 350 & n, 354, 382, 383, 413; liberal Calvinism of Saumur, 48n.
Cambridge, England, 271 & n.
Canon of Scripture, 49 & n, 63-65.
Card playing, see Gambling.
Cartesians, 42.
Carthage, Council of (of 399), 49n.
Causes of justification, 132.
Censure, 373.
Ceremonies, 301, 311, 314, 322, 331, 338, 341-343, 346-356, 359-361, 414, 415, 419, 435.
Certitude of God, 415.
Chaining down, of evil, 206; of human element and human wisdom, 250; of man's natural part or wisdom, 251.
Chalcedon, Council of (451), 379 & n.
Character of a Christian life of temperance, righteousness, and godliness, 112.
Characterem Christianitatis, 322.
Charity, 223, 425.

Charles II, dedicatory address to, vii n; required to renounce episcopacy, 376 & n.
Charles V, 295 & n.
Charles IX, of France, 396.
Chastity, 112.
Children of Darkness, 160, 402.
Children of Light, 160.
Children's Communion, 359 & n.
Christ (see also Christology, Christian, etc.), 318, 329, 357, 367-371, 376, 379, 383, 386, 387, 390, 393, 397, 398, 407, 412-417, 422, 425-431, 435, 438, 439; misunderstood by the apostles and Mary, 116-117; profession of, 173; doctrine and preaching of, 225-226; his baptism, 306; presence in Eucharist, 336.
Christian(s), should have a living sense of reverence, 12; and inward revelation, 17; defined, 22, 25; role of Spirit for, 31-36, 43; nominal, 44; inward grace the rule and guide for, 51-52; role of scripture for, 60; righteousness, 148; in name only, 164; 168, 171-172, 179, 184, 196, 209; ministers would starve under hard-hearted, 225; defection greatest in worship, 240; 246; surest way to become a, 255; most important thing for a, 265; 270, 273; mysticism and perfection, 275-277; to pray frequently, 286; 294; and Lord's Supper, 296; outward worship of, 313; and circumcision, 315; 357, 359, 365, 370-373, 376, 381, 390-398, 402-408, 417, 420, 423-428, 431-438.
Christianity, 1-2, 17; role of Spirit for, 32, 34; and canon of scripture, 49; scripture contains principal doctrines of, 63; and universal redemption, 78-84; notion of, 163; 183-185, 191; innovations, 302; obnoxious to Jews, Turks, and pagans, 334; 344, 408.
Christology (see also Christ, Christ Within, Light, Holy Spirit, Inward Light, Inward Teacher, Inward work), 86 & n, 89-92, 330-332, 337, 339, 367, 368; Just One, 409, 439; Substance, Eternal Word, Essential Oath and Amen, 414, 419-420; Prince of Peace, 425; spiritual appearance, 438.